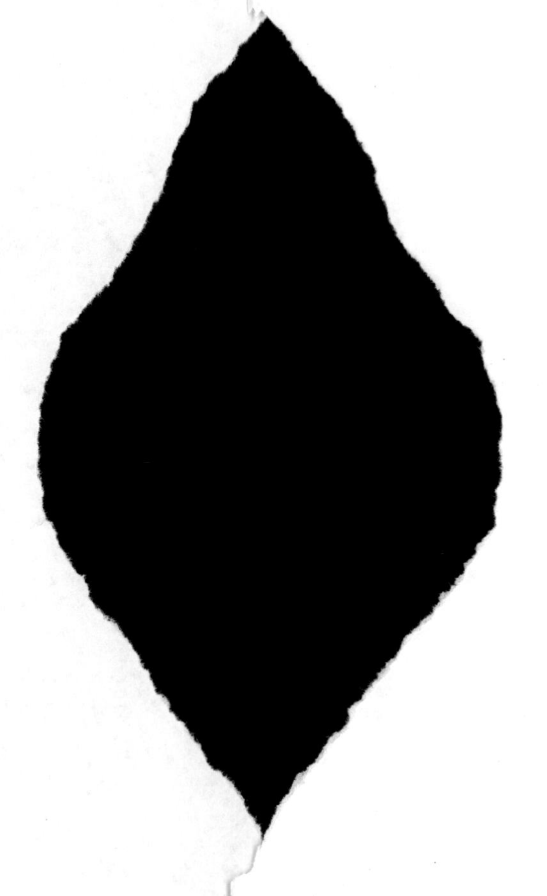

中国城市发展报告

（2011）

主 办

中 国 市 长 协 会

承 办

国际欧亚科学院中国科学中心

《中国城市发展报告》编委会 编

中国城市出版社

·北 京·

图书在版编目（CIP）数据

中国城市发展报告．2011/《中国城市发展报告》编委会编．—北京：中国城市出版社，2012.4

ISBN 978－7－5074－2571－0

Ⅰ.①中…　Ⅱ.①中…　Ⅲ.①城市经济—经济发展—研究报告—中国—2011　Ⅳ.①F299.21

中国版本图书馆 CIP 数据核字（2012）第 061388 号

责任编辑　孙湛波　陈夕涛　宋　凯

装帧设计　美信书籍设计工作室

责任技术编辑　张建军

出版发行　中国城市出版社

地　　址　北京市西城区广安门南街甲 30 号（邮编　100053）

网　　址　www.citypress.cn

发行部电话　（010）63454857　63289949

发行部传真　（010）63421417　63400635

总编室电话　（010）68171928

总编室信箱　citypress@sina.com

经　　销　新华书店

印　　刷　北京圣夫亚美印刷有限公司

字　　数　847 千字　　印张　38

开　　本　889×1194（毫米）　1/16

版　　次　2012 年 5 月第 1 版

印　　次　2012 年 5 月第 1 次印刷

定　　价　398.00 元

《中国城市发展报告(2011)》
机构组成名单

《中国城市发展报告(2011)》总顾问

路甬祥　全国人民代表大会常务委员会副委员长
成思危　全国人民代表大会常务委员会原副委员长
周光召　全国人民代表大会常务委员会原副委员长
徐匡迪　中国人民政治协商会议全国委员会原副主席
罗豪才　中国人民政治协商会议全国委员会原副主席

《中国城市发展报告(2011)》顾问

汪光焘　全国人大环境与资源保护委员会主任委员
王梦奎　国务院发展研究中心原主任
曲格平　全国人大环境与资源保护委员会原主任
刘燕华　国家科技部原副部长
刘　江　国家发展改革委员会原副主任
周干峙　原国家建设部副部长，中国科学院院士，中国工程院院士
赵宝江　原国家建设部副部长
李振东　原国家建设部副部长

《中国城市发展报告(2011)》理事会

理 事 长：蒋正华　全国人民代表大会常务委员会原副委员长
国际欧亚科学院中国科学中心主席
副理事长：陶斯亮　中国市长协会副会长
理　　事：（以下按姓氏拼音顺序排列）
崔衡德　戴　逢　廖幼鸣　马俊如
毛其智　彭公炳　王长远

《中国城市发展报告(2011)》学术委员会

《中国城市发展报告(2011)》编委会

《中国城市发展报告(2011)》研编机构

中国城市经济学会
广州市都市发展研究会
清华大学建筑学院
北京大学数字中国研究院
中山大学城市与区域研究中心
北京师范大学资源学院
北京凯德欧亚咨询中心有限公司
国家遥感应用工程技术研究中心

《中国城市发展报告(2011)》工作委员会

主任委员： 王长远

委　　员： 林家宁　方兆瑞　马海鹰

序　一

蒋正華

（九届、十届全国人大常委会副委员长，国际欧亚科学院中国科学中心主席）

2011 年是我国改革开放继续深入推进的一年，也是纪念中国共产党成立 90 周年和辛亥革命 100 周年的特殊年份。面对复杂多变的国际形势和艰巨繁重的国内改革发展稳定任务，党中央、国务院审时度势，科学决策，全国各族人民同心协力、锐意进取，推动社会主义经济建设、政治建设、文化建设、社会建设以及生态文明建设和党的建设取得新成就，实现了“十二五”时期良好开局。

党的第十七届六中全会审议通过了《中共中央关于深化文化体制改革、推动社会主义文化大发展大繁荣若干重大问题的决定》。《决定》全面总结了党领导文化建设的成就和经验，深刻分析了文化建设面临的形势和任务，历史上第一次阐述了中国特色社会主义文化发展道路，创造性提出了新形势下推进文化改革发展的指导思想、目标任务、政策举措，充分彰显了我们民族的文化自觉和文化自信，是当前和今后一个时期指导我国文化改革发展的纲领性文件。国际欧亚科学院中国科学中心作为活跃在国内外的科技组织，加强我们自身的文化建设是一项极其紧迫的任务。经过多年努力，在中国市长协会的密切合作下，以城市科学研究为基础的《中国城市发展报告》，已经成为中心的学术品牌之一。

2011 年我国在城市发展方面的大事很多，其中两件备受国内外关注：

第一件是城镇化率在统计上突破 50%，实现了中国社会结构的历史性转变。今后，在统筹城乡发展、改变二元经济结构、实现城乡人口转移、优化城镇空间布局、加强城镇产业支撑、跨越“中等收入陷阱”等方面，我们还将面对城镇化持续发展的重大挑战。从世界范围看，中国如此大规模、高速度的城镇化史无前例，没有可以直接照搬的经验，需要探索我们自己的道路。“十二五”规划提出，要探索工业化、城镇化和农业现代化“三化”协调发展的新路，应该具体落实在坚持工业反哺农业、城市支持农村，充分发挥工业化、城镇化对促进农民增收、加强农村基础设施和公共服务的辐射带动作用等方面。

第二件是社会各界针对前段时间在一些大城市出现的长时间灰霾天气，提出了监测微细颗粒物（PM2.5）的呼吁。最近，环境保护部发布了新修订的《环境空气质量标准》，增加了 PM2.5 和臭氧（O_3）8 小时浓度限值监测指标等内容。相信新标准将会更好地为公众提供健康指引，并有助于消除公众主观感观与监测评价结果不完全一致的现象。把 PM2.5 等纳入空气质量常规监测指标，不仅仅是环境保护的一大进步，也是城乡发展、经济结构、消费模式的一大转折。我们绝不能靠牺牲生态环境和人民健康来换取经济增长，我们一定要在中国走出一条生产蓬勃发展、生活富裕美满、生态良好宜居的城乡文明发展之路。

《中国城市发展报告（2011)》的主题定为“十二五”规划构建和谐社会与幸福城市。目前我国人均国内生产总值已超过5 000美元，人民群众憧憬建设美好家园，对提高生活水平和质量有了更多期盼和要求，对保障和改善民生的需求日益增长。在我们的《报告》中如何充分反映这一主题，如何客观记录一年来城市发展进程中的风风雨雨，如何不断总结城镇化的正反两方面经验教训，实现美好人居环境与和谐社会全面建设，是我和《报告》编委会同志们继续努力的方向，希望我们的《报告》能为实际工作提供一点帮助。

序　二

加快转变城市发展方式，提高城市发展质量

（住房和城乡建设部部长，中国市长协会执行会长）

改革开放以来，我国城镇化与经济社会同步快速发展。2011 年年底，我国城镇化率已达到 51.3%，跨过了 50% 的历史门槛。在切身感受到我国城镇化取得巨大成绩的同时，我们应清醒地认识到，我国城镇化的质量还不高。如何在城镇化快速发展的进程中进一步提高人居环境质量、加强和改善民生、统筹城乡区域协调发展、推进农民工市民化、加强自然文化资源保护等，关系我国长远的可持续发展、人民安居乐业和社会稳定和睦。我们要按照“十二五”规划提出的积极稳妥推进城镇化的要求，围绕转变城市发展方式、提高城镇化质量，继续扎实做好一些实实在在的工作。

一、完善住房保障体系，加强和改善民生

2011 年，我们完成了 1 000 万套保障性住房和棚户区改造住房的开工建设任务，落实了中央关于房地产市场调控的要求，使房价稳中有降，为实现广大人民群众“住有所居”的目标奠定了坚实的基础。2012 年计划新开工建设保障性住房和棚户区改造住房 700 万套以上，基本建成 500 万套以上，任务仍十分艰巨。要继续推进保障性安居工程建设，强化质量和分配管理。要继续坚持房地产调控不动摇，加强市场监管，规范市场秩序，引导房地产市场健康稳定发展。当然，还要注意加强制度建设，加快推进个人住房信息系统和住房公积金运行监管系统建设。

二、切实提高城市规划建设和管理服务水平，推进转型发展

要着力提高城乡规划的科学性、严肃性和权威性，完善规划实施监督机制。继续扩大部派城乡规划督察员的派驻城市范围，对规划确定的需要强制性保护的地区，要严格监管。加强对规划实施情况的评估，使城乡规划更好地为不可再生资源保护和城市建设发展服务。要

加强城市综合管理，当前重点是加强城市地下管线的综合管理，保证城市运行安全。要继续加强城市污水、垃圾处理等市政公用设施建设，改善城市人居环境质量。要编制好城市综合交通体系规划，加快城市轨道交通建设和步行、自行车交通系统建设，大力提倡采用绿色交通方式出行。要加快建筑节能改造，大力发展绿色建筑。

三、加大村镇整治力度，改善农村生产生活环境

2011 年，农村危房改造试点的范围已扩大到中西部全部农村，共安排了 265 万户的改造任务，是我国农村危房改造试点工作以来力度最大、进度最快的一年。2012 年要进一步加快推进农村危房改造，研究提高中央补助标准。要着力强化村镇人居环境整治力度，加强对乡村地区建设的规划管理。要继续支持重点小城镇建设，做好历史文化名镇和传统村落的保护。

由中国市长协会和国际欧亚科学院中国科学中心组织编写的《中国城市发展报告》作为年度性专业文献，已成为国内外了解中国城市发展的一个重要品牌和窗口。为此，借《中国城市发展报告（2011）》出版发行之际，我代表中国市长协会对多年来关心和支持《中国城市发展报告》的各位专家和编委会成员表示感谢！特别是吴良镛院士、周干峙院士等老专家、老领导，长期以来为我国城市发展献计献策，尽心尽力为《中国城市发展报告》撰文，我们应该向他们致敬，向他们学习。希望在各位专家的帮助下，编委会的同志们继续努力，把《中国城市发展报告》办得更好，进一步提高其在国内外的影响力。

2012 年 4 月 6 日

前　言

城乡统筹规划从认识中国国情开始
——论中国特色城镇化道路

汪光焘

（全国人大环境与资源保护委员会主任委员，国际欧亚科学院中国科学中心常务副主席）

城市化或城镇化水平是社会发展阶段的一个数量化表述，本质上讲是为了实现城乡共同富裕，是社会发展的根本目标。城乡统筹是党中央和国务院在我国社会经济进入新发展阶段，面临新的机遇和挑战背景下，借鉴国内外历史经验，为致力于突破城乡二元结构、破解“三农”难题、实现全面建设小康社会所作出的重大战略决策。

在城乡统筹的实现过程中，城乡统筹规划必将发挥规划的“龙头”作用，担负起引领城乡一体化发展的重担。这既是城乡统筹的历史使命所要求，也是城乡规划的行业属性所决定，更是2008年开始实施的《城乡规划法》所赋予的不可推卸的责任——《城乡规划法》第一条就开宗明义，提出了“协调城乡空间布局，改善人居环境，促进城乡经济社会全面协调可持续发展”是城乡规划的任务所在。

编制立足发展现状、着眼长远未来、追求统筹协调的城乡统筹规划是城乡规划行业不可推卸的历史责任，如何充分发挥城乡规划的统领作用，需要理解城乡统筹的战略意义，需要掌握城乡统筹的工作特点，需要明确城乡统筹规划的历史责任。

一、要正确理解城乡统筹发展的战略意义

（一）从城乡关系看，我国已经进入到必须实施城市反哺农村、工业反哺农业的关键时期

长期以来，我国始终实施农村支撑城市、农业支持工业的发展思路。新中国成立后，随着重工业优先发展战略的确定，采用计划经济体制、统购统销等经济制度，配合人民公社制度、户籍管理制度等限制人员城乡流动的系列辅助政策，通过工农产品“价格剪刀差”方式，抽取农业剩余迅速建立了新中国现代工业。改革开放后，除了短暂时间外，随着经济建设投资向城市的过度倾斜，以及社会主义市场经济建立后，城乡二元制度下的“土地剪刀

差”和“工资剪刀差”[①]的出现，城市发展仍从农村获取大量支持。虽然这些年农村发展取得一定成绩，但是到2000年左右，“三农”问题已经相当严峻，城乡间的居民收入、公共服务、社会保障形成了巨大差距，如城乡居民家庭人均收入差距，已经从1978年的2.57:1扩大到2002年的3.11:1，城乡恩格尔系数比值，已经从1978年的1.177:1扩大到2002年的1.225:1[②]，这种局面如果不尽快得到扭转，必将对我国社会经济产生一系列的严重后果。

（二）从现实情境看，我国可持续发展所面临的多重危机和内外困境需要依靠城乡统筹发展予以破解

某种程度上，我国很长一段时间以来的持续高速发展是以资源超前消费、环境污染破坏、能源过度消耗、文化丢失为代价。土地方面，粗放用地模式已经严重威胁到我国18亿亩耕地红线；能源方面，我国原油、原煤、铁矿石等主要能源的消耗占世界消耗总量比例远远高于GDP的贡献量；水资源方面，我国600多座城市中有2/3供水不足，其中1/6的城市严重缺水，全国近一半城镇饮用水源地水质不符合标准；环境方面，区域性环境事故频发，污染开始从城市向农村全面蔓延；文化传统方面，文化遗产破坏时有发生，传统文化保护传承举步维艰。此外，我国长期外向型经济受到全球性经济危机和国外贸易保护的双重制约，单一出口导向的经济模式面临严峻挑战。必须全面实施城乡一体化发展，才能发挥农村在保障国家和城市资源安全、环境安全、能源安全、粮食安全的作用，挖掘其在促进经济增长、传承历史文化、建设和谐社会方面的巨大潜力，实现社会经济持续健康发展。

（三）从发展阶段看，我国社会经济已经进入具备实施城乡一体化协调发展条件的时期

正如胡锦涛总书记在党的十六届四中全会上指出的两个“趋势”判断，大部分国家均是在工业化、城市化发展到一定阶段，且具备了相当国家支撑财力后，方才适时启动缩小城乡差距。从产业发展和城市化进程看，中国工业化和城市化均已进入中期阶段：2000年，第一产业增加值占国内生产总值的比重下降到15.1%，第一产业劳动力占全国劳动力比重下降到50.0%，中国城市化水平达到36.22%；到2003年，第一产业增加值仅占国内生产总值的12.8%，全国劳动力中从事第一产业的仅占49.1%，城市化水平达到40.53%；而到2009年，第一产业增加值仅占国内生产总值的10.6%，全国劳动力中从事第一产业的仅占38.1%，城市化水平达到46.59%。按照相关国家经验，我国已经进入了具备实行“城市支持农村，工业反哺农业”政策的发展阶段。从国家财力看，我国财政收入从1993年开始进

---

① 关于工资剪刀差，陆学艺在《当前农村形势和社会主义新农村建设》进行解释和估算：农民工进城打工，因为农民工的户籍是农业户口，所以与有城市户籍职工的待遇不同，干同样的工作，但“同工不能同酬，同工不能同时，同工不能同权”；仅以工资一项比较，据有关部门调查统计，2004年，农民工的月工资要比城镇职工低500~800元。当年农民工1.2亿人，以相差600元/人·月计，这个工资剪刀差就有8400亿元留在用工的城镇了。

② 数据来源《中国统计年鉴》。虽然农村和城镇的恩格尔系数从改革开放后均持续下降，但是城镇下降速度要明显快于农村，1978年农村和城镇的恩格尔系数分别为67.7%和57.5%，到2002年数据分别为43.1%和36.3%，其比值也从1978年的1.177:1扩大到2002年的1.225:1。

入持续高速增长期，到2009年，全国国内生产总值达到33.5万亿元、国家财政收入6.8万亿元、人均GDP达到25 575元（折合3 900美元左右），已经具备全面实施城乡一体化的雄厚国力。

（四）从目标实现看，城乡统筹是全面建设小康社会的根本要求，是构建和谐社会的坚实支撑，是实现科学发展的重要保证

2002年党的十六大报告明确提出城乡统筹概念，2003年党的十六届三中全会《决定》将统筹城乡发展上升为国家战略，2004年党的十六届四中全会《决定》提出了要推动建立“五个统筹”的有效机制，2007年党的十七大报告把统筹兼顾上升为科学发展观的根本方法，中央领导先后在一系列会议和讲话中就城乡社会一体化发展和城乡统筹发表过多次重要论述。回顾这一概念的提出和认识深化的过程，我们可以清晰地看到城乡统筹在党中央、国务院确立的我国长远发展思路中具有重要地位，对其内涵、作用和意义的认知是随着改革深化而日益清晰，其既是构成国家发展目标的组成部分，也是实现国家发展目标的有效路径，更是立足当前、着眼未来的战略选择。

二、要全面掌握城乡统筹的工作特点

（一）城乡统筹是一项系统性工作，其实现方式是通过多领域的公共政策综合作用，引导各种社会经济要素在城乡间的优化重组，最终实现城乡和谐发展

城乡统筹发展是一场涉及思想观念转变、资源配置整合、生产力布局优化、人口大量转移、利益关系调整、管理体制改革、领导方式创新等方面的深刻变革（2010，李迅）。其问题的复杂性和涉及的广泛性决定工作的综合性，必须通过系统性措施探索解决，实现必须通过多领域、多部门的公共政策综合作用，共同引导社会经济要素在城乡之间自由流通和合理配置，进而实现城乡一体协调发展。事实也的确如此，我国从2003年城乡统筹实践启动以来，城乡统筹工作在社会经济的各个领域全面展开，几乎所有的政府部门均动员起来，已经制定和实施了一系列的政策措施，如农业税费的取消、农村基本养老保险制度的建立等，从实施成效看大部分取得良好的效果。未来，城乡统筹公共政策仍需要重点加强以下几个领域：城乡资源的高效综合利用、城乡间生产要素的自由流动、城乡间的公共服务均等化、农村经济扶持和农业现代化提升、农村人才素质提高和农村劳动力转移等。

（二）城乡统筹是一项动态性工作，其实现过程具有时间上的阶段特征和空间上的层次特征，不同时期、不同空间范围的工作重点存在明显差异

作为长期积累而成的并关系到13亿人尤其是9亿农民的庞大工程而言，很难一蹴而就、短时间迅速完成，需要循序渐进的分阶段、分步骤加以解决。就全国而言，城乡统筹不仅与国家总体发展目标的实施过程相互关联，也与各个阶段的社会经济主要矛盾和国内外形势密切相关。现阶段城乡统筹需要重点关注民生问题、资源环境问题、社会公平问题，其中核心是公共服务均等化问题。具体到规划领域，现阶段对大部分地区而言核心任务将突出表现为“保护城乡地域生态、保障城乡聚落安全、保全城乡居民利益”的“三保”、“集中城镇、集聚人口、集群企业”的“三集”、“交通运输圈，基础设施、公共服务、社会管理的服务圈，城乡居民户外运动的休闲圈”的“三圈”规划实现（2010，李兵弟）。另外，城乡统筹发展具有明显的空间层次差异，城乡统筹在全国空间范围、区域空间范围、省域空间范围、市县域空间范围的任务和重点不尽相同，需要注意的是不同空间层次的工作重点会随着地域差异而有所不同，也必然随着时间推移会发生变化和转移。这就需要我们时刻关注、分析不同阶段的工作特点，及时调整不同时期、不同层次和空间范围内的城乡统筹的工作重点。

（三）城乡统筹是一项探索性工作，其实现关键是立足全面科学的城乡差异和地区差别分析，因地制宜、因时而异制定适宜性政策引导

从国外城乡一体化发展历程看，城乡统筹没有普适性模式，需要立足各国国情和发展阶段选择不同的实现路径。对我国这样一个地域范围辽阔、人口数量巨大、发展严重不均衡的国度而言，城乡统筹工作更需要加大探索和创新力度，其成功的关键就在于科学全面地分析城乡差异和地区差异及其内在原因。我国城乡差异主要体现在发展基础差异（家庭收入、社会保障、公共服务等）、社会模式差异、生活习俗方式差异等；需要注意的是与城乡差异相伴生的是地区差异，后者主要表现为发展阶段差异、资源禀赋差异、区位条件差异等，如东部发达的部分地区已经进入城镇化后期阶段，阻止城镇地区无序扩张是当前的突出问题，西部个别地区还处于城镇化起步阶段，城镇发展的培育是未来很长一段时间的主要任务。只有将城乡差异和地区差异结合起来共同分析研究，才能避免被假象所蒙蔽，否则难以正确理解诸如海南城乡收入差距较小、东北地区城镇化水平较高的特殊现象，自然也就无法制定出适宜性、针对性、时效性的政策引导。

三、要切实明确城乡统筹规划的历史责任

（一）编制好城乡统筹规划，切实转变思维方式是前提

转变思维方式是编制好城乡统筹规划的首要前提。一方面，长期的教育、生活和工作经历已经在规划从业人员脑海中留下了“城市中心论”思维定式。现在活跃在工作一线的广大城市规划从业人员在大学期间接受的都是以城市为核心的现代城市规划教育，长久形成的城乡分离、城市中心的思维习惯根深蒂固，而从业以后受到整个社会对城乡关系认知和工作经历的影响，观察视角、分析思路、工作习惯、判断标准均打下了深深的“城市中心论、城市优越论”烙印。另一方面，我们要清晰地看到新时期城乡统筹是源于“三农”问题、从农村视角而提出，是以构建和谐城乡一体化为目标，这一背景就决定了以往重城市轻乡村、从城市看农村的传统规划思维方式必然难以满足城乡统筹发展的要求、难以支撑城乡统

筹规划的编制，需要尽快加以转变。

（二）编制好城乡统筹规划，深入调查农村社会是关键

从现代城市规划奠基人之一迪格斯提出规划的基本工作方法开始，社会调查始终是城市规划的重要工作内容和基础，其重要性随着20世纪60年代西方社会思潮对城市规划的影响而愈发重要。十分遗憾的是，由于现代规划以城市发展建设为中心，农村社会调查随着规划重心的偏移已经逐渐被规划行业所淡忘，规划从业人员对农村的认知远不及对城市的深入。更为关键的是，20世纪70年代之后城市出生的规划从业者基本没有农村生活经历，既是年长一些的、出生在农村的规划从业人员对农村的认识也日渐模糊，而农村社会相对城市而言有其自然独特性，以城市模式规划农村难免水土不服，这也是很多农村规划缺乏可操作性的根源所在，显然不利于城乡统筹规划工作的开展。此外，中国历史上长期是农业社会国家，正如费孝通先生指出的一样，农村中蕴涵着中国社会经济变迁的一切基因，深入了解农村不仅有利于把握农村特征，也有利于全面正确的了解中国社会特征和城乡关系。未来对农村社会调查除了关注农村社会经济发展条件和问题外，要重点加强对农民意愿、社会模式、传统文化的了解和关注，提高规划的针对性和可操作性。

（三）编制好城乡统筹规划，规划理论制度研究是基础

从现代城市规划发展历程看，虽然在各个阶段始终存在追求城乡一体和谐发展的美好愿景和理想模式，但是这些理论均是以解决城市问题作为出发点，规划理论发展中以城市为中心的主流发展态势始终没有改变。虽然，近几十年，随着生态环境等问题的凸显，城市规划界开始反思传统规划理论，但是尚未形成完善的城乡一体规划理论体系。作为世界上人口最多、城乡关系复杂的国家，我国需要结合城乡统筹实践和中国传统规划理论，探索新时期城乡一体化规划基础理论，这既是我国城乡统筹发展的现实需求，也将成为中国对世界规划理论的贡献。在规划理论探索，要重视以下几个方面：重视对规划学科基础理论补充，重视与中国传统规划结合，重视与城镇化理论完善的互动，重视与城乡统筹其他学科理论的联系。此外，还应加强规划制度体系的研究，加强对城乡规划的法定地位、规划程序、配套政策、实施保障等一系列问题研究，为今城乡规划体系的调整和完善作好铺垫。

（四）编制好城乡统筹规划，规划技术方法创新是重点

作为应用型学科，通过技术手段创新让学科理论更好地服务社会经济是城乡规划的现实价值所在。寻找运用现代科技创新、契合中国现实国情、满足地域差异现实、涵盖不同发展阶段、传承中国传统规划理念、符合规划发展趋势的规划方法技术是编制好城乡统筹规划的重点。规划技术方法创新，不仅要加强规划编制阶段的前期研究和规划编制的技术支撑，还应当关注规划实施管理和后期评估的技术保证；不仅要重视规划核心技术，还应当关注规划支撑技术的创新；不仅应加强学科交叉引入技术方法，还应当立足规划自身寻求技术变革，例如将生态、低碳、交通等专项规划的新技术方法引入进来。

四、结语

城乡统筹是我国在实施长期“城市偏向”发展政策之后，在新的发展背景和形势下作出的战略选择，是关系到我国全面建设小康社会、构建和谐社会、实现社会经济可持续发展的重要举措。城乡统筹的实现将需要综合措施的共同作用，将是一个动态发展、不断地创新和探索过程。在这一过程中，城乡统筹规划将担负统领发展的重大使命，这就需要加快思维方式转变、开展农村社会深入调查、积极创新规划理论方法和技术。

参考文献

[1] 韩俊．中国城乡关系演变60年：回顾与展望［J］．改革，2009（11）：5－14.

[2] 李兵弟．城乡统筹规划：制度构建与政策思考［J］．城市规划，2010（12）：24－32.

[3] 李兵弟．关于城乡统筹发展方面的认识与思考［J］．城市规划，2004（8）：9－19.

[4] 李迅．以城乡规划引领城乡统筹发展［J］．上海城市管理，2010（3）：2－3.

[5] 陆学艺．当前农村形势和社会主义新农村建设［J］．江西社会科学，2006（4）：7－21.

[6] 孙津．城乡统筹：城乡协调发展的政策机制［J］．中国发展，2004（2）：10－12.

[7] 汪光焘．认真研究社会主义新农村建设问题［J］．城市规划学刊，2005（4）：1－3.

[8] 汪光焘．中国城市规划理念［M］．北京：中国建筑工业出版社，2008.

[9] 赵英丽．城乡统筹规划的理论基础与内容分析［J］．城市规划学刊，2006（1）：32－38.

[10] 周天勇，张弥．城乡二元结构下中国城市化发展道路的选择设计［J］．财经问题研究，2011（3）：3－8.

[11] 祝华军．对我国城市化健康发展的理论思考［J］．科学发展，2010（1）：35－46

目 录

综论篇

论坛篇

观察篇

专题篇

案例篇

附录篇

综论篇

2011中国城市发展综述

2011年是我国“十二五”时期经济社会良好发展的开局之年。面对复杂多变的国际形势和国内经济运行出现的新情况新问题，党中央、国务院以科学发展为主题，以转变发展方式为主线，坚持实施积极的财政政策和稳健的货币政策，着力稳增长、控物价、调结构、惠民生、抓改革、促和谐，国民经济继续朝着宏观调控预期方向发展，城镇就业进一步扩大，人民生活水平有了新的提高，在全面建设小康社会进程中写下不平凡的一页。

据初步测算，全年国内生产总值471 564亿元，按可比价格计算，比上年增长9.2%，三次产业的比重为10.1:46.8:43.1，结构与上年基本持平。在“十二五”开局之年，全国1 000万套保障房顺利开工，国家扶贫标准大幅上调，社会保障体系不断完善，结构性减税持续推进……一系列力度更大、覆盖更广的惠民政策，让人民群众充分享受到改革发展成果，既为保障和改善民生奠定了更加坚实的基础，也为进一步深化改革开放、加快转变经济发展方式创造了更加有利的环境。

十七届六中全会审议通过了《关于深化文化体制改革推动社会主义文化大发展大繁荣若干重大问题的决定》，这是中国共产党90年来第一次系统谋划文化发展战略。《决定》成为当前和今后一个时期指导我国文化改革发展的纲领性文件——从中国特色社会主义事业四位一体总体布局出发，以高度的文化自觉和自信，对中华民族未来的文化改革发展做出了全面部署，提出了“努力建设社会主义文化强国”的宏伟目标，指出了文化繁荣发展的前进方向、根本任务、出发点落脚点、发展动力以及发展路径。

一、城镇化进入历史新阶段

城镇化是经济社会发展的必然趋势，也是现代化的重要标志。2011年3月14日，第十一届全国人民代表大会第四次会议决议通过的《国民经济和社会发展第十二个五年规划纲要》指出：2010年全国城镇化率47.5%，较2005年增长4.5%；同时提出“十二五”时期经济社会发展主要指标中2015年的全国城镇化率预期性指标为51.5%，较2010年增长4个百分点。然而，由于统计等各方面原因，这一指标在2011年的一年时间内发生了较大变化，将中国的城镇化推入一个新的历史阶段。

(一) 人口与社会结构的历史性变化

第六次全国人口普查以2010年11月1日零时为标准时点，普查登记的我国大陆31个省、自治区、直辖市和现役军人的人口共133 972万人，其中居住在城镇的人口为66 558万人，占49.68%。全国流动人口（人户分离人口中不包括市辖区内人户分离的人口）达22 143万人。同第五次全国人口普查相比，10年间城镇人口增加20 714万人，乡村人口减少13 324万人，城镇人口比重上升13.46个百分点。

2012年1月17日，国家统计局公布了2011年的人口变化情况。全国人口及社会结构变化的基本情况是：人口总量继续保持低速增长，劳动年龄人口比重出现下降，城镇化率历史性地首次超过50%，流动人口继续增加。

2011年末，我国大陆总人口134 735万人，比上年末增加644万人，人口自然增长率为4.79‰。从年龄构成看，65岁及以上人口12 288万人，占总人口的9.1%，比上年末增加0.25个百分点；15~64岁劳动年龄人口100 283万人，占总人口的比重为74.4%，比上年末微降0.10个百分点。

从城乡结构看，2011年城镇人口69 079万人，比上年末增加2 100万人；乡村人口65 656万人，减少1 456万人；城镇人口占总人口比重达到51.27%，比上年末提高1.32个百分点。全国人户分离的（居住地和户口登记地所在乡镇街道不一致且离开户口登记地半年以上的）人口为27 100万人，比上年增加977万人；其中，流动人口（人户分离人口中不包括市辖区内人户分离的人口）为23 000万人，比上年增加828万人。

(二) 人口城镇化的问题凸显

2011年12月27日，温家宝在中央农村工作会议上的讲话指出：“30多年来，城镇常住人口增加了5亿人，其中有相当数量是进城的农民工。大规模的人口迁徙，史无前例，世所罕见，既改变了亿万农民的命运，更为经济发展注入了强大动力。需要注意的是，推进城镇化涉及面广、政策性强，对存在的问题要有清醒认识，对今后可能遇到的矛盾、困难甚至风险要有充分估计。”

温家宝提出，要把促进人口城镇化作为重要任务。他说，近些年来，城镇建设日新月异，规模迅速扩大，人口明显增加。但进入城镇的农民工，绝大多数还只是有就业而难以安家。如何促进人口城镇化，至少有这样两个关系长远的重大问题必须考虑：一要合理引导人口的流向。大量农民工向少数大城市、特大城市和沿海发达地区集中，极大地推动了这些地方的经济增长，但同时也提高了这些地方人口城镇化的成本，甚至超越了这些地方资源环境的承载能力。我国是世界上人口最多的国家，不可能只靠几个城市圈和少数经济发达地区来完成规模巨大的人口城镇化。因此，必须一方面采取措施让具备条件的农民工在就业所在地逐步安家落户，另一方面，加快调整地区生产力布局，引导产业向内地、向中小城市和小城镇转移，让更多农民就地就近转移就业。这既是促进人口城镇化的重大举措，也是转变经济发展方式、调整经济结构、实现区域经济协调发展的重大任务。二要充分考虑农村转移人口的当前利益和长远生计。土地承包经营权、宅基地使用权、集体收益分配权等，是法律赋予农民的财产权利，无论他们是否还需要以此来作基本保障，也无论他们是留在农村还是进入城镇，任何人都无权剥夺。在任何情况下都要尊重和保护农民以土地为核心的财产权利，应当让他们带着这些权利进城，也可以按照依法自愿有偿的原则，由他们自主流转或处置这些权利。

二、城乡建设的新进展

随着城乡建设的快速发展，城镇建制在 2011 年又有了新的调整。根据国务院的批复，撤销安徽省地级巢湖市，设立县级巢湖市；撤销贵州省毕节地区和县级毕节市，设立地级毕节市；撤销贵州省铜仁地区和县级铜仁市、万山特区，设立地级铜仁市；撤销江苏省县级江都市；同意新疆维吾尔自治区设立县级北屯市。至 2011 年末，全国共有 657 个设市城市，建制镇增加至 19 683 个。根据已公布的“六普”数据，全国有 30 个城市的常住人口超过 800 万人，其中 13 个城市超过 1 000 万人。按照全国设市城市市区户籍非农业人口统计，2010 年末全国有 200 万人口以上城市 24 个，100 万～200 万人口城市 39 个，50 万～100 万人口城市 94 个，20 万～50 万人口城市 239 个，20 万以下人口城市 261 个。

《民政事业发展第十二个五年规划》提出，为适应区域协调和城镇化健康发展的要求，在“十二五”期间将修订设市、设镇标准，制定市辖区设置标准，支持民族地区、边境口岸和新疆生产建设兵团发展中小城市；同时稳步推进省直管县（市）试点工作，并逐步开展城市内部行政区划体制、县城行政区划体制、经济发达镇行政管理体制等改革试点工作。

（一）城市建设

根据住房和城乡建设部统计，2010 年末，全国 657 个设市城市的城区人口共 3.54 亿，暂住人口 0.41 亿，建成区面积 4 万平方公里。城市市政公用设施固定资产完成投资 14 305.9 亿元，占同期城镇固定资产投资总额的 5.9%。

2010 年全国城市用水人口 3.8 亿人，用水普及率 96.7%，人均日生活用水量 171.43 升；用气人口 3.63 亿人，燃气普及率 92%；集中供热面积 43.6 亿平方米；城市道路长度 29.4 万公里，人均城市道路面积 13.21 平方米，城市道路机械清扫率 34%；全国有 12 个城市已建成轨道交通线路，长度 1 429 公里，配置车辆数 7 635 辆，有在建轨道交通线路长度 1 741公里；城市共有污水处理厂 1 444 座，污水处理厂集中处理率 73.8%；城市生活垃圾无害化处理率平均为 72.91%；全年清运生活垃圾、粪便 1.78 亿吨；建成区绿化覆盖率 38.6%，建成区绿地率 34.5%，人均公园绿地面积 11.2 平方米。2010 年末，全国共有 208 处国家级风景名胜区，根据其中 201 处统计，风景名胜区面积 8.3 万平方公里，可游览面积 3.4 万平方公里，全年接待游人 5 亿人次。国家投入 47.4 亿元用于风景名胜区的维护和建设。

经有关省、自治区、直辖市建设主管部门推荐，专家考查评审和社会公示，山东省潍坊市、江苏省江阴市、江苏省常熟市被授予2011年中国人居环境奖；“北京市城乡规划社区参与实践”等39个项目被授予2011年中国人居环境范例奖。

（二）县城建设

2010年末，全国有县城1 633个，据其中1613个县、1个县级市、10个特殊区域及148个新疆生产建设兵团师团部驻地统计汇总，县城人口1.26亿人，暂住人口1 236万人，建成区面积1.66万平方公里。全国县城市政公用设施固定资产完成投资2 569.8亿元。

2010年，全国县城用水人口1.18亿人，用水普及率85.1%，人均日生活用水量118.9升；用气人口0.9亿人，燃气普及率64.9%；集中供热面积6.1亿平方米；县城道路长度10.6万公里，人均城市道路面积12.7平方米，道路机械清扫率18.4%；全国县城共有污水处理厂1052座，污水处理厂集中处理率54.2%；县城建成区绿化覆盖率24.9%，建成区绿地率19.9%，人均公园绿地面积7.7平方米。

（三）村镇建设

2010年末，全国共有建制镇19 410个，乡（苏木、民族乡、民族苏木）14 571个。据16 774个建制镇、13 735个乡（苏木、民族乡、民族苏木）、721个镇乡级特殊区域和272.98万个自然村（其中村民委员会所在地56.35万个）统计汇总，村镇户籍总人口9.44亿人，其中，建制镇建成区1.39亿人，乡建成区0.324亿人，镇乡级特殊区域建成区0.037亿人，村庄7.688亿人。全国建制镇建成区面积317.9万公顷，人口密度5 215人/平方公里；乡建成区75.1万公顷，人口密度4 645人/平方公里；镇乡级特殊区域建成区10.4万公顷，人口密度4 059人/平方公里。全国有总体规划的建制镇14 676个，有总体规划的乡8 448个，有总体规划的镇乡级特殊区域466个，有规划的行政村269 849个。

2010年全国村镇建设总投入10 808亿元。按用途分，房屋建设占总投入的78.6%，市政公用设施建设占总投入的21.4%。全国村镇房屋竣工建筑面积9.74亿平方米，年末全国村镇实有房屋建筑面积355.5亿平方米，人均住宅建筑面积31.62平方米。

据统计，全国建制镇建成区用水普及率79.56%，人均日生活用水量99.3升，燃气普及率45.05%，人均道路面积11.4平方米，排水管道暗渠密度5.29公里/平方公里，人均公园绿地面积2.03平方米。乡建成区用水普及率65.64%，人均日生活用水量81.4升，燃气普及率18.98%，人均道路面积11.24平方米，排水管道暗渠密度3.12公里/平方公里，人均公园绿地面积0.88平方米。镇乡级特殊区域建成区用水普及率85.02%，人均日生活用水量86.65升，燃气普及率45.66%，人均道路面积13.25平方米，排水管道暗渠密度4.59公里/平方公里，人均公园绿地面积2.58平方米。2010年末，全国52.3%的行政村有集中供水，6%的行政村对生活污水进行了处理，37.6%的行政村有生活垃圾收集点，20.8%的行政村对生活垃圾进行处理。

自从开展社会主义新农村建设以来，各地积极探索，取得了一定的成效。但必须清醒看到，我国最大的发展差距仍然是城乡差距，最大的结构性问题仍然是城乡二元结构。城镇化不可能取代新农村建设，不能把城镇建设的做法简单地套用于农村建设。如何统筹城乡发展，有利于农民生产生活；如何保持广大乡村的良好生态环境，建设农民幸福生活的美好家园，将始终是中国发展中必须面对的重大挑战。

三、发展中的几个关注焦点

（一）区域规划对经济空间的拓展与整合

《国民经济和社会发展第十二个五年规划纲要》提出了实施区域发展的总体战略。要求“充分发挥不同地区比较优势，促进生产要素合理流动，深化区域合作，推进区域良性互动发展，逐步缩小区域发展差距”的总体要求，不断优化空间布局，促进区域协调发展和城镇化的健康发展。

根据《“十二五”规划纲要》，推进新一轮西部大开发应坚持以线串点、以点带面，推进重庆、成都、西安区域战略合作，推动呼包鄂榆、广西北部湾、成渝、黔中、滇中、藏中南、关中—天水、兰州—西宁、宁夏沿黄、天山北坡等经济区加快发展，培育新的经济增长极。

全面振兴东北地区等老工业基地时要积极促进资源枯竭地区转型发展，增强资源型城市可持续发展能力。重点推进辽宁沿海经济带和沈阳经济区、长吉图经济区、哈大齐和牡绥地区等区域发展。

在大力促进中部地区崛起的过程中要加快构建沿陇海、沿京广、沿京九和沿长江中游经济带，促进人口和产业的集聚，加强与周边城市群的对接和联系。重点推进太原城市群、皖江城市带、鄱阳湖生态经济区、中原经济区、武汉城市圈、环长株潭城市群等区域发展。

努力发挥东部地区率先发展对全国经济发展的重要引领和支撑作用，在更高层次参与国际合作和竞争，在改革开放中先行先试，在转变经济发展方式、调整经济结构和自主创新中走在全国前列。推进京津冀、长江三角洲、珠江三角洲地区区域经济一体化发展，打造首都经济圈，重点推进河北沿海地区、江苏沿海地区、浙江舟山群岛新区、海峡西岸经济区、山东半岛蓝色经济区等区域发展，建设海南国际旅游岛。

进一步加大对革命老区、民族地区、边疆地区和贫困地区的扶持力度，加强基础设施建设，强化生态保护和修复，提高公共服务水平，切实改善老少边穷地区生产生活条件。在南疆地区、青藏高原东缘地区、武陵山区、乌蒙山区、滇西边境山区、秦巴山—六盘山区以及中西部其他集中连片特殊困难地区，实施扶贫开发攻坚工程，加大以工代赈和易地扶贫搬迁力度。支持新疆生产建设兵团建设和发展。推进三峡等库区后续发展。实行地区互助政策，开展多种形式对口支援。

2011年，国务院先后批复了《山东半岛蓝色经济区发展规划》、《浙江海洋经济发展示范区规划》、《广东海洋经济综合试验区发展规划》、《河北沿海地区发展规划》、《成渝经济区区域规划》和《平潭综合实验区总体发展规划》；印发了《关于浙江省义乌市国际贸易综合改革试点总体方案的批复》、《关于同意设立浙江舟山群岛新区的批复》、《关于横琴开发有关政策的批复》、《关于支持河南省加快建设中原经济区的指导意见》、《关于厦门市深化两岸交流合作综合配套改革试验总体方案的批复》等。自2005年6月至2011年末，国务院共批准设立了11个国家级综合配套改革试验区。

随着各类区域规划的陆续出台，如何避免盲目上马、重复建设、以邻为壑、以损害环境为代价谋求经济增长等长期存在的问题再度出现，如何加强对规划实施的督促和指导，如何充分激发市场力量进行规划建设，都需要在制度和政策设计上不断进行体制机制创新，以实现区域统筹与可持续发展的长远目标。

（二）开工建设1 000万套保障性住房

住房水平是社会发展的重要指标。让绝大多数城镇家庭都能够居住在符合文明、健康标准的成套住房中，是中央提出到2020年实现全面建成小康社会的主要目标之一。

近年来，各级政府在推进城镇住房制度改革和住房商品化的同时，也在积极探索和推进住房保障工作。我国城镇人均住房建筑面积由1998年的18.7平方米提高到2010年的31.6平方米。“十一五”期间，全国开工建设各类保障性住房和棚户区改造住房1 630万套，基本建成1 100万套。到2010年底，全国累计用实物方式解决了近2 200万户城镇低收入和部分中等偏下收入家庭的住房困难，实物住房保障受益户数占城镇家庭总户数的比例达到9.4%，还有近400万户城镇低收入住房困难家庭享受廉租住房租赁补贴。保障性住房建设，改善了低收入家庭住房条件，对促进经济增长与社会和谐发挥了重要作用。

但是，到2010年底，我国仍有2 000多万户城镇低收入和少量中等偏下收入家庭的住房不成套，设施简陋。其中1 000多万户居住在棚户区中。棚户区房屋破旧拥挤，厨卫设施不全，有的甚至存在安全隐患。另外，城镇新就业职工和常住外来人口由于积累少，住房支付能力弱，他们中的一部分租住在地下室、城中村里，住房条件十分困难。这一群体是城镇经济发展的重要力量，帮助他们解决基本居住问题，对促进经济发展和社会稳定十分重要。

按照国务院关于大幅度增加保障性安居工程建设的要求，住房和城乡建设部住房保障司、国家发展和改革委员会固定资产投资司、财政部综合司于2010年11月23日联合下发《关于报送城镇保障性安居工程计划任务的通知》，提出2011年计划安排建设保障性住房和各类棚户区改造住房1 000万套，并要求各地2011年的计划任务要在原有保障性住房建设规划的基础上进行调整，并确保将计划落实到市县。

2011年2月27日，温家宝总理在中国政府网与网友在线交流时宣布：今年将要计划建设保障性住房和棚户区改造住房1 000万套。国务院主持各地与中央签订了保障性住房的责任书，计划在今后五年，新建保障性住房3 600万套。保障性住房应当以公租房和廉租房为主，再加上棚户区改造，不要走偏方向。

十一届人大四次会议上的政府工作报告提出：今年要再开工建设保障性住房、棚户区改造住房共1 000万套，改造农村危房150万户。重点发展公共租赁住房。中央财政预算拟安排补助资金1 030亿元，比上年增加265亿元。各级政府要多渠道筹集资金，大幅度增加投入。抓紧建立保障性住房使用、运营、退出等管理制度，提高透明度，加强社会监督，保证符合条件的家庭受益。在新增建设用地计划中，单列保障性住房用地，做到应保尽保。稳定房价和住房保障工作实行省级人民政府负总责，市县人民政府负直接责任。有关部门要加快完善巡查、考评、约谈和问责制度，对稳定房价、推进保障性住房建设工作不力，从而影响社会发展和稳定的地方，要追究责任。

2011 年保障性安居工程建设规模之大、任务之重，史无前例。考虑到各地区经济社会发展水平、城镇化进程，以及住房市场状况差异较大，住房保障方式不搞一刀切。实践中，由各地区结合本地实际情况，因地制宜地确定保障房类型。2011 年 1 000 万套保障性住房的构成是，廉租住房 165 万套、公共租赁住房 227 万套、经济适用住房 110 万套、限价商品住房 83 万套，以及各类棚户区改造 415 万套。此外，还计划新增发放廉租住房租赁补贴 60 万户。同时再次重申保障性住房的开工标准是，规划设计的永久性建筑工程已进入地基基础的结构施工。对于仅是搭建施工现场围护设施，或仅是开挖基坑的，不计入已开工的项目和套数。

初步计算，2011 年保障性住房建设需投入资金 1.3 万多亿元。其中，经济适用住房、限价商品住房建设投资 4 000 多亿元，这类保障性住房主要由社会投资，通过销售实现资金平衡；各类棚户区改造投资 5 000 亿元，这部分投资由政府补助一部分，主要通过企业筹一点、住户拿一点等办法解决；廉租住房和公共租赁住房建设投资 4 000 多亿元，这类保障性住房主要由各级政府、用工企业、社会机构投资等解决。中央财政分批下达了 1 522 亿元补助资金，相关各部门制定了加强建设资金管理的措施，督促各地切实落实配套建设资金，规范利用企业债券融资，加大信贷支持力度，扩大住房公积金贷款试点等，多渠道筹措建设资金。此外，各省（自治区、直辖市）也加大了投入力度，较好落实了保障房建设用地，不少地方还对保障性住房使用管理进行了动态监测。

为了完成国务院关于今年计划的保障性住房和棚户区改造项目在 11 月底前保质保量地开工，国务院办公厅组织 8 个督查组，对北京、辽宁、上海等 16 个省（自治区、直辖市）推进保障性住房建设情况进行了督查。住房和城乡建设部向每省派出了巡查联络员，常驻各地促开工、促质量、促后期管理。财政部、国土资源部、国家发展改革委、农业部、林业局等各有关部门也加强了督促检查。

2011 年 12 月 23 日，姜伟新同志在全国住房城乡建设工作会议上宣布，在各地方、各部门的共同努力下，今年提前、超额完成了开工建设保障性住房和棚户区改造住房 1 000 万套的任务。但从总体上看，我国住房保障工作还处于探索阶段，存在不少矛盾和问题，既有住房保障制度不够健全、政策不够完善的问题，也有管理不到位和实施过程中操作不规范的问题，需要及时总结经验，完善制度，加强管理。

（三）缓解交通拥堵，保障出行安全

根据国家统计局的数据，2011 年末全国民用汽车保有量达到 10 578 万辆，比上年末增长 16.4%，其中私人汽车保有量 7 872 万辆，增长 20.4%。民用轿车保有量 4 962 万辆，增

长23.2%，其中私人轿车4 322万辆，增长25.5%。北京、上海、广州、深圳、天津、重庆、成都、沈阳、武汉、西安等14个城市的汽车保有量超过100万辆。总体上，城市交通供需矛盾更加尖锐，以交通拥堵频发为主要表现形式的城市交通发展形势更加严峻，拥堵范围有局部向整体扩张，拥堵时间由高峰向全天扩散，且周期更短、更快、更顽固，行车难、停车难、行人过街难、秩序乱等问题仍将在一定时期内影响我国城市交通发展。积极创新，探索缓解城市交通拥堵之路，成为我国城乡规划建设管理工作的“重中之重”。

据公安部交通管理局统计，2011年全国机动车总量已达2.25亿辆，驾驶人2.36亿人。一年来涉及人员伤亡的道路交通事故210 812起，共造成62 387人死亡，事故起数、死亡人数同比分别下降4%和4.4%，道路交通万车死亡人数为2.8人，下降12.5%。但仍发生了一些令人痛心的重特大事故，尤其是7月23日甬温线在温州市境内发生的动车组列车追尾事故，造成40人死亡、172人受伤，中断行车32小时35分，直接经济损失19 371.65万元；10月7日唐山市交通运输集团有限公司一辆大客车（核载53人、实载55人），自河北省保定市开往唐山市途中与一辆小客车剐蹭，致使大客车向右侧翻，造成35人死亡、19人受伤，死者多数为保定籍在唐山上学的大学生；11月16日甘肃省庆阳市正宁县榆林子小博士幼儿园运送幼儿的校车（核载9人、实载64人）与重型自卸货车发生正面相撞，造成21人死亡（其中幼儿19人）、43人受伤。

1. 各级政府缓解交通拥堵的努力

住房和城乡建设部城市建设司提出，2011年要认真研究预防和缓解城市交通拥堵的措施的具体任务。要求全面梳理我国城市交通发展存在的问题，从城市交通基础设施规划、建设及与设施有关的管理方面，预防和缓解城市交通拥堵。研究制定《关于切实加强城市交通基础设施规划建设的指导意见》、《城市轨道交通线网规划编制办法》和《关于城市步行、自行车交通系统规划建设的指导意见》，进一步加大推动绿色交通工作的力度，加快各地步行、自行车交通系统的建设。

公安部、教育部、住房和城乡建设部和交通运输部联合下发的《关于深入实施城市道路交通管理畅通工程的指导意见》，提出了健全城市交通管理体制、发挥规划引导作用、落实公交优先发展战略、运用综合调控手段、改善城市道路通行条件、实施科学的交通组织管理、综合治理交通秩序等七个方面20条工作任务和措施。

首都北京除继续实施工作日高峰尾号限行、错时上下班等措施之外，市政府发布全面部署缓堵的66项工作任务。总的工作思路和目标是综合运用科技、经济、必要的行政和法律等手段，大力推进优先发展公共交通、加快交通基础设施建设、提高交通综合管理水平、开展文明交通建设等工作；并提出着力实施公交提速、地铁运力保障、交通秩序整治、停车秩序综合整治、小客车数量调控等五项重点措施。此外，北京市还陆续开通了20组社区通勤快车、10条“袖珍公交”线路，解决天通苑、回龙观等大型居住区市民“最后一公里”出行问题。2011年北京市公共交通出行比例上升至42%，小汽车出行比例首次出现1.2个百分点的下降。

在“十二五”规划中，深圳、杭州、武汉、济南、西安、长沙、宁波等诸多城市将缓解城市交通拥堵、加大力度建设公共交通体系、完善停车规划与管理、保障慢行出行环境等作为“十二五”期间的重要任务实施。进一步加强公共交通的建设和投入，逐步采取较为严格的交通需求管理措施，同时重视慢行交通出行环境，已经成为全社会的共识，也是今后我国城市交通发展的必然趋势。

2. 保障交通安全任重道远

2011 年 4 月 22 日，第十一届全国人民代表大会常务委员会第二十次会议通过《关于修改〈中华人民共和国道路交通安全法〉的决定》。从 2011 年 5 月 1 日零时起实施新的《道路交通安全法》，对醉酒驾驶机动车、因饮酒后驾驶机动车被处罚而再次饮酒后驾驶机动车、饮酒后驾驶营运机动车等严重危害群众利益行为，吊销机动车驾驶证，依法追究刑事责任，并设定了相应的刑事处罚措施。据统计，至 10 月 31 日，全国共查处酒后驾驶机动车 148 651起，比 2010 年同期下降 47.9%。其中，醉酒驾驶机动车 26 617 起，比 2010 年同期下降 42.7%；因酒后驾驶造成交通事故死亡 467 人，比 2010 年同期减少 175 人，下降 27.3%；因醉酒驾驶造成交通事故死亡 410 人，较 2010 年同期减少 94 人，下降 18.7%。查处酒后驾驶机动车在社会上取得了广泛的支持和反响，有效预防和遏制了醉酒驾驶行为，降低了交通事故发生的可能性。

2011 年 11 月 23 日，国务院安全生产委员会办公室通报甘肃省庆阳市“11·16”重大道路交通事故，要求各地高度重视中小学和幼儿园校车交通安全工作，建立完善校车交通安全监管的长效机制；全面开展中小学和幼儿园校车安全隐患大排查，严查校车超速、超员等违法行为，对违法行为实行“零容忍”，发现一起处理一起；进一步加大对中小学和幼儿园校车安全的宣传教育力度，教育中小学生坚决不乘拼装车、报废车、农用车、货运车等非法运营车辆和超员车辆上下学，教育提醒步行上下学的中小学生遵守交通规则，主动安全避让行驶车辆，并要提醒学生家长提高安全意识和监护人责任意识，不得租用不符合安全规定的车辆接送学生；认真执行事故查处挂牌督办制度，严肃事故查处，吸取事故教训，举一反三，切实搞好道路交通安全尤其是中小学和幼儿园校车安全工作。

为了加强校车安全管理，保障乘车幼儿、学生的人身安全，国务院法制办公室会起草了《校车安全条例（草案征求意见稿）》，并于 2011 年 12 月 11 日将征求意见稿及其说明全文公布，征求社会各界意见。征求意见稿对学校和校车服务提供单位、校车使用许可、校车驾驶人、校车通行安全、校车乘车安全、法律责任等方面作出了详细规定；并赋予校车最高路权，以进一步保障乘车幼儿、学生的人身安全。

（四）加快建设社区服务体系

社区和谐是社会和谐的基础，发展社区服务，健全社区服务体系是社区和谐的重要前提和保障。社区服务体系，是指以城乡社区为基本单元，以各类社区服务设施为依托，以社区全体居民、驻社区单位为对象，以公共服务、志愿互助服务、便民利民服务为主要内容，以满足社区居民生产生活需求、提高社区居民生活质量为目标，党政引导支持、社会多元参与的服务网络及运行机制。

目前，全国有7 194个城市街道办事处，8.9万个城市社区。“十一五”期间，各地认真贯彻落实《国务院关于加强和改进社区服务工作的意见》和国家发展改革委、民政部《“十一五”社区服务体系发展规划》，城乡社区服务体系建设取得显著成效。

一是社区服务设施建设取得初步进展。“十一五”期间全国共建成街道社区服务中心3 515个，便民利民服务网点69.3万个，还建有社区卫生服务中心（站）、社区文化中心（室）等专项社区服务设施。

二是社区服务内容不断拓展。劳动就业、社会保障、社会服务、生活救助、文化娱乐、社会治安等政府公共服务事项逐步向社区覆盖，广泛推行社区志愿者注册登记制度，社区志愿互助服务蓬勃开展。超市、菜场、早餐等生活保障性商业网点得到重点配套，家政服务、物业管理、养老托幼、食品配送、修理服务、废旧物品回收等便民利民服务项目逐步进入社区，极大地方便了社区居民生活，提高了生活质量。

三是社区服务队伍不断壮大。依法选举产生一批社区居委会成员，逐步面向社会公开招聘专职社区工作人员。截至2010年底，全国共有各类社区服务设施15.3万个，其中社区服务中心12 720个，社区服务站44 237个，其他社区服务设施9.6万个。城镇便民、利民服务网点53.9万个。社区共吸纳从业人员105.9万人。全国共有社区居民委员会成员43.9万人，社区公共服务从业人员105.9万人。有社区志愿服务组织10.6万个，507.6万社区居民成为社区志愿者，活跃在社区服务各领域，成为推动社区建设和社区服务的重要力量。

四是社区服务方式不断改善。不少地方依托街道社区服务中心、社区服务站，实行“一站式”服务；利用现代信息技术，推动社区信息化建设，方便快捷地满足了居民多样化需求。有的地方通过政府购买服务、设立项目资金、开展项目补贴等方式，引导社会组织、企事业单位和居民参与社区管理和服务活动，增强了社区服务的活力和社会组织的服务能力。

五是社区服务制度环境初步形成。中央政府围绕老年人、未成年人、残疾人权益保护工作出台了法律，围绕社区卫生、社会救助、劳动就业、文化教育、社区服务设施等内容出台了相关政策，各地也相继出台了积极推进社区服务的政策措施，社区服务的政策法规逐步完善，各级党委政府对社区服务的重视程度越来越高，社区居民对社区服务的认同感和归属感越来越强。

实践证明，加强社区服务体系建设是保障和改善民生、提高居民生活水平和生活质量的民心工程，是拉动内需、扩大就业、促进经济发展方式转变的助力工程，是加强和创新社会管理、维护社会和谐稳定的基础工程。

但就总体情况而言，我国社区服务体系建设仍然处于初级阶段，仍然存在许多困难和问题，也面临许多机遇和挑战。存在突出问题是，城乡社区服务发展严重失衡，社区服务设施严重短缺，街道、社区仍然缺乏服务场所，农村社区服务设施建设刚刚起步。社区服务内容亟待丰富，社区公共服务城乡差距巨大，需求和供给脱节，供给方式单一。社区服务人才短缺、素质偏低，结构亟待优化。社区服务体制机制不顺畅，缺乏统一规划，投入不足、各自为政、重复建设的问题较为突出，资源整合不够，社会参与机制亟待完善。

为适应统筹城乡经济社会发展、加强和创新社会管理需要，强化社区自治和服务功能，保障和改善民生，促进社会和谐稳定，国务院办公厅发布了《社区服务体系建设规划（2011—2015 年）》，提出了把城乡社区建设成为管理有序、服务完善、文明祥和的社会生活共同体的总体思路。

“十二五”期间社区公共服务发展的具体目标任务是：发展多层次、多样化的社区劳动就业、社会保险和社会服务，社区医疗卫生和计划生育服务，社区文化、教育、体育服务，社区法律、治安服务，社区便民利民服务，到 2015 年初步建立起较为完善的社区服务设施、服务内容、服务队伍、服务网络和运行机制。同时。要建立健全政府投入与社会投入相结合的社区服务经费保障机制，发挥市场多元主体作用，加强社区服务设施建设，特别是城中村、新建小区、特殊人群相对集中小区、流动人口聚集小区的社区服务设施建设，加快形成以综合服务设施为主体、专项服务设施相配套的社区服务设施网络。以居民需求为导向，整合社区服务资源，加快社区信息化建设，构建社区综合管理与服务平台。大力发展面向全体居民特别是困难群众、优抚对象、老年人、残疾人、未成年人和农村进城务工人员的社区服务。

四、探求未来的包容性发展之路

（一）倡导和实践包容性增长

2010 年 9 月，国家主席胡锦涛在亚太经合组织会议上指出：“中国是包容性增长的积极倡导者，更是包容性增长的积极实践者。中国强调推动科学发展、促进社会和谐，本身就具有包容性增长的含义。我们既强调加快转变经济发展方式、保持经济平稳较快发展，又强调坚持把发展经济与改善民生紧密结合起来，以解决人民最关心最直接最现实的利益问题为着力点，大力推进以改善民生为重点的社会建设。”对此，他首次提出了“优先开发人力资源，实施充分就业，提高劳动者素质和能力，构建可持续发展的社会保障体系”等实现包容性增长的四点建议。

2011 年 4 月，博鳌亚洲论坛以“包容性发展：共同议程与全新挑战”为主题，再次探讨包容性发展的内涵，拟通过高速以及可持续的经济增长，争取最大限度地创造发展与就业机会，确保民众基本福利保障和在整个发展过程中民众的机会平等、公平参与，为亚洲经济、社会的适时转型提供前瞻性的思路和引导。

博鳌亚洲论坛中方首席代表曾培炎在演讲中指出，今天，全世界的财富正在迅速增长，但繁荣并没有光临地球的每一个角落。探究其背后的原因，传统的发展道路在一定程度上具有排他性，或其他各种原因，使不同国家在参与国际事务上，不同人群在参与政治、经济活动上出现了不公平，无法共享文明进步的成果。他主张应从四个方面来理解包容性发展的理念：第一，包容性发展是所有人机会平等、成果共享的发展；第二，包容性发展是各个国家和民族互利共赢、共同进步的发展；第三，包容性发展是各种文明相互激荡、兼容并蓄的发展；第四，包容性发展是人与自然和谐相处、良性循环的发展。

曾培炎认为，包容性思想是中华文化的重要体现。中国传统文化强调天人合一、道法自然，主张人与自然和谐共存。早在两千多年前的春秋战国时代，中国就出现了多种思想学派"百家争鸣"的辉煌时期。时至今日，兼容并蓄、海纳百川仍是中国人文精神的重要特征之一，可以说包容性是中华文明绵延数千年的重要原因。

（二）与城市未来的对话和展示

第六届世界城市论坛将于2012年9月1日至7日在意大利的那不勒斯市举办。"城市未来"取代原来确定的"城市繁荣"成为本次论坛的主题，旨在探讨当今世界面临的最紧迫问题之一：快速城市化及其对社区、城市、经济、气候变化和政策的影响。

联合国秘书长潘基文说："人类追求的、未来的理想城市是美丽、绿色、可持续、充满人文气息的，理应为我们所有人瞩目。想象未来的城市就是想象人类的未来及我们将来生活的城市，因为我们的世界正在日益城市化。"

联合国人居署执行主任霍安·克洛斯说："在所有以城市为议题的大会中，世界城市论坛已经成为举足轻重的一个。人们齐聚一堂，共同探讨城市化带来的问题和机遇，互相交流借鉴。"

本次论坛包括公开辩论，青年、性别和商业集会，核心小组会议，特别会议，圆桌会议，培训研讨会和一系列周边活动、展览和文化活动。为论坛设定基调的高端活动，是有关城市未来的六个大型对话会议，对话主题分别是：富于生产力的城市：城市就业；宜居城市和生活质量；城市规划：机构和规章；城市公正和繁荣；城市文化和繁荣；环境、城市交通和能源。

论坛筹办者呼吁，目前全球人口已有超过半数居住在城镇城市，预计再过一代人时间，全人类将有三分之二人口居住在城市。这意味着，我们必须更好地规划城市，保障优良的城市立法和治理，改善基本服务供应和住房。同时，我们必须比以往任何时候都更努力地节能，保护环境，减少污染，严肃处理城市气候变化的问题。我们需要整合资源、协调配合，以期建设更美好、更宜居、更节约、更智能、更具包容性的未来城市。这是我们应当为子孙做的，尤其是为全球贫民窟和低于标准住房的近10亿居民做的。

五、结语

回顾过去，展望未来，新的一年将是我国发展进程中具有重要意义的一年。2011年12月召开的中央经济工作会议深入分析国内外经济形势，明确提出了稳中求进的总基调，要求把握扩大内需这一战略基点，把握发展实体经济这一坚实基础，把握加快创新这一强大动力，以更大的决心和气力推进改革开放，着力解决影响经济长期健康发展的体制性、结构性矛盾，在转变发展方式上取得新进展，在深化改革开放上取得新突破，在改善民生上取得新成就。在发展思路上，必须走出一条创新发展之路、跨越发展之路、融合发展之路和可持续发展之路。

在2012年2月14日召开的国家科学技术奖励大会上，中国人居环境科学的创建者吴良镛教授荣获2011年度国家最高科学技术奖。吴教授在其漫长学术生涯中所取得一系列具有前瞻性、示范性的理论与实践成果，为中国城乡规划建设写下绚丽的篇章。

2012年6月，联合国可持续发展会议（又称“里约+20”峰会）将在巴西名城里约热内卢举行。在这次峰会上，世界各国领导人以及数千名来自各方面的参与者将共聚一堂，商讨在一个人口越来越拥挤的星球上如何减少贫困、促进社会公平，并合理使用资源、保护环境等议题。正如峰会秘书长沙祖康所说，可持续发展不是任由取舍的选择！全人类要在这一个星球上过像样的生活，这是唯一的途径。

（作者：毛其智，清华大学教授，国际欧亚科学院院士）

An Introduction of Urban Development in China: 2011

The year 2011, as the beginning of the China's Twelfth Five-year Plan, has experienced a sound development in economy and society. Facing both the complicated international situation and the new conditions and problems in domestic economic operation, the Central Party Committee and State Council, upholding the theme of scientific development and taking transforming the pattern of development as the main thread, have steadfastly implemented a proactive fiscal policy and a prudent monetary policy, and exerted all efforts to steady growth, control prices, adjust the economic structure, improve the people's wellbeing, implement reform, and promote harmony. The national economy could continue to move in the expected direction of macro-controls, urban employment was expanded, and the people's living standards were improved to a new level, all of which have left an extraordinary mark in the process of building a well-off society in an all round way.

According to preliminary estimation, the gross domestic product (GDP) of the year reached 47.1564 trillion yuan, an increase of 9.2% over the previous year calculated by constant prices. The ratio of the three industries was 10.1:46.8:43.1 and basically remained flat compared with the previous year. At the beginning of the Twelfth Five-year Plan, the country successfully launched the construction of 10 million units of low-income housing; the national standards for poverty alleviation were remarkably raised; the social security system were constantly improved; and the structural tax deduction were promoted continuously, ..., a series of policies benefiting the people with more support and wider coverage have enabled the masses to fully enjoy the fruits of reform and development, which not only lay a more solid foundation for ensuring and improving the people's wellbeing but also create a more favorable environment for further deepening the reform and opening-up and accelerating the transformation of the pattern of economic development.

The Sixth Plenary Session of the Seventeenth CPC Central Committee considered and adopted the *Decision of the CPC Central Committee on Major Issues Pertaining to Deepening Reform of the Cultural System and Promoting the Great Development and Flourishing of Socialist Culture*. This was CPC's first systematic scheme for cultural development strategy since its foundation 90 years ago. The decision, which has become a programmatic document guiding the national cultural reform and development now as well coming future, based on the quaternity overall cause of socialism with Chinese characteristics, makes comprehensive arrangements for the reform and development of Chinese nation with a high degree of cultural self-awareness and self-confidence. It sets the grand objective of "striving to build a country with a strong socialist culture" and points out the guide, the fundamental task, the starting and end point, the motive force and the development path of promoting cultural flourishing and development.

Ⅰ. New Historic Stage of Urbanization

Urbanization is an inevitable trend of economic and social development and also an important benchmark for modernization. As is mentioned in the *Outline of the Twelfth Five-Year Plan for National Economic and Social Development* approved by the Fourth Session of the Eleventh National People's Congress on March 14, 2011, China's urbanization level reached 47.5% in 2010, an increased 4.5% since 2005. It is also proposed that among the major indicators of economic and social development during the Twelfth Five-year Plan period, the target of the national urbanization level is 51.5% by 2015, a four percent increase over 2010. However, for some reason from official statistics, that indicator has experienced a remarkable change during 2011, which has brought China's urbanization into a new historic stage.

(Ⅰ) Historic changes of population and social structure

With zero hour of November 1 2010 as the reference time, the population of the 31 provinces, autonomous regions and municipalities and of servicemen on the mainland of China through the Sixth National Census was 1 339.72 million. Of the total population 665.58 million were urban residents, accounting for 49.68%. The nation's migrant population (people living in places other than the towns (townships or streets) of their household registration don't include those with current residence different from the place of their household registration in the same city) reached 221.43 million. Compared with the Fifth National Census, over the past ten years the number of urban residents had increased by 207.14 million, and the number of rural residents had dropped by 133.24 million. The proportion of urban residents rose by 13.46%.

The National Bureau of Statistics announced the demographic changes of 2011 on January 17th, 2012. The basic facts of the national population and social structure change were as follows: the total population maintained a low growth rate, the proportion of working-age population declined, the urbanization level exceeded 50% for the first time in history and the migrant population continued to grow.

By the end of 2011, the total population on the mainland of China had reached 1 347.35

million, an increase of 6.44 million over the end of the previous year. The natural population growth rate was 4.79 ‰. As regards the age composition, 122.88 million persons were in the age group of 65 and over, accounting for 9.1% of the total population, an increase of 0.25 percentage over the end of the previous year; 1 002.83 million were in the working-age group of 15 ~ 64, accounting for 74.4%, a slight decrease of 0.10 percent over the end of the previous year.

As regards the urban and rural population, 690.79 million persons were urban residents, an increase of 21 million over the end of the previous year; 656.56 million persons were rural residents, a decrease of 14.56 million. The proportion of urban residents reached 51.27%, an increase of 1.32 percentage points over the end of the previous year. 271 million persons lived in places other than the towns (townships or streets) of their household registration where they had left for over 6 months, an increase of 9.77 million over the previous year. Of that total 230 million were migrant population (with people with current residence different from the place of their household registration in the same city excluded), an increase of 8.28 million over the previous year.

(Ⅱ) Increasingly serious problems of population urbanization

Premier Wen Jiabao said at the Central Rural Working Conference on December 27th, 2011: "over the past more than 30 years, the permanent urban residents had increased by 500 million, many of which were rural migrant workers. This population flow on such a large scale seldom seen at any time in history and anywhere in the world not only changed hundreds of millions of peasants' fate but gave considerable impetus into the economic development as well. It is worthy to note that the promotion of urbanization involves a wide range of issues and is remarkably policy-oriented, which requires a high level of awareness of the existing problems and fully consideration of the potential conflicts, difficulties and even risks in future."

Wen Jiabao also proposed that the promotion of population urbanization should be taken as an important task. He said that recently the urban construction was expanding at an accelerating pace, with the population increasing noticeably. But a majority of the rural migrant workers in the urban areas was merely able to find employment rather than settle down. There were at least two far-reaching issues on promoting population urbanization that should be taken into consideration. First was to guide the rational flow of the population. Most migrant workers converged on several large and super-sized cities and developed coastal areas, which had stimulated economic growth there significantly, but meanwhile raised the cost of population urbanization of these areas to the level even beyond the carrying capacity of the resources and environment. China, with the largest population in the world, couldn't depend on only a few metropolises and limited developed areas to realize such large-scale population urbanization. Therefore, on one hand, we should take measures to settle those migrant workers whose conditions permitted at where they worked step by step; on the other, we should speed up improvement of the distribution of the productive forces between places through guiding industries to inland and medium or small-sized cities, in order to enable more surplus rural workers to find nonagricultural employment in nearby towns and cities. Those were the significant measures not only to promote population urbanization, but also to transform the pattern of economic development, to adjust the economy structure and to enhance balanced development among regions. Second was to fully consider both the current and long-term benefits of the rural migrant residents. The peasants were entitled to such property rights as land contractual management right, homestead right, the collective revenue distribution right and so on by law. No matter whether they needed them as basic security or whether they choosed to stay in rural or urban areas, no one had the access to depriving them of their rights. We should respect and protect the peasants' property rights that centered around the land under any circumstance. They should be allowed to retain these rights when coming to the cities, and to transfer or dispose them on their own on a compensated and voluntary basis by law.

Ⅱ. New Progress of Urban and Rural Construction

With the rapid growth of urban and rural construction, the urban system was rearranged in 2011. Approval by the State Council, Anhui Province revoked the Prefecture-level City of Chaohu and established the County-level City of Chaohu; Guizhou Province revoked Bijie Prefecture and the County-level City of Bijie, and established the Prefecture-level City of Bijie; revoked the Tongren Prefecture, the County-level City of Tongren and Wanshan Special Zone, and established the Prefecture-level City of Tongren; Jiangsu Province revoked the County-level City of Jiangdu; Xinjiang Uygur Autonomous Region established the County-level City of Beitun. By the end of 2011, there had been 657 cities officially designated across the country, and the number of county seats had reached 19 683. According to the published data from the Sixth National Census, 30 cities had more than 8 million permanent residents and 13 of them had over 10 million. Based statistics on the nonagricultural population of the cities officially designated, by the end of year 2010, 24 cities had more than 2 million permanent residents, 39 cities had 1 ~ 2 million, 94 cities had 0. 5 ~ 1 million, 239 cities had 0. 2 ~ 0. 5 million, and 261 cities had less than 0. 2 million.

As was proposed in the *Twelfth Five-Year Plan for Development of Civil Affairs*, in order to meet the requirements of promoting coordinated regional development and healthy urbanization development, during the twelfth five-year period, it is necessary to revise the standards of the establishment of cities and counties, set the standards of the establishment of municipal districts, and support the development of medium and small-sized cities in ethnic minority areas, border crossings and Xinjiang Production and Construction Corps. Meanwhile we would steadily promote the pilot schemes for the direct provincial supervision of counties, and gradually launch the reform of the administrative division systems of cities and counties and the administrative management systems of developed towns.

(Ⅰ) Construction of cities

Based on statistics of the Ministry of Housing and Urban-rural Development, there were 657 cities officially designated across the country at the end of 2010 with 354 million urban residents and 41 million temporary population wherein, and the urban built-up areas amounted to 40 000 square kilometers. The total fixed assets investment in the urban municipal facilities reached 1 430. 59 billion yuan, accounting for 5. 9% of the total urban fixed assets investment in the same period.

In 2010, the water supply served a population of 380 million with a coverage rate of 96. 7% and daily per capita consumption of domestic water being 171. 43 liters; the gas served a population of 363 million with a coverage rate of 92% ; the central heating area extended to reach 4. 36 billion square meters; the total length of urban road was 294 000 kilometers with per capita area of 13. 21 square meters and the mechanical cleaning rate of 34% ; 12 cities had rail transit lines completed with the length up to 1 429 km with 7 635 vehicles, and another 1 741 km of rail transit lines were under construction; there were a total of 1 444 wastewater treatment plants in cities with a central treatment rate of 73. 8% ; the urban domestic garbage harmless treatment rate was 72. 91% , and total 178 million tons of garbage was cleared and transported; the greenery coverage of urban built-up areas was 38. 6% , and the green space coverage rate of built-up areas was 34. 5% with per capita public green space 11. 2 square meters. By the end of 2010, there were 208 national parks in China, and according to the statistics of 201 places wherein, they covered an area of 83 000 square kilometers with 34 000 square kilometers open to visitation which added up to 500 million person times for the whole year. The state invested 4. 74 billion yuan for maintenance and development of national parks.

Upon the recommendation of the construction authorities of relevant provinces, autonomous regions and municipalities, reviews of experts and social publicity, Weifang in Shandong Province, Jiangyin and Changshu in Jiangsu Province were conferred the China Habitat Award of 2011; 39 projects including *Beijing Communities' Participation in Urban and Rural Planning Practice* were awarded for Best Practices to Improve the Human Settlements in China of 2011.

(Ⅱ) Construction of county seats

There were 1 633 county seats across the country at the end of 2010. Based statistics on 1 613 counties, 1 county-level city, 10 special regions and 148 Xinjiang Production and Construction Corps, there were total population of 126 million and temporary residents of 12. 36 million, and built-up areas in accounted for 16 600 square kilometers. The fixed assets of investment in the county seats reached 256 980 million yuan.

In 2010, the county seats supplied water to 118 million residents and the water coverage rates was 85. 1% ; daily per capita water consumption was 118. 9 liters; the population supplied with gas was 90 million with a coverage rate registering 64. 9% ; The centrally heated area extended to reach 610 million square meters; the length of roads in county seats was 106 000 kilometers, the average road area per capita was 12. 7 square meters, and the mechanic cleaning rate was 18. 4 % ; there were total 1 052 wastewater treatment plants with a central treatment rate of 54. 2% in county seats; the green coverage rate in built-up area in county seats was 24. 9% , the green space coverage rate reached 19. 9% , and per capita public green space reached 7. 7 square meters.

(Ⅲ) Construction of villages and small towns

By the end of 2010, there were 19, 410 designated towns and 14 571 townships (including sumu, ethnic township and ethnic sumu) in China. Based on the data collected from 16 774 designated towns, 13 735 townships (including sumu, ethnic township and ethnic sumu) , 721 township level special regions and 2. 73 million villages (563 500 villages accommodated villagers' committees) , the total household registered population was 944 million. Among them, there were 139 million people living in towns, 32. 4 million in built area of townships, 3. 7 million in the township level special regions and 768. 8 million villagers. The total built-up area of the designated towns was 3. 179 million hectares, and the population density was 5 215 persons per square kilometer; the township built-up area was 0. 751 million hectares, and the population density was 4 645 persons per square kilometer; the special township level built-up regions was 0. 104 million hectares, and the population density was 4 059 per square kilometers. 14 676 towns, 8 448 villages, 466 township level special regions and 269 849 administrative villages had made master plans.

In 2010, the total investment of towns and townships was 108. 08 million yuan. Classified by purposes, 78. 6% had been invested in housing construction, and 21. 4% in municipal public utilities. The floor space of buildings completed in towns and villages across the country was 974 million square meters; at the end of the year, the total floor space of buildings in towns and villages was 35. 55 billion square meters, and the per capita average floor space of residential buildings was 31. 62 square meters.

Based on statistics, the designated town water popularity rate was 79. 56% , the average daily water consumption per capita was 99. 3 liters, the gas popularity rate was 45. 05% , the average road area per capita was 11. 4 square meters, the drainage & channel density was 5. 29 kilometers per square kilometer, and the average per capita public green space was 2. 03 square meters. The water popularity into rural areas was 65. 64% , the average daily water consumption per capita was 81. 4 liters, gas popularity rate was 18. 98% , the average road area per capita was 11. 24 square meters, drainage & channel density was 3. 12 kilometers per square kilometer, and the average per capita public green space was 0. 88 square meters. The water popularity of township level special region was 85. 02% , the average daily water consumption per capita was 86. 65 liters, the gas popularity rate was 45. 66% , the average road area per capita was 13. 25 square meters, the drainage & channel density was 4. 59 kilometers per square kilometer, and the average per capita public green space was 2. 58 square meters. At the end of 2010, among the administrative villages 52. 3% had central water supply system, 6% had domestic wastewater treatment, 37. 6% had garbage collection stations and 20. 8% had domestic waste treatment.

Ever since to launch the building new socialist countryside, there have been a lot of active exploring from place to place and some achievements as well. However, it should be soberly aware that the widest gap of development in China still remains between urban and rural, and the most serious structural problem still remains to be the urban-rural dual structure. Building new socialist countryside cannot be replaced by the urbanization; neither can we simply apply urban construction methods to the rural development. How to balance the urban and rural development in favor of peasants' production and life, and how to maintain the pleasant ecological environment in the vast countryside and to build a better home for peasants will always be inevitable challenges China has to confront during the process of modernization.

Ⅲ. Focused Points and Issues in Urban Development

(I) Regional planning for the expansion and integration of the economic space

The *Outline of the Twelfth Five-Year Plan for National Economic and Social Development* proposed to implement an overall strategy for regional development. It generally required to "give full play to the relative advantages of different regions, promote the rational flow of the factors of production, deepen regional cooperation, promote the virtuous interactive development between various regions, and gradually reduce the gap of regional development" in order to continually optimize setup and promote coordinated regional development and healthy urbanization.

According to the *Outline*, to promote a new round of the great development of western regions development, it is necessary to promote regional strategic cooperation between Chongqing, Chengdu, and Xi'an in an all-encompassing manner, as well as the accelerated economic development in the economic zones in Hohhot, Baotou and Ordos area, Guangxi's Beibu Gulf, Central Guizhou, Central Yunnan, Central and Southern Tibet, Guanzhong-Tianshui, Lanzhou-Xining, Ningxia along the Yellow River, North Slope of the Tian Mountain. There is a need to nurture a new economic development pole.

To comprehensively invigorate old industrial bases in China's northeastern regions and in other areas, we will promote the transformation and development at resources-depleted regions, and enhance the sustainable development capabilities of cities that have abundant resources. Key emphasis will be given to the regional development of the economy in coastal Liaoning, Shenyang economic zone, Changchun-Jilin-Tumenjiang Economic Zone, Harbin-Daqing-Qiqihar and Mudanjiang-Suifenhe areas.

To greatly promote the emergence of central China area, steps will be quickened to establish an economic belt in areas along the Longhai Railways, the Beijing-Guangzhou Railways, the Beijing-Kowloon Railways, and along the Yangtze River. We will promote the convergence of population and industries and enhance the link and ties with neighboring city clusters. Major efforts will be made to promote the regional development in the Taiyuan City Group, Wanjiang City Belt, Boyang Lake Ecological Economic zone, Zhongyuan Economic Zone in Henan, Wuhan City-Region, and the Changsha-Zhuzhou-Xiangtan City Group.

We will give play to the eastern regions' major guiding and supporting role on the nation's economic development, take part in an even higher level international cooperation and competition, play a pioneering role in reforms and opening up, and advance ahead of the nation in the transformation of the economic development model, in economic structural readjustment, and in indigenous innovation. We will promote the integrated development of the regional economies of Beijing, Tianjin, Hebei, the Yangtze River Delta, the Pearl River Delta, create the Beijing-Tianjin-Hebei economic circle, and give emphasis on promoting the regional development in coastal regions of Hebei, in Jiangsu's coastal regions, Zhoushan Islands in Zhejiang, in western coast economic zone of Taiwan Strait's, and in Shangdong Peninsula's blue economic zone. We will build Hainan Province into an international tourist island.

To further intensify support to old revolutionary base areas, to areas inhabited by various ethnic groups, to border regions, and to impoverished regions, we will enhance infrastructure construction; strengthen ecological protection and restoration; raise public service level; and earnestly improve the production and living conditions in these areas. We will implement projects on tackling poverty in such particularly difficult areas as in Southern Xinjiang, Eastern Areas of Qinghai-Tibet Plateau, Wuling Mountainous Areas, Wumeng Mountainous Areas, Western Yunnan Mountainous Border Areas, Qinba Mountains-Liupan Mountains, and others in Central and Western Regions. The efforts to create jobs instead of providing relief funds for impoverished people and the efforts on relocating impoverished people to other places will be intensified. The building and development of the Xinjiang Production and Construction Corp will be supported. The follow-up development of the Three Gorges Dam area and other dam areas will be promoted. It is necessary to implement the regional mutual assistance policy, and carry out counterpart assistance in various forms.

In 2011, the State Council has approved the *Shandong Peninsula Blue Economic Zone Development Plan*, the *Plan for Demo Marine Economic Zone of Zhejiang*, the *Guangdong*

Marine Economy Comprehensive Experimental Zone Development Plan, the *Hebei coastal development plan*, the *Chengdu-Chongqing Economic Zone Regional Plan*, and the *Pingtan Comprehensive Experimental Zone Overall Development Plan* in sequence; published the *Approval of the Comprehensive Reform of the Overall Program of Zhejiang Yiwu International Trade*, the *Agreement to Set up the Zhoushan Islands New District*, the *Approval of the Relevant Policies for Hengqin Development*, the *Guiding Opinions on Speeding up Construction of the Central Economic Zone in Henan*, the *Approval of the Overall Plan for the Comprehensive Experimental Coordinated Reform to Deepen Cross-strait Exchanges and Cooperation in Xiamen City*. From June 2005 to the end of 2011, the State Council has approved the establishment of 11 national experimental zones for comprehensive coordinated reforms.

As various regional plans appeared successively, we should be aware how to avoid the reappearance of such long-standing problems as the blind launching, the redundant construction, the "beggar my neighbor" policies, and the pursuit of economic growth at the cost of much damage to the environment, how to strengthen the supervision and guidance over the implementation of these plans, and how to fully mobilize the market force to promote planning and construction. In order to achieve the long-term goals of regional coordination and sustainable development, we need to constantly promote the institutional innovation of system and policy design in front of these problems.

(Ⅱ) Launching the construction of 10 million units of low-income housing

Housing standard is an important indicator of social development. Enabling majority of urban households to live in the complete sets of housing which meet the standards of civilization and health is one of the main objectives of building a well-off society in an all-round way by 2020 proposed by Chinese Government.

In recent years, while promoting the urban housing system reform and the commoditization of housing, governments at all levels are actively exploring and improving the housing security system as well. China's per capita floor space of residential buildings has increased from 18.7 square meters in 1998 to 31.6 square meters in 2010. During the Eleventh Five-Year period, construction of 16.3 million units of low-income houses and houses for slum redevelopment was launched, among which 11 million had been completed basically. By the end of 2010, the total number of low-income and part of lower-middle-income urban households whose housing difficulty had been addressed in kind added up to nearly 22 million, and these households who benefited from housing security in kind accounted for 9.4% of the total number of urban households. Besides, there were nearly 4 million low-income urban households with housing difficulty receiving rental subsidies for low-rent housing. The construction of low-income housing has improved the housing conditions of low-income households and played an important role in promoting economic growth and social harmony.

However, by the end of 2010, there were still more than 20 million low-income and a small part of lower-middle-income urban households who were living in incomplete sets with poor facilities. More than 10 million of them lived in slums, which were dilapidated, crowded, with incomplete kitchen and bath facilities and even hidden safety trouble. In addition, the newly employed workers and permanent migrant residents in urban areas with few savings and low housing affordability had to live in basements or urban villages with poor housing conditions. Helping that community who plays an important part in urban economic development to solve the basic living problems will make significant difference to the promotion of economic development and social stability.

According to the requirements of the State Council to increase the construction of low-income housing considerably, the Department of Housing Security of the Ministry of Housing and Urban-Rural Development, the Department of Fixed Asset Investment of the National Development and Reform Commission, and the Comprehensive Department of the Ministry of Finance jointly issued the *Notification of Submitting the Scheduled Tasks of Low-income Housing Projects* on November 23 2010, which proposed a plan to construct 10 million units of low-income houses and houses for slum redevelopment in 2011, and required local authorities to adjust their tasks of 2011 on basis of the original plans for construction of low-income housing and to ensure those plans being implemented by all cities and counties.

On February 27 2011, Premier Wen Jiabao announced during the online communication with netizens on the Chinese Government Network that the government planned to build 10 million units of low-income houses and houses for slum redevelopment that year. The State Council presided over the liability agreements on low-income housing between localities and the central government. 36 million units of low-income housing were scheduled to be constructed in the next five years. The low-income housing would be dominated by low-rent houses and public rental houses, with houses for slum redevelopment included, which was the right direction to go.

As was pointed out in the Report on the Work of the Government at the Fourth Session of the Eleventh National People's Congress, in that year the total number of units of new low-income houses and houses for slum redevelopment would reach 10 million, and 1. 5 million dilapidated rural houses would be renovated. We would give priority to developing public rental housing. The central government was allocating 103 billion yuan in that year's budget for subsidies to support this work, an increase of 26. 5 billion yuan over the previous year. Governments at all levels needed to raise funds through various channels and substantially increased spending in these areas. We would promptly establish an administrative system for the use, operation and return of low-income housing; increase transparency; and strengthen public oversight to ensure that eligible families benefit from low-income housing. Provincial governments had general responsibility and municipal and county governments had direct responsibility for stabilizing housing prices and guaranteeing the availability of low-income housing. Relevant government authorities need to more quickly improve inspection, appraisal, admonition and accountability systems. Localities that put insufficient effort into stabilizing house prices and promoting the construction of low-income housing and thereby affect social development and stability will be held accountable.

Both the scale and difficulty of the construction of low-income housing project in 2011 are unprecedented. Considering the differences in economic and social development, urbanization and housing market conditions from place to place, housing security practices are not encouraged to be the same. Localities should determine housing types according to their own conditions. In 2011, 10 million units of low-income housing consisted of 1. 65 million units of low-rent houses, 2. 27 million units of public rental houses, 1. 1 million units of affordable houses, 830 000 units of capped-price houses, and 4. 15 million houses for slum redevelopment. Besides, another 600 000 households would receive rental subsidies of low-rent housing. At the same time, it was reiterated that the criteria of starting a low-income house project was that the permanent building which had been planned and designed had entered the phase of the structural construction of the foundation. Those only with the construction site enveloped or the foundation pit excavated should not be included in the total amount.

According to preliminary calculations, the construction of low-income housing of 2011 needed an investment of over 1. 3 trillion yuan. Wherein 400 billion would be invested in affordable housing and capped-price housing, which was raised mainly through social investment and balanced with sales; 500 billion would be invested in houses for slum redevelopment, which was partly funded by the government and mainly raised through enterprises and households themselves jointly; over 400 billion would be invested in low-rent housing and public rental housing, which was raised through government at all levels, enterprises, social institutions and so on. The central government had allocated 152. 2 billion yuan in that year's budget for subsidies in batches. Relevant departments had taken measures to strengthen the management of the construction funds, to urge localities to realize the relevant funds effectively, to standardize the application of corporate bond financing, to increase credit support, to promote the pilot projects of housing provident fund loans, and finally to raise construction funds through these multiple channels. In addition, all provinces (autonomous regions and municipalities) had also expanded investment, realized the construction sites of low-income housing, and many localities had dynamically monitored the use and management of low-income housing.

In order to launch the construction of low-income houses and houses for slum redevelopment with the quality and quantity required before the end of November, the General Office of the State Council had organized eight inspection teams to supervise the construction of low-income housing in 16 provinces (autonomous regions, municipalities) including Beijing, Liaoning and

Shanghai. The Ministry of Housing and Urban-Rural Construction had sent permanent inspection officers to each province, who would supervise the starting date, the quality, and the final-period management of the construction. The Ministry of Finance, the Ministry of Land and Resources, the National Development and Reform Commission, the Ministry of Agriculture, the Forestry Bureau and other relevant departments had also strengthened the supervision and inspection.

Minister Jiang Weixin announced at the National Housing and Urban and Rural Construction Working Conference on December 23, 2011 that, under the joint efforts of various localities and departments, the task of constructing 10 million units of low-income houses and houses for slum redevelopment had been overfulfilled ahead of schedule. But in general, since China's low-income housing program still remains in the exploratory stage, there are plenty of conflicts and problems including not only the imperfect housing security system and unsound policies, but also the insufficient management and less than standard implementation. The governments need to summarize this experience in time, improve the system and strengthen management.

(Ⅲ) Moderating traffic congestion and realizing safe travel

Based on the data from the National Bureau of Statistics, till the end of 2010, the total number of motor vehicles for civilian use reached 105.78 million (including 12.28 million tri-wheel motor vehicles and low-speed trucks), up 16.4 percent, of which private-owned vehicles numbered 78.72 million, up 20.4 percent. The total number of cars for civilian use stood at 49.62 million, up by 23.2 percent, of which private-owned cars numbered 43.22 million, up by 25.5 percent. There fourteen cities, including Beijing, Shanghai, Guangzhou, Shenzhen, Tianjin, Chongqing, Chengdu, Shenyang, Wuhan and Xi'an, had over one million motor vehicles. In general, the gap between supply and demand of urban transport has been widened, and the situation of urban transport development mainly featuring frequent traffic congestion became even more severe; the congestion range had expanded from local to the whole area, and the congestion time had spread from rush hours to the whole day with shorter cycle and more intractable nature; driving difficulty, parking difficulty, pedestrian crossing difficulty, disorder and so on will continue to impact China's urban transport development in a certain period. Active innovation and exploration of the ways of moderating urban traffic congestion are of top priority in the management of urban and rural planning and construction in China.

On the statistics of the Traffic Management Bureau of the Ministry of Public Security, the total number of motor vehicle across the nation reached 225 million in 2011, with 236 million drivers. There were 210 812 road traffic accidents involving casualties in the whole year, killing 62 387 persons. The numbers of accidents and deaths dropped by 4% and 4.4% year on year respectively. The deaths of road traffic accidents per 10 000 vehicles were 2.8 persons, a decrease of 12.5%. However, there were still some distressing extraordinarily serious accidents, especially the rear-end accident of electric multiple unit (EMU) trains along the Ningbo-Wenzhou Railways in the territory of Wenzhou City on July 23rd, which killed 40 passengers and injured 172; the train services were suspended for 32 hours and 35 minutes, causing a direct economic loss of 193.7 million yuan. On October 7, a bus (with the design capacity of 53 persons and the actual load of 55) of Tangshan City Transportation Group Co., Ltd. heading from Baoding to Tangshan in Hebei Province scraped against a minibus, which caused the bus to roll over to the right side and ended in 35 deaths and 19 wounded, most of whom were college students of Tangshan with families in Baoding. On November 16th, a school bus (with the design capacity of 9 persons and the actual load of 64) of Little Doctor Kindergarten which was carrying children crashed head-on with a heavy-duty dump truck in Yulinzi, Zhengning County, Qingyang City, Gansu Province, which killed 21 persons (including 19 children) and injured 43.

1. Efforts of the governments at all levels to moderate traffic congestion

The Urban Construction Department of the Ministry Housing and Urban-Rural Development proposed the specific tasks of 2011 that measures to prevent and moderate the urban congestion should be earnestly studied. We should well analyze the existing problems in China's urban transport development and propose measures on the aspects of planning, construction and management of urban transportation infrastructure. Such policies as the *Guiding Opinions on Effectively Strengthening the Planning and Construction of Urban Transport Infrastructure Planning and Construction*, the *Measures for Planning Urban Rail Transit Networks* and the *Guiding Opinions on Planning of Urban Pedestrian and Bicycle Transport Systems* have been researched and formulated, which helps to promote the environment friendly transport and accelerate the construction of pedestrian and bicycle system.

The Ministry of Public Security, the Ministry of Education, the Ministry of Housing and Urban-Rural Construction and the Ministry of Transportation jointly issued the *Guiding opinions on the In-depth Implementation of the Urban Road Traffic Management and Smooth Traffic Project*, proposing 20 items of tasks and measures on seven aspects such as improving the urban traffic management system, giving play to the guiding role of planning, giving priority to the development of public transport, applying integrated controls, improving urban road conditions, implementing scientific traffic organization and management, and synthetically treating the traffic order.

The Beijing municipal government promulgated 66 tasks aiming to moderate the congestion except for such measures as the licensed plate management in rush hours on workdays and staggered rush hour plan which continued to be implemented. The general ideas include giving priority to the development of public transport, accelerating the construction of transport infrastructures, improving the integrated traffic management, and carrying out civil transport construction with comprehensive mobilization of technological, economic, and necessary administrative and legal methods; five major measures including raising the speed of public transportation, securing the capacity of subways, treating traffic order, regulating the order of parking, implementing quantity control to minibuses are proposed as well. Besides, Beijing launched 20 sets of community commuter express, 10 mini bus lines in succession, aiming to solve "the last mile" problem for residents living in the large residential communities such as Tiantongyuan and Huilongguan. In 2011, Beijing's public transport proportion rose to 42%, while the car proportion declined by 1.2 percent for the first time.

During the Twelfth Five-Year Plan period, many cities including Shenzhen, Hangzhou, Wuhan, Ji'nan, Xi'an, Changsha, Ningbo, and so on will take the tasks of moderating urban traffic congestion, speeding up the construction of public transport system, improving the planning and management of parking and protecting a slow travel environment as the important goals of the Twelfth Five-Year. Further strengthening the construction and investment of public transport, taking stringent measures of transportation demand management step by step, and at the same time paying attention to the slow traffic environment have all become the consensus throughout the society and an inevitable trend in future development of China's urban transportation.

2. A long way to go to realize the traffic safety

The Twentieth Plenary Session Meeting of the Standing Committee of the Eleventh National People's Congress on April 22, 2011 adopted the *Decision on the Amendments to the Law of the People's Republic of China on Road Traffic Safety*. The new *Law of Road Traffic Safety* would go into effect as of zero hour of May 1, 2011. According to the new law, whoever drives a motor vehicle after drinking alcohol, or drives a motor vehicle after drinking alcohol again after being punished for such act, or drives an operating motor vehicle after drinking alcohol, or conducts such activities as seriously do harm to the masses, shall be revoked his motor vehicle driving license, and be subject to criminal liability according to law. The corresponding criminal penalties are also ruled in the law. Based on statistics, up until October 31, total 148 651 cases of driving a motor vehicle after drinking alcohol had been investigated, and a decrease of 47.9 percent over the same period of the previous year. Wherein the cases of drunk driving amounted to 26 617, a decrease of 42.7 percent over the same period of the previous year; the deaths in the traffic accidents caused by driving a motor vehicle after drinking alcohol amounted to 467 persons, a decrease of 175 persons and 27.3 percent over the same period of the previous year; the deaths in the traffic accidents caused by drunk driving amounted to 410 persons, a decrease of 94 and 18.7 percent over the same period of the previous year. The investigation of driving a motor vehicle after drinking alcohol has received wide support and response from the society, and has effectively prevented the behavior of drunk driving, and decreased the possibility of accident occurrence.

On November 23, 2011, the Safety Commission Office of the State Council announced the "11.6" major road traffic accident in Qingyang City, Gansu Province, calling on all localities to attach great importance to the school bust traffic safety of primary and middle schools and kindergartens, and to establish the long-term mechanism improving the supervision over school bus traffic safety; to carry out thorough investigation into the hidden safety trouble of school buses and into such violations as overspeed and overload of school buses with "zero tolerance"; to promote the school bus safety publicity and safety education, to educate primary and middle school students to refuse taking the assembled vehicles, scrap vehicles, agricultural vehicles, cargo vehicles and other illegal vehicles and overloaded vehicles before or after school, to remind the students on foot to obey traffic rules and avoid driving vehicles, to remind the parents as well to improve their safety awareness and sense of responsibility as guardians and not to lease vehicles not in line with the safety standards to pick up students; and to implement the accident investigation supervision system, to draw lessons from the accidents, and to effectively realize the road traffic safety, especially the safety of school buses of primary and middle schools (kindergartens).

In order to strengthen the management of school bus safety and to protect the personal safety of traveling children and students, the Legislative Affairs Office of the State Council drafted the *School Bus Safety Bill (draft)*, which was published in full with its specifications for the community comments on December 11, 2011. The Draft gives specific instructions on the school bus service companies, school bus license, school bus drivers, school bus travelling safety, and school bus riding safety, liability and so on; and endows school bus with the supreme right of way so as to protect the personal safety of traveling children and students.

(Ⅳ) Accelerate the construction of urban-rural community service system

Community harmony is the foundation of social harmony. Developing community services and improving the community service system are the important prerequisites for community harmony. Community service system, taking the urban and rural communities as its basic units, the various community services facilities as its foundation, the whole residents and units in communities as its subject, the public services, voluntary mutual aid services and convenient services as its main content, meeting the production and living needs of the residents and improving their quality of life as its goals, is a service network and operating mechanism with the guidance and support of governments and the multiple participation of society.

At present, there are 7 194 urban street offices and 89 000 urban communities across the country. During the Eleventh Five-Year period, localities had implemented the *State Council's Opinions on Strengthening and Improving the Community Service Work* and the *Eleventh Five-Year Plan for Community Service System Development* jointly issued by the National Development and Reform Commission and the Ministry of Civil Affairs, and had made achievements in the construction of urban and rural community service system.

Firstly, we have made some progress in the construction of community service facilities. During the Eleventh Five-Year period, 3 515 Neighborhood Community Service Center and 93 000 Community Service outlets had been completed across the country. There were also some other special community service facilities such as community health service centers (stations) and community cultural centers (rooms) to be constructed.

Secondly, community service items have been continuously expanded. The government public service items including labor employment, social security, social service, living assistance, culture and entertainment, social order and so on are reaching all over the communities step by step. The registration system of community volunteers and community mutual assistance services are also promoted considerably. The arrangement of life support commercial networks including supermarkets, groceries, breakfast outlets received significant attention; such services as housekeeping services, property management, the service of caring the aged and children, food delivery, repair services, waste recycle all gradually enter the communities, which greatly facilitate the residents and improve the quality of their life.

Thirdly, the community service team is growing. The community neighborhood committees whose members were elected according to law are gradually open to the whole society and recruit full-time community service workers. By the end of 2010, there were 153 000 community service facilities across the country; wherein there were 12 720 community service centers, 44 237 community service stations, and 96 000 other community service facilities. There were also 539 000 facilitating service networks in urban areas. There were 439 000 community neighborhood committee members, 1.059 million community service workers, 106 000 volunteer service organizations and 5.076 million volunteers from community residents who were active in various fields of community service and played an important part in promoting community construction and community service.

Fourthly, the measures of community services are continually improved. Based on the street community service centers and stations, many localities have carried out the "one-stop" service; they mobilize the modern information technology to promote the informatization of communities and meet the diverse needs of residents more easily and efficiently. Some localities have guided the social organizations, enterprises and public institutions and residents to participate in the community management and service through the government's purchase of services, the establishment of project funds and the promotion of projects subsidies, which has enhanced the vitality of community service and the capabilities of social organizations.

Fifthly, the preliminary institutional environment of community service has been established. The central government has promulgated laws focusing on the protection of the benefit of the elderly, minors and the disabled, and introduced relevant policies focusing on community health, social assistance, labor employment, cultural education and community service facilities; the local governments have also issued policies and measures which actively promote community service one after another; the policies and regulations of community service have received gradual improvement and increasing attention from the party committees and the governments at all levels; the residents' sense of identity and belonging to the community services is growing.

Practice has proved that strengthening the construction of community service system is a morale project to ensure and improve people's wellbeing and to increase people's living standards and quality of life, a supporting project to stimulate domestic demand, to expand employment and to promote the transformation of the pattern of economic development, and a fundamental project to strengthen and innovate social management and to ensure social harmony and stability.

However, in general, the community service system in China still remains in the primary stage; there are still many difficulties and problems, and opportunities and challenges as well. The prominent problems include the serious imbalance between urban and rural community service development, the severe shortage of community service facilities, the lack of service establishments in streets and communities and the immaturity of rural community service facilities construction. The content of community services urgently needs enrichment, the gap between the community public service of urban and rural areas remains huge, the supply can't meet the demand, and the methods of supply are lack of change; the community service team is short of talent and of low quality, whose structure urgently needs to be optimized. The institution and mechanisms of community service are not smooth enough and lack unified planning with such prominent problems as insufficient investment, fragmented administration and repeated construction; resource integration is far from enough, and the social participation system urgently needs to be improved.

To meet the needs of integrating the urban and rural economic and social development and strengthening and innovating the social administration, to strengthen community self-government and service functions, to ensure and improve people's wellbeing and to promote social harmony and stability, the State Council issued the *Plan for the Construction Community Service System (2011—2015)* which proposed the general idea of building urban and rural communities into a well-managed unified structure of social life featuring perfect service, and civility and harmony.

The specific objectives and tasks of developing community public service during the Twelfth Five-Year period are developing the multi-layered and diversified community labor employment, the social insurance and social services, the community health care and family planning services, the community culture, education and sports services, and the community law and public order services, and making the first step towards the perfect community service facility, service content, service team, service network and operation mechanism till 2015. At the same time, we should establish a mechanism to ensure community service funds which should coordinate with the government investment and social investment, give play to the multiple market subjects, strengthen the construction of community service facilities especially in the city villages, new neighborhoods and communities where special population and migrant population concentrate, and accelerate the formation of community service facility network with the integrated service facility dominating and the special service facility supporting. We should be guided by the residents' demand, integrate community service resources, speed up the informatization of communities, and establish a platform of the community integrated management and service. We should vigorously develop the community service geared to the needs of the whole residents, especially those with financial difficulties, the entitled groups, the elderly, the disabled, minors and rural migrant workers.

Ⅳ. Exploring the Future Path for Inclusive Development

(I) Advocating and practicing the inclusive growth

In September 2010, President Hu Jintao remarked during the APEC meeting that: "China is a strong supporter and follower of inclusive growth, a concept that is consistent with our pursuit of scientific development and social harmony. While speeding up the transformation of economic growth pattern and maintaining stable and relatively fast economic growth, China is committed to integrating economic development with improvement of people's lives. We focus on addressing issues that directly concern people's biggest and most immediate interests, and endeavor to promote social progress designed to improve people's livelihood".

In this regard, he made the four proposals of "giving priority to human resources development, implementing the strategy of full employment, improving the quality and competence of our workers and building a social security system that ensures sustainable development" for the first time to realize inclusive growth.

In April 2011, the Boao Forum for Asia themed by "Inclusive Development: Common Agenda & New Challenges" again discussed the connotation of inclusive development. It sought to maximize the opportunity of development and employment through rapid and sustainable economic growth, and to ensure the basic welfare and equality of opportunity of the people during the entire development process, which provided insight and guidance for the timely transition of the Asian economy and society.

Mr. Zeng Peiyan, the Chief Representative of China at the Boao Forum for Asia, pointed out in his speech that nowadays, the wealth of the whole world was experiencing a rapid growth, but the prosperity did not arrive at every corner on the earth. The reason for that was that the path of traditional development was exclusive to some extent, or, due to some other reasons, created inequality in the participation of different countries in international affairs, and of different groups in political and economic activities, which didn't allow the fruits of civilization progress to not be shared by everyone. He advocated to understand the concept of inclusive development from four aspects: firstly, inclusive development was the development which provided the equal opportunity and share in the fruits for everyone; secondly, inclusive development was the development which promoted the mutual benefit and common progress of all the countries and nations; thirdly, inclusive development was the development which allowed the interaction and compatibleness of various civilizations; fourthly, inclusive development was the development with a virtuous cycle which protected the harmony between human and nature.

Zeng Peiyan believed that inclusive ideology reflected Chinese culture. Traditional Chinese culture emphasizes the oneness of man and nature and following the law of nature, and advocates harmonious coexistence of human and nature. As early as the Warring States period 2 000 years ago, there had already been the brilliant period in which "a hundred schools of thought contended" in China. To date, Chinese humane spirit still features the inclusiveness of and tolerance for diversity. As it were, it is with the inclusiveness that the Chinese civilization can be continuous for thousands of years.

(Ⅱ) Dialogue and exhibition with the urban future

The Sixth session of the World Urban Forum will be held on 1—7 September 2012 in Naples, Italy. The Urban Future replaced the original theme of The Prosperity of Cities of this forum, aiming to discuss one of the most urgent issues faced by the world today: the rapid urbanization and its impact on communities, cities, economy, climate change and policies.

United Nations Secretary-General Ban Ki-moon said: "Humanity's pursuit of dream cities of the future which are beautiful, green, sustainable and humane places, is deserving of all our attention. Imagining the cities of the future, is imagining the very future of humanity, and the cities in which we will be living as our world becomes more and more urbanized."

UN-HABITAT Executive Director Joan Clos said: "the Forum has become the preeminent conference on all things urban. People come together at these events to exchange notes and learn from each other about the problems and opportunities offered by urbanization".

The Forum includes open debates, youth, gender, and business assemblies, caucus meetings, special sessions, roundtables, training seminars and an exciting array of side events, exhibitions and cultural events. The high profile events which will set the tone for the Forum are six dialogues, whose themes are as follows: Productive Cities: Urban job creation, Livable cities and Quality of life; Urban planning: Institutions and Regulations; Equity and prosperity of cities; Culture and prosperity of cities; and Environment, Urban mobility and Energy.

Forum organizers appeal that already more than half the global population lives in towns and cities, and projections now show that cities will be home to two-thirds of humanity in little over a generation from now. This means we have to plan our cities better, ensure sound urban legislation and governance, and improve basic service delivery and housing. At the same time, we have to save energy harder than ever before, conserve our environment, reduce pollution and tackle the urban dimension of climate change very seriously. We need to coordinate these actions and resources for smarter, more livable, less wasteful cities of the future. We owe it to future generations and we owe it especially to the estimated 1 billion people living in slums and other sub-standard housing around the world.

Ⅴ. Conclusion

In retrospect and looking ahead, the following year will be of great significance to China's development process. The Central Economic Work Conference before the new year thoroughly analyzed the domestic and international economic situation, clearly set the tone of making progress while ensuring stability, and required to take the strategic stronghold of domestic demand expansion, to lay the solid foundation of the real economy development, to grasp the powerful motive force of accelerating the innovation, to promote the reform and opening up with greater determination and effort, to solve the institutional and structural conflicts exerting impact on the long-term sound economic development, to make new progress in the transformation of the pattern of development, to strengthen the breakthroughs in reform and opening up, and to realize new achievements in improving people's wellbeing. As regards of the development ideas, we should find out a way of innovative development, leap development, inclusive development and sustainable development.

At the National Science and Technology Award Conference on February 14, 2012, the creator of the Sciences of Human Settlements of China, Professor Wu Liangyong won the 2011 National Top Science and Technology Award. Professor Wu made a series of foresighted and demonstrative achievements in theory and practice during his long academic career and wrote a brilliant chapter for China's urban and rural planning and construction.

The United Nations Conference on Sustainable Development (also known as "Rio + 20" summit) will be held in June 2012 in the famous Brazilian city Rio de Janeiro. At the summit, state leaders and thousands of participants from all sides across the world will come together and discuss how to eliminate poverty, promote social equality, make rational use of resources and protect the environment on a more and more crowded planet. As is pointed out by the Summit Secretary-General Mr. Sha Zukang, "Sustainable development is not an option! It is the only path that allows all of humanity to share a decent life on this, one planet."

(Author: Mao Qizhi, Professor of Tsinghua University, Academician of International Eurasian Academy of Sciences)

2011中国城市发展十大事件

2011年是具有特殊意义的一年，在纪念中国共产党成立90周年和辛亥革命100周年之际，我国的社会结构出现了重大的历史性变化——全国城镇人口首次超过农村人口，城镇化率达到51.27%，标志着中国从一个具有几千年农业文明历史的农民大国，进入以城市社会为主的新成长阶段，这不是简单的城镇人口百分比的变化，它意味着人们的生产方式、职业结构、消费行为、生活方式、价值观念等都将发生极其深刻的变化。

2011年，国务院批复山东半岛蓝色经济区、浙江海洋经济发展示范区、广东海洋经济综合试验区、河北沿海地区、成渝经济区等规划，提出支持河南省加快建设中原经济区的指导意见，有利于促进我国的区域协调和城乡统筹发展；国务院批准设立首个以海洋经济为主题的国家级新区——舟山群岛新区和首个县级市综合改革试点——义乌市国际贸易综合改革试点，有助于进一步探索深化改革、扩大开放的更有效路径。

2011年，备受国人关注的个人所得税、城市房屋拆迁、房地产价格等涉及民生问题有了重大进展。全国人大审议通过个人所得税法修正案，提高了个人所得税的起征标准，调整了税率结构，减轻了中低收入阶层的税负；国务院颁布《国有土地上房屋征收和补偿条例》，为维护公共利益，保障被征收房屋所有权人的合法权益提供了法律依据；中央持续出台房地产市场调控政策，有效遏制了房价持续上涨的势头，全国房价平均环比指数出现下降，调控成效初步显现。

2011年，我国成功举办了国际生态园林盛会，推动了城市生态园林建设。在西安浐灞生态区举行的世界园艺博览会生动演绎了“城市与自然和谐共生”的主题。

2011年，我国发生高铁“7·23”甬温线特别重大交通事故，造成了严重的人员伤亡和财产损失，国务院组成调查组严查事故原因，对相关责任人进行了严肃处理。

一、我国城镇化进入了新的历史进程

2011年12月15日，国务院副总理李克强同志在全国发展和改革工作座谈会上指出：2011年我国城镇人口占总人口的比重超过50%，这是巨大的历史性变化。但总的看，我国城镇化依然明显滞后，不仅远低于发达国家，而且也低于世界平均水平。据有关方面统计，发达国家城市化率一般达到80%，人均收入与我国相近的一些发展中国家城市化率也在

60%以上。我国正处于城镇化快速发展阶段，城镇化不仅可以扩大投资，而且能够促进消费，对扩大内需具有重要推动作用。国际上有经济学家曾经预言，中国的城镇化和美国的高科技是21世纪带动世界经济发展的“两大引擎”。有关方面数据表明，2010年我国农村居民消费水平为4 455元，城镇居民为15 900元，城镇居民消费水平是农村居民的3.6倍。按此测算，一个农民转化为市民，消费需求将会增加1万多元。城镇化率每年提高1个百分点，可以吸纳1 000多万农村人口进城，进而带动1 000多亿元的消费需求，而相应增加的投资需求会更多。目前我国农民工总量达2.4亿人，其中外出农民工约1.5亿人，农村还有相当数量的富余劳动力，城镇化蕴涵的内需潜力巨大。在城乡之间二元结构还没有得到根本改变的同时，城镇内部“二元结构”现象又在显现，后者既包括城镇居民与进城农民工及其家属之间在生产生活条件上形成的差异，也包括城镇历史遗留的棚户区困难群众与大多数市民之间在居住条件上的差异。这是我们面临的矛盾和困难，也是潜力所在。推动解决这种“双二元结构”问题，有利于促进城乡协调发展，减少社会矛盾，释放出城镇化带来的需求潜力。

稳步推进城镇化，必须在充分尊重农民意愿、切实维护农民权益、严格保护耕地的基础上进行。要研究制定我国城镇化发展的中长期规划，出台综合性的政策措施。加强城镇规划和管理，遵循城市发展的客观规律，考虑不同规模和类型城镇的承载能力，合理引导人口流向和产业转移，促进大中小城市和小城镇科学布局、合理分工、功能互补、集约发展。要抓紧制定并有序实施促进农民工融入城市的政策措施，推动城镇社会保障、医疗卫生、教育、文化等基本公共服务覆盖农民工并逐步实现均等化，帮助他们逐步解决就业、住房、医疗和子女教育等方面实际问题，放宽中小城市落户条件，把在城镇已稳定就业和居住的农民工有序转变为城镇居民。要研究出台规范的市政建设投融资政策，进一步完善土地管理制度，搞好综合交通运输体系与城镇化布局体系的衔接，加强公共交通、污染防治、水电气热供应等城镇基础设施建设。应当指出，房地产市场能否健康发展是我国城镇化进程中必须解决好的重大问题。要继续搞好房地产市场调控，巩固调控成果，积极推进保障性安居工程建设，有效增加普通商品住房供给，加快建立促进房地产市场平稳健康发展的长效机制，使城镇化稳步向前推进。

2010年全球城市人口首次超过农村人口

国际红十字会报告称，城市化进程加快正面临巨大风险，10多亿城市人口将被“边缘化”。

西班牙《世界报》2010年9月23日报道，红十字会与红新月会国际联合会发表了2010年世界灾难报告，报告指出，到2020年，全世界将有大约14亿城市人口生活在边缘化状态，居住在非正式聚居区，缺少可降低灾害风险的基础设施和基本服务。

西班牙红十字会总协调员安东尼·布鲁埃尔指出，2010年的灾难报告集中关注城市问题，并对“不可接受的城市风险水平”发出警告，指出历史上城市人口首次超过农村人口，到2050年将超过69%。

报告强调，中低收入国家的25.7亿城市人口是这些高风险面前最为脆弱的人群。随着城市化的快速发展、当地城市管理不善、人口增长、卫生服务欠缺和很多地方城市暴力的日益加剧，这些风险与日俱增。

此外，这些城市人口中相当一部分是气候变化的受害者。布鲁埃尔提醒决策者，要么阻止大量人口涌入城市，要么将会出现越来越难以应对的局面。

一些负责国际合作的组织正在努力阻止人口离开农村，因为对农村地区的管理比城市要容易得多。

布鲁埃尔强调，这种城市新环境迫使人们必须推行新一代国际合作模式。以海地为例，该国首都太子港遭遇地震灾害后，重新安置灾民的难度远不及确认安置点所在土地所有权的难度，这就大大延误了援助工作的进度。

布鲁埃尔称，无论在正常情况还是紧急状态下，土地都已经成为一个重要因素。边缘化聚居区的快速增加也推动了与预防暴力有关的新合作项目，例如红十字会在拉美开展的项目，这在几年前还是无法想象的，因为当时类似的项目大多在农村地区开展。

报告强调，2000—2008年平均每年有5万多人死于地震，还有1亿多人可能受到洪水的侵害，并成为受害最严重城市中的脆弱群体。

红十字会认为，一个好的政府必须保障城市居民都接受教育，并参与到城市环境的发展中来，而不是将他们边缘化，让他们暴露于灾害、气候变化、暴力和卫生条件恶化的危害之下。

报告还指出，强制拆迁是城市贫困人口面临的持续威胁。报告透露，每年都有数以百万计的人口被施政当局强行迁徙，有的是为了实施改造或美化计划，有的只是为了将这些当局不欢迎的群体赶走。

关于千年发展目标框架内开展的一些让人们留在农村、让他们更好地发展、吃的更好、拥有更好的未来的行动，布鲁埃尔予以高度评价。

他说："从农村来到城市缺乏生活条件的人，从来到城市第一天开始就直接成为脆弱群体。"

（资料来源：《参考消息》2010年9月26日发表的文章）

二、国务院批准设立浙江舟山群岛新区

2011年6月30日，国务院下发了《关于同意设立浙江舟山群岛新区的批复》（国函〔2011〕77号），原则同意设立浙江舟山群岛新区。这是继上海浦东新区、天津滨海新区和重庆两江新区后，党中央、国务院决定设立的又一个国家级新区，也是国务院批准的我国首个以海洋经济为主题的国家战略层面新区。

浙江舟山群岛新区范围与舟山市行政区域一致，包括舟山1 390个岛屿，陆域面积1 440平方公里、内海海域面积2.08万平方公里，区位条件、海洋资源、海洋产业等综合优势明显，在全国沿海开发开放中具有重要地位。

国务院批复要求，舟山群岛新区建设要以改革为动力，以先行先试为契机，坚持高起点

规划、高标准建设、高水平管理。舟山群岛新区作为浙江海洋经济发展的先导区、海洋综合开发试验区和长江三角洲地区经济发展的重要增长极，要加强体制机制创新，扩大对外开放，逐步建成中国大宗商品储运中转加工交易中心、东部地区重要的海上开放门户、海洋海岛科学保护开发示范区、重要的现代海洋产业基地、陆海统筹发展先行区，在推动浙江经济社会发展、推进东部地区发展方式转变、促进全国区域协调发展中发挥更大作用。

国务院批复认为，设立并建设好浙江舟山群岛新区，对于深化海洋管理体制改革、创新海洋海岛综合保护开发方式、加快转变经济发展方式具有重要意义。各有关方面要统一思想，密切配合，开拓创新，扎实工作，共同推动浙江舟山群岛新区又好又快发展。

浙江舟山海岛新区的设想源于2010年2月启动的中国工程院、国家开发银行和浙江省人民政府合作的重大咨询项目——“浙江沿海与岛屿综合开发战略研究”。该项目研究认为：舟山群岛是我国开拓走出大陆通道、开发西太平洋资源的战略前进基地，具有重要的资源和区位优势。建议将“建设舟山群岛新区”作为国家战略列入国家“十二五”规划。该建议得到国务院及有关部门的高度重视。

2011年3月14日，十一届全国人大四次会议审议通过的《国民经济和社会发展第十二个五年规划纲要》中，明确提出要重点推进浙江舟山群岛新区发展。2011年4月1日，国务院总理温家宝在听取中国工程院《浙江沿海及海岛综合开发战略研究综合报告》的汇报后说：报告基础研究扎实，战略目标清晰，发展重点明确，政策建议具体可行，对于科学编制发展规划、研究制定相关政策有重要的参考价值。

舟山十大历史事件

舟山的历史大多与海有关，因海兴衰，与海起伏，因此也可以说是中国近代海洋历史的一个缩影。

1. 6000年前，“海上河姆渡”发祥

这是舟山最早的历史印记。20世纪70年代以来，舟山马岙发现了大量的陶器、石器，经专家鉴定，是早在6000年前舟山古人类活动的遗迹，史称“海上河姆渡”。舟山的海洋文明可谓源远流长，岱山衢山孙家山遗址、定海白泉十字路遗址、岱山大舜庙后墩遗址等一大批新石器时代遗址，都证明了舟山有着光辉的史前文明，这正是舟山海洋文化发展的源头，舟山也成为人类最早走向海洋的地方之一。

2. 始皇帝遣徐福东渡途经舟山

徐福东渡的故事在舟山的许多旧志上都可以找到记载。而徐福东渡的历史意义不仅在于此，这是舟山历史上对外交流的一个开端，古有“海上丝绸之路”，舟山就是其中一个重要节点，鉴真东渡、郑和下西洋以及无数次的东南亚贸易都以舟山为起点或中转站，这是舟山海洋文明最重要的一段见证。

3. 公元738年，设翁山县

唐开元二十六年（738年），舟山设翁山县，这是国家第一次为舟山命名。舟山建立县治后，建造了城墙，秩序安定，人口增长，社会繁荣。但仅过了33年，随着袁晁起义，占领翁山县，翁山县被废，300年后，才又重新设立县治，名昌国，而国家已经改朝换代，是为北宋时期。翁山县虽然只有33年，但是对于舟山的意义非常，舟山从此告别了“蛮荒时代”。

4. 宋高宗避金兵至昌国

北宋建炎三年（1129年），当时的皇帝宋高宗为避金兵至舟山（昌国），从舟山出海至南方。宋高宗也成为封建时期唯一一位到过舟山的皇帝，而当时选择从舟山出海，亦体现了当时的历史社会环境。当时舟山是明州的一部分，是重要的港口，也是江南的富庶之地，造船业发达。这足以证明舟山当时已经在国家中有了一定的地位。

5. 双屿港兴衰荡气回肠

明嘉靖年间，有一群崇尚自由贸易的海商活跃在舟山的六横岛双屿港，他们由葡萄牙商人、日本浪人和以王直为首的海商组成，不过当时国家对他们的定位是“海盗”，这群人成就了当时东亚最大的自由贸易港——双屿港，鼎盛一时。当然，双屿港在当时统治者的眼里是走私贸易的基地，因此朝廷出兵进行围剿，“海盗”溃败，双屿港被填。有史学家称，双屿港的消失，让中国错失了一次走向海洋的机会，让中国的海洋经济延后了数百年。

6. 南明鲁王移驻舟山

李自成占领北京，明朝宣告灭亡，朱氏王朝的残余势力纷纷在南方建立政权，以图东山再起，这就是历史上所谓的“南明”，鲁王朱以海便是其中的一支。1649年，鲁王自闽移驻舟山，建鲁王行宫，号召“反清复明”，一时声势浩大。清政府也组织重兵进攻舟山，当时舟山城内的军民进行了永载史册的抗清斗争，清军屠城，史称“辛卯之乱”。至今，舟山仍有南明抗清的三处遗址，分别是定海海山公园的“同归域”、六横悬山岛的张煌言蒙难处、舟山警备区司令部院内的宫井。

7. 康熙颁布“展海令”，赐“定海山”

明清时期的两次“海禁”让舟山一度荒废，直到康熙二十三年（1684年），朝廷颁“展海令”，开海禁，舟山开始展复，渔业农业渐兴。两年后，康熙接受了总兵黄大来的上疏，恢复县治，并把舟山改名“定海山”，并题写匾额，如今匾额存于昌国路上的御书楼。从此，舟山的历史再无因为动乱和海禁的影响而断代，舟山也走上了繁荣发展的道路，定海的地名也沿袭至今。

8. 第一次鸦片战争三总兵激战舟山

舟山是第一次鸦片战争中的主战场。1840年，英军入侵定海港。定海总兵张朝发率军应战，重伤回城，定海城陷。知县姚怀祥投梵宫池殉职。舟山人民自发保卫定海，英军伤亡惨重。一年后，英军退而重犯，定海镇总兵葛云飞、寿春镇总兵王锡朋、处州镇总兵郑国鸿英勇反击，激战6昼夜，三总兵及大部兵卒阵亡。定海再次沦陷。1846年，钦差大臣耆英与英国代表德庇时签订《退还舟山条约》。七月，英军退出舟山。史学家称“中英开战以来，定海抵抗最力，英军受创不小”。

9. 1950年，舟山解放

解放战争后期，国民党十万大军退败至舟山。中国人民解放军经过一年的艰苦战争，历经登步岛战役在内的数次血战，终于在1950年5月17日，分东、西、中三路解放舟山岛。舟山从此走上了崭新的发展道路。

10. 浙江舟山群岛新区被纳入国家战略

2011年3月14日，舟山群岛新区正式写入全国“十二五”规划，规划瞄准新加坡、香港世界一流港口城市，要拉动整个长江流域的经济。6月30日，国务院下发了《关于同意设立浙江舟山群岛新区的批复》，原则同意设立浙江舟山群岛新区，舟山成为中国继上海浦东、天津滨海和重庆两江后又一个国家级新区，也是首个以海洋经济为主题的国家级新区。

（资料来源：据舟山新区网站整理）

2011年国务院批复的沿海地区发展规划

1. 山东半岛蓝色经济区发展规划

2011年1月，国务院正式批复《山东半岛蓝色经济区发展规划》。这是我国第一个以海洋经济为主题、兼顾海陆统筹的区域发展的战略，也是“十二五”开局之年的首个国家战略。

规划的主体区范围包括：山东全部海域和青岛、东营、烟台、潍坊、威海、日照6市及滨州市的无棣、沾化2个沿海县的陆域，共涉及51个县市区，海域面积15.95万平方公里，陆域面积6.4万平方公里。

规划的战略定位是：建设具有较强国际竞争力的现代海洋产业集聚区、具有世界先进水平的海洋科技教育核心区、国家海洋经济改革开放先行区和全国重要的海洋生态文明示范区。

2. 浙江海洋经济发展示范区规划

2011年2月，国务院正式批复《浙江海洋经济发展示范区规划》。这是继山东蓝色半岛经济区上升为国家战略后，又一个主打海洋经济的国家级区域发展规划，有利于提升浙江的海洋生产力。

示范区规划范围包括：杭州、宁波、温州、嘉兴、绍兴、舟山、台州7个市47个县（市、区），海域面积26万平方公里，陆域面积3.5万平方公里。

示范区规划的战略定位是：建成我国重要的大宗商品国际物流中心、现代海洋产业发展示范区、海陆协调发展示范区、海洋生态文明和清洁能源示范区。

3. 广东海洋经济综合试验区发展规划

2011年7月，国务院正式批复《广东海洋经济综合试验区发展规划》。这是我国第三个主打海洋经济的国家级区域规划。广东省海岸线长，海域面积广，优质港口众多，同时紧邻港、澳地区和东南亚，有着优越的区域开发优势。

综合试验区规划的主体区范围，涵盖了广东省全部海域和广州、深圳、珠海、汕头、惠州、汕尾、东莞、中山、江门、阳江、湛江、茂名、潮州、揭阳14个市，海域面积41.9万平方公里，陆域面积8.4万平方公里。

综合试验区的战略定位是：建设成为我国提升海洋经济国际竞争力的核心区、促进海洋科技创新和成果高效转化的集聚区、加强海洋生态文明建设的示范区和推进海洋综合管理的先行区。

4. 河北沿海地区发展规划

2011年11月，国务院批复《河北沿海地区发展规划》。这标志着河北省沿海地区发展正式上升为国家战略，至此，我国1.8万公里海岸线实现了国家规划的“全覆盖”。

河北沿海地区毗邻京津，东临渤海，面向东北亚，是京津城市功能拓展和产业转移的重要承接地，是华北、西北地区重要的出海口和对外开放门户。规划范围包括秦皇岛、唐山、沧州三市所辖行政区域，陆域面积3.57万平方公里，海岸线487公里，海域面积0.7万平方公里。

河北沿海地区的战略定位是：环渤海地区新兴增长区域、京津城市功能拓展和产业转移的重要承接地、全国重要的新型工业化基地、我国开放合作的新高地、我国北方沿海生态良好的宜居区。

（资料来源：摘自相关的区域规划）

三、国务院批复成渝经济区区域规划

2011年4月24日，国务院正式批复《成渝经济区区域规划》。这是国家推动科学发展、加快转变经济发展方式的重要战略部署，也是深入实施西部大开发、促进区域协调发展的又一重大举措。

成渝经济区位于长江上游，地处四川盆地，面积20.6万平方公里，是我国重要的人口、城镇、产业集聚区，包括重庆市31个区县和四川省15个市，自然禀赋优良，产业基础较好，城镇分布密集，交通体系完整，人力资源丰富，是我国重要的人口、城镇、产业集聚区，是引领西部地区加快发展、提升内陆开放水平、增强国家综合实力的重要支撑，在我国经济社会发展中具有重要的战略地位。

国务院要求，《规划》实施要以科学发展为主题，以加快转变经济发展方式为主线，着力推动区域一体化发展，着力推进统筹城乡改革，着力提升发展保障能力，着力保障和改善民生，着力发展内陆开放型经济，着力构建长江上游生态安全屏障，努力实现居民收入增长与经济发展同步提高，经济发展更多依靠科技创新驱动，在带动西部地区发展和促进全国区域协调发展中发挥更重要的作用。

依据《规划》，成渝经济区的战略定位是：建成西部地区重要的经济中心、全国重要的现代产业基地、深化内陆开放的试验区、统筹城乡发展的示范区和长江上游生态安全的保障区。

在总体布局上，要根据资源环境承载能力和发展基础，统筹区域发展空间布局，依托中心城市和长江黄金水道、主要陆路交通干线，形成以重庆、成都为核心，沿江、沿线为发展带的“双核五带”空间格局，即重庆成都双核、沿长江发展带、成绵乐发展带、成内渝发展带、成南（遂）渝发展带、渝广达发展带，推动区域协调发展。

在城乡统筹上，要加快新型城镇化进程，加强社会主义新农村建设，形成城镇化和新农村建设互促共进机制，构建城乡经济社会一体化发展的新格局。推进统筹城乡综合配套改革试验，完善有利于科学发展的体制机制，建立内陆开放型经济体系。

在产业发展和基础设施建设上，要推动产业结构优化升级，加快农业现代化，走新型工业化道路，提升服务业发展水平，建成特色鲜明、优势突出、具有竞争力的现代产业基地；要按照统筹规划、合理布局、适度超前、安全可靠的原则，推进交通、水利、能源、信息等重大基础设施一体化建设，形成分工合理、功能完善、保障有力的基础设施体系，增强区域发展支撑能力。

《规划》明确了发展的近期目标和远期目标，到 2015 年，经济实力显著增强，建成西部地区重要的经济中心。地区生产总值占全国的比重达到 7%，人均地区生产总值达到 39 000元，城镇化率达到 52%，城乡居民收入差距由目前的 3. 3:1 缩小到 2. 8:1。到 2020 年，经济社会发展水平进一步提高，成为我国综合实力最强的区域之一。人均地区生产总值达到 65 000元，城镇化率达到 60%。

成渝经济区区域性中心城市发展定位

万州：能源化工、新型建材、轻纺食品、机械电子、商贸物流基地，经济区东北部的中心城市、综合交通枢纽和重要的港口城市。

涪陵：天然气精细化工、生物制药、机械制造、轻纺食品、商贸物流基地，经济区东部的中心城市。

长寿：石油天然气化工、冶金建材、合成材料基地，区域性专用物流节点城市。

江津：先进制造、能源建材、食品加工、商贸物流、休闲旅游基地，重要的港口城市。

合川：能源建材、机械制造、电子信息、轻纺食品基地，重要的物流节点和旅游城市。

永川：装备制造、电子信息、商贸物流、休闲旅游基地，西部职业教育城。

德阳：全国重要的重型装备制造业基地，重要的新材料、精细化工、食品加工基地，现代工业城市。

绵阳：电子信息、科研生产基地，经济区西北部的中心城市和国家科技城。

眉山：机车制造、冶金建材、精细化工、特色农产品加工基地和国家粮食储备基地，重要的交通节点城市。

资阳：全国重要的机车制造及出口基地，汽车与零部件制造、节能产品生产、食品生产配送、会展基地和旅游休闲度假目的地，新兴工业城市。

遂宁：精细化工、电子信息、食品饮料、商贸物流基地，重要的交通节点城市。

乐山：清洁能源、新材料、冶金建材产业基地，生态和文化旅游胜地，重要的交通节点和港口城市。

雅安：农产品加工、清洁能源产业基地，交通节点和生态旅游城市。

泸州：饮料食品、天然气和煤化工、能源、装备制造基地和商贸物流中心，重要的交通节点和港口城市。

自贡：盐卤化工、机械制造、新材料、物流配送基地，现代工业城市。

宜宾：饮料食品、能源轻纺、机械制造和商贸物流基地，重要的交通节点和港口城市。

内江：农产品加工、冶金建材、汽车零部件生产、再生资源综合利用基地，重要的商贸物流节点城市。

南充：石油天然气精细化工、汽车及零部件、轻纺服装、有机农产品加工、能源基地和商贸物流中心，经济区北部的中心城市、重要交通节点和港口城市。

广安：精细化工、新能源、新材料、有色金属加工、汽车及汽摩零部件制造、特色农产品加工和供应、红色旅游基地，重要的交通物流节点和港口城市。

达州：天然气和磷硫化工、冶金建材、农产品加工基地，重要的商贸物流节点城市。

（资料来源：摘自《成渝经济区区域规划》）

四、国务院支持河南省加快建设中原经济区

2011年9月28日，国务院出台《国务院关于支持河南省加快建设中原经济区的指导意见》（国发〔2011〕32号），提出了包括“总体要求”在内十个方面共45条指导意见，标志着建设中原经济区作为国家战略已进入实施阶段。

中原地处我国中心地带，是中华民族和华夏文明的重要发源地。中原经济区是以全国主体功能区规划明确的重点开发区域为基础、中原城市群为支撑、涵盖河南全省、延及周边地区的经济区域，地理位置重要，粮食优势突出，市场潜力巨大，文化底蕴深厚，在全国改革发展大局中具有重要战略地位。

《指导意见》认为：河南省是人口大省、粮食和农业生产大省、新兴工业大省，解决好工业化、城镇化和农业现代化（以下简称“三化”）协调发展问题具有典型性和代表性。积极探索不以牺牲农业和粮食、生态和环境为代价的“三化”协调发展的路子，是中原经济区建设的核心任务。支持河南省加快建设中原经济区，是巩固提升农业基础地位，保障国家粮食安全的需要；是破除城乡二元结构，加快新型工业化、城镇化进程的需要；是促进“三化”协调发展，为全国同类地区创造经验的需要；是加快河南发展，与全国同步实现全面建设小康社会目标的需要；是带动中部地区崛起，促进区域协调发展的需要。

《指导意见》要求，坚持以科学发展为主题，以加快转变经济发展方式为主线，探索不以牺牲农业和粮食、生态和环境为代价的工业化、城镇化和农业现代化协调发展的路子，进一步解放思想、抢抓机遇，进一步创新体制、扩大开放，着力稳定提高粮食综合生产能力，着力推进产业结构和城乡结构调整，着力建设资源节约型和环境友好型社会，着力保障和改善民生，着力促进文化发展繁荣，以新型工业化、城镇化带动和提升农业现代化，以农业现代化夯实城乡共同繁荣的基础，推动中原经济区实现跨越式发展，在支撑中部地区崛起和服务全国大局中发挥更大作用。

《指导意见》确定的战略定位是：

——国家重要的粮食生产和现代农业基地。集中力量建设粮食生产核心区，巩固提升在保障国家粮食安全中的重要地位；大力发展畜牧业生产，建设全国重要的畜产品生产和加工

基地；加快转变农业发展方式，发展高产、优质、高效、生态、安全农业，培育现代农业产业体系，不断提高农业专业化、规模化、标准化、集约化水平，建成全国农业现代化先行区。

——全国工业化、城镇化和农业现代化协调发展示范区。在加快新型工业化、城镇化进程中同步推进农业现代化，探索建立工农城乡利益协调机制、土地节约集约利用机制和农村人口有序转移机制，加快形成城乡经济社会发展一体化新格局，为全国同类地区发展起到典型示范作用。

——全国重要的经济增长板块。提升中原城市群整体竞争力，建设先进制造业和现代服务业基地，打造内陆开放高地、人力资源高地，成为与长江中游地区南北呼应、带动中部地区崛起的核心地带之一，引领中西部地区经济发展的重要引擎，支撑全国发展的重要区域。

——全国区域协调发展的战略支点和重要的现代综合交通枢纽。充分发挥承东启西、连南贯北的区位优势，加速生产要素集聚，强化东部地区产业转移、西部地区资源输出和南北区域交流合作的战略通道功能；加快现代综合交通体系建设，促进现代物流业发展，形成全国重要的现代综合交通枢纽和物流中心。

——华夏历史文明传承创新区。传承弘扬中原文化，充分保护和科学利用全球华人根亲文化资源；培育具有中原风貌、中国特色、时代特征和国际影响力的文化品牌，提升文化软实力，增强中华民族凝聚力，打造文化创新发展区。

《规划》明确了发展的近期目标和远期目标，到 2015 年，粮食综合生产能力稳步提高，产业结构继续优化，城镇化质量和水平稳步提升，“三化”发展协调性不断增强，基本公共服务水平和均等化程度全面提高，居民收入增长与经济发展同步，生态环境逐步改善，资源节约取得新进展，初步形成发展活力彰显、崛起态势强劲的经济区域。到 2020 年，粮食生产优势地位更加稳固，工业化、城镇化达到或接近全国平均水平，综合经济实力明显增强，城乡基本公共服务趋于均等化，基本形成城乡经济社会发展一体化新格局，建设成为城乡经济繁荣、人民生活富裕、生态环境优良、社会和谐文明，在全国具有重要影响的经济区。

《指导意见》空间布局：按照“核心带动、轴带发展、节点提升、对接周边”的原则，形成放射状、网络化空间开发格局。“核心带动”，提升郑州交通枢纽、商务、物流、金融等服务功能，推进郑（州）汴（开封）一体化发展，建设郑（州）洛（阳）工业走廊，增强引领区域发展的核心带动能力。“轴带发展”，依托亚欧大陆桥通道，壮大沿陇海发展轴；依托京广通道，拓展纵向发展轴；依托东北西南向、东南西北向运输通道，培育新的发展轴，形成“米”字形重点开发地带。“节点提升”，逐步扩大轴带节点城市规模，完善城市功能，推进错位发展，提升辐射能力，形成大中小城市合理布局、城乡一体化发展的新格局。“对接周边”，加强对外联系通道建设，促进与毗邻地区融合发展，密切与周边经济区的合作，实现优势互补、联动发展。

《指导意见》从“着力提高粮食生产能力，积极推进农业现代化；加快新型工业化进程，构建现代产业体系；积极推进城镇化，促进城乡一体化发展；加强基础设施建设，提高发展保障水平；加强资源节约和环境保护，大力推进生态文明建设；全面提升公共服务水平，切实保障和改善民生；弘扬中原大文化，增强文化软实力；推进体制机制创新，扩大对内对外开放”等八个方面部署了重点任务，并提出了强化组织实施、加大政策支持和加强指导协调等三条保障措施。

《指导意见》最后指出，建设中原经济区，事关促进中部地区崛起和区域协调发展总体战略，是一项重大而艰巨的历史任务。国务院有关部门和有关地方要进一步统一思想，提高认识，锐意进取，扎实工作，全面落实意见提出的各项任务，推动中原经济区实现跨越式发展，为服务全国发展大局做出更大贡献。

五、国务院批准义乌国际贸易综合改革试点

2011 年 3 月 4 日，国务院下发了《关于浙江省义乌市国际贸易综合改革试点总体方案的批复》(国函〔2011〕22 号)。这是继国家设立 9 个综合配套改革试验区之后，经国务院批准设立的又一个综合改革试点，是浙江省第一个国家级综合改革试点，也是全国首个由国务院批准的县级市综合改革试点。

浙江省义乌市拥有我国最大的小商品市场，是重要的国际贸易窗口。改革开放以来，义乌市积极探索对外贸易新模式，在扩大出口、增加就业、带动中小企业发展等方面取得积极成效。在义乌开展国际贸易综合改革试点，通过大胆探索、先行先试，充分发挥市场在资源配置中的基础性作用，充分发挥义乌市场在全球分工体系中的独特作用，通过大胆探索、先行先试，加快转变外贸发展方式，推动内外贸协调发展，形成经济全球化条件下参与国际经济合作和竞争新优势。

根据《规划》，义乌将承担起探索建立新型贸易方式、优化出口商品结构、加强义乌市场建设、探索现代流通新方式、推动产业转型升级、开拓国际市场、加快“走出去”步伐、推动内外贸一体化发展、应对国际贸易摩擦和壁垒 9 方面的试点主要任务。

《规划》进一步提出了优化国际贸易发展环境、健全金融机构体系、提升金融服务能力、改善金融生态环境、构筑区域合作优势和新型公共服务体系 6 方面的保障措施。

义乌试点的目标是，到 2015 年，基本形成有利于科学发展的新型贸易体制框架。到 2020 年，率先实现贸易发展方式转变，提升义乌在国际贸易中的战略地位，使义乌成为转变外贸发展方式示范区、带动产业转型升级的重要基地、世界领先的国际小商品贸易中心和宜商宜居宜游的国际商贸名城。

2011 年 5 月 6 日，义乌市召开国际贸易综合改革试点工作动员大会，研究义乌市国际贸易综合改革试点三年实施计划，对义乌市国际贸易综合改革试点工作进行部署。义乌市将通过三年努力，基本确立“市场采购”新型贸易方式，形成贸易便利化的政策支撑体系；初步建成展示交易、交通物流、产业升级、区域合作、公共服务五大平台，形成出口、进口、转口和服务贸易协调发展新优势；率先建立适应国际贸易发展需要的行政管理体制和公共服务体制，形成良好的制度环境和政策保障，为加快转变外贸发展方式奠定坚实的体制基础。

国家设立的综合配套改革试验区

国家综合配套改革试验区的设立是我国在经济社会发展的新阶段，在科学发展观的指导下，为促进地方经济社会发展而推出的一项新的举措。它是我国改革开放后继深圳等第一批经济特区后建立的第二批经济特区，即中国的“新特区”。

国家设立综合配套改革试验区的目的，是为了探索建设和谐社会、创新区域发展模式、提升区域乃至国家竞争力的新思维、新思想、新路径、新模式和新道路，通过选择一批有特点和有代表性的区域进行综合配套改革，以期为全国的经济体制改革、政治体制改革、文化体制改革和社会各方面的改革提供新的经验和思路。

综合配套改革试验区设立的核心在于“综合配套”，其宗旨是要改变多年形成的单纯强调经济增长的发展观，要从经济发展、社会发展、城乡关系、土地开发和环境保护等多个领域推进改革，形成相互配套的管理体制和运行机制。

实施综合配套改革试点是我国改革向纵深推进的战略部署。实施综合配套改革，能够合理解决经济体制改革的系统性和配套性，增强各方面、各领域、各层次改革的协调性、联动性和配套性，有利于建立健全充满活力、富有效率、更加开放的体制机制，建立起完善的社会主义市场经济体制。

截至2011年底，国家已批准设立了12个综合配套改革试验区：

1. 2005年6月，国务院批准成立上海浦东新区综合配套改革试点；

2. 2006年5月，国务院批准设立天津滨海新区综合配套改革试验区；

3. 2007年6月，国务院批准设立重庆市全国统筹城乡综合配套改革试验区；

4. 2007年6月，国务院批准设立成都市全国统筹城乡综合配套改革试验区；

5. 2007年6月，国家发改委批准设立武汉城市圈全国资源节约型和环境友好型社会建设综合配套改革试验区；

6. 2007年6月，国家发改委批准设立长株潭城市群全国资源节约型和环境友好型社会建设综合配套改革试验区；

7. 2009年5月，国务院正式批复《深圳市综合配套改革总体方案》；

8. 2010年4月，国家发改委批准设立沈阳经济区国家新型工业化综合配套改革试验区；

9. 2010年12月，国家发改委批准设立山西省国家资源型经济转型综合配套改革试验区；

10. 2011年3月，国务院正式批复《义乌市国际贸易综合改革试点总体方案》；

11. 2011年6月，国务院下发了《关于同意设立浙江舟山群岛新区的批复》，原则同意设立浙江舟山群岛新区；

12. 2011年12月，国务院正式批复《厦门市深化两岸交流合作综合配套改革试验总体方案》。

（资料来源：摘自国家发布的相关文件）

六、全国人大审议通过个人税所得法修正案

2011年3月1日，国务院总理温家宝主持召开国务院常务会议，讨论并原则通过《中华人民共和国个人所得税法修正案（草案）》。这标志着自1980年施行以来的个人所得税法将与时俱进，作重大修改。

4月20日，十一届全国人大常委会第二十次会议初次审议了《中华人民共和国个人所得税法修正案（草案）》。草案将工资薪金所得减除费用标准由现行的每月2 000元提高到每月3 000元；调整了工资薪金所得税率级次级距，将现行工薪所得9级超额累进税率修改为7级，加大了对高收入者的调节力度；相应调整个体工商户生产经营所得和承包承租经营所得税率级距；延长了申报缴纳税款时间。

4月25日，全国人大常委会办公厅将《中华人民共和国个人所得税法修正案（草案）》及草案说明在中国人大网公布，向社会公开征集意见。在36天时间内，共收集到23.8万条意见。同时书面征求了各地方、中央有关部门和部分企业、高等院校、研究机构的意见，还专门召开座谈会直接听取专家和公众代表的意见。

5月10日和20日，全国人大法律委员会、财政经济委员会和全国人大常委会法制工作委员会联合召开座谈会，分别听取了11位专家和16位来自不同地区、不同职业、不同收入群体具有一定代表性的社会公众对草案的意见。

6月30日，全国人大常委会表决通过了修改的《个人所得税法》，同日，国家主席胡锦涛签署第48号主席令予以公布，自2011年9月1日起施行。

《个人所得税法》修改的主要内容是：将工资、薪金所得项目减除费用标准由每月2 000元提高到每月3 500元；税率由9级调整为7级，取消了15%和40%两档税率，将5%最低税率改为3%，并拉大了6个税率档次的级距；调整了对企事业单位的承包经营、承租经营所得的税率级距，对五档税率级距相应作了2～3倍的扩大调整；扣缴义务人每月所扣的税款，自行申报纳税人每月应纳的税款，缴入国库的时间改为“在次月十五日内缴入国库”，与其他主要税种的申报缴纳时间一致。

修改后的《个人所得税法》，通过对个人税收的调整，切实提高了普通工薪阶层的收入水平，同时有效调节了个人的过高收入，更加体现了公平，有利于营造社会的公平环境和防止贫富差距过大引起的社会矛盾，体现了中国特色社会主义经济制度的优越性。

7月19日，温家宝总理签署第600号国务院令，发布了《关于修改〈中华人民共和国个人所得税法实施条例〉的决定》，与新的《个人所得税法》同步施行。个人所得税法实施条例修改的主要内容是：计算对企事业单位的承包经营、承租经营所得的应纳税所得额时，减除必要费用的标准由“按月减除2 000元”修改为“按月减除3 500元”；对在中国境内无住所而在中国境内取得工资、薪金所得的纳税义务人和在中国境内有住所而在中国境外取得工资、薪金所得的纳税义务人，可以根据其平均收入水平、生活水平以及汇率变化情况确定附加减除费用，附加减除费用标准由“每月2 800元”改为“每月1 300元”。

个人所得税税率表一
（工资、薪金所得适用）

级数	全月应纳税所得额		税率（%）	速算扣除数
	含税级距	不含税级距		
1	不超过 1 500 元的	不超过 1 455 元的	3	0
2	超过 1 500 元至 4 500 元的部分	超过 1 455 元至 4 155 元的部分	10	105
3	超过 4 500 元至 9 000 元的部分	超过 4 155 元至 7 755 元的部分	20	555
4	超过 9 000 元至 35 000 元的部分	超过 7 755 元至 27 255 元的部分	25	1 005
5	超过 35 000 元至 55 000 元的部分	超过 27 255 元至 41 255 元的部分	30	2 755
6	超过 55 000 元至 80 000 元的部分	超过 41 255 元至 57 505 元的部分	35	5 505
7	超过 80 000 元的部分	超过 57 505 元的部分	45	13 505

个人所得税税率表二
（个体工商户的生产、经营所得和对企事业单位的承包经营、承租经营所得适用）

级数	全年应纳税所得额		税率（%）	速算扣除数
	含税级距	不含税级距		
1	不超过 15 000 元的	不超过 14 250 元的	5	0
2	超过 15 000 元至 30 000 元的部分	超过 14 250 元至 27 750 元的部分	10	750
3	超过 30 000 元至 60 000 元的部分	超过 27 750 元至 51 750 元的部分	20	3 750
4	超过 60 000 元至 100 000 元的部分	超过 51 750 元至 79 750 元的部分	30	9 750
5	超过 100 000 元的部分	超过 79 750 元的部分	35	14 750

资料来源：《个人所得税法》。

七、国务院颁布房屋征收和补偿条例

2011 年 1 月 19 日，国务院第 141 次常务会议讨论并原则通过了《国有土地上房屋征收与补偿条例》。

1 月 21 日，国务院总理温家宝签署第 590 号国务院令，公布《国有土地上房屋征收与补偿条例》，并自公布之日起施行。2001 年 6 月 13 日国务院公布的《城市房屋拆迁管理条例》同时废止。

《条例》共分五章三十五条，制定的目的是为了规范国有土地上房屋征收与补偿活动，维护公共利益，保障被征收房屋所有权人的合法权益。《条例》以取消行政强拆为标志，宣布野蛮暴力拆迁的终结，呈现出统筹兼顾、公平补偿、阳光征收的特点。

《条例》明确了政府是唯一征收和补偿主体。《条例》废除了拆迁许可证的方式，规定市、县级以上地方人民政府为征收与补偿主体，所有的国有土地上房屋征收行为都是政府行为，政府对此负责，从制度上保证了征收、补偿工作的规范化。

《条例》界定了公共利益的范围。《条例》规定市、县级人民政府作出房屋征收决定，必须以为了保障国家安全、促进国民经济和社会发展等公共利益的需要为前提，并以列举的方式对公共利益进行了界定，明确了因公共利益征收的范围。公共利益征收与商业开发征收混为一谈的拆迁模式已成为历史。

《条例》强调尊重被征收人意愿，并明确征收过程程序化。《条例》提高了对征收补偿方案的公众参与程度，规定征收补偿方案应征求公众意见，多数被征收人认为征收补偿方案不符合本条例规定的，应当组织听证会并修改方案；政府作出房屋征收决定前，应当进行社会稳定风险评估；房屋征收决定涉及被征收人数量较多的，应当经政府常务会议讨论决定；被征收房屋的调查结果和分户补偿情况应当公布；被征收人对征收决定和补偿决定不服的，可以依法申请行政复议或者提起行政诉讼。征收过程的程序化为规范政府征收行为、维护被征收人合法权益提供了重要保障。

《条例》明确了征收补偿标准。《条例》规定，对被征收房屋价值的补偿，不得低于房屋征收决定公告之日被征收房屋类似房地产的市场价格。以市场价格作为补偿标准，使得被征收人的基本利益得到保障。

《条例》规定了由被征收人协商选评估机构。《条例》规定，房地产价格评估机构由被征收人协商选定；协商不成的，通过多数决定、随机选定等方式确定，改变了过去通常由政府指定评估机构的做法，有利于房屋评估的公平和公正，维护了被征收人的权益。

《条例》要求征收房屋实行先补偿后搬迁。《条例》规定，实施房屋征收应当先补偿、后搬迁，并进一步明确作出房屋征收决定前，征收补偿费用应当足额到位、专户存储、专款专用。由政府发放补偿款可以增加公信力，使被征收人安心、放心，也便于依法征收的顺利进行。

《条例》废除了行政强制拆迁。《条例》规定，被征收人在法定期限内不申请行政复议或者不提起行政诉讼，又不履行补偿决定的，由作出房屋征收决定的市、县级人民政府依法申请人民法院强制执行。改变了以往由政府直接进行强制拆迁的做法，明确法院为实施强制搬迁的唯一主体，有利于强制搬迁依法、规范进行。另外规定，本条例实施之前已依法取得房屋拆迁许可证的项目，继续沿用原有的规定办理，但政府不得责成有关部门强制拆迁。

《条例》规定了暴力迫使搬迁可追究刑事责任。《条例》规定，禁止建设单位参与搬迁活动，任何单位和个人不得采取暴力、威胁或者违反规定中断供水、供热、供气、供电和道路通行等非法方式迫使被征收人搬迁，构成犯罪的，依法追究刑事责任。

《国有土地上房屋征收与补偿条例》把公共利益同被征收人个人利益统一起来，通过保护被征收群众的利益、完善征收程序、加大公众参与、明确补偿标准、补助和奖励措施、禁止建设单位参与搬迁、取消行政机关自行强制拆迁的规定，充分显示了维护公共利益，保障被征收人的合法权益的鲜明特色，彰显了以人为本的立法精神，推动了和谐社会的建设与发展。

我国城市房屋拆迁制度变化历程

我国城市房屋拆迁制度始于20世纪90年代。

1991年6月1日，国务院发布我国第一部系统规范城市房屋拆迁行为的行政法规《城市房屋拆迁管理条例》，以配套当时的《城市规划法》。

1994年7月5日，我国出台《城市房地产管理法》，由此拉开了房地产市场化序幕，开发商成为我国城乡建设的主力军。就在当年我国开始推行分税制改革，地方政府开始逐渐倚重土地财政。

2001年6月7日，国务院常务会议通过了对《城市房屋拆迁管理条例》的修改，并于当年7月1日起实施。修改后的《条例》，仍然没有区分公益和商业拆迁，其运作模式依然是建设单位向政府申请拆迁许可，获批后实施拆迁，发生纠纷由政府裁决；被拆迁人拒绝拆迁的，实行强制拆迁。

2007年3月16日，全国人大通过《物权法》，该法明确了公共利益征收问题。当时，未体现公共利益征收原则的《城市房屋拆迁管理条例》面临和《物权法》的冲突，《物权法》正式实施后拆迁将“无法可依”。

2007年8月30日，全国人大常委会修改了《城市房地产管理法》，其中规定：为了公共利益需要，国家可以征收国有土地上单位和个人的房屋，并依法给予拆迁补偿，维护被征收人的合法权益；征收个人住宅的，还应当保障被征收人的居住条件。具体办法由国务院规定。

2007年12月14日，在国务院第200次常务会议上，《国有土地上房屋征收与拆迁补偿条例(草案)》是一项重要议题。会议认为，这个条例直接关系人民群众切身利益，要求有关部门广泛听取意见进一步修改后，再次提请国务院常务会议审议，然后公开征求群众意见，再由国务院决定公布施行。

2010年1月29日和12月15日，国务院法制办两次就征收条例公开征求意见，开了行政立法两次征求意见的先例。

2011年1月19日，国务院总理温家宝主持召开国务院常务会议，原则通过了《国有土地上房屋征收与补偿条例》。

2011年1月21日，国务院总理温家宝签署第590号国务院令，正式公布《国有土地上房屋征收与补偿条例》。

(资料来源：法制网)

八、中央房地产调控政策成效显现

2011年1月26日，国务院总理温家宝主持召开国务院常务会议，研究部署进一步做好房地产市场调控工作。会议指出，自2010年4月份《国务院关于坚决遏制部分城市房价过快上涨的通知》印发后，房地产市场出现积极变化，房价过快上涨势头得到初步遏制。为巩固和扩大调控成果，逐步解决城镇居民住房问题，继续有效遏制投资投机性购房，促进房地产市场平稳健康发展，必须进一步做好房地产市场调控工作。同日，国务院办公厅下发了《关于进一步做好房地产市场调控工作有关问题的通知》（国办发〔2011〕1号），落实了国务院会议精神，提出了八条措施，简称“新国八条”。

3月13日，在国务院常务会议上，国务院总理温家宝对于房地产调控提出了“巩固和扩大房地产市场调控成效”的要求，要求各地政府坚持调控方向不动摇、调控力度不放松，严格控制投机投资性购房需求，努力增加市场供应，稳定市场预期，把房价控制在一个合理水平。同时还应切实抓好保障性住房建设，今年全国要开工建设1 000万套保障性住房。各级政府都要切实负起责任，多渠道筹措资金，切实加大投入，并优先保证用地供应。

7月12日，国务院总理温家宝主持召开国务院常务会议，分析当前房地产市场形势，研究部署继续加强调控工作。会议认为，当前房地产市场调控正处于关键时期，必须坚持调控方向不动摇、调控力度不放松，坚定不移地抓好各项政策措施的落实，不断巩固和加强调控效果。要求房价过高的地区要加大调控力度，确保2011年1 000万套的保障性住房11月底前全部开工建设，继续严格实施差别化住房信贷、税收政策和住房限购政策，遏制投机投资性购房。

8月17日，住房和城乡建设部公布对各地列入新增限购城市名单的5项建议标准，并建议将符合2条以上标准的城市列入新增限购城市名单。

11月18日，国家统计局公布了10月份70个大中城市住宅销售价格指数，房价环比出现下降的城市达到了34个，接近一半。此次公布的数据中最具转折性意义的变化在于，长久以来都持续上涨的全国房价平均环比指数开始出现下降，下降幅度达到0.14个百分点。虽然这一数据在2011年4月份之后就始终保持着回落的趋势，但由正增长转为负增长在年内还是首次。

12月9日，中共中央总书记胡锦涛主持政治局会议，分析研究2012年经济工作。要求2012年实施积极财政政策和稳健货币政策，根据形势变化作出预调、微调；坚持房地产调控政策不动摇，促进房价合理回归，保证物价总水平稳定。

12月23日，住房和城乡建设部部长姜伟新在全国住房城乡建设工作会议上指出，2011年保障性安居工程建设规模之大、任务之重，是史无前例的。在党中央、国务院的坚强领导下，在各地方、各部门的共同努力下，2011年提前、超额完成了开工建设保障性住房和棚户区改造住房1 000万套的任务。2011年以来，各地区、各部门加大了落实中央房地产市场调控政策的力度，多数地区涨幅回落，房地产市场总体运行平稳，调控成效已经显现。

回顾2011年的房地产调控政策，除了国务院及有关部门的行政措施外，金融手段也发挥了重要作用。中国人民银行分别从1月20日、2月24日、3月25日、4月21日、5月18日、6月20日起，先后6次上调存款类金融机构人民币存款准备金率0.5个百分点；还分别从2月9日、4月6日、7月7日起，3次上调金融机构人民币存贷款基准利率，金融机构一年期存贷款基准利率分别上调0.25个百分点，其他各档次存贷款基准利率相应调整。这些金融措施的连续出台，提高了房地产商和购房者的融资成本，在一定程度上也有助于遏制购房者的投资和投机需求。

近两年我国主要房地产调控政策一览表

时间	调控措施要点
2009－12－14	国务院提出四措施遏制房价：一要增加普通商品住房的有效供给；二是继续支持居民自住和改善型住房消费，抑制投资投机性购房；三要加强市场监管；四要继续大规模推进保障性安居工程建设
2010－01－10	国务院办公厅发出通知，要求进一步加强和改善房地产市场调控，稳定市场预期，促进房地产市场平稳健康发展
2010－03－10	国土资源部发出通知：一、加快住房建设用地供应计划编制；二、促进住房建设用地有效供应；三、切实加强房地产用地监管；四、建立健全信息公开制度；五、开展房地产用地突出问题专项检查
2010－03－18	国资委要求，除已确定的16家以房地产为主业的央企外，78家不以房地产为主业的央企正在加快调整重组，在完成自有土地开发和已实施项目后要退出房地产业务
2010－04－14	国务院常务会议要求，对贷款购买第二套住房的家庭，贷款首付款不得低于50%，贷款利率不得低于基准利率的1.1倍；对购买首套住房且套型建筑面积在90平方米以上的家庭，贷款首付款比例不得低于30%
2010－04－17	国务院要求，商品住房价格过高、上涨过快、供应紧张的地区，暂停发放购买第三套及以上住房贷款；对不能提供1年以上当地纳税证明或社会保险缴纳证明的非本地居民暂停发放购买住房贷款
2010－06－04	住房和城乡建设部、中国人民银行、中国银行业监督管理委员会发出通知规定，商业性个人住房贷款中居民家庭住房套数，应依据拟购房家庭（包括借款人、配偶及未成年子女）成员名下实际拥有的成套住房数量进行认定
2010－11－03	住房和城乡建设部、财政部、中国人民银行、中国银监会等四部委再次发出通知，全面叫停第三套住房公积金贷款，并将第二套住房公积金个人住房贷款首付提至五成
2011－01－26	国务院召开常务会议研究部署进一步做好房地产市场调控工作。会议提出8条政策，包括二套住房首付款比例不低于60%、贷款利率不低于基准利率的1.1倍、地方政府问责、调整个税和加强土地增值税、普遍实施限购令等
2011－07－14	国务院召开会议部署房地产调控。部分城市房价上涨压力仍然较大，要求继续严格执行限购政策，上涨过快的二、三线城市也要采取限购
2011－08－17	住房和城乡建设部公布对各地列入新增限购城市名单的5项建议标准，建议将符合2条以上标准的城市列入新增限购城市名单
2011－12－09	中共中央总书记胡锦涛主持政治局会议，要求2012年实施积极财政政策和稳健货币政策，根据形势变化做出预调、微调；坚持房地产调控政策不动摇，促进房价合理回归；保证物价总水平基本稳定

资料来源：据新华网资料整理。

九、西安世界园艺博览会隆重举行

2011年4月28日至10月22日，西安世界园艺博览会暨第41届世界博览会在西安浐灞生态区举行。这是继1999年昆明、2006年沈阳之后，世界园艺博览会第三次来到中国。2011西安世界园艺博览会由陕西省政府、国家林业局、中国贸促会、中国花卉协会共同主办，西安市政府承办。

西安世园会以“天人长安·创意自然——城市与自然和谐共生”为主题，“绿色引领时尚”为宣传口号。世园会的主会址是广运潭，位于史称“灞上”的浐灞之滨，园区总面积418公顷，其中水域面积188公顷，总体结构为“两环、两轴、五组团”。其中，“两环”分为主环和次环。主环为核心展区，主要分布有室外展园和园艺景点；次环为扩展区，布置世园村、管理中心等服务配套设施。“两轴”是指园区内的两条景观轴线，南北为主轴，东西为次轴。"五组团" 分别为长安园、创意园、五洲园、科技园和体验园。四大标志性建筑有长安塔、创意馆、自然馆和广运门；五大主题园艺景点分别是长安花谷、五彩终南、丝路花雨、海外大观和灞上彩虹；三大特色服务区是灞上人家、椰风水岸和欧陆风情，此外，园区还设置了展示来自国内外的精美艺术品、雕塑以及珍禽、珍稀动物等展出，可以让人们充分领略园林、园艺、建筑、艺术之美。

2011 年 4 月 28 日，伴随富于长安古韵的简短歌舞表演，西安世园会正式开园迎宾，全国政协副主席王刚出席开园仪式并宣布 "2011 西安世界园艺博览会开幕"，近千名来自世界各地的嘉宾参加了开园仪式。开园仪式上，唐代宫廷舞蹈《霓裳羽衣舞》，秦腔戏曲绝技绝活大展演、生旦净丑大亮相的《秦腔颂》、舞蹈《延河喊春》、啦啦操《魅力四射》，表现了陕西古老和现代交融的文化特色。开园仪式上还举行了授冠仪式，由国际园艺生产者协会主席杜克・法博为一位美丽的西安女孩戴上花冠，象征着世界园艺博览会花落西安。

西安世园会的主要特点是，把游览区分为天人长安岛、创意自然岛、丝绸之路岛、花之岛、未来岛、世园岛、冒险岛和乐活岛，建造 7 大特色主题展园，即：体现西安历史文化特色的 "人文山水、诗意长安园"；反映陕西生态环境及动植物特色，包括羚牛、大熊猫、金丝猴、朱鹮等秦岭四宝的 "秦岭园"；反映陕西及西安航天科技和农业科技最新成果的 "航天科技园"；体现世园会和浐灞生态区地域特色的 "柳园"；反映中国古代庭院建筑风格的 "天籁庭园"；反映古丝绸之路沿途异域风情的 "丝绸之路园"；反映珍稀植物及药材品种的 "药草园"；同时建造一个零排放、零能耗的乌托邦式生态科技示范建筑，以体现世园会绿色、生态、环保的主旨。

西安世园会不仅是一场园林盛会，也是一场文化盛事。据统计，世园会期间园区文化演艺活动日均 50 余场次，累计演出 8 600 场次，成功举办国内外活动周 34 个，来自美国、法国、巴西等 41 个国家以及北京、云南、山西等 24 个省市的 320 家表演团队参与演出。

西安世园会期间，世园会组委会先后与北京大学、清华大学等 20 余所高校联合举办 "青春为世园喝彩" 大学生演出季活动；邀请姚明、闫妮、谭晶等 81 位明星参加 "我和明星游世园" 等公益活动；成功举办第 63 届国际园艺生产者协会年会、城市与会展高峰论坛等 9 项国际性论坛，以及国际兰花、菊花等 6 项专业竞赛和国际月季、杜鹃花等 6 项专业展览等重大活动，有效扩大了世园会在国内外的影响力和美誉度。

西安世园会共接待国内外游客 1 572 万人次，实现旅游业总收入 339 亿元，开创了历届世园会之最。西安世园会先后获得 "国际项目管理大奖"、"2011 亚洲都市景观奖"、"绿色特别贡献奖" 等奖项。

10 月 22 日，历时 178 天的西安世园会，在西安浐灞正式落下帷幕。闭幕式上举行了简短隆重的颁奖仪式，授予上海展园 2011 西安世界园艺博览会国际园艺生产者协会大奖，汉中园、成都园获 2011 西安世界园艺博览会特等奖。在淅沥秋雨中，闭幕式演出的《天人长安》精彩呈现，通过《广运传奇》、《万花来仪》和《绽放未来》三个部分，以大型歌舞《送你一个长安》、50 国模特服装秀《长安花》等一批精心节目，诠释了古都西安对天人合一理念的一贯追求，展现了现代西安建设生态文明的美好构想。

历届世界园艺博览会概况

界次	年份	地点	全称
第一届	1960	荷兰鹿特丹	鹿特丹国际园艺博览会
第二届	1963	德国汉堡	汉堡国际园艺博览会
第三届	1964	奥地利维也纳	奥地利世界园艺博览会
第四届	1969	法国巴黎	巴黎国际花草博览会
第五届	1972	荷兰阿姆斯特丹	芙萝莉雅蝶园艺博览会
第六届	1973	德国汉堡	汉堡国际园艺博览会
第七届	1974	奥地利维也纳	维也纳国际园艺博览会
第八届	1976	加拿大魁北克	魁北克国际园艺博览会
第九届	1980	加拿大蒙特利尔	蒙特利尔国际园艺博览会
第十届	1982	荷兰阿姆斯特丹	阿姆斯特丹国际园艺博览会
第十一届	1983	德国慕尼黑	慕尼黑国际园艺博览会
第十二届	1984	英国利物浦	利物浦国际园林节
第十三届	1990	日本大阪	大阪万国花卉博览会
第十四届	1992	荷兰路特米尔	海牙国际园艺博览会
第十五届	1993	德国斯图加特	斯图加特国际园艺博览会
第十六届	1994	法国圣·丹尼斯	圣·丹尼斯国际园艺博览会
第十七届	1995	德国哥特布斯	哥特布斯国际园艺博览会
第十八届	1996	意大利热那亚	热那亚国际园艺博览会
第十九届	1997	比利时利戈	利戈国际园艺博览会
第二十届	1997	加拿大魁北克	魁北克国际园艺博览会
第二十一届	1999	中国昆明	昆明国际园艺博览会
第二十二届	2000	日本淡路	淡路花卉博览会园艺博览会
第二十三届	2002	荷兰阿姆斯特丹	芙萝莉雅蝶园艺博览会
第二十四届	2003	德国罗斯托克	罗斯托克国际园艺博览会
第二十五届	2004	日本静冈	滨名湖国际园艺博览会
第二十六届	2005	德国慕尼黑	慕尼黑联邦园艺展
第二十七届	2006	泰国清迈	清迈国际园艺博览会
第二十八届	2006	中国沈阳	沈阳国际园艺博览会
第二十九届	2010	中国台北	台北国际花卉博览会
第三十届	2011	中国西安	西安国际园艺博览会

资料来源：2011 西安世界园艺博览会网。

十、高铁甬温线发生“7·23”特大交通事故

2011 年 7 月 23 日 20 时 30 分 05 秒，甬温线浙江省温州市境内，由北京南站开往福州站的 D301 次列车与杭州站开往福州南站的 D3115 次列车发生动车组列车追尾事故，造成 40 人死亡、172 人受伤，中断行车 32 小时 35 分，直接经济损失 19 371.65 万元。

事故发生后，党中央、国务院高度重视，胡锦涛总书记、温家宝总理等中央领导同志分别作出重要指示，要求务必把救人放在第一位，全力以赴组织好抢险救援工作，同时要尽快查明事故原因，做好善后处理等工作。

7 月 24 日，国务院副总理张德江率有关方面负责人紧急赶赴事故现场，指导抢险救援、伤员救治、善后处理和事故调查工作，对相关工作作出全面部署。

7 月 25 日，国务院批准成立了国务院“7·23”甬温线特别重大铁路交通事故调查组。

7 月 27 日，国务院总理温家宝主持召开国务院常务会议，会议要求，要继续全力救治受伤人员，全力减少因伤死亡、因伤致残；要按照科学、严谨、依法和实事求是的原则，严肃认真地对事故进行调查处理；抓紧查清事实，依法依规追究责任。

7 月 28 日，国务院总理温家宝亲临浙江省温州市，查看事故现场，悼念遇难者，亲切慰问遇难者家属和受伤人员，对事故调查工作提出明确要求，强调要通过现场勘察、技术鉴定、调查取证、综合分析和专家论证等，得出一个实事求是、经得起历史检验的结论。

8 月 10 日，国务院总理温家宝主持召开国务院常务会议，决定开展高速铁路及其在建项目安全大检查，适当降低新建高速铁路运营初期的速度，对拟建铁路项目重新组织安全评估。会议对事故调查工作提出明确要求，强调不仅要查清直接原因，还要追根溯源，查清设计、制造、管理等方面的源头性问题，依照法律法规严肃追究直接责任者和有关领导的责任。根据调查工作需要，会议决定对事故调查组进行充实、加强，调整了人员结构，完善了调查制度。

事故调查组由国家安全监管总局局长任组长，国家安全监管总局、监察部、工业和信息化部、电监会、全国总工会、浙江省人民政府各 1 名负责同志和 3 位曾担任过国家有关部门（单位）或地方政府主要负责人且熟悉铁路工作的老同志任副组长。事故调查组下设技术组、管理组、综合组。同时，聘请了 12 名铁路运输、电力、电气、自动化、通信、信号、安全管理、建筑等专业领域的专家组成专家组，其中有全国人大代表 2 名、全国政协委员 1 名、“两院”院士 2 名。邀请最高人民检察院派员参加了事故调查工作。

12 月 28 日，国务院总理温家宝主持召开国务院常务会议，听取“7·23”甬温线特别重大铁路交通事故调查情况汇报。经调查认定，“7·23”甬温线特别重大铁路交通事故是一起因列车控制中心设备存在严重设计缺陷、上道使用审查把关不严、雷击导致设备故障后应急处置不力等因素造成的责任事故。

会议作出了对“7·23”甬温线特别重大铁路交通事故的处理决定：给予 54 名责任人相应的党纪、政纪处分；责成铁道部和铁道部部长盛光祖分别向国务院作出深刻检查；责成

通信信号（简称通号）集团向国务院国资委作出深刻检查；责成国资委对通号集团公司、通号股份公司及下属通号设计院依法进行整顿，重新组建通号设计研究院列控所；对相关单位及其主要责任人给予规定上限的行政处罚。

12 月 28 日，铁道部分别召开了党组会和全国铁路系统电视电话会议，要求全国铁路系统干部职工，坚决贯彻国务院常务会议决定，认真落实责任追究，深刻吸取事故教训，切实加强安全管理，维护职工队伍稳定，推进铁路安全发展。

我国高速铁路规划

我国高速铁路发展规划，是2004 年 1 月国务院常务会议讨论并原则通过的《中长期铁路网规划》确定的。《规划》提出，到2020 年，全国铁路营业里程达到 10 万公里，主要繁忙干线实现客货分线，建设客运专线 1.2 万公里以上。2008 年，国务院根据我国综合交通体系建设的需要，对《中长期铁路网规划》进行了调整，确定到 2020 年，全国铁路营业里程达到 12 万公里以上，建设客运专线 1.6 万公里以上。

根据《中长期铁路网规划》，我国高速铁路发展以“四纵四横”为重点，构建快速客运网的主要骨架，形成快速、便捷、大能力的铁路客运通道，逐步实现客货分线运输。

“四纵”：一是北京—上海高速铁路，全长 1 318 公里，贯通环渤海和长三角东部沿海经济发达地区；二是北京—武汉—广州—深圳（香港）高速铁路，全长 2 350 公里，连接华北、华中和华南地区；三是北京—沈阳—哈尔滨（大连）高速铁路，全长 1 612 公里，连接东北和关内地区；四是上海—杭州—宁波—福州—深圳高速铁路，全长 1 650 公里，连接长三角、东南沿海、珠三角地区。

“四横”：一是青岛—石家庄—太原高速铁路，全长 906 公里，连接华北和华东地区；二是徐州—郑州—兰州高速铁路，全长 1 346 公里，连接西北和华东地区；三是上海—南京—武汉—重庆—成都高速铁路，全长 1 922 公里，连接西南和华东地区；四是上海—杭州—南昌—长沙—昆明高速铁路，全长 2 264 公里，连接华中、华东和西南地区。

同时，以环渤海地区、长三角地区、珠三角地区以及辽中南、山东半岛、中原地区、江汉平原、湘东地区、关中地区、成渝地区、海峡西岸等经济发达和人口稠密地区为重点，建设城际高速铁路，覆盖区域内主要城镇。

（资料来源：《中长期铁路网规划》）

（作者：邵益生，中国城市规划设计研究院副院长、研究员，国际欧亚科学院院士；周长青，中国城市规划设计研究院高级工程师）

2011中国城市经济发展述评

2011年是第十二个五年规划的开局之年，面对严峻复杂的国际国内形势，坚持以科学发展为主题、以加快转变经济发展方式为主线，实施“十二五”规划，国民经济继续朝着宏观调控的预期方向发展，呈现增长较快、物价趋稳、效益较好、民生改善的良好态势。城市经济作为国民经济的中心、工业化和城镇化的坚实基础，发扬创新精神，积极探索发展道路，不断推进经济体制改革，出现经济总量增长较快，中心作用显著，经济结构逐步调整，生活质量明显改善的新局面和新发展。

一、城市经济总的发展态势

2011年，国际方面，欧债危机阴霾笼罩，欧美经济复苏艰难，全球经济不确定因素增多；国内方面，经济增长开始减速，深层次矛盾逐渐暴露，经济发展中的不平衡、不协调、不可持续问题日益突出。在国际和国内的挑战和机遇并存的经济环境下，各类各级城市经过奋力拼搏，克服种种困难，其经济仍然得到了平稳、健康和较快的发展，并且在国家和地区经济发展中发挥了重要的中心的作用，经济发展质量明显改善。表现为以下方面：

（一）城市经济总量仍有较快增长

国家统计局发布的数据显示，2011年全年国内生产总值471 564亿元，按可比价格计算，比上年增长9.2%。分产业看，第一产业增加值47 712亿元，比上年增长4.5%；第二产业增加值220 592亿元，增长10.6%；第三产业增加值203 260亿元，增长8.9%。三次产业的比例为：10.12:46.78:43.10。虽然遇到诸多不确定因素，但是，全年经济运行比较平稳。一季度同比增长9.7%，二季度增长9.5%，三季度增长9.1%，四季度增长8.9%。全国国内生产总值9%的增长幅度不仅属于平稳、健康和较快发展，而且远远高于全球GDP3.2%的增长总水平，更是一些西方国家所不可能比拟的。2011年的GDP增长，美国约2.5%，欧元区约1.8%，日本约1.5%，个别国家甚至出现负增长。

在GDP总的增长中，城市特别是大中城市做出了积极的贡献。在全国GDP总量中，第二产业和第三产业占90%，而以农业为主的第一产仅占总量的10%，也就是说，90%以上的国内生产总值基本上是由城镇创造和提供的。

数据显示，全国主要城市 2011 年的 GDP 增长速度一般都达到两位数，多数在 11% ~ 14%，少数城市超过 15%，如重庆市 16.7%、天津市 16.5%、合肥市 16.0%、长春市 15.2%、成都市 16.0%……当然，也有一些城市 GDP 的同比增长低于全国的平均水平，如上海 8.2%、北京 8.1%。这些城市经济发展速度放慢与国际环境、结构调整、发展阶段、出口导向等因素有关，是我国局部地区和部分城市从中等收入阶段向高收入阶段转型发展的典型现象。

随着经济总量的增长和经济实力的增强，人均 GDP 不断提高，经济发展质量明显改善，从而使城市经济发展进入一个新时期和新阶段。许多城市已经全面实现了小康社会，并向基本现代化迈进，在国家的现代化进程中发挥引领和率先作用。

2011 年上海实现生产总值 19 195.69 亿元，按可比价格计算，比上年增长 8.2%。按常住人口计算人均 GDP 是 82 560 元，折合 12 784 美元；北京市实现生产总值 16 000.4 亿元，比上年增加 8.1%，人均 GDP 80 394 元，折合 12 447 美元；天津生产总值完成 11 190.99 亿元，比上年增长 16.4%，参考相关的人口数据，人均 GDP 已经超过 8 万元大关。重庆人均 GDP 已达 34 705 元，上升至全国第 12 位。除了中央直辖市，许多省会城市、计划单列市、地级市和县级市的经济发展也达到新的较高水平，如，按照全市常住人口计算，杭州市人均生产总值突破 8 万元。2011 年苏州市实现地区生产总值达到 10 500 亿元，比上年增长 12%。按世界银行划分各国贫富程度的标准，上海、北京、天津、苏州、杭州等诸多城市已经达到中上等富裕国家水平。

各城市经济发展是不平衡的，有的城市发展速度较快，也比较平稳，而有的城市，面临的不确定因素较多，或遇到更多的困难。如，沿海少数城市对外的依存度较高，因此受国际经济危机的直接影响较深，以国际市场为主要对象的产品的生产和出口出现萎缩，从而对 GDP 增长产生一定影响。相反，中部的一些城市，由于国家支持中部崛起和西部开发的一系列政策措施的实施和作用，其经济发展明显加快，甚至快于东部城市。从地区上分析，2011 年经济增速最快的是中部城市，其次是西部城市，如成都市在 2011 年 GDP 总量跻身于中国城市 GDP 前十大城市的行列，而原来前 10 名内的东部城市可能被挤出前 10 名。从规模上说，中小城市的经济增速要快于大城市和特大城市。

（二）城市经济中心作用进一步增强

2011 年全国城市化进一步推进，城镇人口首次超过农村人口，达到 69 079 万人，比上年末增加 2 100 万人；城镇人口占总人口比重达到 51.27%，比上年末提高 1.32 个百分点。伴随人口的增长，经济实力进一步增强。据统计，全国 655 个城市中，GDP 达到 3 000 亿以上的城市已经超过 39 个，其国内生产总值为 231 323 亿元，接近全国经济总量的一半，占全国国内生产总值的 49.05%。其中 GDP 进入万亿元行列的城市从 2010 年的 3 个，发展到 7 个，比上年增加了 4 个。除了上海、北京、广州 3 市外，天津、深圳、苏州、重庆 4 城市也加入万亿元城市俱乐部。7 个城市的 GDP 却占全国的 17%。GDP 在 5 000 亿 ~ 1 万亿元的城市达到 12 个，GDP 总量为 75 603 亿元，占全国 GDP 的 16.03%。它们主要是省会城市或计划单列市。如，杭州、成都、青岛、武汉、大连、宁波、沈阳、长沙等城市。所有这些大中城市是我国国民经济的中流砥柱，决定国家经济命脉和态势。详见下表。(表1)

表1 2011年大中城市GDP的总量、分布及比重

GDP分布	城市数	GDP总量	占全国GDP总量比例	主要城市
10 000亿以上	7	80 180	17.00	上海、北京、广州等
5 000亿~10 000亿元	12	75 603	16.03	杭州、成都、无锡等
3 000亿~5 000亿元	20	75 540	16.02	潍坊、常州、徐州等
总计	39	231 323	49.05	

城市对地区，特别是对省（区）经济发展的作用更是明显，无论是广东、江苏、浙江、山东等经济较发达的省（区），还是像河北、湖北、四川等发展较快的省（区），以及某些一般的省（区）都是如此。大量数据表明，城市经济是地区或省市经济的主力和支柱。省（区）经济的兴旺繁荣决定于城市经济的发展和繁荣。

（三）进一步调整和优化经济结构，加快城市转型发展

2011年是转变经济发展方式和优化产业结构之年。年初，公布了《中华人民共和国国民经济和社会发展第十二个五年规划纲要》。4月国家公布了2011年版的《产业结构调整指导目录》，明确划分鼓励类、限制类、淘汰类行业、企业和产品。2010年12月21日《国务院关于印发全国主体功能区规划的通知》，以及其他许多文件，对城市编制五年规划，制定年度发展计划，确定年度发展目标，采取一定的发展措施和政策，以及城市经济产业结构和地区结构的调整、优化和升级，产业在不同地区的布局和落地，都具有重要的指导意义和强制约束作用。经过一年的发展，经济结构的调整、优化和升级取得了明显成绩。

一是在三次产业中，许多城市以工业为主的第二产业有所下降，而第三产业却明显上升，特别是现代服务业发展更为显著，使城市的定位和性质发生了转变。整个城市结构由二三一向三二一转变化，使城市产业结构更符合现代科学技术进步、社会生产力发展和保持良好的生态环境的要求，在推进城市现代化的道路上有了明显的进步。北京第三产业继续占绝对优势，超过了75%。上海、广州等城市的第三产业均已超过第二产业，接近甚至超过经济发达国家和城市第三产业的水平。深圳市2011年农业在三产结构中占比首度为“零”（农业增加值实为5.7亿元左右，在万亿元GDP中，占比已在0.05%以下）。而第三产业的比重进一步提高，由2010的52.7%提高到53.7%。无锡市服务业增加值占GDP比重达到44%，比去年提高1.2个百分点；文化产业增加值占GDP比重达到3.1%，比去年提高1.03个百分点。

杭州市2011年服务业等第三产业以11%的增速，继续快于第一和第二产业，已明显超过第二产业所占比例，并继续扩大，占GDP的49.3%，其中，电子商务服务增长63.9%，领跑第三产业。

二是以高新技术为支撑的战略性新兴产业、现代装备工业和现代服务业得到飞速的发展。城市在经济发展中大力推进新型工业化，先进的新兴高科技产业替代了传统的工业产业和行业，淘汰了粗放的、落后的工业，使整个城市逐步成为创新型城市。

三是在节能减排、低碳发展和注重生态的推动下，许多三高一低的产业和企业或者被代之以高新技术的新型工业企业或第三产业，或者通过技术改造和更新，不仅实现了清洁生产，而且使城市整个产业结构发生了变化。杭州市金融和文化创意产业发展势头迅猛。去年一年杭州市新增金融机构 17 家，新增上市公司 10 家，全年募集资金达 101.3 亿元，全市文化创意产业收入增长 24.1%。

四是在文化大繁荣大发展中，文化产业，特别是文化创意产业得到前所未有的发展。城市不仅是国家的经济中心，同时是国家的文化中心。我国绝大部分文化事业单位和文化企业都聚集于城市。2010 年，全国文化产业法人单位实现增加值 11 052 亿元，占国内生产总值的比重达到 2.75%。在此基础上，2011 年得到进一步的发展，文化产业成为城市经济增长的动力源和增长点。以城市为主体的结构合理、门类齐全、科技含量高、富有创意、竞争力强的现代文化体系正在形成，文化产业逐步成为国民经济的支柱性产业，并成为推动经济结构调整、加快转变经济发展方式的重要抓手。许多城市确立或实现了文化中心的地位。

（四）进出口贸易在波动中保持一定增长

2011 年是我国加入世贸组织的 10 周年。在国际经济复苏乏力、人民币持续升值、国内外需求明显趋弱、国际贸易摩擦升温的大背景下，2011 年中国外贸仍平稳增长，进口、出口协调发展，外贸顺差逐年收窄。

据海关总署公布的数据，2011 年，我国外贸进出口总值 36 420.6 亿美元，比 2010 年同期（下同）增长 22.5%，外贸进出口总值刷新年度历史纪录。其中，出口 18 986 亿美元，增长 20.3%；进口 17 434.6 亿美元，增长 24.9%，贸易顺差 1 551.4 亿美元，比上年净减少 263.7 亿美元，收窄 14.5%。

在进出口总额中，广东、江苏等 7 个省市对外贸易合计占 81.5%，中西部对外贸易发展动力较强，其中城市的作用功不可没。2011 年，上海、北京、天津三个直辖市进出口值分别为 4 373.1 亿美元、3 894.9 亿美元和 1 033.91 亿美元，分别增长 18.5%、29.1% 和 25.9%。天津市进出口总额首次突破千亿美元，标志着天津市外贸踏上了新的台阶。从出口方面看，2011 年，上海市、北京市出口 2 096.9 亿美元、590.3 亿美元，增长 16%、6.5%。身居西部地区的重庆市虽然外贸的绝对值尚不能与沿海的省市相比，但增长势头强劲，2011 年的出口比上年增长 1.6 倍。在广东、江苏、浙江、山东和福建等省的进出口总值中，主要是所属的城市所创造的。如，2011 年广东省进出口总值 9 134.8 亿美元，增长 16.4%，其中深圳市 4 141.00 亿美元，增长 19.4%，占全省的 45.3%；广东省出口 5 319.4 亿美元，增长 17.4%，深圳市出口 2 455.25 亿美元，增长 20.25%，占全省出口的 46.16%。而中西部地区出口的增速明显高于全国同期总体出口增速，也主要是所属城市的对外贸易的增长。

由于众所周知的原因，近几年出口对中国经济增长的贡献率有所下降。2008 年前若干年，出口对中国经济增长的贡献率一般达到2到3个百分点，2009年出口对中国经济增长的贡献率下降到负3.9个百分点，2010年只有0.8个百分点。2011年也没有完全恢复2009年以前的水平。这在一定程度上影响外贸依赖度偏高的城市经济的更快增长。

在对外出口中，产品结构进一步改善。2011年，我国机电产品出口10 855.9亿美元，增长16.3%。其中电器及电子产品出口4 457.9亿美元，增长14.7%；机械设备出口3 537.7亿美元，增长14.2%。传统大宗商品出口稳定增长，其中服装出口1 532.2亿美元，增长18.3%；纺织品出口946.7亿美元，增长22.9%；鞋类出口417.2亿美元，增长17.1%。

（五）城市民生工程进一步受到重视和发展

1. 全面提高城市居民的经济收入和生活水平。由于在2011年调整城市分配结构，提高初次分配中的劳动收入比重，着力提高最低工资标准，提高最低生活保障线，使城镇居民的经济收入明显提高。据统计，2011年全国城镇居民人均可支配收入21 810元，比上年实际增长8.4%。城市普遍高于全国平均水平。如，北京市全市城镇居民人均可支配收入30 016元，同比增长12.3%，增幅逐月提高。统计显示，苏州2011年城乡居民收入也保持了较快增长，市区居民人均可支配收入33 070元，同比增长13.2%。无锡市全市城镇居民人均可支配收入达到31 350元，同比增长13%。在居民收入提高的基础上，2011年全年城镇社会商品销售总额达156 908亿元，增长17.2%。

2. 城市政府财政中增加了与民生相关的支出。在国家和城市的财政支出中，积极调整优化支出结构，压缩一般性项目支出，提高了关系居民衣食住行、生活、福利、教育、健康等事业的支出比重。2011年天津市全市一般预算和政府性基金预算用于民生领域支出共计1 940亿元，增长26.2%，占财政总支出的比例达到75.2%。实施更加积极的财政就业政策，完善社会保障制度，连续七年提高企业退休人员养老金待遇，增加城乡居民基础养老金、城乡低保和困难家庭生活补贴，落实社会救助和保障标准与物价上涨挂钩的联动机制。

3. 大力建设保障性住房，切实改善中低收入住房条件。2011年从中央财政到各城市，从资金筹集到土地供应，切实解决城镇居民住房问题，大力建筑和分配保障性住房，全年投资开工建设廉租房1 000万套，并且层层落实到各个城市和居民。天津市多渠道筹措财政资金，建设保障性住房1 600万平方米、23.8万套，发放租房补贴8.5万户。保障性住房的建设对调整房地产结构、稳定房地产业发挥了积极作用。

4. 减轻城市居民的税负负担。为了提高居民的收入，国家调整税收政策，从9月1日起，新修订的个税法实施，起征点从2 000元提高到3 500元，全国个税收入全年将减收1 600亿元。也就是说，城市居民的实际的经济收入得到了相应的提高。同时实施税制改革，降低或取消许多对中小企业、个体经营户或居民的收费。如免费开放公园、博物院（馆）、公共场所等。

5. 建设重要的民生工程和公共事业设施。如大力发展和建设各种类型，特别是基层和社区的福利、文化、体育等设施和事业单位，改善医疗条件和设施。

除了上述以外，城市在积极解决劳动力就业，扩大国内市场等方面做出努力。如，对家电等耐用消费品实行优惠补贴和促销等措施。这些都有利于城市居民经济收入的增长和物质文化水平的提高。

二、城市经济发展的特点

（一）国内外经济发展环境和因素复杂多变

城市经济始终处于复杂多变环境下和异常激烈的竞争中运行和发展。2011 年，是国际经济环境极其复杂、极具挑战、竞争激烈和不确定的一年。改革开放以来，我国许多城市已经是外向型城市，甚至是国际性城市，受国际市场的影响明显，对出口的依存度较强，所以国际经济市场形势和政府政策，特别是进出口和关税政策，对城市的影响非常之大。主要表现为：

一是，城市经济总的增长速度受到影响，少数城市，特别是沿海开放的大城市，其经济增长趋缓；

二是，城市间经济增长态势更为复杂。一些城市仍处于高增长的态势，增长率仍在两位以上，甚至高达 20%，特别是中西部的一些中小城市，如内蒙古自治区的鄂尔多斯市，2011 的 GDP 上了 3 000 亿元的台阶，达 3 300 亿元，增长 14.5%，进入全国 GDP 五十强的行列，成为内蒙古自治区 GDP 最高的城市。相反，有的城市受国际经济形势的影响，GDP 增长趋缓，回落到个位数；

三是，城市转型发展成为一些城市的主线。在新的国际国内环境下重新审视和确定了城市的发展方向、定位和产业结构，以及发展方式，导致 2011 年将市场从国际转向国内，或国际与国内并重，扩大内需成为城市经济的主要动力，经济发展重心确定为转变经济发展方式、以调整和优化产业，提高城市发展质量为主要目标。

（二）城市经济发展面临深层次的矛盾和问题

改革开放 30 多年来，我国城市经济已经取得世人瞩目的巨大成就。但是，过去 30 多年，基本上是粗放的、外延的发展。由于国际经济格局的变化和经济危机的冲击，国家经济发展方针和战略的调整，使城市经济在新的时空环境下，产生了大量的新情况和新问题，暴露出深层次的矛盾和问题。突出的表现为：

一是城市工业的发展速度有所减慢。工业是城市的主导产业或支柱产业，而 2011 年城市工业的发展受不同程度的影响。2011 年 1—12 月，工业同比增速回落至 12.4%，创下 2009 年 9 月以来的新低，其中重工业成为工业生产下滑的主要原因。1—12 月份，规模以上工业增加值同比增长 13.9%，比 1—11 月份回落 0.1 个百分点。

二是中小企业遇到前所未有的困难。由于原材料价格上涨，劳动力费用提高，资金紧张，甚至资金链断裂，加上以出口为主的中小企业受国际经济危机和债务的影响，国际市场缩小，甚至退出关闭。一些中小企业不能正常的运行和经营，或者造成亏损，或者倒闭，或者转行，严重的甚至导致企业业主纷纷外逃，不仅对城市GDP的增长产生影响，而且带来许多经济社会问题。南方一些城镇企业受电力供应限制，成本骤增，停工停产，被迫关闭。

三是金融制度和体制滞后的矛盾凸显。金融是市场经济的核心，更是城市经济的核心，由于金融制度和体制改革滞后，与市场经济不相适应，金融机构及业务不能灵活地满足城镇企业对资金的需要，因此导致民间金融的滋生和蔓延，而国家又缺乏必要的法律和制度进行规范，于是出现的问题越来越突出和严重，资金流向失控，非法集资、违规揽储屡见不鲜，金融犯罪层出不穷，金融生态严重恶化。

四是社会分配结构不合理，收入分配不公，成为城市经济进一步健康、平稳和较快发展的突出问题。

（三）股市、楼市成2011年城市经济运行的重点

市场是城市的内核，是城市经济的支撑，没有市场就没有城市，同时市场也是城市经济兴衰的标志。而股市、楼市不仅是现代市场经济的最重要的市场组成部分，而且是反映最敏感，交易额最巨大的要素市场。2011年股票走势，无论是其直线趋势还是平均趋势，都处在下滑阶段，至年底，尚未改变。所以，对于投资界来说是艰难的一年，对投资主体面临巨大挑战。A股2011年年初2808点，年底已跌破2200点，暴跌近20%，成为全球跌幅最大的股市。

由于股市下挫，不仅对投资者，特别是一般股民造成不同程度的影响，甚至带来利益的损失，而且使居民的部分资金流向理财产品，从而使2011年理财产品比较活跃，呈现发行数量和发行规模不断创新高、收益率偏高等特点。不仅如此，股市的波动和变化对城市经济必然产生一定的不利影响。

楼市不仅是房地产业兴衰的标志，而且直接关系城市经济的发展。房地产业是城市的支柱产业。前几年是拉动城市经济的引擎。2011年是强化对房地产业和房地产市场宏观调控的一年，在一些城市实施限购住房、信贷限制、税收试点等较严厉措施，加上国际国内的环境，房地产业受到一定的冲击，出现房地产开发和房地产市场与前几年不同的情况。统计数字显示，2011年房地产开发投资、房地产建筑面积、商品房销售额、开发企业资金筹措的增幅存在不同程度的下降。2011年全国房地产开发投资61 740亿元，比上年增长27.9%，增速比上年回落5.3个百分点，商品房销售面积10.99亿平方米，比上年增长4.9%，增速比上年回落5.7个百分点；房地产开发企业全年资金来源83 246亿元，比上年增长14.1%，增速比上年回落12.1个百分点。进入年底，其回落趋势仍在继续，甚至更突出，直接影响到2012年初房地产业的开局，使整个房地产景气指数下降。据国家统计局公布的数据，2011年12月份，全国房地产开发景气指数（简称“国房景气指数”）为98.89，比11月份回落0.98点。

国家在前几年加强和完善对房地产宏观调控的基础上，进一步加强了对房地产调控的力度，1月26日，以国办发一号文件的方式，发布了《国务院办公厅关于进一步做好房地产市场调控工作有关问题的通知》，开始了全年的对房地产业发展和房地产市场的调控。经过

一年的调控，已经取得了明显的成效，房价快速上涨的势头初步得到遏制。

12 月 1 日，中国指数研究院发布的百城价格指数对 100 个城市的全样本调查数据显示，2011 年 11 月，全国 100 个城市住宅平均价格为 8 832 元/平方米，与 10 月相比下降 0.28%。其中，43 个城市房价环比上涨，57 个城市环比下跌。

（四）抑制通胀预期是 2011 年城市经济管理的中心

物价稳定，特别是消费品销售价格的稳定是城市经济健康发展的标志，也是社会稳定的物质保证，从而使物价成为居民关注的重点。由于国际国内一系列经济因素的影响和作用，从年初开始国家和城市面临通胀预期的压力。2011 年 5 月份全国居民消费价格指数（CPI）同比上涨 5.5%，创 34 个月以来新高，7 月份居民消费价格同比涨幅达到高点 6.5%。随着稳定物价、遏制通胀的调控措施不断出台，力度进一步加强，高企的物价出现回落。12 月份，居民消费价格同比上涨 4.1%，环比上涨 0.3%。从全年分析，居民消费价格比上年上涨 5.4%。其中，城市上涨 5.3%，食品上涨 11.8%。全年工业生产者购进价格比上年上涨 9.1%，12 月份同比上涨 3.5%，环比下降 0.4%。

当然，各城市物价水平和波动烈度是不完全相同的。北京市统计局发布的 1—11 月北京经济主要指标数据显示，1—11 月，居民消费价格比上年同期上涨 5.7%，涨幅比 1—10 月回落 0.2 个百分点。

（五）开发区和新城建设成为城市经济发展新的增长极

2011 年是我国第十二个五年规划的开局之年，各个城市都编制了宏伟的第十二个五年经济建设和社会发展五年规划，不同程度地扩大城市规模，制定了较快的经济发展目标，争取在第十二个五年规划期间，让城市经济更上一个台阶。与此同时，国家制定和颁布了一系列区域和地区发展规划、规划纲要、指导意见、实施原则等。如长三角经济区、珠三角经济区、环渤海湾经济区、中原城市群、天津滨海新区、皖江城市带、沈阳经济区、武汉城市圈、长珠潭城市群、环鄱阳湖城市群、太原城市圈、重庆两江新区、成渝经济区、天府新区、江西省鄱阳湖生态经济区等。通过高层协商、多级合作、建立机构、编制规划、共建设施等措施和手段，加强了城市间的竞争、协调与合作，促进了地区间的优势互补、互通有无、资源共享、资金融通、产品交易、人员来往，实现地区或城市群的一体化发展，使城市从个体孤立发展转变为群体性发展。这不仅是城市经济发展的必然趋势和规律，而且成为城市和地区的经济增长极，其经济基础增长速度和发展质量，远远超过城市的单体发展。这有利于科学的、合理的城市体系的建立与发展，有利于实现具有中国特色的城乡一体化建设。

三、2012 年城市经济发展前景展望

2012 年中国城市经济发展仍然面临着严峻的挑战、深层次矛盾和诸多压力，同时提出一系列新的发展任务。如：（1）加速城市转型发展，在进一步优化经济结构的基础上，促

使社会结构与经济结构和谐发展；(2) 加强城市空间布局和规划，克服城市的无序扩张和无限膨胀，高效、集约、合理利用土地；(3) 全力提高城市发展质量，节约资源，加强生态建设，强化社会管理，创造安全、宜居、和谐的环境；(4) 建立住房制度的顶层设计和长效机制，健康发展城市房地产，切实解决居民住房问题；(5) 从城市经济发展和生活质量等多视角重视和解决城市交通难题；(6) 改革和完善城市财政体制、摆脱城市财政对土地的依赖。

2012 年是实施“十二五”规划承上启下的重要一年，国家总的发展方针是稳增长、调结构、保民生、促稳定。城市经济继续为实现国家 2012 年的经济发展目标、任务和战略作出努力。

(一) 保持一定的经济发展速度

中国城市经济仍然拥有明显的优势、巨大的潜力和充分的活力，2012 年城市经济仍将努力实现持续、平稳和较快的增长，但有的城市的经济总量增长速度可能会趋缓，而且各城市的经济发展速度、经济增长水平可能有所不同，出现较大差异。相对而言，大城市，尤其是特大城市，其经济增长速度可能会缓慢一些，更多注重增长的质量和协调经济结构和社会结构，而中小城市的增长速度会更快一些。不仅经济增长速度存在差别，而且不同城市的增长极或增长点也会不同，显示出更明显的城市发展特点。

(二) 城市经济转型成为发展重心

经过改革开放 30 多年的发展，我国城市的总规模已经达到一定的水平，但是城市的发展质量、经济结构的缺陷和短板，严重影响城市经济的发展和竞争力。一些资源型城市面临资源的不断减少，甚至枯竭；工业型城市，传统工业产品面对出口的困难和国内市场的限制，以及城市间竞争的激化，必须实现城市的经济转型，加速产业结构的调整，从资源型向创新型城市转变，从工业型城市向服务型城市前进。所以，2012 年城市会更加重视城市经济结构、社会结构的调整，以及两者之间的和谐。特别是经济发达的城市，在保持一定的增长速度的前提下，更加重视发展自主创新，发展新兴产业和文化产业，为全面执行“十二五”规划打好坚实的基础。

(三) 继续加强和完善对市场的宏观调控

2012 年城市市场依然动荡不定，因为不确定因素不断增多，市场主体变化万千，市场环境不稳定，市场掌控难度增加。股市、楼市、车市、能源以及进出口市场仍是城市企业和居民关注重点。股市难以摆脱低迷状态，楼市的不景气现象还将继续或加深，并向二三线城市蔓延。房产价格总的是稳中有降，同时不排斥少数城市出现小幅的涨价。城市的交通拥堵以及部分城市的限购政策会直接影响车市。部分城市的能源紧缺、供应不足，甚至拉闸限电会直接困扰城市经济，甚至居民生活。由于受国际经济的种种影响，出口贸易难以较大改变。所以，2012 年政府必然继续加强和完善宏观调控，以引导城市市场的健康、有序、正确的发展。

（四）经济体制改革进一步深化和推进

已有的城市经济体制成为城市经济进一步发展和实现城市社会公平正义的制度性障碍。所以，城市经济的进一步发展必然触及诸多制度、体制和机制，以及相关的政策、规章和条例。如果不解决这些问题，不仅 2012 年城市经济发展受到影响，而且关系到“十二五”规划的全面实现。所以，2012 年对关系城市经济较快、稳定和和谐发展的收入分配、税收制度、土地供应、住房制度、资源配置、教育医疗、社区发展、养老保险等方面深化改革。不仅中央会出台一些改革措施，而且一些城市，特别是大中城市将会有所创新和突破。

（作者：杨重光，中国社会科学院研究员，中国城市经济学会原副会长）

2011 中国城市土地利用

2011 年是“十二五”规划的开局之年，面对国内外宏观经济运行的不确定性，中央明确全年宏观经济的基调为积极的财政政策和稳健的货币政策，保持了宏观经济政策的连续性和稳定性。全年土地利用管理围绕“稳供应，保民生；控价格，防地王；严监管，促开发”的基本要求，在重点保证保障性安居工程等民生用地的同时，强化了一系列政策措施，城镇土地出让方式不断创新，监测监管日趋完善，调控能力切实增强，工作重点更为突出，房地产市场用地调控效果明显，保障房建设用地实现应保尽保，有力地促进了城市土地利用的良性发展，也为“十二五”时期房地产市场平稳健康有序运行打开了良好局面。

一、2011 年城市土地利用的基本情况

（一）持续保障发展，用地计划指标大幅提升，土地供应总量持续增长

2011 年，全国新增城镇建设用地计划指标安排同比增加 21.9%，各地积极开展批而未用土地都清理，加快推动存量土地的盘活，确保了全国建设用地供应持续增长。全年供应 58.77 万公顷，同比增长 37.2%，增速较 2010 年同期扩大 3 个百分点，有效满足了各项土地需求。分季度看，第三季度为供地高峰，同比增加 79.1%，环比增加 54.9%，第四季度增幅明显收窄，同比增加 30.1%，环比减少 4.6%，与往年相比，供地高峰有所提前。

从土地供应分用途看，基础设施用地占比显著提高。工矿仓储用地、房地产用地和基础设施等其他用地（包括公用设施、公共建筑、交通运输、水利设施和特殊用地）分别供应 19.27 万公顷、16.72 万公顷和 22.78 万公顷，同比分别增加 26.2%、9.2% 和 86.1%，占土地供应总量的比重分别为 32.7%、28.5% 和 38.8%。在实施国家区域发展战略和加快发展水利等政策作用下，交通、水利等基础设施用地占比同比提高 10.2 个百分点，而随着限购等房地产调控政策持续作用，房地产用地占比有所回落。

（二）积极参与调控，住宅用地价格调整合理，高价地异常情况趋稳

住宅地价涨幅持续回落，宏观调控效果明显。2011 年末，全国主要城市住宅用地价格为 4 518 元/平方米，同比增长 6.58%，增幅较 2010 年同期下降 6.11 个百分点。环比增幅持

续回落，1—4 季度，住宅用地价格环比增幅分别为 2.68%、2.19%、1.74%和 0，住宅用地价格环比负增长的城市由 2 个增加 37 个。

“高价地”数量明显减少，土地市场进一步降温。2011 年各地共上报招拍挂出让中溢价率超过 50%、成交总价或单价创历史新高的房地产交易异常地块 596 宗。其中，1—12 月份分别上报 115 宗、41 宗、81 宗、57 宗、76 宗、81 宗、62 宗、29 宗、27 宗、16 宗、8 宗和 3 宗，从下半年开始，高价地数量逐月减少，土地拍卖底价成交开始增多，一些地方甚至出现流拍流标，市场热度持续降温。

溢价率和竞价轮次持续走低，市场选择更趋理性。全年异常地块平均溢价率为 153%，到 12 月，溢价率为均值 136%，低于除 2 月、4 月和 10 月外的其他各月水平；竞价轮次均值为 62 次，到 12 月，竞价轮次均值为 34 次，低于除 4 月外的其他各月水平，房地产市场用地竞争程度明显减弱，市场选择回归理性。

（三）有效服务民生，住房供地计划执行好于往年，保障房用地应保尽保

住房供地计划大幅提升。2011 年计划供应住房用地 21.8 万公顷，与 2010 年全国住房用地供应计划（18.47 万公顷）和实际供地量（12.63 万公顷）相比，分别增加 18% 和 72.6%，超过前两年年均实际供地量（10.17 万公顷）。其中，保障性安居工程用地计划供应 7.74 万公顷，占住房用地供应计划的 35.5%，与 2010 年计划（6.58 万公顷）和实际供地量（3.34 万公顷）相比，分别增加 17.6% 和 138.9%。商品住宅用地计划供应 14.05 万公顷，比 2010 年实际供应增加 51%。

住房实际供地 2011 年全国房地产用地供应继续增长，用地结构进一步优化。全年房地产用地供应 16.72 万公顷，同比增长 9.2%，超过前两年年均实际供地量（10.17 万公顷）。住房用地占房地产用地的比例为 74.9%，同比上升 0.2 个百分点。在调控政策作用下，普通商品住房用地供给力度加大，达 9.67 万公顷，同比增加 3.2%，为前两年平均供应量（7.79 万公顷）的 1.24 倍。各地保障性安居工程建设力度加大，保障性住房用地供应持续增加，占比显著提高。保障性住房全年实际用地量达 2.84 万公顷，同比增加 37.7%，占住房用地总量 22.7%，创历史新高。

保障性安居工程用地优先供应，提前两月完成任务。2011 年，配合国家住房市场调控政策需要，国土资源部对 1000 万套保障性安居工程实行新增建设用地计划指标单列，并先后下发了《关于加强保障性安居工程用地管理有关问题的通知》（国土资电发〔2011〕53 号）、《关于开展保障性安居工程建设任务用地落实情况月调度工作的通知》（国土资电发〔2011〕125 号）等一系列文件，对保障性安居工程用地供应的计划、规模、结构、时序、开发建设、监测监管、检查、考核等作了明确的部署和要求，跟踪政策执行，确保任务落地。2011 年初，经多方协调、科学测算，1000 万套保障房用地需求约为 4.18 万公顷。截至 2011 年 10 月 14 日，各地已落实用地 4.26 万公顷，供地计划提前完成。到 10 月底，全国共落实用地 4.36 万公顷，落实率超过 100%，提前、超额完成中央任务。

（四）强化融资监管，城镇土地抵押增速放缓，土地抵押贷款率大幅回落

土地抵押面积和贷款总量增速回落明显。2011 年，全国土地抵押面积净增 419 平方公里，抵押贷款净增 12 627 亿元，比年初的土地抵押面积（2 589 平方公里）、土地抵押贷款金额（3.54 万亿），分别增加了 16.2% 和 35.6%，增速与 2010 年相比分别下降 1 和 0.4 个百分点，与同期人民币各项存贷款增幅回落趋势一致。

土地抵押贷款率大幅回落。2011 年，全国土地抵押贷款率总体保持在 50% 左右，但受稳健货币政策和日趋严厉的房地产调控政策影响，加上政策执行的滞后效应，分季度看，2011 年新增土地抵押贷款率，第一季度为 52.7%、第二季度为 52.3%、第三季度为 56% 和第四季度为 49%，第四季度有较大幅度回落。

储备用地抵押贷款占比稳步上升。在土地抵押贷款中，住宅用地和商服用地分别占 40% 和 28%；其次是储备用地和工矿仓储用地，分别占 17% 和 12%。特别是储备用地抵押贷款占比稳步上升，2011 年末储备用地抵押贷款占比为 16.7%，与一季度末的 15.3%、二季度末的 16.1% 和三季度末的 16.4% 相比，呈逐步增长趋势。说明中央规范地方投融资平台、严格土地抵押贷款管理的政策措施下，储备土地抵押越来越被地方政府倚重。

二、存在的主要问题及原因分析

总体来看，2011 年全国城镇土地供应落实总量平稳增长，用地结构更趋合理，住房用地管理和调控供应计划引导作用明显，对促进房地产市场平稳健康发展发挥了积极作用。但是，在城市土地利用过程中，仍暴露出一些不利于城市持续发展的问题，有的可能会直接影响下一阶段调控政策的落实，需要重点关注。

（一）土地供需求持续放大，结构性矛盾逐步显现

土地供需矛盾在“十二五”乃至今后相当长一个时期将更加突出。伴随着“时空压缩式”的工业化、城镇化和农业现代化同步快速推进，经济社会发展对土地需求的刚性增长趋势不会改变。工业化发展重点由东部向中西部转移，靠投资拉动、资源要素投入为主的发展方式在一定时期内不会有根本改变；18 个区域发展规划、8 个综合配套改革试验区和 14 个促进经济社会发展的政策文件实施与政府换届效应相互叠加，各地扩张用地势头不减；推进城镇化作为最大的内需，将成为明年和今后稳定经济增长的重要着力点，建设用地需求将集中释放。

土地供给的结构性矛盾逐步显现。“十二五”开局产业布局和投资快速扩张，区域发展战略的相继实施，以交通、水利为主的基础设施用地在供地节奏和时序调整上迹象明显，工矿、房地产和基础设施类用地同比分别增加 30.1%、12.5% 和 85.5%，三类用地占比分别为 33.5%、29.1% 和 37.4%，基础设施用占比增幅较大，同比提高 9.3 个百分点，土地供给的结构性矛盾已经开始显现。

低效利用和盲目扩张进一步加剧了土地供需矛盾。近年来，中、西部在加大招商引资力度、承接产业转移中，随意选址占地，宽打宽用，低价供地现象持续存在，部分地区“两高一资”、产能过剩、低水平重复建设有所抬头，维护良好的土地管理秩序，遏制违法用地反弹、严格耕地保护压力增大。一些地方城市新区建设盲目扩张，部分工业园区、交通基础设施等过度超前超标建设、重复布局，用地粗放浪费现象依然比较普遍，以资源利用方式转变促进发展方式转变的任务十分艰巨。

（二）住房用地集中放量，市场管理调控难度加大

住宅用地集中放量，房地产用地供后开发利用监管面临压力持续增大。近年来，住宅用地供应持续增加，但房屋竣工率持续下降，已供土地未能全部形成有效住房供给。截至2011 年 12 月底，全国未竣工房地产项目面积约 48 万公顷，与近 3 年（2009—2011 年）房地产用地平均供应量比值为 3.4，随着房地产用地供应量的增加和供应速度的加快，未来一段时间内，待监管房地产用地将继续增长。但是，受适度从紧的财政政策和持续深化的住房调控政策影响，开发商资金链紧张，已供土地的开发利用进度势必受到影响，合同违约和闲置土地在一定程度上将会增加，监管难度和压力将进一步加大。

前期易征易拆存量用地消耗较多，后期保民生住房用地供应压力增大。近两年来，全国上下将落实保障性安居工程建设用地列为工作重点，实行应保尽保，已经消耗了大量净地和易征易拆存量用地，今年将更多地选择新征地和难拆迁的存量土地。同时，不少地方为缓解财政压力，土地出让由住宅转向商服综合优质地块，商服用地价格增速加快，结构性升温对土地供应和价格产生一定的影响。同时，《国有土地上房屋征收和补偿条例》出台后，集体土地征地拆迁问题更加突出，成本高，周期长，供地压力明显增大。此外，防止违法征地拆迁损害群众的合法权益，维护社会稳定的任务更加突出，保民生压力进一步增大。

国内外经济形势复杂多变，住房用地管理和调控的不确定性进一步增大。当前和今后一段时期，世界经济复苏的艰巨性和复杂性对我国经济的不利影响逐步加深，这种影响势必牵制下一步住房用地管理和调控的政策效果：高压调控下，锐减的土地财政和换届效应带来的新一轮土地出让冒进风险；货币政策微调中，房地产业资金压力一旦缓解市场反弹力度将会更大；负利率困境仍未改变，民间投资渠道不足时，房地产投资资金从一、二线城市向三、四线城市不断蔓延加剧等。

（三）地方发展过度依赖土地出让，影响土地节约利用目标实现

制约产业升级和经济发展方式转变。工业化的快速发展严重依赖土地的大规模、低成本投入，不利于产业结构的转型升级。过低的成本不仅使企业缺乏土地成本意识，工业与商住用地间巨大的价格差形成的潜在土地收益，激发了企业隐性囤地行为，一些传统企业所占土地潜在升值已远远超过多年来的工业产出，阻碍了企业产业转型升级的积极性。这种建立在政府强力动用资源的组织能力、不合理的定价机制和低成本大范围外延式扩张基础上的对土地财政高度依赖的经济发展方式既不合理，也不持续，亟待转变。

引起带来金融经济运行潜在风险。2008年后，各地为应对金融危机影响，纷纷搭建融资平台，将公共建筑和基础设施用地以及集体土地抵押融资。一方面，土地融资建立在未来土地收益增长的预期上，一旦土地及房地产市场出现波动，可能引发金融风险，同时，债务的偿还，过度依赖土地、住房价格上涨的预期，影响房地产价格调控目标的实现；另一方面，出让土地年限为40~70年，土地收益一次性收取，以透支未来谋求眼前发展，带来国家经济运行风险，违法用地抵押融资存在的风险更大。

影响耕地保护和集约节约用地目标的实现。依赖出让土地促进经济增长和城市发展的模式，刺激了新增建设用地需求，不少地方突破规划计划征占土地甚至违法用地，政府储备用地和企业囤地规模不断增长，不利于最严格的节约用地政策的落实。长期以来，由于工业用地低价出让甚至低于成本出让的现象较为普遍，使得用地者普遍通过土地来取代资金，不少工业用地宽打窄用、优地劣用。此外，部分交通基础设施和高校园区等过度超前超标建设、重复布局，一些达标评比提出的用地标准脱离国情，宽马路、大广场、大水景等形象工程建设屡禁不止。土地粗放浪费在一定程度上加剧了建设用地供需矛盾。

在城市土地利用过程中暴露出来的以上不适应、不完善、不协调问题的深层次原因是：

第一，土地参与宏观调控的优势尚未充分发挥，差别化政策落地难。目前土地调控过多注重总量，并且与保护耕地等长远目标绑定在一起，调控的动态性和有效性受到制约。实际上，土地政策在产业布局、区域协调、空间时序等结构性调控方面，相比货币财政政策而言更具优势，但由于部门间信息共享和政策协调不充分，这种差别化调控的优势还未得到有效发挥，调控的针对性还不强。特别是由于国土规划的缺位，各相关空间规划不衔接，国土空间划分过于粗略，缺乏针对不同发展阶段和资源禀赋地区的空间管控和分类指导，难以满足土地政策实施差别化和精细化调控的需要。

第二，建设用地审批制度不适应转变政府职能的要求，深化改革难。现行的建设用地审批制度总体上符合用途管制的要求，但在我国工业化、城镇化进程持续快速发展的背景下，已不完全适应当前建设法治政府和服务型政府的需要：单独选址项目用地审批承载过多其他审批事项，造成审批周期长。土地审批处于基本建设程序的末端，对项目的把关作用形式大于内容。出现应该批、能够批，但因为审批程序原因，导致地方政府“未报即用”、“未批先用”等行为大量存在，因为审批问题阻碍项目建设，造成土地违法行为，既影响土地执法权威，也危及土地管理秩序。现行的报国务院批准的城市分批次用地，需要地方将一年的用地年初一次性落实到具体地块上，一方面程序烦琐，另一方面实际用地区位、用途存在着不确定性，操作性差，不利于发挥城市政府用地的主动性和灵活性。特别是由于法律规定的审批层级较高，中央与地方事权划分不尽合理，中央政府审批内容过细，难以腾出更多的精力加强监管，地方政府责任难以落实。

第三，基础制度建设不适应加强服务监管的要求，理顺体制难。落实转变政府职能的要求，把权力和责任放下去，把服务和监管抓起来，必须有及时、准确的土地利用和管理基础信息作为支撑，但现行的土地调查统计、产权登记等管理体制机制难以适应这一要求。土地登记多头管理，林地、草地、农地承包经营权与其他土地产权分别登记管理，土地和房产登记缺乏衔接，难以形成统一、共享的土地登记信息，推进不动产统一登记面临体制性障碍，制约了土地管理在产权保护与公共服务等方面的功能。全国土地统一调查制度虽已建立，但由于缺乏专业专职的调查机构和队伍，日常监管所需要的快速反应能力不足，加上土地调查结果逐渐与落实耕地保护责任、分配规划计划指标、考核管理绩效等挂钩，土地调查数据已经成为地方和中央政府博弈的工具。

第四，对违法用地的查处缺乏有效的协同机制，土地执法难。查处各类土地违法案件是《土地管理法》赋予国土资源主管部门的职责，但法律设定的制止等措施不明确，同时行政执法和司法执行缺乏有效的对接与协同，造成土地违法行为制止难、调查难和处理难。一方面，法律未就制止土地违法行为规定明确、具体的措施，制止往往流于形式，很难达到及时、有效制止违法行为的效果。另一方面，法律未赋予国土资源主管部门行政强制权，当事人如果不配合调查，调查工作往往陷入停顿；涉及拆除建筑物构筑物的，则必须依法申请人民法院强制执行。不仅周期长而且执行率很低，执法效果难以保证。

三、对策和建议

2012 年是“十二五”规划承上启下的关键年，今后一段时期也是土地参与宏观调控的关键时期。城市土地供给和利用应继续落实民生优先的供地方向，更加重视保障和改善民生，合理增加普通商品住房用地供应。

（一）改进土地参与宏观调控手段，促进差别化政策落地

完善土地规划计划手段，加强用地总量、时序调控和动态管理。探索建立土地规划五年定期评估和滚动修编制度，确保规划及时反映经济社会发展最新要求，增强土地规划控制和引导的有效性和可操作性；建立土地利用计划指标与年度经济社会发展指标相挂钩的联动机制，从供需双向适时、适度调整计划控制指标总量。

加快编制国土规划，落实差别化土地政策。在整合相关空间规划基础上加快编制国土规划，统筹城乡区域发展战略、国土空间格局与土地利用相关政策，明确差别化政策分区和要求，为落实土地差别化政策落地提供政策平台和依据。发挥土地在结构化调控和差异化调控方面的优势，强化空间管制和区域差别化用地政策，实现从资源供给总量约束向空间配置约束的转变，确保调控政策落地。

加强部门间信息共享与政策协同，创新土地调控工具，提高调控的有效性。加快土地信息平台与投资、产业、金融、人口等信息平台的对接与互通共享，提升土地调控决策水平。建立土地政策与货币、财政、产业政策的联动和协同机制，探索土地金融、土地财税等方面的差别化调控工具，丰富土地调控的方式和手段。

（二）健全土地市场监测监管，促进已供土地形成住房有效供给

强化土地市场动态监测监管和城市地价动态监测分析。密切关注市场波动，适时对调控

措施进行预调微调。加强城市地价动态监测，完善异常交易情况备案制度，及时掌握地价异常变动。深化土地市场动态监测监管，对各地反应的问题，及时进行汇总分析，快速应对。同时，做好政策储备和预评估，防患未然，疏导控制下一步市场降温可能带来的负面效应。

加强住房用地供应前后的全程监管。强化供后开发利用的跟踪监管，以供地政策落实和合同履行为重点，切实把握土地供应和开发利用的关键环节。严格实施建设项目开竣工申报制度，督促各地落实开竣工申报制度，探索建立项目开发建设的动态巡查机制。进一步细化批而未用土地的处置意见，督促已批未建的住房建设项目尽快开工，打击囤地、炒地行为，推进已供土地的开发建设。

健全房地产用地市场信息披露制度。采取多种方式和渠道适时向社会公布住房用地供应计划、已供土地的数量、结构、分布和开发建设进展等情况，增强市场信息透明度，稳定市场心理预期，促进市场理性发展。及时向社会公布住房供地计划执行情况和保障性安居工程用地落实情况，适时向社会通报违法违规违约房地产用地查处情况。密切关注土地市场苗头性、倾向性问题，及时分析研判形势，认真研究跟进措施，做好正面宣传，积极引导舆论。

（三）深化土地有偿使用制度改革，促进土地节约集约利用

推动完善土地收益分配制度。规范国有土地使用权出让收支管理，确保土地增值收益主要用于农业、农村和农民；建立国有土地收益基金，遏制片面追求土地收益的短期行为；改革土地出让批租制，探索年租制；建立耕地保护补偿机制，从根本上调动耕地保护的积极性。

进一步显化土地市场主体。处理好政府与市场的关系，强化政府的土地管理的公共服务职能，弱化政府的土地经营职能，增强市场主体在土地资源配置中的动力和活力。逐步实现从政府主导的土地资源配置方式向以产权为基础的市场配置方式转变，规范集体土地入市，加快建立城乡统一的土地市场，完善市场规则、丰富资源配置手段，坚持和完善招拍挂制度，提高土地市场运行的规范性。

深化土地有偿使用制度改革。更好地发挥市场在土地资源配置中的基础性作用，建立完善反映市场供求状况、资源稀缺程度和环境损害成本的资源价格形成机制，推进国家机关办公和交通、能源、水利等基础设施（产业）、城市基础设施以及各类社会事业用地的有偿使用。加快土地税费制度改革，提高土地保有成本，探索将土地闲置费改为土地闲置税，促进土地节约集约利用。

（作者：田彦军，中国土地勘测规划院地价所主任工程师，研究员；郑伟元，国土资源部耕地保护司研究员）

2011中国城市交通发展进程

2011年是“十二五”开局之年，也是我国城市交通发展具有重要意义的一年。截至2011年11月，我国汽车保有量达到1.04亿辆，仅次于美国，居世界第二位。2006年以来年均增加汽车951万辆，占机动车增加总量的45.88%，北京、深圳、上海、成都、天津等14个城市汽车保有量超过100万辆。总体上，城市交通供需矛盾更加尖锐，以交通拥堵频发为主要表现形式的城市交通发展形势更加严峻，从关注民生的角度坚决落实公交优先发展的呼声更加强烈，通过城市交通发展模式转型来缓解城市交通的任务也变得更加紧迫。

一、城市交通可持续发展面临严峻考验

近年来，大城市交通拥堵迅速扩展，拥堵范围有局部向整体扩张、拥堵时间由高峰向全天扩散。部分二三线城市高峰期交通拥堵已成为常态，甚至部分发达地区中小城市中心区高峰期也出现了严重拥堵，且周期更短、更快、更顽固，行车难、停车难、行人过街难、秩序乱等问题仍将在一定时期内影响我国城市交通发展。

（一）城市规划没有充分预见交通需求的增长，交通网络优化难度大

城市规划与交通规划的统筹和协调不仅体现在城市功能布局和用地开发强度方面对交通的影响，还体现在路网结构和交通设施之间的配套衔接上。为紧跟城镇化和机动化快速发展的步伐，目前无论是城市规划、交通规划还是基础设施建设，其决策周期、建设效率和更新速度都非常快，但城市规划与交通发展脱节，城市功能布局与交通设施不匹配的情况依然较为突出。普遍强调城市的功能分区和交通性的“大通道”建设，忽视用地的混合开发和生活性道路的建设，结果造成路网密度偏低，东京和纽约2005年的路网密度分别为18.74公里/平方公里和17.01公里/平方公里，而目前我国36个大城市的平均路网密度仅为6.18公里/平方公里。一方面，交通供需严重不平衡，而另一方面，已有的城市布局和道路网结构短期内难以改变，不仅没有起到很好的疏散和缓解作用，反而造成了更大范围的拥堵。

（二）小汽车发展呈“三高”趋势，公共交通出行比例提升艰难

我国各城市小汽车高速发展、高密度聚集、高强度使用的特点显著。截至2011年6月

底，全国私家车保有量达7 206万辆，占汽车保有量的73.2%，北京、上海、广州出行比例较20年前分别增长了29%、30%和14%，私人小汽车交通发展大大超出了现有城市道路的供给能力。发达国家城市人口密度越高的区域，人均机动车拥有量越低，但我国的情况恰恰相反，北京市核心区人均机动车保有量达0.31辆/人，是纽约曼哈顿地区的2.06倍，是东京新宿等人口密度最高中心城区的1.8倍。个人汽车拥有率不断提高，私家车主要用于上下班通勤交通，且使用频率较高，北京市小汽车年均行驶1.5万公里，是伦敦的1.5倍、东京的2倍多。

虽然近年来，各地不断加大轨道交通的投入和建设力度，取得了长足的进步，截至2011年8月，全国已有北京、上海、天津等13个城市开通城市轨道交通，运营线路51条、总里程达1 568公里，运营车站总数995座，与此同时，还有31个城市轨道交通近期建设规划获得批准。但是与小汽车的快速发展相比，全国36个大城市公交分担率平均约为20%，且增长缓慢，远低于发达国家60%以上的平均水平，城市交通向个体机动化发展的趋势仍然非常明显。2011年北京市采取小客车摇号、提高停车收费、开通快速路公交专用道、优化公交网络、加速开通新的轨道交通线路等多项措施以后，公共交通出行比例才艰难地提高了1.9个百分点，达到了42%的目标。

（三）停车资源供需严重不协调，停车问题集中显现

按照国际惯例“一车一基本停车位，15辆车一公共停车位”，我国城市停车位缺口普遍达到50%以上。据统计，目前北京市近500万辆小汽车，只有248万个停车位，基本停车位缺口约300万个；杭州主城区50多万辆小汽车仅有22万个停车位；厦门市汽车年增长率20%以上，而停车位年增长率仅约4%，仅岛内基本停车位缺口就达23万个；南宁69万辆小汽车仅有40.5万个停车位。停车位缺口尤其以医院、商业中心、中小学校、中心城区的老社区等最为严重，部分时段的路边停车极易引发区域性的交通拥堵。

停放一辆小汽车占用土地面积是30~40平方米，截至2009年底，我国城市人均住宅建筑面积仅为30平方米。停车空间缺乏也决定了大城市中心区不能选择过度发展小汽车交通模式。在大多数居民居住空间尚未得到有效满足的情况下，为小汽车提供大量的停车空间不仅不经济，也不公平。此外，将停车公建挪作他用的情况也较为普遍。停车位数量和汽车保有量形成的巨大反差和缺口，一方面说明我国停车设施建设严重滞后，反映出城市公共资源的供需失衡，另一方面也表明我国机动车发展缺乏有效引导和控制，两者之间缺乏制度约束。

（四）交通参与者文明习惯尚未养成，城市交通问题更加复杂

我国城市机动车不按规定让行、随意变更车道，电动自行车进入机动车道行驶，行人闯红灯等不文明交通行为比比皆是，各类交通方式不能各行其道，争抢道路资源，交通流互相干扰大，道路通行能力差，严重影响道路交通安全和秩序。更重要的是，如果出行者交通行为得不到有效改善，再先进的智能交通手段在整个系统中也很难发挥应有的作用。

交通参与者守法意识薄弱，一方面是由于长期的侥幸心理和不良交通习惯造成的，另一方面是长期以来对于不文明驾驶行为与交通陋习的制约惩处力度不够，这些都与机动化社会的要求有很大差距。通过改变出行者的“习惯性陋习”，挖潜城市交通时空资源是一项十分紧迫的任务，也需要将宣传教育与严格执法相结合。

交通拥堵是大城市现代化和机动化过程中难以逾越的阶段。纽约、伦敦、巴黎、东京、首尔先后于20世纪经历了严重的交通拥堵，虽然经过多年努力，拥堵有所缓解，但至今仍难以真正摆脱交通拥堵的困扰。当前我国城市正处于社会经济高速发展阶段，同时我国城市基础比较薄弱、各类矛盾更加突出，决定了我国城市交通拥堵问题将在今后一段时期持续存在，如不切实采取有效的措施，还有可能进一步加剧。近年来，各城市不懈的努力取得了一定成效，但多为弥补道路基础设施建设的不足，偿还历史旧账。在老问题尚未完全解决的情况下，新的问题又在不断涌现，交通拥堵的局面未能根本扭转。

二、积极创新探索缓解城市交通拥堵之路

（一）国家层面积极推进城市交通健康发展

1. 四部委联合发布指导意见。2011年9月1日，公安部、教育部、住房和城乡建设部、交通运输部四部委联合发布《关于深入实施城市道路交通管理畅通工程的指导意见》。《意见》回顾了“畅通工程”实施10年来取得的成绩和面临的严峻形势与挑战，提出了健全城市交通管理体制、发挥规划引导作用、落实公交优先发展战略、运用综合调控手段、改善城市道路通行条件、实施科学的交通组织管理、综合治理交通秩序等7个方面20条工作任务和措施。

2. 继续开展“无车日”活动。2011年9月22日，住房和城乡建设部启动了第五个中国城市无车日，本次无车日的主题为“绿色交通，城市未来”，除继续“围绕活动主题开展宣传”、“至少实施两项新的改善绿色交通出行安全和服务的措施”、“划设一定区域作为无小汽车区域”三项承诺活动内容之外，还包括给“汽车放个假”、“员工自行车或步行日”、“居民的安全街道”等特色内容。自2007年中国城市无车日启动以来，五年内先后有134个中国城市承诺开展这一活动，在全社会建立发展绿色交通体系的认识，鼓励政府完善公交服务，提高公众对使用小汽车出行带来环境问题和交通拥堵的认识，鼓励绿色出行。

3. 着手“公交都市”示范。2011年11月9日，交通运输部将在“十二五”期间组织开展国家“公交都市”建设示范工程，优先选择城市人口较为密集、公共交通需求量大、城市公共交通发展水平较高、城市轨道交通或快速公交系统发展较快、城市人民政府对城市公共交通发展有明确的扶持政策的大中城市作为示范，发挥轨道交通、快速公交在城市交通运输系统中的骨干作用，缓解中心城市交通拥堵。在2013年底前，启动30个城市示范工程试点工作。

4. 实施“醉驾入刑”。根据《刑法修正案（八）》及《中华人民共和国道路交通安全法

修正案》，2011年5月1日零时起，将醉酒驾驶机动车等严重危害群众利益行为定为刑事犯罪。“醉驾入刑”实施以来至2011年11月30日，全国共查处酒后驾驶机动车违法行为20余万起，同比下降了44.5%，在社会上取得了广泛的支持和反响，有效预防和遏制了醉酒驾驶行为，降低了交通事故发生的可能性。

5. 拟出台《校车安全条例》。针对多个地方出现的校车安全问题，国务院总理温家宝2011年11月27日在出席第五次全国妇女儿童工作会议时强调，国务院已经责成有关部门迅速制定校车安全条例，抓紧完善校车标准。2011年12月，《校车安全条例》草案公开征求意见，征求意见稿共八章五十九条，分别对学校和校车服务提供单位、校车使用许可、校车驾驶人、校车通行安全、校车乘车安全、法律责任等方面作出了详细规定，并赋予校车最高路权，进一步加强校车安全管理，保障乘车幼儿、学生的人身安全。

（二）首都北京加大力度缓解城市交通拥堵

2011年是北京全面实施《北京市关于进一步推进首都交通科学发展　加大力度缓解交通拥堵工作的意见》的第一年，在继续实施工作日高峰尾号限行、错时上下班等措施之外，为进一步落实《意见》提出的28项综合措施，5月4日，北京市政府发布《缓解北京市区交通拥堵第八阶段（2011年）工作方案》全面部署缓堵66项工作任务。《方案》总的工作思路和目标是综合运用科技、经济、必要的行政和法律等手段，大力推进优先发展公共交通、加快交通基础设施建设、提高交通综合管理水平、开展文明交通建设等工作，着力实施公交提速、地铁运力保障、交通秩序整治、停车秩序综合整治、小客车数量调控等5项重点措施，实现2011年公共交通出行比例达到42%，中心城交通拥堵指数控制在6.0以下。

1. 小客车保有量增量调控。自2011年1月1日正式实施小客车数量调控政策以来，截至2011年12月初，共进行11轮摇号（每月发放2万个指标，其中个人占88%，单位占10%，运营小客车占2%），共摇出个人小客车配置指标19.36万个；单位小客车配置指标2.2万个。目前，北京市共新增机动车24.6万辆（含报废更新车辆），全市机动车保有量达到497.3万辆，机动车增长得到有效控制。

2. 非居住区停车收费调整。4月1日起，按照“中心高于外围、路内高于路外、地上高于地下”的原则，北京市正式提高非居住区停车场白天（7至21时）收费标准。据统计，停车价格调整后，路外地上停车场每车位平均停放车辆数总体下降19%，其中一类地区（三环以内，含三环）下降22%，二类地区（三环至五环，含五环）下降21%，三类地区（五环外）下降10%。

3. 京通快速路公交专用道。5月24日，京通快速路公交专用道正式启用，京通快速路是高峰期有名的“堵路”，启用后的京通快速路高峰时段公交车速度由原来的每小时24公里提高到每小时52公里，沿线地面公交线路日均客运量提高了10%左右，同时缓解了轨道交通的客流压力，京通快速路周边路网使用效率平均上升7.2%，路网分流效果明显。

4. 加快城市轨道交通开通。12月底，北京市轨道交通9号线南段、8号线二期北段和15号线一期东段3条地铁新线提前试运营，北京地铁总里程增至372公里，每天可净增客流 50 万人次。

此外，北京市还陆续开通了 20 组社区通勤快车、10 条“袖珍公交”线路，解决天通苑、回龙观等大型居住区市民“最后一公里”出行问题。再加上公交调整优化，2011 年北京市公共交通出行比例上升至 42%，小汽车出行比例首次出现下降，降幅达 1.2 个百分点。

（三）各地多措并举不断创新探索缓堵之路

1. 上海市公交网络优化。上海市延续世博公交服务理念，以“消除重复线路，提高营运效率”为重点，进一步梳理优化线网，第一批调整 283 条公交线网，在满足供应的前提下，提高车辆使用效率，全面提升巴士公交整体服务质量。2011 年 3 月 10 日，上海市召开新闻发布会公布了全市第四次综合交通调查结果，中心城（外环线以内）42% 的居民从家步行 10 分钟以内可到达轨道站点，内环线内这一比例达到 71%，均较 2004 年的 16% 和 28% 显著提高。全市轨道交通（含磁浮线）线路 12 条、运营线路总长 452.6 公里，公交线路 1 100 余条，中心城公交站点 500 米服务半径覆盖率达到 86%，郊区行政村公交通达率达到 95%，基本形成了覆盖全市的地面公交网络，公共交通网络服务范围扩大，居民乘坐公共交通更加方便，市中心城区的公共交通出行比重达到 47%，轨道交通的出行比重比 2004 年提高了 3%。

2. 贵阳市小汽车摇号政策。2011 年 7 月 11 日，贵阳市政府发布了《贵阳市小客车号牌管理暂行规定》，要求从 7 月 12 日起，对在贵阳市新入户的小客车核发“专段号牌”和“普通号牌”两种号牌，以达到控制车流量，缓解老城核心区交通压力的目的。其中，“专段号牌”有入户限制，需要通过向市交警部门申请，以摇号方式无偿分配，该号牌可以在贵阳市所有道路通行；“普通号牌”入户不受限制，但该号牌车辆不能在贵阳市一环路（含）以内的道路上行驶，电子监控设备将全天 24 小时对违法驶入一环线内的普通号牌小客车进行违法取证，予以处罚。贵阳也成为继北京之后，全国施行汽车摇号的第二座城市。

3. 杭州市公共自行车和中心区高峰限行措施。2011 年 4 月，杭州公共自行车交通系统工程通过了住房和城乡建设部科技示范项目的验收。杭州是国内首个将公共自行车纳入城市公共交通系统的城市，也是解决了公交出行“最后一公里”的有效保障。2011 年 10 月 8 日，杭州城区部分区域正式实施高峰时段区域按机动车尾号“错峰限行”交通管理措施，“错峰限行”时段为工作日的 7 时至 8 时 30 分、17 时至 18 时 30 分的早晚高峰时段。机动车按号牌最后一位阿拉伯数字对应，在“错峰限行”的区域和时段禁止通行。同时，从 9 月底开始陆续增加公交车 377 辆，在主城区内大型的社区附近，总共有 52 个公共自行车点并增多储车，总共储车量已达到了 3 000 辆以上。

4. 济南市慢行交通示范。2010 年，济南市、杭州市、昆明市、重庆市、常熟市、昆山市 6 个城市通过编制专项规划和建设示范工程两种方式发展步行和自行车交通系统，并经住房和城乡建设部批准签订了“示范项目合作备忘录”。济南成为全国步行和自行车系统第一批示范项目建设城市。目前，济南市在多条步行和自行车交通系统示范道路的基础上对慢行交通条件进行提升与细化，历山路、经一路、经十路、大纬二路合围区域作为慢行交通试点，划出专门的自行车道、步行道，在有条件的地方调整机动车道，将更多的路权分配给行人和自行车，在机动车道与自行车道之间以绿化带相分割，起到隔离作用，让行人和骑自行车者都拥有充分的行走空间。自行车道还以彩色沥青敷设，清晰界定边界，交叉口转弯半径进一步减少，降低机动车速，保证自行车和步行的通行安全。济南还将结合泉城风貌，在现状护城河滨河步道的基础上，完善滨河步道专用道，将大明湖、趵突泉、环城公园等串起来，形成环古城赏泉步道系统。

5. 成都市交通影响评价管理制度。成都市规划局会同市交委、建委、公安交管局共同研究制定了《成都市建设项目交通影响评价规划管理暂行规定》，并从 2011 年 9 月 1 日正式实施。《规定》要求中心城区内用地面积超过 1 万平方米，商业建筑面积超过 3 万平方米的商业、服务、办公等建设项目，在申请规划审批时必须进行交通影响评价，市规划局把交通影响评价结果作为依据之一，对建设项目提出规划条件。《规定》的出台把交通影响评价的重点从项目阶段转向了规划阶段，针对具体项目对交通需求产生的负面影响提出改善和应对措施，如设置出租车下客点、公共港湾站、限制出入口、车位数的配备比例等具体要求。

此外，成都采取“淘宝体——亲，注意避让行人哦”、“爱情斑马线”等创新交通管理措施提示交通参与者遵守交通规则、文明出行。杭州坚持“礼让斑马线”，不仅赢得了市民百姓口碑，也为杭州创建文明城市加分添彩。同时，上百个城市利用微博平台及时将城市交通管制、交通出行提示、天气预报等交通资讯向市民发布。

6. 广州市的“快速通道 + 灵活线路”模式。近年来，快速公交在我国迅速发展，目前已有 10 多个城市建成快速公交并开通运营，虽然快速公交带来快速、舒适的公交服务，但往往需要开辟专用车道供 BRT 车辆服务，占用地面道路空间，在城市道路资源紧缺的条件下，快速公交的推广应用受到较大阻力。广州市采用了“快速通道 + 灵活线路”的系统模式，体现了高效灵活的公交优先理念。该系统主要由道路、场站、车辆、票务、运营、管理六个要素构成。BRT 服务一般有两种基本类型：干支接驳式服务和直达式服务，干支接驳服务的 BRT 一般采用固定线路；直达式采用常规公交的直达线路运营。广州市结合两种运营方式的特点，不仅设置全线在走廊内行驶的 BRT 线路，也设置多条部分在走廊内行驶并直接连接走廊外公交产生、吸引点，具有专用车道内线路组织、乘客换乘相对灵活的特点。

7. 深圳市的“区域性全天候步行系统”规划。目前，我国一些城市已从大规模道路设施建设阶段逐步迈入以步行改善、交通稳静化及更高品质系统引入为主的发展阶段。同时伴随轨道交通建设速度的加快，出行方式逐步向“轨道 + 步行”转变，步行周转量呈几何级数增长。全天候步行系统的建设在拓展片区步行空间、改善道路交通瓶颈、提高居民生活品质等具有很强的推动力。全天候步行交通系统，指能够将天气（如雨、雪、风）变化对人的出行活动的影响减至最低的一系列步行交通总称。罗湖金三角是深圳市主要的商业区、商贸片区，面积约 3.1 平方公里，片区日均人流量 80 万 ~ 100 万人次，节假日达 150 万 ~ 160 万人次。规划全天候步行系统由 10 公里高架系统、12 公里地面系统以及 4 公里地下系统组成，三种步行系统共形成 100 余个衔接点，连接 58 座建筑。近期（2010—2012 年）为重点启动阶段，主要是片区内部融合，结合近期开发项目建设以及主要交通瓶颈点确定建设项目库。

在“十二五”规划中，深圳、杭州、武汉、济南、西安、长沙、宁波等诸多城市将缓解城市交通拥堵、加大力度建设公共交通体系、完善停车规划与管理、保障慢行出行环境等作为“十二五”期间的重要任务实施。由此可见，进一步加强公共交通的建设和投入，逐步采取较为严格的交通需求管理措施，同时重视慢行交通出行环境，已经成为全社会的共识，也是今后我国城市交通发展的必然趋势。

三、城市交通发展模式转型成为重中之重

当前，我国正处于“十二五”社会经济结构转型时期，同时也是城市交通结构调整的敏感期。可以预见，在“十二五”期间，城市布局和道路结构不会发生根本性改变，汽车产业政策仍将维持不变。因此，城市人民政府不仅需要优化城市布局、完善路网结构、加强城市交通管理，更需要坚决采取有效的措施，在引导城市交通发展模式转型，确立公共交通的主体地位方面做出更大的努力。

（一）从关注民生的高度落实优先发展公共交通战略

自 2004 年公共交通优先战略推进了 7 年多的时间里，取得了相当大的成绩和进展，然而“以车为本”、重点考虑小汽车的通行空间，竭力缓解小汽车拥堵仍然是城市交通规划与管理的主流思想，公共交通的主体地位在资金投入、土地划拨、路权分配以及财税政策等方面没有得到充分保障。小汽车出行需求不等同于城市居民的基本出行需求，城市交通体系应保障所有的公民出行和交通公平，每一个人都应该拥有多种交通工具选择的权利，都能在经济和体力可承受范围内方便、通顺到达城市任意一个地方，都可以了解并支付其全部的交通成本，从我国人口多、土地资源缺乏、城市交通资源有限的实情出发，优先发展公共交通是解决城市交通问题的必然选择。胡锦涛总书记指出：“交通问题是关系群众切身利益的重大问题，要解决城市交通问题，必须充分发挥公共交通的重要作用，为广大群众提供快捷、安全、方便、舒适的公交服务，使广大群众愿意乘公交、更多乘公交。”温家宝总理批示：“优先发展城市公共交通是符合中国实际的城市发展和交通发展的正确战略思想。”由此可见，优先发展公共交通不仅仅是交通需求，更是改善民生和城市发展的迫切要求，必须成为城市交通发展模式转型指导方针和目标，必须成为土地分配、财政、税收等政府决策的重要依据，必须贯彻在城市规划与建设的全过程。

（二）充分认识停车管理在城市缓堵中的关键作用

目前，很多大城市在停车问题上基本采取了听之任之的做法，停车场建设尤其是配建停车场建设历史欠账过多，停车管理混乱、价格体系不合理现象非常普遍。小汽车使用成本和违法成本较低，在很大程度上刺激了小汽车的无序增长，也进一步促使了交通拥堵的加剧。

而国际大城市如东京、伦敦，都非常重视停车问题，通过加强停车秩序管理、实行差别化停车供给、完善停车法律等手段，有效发挥了停车在缓解交通拥堵中的作用。当前，停车管理的迫切任务是制定路内停车泊位、公共停车场以及配建停车泊位的标准与指标，明确停车泊位与机动车保有量之间的相互制约和量化关系，有效遏制机动车保有量的迅猛增长，加强配建停车的监管，制止停车位挪用行为，推动停车产业的发展，加快缓解停车难、行车难问题。

（三）切实保障居民慢行交通出行环境

在城市交通机动化发展的早期，慢行交通系统尤其是自行车是交通方式转化的重点。各大城市分别制定相关措施鼓励自行车向其他方式转化，甚至将自行车出行比例下降看做是城市发展水平高低的重要标志。在路权分配上，非机动车和行人交通的出行空间和路权也没有得到充分的尊重和保障，甚至正在逐渐被蚕食和压缩。事实上，交通出行，不论是小汽车、公共交通还是步行、自行车，都是城市居民的基本权利，为居民提供基本交通出行保障也是政府的责任所在。不论城市规模和类型如何，城市步行出行比例都会保持在30%左右，步行系统的规划建设与管理不容忽视，尤其是随着城市交通拥堵问题日益严重，慢行交通系统更应重新得到交通政策制定者的重视，应鼓励并切实保障城市慢行交通的出行环境。

（四）加强城市交通科学管理与服务

应进一步加强城市主干道、微循环以及交通枢纽等重点区域交通组织，通过精细化交通组织提升道路通行能力，排查整治交通堵点乱点，加强交通秩序管理。同时，充分发挥城市交通信息采集和信息发布平台的作用，完善交通管理信息服务与诱导系统，推动构建诱导标志、交通广播、微博、手机、移动电视、交通诱导屏、互联网等交通诱导系统，为群众及时提供交通信息服务。通过“文明交通行动计划”和“122交通安全日”活动，广泛开展“遵守交通信号”、“各行其道”和“情系安全带”等主题宣传活动，引导市民有序参与交通。

四、小结

2011年11月17至18日，以“城市交通发展模式转型与创新”为主题的中国城市交通规划年会暨第25次学术研讨会在武汉召开。会议回顾了20多年来城市交通发展历程，总结了2010年苏州会议上在发展理念、发展策略方面达成的共识，提出把调整城市布局、优化城市交通出行结构、转变城市交通发展模式等作为城市交通的主要工作重点，完善交通规划工作的编制机制和协调机制，加快推进城市交通规划和城市规划的融合，在规划建设中高度重视公共交通在城市空间发展中的主导作用，在城市交通需求多样化的趋势下统筹规划建设城市交通系统。在今后相当长的时间里，城镇化和机动化发展对城市交通演变的影响和作用是巨大的，需要用更宽的视野、更高的站位来审视城市交通问题，用更严谨的态度来研究缓解城市交通的深层次问题，用务实的工作来切实解决面临的紧迫问题，用科学的体制机制和法律政策来保障各项工作的切实得到落实，这也正是现阶段我国城市交通发展的基本目标和重要任务。

（作者：王静霞，住房和城乡建设部城市交通工程技术中心　教授级城市规划师，国务院参事）

2011中国城市建设新进展与趋势

2011年是“十二五”规划开局之年，各地城市建设部门坚持以科学发展观为指导，以保障和改善民生为目标，全力落实节能减排任务，努力提升市政公用事业服务质量和安全运行水平，加强城市管理工作，推动城市建设事业健康发展。

一、2011年城市建设工作进展

（一）城市生活垃圾处理工作全面推进

一是城市生活垃圾处理政策逐步完善。针对城镇化快速发展中许多城市面临“垃圾围城”的困境，2011年4月，国务院下发了《关于进一步加强城市生活垃圾处理工作的意见》（国发〔2011〕9号），提出“十二五”期间全国生活垃圾处理发展目标，要求各地区、各有关部门提高对加强城市生活垃圾处理工作重要性紧迫性的认识，加快提升城市生活垃圾处理水平。《意见》的出台，为今后城市生活垃圾处理工作奠定了坚实的基础。

二是大力推动生活垃圾处理设施建设。国家相关部门共同组织编制完成全国城镇生活垃圾无害化处理设施建设“十二五”规划，中央预算内支持地方生活垃圾处理设施建设力度进一步持续加大，城市生活垃圾分类试点和餐厨废弃物资源化利用和无害化处理试点工作稳步推进。召开全国城镇生活垃圾处理设施建设及运营经验交流会，启动了第三次生活垃圾填埋场等级评定和第一次焚烧厂等级评定工作，指导各地提高设施运行水平。

（二）供热计量改革和城市照明节能取得积极进展

一是不断推进北方采暖地区供热计量改革工作。各地全力落实国务院《“十二五”节能减排综合性工作方案》，建立健全供热计量工程监管机制，全面落实两部制热价制度，实行按用热量计量收费，扎实做好既有居住建筑供热计量和节能改造工作。

二是印发了《关于加强夏热冬冷地区居住建筑采暖方式管理的通知》，对夏热冬冷地区居住建筑采暖方式的选择、建筑围护结构保温隔热等工作做出明确要求，促进了夏热冬冷地区居住建筑采暖节能工作。

三是积极推动城市照明领域节能减排。2011年，住房和城乡建设部制定了《“十二五”城市绿色照明规划纲要》，提出了“十二五”期间城市照明节能任务目标，提高城市照明质量和节能水平。各地积极采取有效措施，进一步加强城市照明专项规划的编制。全面淘汰低效照明产品，并对新型照明产品，如 LED 路灯等进行了试点或示范应用。主动控制景观照明规模和照明能耗，落实城市照明建设项目的设计、施工、监理、验收等环节的责任制度，地方性城市照明节能管理制度和技术规范逐步完善，全社会的城市照明节能意识得到了明显提升。

（三）城镇节水和污水处理设施建设运行监管不断加强

一是不断加强对城镇污水处理设施建设和运行的监管。组织编制了《全国城镇污水处理及再生利用“十二五”规划》，城镇污水处理配套管网建设有中央专项资金支持，各地建设任务进展顺利。开展了污泥安全处理处置示范项目试点，积极推进城镇生活污水处理厂污泥安全处理处置。《城镇排水与污水处理条例》的立法工作取得积极进展，制定完成污水处理收费管理办法，为城镇污水处理设施建设运行提供资金保障。

二是进一步强化城镇节水减排工作。总结了“十一五”城市节水工作，组织召开“节水型城市创建工作会议”，提出了下一步城市节水工作目标和任务；组织开展了以“建设节水型城市，改善城市水生态”为主题的城市节水宣传周活动；完成第一批和第三批共计 21 个国家节水型城市的复查工作；研究修订《节水型城市考核标准》，研究制定《城市节水评价标准》。

（四）缓解城市交通拥堵的政策措施不断完善

一是加强城市交通政策研究。完成了《城市交通基础设施规划建设专题调研报告》，研究起草了加强城市步行和自行车交通系统规划建设工作和城市交通基础设施建设的指导意见，起草了《城市轨道交通线网规划编制办法》。

二是各地综合交通体系规划和城市轨道交通规划建设进一步加强。湖南、海南等地的城市综合交通体系规划的编制工作大力推进，各地构建城市综合交通体系工作进一步加强；2011 年，加大了城市轨道交通建设规划技术审查力度，共完成广州、深圳、苏州、沈阳、常州、厦门、天津等 7 个城市的轨道交通建设规划技术审查工作。

三是开展城市步行和自行车交通系统示范项目和“无车日”工作，促进城市绿色交通系统的发展。完成了首批 6 个“示范项目”进行阶段性验收工作，研究确定了第二批 6 个“示范项目。2011 年新增 16 个城市签署了“无车日”活动承诺书，承诺开展“无车日”活动的城市达到 148 个，取得良好效果，“无车日”活动影响力进一步扩大。

（五）市政公用事业安全管理有序开展

一是加强城镇供水安全保障。组织开展了对全国设市城市和县城的 4457 个自来水厂进行了全面调查，摸清了城市供水存在的问题；对全国设市城市的公共供水厂出厂水进行全部 106 项水质指标普查，加强城市供水水质管理和卫生监督。组织编制《全国城镇供水设施改造和建设规划（2011—2020 年）》，通过规划引导，加强对城镇水务行业指导和监管；逐步建立了城镇供水绩效考核制度，研究修订了《城市供水价格管理办法》，城镇供水设施建设运行保障的制度逐步完善。

二是重点抓好燃气、道路桥梁、下水道作业安全管理。全面贯彻落实《城镇燃气管理条例》，印发《关于〈燃气经营许可证〉格式的通知》，起草了燃气经营许可、相关人员考核等方面的实施细则，制定了相应的配套政策文件；组织开展城镇燃气"十二五"发展规划编制工作。开展了全国城市桥梁安全检查工作，选派专家对涉及24个省（自治区、直辖市）的125座既有城市桥梁进行检查，印发《加强城市桥梁安全管理的通知》；针对城市内涝灾害频发的问题，对351个城市内涝情况进行调研，组织修订了《室外排水设计规范》，提高了城镇排水设施设计标准。

（六）城镇人居生态环境持续改善

一是引导和推动城市人居环境的改善。各地以人居环境奖、国家园林城市、生态园林城市等创建工作为平台和抓手，加强城镇园林绿化建设监督管理，指导各地提高园林绿化建设管理水平，提升城市建设规划和管理水平，加强公共服务能力建设，关注保障城市中弱势群体的利益；2011年共有山东潍坊、江苏江阴、常熟3个城市获得"中国人居环境奖"，有北京市城乡规划社区参与实践项目、陕西省西安市大明宫遗址保护项目、湖北省鄂州市洋澜湖综合治理项目等39个项目获得"中国人居环境范例奖"，通过树立典型，发挥引导示范作用，指导推动城市人居环境水平持续提升。

二是抓好城镇园林绿化管理工作。加强了政策研究，完善城市园林绿化行业法规、标准体系，起草了《城市园林绿化管理办法》、《国家园林县城标准》，编制了《动物园设计规范》、《公园设计规范》及《城市绿线划定技术规程》。举办中国国际园林博览会，扩大行业认知度和社会影响力；加强调查督办，组织开展动物园行业规范化管理专项检查，切实规范动物园行业管理。进一步规范园林绿化企业资质管理，印发了《城市园林绿化企业资质申报指南》，完成了两批共270家城市园林绿化企业一级资质升级和资质延续核准工作，城市园林绿化企业资质信息核准系统进一步完善。

（七）风景名胜区和世界遗产保护得到加强

一是加强风景名胜区保护和管理。认真抓好风景名胜区规划建设项目管理工作，指导地方妥善处理好风景名胜区保护与利用的关系。风景名胜区规划和重大建设项目选址核准的审查审批工作规范开展，推进风景名胜区有序建设与发展，2011年组织审查风景名胜区总体规划31处，其中13处经国务院批准实施；审查详细规划21处，完成10处；审查重大建设项目选址23处，完成19处；开展了国家级风景名胜区规划实施和资源保护状况年度报告的汇总上报工作，对风景名胜区动态监测核查，2011年分两期完成了45处国家级风景名胜区的遥感动态监测。

二是积极做好世界遗产申报与管理。云南澄江古生物化石群、新疆天山等申遗项目的申报工作有序推进；完成对云南三江并流世界自然遗产地保护管理状况审议及亚太地区世界遗产第二轮定期报告的组织、部署、协调和汇总上报。研究中国世界自然遗产、自然与文化双遗产申报战略，推进我国世界遗产事业有序发展；与联合国教科文组织世界遗产中心、联合国教科文组织驻北京办事处、世界自然保护联盟（IUCN）等国际机构的合作交流更加紧密。

二、城市建设工作面临的形势与挑战

2011 年，全国城镇化水平已经达到 51.3%，城镇人口比重首次超过 50%。我国的城镇化已进入全面提升发展质量的阶段，成为影响世界经济发展的重要因素，在国民经济和社会发展中的作用日益凸显。“十二五”时期及以后，我国将由城乡二元分割的农村社会向城乡统筹的城市社会转型。与此相适应，城市建设和管理也将面临一系列转型或变化。如城市建设将从发展经济为主向发展经济、提高城市经济实力兼顾注重改善城市生活环境、提高居民生活水平方向转型；城市发展战略将从考虑单个城市向统筹区域城市协调发展转型；城市发展模式要从高消耗、高排放、高污染向低碳、生态、绿色的发展方向转型。

当前，做好我国的城市建设工作还面临着一系列压力与挑战，主要表现在以下几个方面：

（一）城市人地关系更加紧张

随着城镇化快速发展，每年有 1 000 多万人进入城镇，城市建设用地需求将在相当长时期内保持较高水平，城镇市政基础设施、公共服务设施水平面临严峻挑战，大城市中心城区压力尤其突出。截至 2010 年底，59 个城区人口超过 100 万的城市的城区人口之和占到全国城市城区人口总量的 50.82%。我国可用作新增建设用地的土地资源十分有限，到 2020 年，全国新增建设用地规模控制目标为 5.85 万平方公里；新增建设用地中工矿用地比例占到 40%，部分地区高达 60%，改善城镇居民生活条件的居住、休闲等用地供应相对不足，各项建设用地，特别是城市建设用地的供给面临前所未有的压力。

（二）城市安全运行面临严重威胁

当前，部分城市的建筑、市政基础设施等在设计建造过程中对防灾减灾考虑不够，防灾减灾设施建设滞后，同时，由于缺乏必要的应急预案、应急队伍、设备装置和应急演练等，导致城市防灾减灾能力不足，不能很好地应对自然灾害、突发污染等情况，往往造成巨大的经济损失，严重影响城市健康发展。2010 年入汛以来，北京、武汉等多个城市发生了不同程度的内涝灾害，造成了巨大的经济损失，严重威胁城市运行安全。此外，城市地下管线安全问题凸显，事故频发，安全隐患突出，成为城市安全运行的重大隐患。据不完全统计，全国每年因施工而引发的路面塌陷、管线爆炸等事故所造成的直接经济损失达 50 亿元，间接经济损失达 400 亿元。

（三）部分城市“城市病”已经开始蔓延

当前，城市交通拥堵状况日趋严重。全国约有 2/3 的城市，包括大部分特大城市、大城市以及一些中小城市，高峰时段都出现了交通拥堵问题。2010年和2011年对全国28个城市开展的城市人居环境居民满意度调查表明，约有1/3的受访者都认为人居环境建设最急需改善的方面是城市交通拥堵问题。此外，城市面临“垃圾围城”困境。根据有关专项调查，截至2010年底，全国约有30%的城市，即200多个城市还没有生活垃圾无害化处理设施，再加上大量已累积的未经处理的城市生活垃圾、每年新增的餐厨垃圾和建筑垃圾等，全国近2/3的城市都已面临“垃圾围城”的困境。

（四）部分城市人居环境形势严峻

当前，部分城市空气质量状况较差，城市环境质量恶化趋势明显。环境保护部2010年监测的471个城市中，17.2%的城市空气质量为三级或劣于三级，达到一级标准的城市仅占3.6%。对494个城市（县）的酸雨监测结果显示，出现酸雨的城市249个，占50.4%，酸雨程度严重或较重（降水年均pH值小于5.0）的城市有107个，占21.6%。部分城市社区服务和居住环境较差。根据住房和城乡建设部2010年和2011年对全国28个城市开展的城市人居环境居民满意度调查，城市社区服务与城市发展水平不同步，硬件设施和软性服务之间没有做到协调发展，市民对小区环境（包括卫生、绿化、美化等）、物业服务、配套设施齐全程度和小区安保等满意度不高。

三、今后城市建设工作设想

为做好新时期城市建设工作，解决“城市病”等主要城市问题，要遵循城市建设发展的客观规律，以改善城市人居环境和提高城市综合承载能力为重点，着力解决与人民群众密切相关的热点难点问题，提高城市建设质量，推动城市发展向低碳、生态、安全方向转变。

（一）强化规划调控作用，合理控制城市规模

要继续强化规划调控，优化城市空间结构和功能格局，提高城市运行效能，增大城市的承载力，有助于解决目前大多数城市“蔓延式”发展所带来的一系列“城市病”。城市建设发展必须以编制和执行城市总体规划和控制性详细规划为前提。完善城镇化布局和形态，科学编制城市总体规划，严格实施规划管理，促进城乡、区域良性互动，引导城市发展模式从粗放型向集约型转型，提高土地、水、能源等资源的使用效率和效益，妥善处理发展与保护、近期与长远、局部与整体的关系，积极稳妥推进城镇化。

加强对城镇的分类指导。做好城镇体系规划，优化城镇布局，促进大中小城市和小城镇协调发展。综合考虑人口、土地、资源环境等条件，防止特大城市面积过度扩张。缓解特大城市中心城区压力，重点解决一些大城市中心功能区过于集中、人口增长过快、土地占用过多、交通拥挤、环境恶化等问题。积极发展中小城市，强化产业功能，增强小城镇公共服务和居住功能。

（二）拓展城市建设资金渠道，加强市政基础设施建设

随着城镇化进程的加快，对基础设施的需求越来越大，但是供给却存在很大缺口。近年来，尽管我国城市基础设施投资占 GDP 百分比始终保持增长势头，但总量上还是存在较大的缺口，城市市政基础设施投资比例太低在一定程度上促成了我国城市产生“城市病”。一方面，我们要积极改进现有陈旧和落后的基础设施，尽量发挥其可持续发展能力；另一方面，应对不同等级和规模的城市，重新制定更加科学合理的新建和改造设施标准体系；紧紧抓住重点环节、关键环节、薄弱环节和容易影响全局的环节，优先提高城市生命线工程以及学校、医院、大型商场等人员密集场所抗灾设防标准。

要继续强化中央资金的引导作用。加大中央财政转移支付和对城市建设中的薄弱环节和重点领域的支持力度，如保障性住房、污水垃圾处理设施、公共交通设施、地下管线工程、城市安全和应急体系建设。明确地方政府城市建设的责任主体地位。加大地方财政投入，研究建立稳定的城市建设融资平台，吸引社会资金和外资，缓解当期资金不足的问题，改变城市建设、管理和发展完全依靠土地出让的现状。完善城市建设投融资政策。针对城市建设的特点和不同时期的需求，研究专项支持城市建设的税收、金融政策，如市政债券、贷款担保制度、专项金融工具等，积极拓宽融资渠道，吸引社会资金有序参与城市建设。

（三）加强地下管线管理，提升城市综合承载能力

要围绕破解城市地下管线综合管理难题，促进城市安全运行。进一步健全和完善有利于地下管线综合管理的法制和标准规范体系，逐步建立城市地下管线规划、建设、运行、维护、应急等方面的规章制度，健全城市地下管线规划、勘察、设计、施工、质量、安全、验收、测量、维护、拆除、档案、信息等综合技术标准规范体系。积极推进城市地下管线综合管理协调机制的建立和应急管理体制机制建设，完善企业与政府应急预案衔接机制和事故处置灾害应对协调联动工作机制；提高地下管线灾害预警预测能力，提高地下管线抗灾设防和灾时保障能力，严防灾害引发管线事故灾难。编制城市地下管线综合规划，加强城市地下管线规划建设的监管，充分发挥城市地下管线社会组织的作用。

建立健全地下管线信息资源共享机制，通过定期开展城市地下管线普查工作、构建城市地下管线综合信息管理系统等，建立城市地下管线信息综合管理机制，从信息技术方面切实加强城市地下管线安全保障。建立适应地下管线安全管理需要的技术创新和应用机制，在地下管线建设管理、运行维护、防灾减灾及应急处置等环节广泛采用新技术、新工艺。将数字化城市管理平台功能向地下管线、城市安全等领域拓展和延伸。推动城市地下综合管廊建设，研究制定管线综合管沟（廊）发展的相关政策，开展城市地下管线综合管沟（廊）规划建设试点，推进地下管线的科学管理和提高地下管线的安全水平。

（四）深化市政公用事业改革，提高运营效率和服务质量

我国的市政公用事业改革经历了引入民间资本建立现代企业制度、民间资本全面渗透市

政公用事业和加强政府对市政公用事业的监管，避免市场化过程中产生的市场失灵等三个阶段，改革不断深化和规范，已产生一定的成效。据有关单位调研统计分析表明，通过以市场化为主要内容的市政公用事业改革，打破了城市公用行业的垄断格局，促进了竞争；较好地满足了城市化过程中公众对市政公用产品的需求；促进了市政公用事业的政企分离，提高了市政公用企业的生产效率。但也存在政府监管体制改革的滞后，一些地方政府对市政公用事业改革的盲目性而产生国有资产流失、政府责任缺失等负面效应，特许经营制度有待规范和市政公用事业的普遍服务难以得到保障等问题。

针对城镇化快速发展的实际，要进一步加强对城市建设和管理的专题研究，剖析问题和原因，研究相关对策措施。积极构建市政公用事业的法规政策体系，推进市政公用事业结构重组，对市政公用事业实行分类市场化政策，选择市政公用事业市场化的有效途径，加强市政公用事业市场化的政府责任。要进一步研究民间资本进入市政公用事业领域有关情况，为进一步完善鼓励和引导民间投资健康发展的有关措施提供政策依据；大力推进供热计量改革工作，积极推进北方采暖地区既有建筑供热计量和节能改造。督导各地尽快出台供热计量价格与收费办法。研究供热能耗定额管理试点工作，推进供热合同能源管理工作的开展。完善供热计量分配表等质量监管，尽快研究出台相关产品标准和配套政策。切实做好《关于进一步加强城市生活垃圾处理工作的意见》的贯彻落实工作；指导各地加快城市生活垃圾处理设施建设，积极开展城市生活垃圾示范城市与示范项目、餐厨垃圾资源化利用和无害化处理、建筑垃圾处理等方面的试点工作。

（五）逐步理顺管理体制，推进城市综合管理

一些地方对城市的整体性、特殊性、复杂性等认识不够，忽视城市建设的整体性，大大降低城市建设的统筹协调力度，部分城市市政基础设施管理部门多达十几个，存在着政出多门，各自为政，管理不善等弊端，结果是低水平建设、低效益运行，规模不经济，造成人为的资源闲置与浪费。要进一步优化城市市政基础设施部门的管理机制，应该坚持建设和管理并重，理顺城市建设的管理体制，要研究建立完善适应现代城市发展需要的市政公用行业管理体制机制，强化城市市政公用行业整体化管理，提高服务和管理整体效益，避免部门分割、分散管理造成质量效能低下的状况。加强城市基础设施各部门的统一协调，加强其社会化管理，提高其运行效率，坚决杜绝重复建设、零散建设和建而不用、用而不全的现象发生，使有限的物力、财力发挥最大的效用。总结推广数字化城市管理模式，提高城市综合管理效率和水平，促进多个政府部门城市管理指挥职能的整合，促进城市管理的标准化、精细化和动态化，积极发挥数字化城市管理在提高城市质量、改善城市环境、促进和谐社会建设等方面的积极作用。

（作者：李如生，住房和城乡建设部城市建设司副司长；严盛虎，住房和城乡建设部城市建设司主任科员）

2011 中国城市信息化进展

2011 年是我国“十二五”开局之年，城市信息化发展开始悄然变化。随着信息技术的发展（诸如物联网、云计算、移动通信等）、信息产品的丰富（诸如智能手机、平板电脑、智能传感器等）以及人们对信息化建设的思考，城市信息化从注重技术层面，转入关注业务流程、应用模式和机制等应用层面；从注重管理层面，转入关注服务居民的日常生活和活动等行为层面，乃至关注人的社会和心理因素对城市信息化的影响等社会层面，进而进一步从技术向应用发展，从面向政府向面向社会发展。

一、“十二五”规划部署城市信息化新战略

“十二五”时期是我国全面建设小康社会的关键时期，是深化改革开放、加快转变经济发展方式的攻坚时期。信息化无疑将为我国未来的发展提供有力的支撑。在已经发布的《中华人民共和国国民经济和社会发展第十二个五年规划纲要》和有关领域及地方的“十二五”规划中，信息技术及其应用方面的内容，为城市信息化发展提供了指南和保障。

（一）国家“十二五”规划纲要指明城市信息化方向

在 2010 年 10 月《中共中央关于制定国民经济和社会发展第十二个五年规划的建议》的基础上，2011 年 3 月全国人民代表大会通过的《中华人民共和国国民经济和社会发展第十二个五年规划纲要》（以下简称《国家“十二五”规划纲要》），对未来五年我国国民经济和社会发展做出了总体部署。在规划纲要中，信息化得到了前所未有的重视，总体上可以概括为三大方面：一是大力发展信息技术及信息产业；二是积极推进城乡管理的信息化建设；三是全面提高各行各业的信息化水平，为国民经济和社会发展提供强有力的支持。

（1）大力发展信息技术及信息产业。《国家“十二五”规划纲要》在“培育发展战略性新兴产业”方面，提出要大力发展节能环保、新一代信息技术、生物、高端装备制造、新能源、新材料、新能源汽车等战略性新兴产业，其中，新一代信息技术产业重点发展新一代移动通信、下一代互联网、三网融合、物联网、云计算、集成电路、新型显示、高端软件、高端服务器和信息服务。在“增强科技创新能力”方面，提出要在空间科学、地球科学等领域抢占未来科技竞争制高点；在生态环保、能源资源、信息网络、公共安全和健康等

领域取得新突破。在“加快发展生产性服务业”方面，指出要培育壮大高技术服务业，包括加强信息服务，提升软件开发应用水平，发展信息系统集成服务、互联网增值服务、信息安全服务和数字内容服务，大力发展地理信息产业等。

(2) 积极推进城乡管理的信息化建设。《国家“十二五”规划纲要》在“积极稳妥推进城镇化”方面，提出要统筹地上、地下市政公用设施建设，全面提升交通、通信、供电、供热、供气、供排水、污水垃圾处理等基础设施水平，增强消防等防灾能力；加强城市综合管理。特别提出“推动数字城市建设，提高信息化和精细化管理服务水平”。在“提高住房保障水平”方面，提出要加强市场监管，规范房地产市场秩序；加快住房信息系统建设，完善信息发布制度。此外，规划纲要在“强化城乡社区自治和服务功能”方面，提出要以居民需求为导向，整合人口、就业、社保、民政、卫生、文化以及综治、维稳、信访等管理职能和服务资源，加快社区信息化建设，构建社区综合管理和服务平台。

(3) 全面提高各行各业的信息化水平。《国家“十二五”规划纲要》在“全面提高各领域信息化”方面，首先提出要构建宽带、融合、安全、泛在的下一代国家信息基础设施，加快经济社会各领域信息化，加强网络与信息安全保障，并进一步提出要积极发展电子商务，完善面向中小企业的电子商务服务，推动面向全社会的信用服务、网上支付、物流配送等支撑体系建设；大力推进国家电子政务建设，推动重要政务信息系统互联互通、信息共享和业务协同，建设和完善网络行政审批、信息公开、网上信访、电子监察和审计体系；加强市场监管、社会保障、医疗卫生等重要信息系统建设，完善地理、人口等基础信息资源体系，强化信息资源的整合，规范采集和发布，加强社会化综合开发利用。此外，还涉及农业生产、交通运输、灾害防治、企业管理等信息化方面的内容。

“十二五”规划纲要指明了城市信息化发展方向。可以预期，未来五年，我国的信息化建设和应用将会有大的发展，城市信息化也必将呈现新的气象。

（二）行业和地方“十二五”规划突出城市信息化地位

2011 年 7 月，科技部发布了《国家“十二五”科学和技术发展规划》。规划对未来五年我国科技发展和自主创新的战略任务进行了部署，突出包括加快实施国家科技重大专项、大力培育和发展战略性新兴产业、推进重点领域核心关键技术突破等一系列重点任务。实施的国家科技重大专项大多与信息化密切相关。而战略性新兴产业中的新一代信息技术则包括：推动下一代互联网、新一代移动通信、云计算、物联网、智能网络终端、高性能计算的发展；实施新型显示、国家宽带网、云计算等科技产业化工程；积极推进三网融合，加快网络与信息安全技术创新，保障网络与信息安全；着力发展集成电路、智慧城市、智慧工业、地理信息、软件信息服务等相关技术，促进信息化带动工业化。此外，还将加强信息产业关键技术和基础软硬件的研发，重点突破高性能网络、宽带无线移动通信技术、网络与信息安全技术、导航与位置服务技术等关键技术；加强信息与空间技术产品的集成创新，培育新技术和新业务，推动信息与空间产业发展，全面提高国民经济和社会信息化水平；重点发展电子商务等，改造提升生产性服务业；重点发展数字生活、数字旅游、空间位置信息服务等，大力培育和发展新兴服务业。在“十二五”科技发展规划中，与城市信息化密切相关的许多技术得到充分重视，同时“智慧城市”被单独列出，也显示城市信息化将会得到进一步的关注和支持。

2011 年 6 月，国家测绘地理信息局制定发布了《测绘地理信息发展“十二五”总体规划纲要》。《规划纲要》提出了“构建数字中国，监测地理国情，发展壮大产业，建设测绘强国”的总体战略和一系列重点任务，其中包括加快推进地理信息资源整合和数字城市建设。《规划纲要》明确提出，要全面总结数字城市建设试点工作，“十二五”期间，在全部地级城市和有条件的县级市开展数字城市建设，基于互联网、物联网技术，实现数字城市的互通互联，并开展数字省区地理空间框架建设推广和普及，推动数字中国、智能中国的建设。

《北京市国民经济和社会发展第十二个五年规划纲要》提出，“十二五”时期要加强信息通信高速网络和枢纽建设，促进资源共享和互联互通，构建城乡一体、全面覆盖的现代化信息基础设施网络，推动首都全面迈进信息高速时代；建设面向公众和产业服务的城市基础空间地理信息服务平台，推进数据交换中心、数据中心和信息处理中心建设；运用现代信息技术，推进城市精细化管理，实现城市运行智能感知，让市民享受城市信息化建设成果。特别是要深化城市管理网格化，推进网格化管理应用范围扩展到郊区县，应用领域扩展到生产、消防、食品卫生、房屋管理、社会管理等领域，推进城市运行监测平台和网格化管理平台相结合，完善城市综合运行监测管理，提供智能民生服务。

《上海市国民经济和社会发展第十二个五年规划纲要》明确提出，要大力实施信息化领先发展和带动战略，构建实时、便捷的信息感知体系，提升网络宽带化和应用智能化水平，推动信息技术与城市发展全面深入融合，建设以数字化、网络化、智能化为主要特征的智慧城市。包括：（1）构建宽带、泛在、融合、安全的信息基础设施体系，成为国内带宽和服务最具竞争力的地区之一；（2）以需求为导向，运用先进传感、网络传输和信息处理技术，实施智能交通、智能电网、智能水网、数字城管、数字健康、数字教育、数字社区和电子政务等重大信息化工程，推进城市管理和公共服务信息化，提升城市运行效率和管理服务水平。

《宁波市国民经济和社会发展第十二个五年规划纲要》对“加快创建智慧城市、提升信息化水平”做了明确规划，提出把握物联网等新一轮信息技术发展的新机遇，以全国电子商务试点城市建设为契机，以智慧应用为导向，以智慧产业发展为重点，促进信息化与工业化、城市化的融合，力争到 2015 年，智慧应用体系、智慧产业基地、智慧基础设施等建设取得明显成效，智慧城市模式创新和标准化建设走在前列。规划纲要提出的十大智慧应用体系包括：智慧制造、智慧物流、智慧贸易和智慧能源等产业体系，智慧公共服务、智慧健康保障、智慧交通、智慧安居服务、智慧文化服务和智慧社会管理等应用体系。

除上述领域和城市外，其他很多领域及几乎所有城市在其“十二五”发展规划或国民经济和社会发展规划纲要以及各种专项规划中，都对城市信息化建设和应用进行了规划部署。

二、三网融合与无线城市发展迅猛

(一) 三网融合步伐加快，试点成果逐步显现

根据2010年初国务院发布的“三网融合整体方案”，2010年到2012年为三网融合试点阶段。继2010年6月国务院确定第一批“三网融合”试点的北京、上海、南京、武汉等12个城市之后，进一步确定在2012年初正式发布第二批试点城市，包括了天津、重庆、成都、广州、西安在内的42个城市。不仅4个直辖市及所有省会城市全部纳入试点工作中，20多个其他城市也进入试点范围。三网融合将催生新的产业和应用模式。2011年的发展状况表明，三网融合的推进速度基本符合预期，电信及广电网的改造和提速使得加载更多业务成为可能，虽然试点城市的双向进入业务模式以及执行细节仍有待完善，但IPTV已经成为三网融合较为典型的应用。

2011年10月，广电总局发布《持有互联网电视牌照机构运营管理要求》文件，正式将互联网电视机顶盒纳入互联网电视一体机的管理范围。2011年11月，央广互联网电视集成播控平台中央银河互联网电视集成运营平台正式通过广电总局验收，互联网电视七大国有播控平台布局完毕。中国互联网电视（CNTV）是以视听互动为核心、融网络特色与电视特色于一体的全球化、多语种、多终端的国家网络视频公共服务平台。同时，CNTV与三网融合试点地区广电运营商合建的IPTV播控分平台已经陆续建设完成并开播，将建成全国性的运营传播网络平台。

作为中国国际广播电台新媒体战略下的重要业务，其互联网电视平台“中国国际广播电视网络台”于2011年12中旬投入试运营，并力求不断创新运营模式，以多语种、多类型、多终端的形态，面向全球受众提供服务。与此同时，几乎所有的国内电视机厂商都开始批量生产内置网络平台的电视一体机，主流电视终端生产商都把互联网电视一体机作为替代普通电视机的主打产品。

作为北京三网融合试点单位中唯一的有线电视运营商，歌华有线正在加速转型，不断拓展新的业务领域和服务内容。2011年6月，歌华有线推出“歌华飞视”。歌华飞视采用自主知识产权的融合网元，利用有线电视网络和WiFi传输技术，实现了有线电视网络向无线覆盖的延伸，用户可以通过智能手机、平板电脑等收看电视节目，而不需要担心上网流量费。

工信部发布的信息显示，截至2011年11月底，全国IPTV用户已超过1 100万户，手机视频用户超过4 000万户。据工信部电信研究院的一份分析报告认为，2010—2012年将是我国三网融合的试点阶段和磨合缓冲期，试点阶段IPTV仍处于非完全市场化的发展和竞争状态。

(二) 无线城市发展迅猛、推动多行业信息化

移动宽带通信与无线网络技术的发展，使得无线高速宽带与水、电、暖、燃气一起，并

列为一个现代化城市所必须具备的五大基础设施，是衡量一个城市信息化程度和国际竞争力、影响力的重要标志。2011 年，众多城市大力推进城市无线网络或“无线城市”建设，并将宽带、3G 或 4G 等技术优势与传统行业相结合，强力推进政府、企业、社区、家庭、学校的信息化建设。

新一代移动宽带通信技术——4G 技术，正全面进入蓬勃发展时期。全球主要运营商均已开始或将要部署 4G 商用网络，4G 网络的最大下载速度超过 100Mbps，约为目前 3G 网络的 20 倍。在美国、欧洲、日本等地区 LTE 已经开展商用，终端产品不断丰富，各种基于移动宽带的新型应用不断涌现。我国研发制造企业从标准制定、技术研发阶段开始，就广泛参与和积极投入到 TD-LTE 技术中。

2011 年 11 月，“北京新一代移动通信技术及产品突破工程”（即“4G 工程”）正式启动。北京“4G 工程”科研经费达 4 000 余万元，涉及创新应用开发、核心产品和关键设备研制、重大技术突破等三方面 11 个项目。“4G 工程”拟培育一批新型应用，研制一批高端产品，突破一批关键技术，搭建一批技术验证平台。“4G 工程”确定了 4 个方面的任务：一是支持运营商及终端生产商建设创新应用平台；二是在芯片、终端和设备方面研制一批国际领先的产品；三是依托市级重点实验室及工程技术研究中心，研建 4G 试验平台；四是支持核心技术攻关，积极参与标准制定，扩大 TD-LTE 标准的国际影响力。

河北省有 11 个地市政府签署了使用 3G（TD-SCDMA）技术建设“无线城市”协议，已有 10 个地市建成无线城市门户网站，并与气象、电力、环保等行业合作，开通了自动雨量采集、企业排污监测、水墒情监控、车辆状态监控、生产设备监控等应用，推动行业信息化应用。2012 年 1 月，“无线城市”平台开通仪式在河北省艺术中心举行，该平台涵盖了政务、公共事业、交通、医疗、教育、就业、生活服务、消费购物等 10 大类近 50 项应用服务。

2011 年，我国主要电信运营商都争相开展无线城市建设工作。截至 2011 年 12 月，大陆 31 个省、自治区、直辖市的 200 多座城市都与相关电信运营商签署了无线城市建设合作协议，其中 25 个省市初步完成平台建设，将陆续上线推广。所推出的“政务、医疗、教育、金融、旅游、生活服务、消费购物”等 10 大门类、50 个重点应用，公众通过手机上网基本上就可以获得所需信息。其中，政府网站、移动执法、校讯通、WLAN 热点查询、车辆定位、移动办公、商家优惠、无线 POS 等应用受到广大用户喜爱，年度累计访问量增长迅速。

中国互联网络信息中心（CNNIC）于 2012 年 1 月发布了《第 29 次中国互联网络发展状况统计报告》。截至 2011 年 12 月底，我国大陆地区网民规模达到 5.13 亿，其中城镇网民占 73.5%；互联网普及率较 2010 年底提升 4 个百分点，达到 38.3%；有 12 个省市的互联网普及程度超过全国大陆地区平均水平，其中北京市互联网普及率达到 70.3%，位列全国大陆地区第一。

（三）移动终端逐步普及，改变信息化应用模式

随着智能手机、平板电脑等移动终端和 LBS 应用的普及，无线城市的加速建设，城市

信息化应用模式正在发生变化。移动终端正在成为随身携带的计算机，通过移动互联网实现数据通信，内置的GPS、摄像头及其他传感装置构成了流动的空间定位装置和传感器，集多种功能于一体成为移动互联网、物联网和云计算的普及率最高和应用范围最广的终端设备，同时也在改变着人们的工作、生活和娱乐方式，如智能手机摄像头与软件的组合，构成条码和二维码识别器，与商品比价网的数据库，为消息者购买商品提供现场的多家价格比对服务。

2011年10月，Google与IPSOS Research发布的联合调查的结果表明，中国城市（主要基于在北京、上海、沈阳、成都等7个城市的调查）已成为全球五大智能手机普及率最高的地区之一，高达35%，仅次于新加坡（62%）和澳大利亚（37%），这个比例在亚太地区是最高的。智能手机的十大用途分别为：浏览网页（50%）、听音乐（43%）、收发电子邮件（包括使用QQ，41%）、使用搜索引擎查询信息（37%）、拍照或录像（37%）、通过报纸或杂志的网页版浏览新闻（35%）、登录社交平台（35%）、浏览微博或其他信息平台（34%）、玩游戏（33%）及查询路线或使用地图（28%）。在电视与智能手机之间，50%的受访者表示宁愿放弃电视而非智能手机，说明智能手机在家庭娱乐方面的重要价值正在急速攀升。

《第29次中国互联网络发展状况统计报告》显示，2011年我国手机网民规模达到3.56亿，同比增长17.5%，手机网民在总体网民中的比例达69.3%，成为中国网民的重要组成部分；2011年我国电子商务类应用继续稳步发展，包括网络购物、网上支付、网上银行、旅行预订在内的电子商务类应用在保持稳步发展态势，其中网络购物用户规模达到1.94亿人，较上年底增长20.8%，网上支付用户和网上银行全年用户也增长了21.6%和19.2%，目前用户规模分别为1.67亿和1.66亿。

2011年12月，中科院计算所研发的“面向盲人的位置服务自动系统”有效地解决了盲人朋友出行难以确知自己所处的具体位置的问题。该系统以通用智能手机为载体，充分利用目前环境中越来越丰富的WiFi无线资源，实现了室内外无缝切换的手机定位与服务模式，可达到室内外2~5米的定位精度。系统既可自动提交盲人活动地点与轨迹，也能通过方便易用的按钮操作，让盲人听到语音提示的自己的位置和周围的建筑物或单位。同时，监护人也可通过绑定的手机获知盲人的当前位置，还可通过指定起始时间，查询到盲人的活动地点、轨迹及停留时间，为盲人及其监护人之间架设了便捷的沟通桥梁。

三、城市空间信息服务呈现新气象

（一）国产卫星导航与遥感技术获得重大突破

城市信息化发展离不开卫星导航与遥感技术等空间信息技术的支撑。2011年，我国自主卫星导航与遥感技术取得了重大突破，将进一步推动城市信息化发展。

2011年12月，国务院新闻办公室举行“北斗卫星导航系统试运行情况”新闻发布会，表明中国的第二代北斗卫星导航系统正式开始提供试运行服务。试运行服务期间，将向中国及周边地区提供连续的导航定位和授时服务，利用已经发射的10颗卫星组网，定位服务精度可达25米；到2012年底，北斗卫星导航系统将有16颗卫星组网提供正式运行服务，定位服务精确度可达10米。

北斗卫星导航系统可在全球范围内全天候、全天时，为各类用户提供高可靠的定位、导航、授时服务，并兼具短报文通信能力，在军事定位导航（飞机、导弹、水面舰艇和潜艇的定位导航等）、民用航空定位导航（飞机在大雾天气情况下的自动盲降）、铁路运输导航（铁路运营安全监控）、公路及城市车辆导航与救灾抢险领域，都可以发挥重要的作用。与美国“GPS”系统、欧洲“伽利略”系统、俄罗斯“格洛纳斯”系统的建设不完全相同，我国的北斗卫星导航系统有“源定位”和“短报文”特色服务，短信服务是北斗卫星导航系统的特色和优势。北斗卫星导航系统除了能够告诉用户“什么时间、在什么地方”之外，还可以将用户的位置信息发送出去。如果在没有手机信号的偏远山区迷路或大海航行迷失，都可以利用这个服务功能将自己的“位置”发送给北斗卫星，这样，搜救队就可轻而易举将用户“定位”。

在国家“十二五”规划中，卫星导航被列入战略性新兴产业之一。相关部门针对行业应用发展也制定了卫星导航产业的具体推进措施和目标，已经有8个部委和6个地方政府出台了强制或鼓励发展卫星导航/北斗系统的“十二五”规划细则。同时，国家已经部署42项重大专项应用示范工程促进北斗卫星导航系统产业化推进，其中“重点运输过程监控管理服务示范系统工程”就是以现有全国重点营运车辆联网联控系统为基础，集中安装兼容北斗的车载终端应用系统。在国家与地方政策力挺之下，北斗卫星导航系统及其应用有望飞速发展，推动城市信息化应用新模式。

2011年12月，我国成功发射“资源一号”02C卫星。这是一颗填补国内高分辨率遥感数据空白的卫星，卫星携带2台2.36米的高分辨率相机和1台5米全色和10米多光谱相机，不仅获取数据的精度大大提高，而且一次扫描的数据覆盖范围也大大增加，是我国遥感技术领域的重大自主创新成果，所获取的数据可以广泛应用于国土资源调查与监测、城乡规划等领域，推动城市信息化发展。

（二）数字城市地理空间框架建设成效显著

数字城市地理空间框架建设是国家测绘地理信息局近年来主导并在全国范围着力推进的主要工作之一，其目标是在全国330多个地级以上城市合和少数条件较好的县级城市建立数字城市地理空间框架。

2011年10月，国家测绘地理信息局在江苏南京召开全国数字城市建设工作会议，提出进一步加大力度推动数字城市建设。据统计，目前数字城市地理空间框架建设已在全国29个省、自治区、直辖市的220个城市开展了建设和应用工作，其中地级市约180个，占我国全部地级市的60%。数字城市地理空间框架建设的成果直接服务于领导决策、经济建设、应急指挥、国土资源、城市规划、房产管理、环境保护、防灾减灾、灾后重建、安全生产、医疗卫生、人口管理、旧城改造、地名管理及交通、海洋、旅游、文物、工商、电力、电信、农业、水利等各个领域，开发的各种典型应用系统已达1 000个以上。该项工作实施以来，取得了显著的效果，受到了广泛的关注。

作为面向公众的地理空间信息服务平台，天地图运行以来受到了中央领导的重视，媒体大量报道，网民广泛关注，境内外反响强烈。2011年10月，国家测绘地理信息局在中国测绘创新基地召开天地图开通一周年暨新产品发布会，发布了天地图2011版和手机版。财政部专项经费支持天地图运营维护，使得包括设备扩容、互联网接入带宽租用、异地缓存服务（CDN）租用、技术支持与服务采购、软件升级、数据补充等方面的天地图主节点运行支持环境扩充，到2011年12月底全部到位并部署运行。经过此次扩容，天地图网站已建成了电信级互联网接入、负载均衡服务器集群、高可用服务器集群、企业级的数据存储备份和基于等级保护第三级的计算机安全系统，天地图主节点整体性能提升了3倍以上。

国家测绘地理信息局正在围绕建设一流的有国际影响力的以在线地图服务为主的综合信息搜索服务网站的总体目标，按照“数据覆盖全球、内容丰富翔实、应用方便快捷、服务优质高效”的要求，精心策划、精益求精，力争将天地图打造成为向政府、企业、公众提供权威、可信、统一的地理信息公共服务平台。

（三）城市信息化应用服务取得丰硕成果

2011年11月，住房和城乡建设部组织在北京召开了第六届中国数字城市建设技术研讨会——数字城市高峰论坛。我国目前已有220多个城市开展了数字城市建设，其中40余个城市已经在一定范围内建成城市建设和管理的信息化应用系统，涉及城市的规划、国土、城管、公安、工商、税务、环保、房产、卫生、药监等30多个领域，其经济效益、社会效益和行政效能十分显著。在数字城市建设的体制、机制、技术政策、产业等方面取得了一定的研究成果和经验，并通过一些项目的实施，取得了丰硕的成果。这些成果包括数字城市建设的标准体系建设、数字城市基础设施建设、数字城市空间数据平台建设、数字城市提高城市管理水平、数字城市提高政府服务水平等多个方面。

随着我国数字城市的建设，形成了一大批针对城市规划建设与经营管理的应用系统，诸如电子政务系统、电子商务系统、环保信息系统、水务管理系统、交通管理系统、灾害防范系统、应急指挥系统、数字城管系统等。住房和城乡建设部不仅倡导与推进全国150多个城市建设了网格化数字城市监管系统，而且已建成覆盖全国的“全国城镇污水处理管理信息系统”，并即将建成“全国个人住房信息管理系统”和“全国个人住房公积金信息管理系统”等。数字城市应用系统涉及城市管理的方方面面，在促进城市科学管理、保障城市安全、改善交通状况、提高政府决策能力等方面作出了巨大贡献，城市管理水平得到明显提高。

与此同时，数字城市的发展提高了城市政府的社会服务水平，如北京推出的“市民主页”，市民可以随时随地随需地获取与政务公开、公共事业服务、个人生活等相关的各种城市服务信息。用户可以通过“我的提醒”、“我的服务”和“我的声音”等栏目实时了解对譬如交通违章提醒、热点新闻、多项公共服务等与日常生活息息相关的信息。厦门推出的

"掌上公交"业务，使得市民不仅可以通过手机查询出行线路并确定所要乘坐的公交车，同时还可根据自己的需要定制公交车到站的预约提醒，为市民节省了60%以上的等车时间，"掌上公交"月访问量已超过160万人次，成为市民低碳出行的首选信息工具。

城市信息化必将推动社会信息化。2011年2月，中央领导同志在省部级主要领导干部专题研讨班上指出，我们要正确面对工业化、信息化、城镇化进程不断加快的新形势；要进一步树立与信息化社会环境相适应的社会管理理念；要积极推进社会管理体制机制制度创新，在人口服务管理方面，要完善居民身份证制度，建立国家人口基础信息库，提高对实有人口的管理服务水平；要建立健全社区信息综合管理平台，使社区管理服务达到全方位、无缝隙、全覆盖；要逐步形成信息共享、工作协调的管理机制，促进社会组织健康有序发展。

2011年，我国的社交网络（SNS）继续保持稳定增长。据报道，截至2011年10月，我国社交网站用户规模已达到2.5亿。从应用主体上，微博仍然是2011年SNS行业的热点，部分博运营商也开始尝试微博商业化之路；从媒介价值上，企业加深对微博、SNS等社交媒体营销的认识，而社会化营销ROI评估体系的产生也促进社会化营销的快速发展；从整体互联网趋势上，SoLoMo概念深入社交媒体领域，而各大运营商也着手布局SoLoMo模式，创造新的生态链。由于移动化和本地化有助于社交网络在时间和空间上的延伸，而用户的地理位置结合真实社交关系使得用户的信息更为精准，从而提升社交网站和微博的营销价值，触发社交网站和微博去探索更多元的盈利模式，改变人们的信息化生活方式。

《第29次中国互联网络发展状况统计报告》显示，微博成了我国2011年最火的互联网应用，微博用户数达到2.5亿，较2011年底增长了296%，网民的微博使用率从2010年的13.8%猛涨到2011年的48.7%。但是，在微博发展过程中，也出现了传播谣言和虚假信息、利用网络进行欺诈等突出问题，损害了公共利益和公众利益，社会各方强烈呼吁加强互联网诚信建设，规范微博服务管理，保障互联网健康发展。2011年12月，北京市发布《北京市微博客发展管理若干规定》出台，要求微博用户必须进行真实身份信息注册后，才能使用发言功能。实名注册将有效减少微博的负面影响，有利于营造健康和谐的网络环境。

随着卫星导航与遥感技术等空间信息技术的突破与应用、城市地理空间框架建设的迅速发展、数字化城市管理系统的应用推广、地理信息公共服务平台推广，城市政府管理逐步向"精细化"和"人性化"方向发展，基于信息技术的多部门业务协同也通过城市信息化得到体现。事实上，城市信息化领域相关的专家已开始分析和探讨城市政府部门之间的业务协同问题，从城市发展和政府管理的主线出发，通过业务流程梳理政府的业务，促进政府的业务协同。显然，城市信息化中的政府业务协同问题将是"十二五"需要解决的关键问题。

四、智慧城市进入规划建设发展阶段

随着传感网、物联网、云计算、4G移动通信、卫星导航定位系统、高分辨率遥感等新型信息技术迅速发展和深入应用，信息化发展正酝酿着重大变革和新的突破，由原来的数字化、智能化向更高阶段的智慧化发展已成为必然趋势，数字城市有了更丰富的内涵，正在向智慧城市迅速发展。无论是国家层面，还是省市层面，无论是学术领域，还是技术领域，无论是政府部门，还是企业部门，都非常重视智慧城市的规划与发展。

（一）云计算与物联网推动智慧城市发展

“云计算”被誉为继个人电脑、互联网之后，信息技术领域的第三次变革浪潮。“云计算”已经从一个模糊的概念变成了整个IT产业清晰的发展方向。“云计算”通过计算资源的集约化和虚拟化，可以实现IT资源的物理集中和逻辑分隔，促进IT资源的整合与共享，以及应用的低成本、高可靠性、可扩展性及业务敏捷，更好地开发利用信息资源，正在改变我国的城市信息化进程。

2011年是我国云计算从云端走向应用的一年。虽然云计算技术应用于城市信息化的顶层设计、应用模式、管理体制还处于摸索阶段，但是，国家高度重视云计算技术对IT产业的影响。2011年3月《国家“十二五”规划纲要》将云计算列为新一代信息技术产业的发展重点。2011年财政部政府采购工作要点，将云计算等新型服务业态纳入政府采购。2011年11月，国家发改委正式授牌北京、上海、深圳、杭州、无锡5个城市为云计算试点城市，开展云计算服务创新发展试点建设。与此同时，多个城市正在实施名目各异的“云计划”，诸如北京的“祥云计划”、上海的“云海计划”、天津的“翔云计划”、重庆的“云端计划”、广州的“天云计划”、武汉的“黄鹤白云”计划、西安“高新云”和“长安云”构成的“双云战略”、宁波的“星云计划”等等。然而，民众感受比较深的云计算应用是“云存储”服务。云存储服务以“安全、省心、方便”的理念将云存储引入到民众的日常生活，具备网络同步、备份和共享功能，给工作和生活带来了便利。

推动城市信息化发展的另一项新技术就是物联网。物联网是“物物相连的互联网”，是在互联网基础之上的延伸和扩展的一种网络，借助于类型多样、功能各异的传感与定位技术，诸如射频识别（RFID）技术、红外感应技术、全球定位系统、激光扫描技术等，把任何物品与互联网相连接，进行信息交换和通信，实现智能化识别、定位、跟踪、监控和管理。物联网的用户端延伸和扩展到了任何物品与物品之间，进行信息交换和通信。物联网用途广泛，遍及智能交通、环境保护、政府工作、智能消防、老人护理、个人健康等多个领域，是继计算机、互联网与移动通信网之后的又一次信息产业浪潮。

我国非常重视物联网的发展，自2009年温家宝总理在无锡视察工作时提出“感知中国”的概念以来，无锡部署了“感知中国中心”（包括：建设传感网创新园、传感网产业园、信息服务园），并规划至2015年总投资40亿元，建成引领中国传感网技术发展和标准制订的中国物联网产业研究院。2011年11月，工业和信息化部印发《物联网“十二五”发展规划》，认为物联网是战略性新兴产业的重要组成部分，对加快转变经济发展方式具有重要推动作用，并提出了到2015年的发展目标，并将在“攻克核心技术、构建标准体系、推进产业发展、培育骨干企业、开展应用示范、规划区域布局、信息安全保障、公共服务能力”等8个方面实施一系列重点工程。这必将加速物联网的建设，从而促进城市信息化的发展。

（二）国家部委力推智慧城市规划与建设试点

2010 年底，武汉与深圳一起，被科技部列为国家“863 智慧城市”主题项目试点城市，开启了我国城市信息化的新阶段，步入智慧城市发展时期。

2011 年 1 月以来，武汉按照“十二五”规划，举全市之力推进智慧城市建设，成立了以市政府主要领导牵头的智慧城市建设领导小组，全面整合科技、发改、城建、电信、广电、交通、卫生、环保、规划、城管等多部门力量，全方位推进智慧武汉建设。武汉市科技局投入 1 000 万元面向全球公开招标，分“概念设计”与“总体规划与设计”两个阶段开展智慧城市顶层设计工作。到 2011 年 10 月，已完成了智慧城市“概念设计”和“总体规划与设计”两个阶段的全球公开招标，并形成了具有理论科学性和战略前瞻性的总体规划与设计方案。武汉市科技局本着“总体规划先行、行业应用并举”的发展思路，努力丰富武汉“智慧城市”建设的内涵和体系，在城市交通、市政管理、医疗卫生、文化教育、公共安全等 12 个重点领域制订未来 5 ~ 10 年发展路线图，并着手实施一批应用示范工程，组建一批行业创新平台，支持一批重大高新技术产业化项目，构建“规划设计——技术创新——示范推广——应用服务”的武汉“智慧城市”建设与发展模式。

深圳充分发挥信息通信产业发达、信息化基础设施优良等优势，推动“智慧深圳”建设。2011 年 10 月，国家超级计算深圳中心、深圳市云计算产业协会与太平洋电信签署战略合作协议，以基础架构云为核心，为云计算落地提供重要的基础支撑，推进深圳市云计算产业发展，加快深圳市“十二五”规划目标“智慧深圳”的实现进程。2011 年 11 月发布的《深圳市“十二五”规划纲要实施方案》中，在“智慧深圳”与信息化建设方面，明确要实施信息基础设施跃升计划，无线宽带网络覆盖率超过 83%，互联网普及率超过 80%，全面推进光纤入户，提高宽带接入能力。一年来，智慧深圳的手机“网上交警”栏目，为市民提供“交警微博、出行提示、业务办理、法规宣传”等便民直通车业务；“网上交警”的“短信敬告执法、我来拍违章、我来报路况、轻微交通事故快处快赔”等特色应用服务，深受市民的欢迎，目前已发展移动用户 110 万，及大地拉近了市民与政府的距离。此外，智慧深圳“城管通”、“警务通”、“智能交通管理”等一系列信息化服务广泛应用于深圳的公安执法、人口管理、环境监测、气象预警、政务公开、应急指挥等各领域，协助政府有效提高城市管理水平。

（三）众多城市积极开展智慧城市规划与建设

在信息技术发展推动、城市管理与服务需求牵引以及国家政策引导下，2011 年我国智慧城市的发展势头强劲，包括北京、上海等直辖市，广州、武汉等省会城市，宁波、扬州等其他城市，都在积极开展智慧城市规划与建设工作。

在“十一五”时期，北京市累计建设 3G 基站约 1.8 万个，具备 20M 宽带接入能力的用户超过 176 万户。在实施“感知北京”示范项目与“祥云工程”行动计划以来，2011 年底北京市整体网民数量接近 1 400 万人，普及率达到 70.3%，位列全国第一，城市信息化建设已达到世界发达国家主要城市的中上等水平，数字北京基本实现。在此基础上，北京在“十二五”期间大力推进智慧城市的建设，包括加快无线物联网专网和无线宽带专网等网络基础设施建设，推进感知北京示范工程项目，建设物联网特色产业园区，积极推进物联网在公共服务、交通管理、卫生医疗等领域的应用。北京计划投资1 000亿元建设城市高速信息网络，培育10个具有国际影响的企业。到2015年云计算的三类典型服务（IaaS、PaaS、SaaS）形成500亿元产业规模，带动产业链形成2 000亿元产值，云技术应用水平居世界各主要城市前列，成为世界级的云计算产业基地。

2011年7月，天津市委提出，“十二五”期间天津要加快构建“智慧天津”的战略部署，推动天津市信息化向更高阶段迈进；并明确了“三步走”的时间表，就是三年打基础、五年大发展、十年成格局。具体而言，就是到2013年，天津市将培育出若干个产值超千亿的战略性新兴产业，“物联网”产业得到起步，智能化城市示范工程基本建成。到2015年，天津市将培育形成若干个接近或达到世界先进水平的战略性新兴产业群，数字化、网络化、智能化、无线化成为市民生活工作的主要方式。到2020年，“智慧天津”基本建成，届时天津将成为智慧基础设施完善、智慧应用水平显著提升、智慧产业领先、具有现代化、智能化的北方经济中心和国际港口城市。

2011年9月，上海市政府公布的《推进智慧城市建设2011—2013年行动计划》，未来3年内，上海规划基本建成真正意义上的宽带城市、无线城市；使信息产业总规模达到1.28万亿元，成为国内新一代信息技术创新引领区和产业集聚区。构筑智慧城市，上海电信从蓝图上做好了准备，超前发展基础通信能力。全面启动建设上海城市光网行动，实现光纤进楼到户，用3年时间达到“百兆到户、千兆进楼、百万兆出口”的网络覆盖和光纤上网。

2011年9月，重庆市“市长国际经济顾问团会议第六届年会”在重庆国际会展中心举行，会议的主题是“城市信息化与信息产业——全球化背景下云端智能城市发展”。会议代表认为：重庆正处于城市化、工业化、信息化的加速发展阶段，需要全力打造云端智能城市，其中重点实施“云端计划”，前景广阔、机遇众多。会议代表建议：重庆要推动智能城市建设，首先应该不断完善通信基础设施，包括安装高速的宽带互联网，为云计算提供技术支撑；其次要进一步发展本地人才库，来提高互联网的普及，播种创新的种子，使重庆成为全球范围内极具竞争力的知识中心。最后要进一步开发IT工具用于城市的规划和管理系统。

智慧广州的建设理念是“智慧技术高度集中、智能经济高端发展、智能服务高效便民”。广州市委市政府在“十二五”规划提出建设新设施、发展新产业、研发新技术、推进新应用、创造新生活等5个“智慧广州”的建设方向。根据“智慧广州”的整体构想，天河智慧广州示范中心以智慧、低碳、幸福为主题，聚集了40个智慧广州基础设施、管理、生活、产业场景，120家全球及广州企业的最新技术，并且着重打造智慧八景：智慧之钥、智慧之球、智慧之核、智慧之舱、智慧之窗、智慧之家、智慧之本、智慧之光。

宁波智慧城市建设目标分两个阶段：第一阶段，到2015年，建成一批成熟的智慧应用体系，形成一批上规模的智慧产业基地，取得显著成效；第二阶段，到2020年，将宁波建设成为智慧应用水平领先、智慧产业集群发展、智慧基础设施完善、具有国际港口城市特色的智慧城市。2011 年 4 月宁波市出台了《加快创建智慧城市行动纲要（2011—2015 年）》，安排了智慧城市实施路线图、计划书、时间表，未来 5 年，宁波智慧城市建设共包括 31 项工程 87 个项目，总投资超过 400 亿元。其中，2011 年的投资额接近 50 亿元，从应用体系、产业基地、基础设施、居民信息应用能力和发展环境等 5 个体系全面展开智慧城市建设。

2011 年 7 月，扬州市政府、扬州市卫生局、神州数码在扬州召开项目启动会，打造"智慧扬州区域卫生信息平台"。通过卫生信息数据交换平台，扬州将为市民建立统一的居民电子健康档案，整合医疗卫生资源，完善各类医疗卫生服务应用，为百姓提供安全、有效、方便、价廉的医疗卫生服务

2011 年 7 月，福建省人民政府和中国电信集团公司在福州签署《共同建设数字福建智慧城市群暨"十二五"信息化战略合作框架协议》，中国电信将力争用 5 年时间，投入 600 亿元，建成由 10 个智慧城市组成的数字福建智慧城市群，使数字福建成为全国信息化建设的标杆。

2011 年 7 月，浙江省有关领导表示要建设"智慧浙江"，认为"智慧浙江"是新时期"数字浙江"建设的全面提升工程，是运用新的信息技术构筑一个感知化、物联化、智能化的浙江，以更高质、更高效、更科学、更精细、更便捷地动态管理城市经济社会各种活动，实现发展更科学、社会更和谐、人民更幸福。

五、结语

概括来说，2011 年城市信息化更加注重"以人为本"，更强调实用性和长效机制，更为关注 IT 技术工具与人的社会关系与行为之间的有机结合，从而利用人的社会关系与行为的本质性规律将信息化无缝嵌入，形成内在的推动力，减少信息化过程的阻力，调动全社会的信息化积极性和促进公众参与。同时，在传感网、物联网、云计算等众多新型信息技术的支持下，数字城市的内涵进一步拓展，智慧城市规划与建设成为 2011 年城市信息化的最强音，城市信息化建设在一定程度上进入了具有"无线、移动、物联、便捷、智能、高效、参与、服务"等特点的新阶段，或者说正在由数字城市阶段走向智慧城市时代。与此同时，如何将社会发展的需求与最新技术发展成果集成构建智慧城市，使得城市政府高效透明、城市环境绿色和谐、城市生活幸福安康，将成为值得关注与探索的城市信息化新课题。在未来的城市信息化进程中，需要进一步关注核心技术创新、信息产业发展、以及民众应用服务等关键问题，使城市信息化真正成为促进城市经济社会科学发展的强有力支撑。

（作者：王丹，建设综合勘察研究设计院有限公司研究员；党安荣，清华大学建筑学院教授；梁军，北京超图软件股份有限公司副总裁；何建邦，中国科学院资源与环境信息系统国家重点实验室研究员，国际欧亚科学院院士）

参考文献

[1] 3sNews 视讯传媒网站：http：//sstb. co. 3snews. net/.

[2] 百度新闻网：http：//news. baidu. com/.

[3] 国家测绘地理信息局网站：http：//fazhan. sbsm. gov. cn/.

[4] 国家基础地理信息中心网站：http：//ngcc. sbsm. gov. cn/Guide/.

[5] 数字城市网：http：//www. d-city. com. cn/.

[6] 新华网北京频道：http：//www. bj. xinhuanet. com/.

[7] 中国互联网络信息中心网站：http：//www. cnnic. net. cn/.

[8] 中华人民共和国工信部网站：http：//www. miit. gov. cn/.

[9] 中华人民共和国国家发展和改革委员会网站：http：//www. sdpc. gov. cn/.

[10] 中华人民共和国国土资源部网站：http：//www. mlr. gov. cn/.

[11] 中华人民共和国科学技术部网站：http：//www. most. gov. cn/.

[12] 中华人民共和国住房和城乡建设部网站：http：//www. mohurd. gov. cn/.

论坛篇

学术前沿议人居

一、世界任纷纭，我自觅转型

“无时代之变，便无历史可写”，① 历史演变的过程本身就是一次又一次转型的过程。在中国古代漫长的历史过程中，因为发展速度缓慢，这种转型是不易察觉的。至后期只沿着既有的轨迹运行，变化又比较缓慢，尤其是康乾以后，失去了丰富的创造力。及至近代，在内忧外患之中忽然发现自身的落后与西方的强大，才想要加以追赶，可谓是缓慢被动地认识到了转变的必要性。

当今的时代发展不断向我们提出新的问题。就世界范围来看，一方面，人类面临着重重危机，如：经济危机、气候变化、自然灾害、环境破坏、南北差异、贫富对立、能源与粮食的短缺、物种绝灭的加速，等等；另一方面，又存在着全球范围的纷乱不安，如：恐怖袭击、武装冲突，等等，威胁着人类的生存和发展，这些都迫使我们对政治、经济、社会、文化、城市等问题进行更多的思考和探索。世界的发展面临转型，今天可称为是“大转型”的时代，这是人居环境科学研究大的时代背景。

中国社会也正处在转型之中。自 1949 年中华人民共和国成立，便建立了一种新体制，虽意图转型但有时仍显力不从心。直至 20 世纪 70 年代末改革开放以后，中国才开始主动的探索转型之路，30 年来既取得了辉煌的成就，也产生了不少问题。“最优越的机遇与最尖锐的矛盾”、“成绩显著但问题严峻”②，与西方相比，中国经济社会、城市化的发展急速，规模浩大，中国对问题的认识及技术的研究却相对滞后，西方的发展模式包括已经证明不合适的模式等仍在中国重演，这迫使我们必须在总结 30 年来经验教训的基础上，多方借鉴、研究，探索中国的转型发展之路。这从学术领域涉及多个重大问题，包括：科学与人文、中与西、古与今、城与乡、发达地区与欠发达地区，等等。

---

① 钱穆．中国历史研究方法［M］．北京：生活·读书·新知三联书店，2001.

② 吴良镛．中国城乡发展模式转型的思考［M］．北京：清华大学出版社，2009.

二、从人类发展前途来领悟人居环境科学

(一) 人居环境科学与人人相关，是普通人的科学

在世界问题的纷纭之中，中国也正处在社会经济的转型期，城市疾速发展，各方面的问题纷繁芜杂，未来的发展方向也难以预料。但是，在人类文明的发展进程中有一点是始终不变的——社会要进步，人类要追求更加健康美好的生活。上海世博会之广受欢迎，正表明了“城市让生活更美好”是人类共同的期待。从人类的发展前途来领悟人居环境科学的发展，使我们得到了更多的信心。

人居环境科学并非高不可攀、玄而又玄的理论，而是普遍存在于大众日常生活之中的“普通常识”。经过化解和归纳，充分认识“普通常识”的科学性规律，便可以成为“平凡真理”，进而又可成为“社会共识”，使大众对基本原理和工作方法产生认同。同时，人居环境科学又是需要通过艰苦的科学研究探索才可以实现的科学理论，它要将“普通常识”、“平凡真理”、“社会共识”从一般感性上升为科学理性，它渗透于各个学科的理论之中，融会贯通成为一个大的学科体系，最终成为渗透于日常生活与建设活动中的“普世哲学”。因此，人居环境与人人相关，是普通人的科学，人居环境建设是全人类共同的事业，但是面对的情况又是错综复杂的，各有特殊性，因而也可视为永远的“学术前沿”。

(二) 人居环境科学的学术领域有“模糊的包容性”

人居环境科学是中国学者基于中国的现实情况所作出的理论探索，在世界上也具有探索性和前瞻性。其发展历程实践了刘易斯·芒福德（L. Mumford）在 1938 年《城市文化》一书前言中所提出的设想：冀图用“综合的、统一的方式来展示城市这个领域”，“构出一些原则，以便遵从这些原则来改造我们的生存环境。”[①]

人居环境科学以关心人为核心，这是人类的共同追求，故而其学术领域具有模糊的包容性，在当代的社会发展中也有普遍的生存空间。对中国发展而言，当今城市规划中的很多现实问题都离不开人居环境的思想，无论规划体系由分散走向整合、城乡关系由对立走向统筹，等等，这之中人居环境中的整体思想是不可或缺的。在国际事务当中，联合国人居署则具有更多的包容性，其工作得到了全球范围广泛的认可和支持。

---

① “一个想法是这个研究领域（指城市）以往始终是由各个学科的专家们从他们各自的角度分别进行论述的，我则想用一种比较综合的、统一的方式来展示城市这个领域；另一种想法是考虑今后城市社区采取协同行动时的需要，我需要为此构出一些原则，以便遵从这些原则来改造我们的生存环境。”见刘易斯·芒福德（L. Mumford）. 城市文化·前言［M］.［出版者不详］，1938.

三、进一步发展人居环境的理论体系

《尚书》有云："民为邦本，本固邦宁。"《管子》亦言："霸王之所始也，以人为本，本治则国固，本乱则国危。""以人为本"是中国传统文化的精华，也是人居环境科学的核心问题，宏观层面上，国家战略与区域发展要以民为本；中观层面上，城乡建设要以人民群众的需求为出发点；微观层面上，广大群众也需要一个良好宜人的生活环境。正是以关怀人为出发点，我们在不断进行着多层次理论的探索与思考，也不断地在实践中检验、展拓理论，取得了一系列实质性进展。其总目标是通过理论研究与建设实践的努力，探索一种交叉的多学科群组，融贯包括自然科学、技术科学、人文科学及艺术等与人居环境相关的部分，形成一个新的科学体系。

（一）理论的不断探索与思考

自从人居环境科学理论提出之后，理论的探索一直没有停息。继 2001 年《人居环境科学导论》出版之后，《人居环境科学进展》一书也即将面世，这之中凝聚了众多学者的智慧和汗水，《人居环境发展趋势论》一文也已于近期发表①。这之中既有自上而下对国家宏观战略的思考，认为应当珍惜国土资源，保护生态环境，合理使用土地；也有自下而上对重建完整社区，建造社会住宅等的研究。

亨利·丘吉尔（Henry Stern Churchill）1945 年出版的《城市即人民》（*The city is the people*）一书，强调人是城市的核心，没有人城市就无从存在，应关注基本的邻里规划。1946 年我应邀来清华，其间有机会了解到邻里单位的理论，很受启发，当读到《城市即人民》一书时，更是顿然领悟。又在学校旁听费孝通先生的《城市社会学》、《乡村社会学》课程，经过多方阅读与思考，写出了我关于城市规划的第一篇习作论文，萌发"完整社会单位的理论"的概念。

社区本身是一个社会学概念，社区规划与建设的出发点是基层居民的切身利益。在社会整体转型的今天，建设"完整社区"（integrated community）正是从微观角度出发，进行社会重组，通过对人的基本关怀，维护社会公平与团结，最终实现和谐社会的理想。例如，社区养老问题；残疾人康复问题；青年工作者的居住问题等等。今天的中国已进入所谓"后单位"时代，由各事业单位的"大院"分头负责渐转向由社会负责，因此必须丰富社区的内涵，建设"完整社区"，承担综合功能，解决社会问题。

从中国当前的社区发展来看，主要是以房地产开发为主的建设经营模式，市场经济起主导作用。这虽然发挥了很大作用，但也存在很多问题。美国学者凯瑟琳·鲍尔（Catherine Bauer）早在 1934 年出版《近代住宅》（*Modern Housing*）一书指责当时住宅经营为奢侈的投机（the luxury of speculative），指出"不好的制度不能产生好的住房，但只有良好的制度也

① 见《城市与区域规划》，总第 9 期。

不一定能产生好的住房”①，“现代住房是用于居住的，而不是用于谋利的，房屋与社会设施一起作为综合性邻里单元的一部分按照现代方式来进行建造。”②。从20世纪初到现在，社会发生了巨大的变化，但我们仍要清醒地认识到市场经济并不是万能的，不能盲目遵循美国房地产的发展途径，而可从借鉴荷兰、新加坡、我国香港等地建设“社会住宅”的成功经验中博采众长。

在我国，1945年林徽因即著文论战后住宅，1947年梁思成提出“住者有其房”，是人民群众普遍的渴望。在社会转型的大背景下，我们更要思考如何利用自身的智慧来解决时代的问题，在住房建设中加强社会主义的内涵。在当前快速城市化的过程中，理论上说每增加一个城市人口，社会建设就要责无旁贷地加多一份责任和义务。住房及社区的多种基础设施建设需要投入更多的力量，但也不是没有新生的萌芽，社区规划还需要积极的倡导与规划，建立良好的居住环境秩序，促进人民安居，这是走向和谐社会的必由之路。

社区和住房问题是关系民众生存的关键问题，也是当今的社会热点问题，目前各个学科领域虽然做了许多工作，但往往缺乏整体的思想，有支离破碎之嫌。需要进行多学科融贯综合的研究，将社区与住房建设置于城市化与城乡统筹发展的宏观背景下来认识，在战略上整合它所涉及的多方面政策问题，在战术上需要在城市规划、建筑设计、园林设计所进行的物质空间规划建设的基础上，融合社会学、经济学、公共管理等领域的科学理论和研究方法，综合探讨住宅设计、环境塑造、制度保障、社会组织等各方面问题，以实现良好住房、完整社区和和谐社会的共同营造。

在若干年研究实践的基础上，我们清华大学已经从建筑学院为基础的学术活动开始，逐步加强与清华大学其他院系如社会学系、水利系、公共管理学院、经济管理学院等的合作，构建这样一个学科群，共同研究人居环境的现实问题，探讨人居理论发展的方向。

（二）在实践中检验理论、展拓理论

多年来我们进行了多层次的人居环境实践，既是检验理论的必需过程，也是展拓理论的重要契机。这之中既有自上而下，从地区城市到区域整体的研究实践，包括长三角、珠三角、滇西北、京津冀等，《京津冀地区城乡空间发展规划研究》已经完成了两期，近十年来发展变化，第三期正在酝酿之中，也有自下而上，注重基层的建设实践，菊儿胡同居住区建设实验项目便是这一领域的尝试。现在在广东省云浮市，我们正与地方领导一起进行着人居环境理论的地方基层实践。

我曾在1999年于北京召开的国际建协第20次大会主旨报告中提出：“美好的人居环境与美好的人类社会共同创造”，就是意图将环境建设与社会进步的目标逐步统一起来，各种设施的建设无不源于美好的人居环境与和谐社会的基本要求。云浮市正在开展一系列这样的

① Although it is not true that any social-economic order which could produce good housing would be ipso facto a good system, it is true that any arrangement which cannot do so is a reactionary and anti-social one.

② 彼得·霍尔（Peter Hall），《明日之城》中介绍鲍尔的学术观点。

实践，一方面，广泛建设以“健康、生态、幸福”为目标的，关系民生的人居环境设施，如：建设全市5条总长500多公里的生态慢行绿道网，整体改善城乡居住环境；另一方面，政府和社会共同参与到人居环境建设中来，如：采用创新的“共谋、共建、共管、共享”[①]的推进模式，提高地方群众的参与主动性和基层组织凝聚力；同时，坚持统筹和整合，以城带乡，探索新型城镇化，如：健全保障机制，推动基本公共服务城乡共同享有。基于此，云浮的实践还将继续发展，从日常生活的物质环境进一步推广到社会文化环境、产业发展环境、农业生产环境的缔造等各个方面。

在此基础之上我们形成了《云浮共识》，进一步强调“美好环境与和谐社会共同缔造”为目标的纲领，全国多个地方都可以作不同的试验，创造不同的经验。

四、人居环境科学的人文境界与哲学智慧

（一）人居环境科学与人文精神的境界

“现代世界能够给我们人类提供的东西是什么？”[②] 现代社会中广泛存在着对现代文明中人文精神缺失的质疑和反思。人居环境科学是对人类生存与发展的关怀，故而必然要具备高远的人文精神境界，我们对城市文化的研究和正在进行的“中国人居环境史”研究，正是试图重新认识东方人居传统中的人文智慧。

中国文化是世界上从未间断且延续至今的文化，漫长的历史中人居环境建设取得了辉煌的成就，从早在7000年前穴居野处，到聚落定居，再到营城建都、地区开发，不同时期、不同地区也遗存有丰富的人居“原创理念与发展方式”，但缺乏系统的理论总结与提升。“中国人居环境史”的研究旨在以文化自觉的精神认知中国体系，通过梳理中国人居环境的发生、发展、变迁的历史过程及其背后所蕴藏的人居思想的演进历程，辨识其特征，挖掘其规律，探索其模式。中国古人认为：“史者，所以明夫治天下之道也。”[③] 意大利历史学家克罗齐（Benedetto Croce）也说：“当生活的发展逐渐需要时，死历史就会复活，过去史就变成现在的。”[④]

中国人居环境史是中国古代文化的组成部分，是中华文明的一个侧面，整个人居环境的发展历史以及其背后的指导思想，从地区发展到名都大邑，以至城镇发展都存在一以贯之的整体思想，对今天融贯的综合研究有重要的启示意义。中国古代是典型的农业社会，城市与乡村并没有真正的文化与制度的差别，经济上也有直接联系，是一元的整体，今天国家提出“城乡统筹”等战略，正可以从古代的城乡关系中得到更深刻的认识。但同时要认识到，中国从农业社会发展到今天，有它内在的缺陷，在社会体制和结构上都有了根本的变化，在

① 即决策共谋，凝聚民意；发展共建，凝聚民力；建设共管，凝聚民智；成果共享，凝聚民心。

② 刘易斯·芒福德．城市文化·前言［M］．［出版者不详］，1938.

③ ［宋］曾巩．南齐书序．

④ 克罗齐．所有历史都是当代史．

“转型”的大形势中，既要汲取历史智慧，又要从西方工业革命以来城市发展中的知识财富和经验教训中创新，我们要面对的实际问题。在东西方对话的基础上探求新的境界，在学习提炼人类文化遗产的基础上探求新的人文复兴。

(二) 人居环境哲学方法论的智慧

涉及人类的生存与发展，问题多种多样，纷繁复杂，因此人居环境是一个复杂的巨系统，人居环境的问题伴随着社会、环境的变化和技术的进步越来越复杂，需要统筹各方面的影响因素，重视各层面的实际问题，淡化学科界限，开展融贯的综合研究。在哲学和方法论上要具备生成整体的思想，这需要最高决策的智慧。其上策可谓“明者远见于未萌，而智者避危于无形”①，以高屋建瓴的预见，避免前进道路上的激流险滩；其下策可谓“勿临渴掘井”，即谚语所谓“临时抱佛脚”，“头痛医头脚痛医脚”，而是需要以辩证综合的思维和综合创新的道路，为未来可能出现的问题有所预警，及早防治。

整体观念的缺失造成了今天城市发展中的很多问题。它提示我们宜运用复杂性科学观念，以人居环境科学为原则，对政治经济、社会文化有关方面，从城市的空间结构、土地利用、产业发展、政策管理各方面进行整体性的战略决策，并具体有效地落实到有关的空间规划中，确保可持续发展。这需要我们对当今规划科学进行改革。首都北京因为日常严重的交通拥堵而被戏称为“首堵”，这不仅仅是一个技术性问题，而是涉及城市空间结构、土地利用、人口规模、产业发展、政策管理等多方面的综合问题，任何纯技术性的措施，临渴掘井，可以收效于一时，关键在求全局性战略。我们应以交通问题的教训思考其他问题，如今天津市所普遍面临的水危机等。

人居环境科学概念的提出一方面源于生活的领悟、社会的需要，另一方面也来自国际的共识。在人居环境科学发展的过程中，我们一直在不断地向国际学者和学术组织吸取营养，寻找大方向，把握大趋势。从个人感悟到学术探索，再到团队建立，并获得学院、学校和社会的支持，是一个由幼小萌芽逐渐发枝长叶的过程。在中国的范围内来看，良好的城市与区域规划体制和思想仍在探索中，我们希望能够在纷繁芜杂的局面中，在转型的大趋势中，继续发展中国的人居环境科学理论，形成有益于实际工作的指导思想。同时，从全球的视角来看，全球化是世界发展的大趋势，但它并不等同于西方化，既有“大趋势”，应鼓励多有“大创造”，人居环境建设的途径应是多种多样的。我们既要挖掘中国传统的人居智慧，也要吸收西方各研究领域的精华，解决中国的现实问题，为全球人居建设贡献智慧和力量。

注：本文系清华大学“2011 年人居环境科学国际研讨会”的主旨报告。

（作者：吴良镛，中国科学院院士，中国工程院院士，清华大学人居环境研究中心主任）

① ［汉］司马相如．上书谏猎．

城市增长与城市发展

城市增长是指投资和人口增加引发的城市规模和基础设施、公共产品的增加；而城市发展不仅包括城市规模和基础设施、公共产品的增加，还包括城市经济结构、管理体制、社会事业、公共服务水平等在内的城市整个经济社会变动过程。有城市发展就有城市增长，但另一方面，有城市增长可能推动城市发展，也有可能出现有增长无发展。城乡规划转型重构的核心，应该是使城市增长更有效地促进城市发展。

一、规划工作的加强和完善为城市自主增长，促进城市同步发展提供了广阔空间

在城市化和城市现代化的快速进程中，有些地方出现一些极端过程，这就是大家经常在热议的“城市无序扩张”、“经营城市”、“以地生财”、“大广场、大马路”、“交通拥堵”、“人居环境差”等问题。但深入观察一下，凡是规划工作得到加强和完善的地方和时段，这种极端过程都可以避免，城市的高速发展依然可以有效地促进城市发展。

（一）区域中心城市的恢复性增长使中心城市及其城市群高速发展

进入城市快速发展时期的各区域中心城市都迫切需要适合自身发展的新的城市规划。20世纪末至本世纪前10年，各区域中心城市基本上都开展了一轮和自己历史相比应该说是最高水平的城市总体规划或总体规划修编，正是这一轮规划有力引导和控制了各区域中心城市的恢复性增长。区域中心城市得到发展是城市化健康发展和经济发展方式转变的重要基础之一。也正是由于这些大城市的较好发展才使“走以城市群为主体形态的城市化道路”有了较为广泛的共识。

过去建设生产性城市和发展小城镇的指导思想及其相应的方针政策束缚了特大城市的发展。以广州为例，1954年，广州提出“在相当的时期内逐步使广州由消费城市基本上改变为社会主义的生产城市”。1955年，国家建委和中央城建部指出：“广州市属旧城改建，应尽量利用原有基础，采取保持和逐步改造方针，对远景发展，可不作过多考虑”。广州从第1个城市规划方案（1954年），人口规模220万人，用地规模177km^2。到1977年完成的第13个城市规划方案、人口规模204万人，近期（至1985年）市区用地规模185.23km^2，基

本没有变化。

2005 年 12 月 22 日，国务院批复广州市城市总体规划。到 2010 年广州市区城镇人口控制在 920 万人以内，其中，中心城区控制在 628 万人以内；市区城镇建设用地控制在 785km^2 以内，其中中心城控制在 549km^2 以内。实际上 2010 年广州市城镇人口 927.12 万人，中心城 749.94 万人；市区城镇建成区 952.03km^2，中心城 533.86km^2。从 1985 年至 2010 年的 25 年间，中心城建成区面积增长 1.96 倍，平均每年增长 4.44%；人口增长 1.92 倍，平均每年增长 4.38%。如果和 1954 年比较，中心城建成区增长 2.13 倍，平均每年增长 2.06%，人口增长 2.41 倍，平均每年增长 2.21%。用现在的话来说，即：人口城市化快于土地城市化。

（二）基础设施基本同步使城市品质发生了翻天覆地的变化

新一轮城市规划的显著特点是各区域中心城市普遍突出了城市基础设施规划。以广州为例，1996 年 3 月编制完成的广州总体规划（第 15 方案）初稿，建议道路建设经费从 1994 年的 9.9 亿元到高峰的 2002 年 26.15 亿元、16 年共投入 326.21 亿元。规划尚未报批，广州市政府已发现如此安排时序适应不了当时广州发展的形势，将规划路网各工程提前实施并增加了一些新的交通工程（主要是地铁）。这才有后来正式报批的第 16 方案。那几年实际执行结果是 1998—2000 三年投入以交通工程为主的市政设施 464 亿元，城市人均道路面积从 1998 年 6.96m^2 提高到 2000 年的 9.76m^2，增加 40.23%，城区机动车平均速度从原来18km/h 提高到 25～30km/h。基本上和城市增长同步。

回忆一下开放改革之后的前 15 年，全国各特大城市仍普遍存在“吃水难”、“用气难”、“住房难”、“通信难”等问题，看看仅近 10 年的时间，由于生产力发展，投资增长和科技进步使城市基础设施和公共产品供给实现了量和质的飞跃，它不单体现在城市的供水供气、人均拥有公交车辆台数、居住面积、污水及固体废物处理、城市绿化等方面，更体现在交通、能源、通讯等基础设施和其他大型公共服务设施的建设上。标志着民族复兴的世界级机场、港口、大型城市基础设施比比皆是。

2010 年世界机场旅客吞吐量排行榜，进入前 20 名的机场隶属 12 个国家，其中美国占了 6 席、中国占了 4 席，其余 10 个国家分别占 10 席。2009 年全球货物吞吐量前十大港口中，中国稳占 8 席。集装箱吞吐量前十大港口中，中国有 6 个。

近年来城市地铁建设的高速度，也是中国城市加速现代化进程颇具代表性和说服力的一个例子。世界第一条地铁 1863 年在英国伦敦营运，132 年后 1995 年上海第一条地铁营运。如今上海地铁营运总长超英国伦敦排名世界第一。只用了 16 年时间，城市拥有地铁按长度排名，进入全球十大城市之列中国占有 4 个席位：上海、北京、广州、香港。

（三）良好的规划和土地有偿使用制度使城市空间再生产发生了划时代的变化

城市品质的提升有赖于良好的规划和城市基础设施的建设。城市品质的提升大大地提高了城市用地的价值。土地出让金的大幅提高有望使城市空间再生产实现良性循环。

近 10 多年来，城市土地有偿出让金数量级的变化为城市基础设施的完善和城市空间再生产提供了强有力的保证。

按照马克思的理论，“因为土地不是劳动产品，从而没有任何价值”，只有投入资本和劳动力才会产生价值。土地有不同用途，一定数量的土地，可以用来种庄稼，也可以用来盖房子、修公路、建公园。用来种庄稼的土地地租就是种庄稼平均利润的余额即超额利润转化而成的价值；盖房子的地租就是房子经营平均利润余额转化而成的价值。在现阶段，一般是盖房子经营的平均利润余额大大高于种庄稼平均利润余额，这就造成了在只能种庄稼的土地上盖房子的“冲动”和社会上各种抨击农地转城市建设用地对农民的“不公平”。在有条件的情况下，盖房子经营的土地收益高于种庄稼土地的收益，是因为这块土地一经变为城市用地，它就和城市的固定资本联系在一起，也就是说，土地的升值是因为城市原有各种投资（基础设施、硬软环境等）在起作用，这块土地价值的货币额构成这块土地所有者的货币收入，并同真正的地租一样，决定着土地的价值，但是，它们并不是真正的地租，而属于租金。在《资本论》里，马克思将地租和租金作了严格的区别。

了解一下城市市政建设的投资额就可以明白城市土地出让金的增加。“八五”期间，全国城市市政投资近 2 600 亿元，是“七五”期间的 5.2 倍；“九五”期间的投资总和约 7 000 亿，是“八五”期间的 2.7 倍；“十五”期间达到 2 万亿，接近“九五”的 3 倍，“十一五”预计将达到 4.0 万亿 ~4.5 万亿，在“十五”的基础上再翻番。“十一五”暂按 4 万亿计算，应该是“八五”的 15.38 倍。市政建设投资的增加使城市建设用地升值，从而推动了土地出让金的增加。以广州为例，广州珠江新城地价“八五”时期挂牌价为 3 500 元/m^2 楼面（1992），近几年珠江新城土地最高拍卖价为 17 933 元/m^2，是“八五”时期的 5.12 倍。

（四）城市的自组织过程和规划的补救性干预使它能较好地克服自己走过的一些弯路

城市是一个开放系统，由于城市增长过程的不可逆性，按照“耗散结构”理论的基本原理，在远离平衡的条件下，可能会发生各种不同类型的自组织过程，从而形成有序的新结构。随着改革开放的逐步深入，各个城市的自组织程度越来越高，实践已经证明，它们能较好地克服自己城市走过的一些弯路。通过城市规划的干预，发挥城市规划促进城市自组织机能的提高，实现城市空间的优化发展。以广州为例，20 世纪 90 年代初划拨土地、城区房屋拆迁过量应该算是严重的，1992—1996 年，共划拨建设用地 176km^2，至 1996 年下半年，政府有关部门共发出 1194 宗拆迁公告，需要动迁户数 41.874 万户，涉及人口 139.74 万人，而当时广州市区人口就是 316.74 万人，非农业户数 98.6471 万户，也就是说需要动迁户数占非农户数的 42.4%，人口占 44%。这就导致了那几年广州市以清理土地为中心的城市系统整治。几年的认真整治化解了这种比较极端的局面，效果还是可以肯定的，2001 年 12 月，广州获“国际花园城市”称号，成为世界上人口最多的国际花园城市，同年 12 月 29 日，建设部授予广州“迎‘九运’城市基础设施及环境综合整治特别奖”称号。2002 年 7 月，广州获 2002 年联合国“改善人居环境最佳范例奖”。

二、可能会成为城市有增长而无发展的几个问题

(一) 农民工的“半城市化”

允许农民工进城打工削弱了长期以来的城乡隔离政策效应，但由于政策导向依然是采取城乡二元结构思维去考虑城市化，本来可以转变为城市居民的这部分劳动力被称为“农民工”，而当城市不需要这部分劳动力时又被称为“返乡农民工”。这些人在城市就业与生活时，劳动报酬、子女教育、社会保障、住房等许多方面并不能与城市居民享有同等待遇，在城市没有选举权和被选举权等政治权利，不能真正融入城市社会，处于一种“半城市化状态”。基于2000年人口普查和2005年的1%人口抽样调查数据计算，这5年城镇人口增量中的71.8%是持农业户籍进城打工的外地农民工和郊区的农业人口。也就是说，现在的城市化有“虚增长”的部分，并且积重难返，为未来城市发展留下很多难题。

(二) 旧城改造

改革开放以来，我国城市在高速度、高强度、大规模建设的过程中，多数城市对老城区改造都是采取拆平老城区破旧房子重盖高楼大厦的做法。原因一是认为老城区破破烂烂，不够现代化；二是对城市中心区土地的需求，这些区域土地不断升值，寸土寸金使这类地区成为房地产商首选的开发对象。政府不用出钱，让房地产商去提高这些地方的容积率，最后是旧房子全部变成新房子，房地产商也赚了钱，何乐不为。有人认为这种“旧城改造”和美国1950—1960年的“旧城更新”有相似之处。这两种形式的城市再发展都是以改善旧城居住条件的名义，运用政府职权和公共补贴去帮助大规模的私人或准私人投资项目。

从世界范围看，这种大规模的“城市更新”运动早就受到来自各方面的质疑和批判。20世纪初，英国就开始了以拆除重建为主要手段的清除贫民窟及内城复兴运动。第二次世界大战以后，西方不少国家的许多城市为了消除战争破坏的影响和发展城市经济，解决居民住房问题，都在原来的城市中心拆除已被战争毁坏和并未毁坏的老建筑，重建各种象征“现代化”的高楼。这种大规模改建摧毁了有特色、有活力的建筑物，摧毁了城市文化和城市资源，同时也导致了城市宜居环境的丧失，理所当然在历史上站不住脚。从20世纪70年代开始，在发达国家，城市改造中以开发商为主导的大规模改造计划逐步退出历史舞台。

20世纪90年代早期划红线让开发商在老城区开发，广州的做法通常是回迁面积与销售面积的比是4:6，即新房子四成用于安置回迁户，六成进入商品房市场。按照4:6模式，如果红线内原有1万m^2的房子，拆除重建后的面积应该是2.5万m^2，其1万m^2用于回迁安置，1.5万m^2进入商品房市场，开发商卖出1.5万m^2回收的资金就是开发商的开发成本和利润。这种模式看来简单合算，政府不出一分钱，城市老房子全部变成新房子。殊不知原来红线内1万m^2现在变成2.5万m^2。老城区本来就密，再这样大幅度地增加容积率，适宜居住还有希望吗？更不用说历史建筑保护和历史文脉延续了。

（三）港式住宅

“港式住宅”是20世纪90年代广州房地产商对他们开发的高层商品房宣传的广告词。实际上是20世纪60年代英国的高层廉价住宅改头换面进入香港，现已为香港多数人或主动或被动接受的高层住宅楼。

开放改革，首先是有香港背景的房地产商把港式住宅带入沿海一些城市，因为提高容积率是房地产商赚钱较具潜力的因素，很快就得到几乎所有房地产商的仿效，自然而然在全国所有城市蔓延。如今，内地的县城，到处都是这种模式的房子。

20世纪70年代，为配合当时港督麦理浩推行的房屋政策，改善香港市民的居住环境，香港政府推行新市镇计划，主要是在新界划出土地兴建公共房屋及其配套设施。1972年香港政府宣布10年建屋计划，目标是为180万人建造理想的固定居所，包括公共屋和居者有其屋，最终目标是在合理的租金（对公共屋而言）和售价（对于居屋而言）之下，为居住在不理想环境的家庭提供房屋，10年建屋计划成了推动新市镇发展的最大动力。1973—1993年，经过20年的努力，在新市镇居住的人数已达250万人，已开拓都市发展用地7 400多 hm^2。

单从城乡规划而论、就城市形象而言，这种港式住宅全在新区建设有可能让它整齐划一，如果放在旧城区建设，则留下很多难堪的城市景观。旧城区里面有很多不能拆和拆不了的房子，能拆的地方拆了一小片建一幢或几幢这样的港式住宅，不能拆和拆不了的地方保留原来状态，哪怕再加上“穿衣戴帽”，也无法追求建筑群的和谐，整个旧城区极不协调。

更大的问题是港式住宅大量挤占了城市空间之后，建设各具特色的城市已显得十分渺茫。历史上从来没有像今天一样，大中小城市大拆大建之后，少了最能代表自己城市特色的街区，多了“千城一面”的港式住宅。一位英国学者在她2000年出版的书中有一番感慨：“现在回顾起来不禁让人震惊的是，二战后的规划和住房发展部门究竟有多大的权力，竟能够毁掉整个历史城市，并将成千万的人们安置在离就业地遥远的住宅区中，1960年代又将人们安排在塔楼构成的高层街区中。”

（四）过分注重城市形象

城市形象综合反映了城市规划、建设、管理水平，虽然它不能像“低保”、“医保”一样量化到人，但它已成为城市居民精神生活的一部分，良好的城市形象有利于促进城市的工商业活动、增加游客，同时也会增加城市居民的幸福感。“一个城市的形象是一个整体的形象，是一个建筑的形象，是一个历史的形象，也是一个生态的形象，是大地上人类生存不断集约的置换的一种现象。”城市形象属于城市文化范畴，必然是通过慢慢积累而形成自己的风格。如果过分强调城市形象，采取短期行为，带有普遍性的事件是把有限的城市发展资金投入可有可无的“形象工程”，结果贻误了城市经济社会发展。

10多年前，周干峙同志在广州就说过：城市形象问题，我个人不赞成搞形象设计，形象不是靠包装出来的，是由提高规划水平决定的，是综合性的。城市是经济社会综合载体，应该是一个完整的艺术品，是人类经过长期时间完成的，城市不一定完全是美观，还包括经济实用问题。我们的责任重大，要正视面对这些问题，在城市建设中尽量减少损失，提高效益。于今，这段话仍然是有益的教诲。

三、建立城市增长推动城市同步发展的内在机制

（一）确定切合实际的城市定位和环境目标

1984 年国务院批复广州市城市总体规划（第 14 方案），市政府 1989 年组织力量对该方案进行修编，先后形成第 15、16 方案，因各种原因国务院在 2005 年 12 月 22 日批复了第 16 方案。此方案的规划从修编、报送、批复用了 15 年，批复后执行的有效时限为 5 年。

这一时期广州对寻求创造何种城市环境目标明确并切合实际。对市民来说——适宜生活和创业发展“两个适宜”；对城市发展的目标定位——区域性中心城市。

为实现这两个层次的目标，广州提出“一手抓适应，一手抓提高”的城市规划建设方针，循序渐进地改善城市环境。为城市创建“两个适宜”的环境更多地体现在“抓适应”这个范畴，实现城市发展的战略目标更多地体现在“抓提高”这个范畴。“两个适宜”从有能力、办得到的实事做起，“提高”从全球定位的角度去考虑广州基础设施的重构。要使高速发展的广州规划建设保持完美，一是先做好城市的战略规划和其他有关的规划，新区按现代化标准成片建设，老城区放缓速度一步步加以改造；二是从质的方面去理解新区建设和老区改造，新老区最终都要现代化，比如地铁、水电气供应、居住环境等。新开工项目都要求高标准，像南洲水厂的自来水，水质标准比欧洲标准还高；三是为尽快跨入国际性区域中心城市的“门槛”，广州必须拥有区域一流的机场、港口、火车站、地铁、会展中心、歌剧院、博物馆、图书馆诸如此类的基础设施和文化设施，全部按世界一流的标准重新规划建设。这些项目的规划不单是项目本身，也包括项目所在地的小区，一个项目带来一片小区和周边交通的改善。高标准建设新城区，量力而为放慢速度改造老城区，这是处理城市建设和历史文化保护矛盾的有效办法，体现了城市的可持续发展。新的城市景观和原来的城市景观如何协调在规划层面就得到明确：一是新区应足够现代化，老区应保留原来风貌，从区域差别中去体现整体协调；二是保留老城区的风貌主要是通过保留广州历史文化名城的基本要素来体现，即自然环境要素、人工环境要素、人文环境要素和城市空间结构要素，并不是要全面“复古”，加进现代化的要素也是必不可少的，比如，老城区珠江两岸的整治建设即达到了这样的境界；三是新区的足够现代化不是要淹没在仿欧学美的浪潮中，也应该和谐地保留广州特色的传统“元素”，广州大学城的规划建设就是成功的一例，小谷围岛作为大学城一期工程除了保留 4 个自然村落外，还把岛东南部的练溪村改为商业文化休闲区。通过对古村原址民居建筑的改造，转换其功能改造成为休闲旅游区、民俗博物馆、商业文化区、娱乐休闲区，但又基本上保留了原来处于自然状态的古村落风貌。保留一个完整的城市发展画卷，这样复杂的系统问题只能从规划方面去寻求出路。

（二）自主增长的积累机制

传统计划经济完全排斥市场机制在资源配置中的作用，大量商品实行计划生产和供应，城市失去了配置资源的基本功能也就失去了自我积累自我增长的活力。加上当时把摆脱"一穷二白"的落后面貌完全寄托在尽快实现工业化身上，政府只能运用超经济手段从非工业经济积累中积累工业化资金，这是一种强制性增长的工业化激进模式，城市增长特别是城市发展受到了严重的制约。"回想新中国成立初期，第一个五年计划开始，城建很困难，每年做计划总盘子只有三四个亿，因为当时是勒紧裤带先搞工业建设。过了很久才达到十几二十亿，城建占全国基本建设的比重，在第一个五年计划时是3%～4%。"

要使城市自主增长，必须有一套自主增长的积累机制，既然认为快速城市化为中国社会经济发展提供了强大的动力，城市的聚集效应和规模经济极大地提高了资源配置效率，有力地促进了经济的快速发展和人民生活水平的提高。照理应保持城市市政建设资金在财政预算中合理的比例。要这样做是有困难的，以中央财政拨款占全国城市基础设施投资比例为例，20世纪80年代占26%，1990年代降至5%，2008年仅有1.1%。投资责任只能落在地方城市政府身上，但城市政府预算内收入现在和未来一段时间都难以对市政建设投资给予更大的支持，政府编制预算内财政支出除按规定保证农业、教育、科技等行业支出增长幅度要高于收入增幅之外，未来对社会福利方面支出比例将大幅提高，可以肯定市政建设资金所占比例只会下降不会提高，因此，城市土地收益将成为城市扩大再生产所需资金的最大来源。应该好好规范此项资金的使用，建立城市自主增长的积累机制。

在市场经济情况下，不同等级、不同档次的城市或同一城市不同区位土地的级差产生了不同的土地价格。从宏观上看，一个城市商品建设用地地价总体水平大体反映了同类地区的城市总体发展水平和人们对这个城市未来发展潜力的估计。从这个角度出发，可以说一个良好的城市规划在城市空间再生产中将起到事半功倍的作用。

政府投入不足自然使人考虑其他来源，不少人喜欢讨论城市基础设施投资的融资模式，比如说政府的城市建设债券、项目融资、资产证券化，设立基础设施投资基金等。按国内目前现实，除银行贷款之外的其他融资模式的时间成本都高于银行贷款。城市基础设施应该是公益性项目，唯一能减轻政府投资的只有让使用者付费，有人付费的项目政府就可以组织市场化经营，除此之外，都要政府出钱，解决之道还是要从预算内和预算外资金安排。人们也在议论城市土地和空间的"无节制扩张"和土地出让金收入的"不可持续性"。土地是城市发展的载体，是不可再生的自然资源，必须认真贯彻"珍惜用地，合理用地，保护耕地"的基本国策。在这基础上，讨论这些问题可以做几个基本判断：

（1）只要大量农村人口需要流入城市，城市就需要增长，扩大城市建设用地不可避免。但城市人口的人均占用国土面积大大的低于农村人口人均占用国土面积。

（2）几千年以农业为主的国民经济使我国除了少数工矿城市之外，城市周边都是农田，城市要扩大建设用地，占用农田不可避免。"占补平衡"的思路是正确的，但不应该局限在一城一地，应该从更高层次去作决策，我国有很多地方，只要有水就会有田，应该通过现代水利基础设施去“坚守18亿亩耕地红线”。

(3) 资料显示，地价总收益和城市经济社会发展水平有关而和出让总面积无关。我国2000年土地有偿出让面积161 190公顷，2005年165 586公顷，大抵相等，2000年土地有偿出让收益625亿元，2005年2 184亿元。

1993年，全国土地有偿收益405.3亿元，当年全国财政收入4 349亿元，土地出让收益占财政收入比例为9.32%。2007年，相应的一组数字是454.4、51 322、8.85%。15年间，百分比最高值是在2002年，达到12.78%。上述全国财政收入只是预算内的财政收入，还有一块预算外收入，如果把预算内和预算外作为政府的总收入，显然土地收益占政府总收入的比例还会更低。我国香港是一个城市规划建设已趋稳定并严格控制政府供地的地区，1993—1994年度土地收益占政府总收入比例为10.88%，2007—2008年度占17.38%，最高的1980—1981年度占35.56%。

(三) 自觉投入的基础设施发展机制

在生产力发展、科技进步日新月异的时代，要保持城市的活力必须使城市有一套自觉投入的基础设施发展机制，未来城市基础设施规划应保持有更多可持续发展的余地。

生产力的实体要素与外部环境是交互作用的，城市基础设施既要适应今日的城市运转，也要适应明日的发展、更新。整体规划、分期实施、适当超前建设城市基础设施成为城市发展的重要基础。

不同级次的城市是通过城市基础设施来体现的。一段时间，提高城市竞争力成为很多城市的口号和市长们的热门话题。其实没有必要把不同级次的城市放在一起去做竞争力的排名，城市功能不同比较优势也应该有不同表现。有研究这方面的学者把城市竞争力概念框架表达为：UC=f（A、B、C、D、E、F、G、I、K、L、M、N)，UC为城市竞争力，A为劳动力，B为资本力，C为科技力，D为结构力，E为设施力，F为区位力，G为环境力，I为秩序力，J为文化力，K为制度力，L为管理力，M为开放力，N为聚集力。如果有人想把函数中的因子扩展到所有的英文字母，也是可以探讨的，因为城市比较优势包罗万象，因子的选择取决于选择者的价值观而已。到目前为止，还没有一个系统而成熟的理论框架，指导人们从经济学的角度探讨竞争力的深层次问题。不能认为拥有世界一流海港、空港、高铁设施的一些中心城市依然是“国际竞争力不强”，也不必去查外国文献，作为城市竞争力的国际比较，国际级海港、空港、高铁、地铁这些硬件及其营运状态是最有说服力的，P. 霍尔在描述世界城市主要特征时就认为这些城市通常拥有大型国际海港、大型国际航空港。不足一百万人口的法兰克福，因拥有法兰克福机场（2010年机场旅游吞吐量5 300万人次）而成为欧洲门户，谁能说法兰克福不是国际中心城市。

城市基础设施对城市发展的影响更多的将体现在未来。随着中国经济的发展和城市现代化，低成本生产状况总会有结束的一天，基础设施将成为将来影响成本和效益的一个主要组成部分。要保证城市经济增长的持续，一般要求基础设施应超前发展。要使城市增长推动城市同步发展，城市政府应该建立自觉投入的基础设施发展机制。

市场经济使城市建设投资主体多元化，但城市政府应该明白，城市基础设施和社会事业主要投资还是要靠政府。只有政府对基础设施的投资才能将城市经济引向新领域。私人投资者在基础设施建设上起着一定的作用，但这种作用很有限。

城市基础设施的发展要把握好“后发性优势”，直接采用跨越式技术、节约相应的开发和积累时间、实现跳跃性发展在很多城市都可以仿效。通讯、地铁、高铁、城际轨道、电网改造、水和燃气供应等方面，如果技术选择正确，一步就可以跨入目前最好的水平。

（四）组织创新机制

传统的规划编制系统是规划行政机关将城乡规划编制的任务下达给自己管辖的城市规划设计部门，设计部门的编制成果经过一系列的评议论证审批后作为规划行政机关审批城市规划建设的法定文件。显然规划行政机关属下的这个规划设计部门的水平决定了这座城市最终的规划建设水平。建设一流城市应该拥有一流的规划人才，但任何一个城市的规划设计部门都不可能把所有的一流人才收归门下。城市规划水平的提高只能是规划编制工作的社会化。由此人们想到了规划设计招标，引进更多的规划设计单位进来参与某一项规划的编制工作。但是，由于编制时间所限，外来单位并不能拥有大量编制工作所需的基础数据和城市相关的深层次信息，编制结果并不能完全反映这些单位的水平。评标后的处理往往是再由规划行政机关原来管辖的设计部门汇总，也还是原来管辖的设计部门的成果。能否设立一个类似于中介机构一样的组织，它能反映政府规划行政机关的意志、熟悉城市规划的各种规章、拥有自己城市规划编制的各种基础数据和有关信息，有能力完成各种规划招标文件的制订和组织对招标方案的公正评审；不以盈利为目的，只追求城乡规划的科学和完善，使城乡规划的编制真正社会化。因此，2000 年广州市成立了“城市规划编制研究中心”。

将城市规划研究和编制“成建制”地从规划行政机关分离出去，除了实现规划编制工作的社会化之外，同时也为规划方案的谋断分离建立了新机制。编研中心作为“谋者”的组织者，由于体制上的“规避”作用，加上对规划项目采用了招投标方式，公开征选规划设计方案，这就为“断者”提供了多个可能的决策方案，这些方案，在行政审批前还须经过公众征询、专家评审，各个备选方案的利弊长短将显示得比较充分，为行政层面的“断者”提供了很好的决策基础。

（五）城乡规划的法制化管理和监督机制

在 20 世纪 50 年代之前，城镇规划基本上被看做一门艺术，而到了 20 世纪 60 年代末，城镇规划基本上已被看作一门科学了。但也有人认为，把城镇规划描述为一门“科学”是一个误导；相反，它应该作为一种旨在实现某种价值目标的政治活动形式。这些大概是规划理论历史上转型与重构重要的阶段性标志。规划理论和实践总是在继承中创新发展，不会因为强调城乡规划的公共政策属性就认为城乡规划不是一门科学或者认为城乡规划不讲艺术。

随着社会主义市场经济的不断完善，城市建设主体多元化、利益群体的复杂化，大众要求城乡规划的民主化会进一步发展。伴随着法制的不断完善，公众对城乡规划的诉求往往也会走法律途径去表达，城乡规划要从体现公平、公开、公正原则的公共政策层面上去作决策，只能不断地完善城乡规划管理的法制化。《城乡规划法》对限制领导者与规划管理人员的自由裁量权，严格规划调整的法定程序作了明确规定，但现在社会议论较多的照样是这些问题。拿城乡行政首长与规划变更为例作一分析，现在已不是几十年前行政首长不重视城乡规划的那种状态了，而是另一个极端，即行政首长过分重视城乡规划，相当一部分人一当领导就想在城乡规划上“露一手”。客观原因一是改善和建设美好居住环境没有标准的价值判断；二是科技、生产力水平进步太快，原规划执行几年后总有不足的地方。从这个角度出发，每一任领导对规划有想法是正常的，但向好的方向变更还是向差的方向变更则很大程度取决于领导对城市发展的眼界和对原有规划的理解。按照《城乡规划法》第19条的要求，“城市人民政府城乡规划主管部门要组织编制城市的控制性详细规划，经本级政府批准后，报本级人大和上一级政府备案”，第34条也明确，“城市、县、镇政府制定近期（5年）建设计划，报总体规划审批机关备案”，这两条加上第47条、48条、49条对总体规划、控制性详细规划、近期建设规划修改应该完成程序的规定，如果能严格依法行政，向好的方向变更只需多花点时间而已，而向差的方向变更，经过这么多程序后相信也可以减少一些程度。

监督方面，虽然《城乡规划法》明确了上级行政部门、人民代表大会以及全社会的公众监督，按目前的社会现实，上级行政机关的“监督”是最有效的，特别是当地方的权威领导对规划法不够了解或有潜意识的违法倾向时，同级城乡规划主管部门的领导往往迫于“位子”和“进步”的双重压力，可能相当一部分人会视而不见、顺其自然，有甚者还可能会曲意奉承，利用自己的专业知识和部门权威为不依法行政或不严格执法的行为寻幌子、找台阶。

（六）启用人才机制

建设一流城市必须有一流的人才，有什么样的人才就能干出什么样的事业。创一流的工作局面、创一流的业绩，需要有一流的具体领导。城市规划建设的竞争，从某一角度去看，实际上是各城市领导人之间、各城市规划局局长之间、各城市建委主任之间的竞争。如果要强调一下集体作用的话，那就是跟规划建设有关的整个系统各城市人才的竞争。

解决城市人才不足除本地抓紧培养外，一是使具体业务工作社会化，用全社会的人；二是尽最大努力引进人才。

广州市在20世纪末21世纪初的那段时间，城市规划工作社会化除了成立城市编制研究中心外，更多的活动还是城市规划、城市设计的国际国内咨询、研讨、讲座等活动，让国内外一流人才都来参与广州城市规划活动。

要使一个地方对人才有吸引力，一是要有好的发展环境，用事业、用发展的新成就去感召人才、吸引人才、留住人才，让各类人才感到这个地方有创业舞台、发展空间、干事氛围和成事环境；二是实行来去自由、进出随意的政策，不求所在，但求所用，不求所用，但求所得；三是尊重知识、承认知识的价值，大力使用高学历人才。

培养和造就大批高层次、高技能优秀人才除了引进，更大工作量还是培养。除了学校正规教育出人才外，工作实践也是培养人才的重要途径。广州城市规划建设自地铁开始，各种大型工程项目接连不断，一个大项目就是一所人才培养学校，不少人就是通过参与大型工程的实践而成为行业中的专家。

起用人才，就城市规划领域而言最重要的是选好用好规划局局长。真正把那些政治上靠得住、业务上有本事、肯干事并干成事、公道正派、敢抓敢管、廉洁自律的一流人才放在规划局局长的位置上，放手让他有职有权履行职责是一个城市规划及其实施管理能否做好的关键。规划局局长选好了再尊重他的意见配备好局的领导班子，构成一个有战斗力的团队。除了配备好规划局领导班子之外，交流和提拔规划局干部到区里行政领导，培养和储备市、区两级熟悉城市规划的行政首长也是那一时期广州市委、市政府较为独特的做法。

规划局局长之后的关键人物就是分管此项工作的副市长和市长。城市规划与城市领导息息相关。吴良镛先生讲过一段话，市长是决策者，在一定程度上，往往又是规划设计的参与者。古代中国，也是世界园艺史上著名的明代园林设计著作《园冶》的作者计成有句话："三分匠，七分主人。"意思是说，园林艺术水平的高下，主人的作用占七分，匠人占三分，关键在于主人的文化艺术品位的高低，在现实生活中也确实如此。这句话引申一下，可借以说明市长作为决策者对城市建设水平所起的作用。地方领导人要想不要给历史留下包袱，一是要认真学习，学习科学知识、经济理论，学习城市规划、建设、管理的法律法规；二是依法行政；三是按照吴良镛先生所说的"必须遵从科学规划，深入调查研究，听取多方面意见，特别是专业工作者的意见，与他们多交朋友，多交'诤友'，互相沟通"。这一点是最现实也是最重要的。

（作者：林树森，中共中央委员，全国政协港澳台侨委员会副主任，曾任贵州省省长、广州市市长、市委书记）

参考文献

[1] [英] 克莱拉·葛利德．规划引介 [M]．王雅娟，张尚武，译．北京：中国建筑工业出版社，2007.

[2] [英] 尼格尔·泰勒．1945年后西方城市规划理论的流变 [M]．李白玉，陈贞，译．北京：中国建筑工业出版社，2008.

[3] P. 霍尔．世界城市 [M]．中国科学院地理研究所，译．北京：中国建筑工业出版社，1982.

[4] 段进．城市空间发展论 [M]．南京：江苏科学技术出版社，1998.

[5] 莱斯特·C·梭罗．中国的基础设施建设问题 [J]．经济研究，1997 (1).

[6] 林本初，冯莹．有关竞争力问题的理论综述 [J]．经济学动态，2001 (3).

[7] 卢惠明，陈立天．香港城市规划导论 [M]．香港：三联书店（香港）有限公司，1999.

[8] 马克思．资本论第三卷 [M]．北京：人民出版社，2004.

[9] 倪鹏飞．中国城市竞争力的分析范式和概念框架 [J]．经济学动态，2001 (6).

[10] 齐康．建筑形象与城市文化 [Z]．广州市现代化城市讲座之二．广州市建委整理，2000. 4.

[11] 沈华嵩．经济系统的自组织理论 [M]．北京：中国社会科学出版社，1991.

[12] 世界机场排行：旅客吞吐量（2010）[J]．综合运输，2011，(4)．

[13] 田莉．我国城镇化进程中喜忧参半的土地城市化 [J]．城市规划，2011（2）．

[14] 吴良镛．城市世纪、城市问题、城市规划与市长的作用［Z］．1999.

[15] 香港统计处．香港统计资料表 193. 政府收入（一般收入账目及各基金）[Z/OL]．http//www. censtatd. gov. hk.

[16] 章岩，方可．是历史在重演吗?：从美国的“城市更新”到中国的“旧城改造”[J]．经济理论与经济管理，2008（12）．

[17] 中国发展研究基金会．中国发展报告 2010：促进人的发展的中国新型城市战略［M］．北京：人民出版社，2010.

[18] 中国疏浚协会．中国世界大港向世界强港之路迈进［J］．长江航运研究，2001（5）．

[19] 周干峙．认真研究做好规划、迎接城市建设的新高潮［Z］．广州市现代化城市建设管理系列讲座之三．广州市建委整理，2000. 7.

城市化与中国经济[①]

引　言

自1978年实行经济改革和对外开放以来，中国的经济发展取得了巨大的成效。中国是当今世界增长最快的经济体——在过去33年里，其年平均增长率达9.8%。中国在如此长的一段时期内能保持如此快的增长速度是史无前例的。从1978年到2011年，中国实际国内生产总值（GDP）增长了约22倍，从3 448亿美元增长到近7.5万亿美元（2011年价格），一跃成为世界第二大经济体，仅次于美国。2011年，美国的GDP（约15.1万亿美元）是中国GDP的2倍。

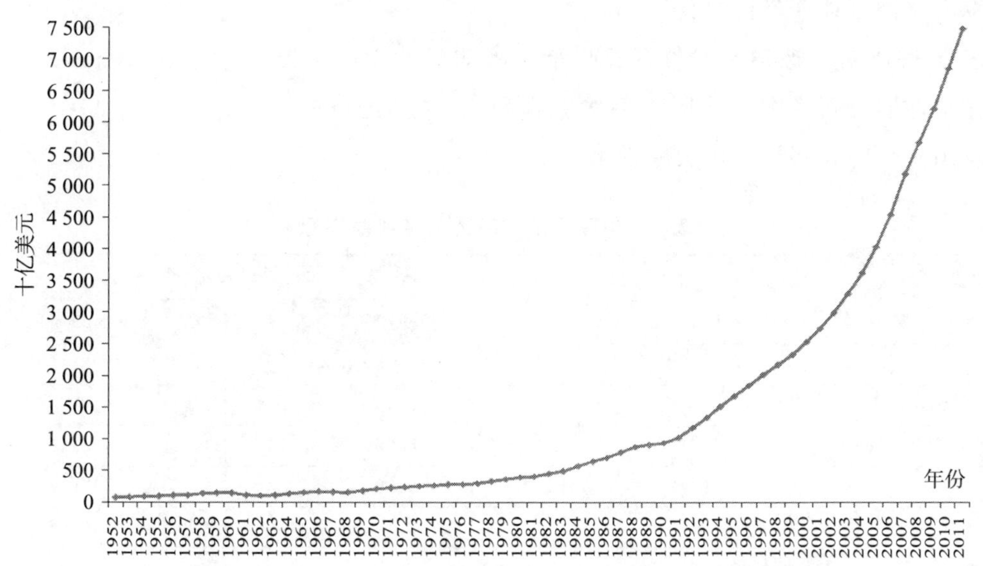

图1　自1952年起的中国实际GDP（单位：美元，按2011年价格）

尽管经济增长迅速，但中国仍然是一个发展中国家。从1978年到2011年，中国人均实际GDP增长了15.5倍，从358美元增长到了5 555美元（2011年价格）。而2011年，美国

① 本文仅为作者观点，并不一定反映该作者所属机构之意见。

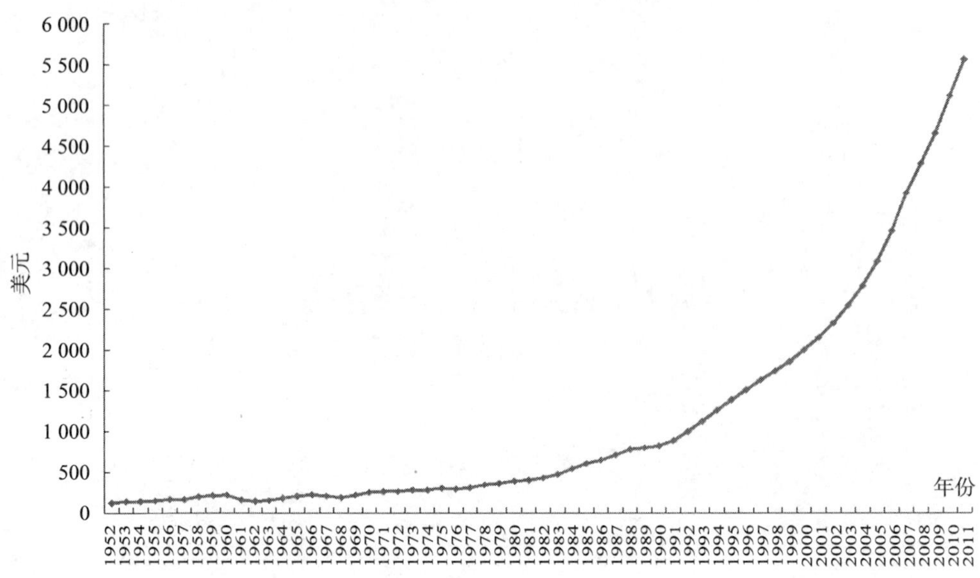

图2　自1952年起的中国人均实际GDP（单位：美元，按2011年价格）

人均GDP（约48 236美元）是中国的8.7倍。

尽管过去10年里中国经济出现了很多问题，例如：区域内和区域间收入差距不断扩大、基础教育和医疗保障分布不均、环境质量下降、基础设施缺乏以及腐败等问题，但可以公平地说，每一位中国公民都从自1978以来的经济改革和对外开放中受益。虽然受益程度不同，但几乎没人想回到计划经济时代。

下表就1978经济改革和对外开放政策实施前后的中国关键绩效指标进行了对比。显而易见，除平均通货膨胀率外（1978后大幅提高），中国经济的各方面因素，如GDP增长率、消费以及国际贸易，都呈现出大幅的增长。

表1　中国经济改革的关键绩效指标

	年增长率	
	第一阶段	第二阶段
	1952—1978	1978—2011
实际GDP	6.15	9.79
实际人均GDP	4.06	8.66
出口	9.99	17.32
进口	9.14	16.63
通货膨胀率(GDP紧缩指数)	0.50	4.24
	1952—1978	1978—2010
实际消费	5.05	8.88
实际人均消费	2.99	7.75

在过去的34年中，中国政府领导人充分展示了其面对重大挑战和解决困难的能力，成功度过了多个经济和金融危机。中国是从计划经济平稳转向市场经济的少数社会主义国家之

一，成为了其他转型经济体（如：越南）和潜在转型经济体（如：古巴、老挝和朝鲜）的学习模范。

2010年，中国GDP产业分布大概为：第一产业（农业）占10.1%，第二产业（制造业、矿业和建筑）占46.7%，第三产业（服务业）占43.2%。（注：其他多数经济体一般将矿业纳入第一产业）。2011年，该分布出现小幅变动，三大产业占比分别为：10.1%、46.8%和43.1%。

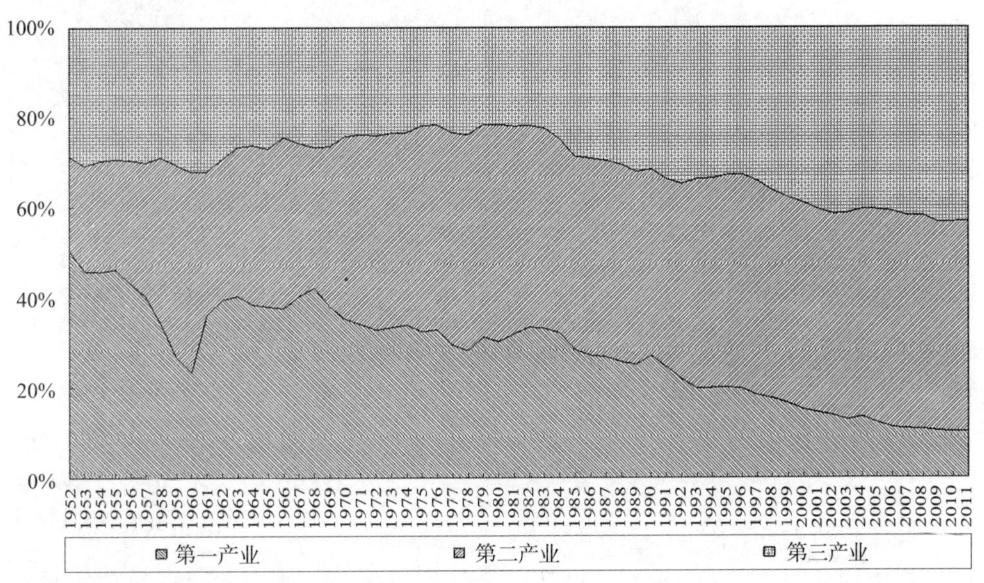

图3 自1952年起中国GDP按三次产业的分配比例

然而，第一产业的劳动力占比仍然超过36%，大批劳动力正有待转移至其他两类生产率更高的产业。但只要第一产业中的劳动力比例仍然大幅超过该产业产出的GDP比例，那么第二产业和第三产业中非技术工人以及初级劳动力的实际工资率就不会面临增长的压力。

中国第一产业中的劳动力占比从1978的70%降低至目前的36%，花费了33年的时间，大约平均每年下降1个百分点。而该比例从目前的36%下降至10%以下（约与目前中国第一产业产出的GDP比例相同）还将花费约25年的时间。到那时，预计中国第一产业GDP占比将不到5%。

因此，在未来20年或更长的时间内，中国仍将有剩余劳动力的存在。在未来很长一段时间内，即使第二和第三产业可能缺乏技术熟练或经验丰富的劳动力，但中国将不缺非技术工人和初级劳动力。

1949年，中国农村人口占比刚刚低于90%；1978年（中国经济改革和对外开放初期）为82%；到2010年，农村人口占比下滑至51%，但仍然约占中国半数人口。预计在“十二五”规划期间（2011—2015），农村人口占比仍将继续降低4个百分点，即下滑至47%。农村人口占比的下降率约为每年下降1个百分点，几乎与第一产业（农业）就业占比的下降率相同。预计农村人口占比将以每年下降1个百分点的速度继续下滑，直至2040年。到那时，农村人口占比将下滑至约30%。

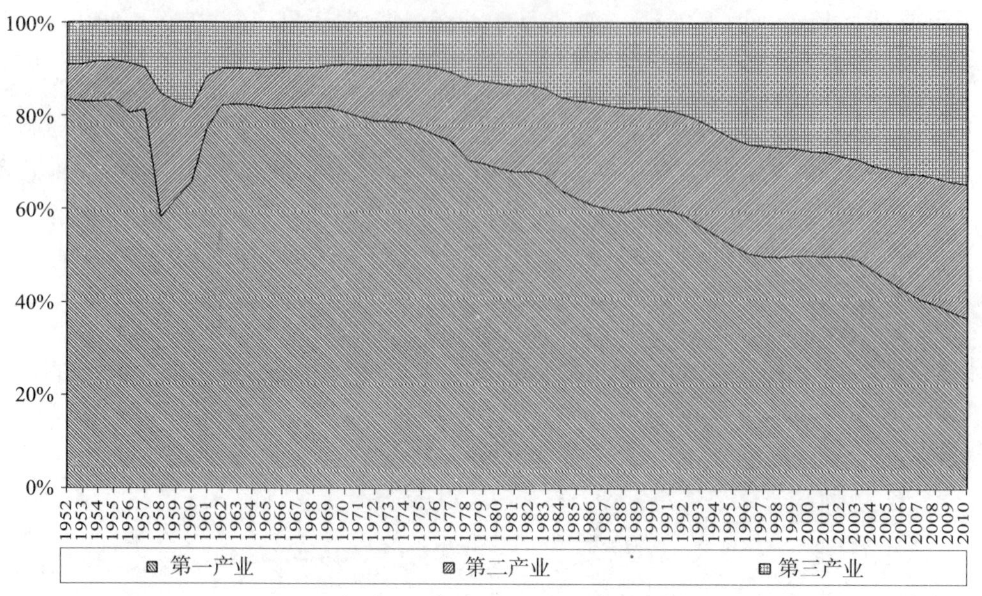

图4 自1952年起的中国各产业的就业分布比例

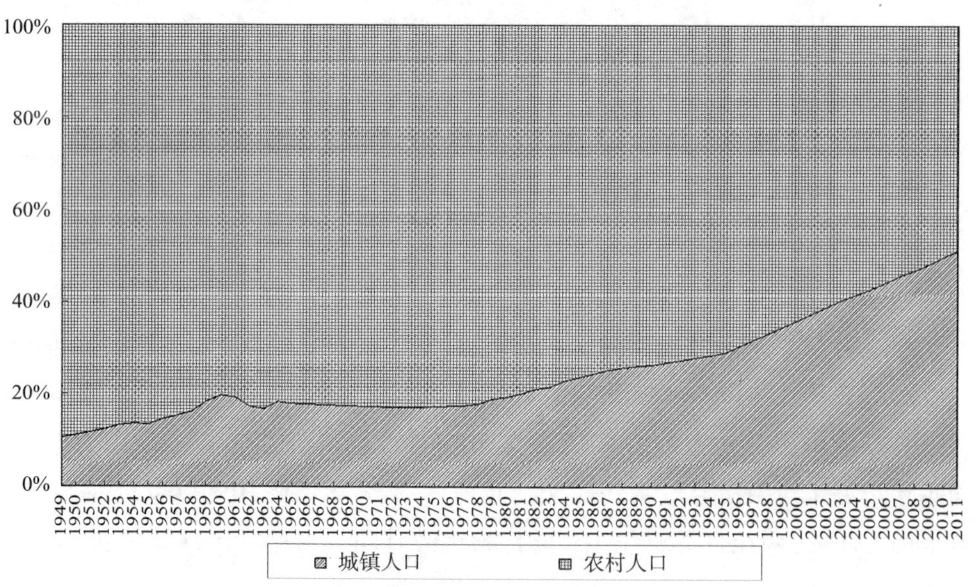

图5 1949年至今的中国农村人口和城镇人口比例

过去30年来，世界经济发展的重心已从美国和欧洲逐渐转移至亚洲，包括东亚和南亚。中国、印度以及其他东亚经济体在2007—2009年全球金融危机和目前的欧洲主权债务危机中的强劲表现正是东亚经济体已同世界其他经济体局部脱钩的佐证。但是，中国和东亚经济体还未强大到足以改变当前世界局势的地步。中美两国组合（G-2）领导世界经济的观念还为时尚早。

一、国民经济和社会发展第十二个五年规划

2010年12月31日，中国国民经济和社会发展第十一个五年规划（2006—2010）正式

结束，实现或远远超越了大多数设立的目标，其中包括单位 GDP 能耗较 2005 年末下降 20 个百分点。“十一五”规划所设实际 GDP 增长率目标为：从 2006 到 2010 年每年增长 7.5%，而实际增长率达到了每年 11.2%。唯一未实现的重大目标是用于研发的 GDP 比例，设立的目标为 2%，而实际只达到了 1.8%。

国民经济和社会发展第十二个五年规划（2011—2015）于 2011 年 3 月中旬经全国人民代表大会同意通过。该规划主要为指示性规划而并非强制性规划。“十二五”规划最显著的特点是将年均实际 GDP 增长率目标从“十一五”规划设立的 7.5% 降低至 7%。（几乎毫无疑问的是，正如“十一五”期间实际年均速率 11.2% 超过目标年均速率 7.5% 一样，这一目标也会被超额完成。）然而，该增长率目标的降低标志着中国政府将重心从定量经济增长转移到提高经济增长质量的决心。同时，年均通货膨胀率将保持在 3% 以下。

“十二五”规划的其中一个主题就是中国经济发展模式的转变：首先，从出口导向型转为内需导向型；其次，从投入驱动型转为技术进步驱动型或创新驱动型。该规划也旨在实现国际贸易的基本平衡。

同时，规划提出了进一步城市化的目标：这一时期，农村人口比重将从 51% 降低到 47%。它还提出要增加教育和医疗（特别是农村地区）、环境保护、空气和水污染控制的支出。它设定了提高能源利用效率和减少碳排放的强制性目标，即将单位 GDP 能耗和碳排放分别降低 16% 和 17%。规划还提出要通过税收、转移支付以及将政府支出转向教育和医疗、改善社会安全网络和养老金制度等公共服务的手段缩小贫富差距。

二、城市化——经济增长的动力

由于中国经济发展正在经历由出口导向型向内需导向型的转变，维持国内巨大的总需求和该需求的持续增长显得至关重要。那什么才是增加国内总需求的主要动力？

中国家庭消费在一定程度上被视为中国国内总需求增长的潜在来源。中国家庭消费实际增长十分迅速，实际零售销售增长速度大于甚至有时远远大于实际 GDP 的增长。然而，如果家庭实际收入继续快速增长，家庭消费的高增长率可能持续一段时间，但从长期来看不太可能一直维持。这是因为中国家庭储蓄率（国民储蓄率远高于家庭储蓄率）目前约为 30%（城镇和农村家庭），已经明显趋于稳定。现今中国大陆家庭的消费－储蓄行为与香港和台湾人均家庭收入相同的华人家庭的消费－储蓄行为基本相同，平均储蓄率为 30%。这样，在可预见的将来，中国家庭储蓄率不太可能出现明显下滑，这就意味着家庭消费率不太可能大幅增长。

因此，只有当中国家庭的可支配收入大幅增长时，中国家庭消费增长速度才可能大幅超过 GDP 的增长速度。而由于某些结构性因素，中国劳动力收入占比（目前低于 50%，而发达经济体一般在 65% 到 70% 之间）在短时期甚至长时期内不太可能实现增长。然而，城市化将无疑增加农村地区的实际收入，尤其是农村人均实际收入。

如此一来，2012 年及之后中国经济的持续增长将不再依赖家庭消费或出口的增长，而

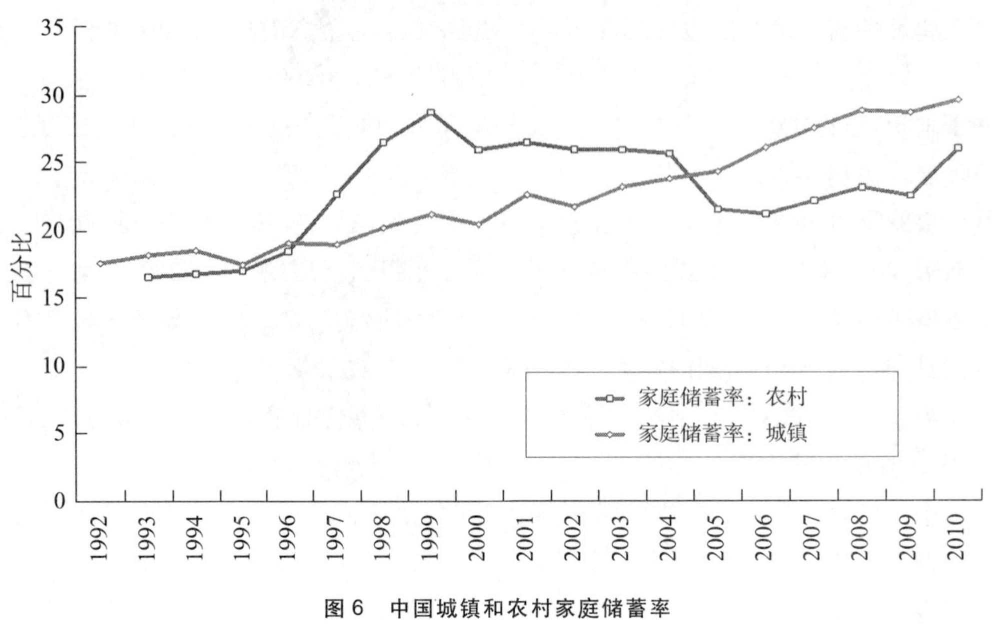

图6　中国城镇和农村家庭储蓄率

主要依赖国内总需求其他方面的增长，如：投资和政府开支。正如国务院副总理李克强所指出：城市化可能成为中国经济增长的最强动力。城市化增加了国内总需求，并且使中国经济从出口导向型转为其他模式成为可能。

第一，城市化本身产生了对公共基础设施投资的需求。公共基础设施可分为两类：连接城市的基础设施，如铁路、高速公路、机场、海港、电网、通信线路等；直接服务于城市自身的基础设施，如发电厂、城市轨道交通（包括地铁）、光纤网络、学校、医院等。两类公共基础设施均需要中央政府以及地方政府进行公共投资。这两类公共基础设施投资均可产生大量国内总需求。但是，该两类投资均需政府进行规划而不能交由市场调配。

城市间通信和交通基础设施需进行进一步的规划和改善，尤其是新城市的建设。超高速火车应代替飞机，成为主要城市间的首选交通模式，既可节省时间，也可减少能源消耗。

为节省稀缺的土地资源，确保城市交通体系的效率和环境友好性，城市建设应强制实行高密度土地利用。新城市建设必须进行集中的规划，包括其位置、布局、土地使用、密度、城市内通信和交通基础设施，否则，全靠市场体系将导致城市扩张和贫民窟的产生，并且城市交通将严重依赖私人汽车，无论是中国还是世界都无法承担这样的能源消耗和碳排放。轨道交通体系应替代汽车，成为现有城市以及新城市内的主要交通方式。否则，“每户一辆小汽车”将成为中国乃至世界的噩梦。完善的城市规划应当使居民无需在日常生活中使用小汽车（尽管他们可以为了周末和休闲使用而拥有一辆小汽车）。

在中国，至少有两百个人口规模超过200万且需要轨道交通体系的城市，因此，轨道交通体系的规划、设计、建设和运营将成为一个新的大型产业，产生大量的国内需求和最终的出口需求。

第二，城市化产生了对住宅建设的大量国内需求。宽带互联网的广泛分布以及超高速火车的运行注定将革命性地改变中国的居住模式。远程办公和乘车上下班将成为可能。他们在产生对住宅建设的新需求同时也大幅减少了主要城市的阻塞和拥挤，并且促进了新的卫星城镇的发展。

住房需求是可持续的国内总需求的重要来源之一。尽管在过去三十余年中国住房建设取得了明显进展，但仍存在巨大的增长空间，特别是对于内陆省份区域以及中低收入家庭来说。这些住房既可以用于自住，也可以用作公共租赁住房（这两者之间还有多种可供选择的住房补贴形式）。对于很多国家和地区来说，自有住房是它们持续几十年的经济快速增长时期的主要增长引擎；毫无疑问，中国存在巨大的潜在住房需求。不仅如此，住房需求还能衍生出对家具、家电（如冰箱、洗衣机和电视机等）、窗帘、地毯、家庭用品和服务的次级需求，从而为企业（不只是大型企业，也包括中小型企业）创造大量的就业岗位和经济活动。

此外，个人的自有住房一般是非投机性质的，不会引起资产价格泡沫。再者，自住者通常更加爱护自己的房子和周边环境。作为自住者，他们也不必面对房租上涨的威胁，因此会感到更加安全。为了将自有住房向全体居民推广，必须使供需双方都受到保障。保障供给，就应当确保土地能够以负担得起的成本获得并被高效利用，如采取高容积率、高密度的土地利用方式。保障需求，就应当确保居民能够获得长期（如35年）固定利率的住房贷款。

政府和私人开发商都可以提供自有住房。按照“十二五”规划的指示，今后五年内将有3 600万套保障性住房竣工。目前已完成432万套，另有1 043万套在建。预计今年将有超过1 100万套破土动工，另有700万套竣工。这些住房既可以用来出租，也可以卖给自住者。

第三，城市化也为服务业的长足发展创造了适宜的环境条件。城市生活需要各式各样由个人或机构提供的服务，包括会计、金融、教育、理发、医疗、住宿、保险、娱乐、餐饮、零售、运输等，这些需求反过来制造了供给。所以说，城市化将引导第三产业的发展。

第四，众所周知，教育、医疗、环境保护、研究与开发（R&D）和测试及认证等公共物品的供给具有规模经济性。城市化为实现规模经济、改善公共服务质量提供了机会。

中国城市化发展的重心不应放在现有大城市的进一步扩张上，尤其是沿海城市，许多大城市扩张已经达到了极限。城市化的发展应在内陆省份和自治区的旧城或新城周边发展城市中心，充分利用传统城镇的自然地理资源，而不是使现有城市变得越来越大，越来越拥挤。与过去不同，资金和技术将被带入剩余劳动力所在的内陆省份和地区，而不是将剩余农村劳动力带入拥有大部分资金和技术的沿海地区。由于中国经济发展模式正在由出口导向型转为内需导向型，这一变化正好适应了沿海地区对传统的“来料加工装配贸易”出口经营的逐步淘汰。

三、城市化和税收政策

省级以下地方政府通过引进可靠稳定的经常性收入来源，能极大地促进城市化。这些市级政府必须提供公共物品及公共服务，例如公共安全、消防、基础教育、公共卫生、医疗服务、交通管控、饮用水等，但同时它们又无可靠专门的收入来源。近几年来，许多市级政府高度依赖于土地买卖和租赁以获取收入，而此类收入既不稳定也不具有长期性。而且，一旦市级政府依赖于土地买卖，则它们会出台激励政策，人为地限制潜在的供需以保持土地价格一路攀升，这反而直接导致产生房地产价格泡沫。因此，引入不动产税作为当地政府稳定长期性收入的来源将能让它们较少地依赖于土地买卖或土地租赁，从而减少对高昂且不断攀升的房价的依赖程度。

城市化必将产生对商业、工业、居住以及其他公共用途的土地的需求。高昂且持续上涨的土地价格将助长投机倒卖活动，妨碍合理有效地使用土地，并且阻碍城市化的成功。城市政府将要采用的增收不动产税的措施将使其无法继续推高房价，从而降低资产泡沫形成的可能性。上海和重庆已经引入不动产税的试点项目。希望最终能在全国范围内得到推广。

如上所述，城市化也将为服务行业供需双方的快速发展创造环境。为了促进服务行业的发展，应考虑用增值税取代当前的营业税（抽取服务企业一定比例的总收入作为营业税），从而让服务企业在纳税前能够从总收入中扣除在提供服务时使用到的商品和服务的成本。这将使第二产业和第三产业之间更加公平合理地分担税收负担，并且为中小型服务企业的发展增加新的动力，反过来为城市人口提供更多的就业机会。

四、城市化和人口政策

中国独生子女政策、城市化和妇女教育水平的提高引起出生率的下降；营养状况的改善和医疗机会的增加则延长了人口的预期寿命。这两项因素使得中国人口正在经历快速老龄化。在城市化背景下，首先应当处理的问题是城市和农村居民在教育、医疗和养老制度等公共服务机会上的不平等待遇。我们需要重新审视城市地区现行的户口登记制度的作用和角色。2012 年 3 月全国人民代表大会通过了一项法律，使城市和农村人口在代表大会中的席位分配更加平等——每 67 万人推选一位人大代表，无论所在地是城市还是农村。这一法律上的改变削弱了北京、上海等直辖市的影响，增强内陆省份的影响，最终将产生深远的作用。

城市化意味着居民从农村地区迁移到城市地区定居。这些新的定居者应当有权利居住在城市地区，享受现有城市居民的所有特权，并承担相应的全部义务。但是在实现完全的迁徙自由之前，处于过渡时期，我们也应当赋予每个在城市地区长期拥有固定职业的农村居民基本的居住权利。此外，尽管仍有争议，我们还应当探寻城市居民在城市之间迁移的可能性，因为它促进了劳动力，尤其是受教育和熟练劳动力的迁移率。这也将鼓励居民从旧城地区向新城地区进行尝试性迁移，从而促进新城地区的发展。

城市化本身也能降低出生率。一般而言，尽管城市地区的污染比农村地区更严重，但通过提供更多的医疗机会、更高质量的教育和更清洁的饮用水，城市化也能提高预期寿命。预计中国人口将在 2035 年达到高峰，此后必将开始下降。这意味着其他条件不变的情况下，随着城市化的进行，中国老龄化速度很可能加快。因此，有必要重新审视退休和养老制度。中国的退休年龄（目前为女性 55 岁、男性 60 岁）并没有根据健康状况的改善和预期寿命的延长做出相应调整。目前退休规定仍是不全面、不完全可靠的。在宏观经济层面，人口老龄化意味着抚养比率、非劳动人口对劳动人口的比例持续上升，这将对劳动人口造成沉重而持续增加的压力。在微观经济层面，一个人在工作寿命内，譬如说到60岁以前所积累的存款，一般不足以支持他（她）长达三四十年甚至更久的退休生活。我们应当在自愿的基础上，让男女退休年龄有更多的上调灵活性。可以规定领导岗位的退休年龄为60岁，比如政府部门的部长、企业的董事长或CEO等，而在另一方面允许个人以不隶属于行政机关的专业人员的身份继续工作。中国还应当考虑转向集中管理的养老基金制度，给予劳动者和退休人员更大的流动性，并最终从固定收益福利制度转变为可提供全部收益型的固定供款制度。

养老金福利的可转移性将成为一个重要问题。一生工作在上海的人，可能喜欢到气候良好、生活成本便宜的云南昆明或其他小城市养老。养老金福利的可转移性将使退休人员在低成本下保持更高的生活质量成为可能，从而使固定供款制度的养老金福利能够维持更长一段时间的生活。

五、城市化和节能环保

城市化可以在几个重要方面降低能耗及单位GDP能耗。第一，独户式住宅每平方米占地面积的采暖和制冷成本要远远高于集合式住宅或者节能效果更好的大型建筑中的居住单元。第二，城市化减少了交通成本，因为小汽车可以不再作为主要的交通工具。不过，为了实现这些预期结果，采取高密度土地利用和公交优先等城市规划手段是十分必要的。第三，在城市地区更容易应用如采暖、制冷、照明、供电和热水等方面的绿色技术。第四，城市化促进了第三产业（服务业）的发展，而第三产业的单位GDP能耗要远低于第二产业（制造业、采矿业和建筑业）。

六、城市化和市场管理

农村地区居民的迁移率较低，买方和卖方一般彼此了解。销售劣质商品、欺瞒诈骗的人即使没受到实际惩罚，也会很快被认出，遭到排斥。城市化改变了这一切。城市化为买方和卖方赋予了一种匿名的属性，人们会被追究责任的可能性大大降低，欺瞒诈骗的利益诱惑更高。城市地区的市场信息一般是不对称的，到处存在着道德危机（隐藏行动）的可能。农村地区的多数交易都是在相同的当事人之间反复进行的，而那些在农村地区毫无必要的做法，到了城市地区，由于一次性交易的普遍存在，为了保护消费者利益，必须进行市场管理与检测认证。高效和起作用的检测认证必须由具备公信力的机构进行，该机构通常由政府组织或得到政府的支持。同时，城市化使很多服务的提供都能充分利用规模经济，因此也促进了劳动力的分化和分工。例如，村里的学校无法达到最佳规模，不能吸引最好的老师或负担最好的设备。一个城市的学校则更有能力做到这些。同样的道理适用于医院和一般意义上的各类基础设施。城市化提高了公共基础设施的利用率，从而提高了效率和回报率。城市化也使群聚效应或聚集经济成为可能。

七、城市化——缩小实际收入差距的手段之一

城市化可以成为缩小经济体系中实际收入差距最有效的手段之一，这是因为城市化能够让农业部门中生产力低下的农村剩余劳动者成为城市地区服务于第二或第三产业且生产力较高的工人。农村剩余劳动者从农村地区搬迁到城市地区，大大地增加了他们的收入。

此外，城市化也使以前的农村居民有机会获得过去无法得到或者质量较好的各种公共物品，如教育、医疗、洁净的空气和水。一般而言，公共物品是所有城市居民都可以自由获取的，无论收入多少。从某种程度上说，公共物品也是实现实际收入再分配的有效手段。例如，通过让所有人能够接触、利用、负担得起互联网，将极大地缩小富人和穷人间教育和信息方面的差距。这在城市地区更容易实现。互联网是一个极好的平衡器，比如通过网络，来自中国最贫困省份之一的青海省的学生可以像上海学生一样获取到差不多的信息；在互联网上大型企业和小型企业将相对公平地进行竞争。城市化将极大地缩小所谓的“数字鸿沟”，从而降低不平等的程度。

八、结论

中国城市化的继续发展是不可避免的。这为中国提供了一个极佳的机会，同时也是一个巨大的挑战。城市化可以成为中国经济增长的动力，可产生大量国内总需求，有助于从出口导向型成功转变为内需导向型。同时，通过让农村地区人口有更多的途径得到或者使用到基础教育和医疗等公共物品、公共交通以及洁净的空气和水，减少城市地区人口和农村地区人口生活水平间的差距，这样一来，城市化便能够促进社会和谐。此外，如果规划正确合理，在城市化的同时并不会出现极端贫困、环境恶化和城市蔓延等诸多发展中国家和发达国家城市的共有现象。

为了取得这些让人满意的成果，规划是绝对必要的。应特别注意的是，不宜将重心放在现有大型城市的进一步扩张，而应落在内陆省份和各自治区中心城市的发展及其周边旧城新镇的发展之上。这与过去三十年发生的情况正好相反，不是将劳动力引入资本和技术所在之处，而是将资本和技术引入劳动力所在之处。最后，如果目前的农村家庭能够得到其依靠谋生的土地产权或使用权的承认，则将会极大地促进城市化进程。

（作者：刘遵义，香港中文大学蓝饶富暨蓝凯丽经济学讲座教授，美国斯坦福大学李国鼎经济发展荣休讲座教授，国际欧亚科学院中国科学中心副主席；译者：贾淑玲，董敏，李秀梅；审校：毛其智，胡若函）

Urbanisation and the Chinese Economy[①]

Introduction

China has made tremendous progress in its economic development since it began its economic reform and opened to the World in 1978. China is currently the fastest growing economy in the World—averaging 9. 8% per annum over the past 33 years. It is historically unprecedented for an economy to grow at such a high rate over such a long period of time. Between 1978 and 2011, Chinese real GDP grew almost 22 times, from US $ 344. 8 billion to nearly US $ 7. 5 trillion (2011 prices) to become the second largest economy in the World, after the U. S. By comparison, the U. S. GDP (approx. US $ 15. 1 trillion) was 2 times Chinese GDP in 2011.

Despite its rapid growth, in terms of its real GDP per capita, China is still a developing economy. Between 1978 and 2011, Chinese real GDP per capita grew 15. 5 times, from US $ 358 to US $ 5 555 (in 2011 prices). By comparison, the U. S. GDP per capita (approx. US $ 48 236) was 8. 7 times Chinese GDP per capita in 2011.

While many problems have arisen in the Chinese economy within the past decade—for example, increasing income disparity—both inter-regional and intra-regional—uneven access to basic education and health care, environmental degradation, inadequate infrastructure and corruption—it is fair to say that every Chinese citizen has benefited from the economic reform and opening since 1978, albeit to varying degrees, and few want to return to the central planning days.

In the following table, the key performance indicators of the Chinese economy before and after the initiation of the economic reform and opening policy in 1978 are compared. It is readily apparent that there has been a huge improvement in every aspect of the economy—rates of growth of GDP, consumption, and international trade—except the average rate of inflation, which has

---

① The author is an Academician of the International Eurasian Academy of Sciences, Ralph and Claire Landau Professor of Economics, The Chinese University. of Hong Kong, and Kwoh-Ting Li Professor in Economic Development, Emeritus, Stanford University. The opinions expressed herein are entirely the author's own and do not necessarily reflect the views of the organisations with which the author is affiliated.

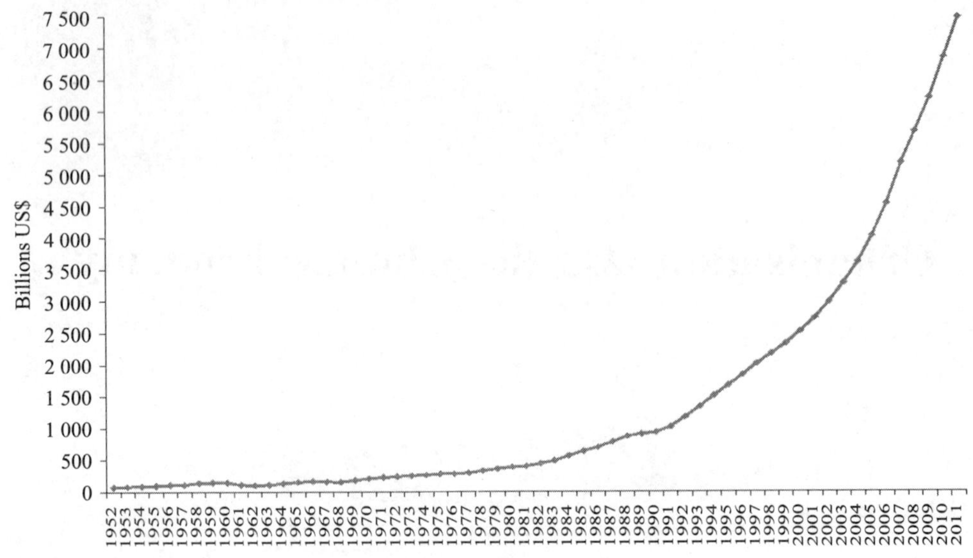

Chart 1 Chinese Real GDP in US $ Since 1952 (2011 Prices)

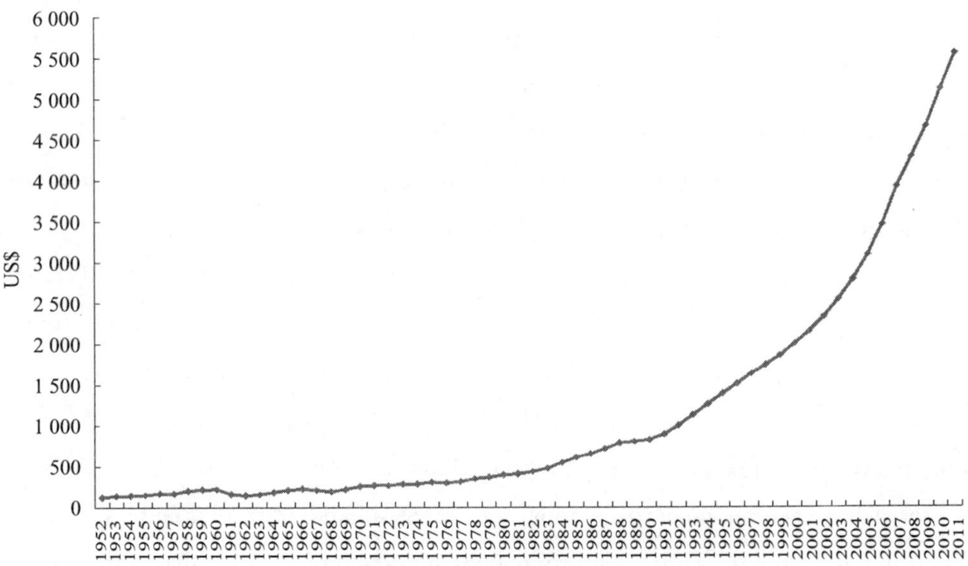

Chart 2 Chinese Real GDP per Capita in US $ Since 1952 (2011 Prices)

become considerably higher in the period since 1978.

The Chinese Government leaders have also amply demonstrated their ability to confront important challenges and solve difficult problems over the past 34 years, surviving various economic and financial crises. China is one of the very few socialist countries that have made a smooth transition from a centrally planned to a market economy. It is a model for other transition economies such as Vietnam and potential transition economies such as Cuba, Laos, and North Korea.

Table 1 Key Performance Indicators of the Chinese Economic Reform

	Growth Rates Percent per Annum	
	Period I	Period II
	1952—1978	1978—2011
Real GDP	6. 15	9. 79
Real GDP per Capita	4. 06	8. 66
Exports	9. 99	17. 32
Imports	9. 14	16. 63
Inflation Rates (GDP defltor)	0. 50	4. 24
	1952—1978	1978—2010
Real Consumption	5. 05	8. 88
Real Consumption per Capita	2. 99	7. 75

The distribution of Chinese GDP by originating sectors in 2010 was approximately: Primary (agriculture), 10. 1% ; Secondary (manufacturing, mining and construction), 46. 7% ; and Tertiary (services), 43. 2% . (Note that mining is normally included in the primary sector in most other economies.) In 2011, the distribution has changed slightly to 10. 1% , 46. 8% and 43. 1% .

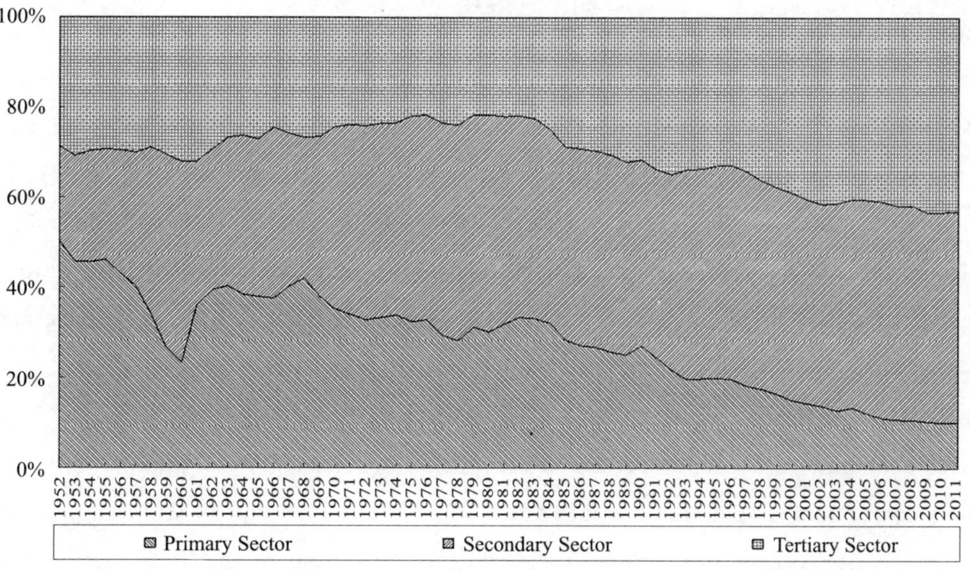

Chart 3 The Distribution of Chinese GDP by Sector Since 1952

But the bulk of the labour force, more than 36% , is still employed in the primary sector, waiting to be transferred to the other two sectors which have higher productivity. As long as the percentage of labour force employed in the primary sector significantly exceeds the percentage of GDP originating from the primary sector, there is little or no upward pressure on the real wage rate

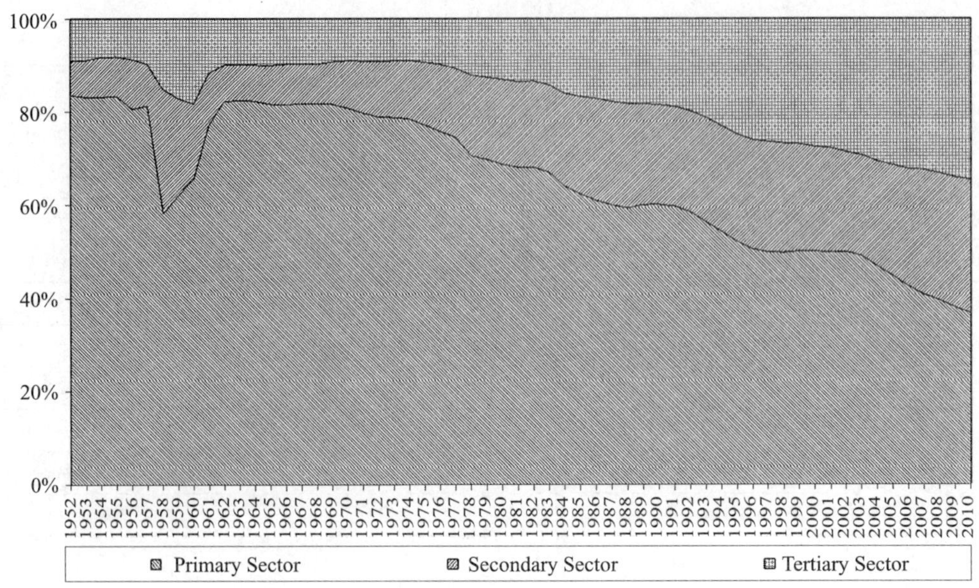

Chart 4 The Distribution of Chinese Employment by Sector Since 1952

of unskilled, entry-level labour in the secondary and tertiary sectors.

It took thirty-three years for the percentage of labour force employed in the Chinese primary sector to decline from 70% in 1978 to its current 36%, at the rate of approximately 1 percentage point per year. It will take approximately another 25 years or so for the percentage of labour force employed in the Chinese primary sector to decline from its current 36% to below 10%, which is approximately the same as the percentage of Chinese GDP produced by the primary sector today. By that time, it is expected that the primary sector will account for no more than 5% of Chinese GDP.

China will therefore continue to have surplus labour for another two decades or even longer. There will not be any shortage of unskilled, entry-level labour for a long time to come, even though there may be shortages of skilled or experienced labour in the secondary and tertiary sectors.

The share of rural population in China was just under 90% in 1949. By 1978, the beginning of the Chinese economic reform and opening to the world, the share of rural population was 82%. By 2010, the share of rural population has fallen to 51%—still almost half of Chinese population lives in rural areas. It is expected to continue to fall during the period of the Twelfth Five-Year Plan, 2011—2015, by 4 percentage points, to 47%. The rate of decline of the share of rural population has been approximately 1 percentage point per year, about the same rate of decline as the share of employment of the primary (agriculture) sector. It is expected that the share of rural population will continue to decline by 1 percentage point a year until 2040, when the share of rural population will have fallen to approximately 30%.

Through the past three decades, the centre of gravity of the world economy has been gradually

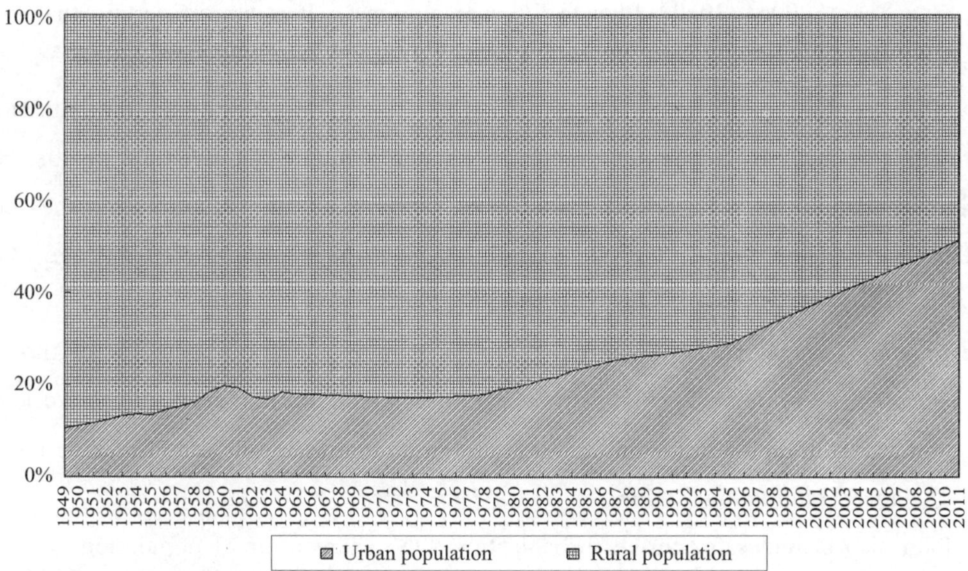

Chart 5 The Shares of Rural and Urban Population in China, 1949-Present

shifting from the United States and Europe to Asia, including both East Asia and South Asia. The East Asian cconomies have become partially de-coupled from the rest of the world economy, as evidenced by the strong performance of China, India and other East Asian economics during the 2007—2009 global financial crisis as well as the current European sovereign debt crisis. However, the Chinese and East Asian economies are not large enough to turn the World around. The idea of a G-2 group of countries consisting of only China and the United States leading the world economy is premature.

Ⅰ. The Twelfth Five-Year Plan for National Economic and Social Development

The Eleventh Five-Year Plan for National Economic and Social Development (2006—2010) officially ended on 31 December 2010. Most of the targets were achieved or exceeded, including the reduction in energy consumption per unit GDP by 20 percent compared to year end 2005. The Eleventh Five-Year Plan provided for a target rate of growth of real GDP of 7.5% per annum between 2006 and 2010. The actual rate of growth achieved was 11.2% per annum. The only major target not achieved was the percentage of GDP expended on R&D—the target was 2% and the actual achieved was 1.8%.

The Twelfth Five-Year Plan for National Economic and Social Development (2011—2015) was approved by the National People's Congress in Mid-March of 2011. It is mostly an indicative plan rather than a mandatory plan. The most remarkable feature of the Twelfth Five-Year Plan was the lowering of the target average annual growth rate of real GDP from 7.5% per annum in the

Eleventh Five-Year (2006—2010) Plan to 7% per annum. (It is almost certain that this target will be exceeded, just as the target average annual rate of 7.5% was exceeded in the Eleventh Five-Year Plan by the actual average annual rate of 11.2%.) However, what the reduction in the target growth rate signals is the determination of the Chinese Government to de-emphasise quantitative economic growth and to focus on improving the quality of the economic growth. During this same period, the rate of inflation is to be kept below an average of 3% per annum.

One principal theme of the Twelfth Five-Year Plan is the transformation in the mode of Chinese economic development—first, from export-oriented to domestic demand-oriented and second, from input-driven to technical progress-driven or innovation-driven. The Plan also aims at essentially balanced international trade.

The Plan also provides for further urbanisation—the share of rural population is to decrease from 51% to 47% during this period. It also provides for increased expenditures for education and healthcare, especially in the rural areas, environmental preservation and protection, and air and water pollution control. It also has mandatory targets for improvement in energy efficiency (energy consumption per unit GDP to decrease by 16%) and reduction in carbon emission (to decrease by 17%). The Plan also provides for reduction in real income disparity through taxation, transfer payments and targeted government expenditures on public goods such as education and health care, the improvement of the social safety net and the pension system.

Ⅱ. Urbanisation as an Engine of Economic Growth

As the Chinese economy undergoes the transformation from an export-oriented to a domestic demand-oriented mode of economic development, the maintenance of a large and growing domestic aggregate demand is of paramount importance. What can be the principal drivers of this domestic aggregate demand?

Chinese household consumption is sometimes viewed as a potential source of growth of Chinese domestic aggregate demand. Chinese household consumption has actually been growing quite rapidly, as indicated by the fact that real retail sales have been growing faster and sometimes much faster, than real GDP. However, such high rates of growth may persist for a while if real household income continues to grow rapidly but are not likely to be sustainable in the long run. This is because the Chinese household savings rate, as distinct from the much higher national savings rate, which currently stands at approximately 30% for both urban and rural households, has apparently stabilised. The consumption-savings behaviour of Chinese households on the Mainland today appears to be little different from ethnic Chinese households in Hong Kong and Taiwan at the same level of per capita household income, with an average savings rate of 30%.

Thus, the Chinese household savings rate is unlikely to fall significantly in the foreseeable future, which means the household consumption rate is not likely to rise significantly.

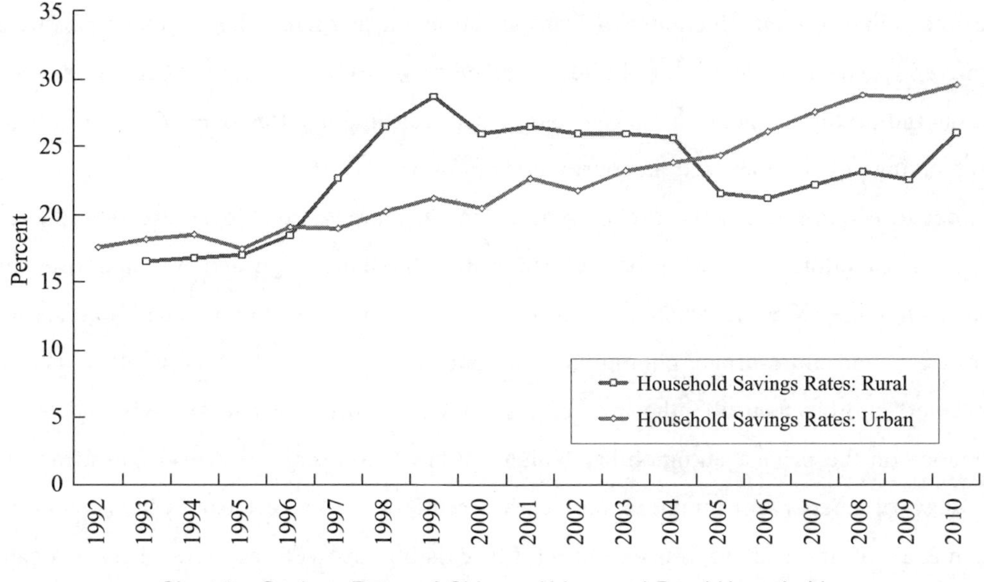

Chart 6 Savings Rates of Chinese Urban and Rural Households

Chinese household consumption can therefore be expected to increase significantly faster than GDP only if the disposable income of Chinese households as a share of GDP rises significantly. There are structural reasons why this is unlikely to occur in the near term even though in the long term, the income share of labour, which currently stands at less than 50%, is likely to rise in China. (The income share of labour in developed economies is typically between 65% and 70%.) Nevertheless, urbanisation will definitely raise the real income of rural areas, especially rural real income per capita.

Continuing Chinese economic growth in 2012 and beyond will therefore have to depend mostly on the growth of other components of domestic aggregate demand, such as investment and government consumption, and not on the growth of household consumption per se, nor on exports. As Vice-Premier LI Keqiang pointed out, urbanisation can be a most powerful engine of Chinese economic growth. Urbanisation enhances domestic aggregate demand and enables the transformation of the Chinese economy from its export orientation.

First, urbanisation per se generates demand for public infrastructural investment. Two types of public infrastructure may be distinguished: infrastructure linking cities, such as railroads, highways, airports, seaports, power grids, telecommunication lines; and infrastructure directly serving the cities themselves, such as power plants, urban mass transit (including subways), optical fibre networks, schools, hospitals, etc. Both types of public infrastructure require public investment from the central government as well as from the provincial and local governments. Both types of public infrastructural investment can generate huge domestic aggregate demand. However, both types of public infrastructural investment require government planning and cannot be left to the market to provide.

The inter-urban communication and transportation infrastructure needs to be further planned and improved, especially with the building of new cities. Super-high-speed trains should be promoted as the preferred mode of transportation between major cities over air travel, resulting in significant savings of time as well as energy consumption.

In order to economise on the use of scarce land resources, and to assure the efficiency and environmental friendliness of the urban transportation system, high-density land use should be mandated in the cities. Central planning of new cities, with regard to their locations, layouts, land use, densities, and intra-urban communication and transportation infrastructure, is absolutely necessary—left entirely to itself, the market system will result in urban sprawls and slums and a heavy reliance on the private automobile, which neither China nor the world can afford from the point of view of energy consumption and carbon emission. Mass-transit systems should be the principal means of intra-urban transportation for existing as well as new cities instead of the automobile. "A car in every garage" would be a nightmare for China and for the world. Cities should be planned so that the residents do not require the use of an automobile in their everyday life (although they may well own an automobile for weekend and leisure use).

With at least a couple of hundreds of Chinese cities of over say 2 million in population and needing mass-transit systems, the planning, designing, building and operating mass-transit systems can become a huge new industry with significant domestic and eventually export demands.

Second, urbanisation generates demand for residential housing which is also largely domestically oriented. The widespread ready access to broadband internet and the availability of the super-high-speed trains are bound to change the residential patterns in China in a revolutionary way. Telecommuting and commuting will become realities. They can generate new demands for residential housing but at the same time greatly reduce congestion and crowding in the major cities and enable the development of new satellite towns.

One important source of sustainable domestic aggregate demand is residential housing. Despite significant development of residential housing during the past thirty odd years, there is still a great deal of room for it to grow, especially in the interior provinces and regions and for the middle-to-lower-middle income households. Such housing can be either owner-occupied or public rental housing (there are many other alternative forms of subsidised housing in between). Owner-occupied residential housing has been a major engine of growth for many countries and regions for decades during their periods of fastest economic growth. There is no question that there is a huge potential demand for residential housing in China. In addition, the demand for residential housing also generates with it the derivative demands for furniture, electric home appliances such as refrigerators, washing machines, and television sets, curtains, carpets, household goods and services and with them a great deal of employment and activities for not only large enterprises but also small and medium enterprises.

Moreover, owner-occupied residential housing is in general non-speculative and does not cause property price bubbles. Furthermore, owner-occupants tend to take better care of their housing units as well as their surroundings. They also feel much more secure as owner-occupants since they are not faced with the threat of rising rents. In order to promote owner-occupied residential housing for all, one has to assure that there is both the supply and the demand. Supply can be promoted by making sure that land is available at an affordable cost and is used efficiently, for example, with relatively high floor-to-area ratios and high densities. Demand can be promoted by making available long-term (say 35 years), fixed interest-rate mortgages.

Owner-occupied residential housing can be provided by both the government and private developers. Under the Twelfth Five-Year Plan (2011—2015), 36 million affordable housing units are supposed to be completed during the next five years. 4. 32 million units have been completed. Under construction are more than 10. 43 million units. It is expected that more than 11 million units will break ground this year with more than 7 million units completed. These units can be rented but also can be sold to owner-occupants.

Third, urbanisation also provides a favourable environment for the broad expansion of the service sector. In the urban context, many services, personal and institutional, are needed—accounting, banking, education, hair-dressing, health care, hotels, insurance, recreation, restaurants, retail services, transportation, etc. —and the demands in turn create their own supplies. Thus, urbanisation will lead to an expansion of the tertiary sector of the economy.

Fourth, there are well-known economies of scale in the provision of public goods, e. g. education, health care, environmental protection and preservation, research and development (R&D) and testing and certification. Urbanisation provides the opportunity for the realization of these economies of scale and for the improvement of the quality of these public services.

As urbanisation proceeds in China, the emphasis should not be on the further expansion of existing large cities, especially those on the coast, many of which have already reached their limits. Instead of making the existing cities larger and more crowded, urbanisation should proceed by the development of urban centres in the interior provinces and autonomous regions around either old cities or new towns, taking full advantage of the natural geography of the traditional market towns. Instead of bringing the surplus rural labour to the coastal regions where the capital and technology were, mostly on the coast, as in the past, capital and technology will be brought to the interior provinces and regions where the surplus labour is. This is also consistent with the gradual phasing out of the traditional "Processing and Assembly" export operations on the coast as the mode of development of the Chinese economy is transformed from export-oriented to domestic demand-oriented.

Ⅲ. Urbanisation and Tax Policy

Urbanisation can be greatly facilitated by the introduction of a dependable and stable source of recurrent revenue for the local governments immediately below the provincial level. These municipal governments have to provide many public goods and services such as public safety, fire fighting and prevention, basic education, public health, hospital services, traffic control, potable water, etc. but do not have any dedicated and dependable sources of revenue. Many of them have become highly dependent on the sale of land and land leases for their revenue in recent years, but such revenue is neither stable nor recurrent. Moreover, the municipal governments, as long as they depend on land sales, have the incentive to keep the price of land high and rising, by artificially restricting potential supply, which unfortunately feeds directly into the property price bubble. Thus, the introduction of a property tax as a source of stable, recurrent revenue for the local governments will enable them to become much less dependent on the sale of land or land leases and hence on high and rising property prices.

Urbanisation will certainly create the demand for land for commercial, industrial, residential and other public uses. High and rising land prices will encourage speculation and prevent the rational and efficient use of land resources and retard successful urbanisation. The introduction of a property tax to be used exclusively by the municipal governments will make it unnecessary for them to promote high and rising property prices and hence reduce the probability of a property price bubble. Pilot programmes for the property tax have been introduced in Shanghai and Chongqing. It is hoped that the property tax will be extended nationwide eventually.

As mentioned above, urbanisation will also create the environment for the rapid growth of the service sector on both the demand and supply sides. To facilitate the growth of the service sector, consideration should be given to replace the current business tax or turnover tax, which is a fixed percentage of the gross revenue of a service enterprise, by the value-added tax, thus allowing the service enterprise to deduct the cost of goods and services used in the provision of the services from its gross revenue before being taxed. This should result in a more equitable sharing of the tax burden between the secondary and tertiary sectors and should provide an additional impetus for the growth of small and medium service enterprises which in turn will provide more employment opportunities for the urban population.

Ⅳ. Urbanisation and Population Policy

The Chinese population is ageing rapidly—caused by rising life expectancy, because of better nutrition and rising availability of health care, and falling birth rate, which is a consequence of the one-child policy, urbanisation and rising level of education of women. The first problem that needs to be addressed in the urbanisation context is the unequal treatment between urban and rural residents in terms of availability of public goods such as education, health care and pension system. The role and function of the household registration system used in the urban areas need to be re-examined. The National People's Congress passed a law in March 2012 which equalises the representation of urban and rural populations at the Congress—one delegate will be elected to the National People's Congress for every 670 000 population, regardless of whether the area is urban and rural. This change in the law will have a profound impact eventually as it reduces the influence of municipalities such as Beijing and Shanghai and enhances the influence of the interior provinces.

Urbanisation means the migration and settlement of residents from the rural areas to the urban areas. These new settlers should have the right to reside in the urban areas and to enjoy all of the privileges and fulfill all of the obligations of the existing urban residents. In the interim, before there is completely free mobility, perhaps every rural resident who has a permanent job in an urban area for an extended period should be granted the right of residence. The possibility of relocation of urban residential rights among urban areas, probably controversial, should also be explored, because it facilitates the mobility of labour, especially that of educated and skilled labour. It will also encourage the potential migration from old urban areas to new urban areas on a trial basis, thus facilitating the development of the latter areas.

Urbanisation in itself will lower the birth rate. Urbanisation will also in general raise the life expectancy, primarily through greater availability of health care, a higher level of education, and cleaner drinking water, despite the fact that the urban areas may be more polluted than the rural areas. Chinese population is projected to reach a peak in 2035 and will begin to decline absolutely. What this means is that ageing is likely to be accelerated in China as urbanisation proceeds, other things being equal. It is therefore necessary to re-examine the retirement and pension system. The Chinese retirement ages, currently 55 for women and 60 for men, have not been changed to reflect the new realities of improved health and lengthened life expectancy. Retirement provision is currently insufficient and not completely dependable. At the macroeconomic level, the ageing population implies that the dependency ratio, the proportion of non-working to working population, will continue to rise, imposing a heavy and rising burden on the working population. At the microeconomic level, the savings accumulated during a person's working life, say, up to 60 years of age, will not in general be sufficient to provide for his or her retired life, possibly for another 30 to 40 years or even beyond. Greater upward flexibility should be introduced for the retirement ages of both women and men, initially on a voluntary basis. It is also possible to mandate retirement at 60 for leadership positions, e. g. , a Minster of a Ministry or a President or CEO of an enterprise, but otherwise allow individuals to continue working as professionals without executive authority. China should also consider moving to a centrally administered pension fund system to enable greater labour and retiree mobility and eventually change to a fully vested defined contributions rather than a defined benefits system.

Portability of pension benefits will become an important issue. Someone who has worked in Shanghai all his life may prefer to retire in Kunming, Yunnan or in other smaller cities because of the better climate and lower living costs. This should be made possible as it will enable the retiree to maintain a higher standard of living at a lower cost, thus allowing the pension benefits from a defined contribution system to last that much longer.

V. Urbanisation and Energy Conservation and Environmental Protection

Urbanisation reduces energy consumption and energy consumption per unit GDP in several important ways. First, heating and cooling costs of individual free-standing houses are much higher per square meeting of floor space than residential units that are clustered together or even better, are all part of a large buildings. Second, transportation costs are also reduced, to the extent that the automobile is not used as the primary means of transportation. However, urban planning is necessary to achieve these desired outcomes—through high density land use and through prior planning and construction of mass transit systems. Third, it is easier to apply green technologies in the urban context in terms of heating, cooling, lighting, provision of electricity and hot water, etc. Finally, urbanisation facilitates the growth of the tertiary (service) sector, which has a much lower energy consumption per unit GDP than the secondary sector (manufacturing, mining and construction).

VI. Urbanisation and Regulation of Markets

In the rural areas, residents are not mobile, and buyers and sellers typically know one another. Those who sell low-quality products, cheat or otherwise commit fraud will be quickly identified and ostracized if not actually punished. Urbanisation changes all that. Urbanisation confers anonymity to both the buyers and the sellers, and the temptation to cheat or commit fraud may be high because the probability that one will be held accountable eventually is much lower. Market information in urban areas tends to be asymmetric and the possibility for moral hazard (hidden action) abounds. Thus, in the rural areas, may not be necessary as most transactions are repeated between the same parties. However, in the urban areas, the transactions are often one-off, and hence market regulation and testing and certification become a must if the interests of the consumers are to be properly protected. Testing and certification, to be effective and useful, must be done by institutions that have public credibility and very often it will have to be a government or government-sponsored organisation.

Urbanisation also enables specialization and division of labour as many services can begin to be provided on an efficient enough scale to take advantage of the economies. For example, a school in a village cannot achieve optimal scale and cannot attract the best teachers or afford the best equipment. But a school in a city will be more able to do so. The same applies to hospitals and in general to all types of infrastructure. Urbanisation enhances the rate of utilization of public infrastructure and hence its efficiency and rate of return. Unbanisation also enables the clustering effect or the economies of agglomeration.

Ⅶ. Urbanisation as a Means of Reducing Real Income Disparity

Urbanisation can be a most effective means of reducing real income disparity in an economy because it allows surplus rural laborers with low productivity in the agricultural sector to become workers in the urban areas in either the secondary or the tertiary sector with a much higher productivity. Their incomes are significantly increased by moving from the rural areas to the urban areas.

Moreover, urbanisation enables the previously rural residents to have access to a range of public goods that were either unavailable or were of inferior quality, such as education, health care, and clean air and water. Public goods are generally freely available to all urban residents without regard to income and to that extent are also an effective means of real income redistribution.

For example, by having the internet accessible, available and affordable to all, the inequality of education (and information) will be greatly narrowed between the rich and the poor. This is much more easily accomplished in the urban areas. The internet is a great equaliser, because on the internet, for examples: a student in Qinghai, one of the poorest provinces in China, will have more or less the same access to information as a student in Shanghai; and large and small enterprises will compete more or less equally on the internet. Urbanisation will greatly reduce the so-called digital divide, and hence reduce the degree of inequality.

Ⅷ. Concluding Remarks

Continuing urbanisation of China is inevitable. It presents a great opportunity for China, as well as a great challenge. Urbanisation can be an engine of growth for the Chinese economy, potentially creating huge domestic aggregate demand and enabling its successful transformation from being export-oriented to domestic demand-oriented. Urbanisation can also promote social harmony by reducing the disparity between the standards of living between urban and rural populations through the increased availability of and access to public goods such as basic education and health care, mass transportation and clean air and water for the latter. Moreover, properly planned, urbanisation does not need to result in the abject poverty, environmental degradation and urban sprawl that characterise many cities in developing as well as developed economies.

However, in order to arrive at these desirable outcomes, planning is absolutely essential. In particular, the emphasis should not be on the further expansion of existing large cities, but rather on the development of urban centres in the interior provinces and autonomous regions around either old cities or new towns. This is the reverse of what has occurred over the past three decades: instead of bringing the labour to where the capital and technology were, capital and technology will be brought to where the labour is. Finally, urbanisation can be greatly facilitated if the rural households currently living on and working with their land can have their property rights or use rights recognised and appropriately valued.

(Lawrence J. Lau)

城市转型与重构进程中的规划调控[①]

我国城镇化已经进行到中期阶段，这就意味着所有的城市在未来20年内仍处于快速发展的阶段，但又由于产业结构的升级、生产要素的流动和国家节能减排要求等方面正推动着我国城市转型，这个阶段城市转型能量的释放与规划的调控之间要相适应，就如同火车要提速，其驱动力已得到快速提升，轨道系统的精密度和刚性也应该适应火车的高速运行。在此期间，我们要认清一个问题，就是既不能用城市规划去压制转型重构的活力，但是又不能让城市转型与重构的活力盲目扩张损害城市可持续长远发展，这是一对矛盾。

这对矛盾应该如何化解？第一，要强化一个总目标来巩固转型过程中的紧凑型的城市发展模式；第二，要推行两类用地混合的布局来注重民生、城市品质和可持续发展；第三，应该严格“三区四线”的管制来保护城乡不可再生资源，为城市的可持续发展保全有生力量；第四，统筹五类交通用地，避免在交通资源分配上犯历史性错误，促进城市的节能减排；第五，要提升“六项”城市的服务功能来奠基和谐社会。

我国从快速城镇化阶段进入城镇化中期阶段，城镇化到了转折的时期。这个时期城市的转型与重构的动力、活力、创造力就会突然迸发出来，此时倘若不在上述五项规划调控的适应性方面下工夫，城市的发展与规划的管制就会成为“两张皮”。一些发展中国家，如拉美、非洲国家出现的严重问题就会在我国各地涌现。可以说，确保我国城镇化健康发展已经到了一个决战的阶段。

一、强化一个节地总目标，巩固紧凑型城市的发展

改革开放30年，我国的城市人口密度变化并不大，城市建设始终坚持每平方公里建成区约1万人的规划标准，这是世界上所有国家的城市建成区中，空间密度比较高的一类，紧凑节约型的发展模式。而美国在近百年城市化的过程中，城市建成区的人口密度下降了三分之二，造成了严重的能源消耗过多、生态环境破坏、耕地减少过快、社会贫富悬殊等问题。美国的人均耕地比我国多20倍，因此可以承受这样的错误，但是我国不行。

正是因为城市蔓延，一个美国人所消耗的汽油相当于5个欧盟人，美国在全世界只占

① 根据作者在2011年9月20日中国城市规划年会上的大会报告材料整理。

5%的人口，但是消耗总的资源和能源占全世界30%多。我国城镇化模式绝对不能步美国的后尘，必须要避免美国式的郊区化，因此，我国的城镇化进程从分散到集中，必须要走向紧凑。但目前，我国城镇化过程中郊区化的动力机制日益强大，其原因如下：

第一，机动化。与美国的城市化特点相似，我国的城镇化与机动化同时发生。小汽车进入家庭，意味着人们获得了空间上的自由选择权，再加上高速公路导向型的城市开发模式，这个时候城市蔓延就会发生，美国代表了失控的车轮上的城市化坏典型。但是，欧洲国家却保持了紧凑型的城市发展模式，这是因为欧洲是城市化在先，机动化在后，是在城市定型之后才出现小汽车普及性进入家庭。在城市空间格局不变的情况下，城市的传统空间结构限制了小汽车的使用，所以，1 000个美国人拥有850辆小汽车，而1 000个欧洲人拥有还不到500辆小汽车，而且实际实用率比美国低许多，结果造成美欧城市能耗和空气污染结果完全不一样。对我国而言，城镇化道路的唯一选择，就是要抛弃美国模式，超越欧洲模式。

第二，小产权房。小产权房就是指规划调控之外的农民或农村集体自建的商品房。这种违背《土地管理法》和《城乡规划法》的开发模式引发郊区化会导致中国式的城市蔓延，小产权房的大量涌现造成优质耕地的占用、城乡规划失控和城市的低密度蔓延。

第三，农村城市化。现代城市规划学的奠基人——霍华德先生在100多年前曾经说过，城市和农村应该像夫妇一般结合，这样一个令人欣喜的结合将萌生新的希望，焕发新的生机，孕育新的文明。如果把农村都建成像城市那样，城与乡就成了“同性恋”，不可能形成互补协调发展的格局。比如，陕北农民以前都是住窑洞的，当地一些干部简单理解新农村建设就是让农民从窑洞里搬出来去住别墅，但结果却是能耗急剧上升，农民以前住窑洞每个采暖季一家只需烧2吨煤，现在却需要10吨煤。有意思的是，当地旅游公司却花钱把这些窑洞买下，改造成三星级宾馆，深受外地旅游者的欢迎。而更多的农村，经过了城市化，已经和城市越来越像，失去了发展“农家乐”乡村旅游业的机遇。

美国在城镇化过程中出现了城乡的同质化发展，同样的城市和农村面貌，不但增加了能耗，也失去了欧盟国家那么多的田园风光。而在欧盟的城市中旅游，越过城市边界一步就是美丽的田园风光，城乡之间差别显著、特色鲜明。中国的城市规划不能步美国后尘，不能让乡村和小城镇成为现代化大都市的牺牲品。要保持城乡之间的差异化特色和阴阳互补性，互补才能协调，协调才能确保城乡和谐。这样一来，农村第一产业就可与第三产业齐头并进，从而保证留驻农村的农民也拥有与进城工作生活的农户共等的富裕机会和幸福指数，这比盲目开展农村城市化更加重要。

第四，征地制度改革。征地制度改革到底往什么方向去？如果朝着土地私有化的方向发展，承包地能够自由地变成房地产项目用地，城郊农民就会竞相向房地产开发公司供地，就将不可避免地导致美国式的城市蔓延。所以，不同道路的选择就影响我国未来城市发展的不同方向，我国能不能保持紧凑型城市发展模式的问题，在城镇化中期阶段就出现了。

对此，应对的基本策略有五条。第一，坚持每平方公里城市建成区1万人的紧凑式用地标准，这是不可动摇的。国际组织的研究表明，在发展阶段，城市密度越高，发展越慢，但是城市发展密度越低的地区，城市用地的扩张就特别快，这就是机动化所带来的一种冲击，也是世界范围内的美国式城市蔓延的错误趋势，这种错误的选择趋势，背后是市场力量和错误的公共政策在推动。也就是说，经济学在节约用地方面基本上是失效的，必须要靠城乡规划调控去弥补。

第二，防止工业用地的粗放发展。城市的发展需要与经济发展相结合，需要足够的就业岗位来支撑城市和谐社会，但是如果工业用地粗放利用，会由于城市空间结构失衡和整体用地的低效而引发城市发展可持续性的受损。从近期来看，许多城市开发了众多用地纯而又纯的工业区，有的还游离于城市总体规划的管制，结果肢解城市的有机空间结构。

第三，构建紧凑型的绿色小城镇来促进节能减排。大中小城市和小城镇协调发展，形成城镇人口规模/城镇数量的正金字塔结构是已被城市化史证实的理想结构。以美国为例，该国直接务农人口仅3%，但却有20%左右的人口是为农业提供产前、产中、产后服务的，这些人往往居住在小城镇，就近为周边的农户提供社会化服务。但我国小城镇的发展一直得不到有效的政策扶持，结果造成了小城镇和小城市人居环境的衰败。为解决这一难题，最近住房和城乡建设部和财政部联合出台了绿色重点小城镇的评选办法，对评为绿色小城镇的将给予中央财政的奖励。

第四，新城市用地尽可能少占或者不占耕地。我国还有很多的盐碱地、石漠化和沙漠化地区。即便美国的人均耕地是我国的20倍，美国也注重在沙漠中建设新城，如凤凰城。我国在盐碱地上、沙漠地上完全可以用现代的技术不占耕地来建设新城市。

第五，南方沿海城市和传统的农产区在城市建设过程中更要注重耕地保护。沿海的耕地都是耕种了几千年的熟地，由于复种指数比北方地区高出250%，南方地区1亩耕地的粮食产出，相当于北方地区的5亩和西北极旱地区的10亩地产出。所以，保护南方沿海地区的1亩耕地，等于保护了北方地区的5亩耕地。

总之，城市发展转型重构需要注重节地，通过两个指标可以衡量城市建设是否节地：一是紧凑，1平方公里建成区人口密度应大于或等于1万人；二是城市扩展方向是否占用了优质耕地。如果少占优质耕地或者不占优质耕地，并且人口密度又很高，就能达到节约用地的目的。对此，我们要学会把复杂的问题简单化，又精准地进行处理。

二、推行两类用地的混合布局，注重民生和城市的品质

第一类混合布局是城镇用地的布局。我国城市建设工业区、开发区过程中，要推行城镇用地的混合布局，即尽快将纯而又纯的工业区、开发区的开发模式转变为综合性的新城建设模式。这里将遇到的主要矛盾就是混合用地与更多专业开发区之间的矛盾。

现在各种各样新类型的开发园区来势汹汹，例如：大学园区、物流园区、特色产业区、软件区、归国人才创业区、环保生态产业园、综合保税园区和文化产业发展园区等每年都有新创造的园区名称，但是万变不离其宗，就是两个字：要地，如任其自行其是，这就会因肢解城市空间有机构成而要了地区可持续发展的命。根据世界城市化和工业化发展的规律，在现行科技水平下，实际上除了危险性、放射性、污染程度高的大型化工产业、炼油产业、钢

铁产业等之外，其他类型的企业用地都可以与文教、商务、居住用地混合安排。

这样的混合安排有什么优点呢？很显然，美国的精明增长（smart growth）、欧盟的可持续发展、联合国人居发展要求，都说明这种用地混合安排能显著地节地、节能，减少了交通流量，改善了景观的多样性，便于创造就业岗位，传承历史的文脉，同时也决定了城市特色。如果是任由功能单纯的园区到处开发，就会造就大江南北和国内国外都一样的城市景观，我国的城市就会失去特色，也就失去了可持续发展的重要资源。

英国在第二次世界大战之后提出了新城运动，并经历了三代新城的教训。第一代建造卧城，即市民们生活休息在一个地方，工作在另一个地方，结果造成很大的社会冲突、能源能耗和交通拥堵。第二代注意到新城的就业问题，一个新城规划10万人口，一半的就业岗位应该在新城内部解决，新城应该有产业的支撑，但在实践中仍不是很成功。最后，规划师们提出第三代新城发展模式，即新城应该基本上能够容纳全部就业，城市单个的规模应该为20万~30万人。在这个过程中，英国不少新城因决策者经历和需求不同，转型重构选择了错误的方向。比如斯蒂文乃奇（Stevenage）新城，到现在为止，人口也不到10万，错过了发展的最好时期。另一个伦康（Run corn）新城，特点是新城中规划了“8”字形的公交车道，是把新城建设和公交建设完美结合的样本，但由于外部政策环境不配套，也落入了城市蔓延的陷阱，成为一种错误的城市扩张所推动的郊区化牺牲品。

第二类混合布局是保障房与商品房必须混合布局。不同收入阶层的市民应由传统的混居——分离——再走向混合，这是一条走向和谐城镇化的正确道路。但是，现阶段贫富阶层分离居住的趋势在我国依然存在，而且还有越演越烈的趋势。例如，各类高档小区争相攀比涌现，高档的、超高档的、超豪华的，一些媒体却把这些当做噱头来宣传，形成了住宅高档化的错误认识；党中央、国务院决定在“十二五”期间要建设3 600万套保障房，但现在每年近千万套的保障房硬任务基本集中在城郊建设，客观上助推了贫富居住的分离；更重要的是郊区化以及小产权房的蔓延也促进了贫富分离化居住的趋势。

在这方面国外已有过深刻的教训。美国在“二战”以后，由政府出钱大量建设保障房，但在后期这些保障房缺乏有效的管理，居住其中的穷人越来越多，而富人都早早搬离了，结果这些小区蜕变为非常萧条的新贫民区，环境非常恶劣。在苏联时期，前东德政府建设了大量形式单调、简陋的板壁式建筑，这类丑陋的板式建筑被讥为“莫斯科的假牙”。原本很漂亮的城市里被安上了一排排假牙似的建筑，看上去非常的不协调。先行国家保障房建设方面的这些不良现象，必须由我国规划师和决策者们通过自身的努力来缓解并消除。

广义的保障房质量观应包括以下几方面的内容：

第一，住宅本身的质量。保障房建设要有统一的质量管理，如建材、住宅结构、施工、装修质量和节能性能等，这些是保障房质量要满足的最基本的方面。

第二，小户型设计质量。当前，小户型的设计质量要提到更重要的位置，因为保障房也是为了低收入阶层可以有尊严的居住，是和谐社会构建的重要保障，所以小户型的设计要更加注重人性化和生态化。

第三，小区规划设计质量。小区规划要注重多样化设计，要注重混合设计和绿化配置，避免出现兵营式整齐、单调、乏味的空间景观。

第四，不同阶层混合或分离所致的包容性质量。《马丘比丘宪章》提出，一个城市最大的魅力就在于它的包容性。如果要缓解甚至消除贫富分离居住的现实问题，实现整个社会的包容性增长，就必须要解决不同阶层混合居住的问题，因为穷人在就业上没有空间选择权，其居住地必须紧靠其就业岗位，但富人可以相对自由地进行选择，所以在居住空间混合与否上，对于贫富阶层而言其意义完全不同。

第五，综合配套质量。现在有些保障房小区建好了，却没有幼儿园、学校、医院，也没有相应的配套公共交通安排，住在这些保障房小区的市民生活极为不方便，更谈不上生活质量问题，这就失去了大量兴建保障性住房的意义。

第六，住宅区整体区域质量。开发房地产非常讲究区位（location），但保障房建设难道就没有区位的问题吗？同样也有。当前正值保障房建设高潮的初期，尤为重要的是要将保障坐落与未来城市发展方向一致起来，与工业区和其他园区掺杂布局，与商品房开发混合搭配。市中心少量土地也可用于保障房，由于区位条件优越，肯定会引发分配难题，要学习新加坡的做法，对此类特别区位的保障房在符合条件的入住户中进行定向拍卖（租），以杜绝腐败。

造成保障房小区低质量的主要因素有以下几个方面：

一是设计者缺竞争性优化动力。为此，建议各学协会和规划学会每年年会上都有针对保障房设计的颁奖内容，同时还要增加保障房混合小区设计的奖项。通过较高层次定期的设计竞赛活动、奖励和评选等方式促进保障房设计优化。

二是开发者无业绩激励动力。建设保障房没有开发商品房的预期利润高，加上政策导向不明确，开发者缺乏提升保障房质量的动力。

三是建造者缺业主过程监督。商品房有预售制度，商品房的业主早早就确定了，在开发过程中业主们会主动参与监督，随时了解所购住房的建造质量。但保障房是建好以后通过摇号确定入围人群，之后再选择具体哪个小区的保障房，住上哪套住房完全是靠碰运气的，与商品房完全不同，保障房在事前、事中都难以做到业主参与监督。

四是配套者缺事先计划与资金。即城市建设的提供者，缺乏事先的规划、计划和过程中的执行。上述几方面的原因共同导致了许多保障房小区的综合质量下降。

在保障房建设质量上应当尽可能做得更好，美国的波特兰就是一个很好的例子。波特兰新城区是一个主要为低收入阶层居住而建设的新的城区，小区环境优美，孩子们在浅浅的水池开心地嬉水。在波特兰的新城区，第一是实现了不同阶层市民居住的混合化；第二是设计的多样化，该新区的每一幢建筑都不一样，但是组合在一起却很和谐，不像我国一些保障房小区，每幢建筑都是一个模子里出来的，呈简单的军营式布局，景观单调枯燥，居住在这样的小区里人们常常会迷路；第三是生活设施的配套非常齐全。在波特兰新区有一条免费的轨道交通，这条免费的轨道交通起点和终点都是由新区直通市中心，这样的公共交通安排让低收入者有免费的交通选择。

解决保障房质量问题的基本对策是什么呢？

第一是要在商品房用地出让合同注明配建保障房比率。建议保障房的配建比率不低于20%，尽管这样设置开发商可能不满意，但为了和谐社会的构建应列为土地出让合同强制性的条款。

第二是提升城市设计与控规编制质量。即要把控制性详细规划做深、做细、做好，重要区段和大型的旧城改造都应事先进行竞争性的城市设计，确保丰富多样化但又具特色的优美社区景观。

第三是学习新加坡经验，强制不同阶层混居比率。事实上不同阶层混居不仅是新加坡，而且是全世界发达国家的共同做法。例如，法国巴黎一些新建的住宅实行经济适用房与商品房混合配建，在具体布局上一幢是经济适用房，另一幢是商品房，两类住房在外观几乎没有区别，只在内部户型的大小上有较大的差异，使得不同收入阶层的人都可以有尊严的共同生活在一起。

三、严格“三区四线”管制，保护不可再生的资源

在城市转型和重构的过程中，市场化的力量非常巨大，城市中许多不可再生的脆弱资源，有可能会消失，被人为破坏，或被小团体所占用，有些房地产项目可能占用风景最好的地方。然而，城市规划学里有句名言，就是“要把最漂亮的景观留给最广大的人群去享受”，这就需要通过“三区四线”的管制来实现。

我国在转型重构过程中面临严峻的挑战：

一是自然资源、人文资源的破坏正从城市向村镇蔓延。随着城市化进程加快，自然资源、人文资源破坏正在从城市向村镇蔓延。

二是城市的面貌又随着“一年一小变，三年一大变”式的过度改造正在变得千城一面，特色丧失。

三是城市的历史文脉遭到中断破坏，历史遗产资源被严重损坏。城市的特色和历史文脉就像祖传的名画那样，保留下来并不消耗能源，但却可以世世代代增值，但是，现在一些无知的决策者和规划师却在做将“珍贵的祖传名画”变成“廉价现代印刷品”的蠢事，这是一个很可怕的常识性错误。

四是邻避效应（NIMBY，not-in-my-backyard）。先行国家出现了类似的情况，即不要在我的后院建设，结果城市的污水处理厂、垃圾中转站、垃圾焚烧厂、变电站等都无法建设，这是一个严重的错误。这些基础设施是公共品，城市的发展和运行需要这些基础设施，但是它们的选址和建设却遭到了强大的利益集团的抵制，一些设施几年甚至几十年都建不成，严重妨碍了城市的可持续发展和防灾能力建设。

所有这些问题我们就要通过“三区四线”来进行控制。三区是指确定不准建设区、非农建设区、控制发展区的控制范围，而四线是指通过绿线保护绿地公园，蓝线保护水资源水景观，黄线保护供电所等市政基础设施用地，紫线保护历史建筑、重点文物和历史街区。即使经科学修编的城市规划，也不可能几十年都不变，但“三区四线”划定的控制范围，可

以也应该百年不变。

在城市转型和重构过程中，我们要守住刚性的底线，相应的应对措施非常重要。第一，将“三区四线”作为基本的城乡规划强制性管理手段。在城镇体系规划、城市总规、控规、详规等层次的规划中要全面执行“三区四线”管理，原来没有的要补充，原来过于粗放的要细化并且强化。第二，要协同好“三区四线”之间的关系，并在城市规划设计中贯彻落实，同时增强它们的强制性和易管性。第三，将“三区四线”扩大到整个规划调控区域，因为“三区四线”是来自于城市的调控需求，是奠基在我国60年城乡规划学术发展的基础之上，它不是无本之木，而是一个内生的制度。任何制度变革都是有成本的，美国经济学家诺斯因发现了变革制度的成本理论而获得了诺贝尔经济学奖。许多人都不明白对原有成熟的制度变更总是附带高昂成本的道理，这就很容易走上盲目冒进式的错误道路。第四，在“四线”管理中还应该划定实线和虚线。比方说历史街区，对实线范围内的历史建筑，应贯彻修旧如旧的原则，让老建筑老街区“延年益寿”；还要划定更大的虚线范围，即在虚线调控范围人的区域内，要保持新旧建筑的风貌协调。在区域规划层面，广东推行的绿道规划就起着很好的作用，通过绿道把自然保护、旅游、体育健身、景观、历史文化遗产保护有机组合在一起。

四、合理安排五类交通用地，推进节能减排

从全世界的范围来看，工业能耗占37.7%，交通能耗占29.5%，而建筑的能耗超出了30%，这是能源结构变化的趋势。我国现在处于工业化时期，交通的能耗最少，仅占10%，建筑的能耗约为26%，其余的60%以上均为工业能耗。但是，建筑和交通的能耗都是刚性的，难以由业主调整治理，如果城市的交通结构已经是以小汽车出行为主，那时再号召城市居民步行、使用自行车或者公交出行就晚了。

表1　世界与发达国家能源部门消费结构

	世界	经济合作与发展组织	美国	日本	英国	法国	德国
工业	37.7	34.6	27.7	42.3	29.7	30.3	33.1
交通	29.5	33.1	40.7	27.1	31.9	31.3	27.4
建筑	32.9	32.3	31.6	30.6	38.5	38.4	39.5

美国总统奥巴马尽管提出要推行绿色经济革命，但是他也无法解决美国郊区化的问题。该国专家分析认为，美国的郊区化道路是历史性刚性的错误，其后果是一百个奥巴马都解决不了的。而工业的能耗会随着技术的革命，以及碳排放税的出台和能源、资源价格的提高，自动地一步步下降，这就是能源结构变化的基本趋势。

先行国家城市转型的历史过程已经证明，在城市交通上以普及小汽车为导向的模式是不可持续的，小汽车用地与步行、自行车、公交的用地之间存在尖锐的矛盾。在这方面由不得

市场自由发挥，而是要通过严格的规划调控合理地分配空间资源，因为交通用地的资源在紧凑式的城市里是极其稀缺有限的。

我国城市现在面临的最大挑战，一是交通的能耗上升最快，我国的交通能耗如果从现在的10%上升到世界平均水平的30%，有着巨大的上涨空间，而且这种能耗结构一旦确立就将是刚性的。

二是城市规划错误地适应小汽车。这个恶果在我国许多城市正在呈现，决策者往往偏好于建更庞大宽广的机动车道来适应小汽车的增加，这也成为了许多城市的错误选择。我国许多城市喜欢造高架桥，这些高架桥仅方便小汽车通行，既不能步行和骑自行车，公交车也无法开上去。据统计，城市的空气污染80%是汽车尾气造成的，而且汽车尾气形成烟雾在密集的城市空间中，就更难以治理，造成市民健康恶化得更加严重，这一定程度上是城市规划适应小汽车带来的恶果。

三是交通的拥堵已经从超大城市扩散到一般城市，从沿海扩散到内地。

四是我国石油的对外依存度已经攀升到很高的水平，严重威胁到我国的能源安全。

从常识上看，应对之策一是必须要编制以绿色交通为主的城市综合交通体系，这是《城乡规划法》所规定的。

二是修建“不可停车”的自行车道，例如，北京采用硬性隔离桩隔离自行车道与汽车道，小汽车根本开不进去，这样就方便了自行车出行。一些城市“禁摩”是有一定道理的，但封杀电动自行车的决策却是“屁股指挥脑袋”。电动自行车在能耗上只有摩托车的七八分之一，并且是零排放的。一些城市一方面对电动汽车给予巨额补贴，每辆车补贴最高超过10万元，而电动自行车不但不补贴，还要对其进行封杀，这是极其短视的。当然，对速度过快、重量过重、又不能脚踩的电动自行车要适当地进行安全性控制。

表2　各种机动化工具能耗比较

机动化工具	每人公里能源消耗(以公共汽车单车为1)
自行车	0
电动自行车	0.73
摩托车	5.6
小轿车	8.1
公共汽车(单车)	1
公共汽车(专用道)	0.8
地铁	0.5
轻轨	0.45
有轨电车	0.4

三是交通用地分配倒三角。从城市规划者来讲，城市合理的交通用地应该呈“倒三角”格式：即步行的空间最多，其后依次是自行车、地铁、公交、小汽车，也就是把行人的需要放在首位。如果颠倒过来，城市交通的发展就走向了洛杉矶的模式。洛杉矶是人类历史上第

一个让城市的规划适应小汽车的城市，城市用地三分之一给了交通，但它仍然是全世界交通最拥堵的城市，也是肥胖症、心脏病发病率最高的城市，由此可见，我国城市交通发展不能走洛杉矶的道路。

四是在城市中还应该设置与可再生能源结合的充电桩，方便电动自行车和新能源车充电。

五是大力推行租赁自行车和租赁电动自行车。租赁自行车和电动自行车目前在我国城市已经有了长足的发展。

六是尽早规划地下交通和公共交通。在厦门，高架桥上跑的不是小汽车，而是BRT，这在当时是一个创举，现在证明这种做法效果非常好，原来设计高架BRT每天的流量为6万人，现在达到20万人。

七是扩大执行“无车日”。逐步增加开展“无车日”活动天数，扩大活动范围，丰富活动内容。广泛宣传优先发展公共交通的政策和措施，加快引导市民出行习惯的转变。更为重要的是，通过“无车日”活动的开展还可以激发民众减少交通排放的参与热情、加快绿色交通的发展。

五、提升“六项”城市服务功能

从《雅典宪章》开始把城市的所有功能定为4类：居住、工作、游憩和交通。但是，这四类传统的城市功能分类与新的城市功能之间存在矛盾，即新的城市必须是低碳生态环保、安全防灾的。在解决这个矛盾时，应该利用城市发展新模式来规划建设生态城。

现在林林总总的生态城很多，一些房地产开发项目也自称是生态城，但是真正的生态城应该满足6个入门条件。第一是紧凑的用地模式，每平方公里建成区居住人口必须大于1万人，以起到节约用地的示范效应；第二是可再生能源应用的比例大于或等于20%；第三是绿色建筑占建筑总数大于或等于80%；因为绿色建筑具有节地、节能、节材、节水，室内空气环保等特征，对外部环境干扰最小，应成为生态城市的基础工程；第四是生物多样性，应通过绿化园林的合理布局和精心设计来确保生物多样性和自然斑痕的保护利用；第五是绿色交通优先，市民出行中步行、自行车与公共交通的使用比例大于65%；第六是拒绝高耗能、高排放工业项目。生态城就是要在用地、可再生能源应用、交通、建筑能耗、城市基础设施和产业类型六个方面去限定，不符合这六个条件的生态城就是“山寨版的生态城”，应及时予以除名。

在城市安全防灾方面，第一是多组团、互补发展城市社区；第二是利用城市的道路和河川的规划建设防灾设施，以便于城镇防灾和在灾难发生时组织救灾；第三是构建具备医疗、福利、行政、避难、储存等多功能的“防灾安全街区”，在一个街区之内储存有足够三天的应急能源；第四是在政府的办公楼、公园、体育场、学校、广场等建立“防灾据点”，储备应急物品。在日本，个人的防灾储备可以支撑3天，防灾据点储备可以支持3天，当地政府的储备也可以支撑3天，总计可以独立应对9天的紧急需求。此外，通过建设公园绿地雨水收集的储存池，既可用于消防，也可节约水资源；采用柔性的管道技术与接口技术提高城市管网抗震性，在日本，城市遇到大地震以后，可以在24小时之内恢复供水，24小时之内实现污水处理正常化，这是非常难得的；第五是编制城镇抗震防灾的规划与防灾应对手册，提供硬件和软件方面的相应国家标准。

总之，通过以上五个方面的规划创新，要达成城市规划的约束和城市转型重构之间的协调。第一，要在城镇化中期规划的调控中防止出现后人难以纠正的刚性错误。第二，要全面正确地汲取先行国家正反两方面经验教训，千万不要将错误当成就。现在有的人认为美国的郊区化好，我国以后就应走这条道路，这是非常错误的。美国的规划界普遍认为美国的郊区化是个巨大的错误，我们不能把它当成效仿的对象。第三，根据我国各地实际的情况“实事求是”地从“问题”出发来积极地创新和应对解决这个问题。第四，勇于从“干中学”，增强城乡规划实际的调控能力，力求与城市转型重构的能量保持平衡。只有这一对总矛盾平衡以后，我国今后30年的城镇化才会是健康有序和可持续的。

（作者：仇保兴，住房和城乡建设部副部长，中国城市科学研究会理事长，中国城市规划学会理事长）

关于中国矿业城市可持续发展战略的思考

2011年是党的十六大作出“支持以资源开采为主的城市和地区发展接续产业”这一战略决策的第10个年头，是《国务院关于促进资源型城市可持续发展的若干意见》实施的第5个年头。以开采资源为主的城市和地区有矿业城市和森工城市两类，缘由开采矿产资源而兴起或发展起来的矿业城市则是资源型城市中的主体。因矿产资源是不可再生的资源，随着时间的推移和矿业开发程度的提高，可采资源的逐渐减少，对矿业生产效益、城市经济状况和矿工生活与社会稳定都不可避免带来不良影响。矿业城市若无非矿产业的支持，就必然会出现由兴起到鼎盛，再到衰败的过程。这是不以人们主观意志为转移的客观规律。目前，我国有一批矿业城市（镇），特别是采矿历史悠久的矿业城市（镇）因探明可采资源逐渐减少以至行将枯竭，城市（镇）也出现各种各样的困难和问题。因此，如何避免“矿竭城衰”，实现矿业城市可持续发展是一个需要解决好的重要战略问题。

一、中国矿业城市的基本情况

矿业城市是城市群体的重要组成部分，是诸多城市中与矿产资源开发关系密切的城市。据中国矿业联合会矿业城市工作委员会余际从、刘粤湘等人结合《中国城市年鉴（2010）》数据资料统计分析结果，我国现有矿业城市（镇）232座（表1）。其中矿业城市数量较多的省（区）依次是：山西、河南、河北、山东、辽宁、吉林、江西、云南、广西、甘肃、新疆、内蒙古、湖南、安徽、贵州、陕西、黑龙江、湖北等省（区）。重庆、福建、广东、江苏、海南、西藏、宁夏、青海、浙江也有少量矿业城市。

表1　我国矿业城市（区）名单

省　名	行政级别	数　量		名　　称
河北	地级市	15	5	唐山、邯郸、邢台、承德、张家口
	县级市		5	鹿泉、迁安、武安、沙河、任丘
	县城		2	易县、曲阳
	市辖区		3	鹰手营子、下花园、井陉矿区

续表 1

省名	行政级别	数量		名称
山西	地级市	16	8	大同、阳泉、长治、晋城、朔州、晋中、临汾、吕梁
	县级市		7	古交、高平、介休、原平、霍州、孝义、河津
	县城		1	垣曲
内蒙古	地级市	9	5	包头、乌海、赤峰、鄂尔多斯、呼伦贝尔
	县级市		3	霍林郭勒、满洲里、锡林浩特
	市辖区		1	石拐区
辽宁	地级市	14	7	鞍山、抚顺、本溪、阜新、盘锦、铁岭、葫芦岛
	县级市		4	海城、凤城、调兵山、北票
	市辖区		3	杨家杖子、南票、弓长岭
吉林	地级市	13	4	辽源、白山、松原、通化
	县级市		8	九台、临江、桦甸、舒兰、磐石、蛟河、珲春、和龙
	市辖区		1	二道江区
黑龙江	地级市	7	6	鸡西、鹤岗、双鸭山、大庆、七台河、黑河
	县级市		1	五大连池
江苏	地级市	2	1	徐州
	市辖区		1	贾汪区
浙江	县城	1	1	青田
安徽	地级市	8	8	淮南、马鞍山、淮北、铜陵、宿州、池州、滁州、巢湖
福建	地级市	4	1	龙岩
	县级市		2	漳平、永安
	县城		1	上杭
江西	地级市	11	5	萍乡、宜春、赣州、景德镇、新余
	县级市		6	乐平、丰城、高安、德兴、瑞昌、大余
山东	地级市	15	6	枣庄、东营、济宁、莱芜、泰安、淄博
	县级市		8	滕州、龙口、招远、莱州、兖州、邹城、新泰、肥城
	市辖区		1	淄川区
河南	地级市	16	6	平顶山、鹤壁、濮阳、焦作、南阳、三门峡
	县级市		8	登封、巩义、新密、禹州、义马、永城、灵宝、汝州
	县城		2	新安、栾川
湖北	地级市	6	2	黄石、松滋
	县级市		4	大冶、潜江、钟祥、应城
湖南	地级市	9	2	郴州、娄底
	县级市		6	冷水江、涟源、耒阳、资兴、常宁、临湘
	县城		1	花垣
海南	县级市	2	1	东方
	县城		1	昌江

续表 1

省 名	行政级别	数 量		名 称
广东	地级市	3	3	云浮、韶关、茂名
广西	地级市	10	3	百色、河池、贺州
	县级市		2	合山、岑溪
	县城		4	环江、南丹、大新、平果
	市辖区		1	平桂管理区
重庆	地级市	5	2	万盛、南川
	县城		3	城口、奉节、铜梁
四川	地级市	14	5	攀枝花、广元、广安、自贡、泸州
	县级市		2	华蓥、绵竹
	县城		7	宝兴、汉源、石棉、荥经、天全、芦山、会理
贵州	地级市	8	2	六盘水、安顺
	县级市		3	福泉、毕节、万山
	县城		3	盘县、水城、六枝
云南	地级市	11	4	曲靖、保山、思茅、临沧
	县级市		3	宣威、个旧、开远
	县城		3	兰坪、富源、易门
	市辖区		1	东川
陕西	地级市	8	4	铜川、渭南、榆林、延安
	县级市		1	韩城
	县城		3	略阳、洛南、潼关
甘肃	地级市	10	6	白银、嘉峪关、金昌、平凉、陇南、庆阳
	县级市		1	玉门
	县城		2	成县、玛曲
	市辖区		1	红谷区
西藏	县城	2	2	曲松、申扎
青海	县级市	1	1	格尔木
宁夏	地级市	2	1	石嘴山
	县级市		1	灵武
新疆	地级市	10	1	克拉玛依
	县级市		4	哈密、库尔勒、阜康、阿勒泰
	县城		5	伊宁、富蕴、托里、和布克赛尔、若羌
合计		232	其中:矿业城市 178 个(地级市 97 个,县级市 81 个),重要资源区 13 个,重要资源县 41 个	

矿业城市的形成有两种情况：一是“因矿而生”，另一种“因矿而兴”。“因矿而生”和“因矿而兴”是按矿业与城市形成先后次序区分的两种矿业城市。新中国成立 50 多年

来，由于广大地质工作者和矿业工作者的辛勤劳动，随着一大批大型矿产地的发现与勘查开发的成功，在那些原本是偏远和人烟稀少的地区，一大批新兴矿业城市拔地而起，如克拉玛依、大庆、白银、攀枝花、平顶山等，均属于由于发现了大矿经过勘查开发建设而逐步发展起来的。"依矿而兴"的城市，即城市或城市雏形已经存在，由于矿业开发而获得新生与发展的城市，如山西大同和新疆库尔勒市等城市就是因为矿业开发的成功而获得新的发展，江西德兴、安徽铜陵等也属于这一种情况。

矿业城市按形成的年代可分古代型、近代型和现代型三种。我国矿业开发的历史久远，一些矿业名城如邯郸、自贡、景德镇等属古代型矿业城市，早已享誉中外。淮南采煤的历史也很悠久，早在17世纪即已开始。近代型矿业城市，如大冶、萍乡、唐山等，这些城市的兴起与19世纪80年代前后的洋务运动有关。但矿业城市大规模蓬勃兴起，则是在新中国成立之后，同社会主义建设高潮的兴起和矿业高速的发展相伴随的，发展起了像大庆、东营、盘锦、乌海、白云鄂博、金昌等一大批现代型矿业城市。

矿业城市按开发的矿产类型划分，可分为以一种矿产和多种矿并重的城市。我国矿业城市多为单一矿业类型的城市，但是也有一部分矿业城市是有多种矿产类型组成的城市。具体情况是：煤城82座、金属矿城51座、建材及非金属矿城10座、化工矿城7座、油气矿城14座、综合矿城（可采主矿种有2种以上）14座。

矿业城市按行政建制划分，可分为地、县、镇三级。全国现有232座矿业城市（镇）中，地（盟）级市矿城有97座，占41.8%；县级矿业城市有81座，占34.9%；县城关镇及建制镇级矿城有54座，占23.2%。

矿业城市按其矿业开发程度和发展阶段划分，可分为成长期、鼎盛期、衰退期3种类型。也可称青年期、壮年期、老年期。在全国现有的地县级178座矿业城市中，成长期有19个，占10.6%；鼎盛期104个，占58.4%；衰退期55个，占30.8%。

一方面由于矿业城市是因矿而生或因矿而兴，随着新的大型矿产地的发现与勘查开发的成功还有一些新的矿业城市出现，这在西部地区尤其如此。另一方面由于矿业城市所拥有的资源有限性和不可再生性。矿业城市的发展必将经历一个产生、发展、成熟和衰退乃至转型的生命周期，所以我国矿业城市的数量和发展状态还会处于不断变化之中。

二、中国矿业城市的历史功勋与主要问题

新中国成立以来，蓬勃兴起与发展起来的矿业城市为国家供给矿产资源、经济实力增强、区域经济发展、文明进步、社会稳定和人民生活水平提高做出了巨大贡献。

（一）矿业城市的历史功勋

1. 矿业城市为国家建设提供了大量矿物能源和原材料

矿业城市的主要功能之一是通过矿业开发向国家提供矿产品和矿产加工制品。新中国成立以来，我国相继建立了克拉玛依、大庆、东营、盘锦、库尔勒等大型石油基地；大同、平

顶山、阳泉、兖州、淮南、鄂尔多斯等大型煤炭基地；鞍山、攀枝花等大型钢铁基地；白银、金川、铜陵、德兴、郴州、赣南大厂等大型有色金属基地；昆阳、荆襄、云浮等大型化工基地，形成了我国能源与原材料的强大供应系统。目前我国已成为体系完整、矿种齐全、矿产资源总量居世界第三位的矿业大国；我国煤炭、铁矿石、钢铁、10 种有色金属、水泥产量居世界第一位；黄金、石油、化工矿产品的产量居世界前列。矿业城市为国家提供了 93.6% 的煤炭、90% 以上的石油、80% 以上的铁矿石和有色金属、70% 以上的天然气和非金属矿产品。

2. 矿业城市增强了国家经济实力

矿业城市的建设与发展，对增强国家经济实力具有举足轻重的作用。2010 年，全国矿业城市国内生产总值约达 75 000 亿元，约占全国 GDP 的 20%。由于矿业的巨大后续效应，矿业产值及矿产品加工业产值则约占全国 GDP 的 30% 以上，矿产品及相关能源、原材料产品进出口总额约占全国进出口总额的 15%。矿业城市向国家交纳了大量利税，为我国财力增强做出重要贡献。可以说矿业城市发展状况直接影响着我国经济发展状况。

3. 矿业城市促进了区域经济发展

矿业城市的兴起与发展，在很大程度上改善了区域经济格局，在促进区域经济协调发展方面发挥了重要作用。由于矿业城市多是在荒无人烟或人烟稀少的穷乡僻壤，如黑龙江的大庆、新疆的克拉玛依、内蒙古的白云鄂博、四川的攀枝花和甘肃的金昌市等都是在偏僻落后地区兴起的。由于矿业城市的发展和区域辐射带动作用，对于促进老少边穷地区脱贫致富、促进区域经济发展起了重要的促进作用。矿业城市不只是众多的人口与资源在地域空间上的简单叠加，而是以人为主体、以自然资源为依托、以经济活动为基础、以社会发展为纽带，相互联系极为紧密的有机整体。同时，矿业城市也是一个区域物质财富、精神文化财富高度聚集的场所，是一个区域人财物的聚集中心和中心市场，它所固有的辐射力、吸引力和综合服务能力，对区域经济社会发展发挥着巨大的带动作用。如四川攀枝花，从 1965 年至今，已发展成为我国重要的钢铁基地、最大的钒钛生产基地，周围辐射 20 万平方千米、2 000 多万人口，成为川滇交界地区经济、科技、社会文化的中心。

4. 矿业城市提供了大量就业机会

矿业城市的兴起，为广大人民群众提供了广泛的就业机会，全国矿业城市吸纳人口 3.1 亿人。仅矿业城市中的矿业职工就约有 827 万。矿业人口占地区人口的比重最高的地级城市为甘肃嘉峪关市，约占 70%，最高的县级区为河南上天梯区约 66%，最高的县级市山西义马市约 54%，最高的镇是青海的芒崖镇约占 52%。由此可见矿业城市为社会提供了大量的就业机会。矿业的发展，带动与促进了矿产品加工业和服务业的发展，为扩大整个社会就业、改善人民群众的物质文化生活、促进社会稳定发挥了重要作用。

5. 矿业城市加速了我国城市化进程

国家城市化水平的高低是国家工业化和现代化程度高低的重要标志之一。我国是一个城市化水平不高的国家，1949 年城市化率仅有 10.6%。由于一大批大型矿产地的发现和勘查开发的成功，先后建起了 232 座矿业城镇，大大加快了我国城市化的进程，据人口普查的结果目前我国城市化率已超过 50%，县以上矿业城市在全国城市中的比例也由 1980 年的 9.8% 上升至目前的 30% 左右。矿业城市为加速城市化进程做出了重要贡献。而且随着西部大开发战略的实施，西部地区还会有一批矿业城市兴起。总之，矿业城市无论过去、现在和将来，在加速我国城市化进程中，都起到积极的促进作用。

6. 矿业城市为提高我国国际地位做出了贡献

新中国成立以来，由于矿业的蓬勃发展，我国已从一个矿业小国一跃而为世界矿业大国。煤炭、铁矿石、十种有色金属、水泥、钢铁等重要矿产品均属世界第一位。中国矿业的发展为世界矿业的发展，为增强国际矿产品市场的活力和国际矿业的合作做出了重要贡献。在这方面矿业城市发挥了重要作用。

（二）矿业城市的主要问题

回顾我国矿业城市的发展历程，矿业城镇在为我国社会主义现代化建设作出巨大贡献的同时，由于支柱产业单一，加上历史和体制方面种种原因，在发展过程中也出现了不少困难和问题。其中主要有以下几个方面：

1. 城市经济滑坡

矿业城市是因矿业开发而兴建或发展起来的城市，矿业在城市产业结构中占据主导或支柱产业的地位。有的矿业城市发展了矿业的延伸产业，即矿产品加工产业，形成了一条以采矿为主导、关联度高的产业链，但这些加工产业对资源的依赖程度也很高。由于矿业开发的对象是不可再生的矿产资源，每个具体矿山总有一天因资源采尽而关闭。改革开放以来，非矿产业在矿业城市中虽有不同程度的发展，但大多数矿业城市产业结构仍比较单一，20 世纪五六十年代建设的老工业基地城市表现尤其突出。由于主导产业衰退，接续产业尚未形成，造成财政收入锐减，经济迅速下滑，下岗人员增多，矿工生活困难，生态环境恶化等一系列不良后果。

2. 后备资源不足

矿业城市存在和发展依托于赋存的矿产资源，矿业城市能否持续发展的根本问题之一是矿城所拥有的矿产资源总量。而矿产资源是不可再生的耗竭性资源，采一点就少一点。矿山企业随着矿产资源的开发进程，由兴起、到鼎盛、再到衰落是客观规律。由于在相当长的一段时间里，重采矿，轻找矿，忽视地质勘查工作，造成地质工作严重滞后，可采资源逐渐减少，以至矿业生产不仅不能扩大而且难以维持持续发展。资源供应不足早已成为制约矿业城市发展的瓶颈。目前，约有 12% 的矿业城市所拥有可供开发的后备矿产资源已经不多，这些城市将面临矿竭城衰的威胁。有 440 多座矿山即将闭坑，这将直接影响到 300 多万矿工和上千万职工家属的生活和社会的稳定。

3. 城市负担过重

矿业城市的社会负担来自矿业企业的社会负担和非矿业的社会负担，由于矿业是矿业城市的支柱产业，矿业人口较大比重，有的占 30%，有的甚至可占 50% 以上。所以矿山企业的社会负担成为矿城的主要社会负担。由于种种原因，矿山企业税赋、债务、社会负担过重。过去，由于历史的和客观环境的原因，可供开发的矿产地往往位于远离城镇的偏僻地区，所以在兴建矿山之时，同时也办起来一个小社会。从幼儿园到中学以至大学，从医院到商店到公安机关等一系列社会服务性机构，大大加重了矿山企业的负担。这种负担往往占矿山企业总支出的15% ~20%，甚至更多。除此之外，社会保障体系建立滞后，矿业城市中企业单位下岗分流再就业问题也带来沉重的负担。

4. 环境压力很大

矿城的环境问题，一是生态建设，二是防治地质灾害，三是固体废弃物、废水和废气处理。矿业的发展就不可避免要占用一些土地和破坏一些土地，矿业生产过程中所产生的废石、废水、废气就必然会对土壤、空气和水体造成一定程度的污染，就会给生态环境造成不良的影响。全国因采矿损毁土地累计达40万公顷。因采空或超采地下水引起地面沉降、塌陷、滑坡、地裂缝及泥石流等地质灾害达千余处。矿产资源开发利用过程中产生的大量废水和废气对生态环境产生的危害和对人民生活带来不良影响，已成为许多矿业城市可持续发展的严重障碍，而矿业城市治理环境的合理机制尚未形成，缺少新的足够的资金来解决环境问题，因此，如何处理开发资源与保护环境的关系，建立与形成有效的治理与保护环境的机制已成为政府亟待破解的一道难题。

5. 城矿关系不顺

一方面，由于历史和体制方面的原因，城市政府和城中矿业企业之间的关系没有完全理顺。矿业城市既是城市，又是矿业工业基地，既承担一般城市经济社会的综合服务，又承担发展工业的产业支柱功能。就矿山企业来说，既要生产经营，又要办社会，履行生产和社会服务的双重职能。从而派生出两个履行城市功能的主体。市政重复建设，效益低下，运行不畅，对城市和企业发展都带来不良影响。大企业小市政，政企不分，既加重了企业负担，又分散了企业抓生产的精力。另一方面，由于“职能错位”，再加上条块分割的管理体制，矿业企业又有中央、省属和地方之分，由于不同利益机制影响，致使城市服务功能畸形化，政府很难发挥城市的带动与辐射功能，不利于矿城政府进行宏观调控，市场不能正确地配置资源，产业和技术不能有效互补，大企业对地方经济的带动力发挥得不充分。由于政府的财政收入主要来自矿山企业，矿山开采后期，经济效益不好，财政收入锐减，不利于城市的建设与发展。

三、推进转型是矿业城市实现可持续发展的必由之路

矿业城市与其他城市有共同之处，又有它自身的特点和发展规律，主要有资源耗竭规律、矿山效益递减规律、环境问题递增规律和城市转型规律。由于矿业资源的不可再生性和矿城范围内的可采资源必然逐渐枯竭。由于资源逐渐减少和开采难度日益加大，开采成本上升，矿山经济效益递减也是客观规律。矿业开发的推进对土地的破坏和开发过程中的三废（废石、废水、废气）对生态环境的影响必会日益加剧，由于矿山企业是提供城市财政的主体，矿山经济差了就必会影响城市财政收入，从而不仅降低了城市自我发展能力，而且会引

起一系列的经济和社会问题。为了实现矿业城市的可持续发展，就必须转变城市功能。变单一支柱产业的矿业城市为多个支柱产业的综合城市。

矿业城市转型包括经济转型、体制转型、文化转型等。经济转型主要是指产业转型，产业转型的本质是摆脱对当地矿产资源开采的过度依赖，但不是彻底抛弃原有矿产资源产业的优势，而是尽可能依托这种优势及影响，来培育发展接续和次生产业，形成新的具有发展实力和潜力的产业结构。体制转型的本质是在理顺城市政府和矿业企业之间关系的前提下，建立以市场为转型动力，企业为转型主体，政府引导的市场经济运行体制。文化转型则主要指转变只有矿产资源才是城市财富，只有矿业企业才是产业支柱的传统发展观，深刻认识人力资源、非矿产业的重要性。

矿业城市转型问题不仅是那些处于资源枯竭状态城市的问题，而且对于那些矿业开发处于青年期和中年期的矿业城市同样重要。因为矿业资源是不可再生的，采一点就少一点，总有一天可采资源会枯竭。所以为了避免“矿竭城衰”，为了不再重复走那些资源枯竭型矿业城市的老路，就要未雨绸缪，及早谋划转型。

矿业城市转型主要依靠4个方面的协调和配合，要处理好4个关系。4个方面的协调和配合，即矿业城市的自身努力、各级政府的支持、发挥市场机制和推动社会关注。要处理好的4个关系即一是要做好《全国资源型城市可持续发展规划》与主体功能区规划、经济社会发展规划、接续替代产业发展规划和资源枯竭城市转型规划的衔接；二是妥善处理好资源勘探开发与生态环境保护之间、矿产业发展与接续替代产业培育之间的关系；三是进一步明确规划的重点任务和阶段性目标，避免面面俱到；四是加强体制机制创新，先行先试有关政策措施，重点解决矿业型城市产业发展融资难、地质灾害治理难度大等问题。

矿业城市加快转变经济发展方式意义深远。矿业城市加快转变经济发展方式是构建国家能源资源安全体系的重要保障，有助于矿业城市建设资源节约型环境友好型社会；是建立健全可持续发展长效机制的重要内容，有助于为矿业城市营造更加合理有利的发展环境；是推动区域协调发展的有效途径。

矿业城市的经济结构转型是一个国际性问题，在世界许多国家都存在，已经积累了丰富的经验和教训。成功的例子有德国的鲁尔工业区，英国西密德兰地区，法国洛林，美国的底特律、休斯敦，日本的九州等，失败的例子如苏联的巴库。国外资源型城市经济结构转型成功的经验主要是：重视相关的立法及规划；政府实施灵活多样的财政税收支持；鼓励扶持中小企业的发展；注重就业转岗方面的培训；制定优惠政策吸引外资进入；利用高新技术促进经济结构转型步伐等。这些措施需要根据不同城市的具体情况综合研究实施，才能发挥最好的效果。

政府财政税收和投资的政策性支持是资源型城市经济结构转型的推动力；切实可行的法制和规划是资源型城市经济结构转型的有效保障；产业结构多元化是实现资源型城市经济结构转型的根本途径；资源的集约高效开发利用则是促进资源型城市经济结构转型的加速器。只有发展才能实现经济结构转型，要从根本上解决资源型城市面临的困难和问题，就必须加快经济结构转型。只有不断系统地总结和分析世界其他国家资源型城市经济结构转型的经验和教训，针对我国资源型城市经济结构转型目前面临的主要问题，在已有试点和研究成果的基础上，就我国资源型城市的科学划分、各城市接续产业的选择、补偿机制的建立等与经济转型密切相关的一系列深层次问题进行全面、系统的研究和研讨。各资源型城市根据自己的实际情况，制定切实可行的经济结构转型与发展规划。

四、中国矿业城市转型的战略选择

矿业城市为了实现可持续发展，就必须推进城市功能转型，对于那些资源枯竭型城市尤其如此。如何有效地推进矿业城市转型，正确地选择转型战略至关重要。

（一）城市转型模式选择

矿业城市转型是指改变城市发展过度依赖矿产资源开发的状况，并解决由此引起的经济、社会、环境问题，实现可持续发展。具体说就是通过培育接续产业，发展替代产业，改变矿业城市主要依赖矿产资源的开采和加工为其主导产业的现状，形成合理的产业结构；通过恢复矿山生态环境，治理矿山地质灾害，改变矿业城市长期以环境为代价的资源开发模式，形成良好的生态环境；通过完善社会保障体系和城市劳动力再就业的技能培训，改变矿业城市长期以来企业办社会的发展状况，形成稳定的社会结构；以发展、稳定、生态为目标带动城市经济形态、经济体制、生产方式、发展战略和发展模式等方面的系列变化，最终实现城市的可持续发展。

根据已有资料，国际上的矿业城市转型模式大致有欧盟的政府主导模式，美、加、澳的市场主导模式，日本的政府主导与市场调节相结合模式等 3 种。我国的矿业城市转型模式不能照搬别国模式，只能根据我国不同矿业城市的资源基础、经济实力、区位条件、技术状况及投资来源等具体情况决定。从近年来的实践来看，我国的城市转型模式可归纳为政府主导与市场调节相结合的 4 种转型模式，即：优势延伸模式、优势互补模式、优势组合模式、优势再造模式。这 4 种转型模式各自的特点如表 2 所示：

表 2　国内外矿业城市转型模式比较

国家(地区)	转型模式		特　点
中国	政府主导与市场调节相结合	优势延伸	优势资源突出，尚有开发前景，保持并延伸甚至壮大这种优势，使资源优势转化为地区发展的经济优势。产业链条延伸，发展关联和接替产业，培育新的增长点及主导产业
		优势互补	优势资源开发与区外的互补资源结合起来。资源优势组合，产业异地衔接，在异地培养增长点及发展自身
		优势组合	资源丰富且配套好，组合优势突出，产业多样化，结构弹性好。多种资源综合开发，优势组合，主导产业关联
		优势再造	优势资源在消减，矿业产业的支柱地位在变化，结构单一，出现衰退现象。重塑优势，利用基础及区位好的特点再造优势，培育新的增长点及主导产业

续表2

国家(地区)	转型模式	特　点
欧盟	政府主导模式	政府成立专门委员会和其他组织,制定详细目标、计划和政策,各部门与各界通力合作促进产业转型
美、加、澳	市场主导模式	政府很少控制矿业城市兴盛衰败,企业投资流向对矿业城市发展起决定性作用。区位好的矿业城市渐渐发展为综合性城市,区位较差的矿业城市则走向衰落或被遗弃。这种模式实施比较简单,但是社会负担的成本过高,必须有完善的社会保障为基础
日本	政府主导与市场调节相结合模式	产业政策和产业援助对产业转型起决定作用。政府根据国内外市场的变化情况和矿区具体实际,制定和修改产业政策,设定目标和措施,各矿区的政府和企业依照日本中央政府的规划实施。这种模式比较易于模仿和实行,但是政府的负担过高,并且需要企业集团和政府有密切的联系,产业政策本身必须代表大部分企业的意志,实施成功的可能性才较大

(二) 产业结构转型模式

在产业结构转型模式方面，不同城市不尽相同。按照我国2003年《三次产业划分规定》划分标准，我国城市的一、二、三次产业范围为：第一产业是指农、林、牧、渔业；第二产业是指采矿业，制造业，电力、燃气及水的生产和供应业，建筑业；第三产业是指除第一、二产业以外的其他行业。目前国内矿业城市接替产业培育和发展出现四种情况：一是依托原有的资源，延长产业链，做深做强，即“保二进二”。二是退出传统的矿业产业，进入以现代农业为主的第一产业，即“退二进一”。三是退出传统的矿业产业，进入以生态、信息、电子、服务等产业为主的第三产业，即“退二进三”。四是根据所处区位以及在区域经济中的地位，摆脱资源基础，发展多元型产业，服务整个地区，使城市向综合性方向发展。

(三) 转型战略方针

自1997年在河南平顶山召开的第一次矿业城市可持续发展论坛以来，历经8次论坛讨论，各矿业城市就转型战略方针取得许多共识。主要有以下8条。

1. 多元发展战略

矿业城市要实行“矿业与非矿业并举”的多元发展战略，第一，加强地质勘查工作，增加资源储备，延长矿山服务年限，支持矿业的持续发展。我国88%的矿业城市资源潜力还比较大。即使处于暮年期的矿业城市也可能有两种情况：一是资源真的快枯竭了，另一种是由于地质勘查工作做得不够，而未能将资源情况全面查明。所以任何矿业城市都应重视加强地质勘查工作，挖掘资源潜力，增加资源储备，以延长矿山服务年限，促进矿城持续发展。第二，实行多元发展战略，延长矿产品深加工链，最大限度地提高资源的附加价值是一个重要的发展方向。第三，鼓励与支持其他非矿产业的发展，特别是鼓励第三产业的发展，以培育新的经济增长点。实行多元发展还有另外一层含义，就是根据中央调整所有制结构的方针，大力发展非国有企业，尤其要注意发展民营企业，这对于发展矿业替代产业，促进城市持续发展具有重要意义。资源枯竭严重的阜新就是以发展现代农业和民营企业迈出了城市转型的可喜的第一步，10 年前主要为煤电工业如今已形成农产品加工、煤化工和新型能源三足鼎立之势。

2. 适度开发战略

所有矿业城市都要注意妥善处理矿业开发强度与矿业长远发展两者之间的关系。既要发挥矿业生产的规模效益，又要考虑矿山的服务年限。应根据矿山拥有的可采资源量，把年度开采量定在一个适当的限度上，进行适度开发，以尽量延长矿山服务年限，以便为矿业城市和矿山企业发展替代产业，实行产业转换与城市转型赢得时间。如果资源丰富，开采条件又好，年产量定得太低，经济效益不好，对矿山企业和城市都不利；如果资源有限而年度产量定得太高，就会影响矿山寿命，或造成生产大起大落，这对矿山和城市也都不利。所以就需要在矿山规模效益与企业持续发展之间寻求一个平衡点，来进行适度开发，如大庆近些年来就注意了这个问题。

3. 集约经营战略

中国矿业的一个显著特征是矿山企业过小、过多。之所以造成这种情况，一是与我国小矿多、大矿少这个资源特点有关，二是与集约化经营程度有关。小而多，造成矿政管理难，资源浪费大，经济效益低，安全隐患多。为了合理开发与保护有限的矿产资源，需要通过改革、改组和改造，组建一批具有国际竞争力的大矿业集团来参与国际竞争，分享全球资源成果。矿城政府从政策上鼓励集约化经营开发，下决心关闭那些浪费资源、破坏环境和安全生产无保障的小矿，这是矿业城市能否长治久安的关键所在。对于那些依法办矿的小矿，也要组织起来实行科学开采、集约化经营，并搞好安全生产。

4. 绿色矿城战略

绿色矿城战略的主要任务是科学规划城市建设，力求布局合理，整齐美观；防治地质灾害，及时治理“三废”，保护土地、大气和水体；加强生态建设，搞好园林绿化；加强清洁卫生等市政管理。实施绿色矿城战略，既需要城市政府负责，又需要矿山企业出力。人类要生存，社会要发展，既需要矿产资源，又需要优良环境。这样就产生了矿业开发与环境保护之间的矛盾。从我国资源条件和国际局势来看，我们不能走停止采矿来保护环境之路，而应实行矿业开发与环境保护并重的方针，在保护中开发，在开发中保护。为了实施绿色城市战略，从城市政府来说就应作好城市环境保护的总体规划，在市政建设、环境卫生和城市绿化三方面进行部署。在矿山建设和矿城建设方面，要按照“矿社分离”的原则来进行，要做到生产区与生活区分开。运用经济的、法律的、行政的多种手段，制订切实有效的保护措施，实行“谁受益、谁污染、谁治理”的政策，创造一个整齐、清洁、优美的城市环境。对于矿山企业来说，要把矿山建设成花园式矿山，实现环境保护与资源开发的双赢目标，这一方面很多矿山和矿城都创造了很好的经验。

5. 科教兴城战略

实施科教兴城战略，走产、学、研结合之路。大力发展教育与推进科技创新对于矿业城市未来的发展，把矿城建设成为高科技现代化的城市具有极大的推动作用。矿城政府和矿山企业都要以科技进步和改革开放为动力，采取有效措施，创造良好环境，提高全民素质，培养与聚集高素质的科技人才、管理人才和经营人才，努力提高矿业城市的科技含量。矿业城市要通过科技创新和体制创新来提高劳动生产率、资源利用率，减少资源浪费，要提高矿产品深加工的科技含量，增加单位矿产品加工的附加值。要运用先进科技进一步提高整个矿业城市的信息化和现代化水平。推动矿城中产业结构的调整和优化，从而对促进各类产业和整个矿城自身的可持续发展也具有长远意义。为了提高城市科技水平，既要加强自主研发与自主创新，又要扩大开放，吸收其他地区和发达国家的新技术、新设备、新工艺，改变矿业开发中传统的粗放经营方式。

6. 筑巢引凤战略

为了扩大开放，吸引外部人才、技术和资金进入矿业城市，就需要在硬环境建设和软环境建设两个方面作出努力。“环境就是生产力”。好的环境能直接促使城市升值，能吸引人才、技术和资金。在环境建设方面，国家在实施西部大开发战略过程中，投入大量资金以加强能源、交通、通讯建设和生态环境建设。许多矿业城市自己也在作出很大努力来改善城市面貌，来改善交通、通讯和生活居住条件，把矿城建设成为一个文明城市、卫生城市、绿色城市。并在提高办事效率、实行一条龙服务等方面来改善软环境。为了筑一个能够引来凤凰的巢，矿业城市在城市建设方面要做好总体规划，合理布局，要充分运用已有条件把城市主体发展与周围小城镇建设结合起来，只要把巢筑好，凤凰就会飞来。

7. 城矿互利战略

矿城因矿业开发而兴起或得到新生。在矿业城市形成之后，矿城通过政府功能的发挥，为矿山企业的生产经营与发展又在多方面提供了有效的服务，并起着极为重要的促进作用。城市与矿业之间存在着极为密切的相互依存、相互促进的关系。此外，在这些城市中的大中型矿山企业，一般都居于重要地位；由于在管理体制上这些企业往往有中央企业和地方企业之分，所以企业与政府之间、中央企业与地方企业之间就有着不同的利益关系。这些利益关系的复杂性，往往不利于城市和矿业的发展。所以建议国家要研究矿业城市发展战略规则，理顺地方政府和企业之间的关系，统筹考虑矿业城市和矿山企业的共同发展问题，把产业发展政策与城市发展政策有机地结合起来，制定有利于城矿双方共同发展的政策，既解脱矿山企业办社会的沉重负担，又能促进企业与城市各方面能协调发展。

8. 矿城扶持战略

鉴于矿业城市在我国经济社会生活中具有重要地位，为了使矿业城市转型实现可持续发展，除了矿城本身要努力外，国家对矿业城市实行特殊的扶持政策甚为重要。第一，国家对矿业城市与可持续发展问题应作为国家21世纪发展战略中的一个特殊问题来加以扶持与指导。第二，从财政和政策上重点支持大中型矿山企业技术改造和产业结构调整，并从宏观上对矿业城市的产业政策、财政政策、投资政策、社保政策和城市政策等多方面给予综合指导，积极推动矿业城市的结构调整与城市转型；第三，建立矿山企业的反哺机制与矿城持续发展的补偿基金，在矿业销售收入中提取一定比例建立暮年矿山的反哺基金，并在分组财政中增加矿城的留成比例以建立补偿基金，为矿山闭坑转产、人员分流再就业和环境治理与保护提供补助与支持；第四，制定有利于城市和矿山企业同步发展的税赋政策、劳动政策和社会保障制度，切实减轻矿山企业的税赋、债务和社会负担，促进矿山企业和城市建设共同发展。

五、中国矿业城市在转型中前进

近10年来，在党中央，国务院的关怀和重视下，我国资源枯竭型矿业城市的转型工作取得显著进展，各矿业城市在可持续发展的道路上迈出了可喜的一步。

（一）矿业城市转型问题被提上议事日程

20世纪90年代初，针对阜新等老矿业城市因可采资源减少，矿业生产下降和城市经济滑坡等情况，原地质矿产部和原国家计委曾派出工作组到东北阜新、抚顺等地矿业城市调研后建议要重视因探明可采资源逐渐枯竭给矿业城市（镇）可能带来的影响。但这个问题在当时并未引起社会各方面应有的重视。

1997年10月19—21日，中国矿业联合会会同中国市长协会、地质矿产部、建设部、河南省平顶山市人民政府在河南平顶山市召开了矿业城市可持续发展研讨会，即第一届中国矿业城市发展论坛。会议第一次对矿业城市（镇）发展的特殊规律、当前存在的主要问题以及如何避免“矿竭城衰”实现可持续发展进行了探讨，第一次向全国矿业城市（镇）敲响了要避免“矿竭城衰”的警钟。会议还就大力发展非矿产业、优化产业结构、转变城市功能、实行多元发展等具有战略意义的可持续发展问题取得一致共识，并得到中央和国务院领导的肯定。

自平顶山会议以来，中国矿业联合会先后会同陕西、河南、安徽、辽宁、吉林等省人民政府和全国有关学会、协会，分别在铜川、淮南、盘锦、阜新、白银、白山等矿业城市召开了8届论坛。交流转型经验，探讨如何成功推进城市转型，坚持可持续发展的战略等一系列问题。期间中国矿业联合会、全国政协人口资源环境委员会和经济委员会多次到一些矿业城市进行调研。通过调研对中国矿业城市面临的严峻形势和发展机遇与挑战进行了深入的思考，形成了一系列报告和文章。其中先后报送给朱镕基总理、温家宝总理和贾庆林主席的调研报告，分别得到他们的批示。除形成一些调研报告报送中央领导外，还形成了一些政协委员提案报送全国政协。此外，在《人民日报》、《人民论坛》、《中国矿业报》、中国工业经济联合会的《工业经济内参》等报刊上和一些会议上发表了一些文章和讲话。呼吁重视与解决好资源枯竭型矿业城市的可持续发展问题。

2001年12月辽宁阜新被国务院批准为第一个转型城市。

2002年3月初，笔者在全国政协九届五次会议第二次全体会议上发言时呼吁，要像重视“三农”（农业、农村、农民）问题一样重视“四矿”（矿业、矿山、矿工、矿城）问题。“四矿”问题主要表现在，我国矿业的基础产业地位没有真正确立。矿业是直接从事自然资源开发利用的初次产业，在联合国制订的标准产业分类中，属于第一层次的有10种，其中第二位即为“矿业和采石业”，位于“农业”之后。世界上大多数国家也把矿业作为一个独立的第一产业来对待。但是，矿业在我国无论在国家产业分类上还是在行政管理上矿业这个地位未被确立，未得到应有的重视，都未作为独立产业，导致无法制定一套统一的、符合矿业经济规律的政策，导致出现一系列经济社会问题，矿城经济滑坡，矿山企业举步维艰，矿工生活困难，在这方面，矿业比农业更具危机。我的发言，引起了李瑞环主席等全国政协领导的高度重视和其他委员的支持，“两会”结束后，全国政协在北京于3月22日和25日召开了两次汇报会，先后邀请中国矿业联合会、国家计委、国家经贸委、国土资源部、全国总工会的同志介绍有关“四矿”情况。4月11—20日，以全国政协副主席孙孚凌任顾问的专题调研组一行28人到辽宁省实地调研。调研组先后到了盘锦市（考察油气）、葫芦岛市（考察有色金属）、抚顺市（考察煤炭）、鞍山市（考察黑色金属）实地调研。同时召开东北三省“四矿”问题座谈会。

2002年5月中旬，全国政协经济委员会和人口资源环境委员会在京主办了“四矿”问题研讨会。邀请中央和国务院有关部门、部分矿业大省、矿业城市、矿山企业、矿业组织和矿业研究机构的负责同志及专家、学者，结合全国政协专题调研组调研的情况对“四矿”问题进行会诊。全国政协副主席李贵鲜、孙孚凌出席会议并发表重要讲话。6月下旬，在全国政协九届常委会第十八次会议上，“四矿”问题成为一项重要议题，会议对专题调研组提交的调研报告《关于采取切实措施缓解“四矿”危机的建议》进行了认真讨论，提出不少修改意见和建议。8月初，经修改定稿的《关于采取切实措施缓解“四矿”危机的建议》，以政协全国委员会的名义正式上报中共中央、国务院。

2002年11月8—14日召开的党的十六大作出一项重大战略决策明确指出“支持东北地区等老工业基地加快调整和改造，支持以资源开采为主的城市和地区发展接续产业。”至此支持资源型城市转型实现可持续发展这一重大问题，终于从国家的层面上被提上议事日程。

（二）国家支持矿业城市转型政策体系初步形成

自党的十六大提出“支持以资源开采为主的城市和地区发展接续产业”以来国务院成立了专门机构制定了相关政策设立财政专项，逐步建立起国家有关部门推动、省级人民政府负总责、资源型城市为主体的上下联动、协调配合机制，形成了较为完善的政策支持体系。

（1）国务院于2007年12月18日发布了《国务院关于促进资源型城市可持续发展的若干意见》（国发〔2007〕38号）。提出了促进资源型城市可持续发展的目标和保障措施，并于2008年、2009年和2011年先后确定了三批69座资源枯竭型矿业城市和9座森工城市（表3）。期间10个省（区）出台了配套政策文件。各资源枯竭型城市抢抓历史和政策机遇，以转型统领经济和社会发展全局，积极探索有中国特色的可持续发展之路，努力促使经济社会保持平稳较快发展，取得明显成效。

（2）中央财政设立的资源枯竭城市财力性转移支付资金，到2011年已累计下达了303亿元。对于资源枯竭型城市解决历史遗留问题、增强可持续发展能力发挥了重要作用。国家发改委同财政部、国土资源部等有关部门，正在研究建立分类指导、有进有出、滚动推进的财政支持机制，帮助资源枯竭型矿业城市尽快步入可持续发展轨道。

(3) 国家发改委将继续组织实施好资源型城市充分吸纳就业、资源综合利用和发展接续替代产业中央预算内投资专项资金，支持资源枯竭型矿业城市建设一批接续替代产业集聚区，培育一批接续替代产业龙头企业，扶持建设一批能够吸纳棚户区和沉陷区回迁居民和下岗失业人员再就业的产业项目。

(4) 财政部会同国土资源部将通过中央分成的探矿权采矿权使用费和价款收入，继续加大对国务院确定的资源枯竭型矿业城市矿山地质环境治理的支持。

(5) 国家发改委会同国家开发银行将继续加大对矿业城市可持续发展的开发性金融支持力度。目前国家发改委会同国家开发银行设立了资源型城市可持续发展专项贷款，国家开发银行出台了《关于进一步支持东北地区等老工业基地全面振兴的意见》，将进一步拓宽资源型城市的融资渠道。

(6) 国家发改委将会同有关部门，继续推动健全资源型城市可持续发展长效机制工作。一是开展资源型城市可持续发展立法工作。《资源型城市可持续发展条例》已列入国家发改委立法规划。二是启动《全国资源型城市可持续发展规划》编制工作。《全国资源型城市可持续发展规划》已列入经国务院批准的《“十二五”期间报国务院审批的专项规划整体预案》。三是推动建立资源型企业可持续发展准备金制度。财政部会同国家发改委等有关部门，开展了大量调查研究工作，初步拟定了资源型企业可持续发展准备金管理办法。四是继大力支持资源枯竭城市转型之后，在资源开采处于青年期或中年期的资源型城市开展可持续发展试点。拟在全国范围内选择一批可持续发展工作基础好、代表性和示范性强、试点作用突出的资源型城市，加强宏观指导和政策支持，探索建立可持续发展的长效机制，先行先试有关政策措施。

（三）矿业城市转型的阶段性成果与差异性分析

2008 年国家发改委同财政部和国土资源部公布了对 12 个资源枯竭型城市的转型给予政策支持，随后于 2009 年、2011 年又先后公布了给予政策支持的 32 座和 25 座资源枯竭型矿业城市的名单（见表 3）。

近些年来，在国家政策的支持和矿业城市的自身努力下，资源枯竭型矿业城市的转型工作取得显著进展。

据国家发改委对第一批 12 个资源枯竭型矿业城市转型评估结果，认为资源枯竭型城市转型已取得阶段性成果，一是经济增长结束了低速徘徊的局面，12 个城市的地区生产总值年均增长 10.5%，略高于全国平均水平；二是资源型产业“一业独大”的局面有所改变，采矿业占地区生产总值的比重由 2006 年 18.3% 下降到 2009 年的 13.6%；三是 4 年间城市沉陷区搬迁、棚户区改造累计完成建筑面积 1423 万平方米，约 28 万住房困难家庭居住环境得到改善；加强矿山环境治理恢复，累计完成治理面积 2.29 万公顷，复垦耕地 1 719 公顷。

国家发改委的评估还认为由于各矿业城市原有的转型基础条件不尽一样，加之区位优势资源禀赋不同，各城市转型发展水平差异较大，除个别城市如盘锦市基本步入可持续发展轨道外，大部分城市历史遗留问题尚未得到根本解决，接续替代产业层次较低，可持续发展能力不强。总体看来，与《国务院关于促进资源型城市可持续发展的若干意见》确立的目标还有较大差距，仍处于爬坡攻坚阶段。

表3　国家公布的三批资源枯竭型城市（地区）统计表

省份	枯竭型矿业城市(地区)			森工城市(地区)	小　计		合计
	首批12座(2008)	第二批32座(2009)	第三批25座(2011)	大小兴安岭林区参照享受政策城市9座	矿业	森工	
河北		张家口市下花园区	石家庄井陉矿区		3		3
		承德市鹰手营子矿区					
山西		孝义市	霍州市		2		2
内蒙古		阿尔山市	乌海市	牙克石市	3	5	8
			包头市石拐区	额尔古纳市			
				根河市			
				鄂伦春旗			
				扎兰屯市			
辽宁	阜新市	抚顺市			7		7
	盘锦市	北票市					
		辽阳市弓长岭区					
		葫芦岛市杨家杖子					
		葫芦岛市南票区					
吉林	辽源市	舒兰市	通化市二道江区		7		7
	白山市	九台市	汪清县				
		敦化市					
黑龙江	伊春市	七台河市	鹤岗市	逊克县	6	4	10
	大兴安岭地区	五大连池市	双鸭山市	瑷辉区			
				嘉荫县			
				铁力市			
江苏			徐州市贾汪区		1		1
安徽		淮北市			2		2
		铜陵市					
江西	萍乡市	景德镇市	新余市		4		4
			大余县				
山东		枣庄市	新泰市		3		3
			淄博市淄川区				
河南	焦作市	灵宝市	濮阳市		3		
湖北	大冶市	黄石市	松滋市		5		5
		潜江市					
		钟祥市					
湖南		资兴市	涟源市		5		5
		冷水江市	常宁市				
		耒阳市					
广东			韶关市		1		1
广西		合山市	贺州市平桂管理区		2		2

续表 3

省份	枯竭型矿业城市（地区）			森工城市（地区）	小计		合计
	首批 12 座 (2008)	第二批 32 座 (2009)	第三批 25 座 (2011)	大小兴安岭林区参照享受政策城市 9 座	矿业	森工	
海南			昌江县		1		1
重庆		万盛区	南川区		2		2
四川		华蓥市	泸州市		2		2
贵州		铜仁市万山特区			1		1
云南	个旧市	昆明市东川区	易门县		3		3
陕西		铜川市	潼关县		2		2
甘肃	白银市	玉门市	兰州市红古区		3		3
宁夏	石嘴山市				1		1
合计	12	32	25	9	69	9	78

（四）我国矿业城市转型的新情况与新问题

一是经济总量快步增长，经济增长速度均快于国家平均增速，城市仍以经济增长为追求的第一目的。

二是以经济结构进一步优化调整为目标，但第二产业比例有变大态势，这说明城市仍是采取走工业强市的发展模式。

三是我国矿业城市经济并没有完全照搬国外“彻底脱资源化”的转型理论，而是探索走着如何有效“利用资源可持续发展”的道路。

四是矿业注重规模生产、清洁生产和循环经济，脏、乱、差的粗放式开采方式在大规模矿业公司得到很大程度改变，开始同时注意经济—环境—生态效益。

五是矿山企业积极“走出去”并购资源，构建本地与异地、国内与国外多源的资源体系，并利用技术创新优势延长集团公司产业链和提高综合利用效益。

六是资源型地区不再是单一利用本地资源发展地区经济，鼓励与支持当地矿业集团（公司）积极开拓外地和国外资源，资源加工业成为了新的支柱产业。

七是《全国资源型城市可持续发展规划》已列入经国务院批准的《“十二五”期间报国务院审批的专项规划整体预案》。这有助于引导资源型城市合理开发资源、科学布局产业、实现可持续发展，是进一步建立健全资源型城市可持续发展长效机制的重要举措。

（作者：朱训，全国政协原秘书长，原地质矿产部部长，国际欧亚科学院院士；刘粤湘，中国矿业联合会矿业城市工作委员会副秘书长，教授）

基于虚拟地理环境的智能城市构建①

摘要： 近几年来，随着科技的不断发展，城市的形态也在发生着变化。在传感器网络、云计算等具有突破意义的技术推动下，数字城市在向智能城市演化。以数据库、模型库和行为库为核心的虚拟地理环境在一定程度上弥补了传统GIS存在的不足，为智能城市的构建与发展提供新的支撑。本文提出基于虚拟地理环境的智能城市构建框架，旨在利用虚拟地理环境的特色与优点来推动与服务智能城市的构建，为智能城市的发展提供一个切实可行的应用平台。

关键词： 虚拟地理环境　智能城市　模型　传感网　社会行为

引　言

数字城市作为社会信息化建设的重要环节，正日益成为国家高科技发展和城市建设关注的重点。数字城市是综合运用GIS、遥感、遥测、网络、多媒体和虚拟仿真等高技术手段，对城市的基础设施、功能机制进行自动采集、动态监测管理和辅助决策支持的技术服务系统[1]。数字城市提供了多种信息，并使用户有身临其境的感觉，为城市规划、智能化交通、网格化管理和服务、基于位置的服务、城市安全应急响应等创造了条件，是信息时代城市和谐发展的重要手段。建设数字城市是城市信息化的系统工程[2-4]。

近年来，随着传感器网络、云计算等具有突破意义的技术的不断发展，数字城市建设正在向智能城市演化。智能城市是通过在城市建立大量的传感网，对城市基础设施与部件状态、建设工程安全质量状况、城市能源供给状况、城市交通状况、水资源与环境状态等进行检测，实施汇集城市各种时空信息，为城市建设、管理与应急响应做出智能决策（龚建雅，2010）。日前，中国三星经济研究院发布报告，对全球智能城市的发展模式进行了比较。报告指出，全球许多城市都在进行智能城市的试验，欧洲和亚洲是智能城市开展较为积极的地区。中国已有近50个城市或地区提出了建设智能城市的目标，智能城市相关市场的规模超过1 500亿元[4,5]。

① 作者感谢研究团队成员车伟涛、胡明远、谭露、孙贵博、张春晓、林天鹏提供成果与文稿。

传统的数字城市、智能城市建设通常基于现有的2D/3D GIS平台。而现有GIS的一些不足也被带入智能城市系统，例如数据更新的问题，对过程模型的表达不足，对人的行为的支持缺失等。对于虚拟地理环境（Virtual Geographic Environment，VGE）的研究为解决这些问题提供了新的支撑环境。

一、基于虚拟地理环境的智能城市

智能城市与数字城市的重要区分，是从城市的数据共享转变为知识和经验的共享。智能包括网络化的数据、知识以及独特经验的共享。智能城市的另外一个核心问题是人在城市中的社会网络以及互动方式，例如工作、学习、生活、旅游等环境。因此，我们认为智能城市应该包括真实城市环境以及与其相对应的虚拟城市环境这两个部分。智能则包括系统化的自我学习、自主决策以及交互启发式的学习与决策。支撑这个转变的平台也需要从经典的GIS走向空间决策支持系统乃至与真实环境相对应的虚拟地理环境。

虚拟地理环境是包括作为主体的化身人类社会以及围绕该主体存在的一切客观环境，包括计算机、网络、传感器等硬件环境，软件环境，数据环境，虚拟图形境像环境，虚拟经济环境，以及虚拟社会、政治和文化环境，其中的化身人类是表示现实世界中的人与虚拟世界中的化身相结合后的集合整体。虚拟地理环境是人类可以生活、工作、生产和消费的一个新的空间世界，它与现实地理环境一样，是一个包含空间系统、生态系统和社会系统的开放、复杂性巨系统[6-8]。虚拟地理环境旨在表达地理现象，模拟地理过程，探索地理规律，提供开展地理学研究和地理问题求解的模拟实验平台；能够提供更接近自然的多感知的空间认知和超越现实的抽象表示与解析理解能力的支持，是一种以用户为中心的、最接近人类自然的交流方式与表达形式的综合表意系统。

本文提出基于虚拟地理环境的智能城市构建，主要包含以下几个方面：1. 基于虚拟地理环境的智能城市模型构建，其中包含精细静态模型与动态的过程模型，静态模型用以表达城市中的静态对象，例如建筑、道路、树木、设施等，而过程模型用以模拟、分析城市中各种动态的环境场与变化；2. 通过分析智能城市中传感器网络的必要性，提出集成传感网的智能城市，并给出传感网服务框架；3. 智能城市中虚实结合的社会行为研究。（图1）虚拟地理环境强调人的参与，基于虚拟地理环境的智能城市虚拟社区能够表达、模拟及分析一系列重要的社会活动行为。

二、基于虚拟地理环境的智能城市模型构建

（一）精细静态模型

传统的单用户三维模型构建系统具有较大的局限性，主要体现在时间消耗、工作空间占用、建模数据提交处理、模型对接等方面。针对这些问题，基于OpenSim的虚拟地理环境平

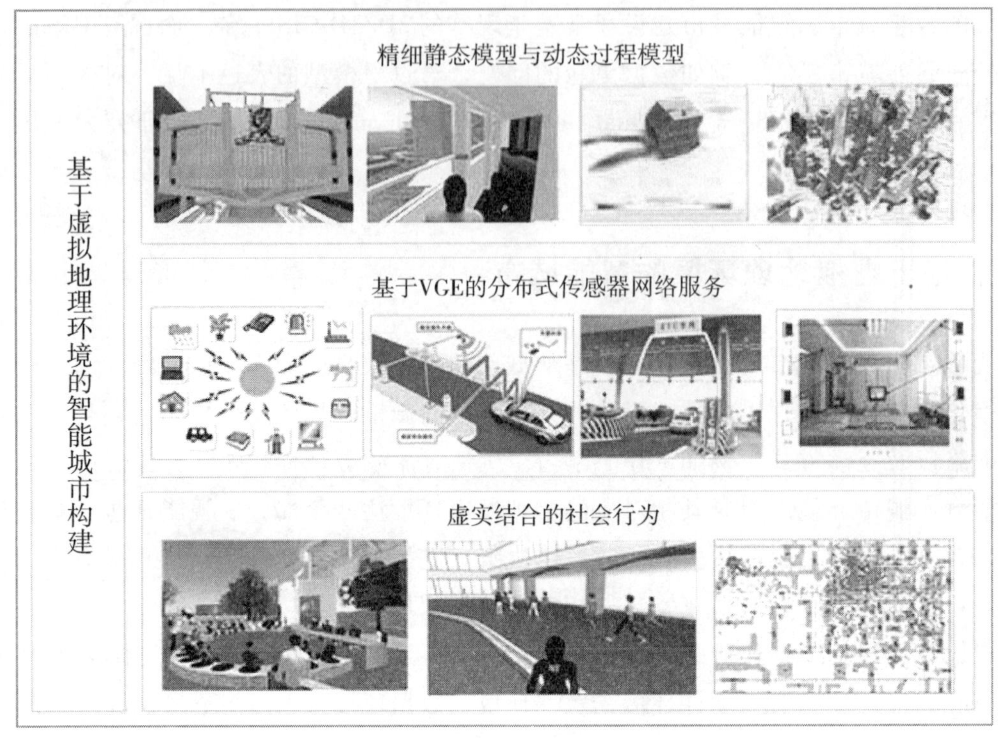

图1 基于虚拟地理环境的智能城市框架

台为智能城市的协同在线建模提供较好的平台。通过该平台，不同用户可以从不同位置接入同一工作场景，进行实时同步的虚拟世界静态模型搭建工作[9]。由于不同用户接入的静态模型基于同一数据库，用户对场景做出的修改可以及时反馈给数据库，从而以模型改变的形式反馈给其他协同工作者。此外，用户可以借助该平台进行沟通交流、共享模型库与材质库，实现用户间各种互动式动态应用，大大提高模型构建效率，解决传统模型构建模式的问题（图2）。另外，基于 Open Simulator 的虚拟地理环境平台还支持多种方式的精细静态模型构建方式，如基于 Open Sim Primitive 的模型，基于 CAD/3D Max/Google SkechUp 的模型以及基于雕刻模式的建模方法（图2）。

基于虚拟地理环境平台的精细模型不仅包含室内、外，还将延伸至地下，如市政管网、地下构造等，从而将二维 GIS 难以表达的三维城市空间信息整合至智能城市中，支持地理环境的多视角显示和全方位分析。

（二）智能城市中的过程/动态模型

随着地学、计算机科学、环境科学等相关学科的发展，城市动态变化过程模型成为智能城市构建与可持续发展的重要组成部分。在基于虚拟地理环境的智能城市研究中，动态变化过程是指地理事物及各种环境场现象随时间的推移和相关地理要素的变化而出现的动态变化过程。根据其在时间、空间上的变化特征，主要可分为地理循环过程、地理演变过程、地理波动性变化过程和地理扩散过程[10]，典型的城市地理过程包括建筑形态、噪音场、风场、热场、空气质量场等动态变化过程。

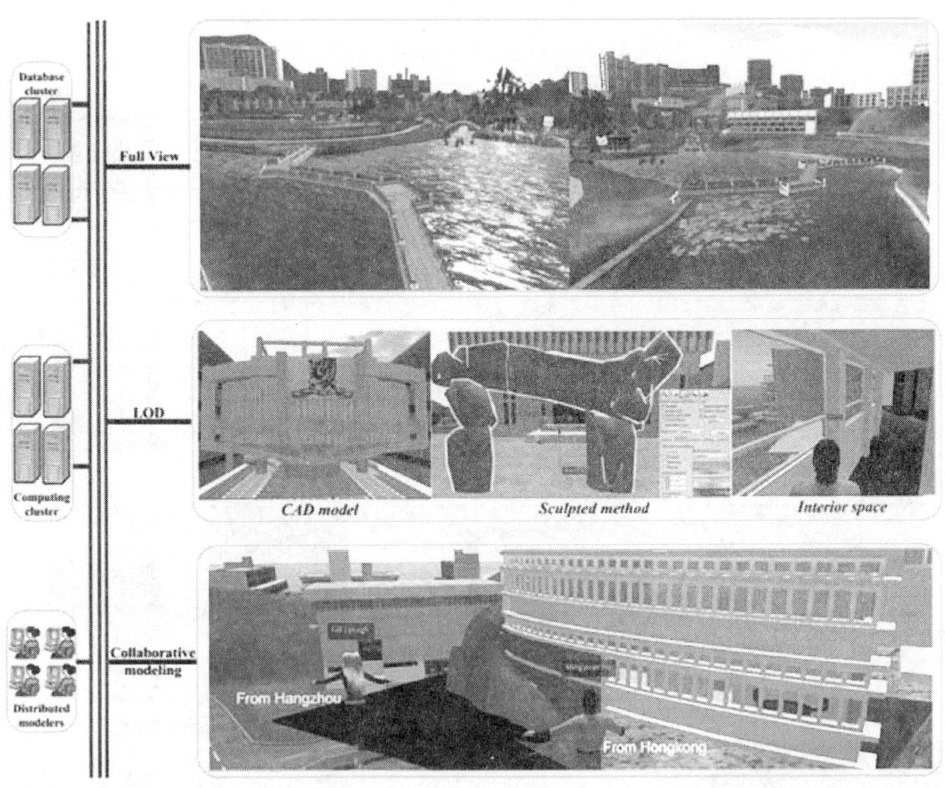

图 2　多用户协同构建虚拟地理环境地理场景示意[8]

虚拟地理环境理论方法应用于智能城市动态过程研究现已取得一定成果，集中体现在城市规划、设施管理、应急模拟、环境模拟等方面。张续红等探讨了虚拟地理环境下城市建模方法，介绍了宁波科技园区的仿真系统[11]。陈驰等基于虚拟现实技术和城市建筑模型数据进行了火灾模拟系统的设计与实现，为城市应急管理提供有力依据[12]。徐丙立等构建协同式虚拟地理环境用于研究珠江三角洲区域的污染物扩散模拟，并进行了系统实现[13]。另一方面，很多学者运用能量守恒、动量守恒、质量守恒等定律研究城市热场、空气污染物扩散等动态变化过程。Vardoulakis 等分析了用于模拟城市空气质量的动态变化模型的优点和不足[14]。Woo 等应用计算流体力学数值模拟方法开发了 AirScope 系统，结合实时传感器数据对微观尺度的空气质量进行了模拟研究[15]。上述虚拟地理环境、守恒定律、传感器网络等构成了智能城市过程模型研究的基础部件，但就研究现状而言，还缺少虚拟地理环境与智能城市结合研究的理论与方法体系，有待进一步的探索。

我们提出基于虚拟地理环境的智能城市过程模型框架。该框架基于云计算平台，提供地理过程模型计算与模拟的服务。各种专业模型例如大气模型、交通模型、污染模型及其他环境模型将会集成在云端来进行科学计算与模拟，而计算结果与模拟结果可用来进行可视化分析与决策支持。

（三）模型应用

在对基于香港中文大学实验区的研究中，我们认为基于虚拟地理环境平台的各种模型可

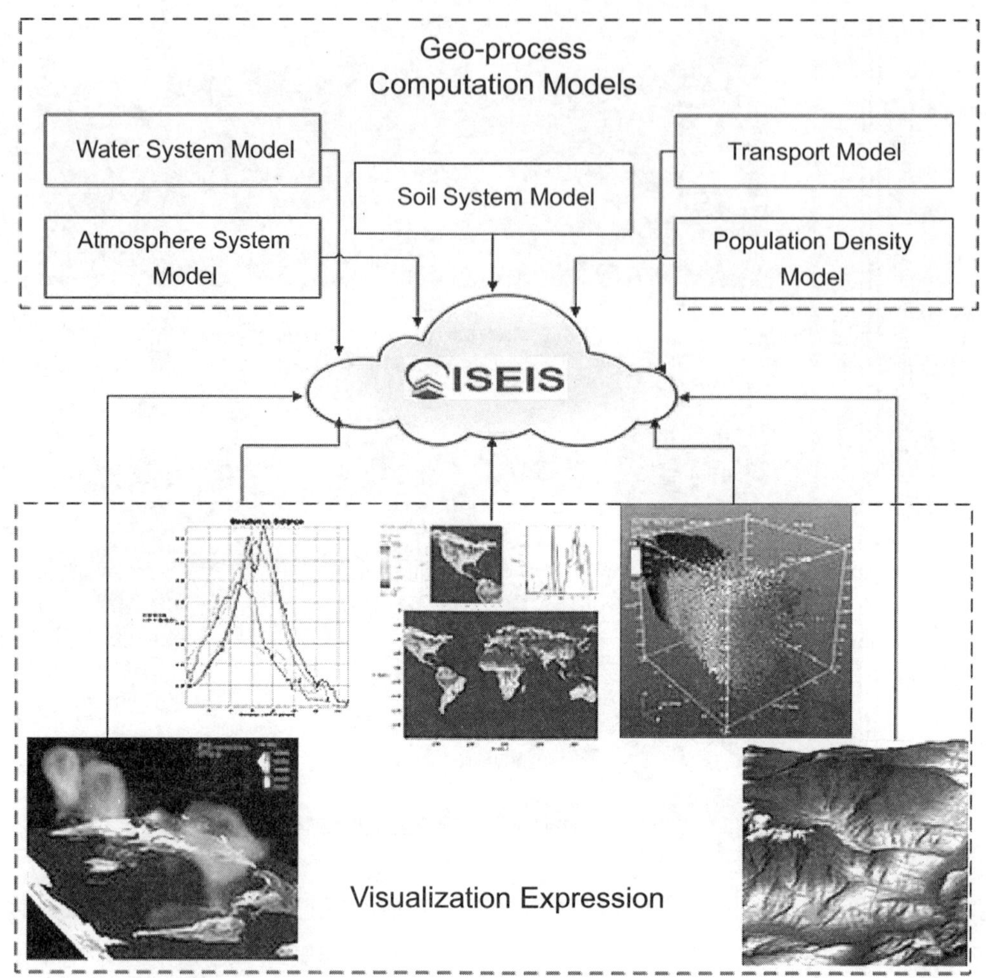

图 3 基于云计算的模型集成与表达

广泛应用于智能城市，从静态模型对现实环境的模拟、分析，到过程模型中物理变量的演示、分析，都展示出其强大而独特的功能。在此，以虚拟规划和建筑设施管理两个方面来说明虚拟地理环境模型在智能城市中的应用。

1. 公众参与的校园规划。规划成果展示始终是城市规划的难点：规划成果平面图缺乏三维效果，透视图不能全方位、多角度展示效果，而沙盘则受比例尺制约，无法全尺度进行展示。通过虚拟地理环境平台展示城市规划成果，则可以在一定程度上避免以上问题。通过在虚拟地理环境中调用规划成果模型，可以以第一人称视角全方位、多角度地查看规划成果，充分展示规划成果的优点与不足。并且，该平台支持模型切换（图 5），从而利于现状与规划的对比分析，及时修改规划以决定最佳规划方案。

2. 校园设施管理。基于虚拟地理环境的精细模型与实物一一对应，通过对建筑模型内部设施进行编号管理，并在真实世界中设置报警装置，可以实现建筑设施的智能化监控。例如，真实世界中某处水管出现故障，监测到的问题可以即时报警并通过网络发送至系统后台，且在虚拟世界中相应的位置显示。管理员可以在虚拟世界中查看该故障的发生地点，从而对该位置有直观清晰的了解，而不需识记复杂的建筑设施编号与其位置的对应关系。每个

图 4　基于 OpenSim 平台规划前后建筑效果对比分析

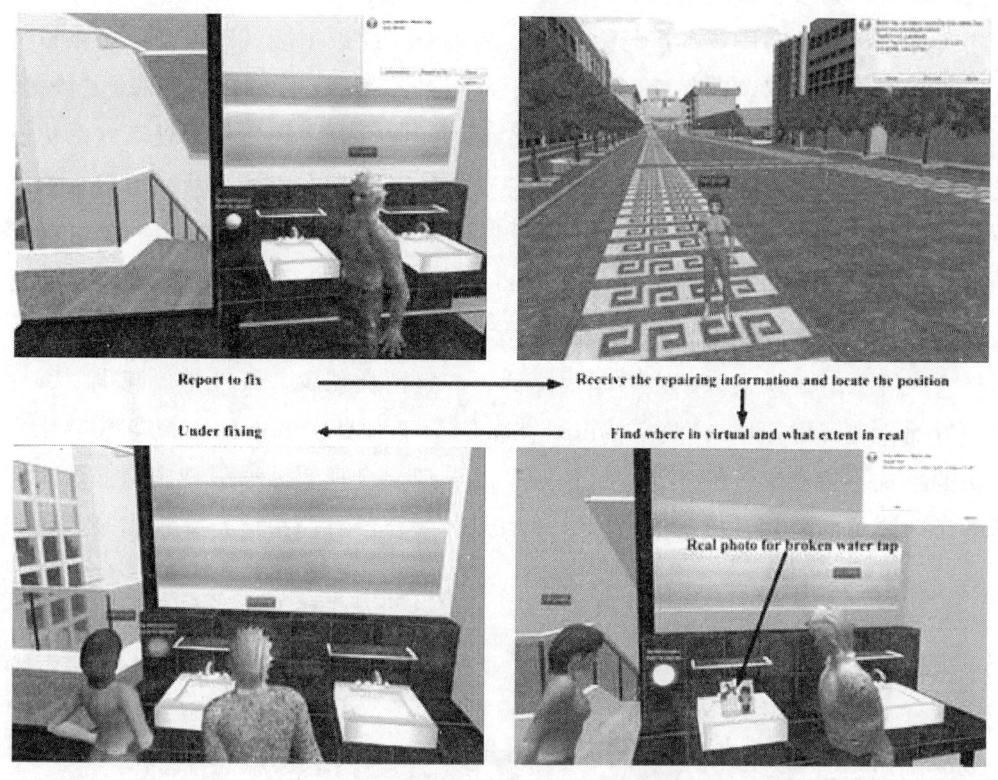

图 5　基于虚拟地理环境的建筑设施智能化监控

故障出现的位置、故障类型均可自动记录在后台数据库中，便于后期统计与分析，从而对解决未来的故障提供充足的数据支持及帮助。

三、智能城市的传感网

传感器网络简称传感网，是由一定数量的传感器节点通过某种有线或无线通信协议连接而成的测控系统，这些节点由传感、数据处理和通信等功能模块构成，安放在被测对象内部或附近，通常尺寸很小，具有低成本、低功耗、多功能等特点。传感器网络综合了传感器技术、嵌入式计算技术、分布式信息处理技术和无线通信技术，能够协作实时监测、感知和采集各种环境或监测对象的信息，并对其进行处理，把结果传送到提供信息的用户。传感器网络将物理世界和虚拟世界连接起来，具有改造社会的潜力。以传感网为核心的物联网将以泛在化的应用为根本目标，感知、网络、智能处理无所不在，任何人在任何时候、任何地点都能享受到任何服务[2,16,17]。

（一）智能城市中传感网的必要性

目前数字城市的数据获取主要包括以遥感技术为代表的大范围数据获取方法和传统的以统计方式的数据获取方法。虽然遥感技术的获取精度和获取能力不断提高，但这主要是一种单向的获取方法，无法和被观测者进行交互。此外，由于天气、气候、地理条件等原因，尚无法达到实时处理和全时段业务运行。而且，其集中式的数据后处理也是一个难以突破的技术门槛。统计方式的数据获取强项则主要在于基于静态数据的数据汇总和历史数据比对等。传感器网络可以为地理环境提供更多的时间方面的元素。真实环境中无处不在的传感器可以捕获空间对象或者地理过程的演变，实现地理现象的实时动态监测，从而可以为智能城市动态地控制和反馈信息，形成新的信息基础设施[2]。例如基于传感器网络的智能交通系统（图6），可实时利用浮动车传感器、交通路口的固定传感器、道路管制数据、视频采集数据、监控中心数据、路况巡查数据、紧急情况定位数据，能有效提高交通运输效益，将能使交通拥挤大大降低、延误损失减少、车祸降低、油料消耗减少、废气排放减少[18]。

另一方面，现有虚拟城市/数字城市研究多侧重于对真实城市的模拟与数字化表达，给用户带来的感觉不够真实。虽然计算机领域早已出现混合现实、增强现实等概念，但目前多由于设备、环境等的限制，使得虚拟与现实的无缝融合没有能很好地体现出来。人们对现实

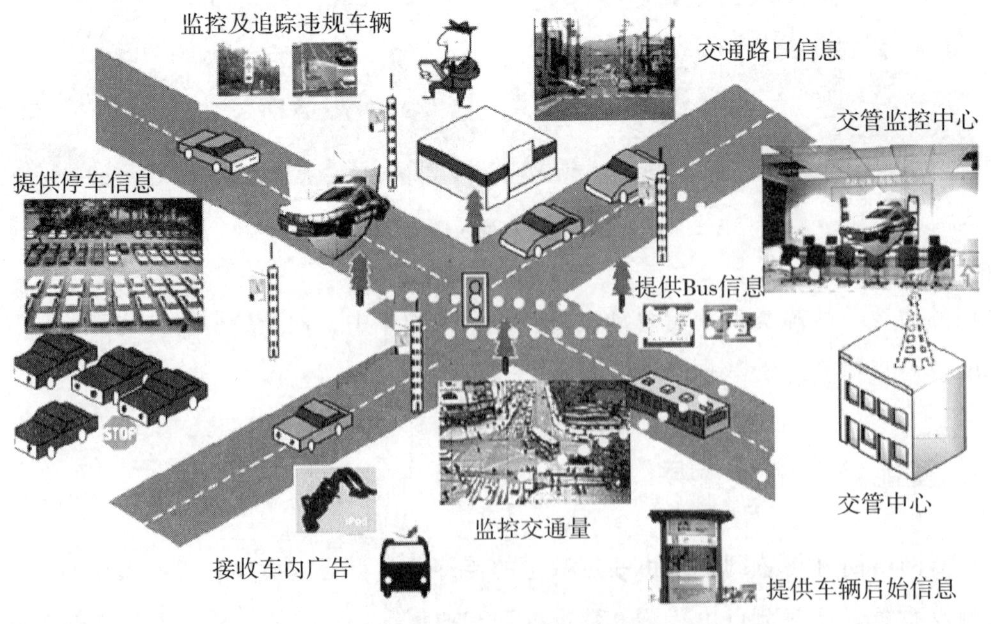

图6 基于传感器网络的智能交通系统[18]

世界进行模拟与数字化表达，其终极目标还是要以虚拟世界的辅助来解决现实中的问题。随着 GIS 应用领域的扩展、计算机软硬件技术的发展，用户越来越渴望获取真实感强的地理空间信息。集成传感网的虚拟地理环境可为用户提供更自然、更真实、更实时、更便捷的虚拟城市环境，消除人们对虚拟与现实认知的两个极端，融合物理世界与虚拟环境[19]。例如日本国立情报学研究所的 Agriculture 项目，利用第二人生（Second Life）游戏平台，结合不同的传感器数据，使得不同的人群可利用化身人来进入系统，进行面对面的交流，感受三维虚拟绿地的场景。真实的传感器可以捕获到绿地的温度、湿度以及实时视频图像数据，然后利用传感器网络传输到虚拟地理环境系统，通过嵌入各种相关信息，从而生成一个虚拟会议空间。这样，不同领域的人（例如专家、草地所有者等）可以在虚拟空间中进行讨论和交流，而不用顾及不同用户的距离问题，通过实时的传感器数据与即时的讨论，可以辅助相关的决策[20]。

图 7　虚实结合的户外环境（温度、湿度和实时监控图像在虚拟世界中的可视化表达）[20]

（二）基于虚拟地理环境的传感网服务框架

如上所述，传感器网络可以有效地连接/融合虚拟环境和现实世界，基于虚拟地理环境的传感网服务可以为智能城市的发展提供诸如噪音、空气污染、能源使用等方面的实时监测信息。图 8 给出了该服务框架。通过组建用于各种环境参数监测的传感器网络，可以实时动态地获取相关的传感器监测数据，用数据库对这些数据进行管理，并通过高性能计算，可以得出各种专业模型的模拟和分析结果，最后在虚拟地理平台中进行显示和表达。各领域不同的用户可根据自身的需求对这些传感器数据和分析模拟结果进行访问。

四、智能城市中虚实结合的社会行为

社区是进行一定的社会活动，具有某种互动关系和共同文化维系力的人类群体及其活动

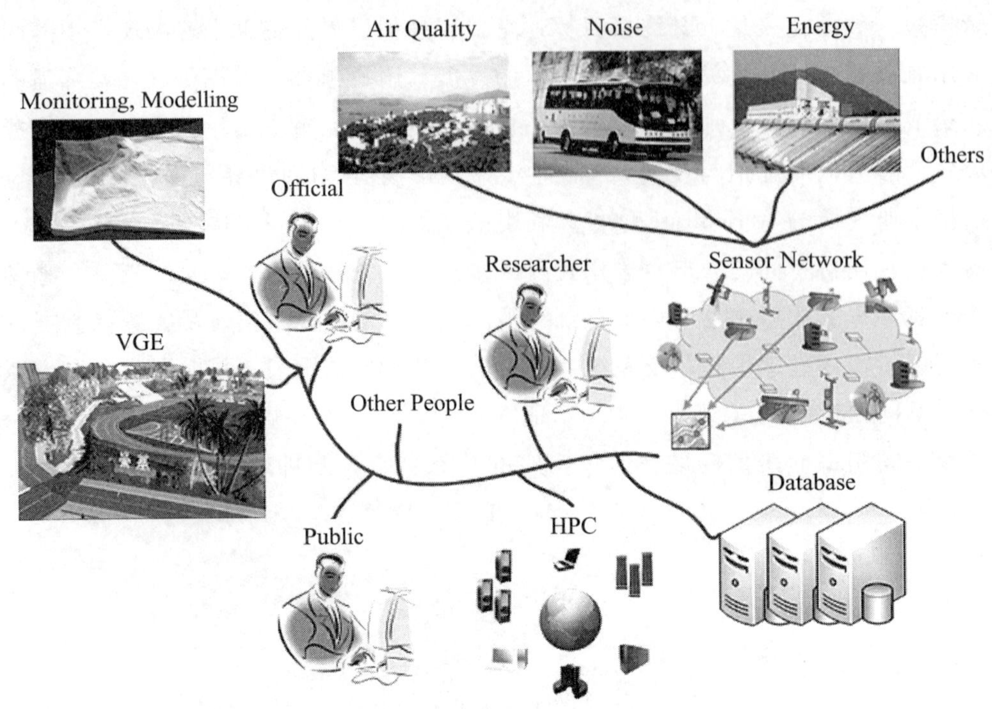

图8 基于虚拟地理环境的传感网服务[19]

区域[21]。虚拟社区（virtual community），也称网上社区（online community），被定义为当足够多的人们带着饱满的情感长期进行公开讨论，以期望在赛博空间（Cyber space）中形成个人的关系网时，在网络中所出现的社会集合体。郑杭生[21]等将虚拟社区定义为由网民在网络空间进行频繁的社会互动形成的具有文化认同的共同体及其活动场所。

（一）基于虚拟地理环境的虚拟社区特征

1. 基于虚拟地理环境虚拟社区的构建

虚拟地理环境是以现实地理环境为基石的一种新的创造，它是一种主体（化身人、化身人群、化身人类）生活的客观实在与现实环境。基于虚拟地理环境的虚拟社区是现实世界的镜像（Mirror world），具有真实的地域表达，并赋予更多真实世界的体验和交互，允许人们以前所未有的丰富细节与深度观察和跟踪真实世界。基于虚拟地理环境的虚拟社区不是静态的，而应该实时反映真实世界的一切动态。这些信息不仅是那些可以观察到的，更是那些不易看到或肉眼看不见的，如市政管理的复杂地下管线。这些信息允许用户自己创建（User Generated Content，UGC）。不同的人根据自己的兴趣可以添加不同的信息层，包括气候、环境、新闻、历史、文化、旅馆、酒店、犯罪数据、学校排名等。

无线传感技术的飞速发展使得虚拟社区更具有真实性。Life Logging（轨迹记录）利用智能手机、移动设备和可穿戴的传感器记录人的声音、兴趣、表情、行动、心跳、睡眠时间。这些无处不在的网络和传感器，使基于虚拟地理环境的虚拟社区具有动态的“层”结构。正如耶鲁大学计算机科学教授戴维·杰勒恩特（David Gelernter）所说的，“人最关心、最感兴趣的始终是自己，在一个真实的世界里，而不是一个虚构的，或者假装的世界”。

2. 虚拟社区人群互动

（1）简易的参与平台

通过简易的参与平台，用户之间的交往可以突破面对面情境的限制、超越时间和空间的界限，也可以进行匿名的交往——“虚拟”的最直接表现；同时这些交流工具和软件系统也成为成员进行互动的共同的活动空间或区域。

（2）足够的参与人群和社会互动

虚拟地理环境是以化身人、化身人群、化身人类为主体的一个虚拟共享空间与环境，它既可以是现实地理环境的表达、模拟、延伸与超越，也可以是指赛博空间中存在的一个虚拟社会（社区）世界。其中的化身人、化身人群、化身人类是表示现实世界中的人与虚拟世界中的化身相结合后的集合体[6]。虚拟社区之所以能称为“社区”，必须有足够的社会互动。参与者在比较固定的网络空间或区域中发生着比较频繁和持久互动，这些互动形成了虚拟社区中的各种社会关系和结构。

（3）社区认同感

在持久的社会互动中形成有共同的社区意识与文化，并建立了成员间的群体认同和心理认同。虚拟社区的信任（reputation）机制引入至关重要[22]。增强现实的核心是对信息的渴望，成为社会的一部分并且感觉到与城市的连接：不仅仅是在社会和商业层面，更包括我们对所生活环境的感受和对我们周围环境的查询。

（二）虚拟社区中的社会活动分析

与Twitter、Facebook、人人网等社交网络相比，基于虚拟地理环境的虚拟社区为用户提供了身临其境的三维空间认知环境，并将生活中的各种场景、细节和体验完全复制到虚拟社区中，是真实世界的虚拟表达。用户以化身（Avatar）的形式进入虚拟社区。化身代表了用户在虚拟社区中的位置，并使用户之间不仅有语言交流，也有一定的“肢体”交流。化身在虚拟社区中的行为将具有与真实世界相似的社会效应（social effect），并有着与真实世界相应的空间特征。因此，虚拟社区为研究社会互动提供了重要平台，通过采集虚拟社区中的行为数据，分析化身的社会活动，将为真实世界的社会活动提供参考。

已有不少学者分析了三维虚拟社区中的化身行为。Friedman[23]通过空间分析，对比了虚拟世界与真实世界的社会互动。La[24]对化身采用时空分析方法，描述了用户在虚拟世界中的空间移动，探索虚拟世界的行为与真实世界的活动的关联。此外，也有研究分析了对化身的人际距离（Interpersonal distance，IPD）和眼睛凝视，发现虚拟世界与现实世界的社会互动遵循相似的规则[25]。Kappe[26]等、Fominykh等[27]对第二人生（Second Life）中化身的互动及交流进行分析，得到用户活动的热点图，即用户访问较为频繁的区域，从而为虚拟世界中的商业布局提供参考，或辅助城市基础设施规划和政策制度制定[28]。

另外，通过召开虚拟会议和虚拟讲座，一方面，管理部门可以实时发布信息，展示规划管理成果；另一方面，社区成员可以共同探讨城市未来的发展，提升城市规划管理的公众参

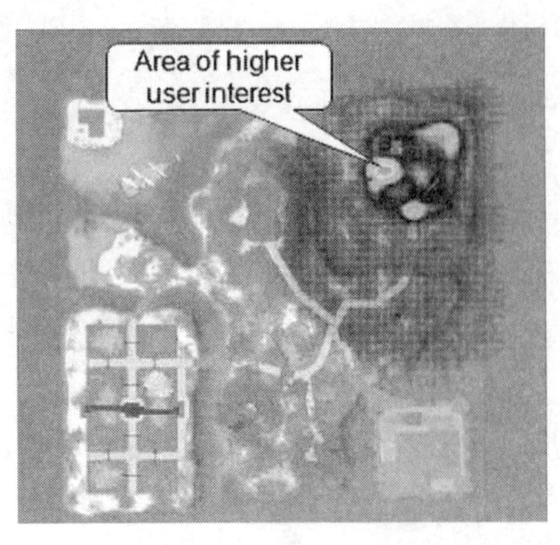

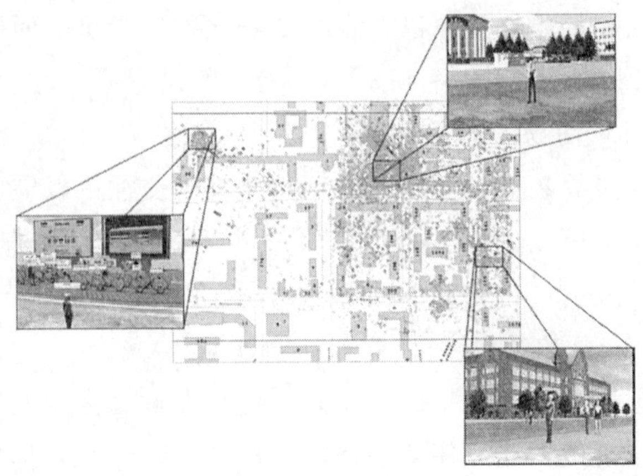

图9 虚拟社区的用户活动热点与分析[26][27]

图10 虚实融合的社区活动[28][29]

与。并且，虚拟社区中的社会活动分析将为城市规划管理提供参考[28-30]。

五、结语

本文以虚拟地理环境的理论为支撑，提出基于虚拟地理环境的智能城市构建，主要涵盖地理模型、传感网与社会行为三个方面的内容。通过文中对虚拟地理环境相关的论述以及现有平台的案例分析可以看出，虚拟地理环境可为智能城市的构建提供精细的静态模型和动态过程模型及场景，提供智能与生态环境感知数据及模拟分析，以及虚实结合的智能城市社会行为研究与分析，从而成为一个更好的新平台为构建智能城市服务。

（作者：林珲，国际欧亚科学院院士，香港中文大学教授）

参考文献

[1] 朱庆，等．数码城市 GIS 的设计与实现［J］．武汉大学学报：信息科学版，2001，26（1）：8－11.

[2] 史文勇，李琦．数字城市：智能城市的初级阶段［J］．地学前缘，2006，13（3）：99－103.

[3] 李博贤，方天培．智能建筑与智能网络集成化及智能城市的技术［J］．工程设计 CAD 与智能建筑，1995（2）．

[4] 秦洪花，李汉清，赵霞．“智慧城市”的国内外发展现状［J］．信息化建设，2010（9）：50－52.

[5] 叶亚芝．智能城市建设及评价体系［D］．北京：北京交通大学，2007.

[6] 龚建华，周洁萍，张利辉．虚拟地理环境研究进展与理论框架［J］．地球科学进展，2010，25（9）．

[7] Lin，Hui，Jianhua，Gong. On virtual geographic environments［J］．Acta Geodaetica et Cartographica Sinica，2002，31（1）：1－6.

[8] Lin，Hui，Huang Fengru，Lu Guonian. Development of Virtual Geographic Environments and the New Initiative in Experimental Geography［J］．Acta Geographica Sinica，2009（1）．

[9] Hu，M.，et al. A virtual learning environment of the Chinese University of Hong Kong［J］．International Journal of Digital Earth，2010，4（2）：1－12.

[10] 李爽，姚静．虚拟地理环境的多维数据模型与地理过程表达［J］．地理与地理信息科学，2005，21（4）：1－5.

[11] 张续红，苏建明，胡庆夕．虚拟现实技术在城市规划仿真中的应用［J］．计算机仿真，2003，20（7）：75－77.

[12] 陈驰，任爱珠，张新．基于虚拟现实的建筑火灾模拟系统［J］．自然灾害学报，2007，16（1）：55－60.

[13] Xu，B.，et al. Collaborative virtual geographic environments：A case study of air pollution simulation［J］. Information Sciences，2011.

[14] Vardoulakis，S.，et al. Modelling air quality in street canyons：a review［J］．Atmospheric Environment，2003，37（2）：155－182.

[15] Woo，J. H.，et al. AirScope：A micro-scale urban air quality management system［J］．Algorithms and Architectures for Parallel Processing，2010：520－527.

[16] Delin，K. and S. Jackson. The sensor web：a new instrument concept. 2001.

[17] Stefanidis，A. and S. Nittel，GeoSensor networks，2003：CRC.

[18] 李德仁，邵振峰．论新地理信息时代［J］．中国科学（F 辑：信息科学），2009.

[19] Che，W.，H. Lin，et al. Reality-virtuality fusional campus environment：An online 3D platform based on OpenSimulator［J］．Geo－spatial Information Science，2011，14（2）：144－149.

[20] von Kapri，A.，et al. Global lab：an interaction，simulation，and experimentation platform based on “second life” and “opensimulator”，2009.

[21] 郑杭生，等．社会学概论新修：第三版［M］．北京：中国人民大学出版社，2003.

[22] Cascio，J.，et al. Metaverse Roadmap：Pathways to the 3D Web［R］．Report on the cross-industry public foresight project，2007. 7.

[23] Friedman，D.，A. Steed，M. Slater. Spatial social behavior in second life［M］．Springer，2007.

[24] La，C. A. and P. Michiardi. Characterizing user mobility in Second Life［M］．ACM，2008.

[25] Yee，N.，et al. The unbearable likeness of being digital：The persistence of nonverbal social norms in online virtual environments［J］．CyberPsychology & Behavior，2007，10（1）：115－121.

[26] Kappe，F.，B. Zaka，M. Steurer. Automatically detecting points of interest and social networks from tracking positions of avatars in a virtual world［C］．2009 Advances in Social Network Analysis and Mining，

2009：89－94.

[27] Fominykh，M.，et al. Virtual Campus in the Context of an Educational Virtual City：a Case Study.

[28] Fulford，C.，Virtual Campus in the Context of an Educational Virtual City：a Case Study.

[29] Virtual 3D worlds or Web 3.0？http：//sudhirsyal. wordpress. com/the-economic-times/.

[30] http：//www. healthlands. org/.

广东节能建筑发展状况与发展趋势的探讨

随着社会经济与城市建设的快速发展，建筑业成为快速发展的行业，也成为社会能耗的主要领域。一方面，在建设过程中能耗比较高；另一方面，在使用过程中，也持续消耗大量的能源。建筑能耗已经占到社会能源消耗总量的32%，此外，加上每年建筑材料的消耗，建筑总能耗将近社会总能耗的45%。因此，建筑物的节能效果对全社会的节能工作将产生重要的影响。国务院在“十二五”节能规划中，明确提出了“大力发展绿色建筑、智能建筑，最大限度地节能、节水、节材、节地”的指导要求。

降低建筑能耗包括建筑节能和节能建筑两个途径。建筑节能与节能建筑是不同阶段、不同概念的节能工作。建筑节能多是在传统建筑基础上加上一些节能元素和技术，也是目前使用较多的方法，但节能建筑却要求节能与建筑在结构设计、建筑材料、供能方式以及施工方法等方面实现一体化，这是全新的建筑理念，也将形成新的产业和产业链。

一、广东省建筑节能发展状况

我国现有建筑总面积430亿 m^2，每年增加16亿~20亿 m^2，预计到2020年将达700亿 m^2,是世界上最大的建筑市场。广东省作为全国经济大省，既有建筑规模大，新建建筑增加速度快于全国平均水平。广东也是能源输入大省，能源调入数量越来越大，到2005年调入比例已经占到了总消耗的74.5%。广东开展建筑物节能工作，有突出的紧迫性和显著的社会意义。

广东省位于中国南部，热量资源丰富，气候温暖，冬无严寒，各地年平均温度在20.4℃~23.1℃之间，最冷月1月份平均温度约为9℃~17℃。相对于北方来说，广东是一个“天然大温室”，气候的影响，决定了广东建筑的节能工作需要得到充分的重视。

长期以来，广东省对建筑的能源消耗情况一直没有进行过系统、全面的统计和调查，没有准确、科学、客观的数据说明建筑能耗的状况，造成社会各界对建筑节能的重要性、紧迫性认识不足，对建筑节能的现状和发展趋势了解不够，相关节能政策的制定缺乏充分的依据，建筑节能产业发展较慢[1]。

《广东省民用建筑条例》指出，要求到2011年，新建建筑节能标准执行率达到97%；新建建筑8%以上应用可再生能源的技术；建成一批绿色建筑、绿色社区；全年节约能源约

60万吨标准煤，减排二氧化碳约160万吨。到2015年，节能标准执行率达到100%；新建建筑30%以上应用可再生能源的技术；30%以上新建建筑和住宅小区达到绿色建筑评价标准要求。5年共节约能源约770万吨标准煤，减排二氧化碳约2048万吨。加上既有建筑的节能改造，总的来说，广东省面临的节能任务比较繁重。

二、广东发展节能建筑存在的一些问题

（一）社会建筑节能意识淡薄，实施过程缺乏监督

建筑总能耗已占了社会总能耗将近45.3%的比例，但许多部门和个人仍然没有意识到，造成的建筑规划设计时只追求外观或只考虑建设投资，没有将节能技术融入设计，或者在施工过程中缺乏监督，出现在实际建设安装过程中，脱离原来节能设计的情况。

（二）相关政策法规不够完善

广东省的深圳市2006年率先出台《深圳经济特区建筑节能条例》，首推12层以下的住宅建筑必须安装太阳能热水系统，为推进城市建筑可再生能源规模化应用奠定了法律基础。2010年8月，广州市建委公示的《广州市民用建筑节能管理条例（征求意见稿）》计划在12层以下新建建筑中强制推广应用太阳能热水，将绿色建筑的规划和推广纳入立法内容。但是，全省大部分地区仍然缺乏相关的政策法规，处于法规滞后或者不完善的状态。

（三）部分节能产品的经济性还需提高

部分新能源节能产品存在节能不节钱的问题，造成推广应用困难。但随着技术的不断革新和产品的规模化生产，产品性价比将越来越高，比如太阳能电池板的成本一直在下降，应用范围将越来越广。

（四）过于依赖设备而忽视了经济性

个别项目偏离根本，过度依赖设备和技术，而忽视了整体经济性。节能建筑事业的出发点应该因地制宜，以人为本，充分利用自然条件，合理应用高新技术，根本目标是综合降低能耗和节省费用。

（五）产业的发展缺乏引导、支持

广大高校、科研院所、大型企业，具有雄厚的技术研究基础和开发能力，但缺乏有效的政策引导和支持，缺乏激励机制，造成节能建筑产业发展缓慢，行业不够规范，缺乏应有的产业氛围和产业配套。

（六）节能建筑技术尚未形成

广东在建筑节能方面已开展了一系列的工作，也取得了一定的成效，但有关节能建筑的理念尚未得到重视，一些节能建筑技术尚在研发中。

三、两项节能建筑技术应用案例介绍

（一）广东科学中心节能建筑技术应用

广东科学中心位于广州大学城小谷围岛西部，作为广东省科技展示的重要建筑，也是典型的节能建筑示范工程之一（见图1）。广东科学中心进行了照明系统节能技术、中庭自然通风技术、建筑围护结构节能技术、太阳能技术和采暖系统节能技术等多种建筑节能措施的研究和应用：

1. 自然采光、通风技术的应用。公共建筑照明能耗约占建筑总能耗的30%。广东科学中心南、北、西侧面向珠江，空间开阔无遮挡，年平均日照时数为1 917.5h，该地区自然光资源丰富，该建筑最大限度的在建筑设计中利用自然光，并且利用智能控制技术，当自然光不足时才启用人工照明，并且按需开启照明。同时，也尽可能的利用健康的自然通风，在夏热冬暖的地区，充分利用自然风以减少对空调的使用，从而实现节能目的。

2. 围护结构节能技术。广东科学中心建筑外围护结构面积非常大，大多采用大面积透明玻璃幕墙等轻质结构作为立面，蓄热能力差、热惰性指标小，导致室内空调系统负荷大，能耗比较高。通过将需要室内人工照明的建筑部分外立面的玻璃幕墙改为铝板幕墙，减少阳

图1　广东省科学中心

光的直接照射，并且合理处理保持建筑外形的协调性，这样既不影响建筑外观，也不影响采光使用，但达到了节约空调能耗的目的。

3. 光伏建筑一体化（BIPV）是太阳能光伏发电的重要趋势。广东科学中心在建筑屋面H区采光天窗部位采用BIPV光电幕墙系统，将光伏组件分布在屋面采光天窗的两侧，共分8个区域，整个系统的安装功率为19.84kW。不仅替代了部分的建筑材料，同时也为科学中心提供了部分的用电[2]。

4. 夏热冬暖地区公共建筑能耗中空调能耗占50%以上，因此空调设备及系统节能对公共建筑节能尤为重要[3]。科学中心在空调系统中采用了分区空调、高大空间分层空调、变风量低温送风、循环水泵变频运行和部分区域热回收等多种节能措施，实现大型空调的节能。

（二）广州某产业园区节能建筑技术示范

该产业园位于广州市，占地约6万m^2，是新建的创意产业和创新科技园区，建成建筑物5万多m^2（见图2）。中国科学院广州能源研究所拟对该园区进行整体低碳建设规划，并为办公大楼的节能建筑开展了多项技术研究与集成应用。

1. 光伏建筑一体化（BIPV）的应用。分别采用265W和190W单晶硅太阳能电池板作为屋面材料，直接代替约200m^2屋面建筑材料，形成建筑一体化。该光伏系统总装机20KW，采用需求侧并网和智能控制技术，减少了蓄电池的投资和安装，智能控制实现建筑的照明等优先使用太阳能绿色电源，节约了大部分的建筑用电，该系统还可以减排二氧化碳约29.2t/a。

2. 在建筑墙立面安装两处非晶硅太阳能幕墙，替代了落地玻璃，建成小规模独立发电

图2 产业园区

系统、离网设计，以此作为建筑物应急备用电源。非晶硅电池吸收光谱范围更广，弱光发电性能比晶体硅电池优越，安装在立面也有显著的发电效果。同时，非晶硅电池颜色均匀，透光率低，投影柔和[6]，既可满足采光又具有良好的隔热性能。

3. 高效太阳能—热泵热水系统。广东省属于我国三类太阳能辐射地区，全年日照时间为2 200～3 000h，年辐射总量为5 016～5 852MJ/m^2，有比较充足的太阳能资源。在宿舍楼顶安装296m^2太阳能平板集热器和3台10P空气能热水器，充分利用日照和空气中的热量，每天为员工宿舍提供30t生活热水，同时也为屋顶起到了良好的隔热作用。该系统每年可节约标准煤35.04t，减排二氧化碳约91.2t。

4. 低辐射节能玻璃。采用铝合金窗安装Low－E低辐射节能玻璃，玻璃的透光率在40%以上，保证了最大限度的自然采光，减少人工照明，同时也能减少热辐射导致空调制冷负荷大的问题。据调查，广东省既有建筑外围护结构各部分的节能潜力分别为：屋面0.3%，外墙6%，外窗11%，外窗气密性12.9%[4]。因此，在窗户材料上选用低辐射节能玻璃是很重要的节能措施。

5. 节能智能控制系统。智能控制系统能为屋顶太阳能电池板和其他屋顶材料进行自动喷水，一方面是给屋顶材料降温，降低夏日时空调的负荷，一方面清洁了太阳能电池板的表面和降低了电池板的温度，有利于提升太阳能电池板光电转换效率。

举例说明：如果电池的最大输出功率Pm是1 000W，在60℃的温度下工作，这时晶硅电池的Pm会降到825W[5]。所以，在强日照情况下，控制电池板不出现过高的温度，将有利于保持电池板较好的光电转换率。

通过智能控制系统，园区道路照明实现光感开、时控关（光感关）功能，最少时间的开启路灯照明，在入夜之后，分级自动调暗灯光照明，实现最低能耗。

6. 应用LED节能灯。室内照明和园区的太阳能草坪灯和路灯采用LED节能光源。LED是一种固态的半导体器件，它可以直接把电转化为光，高光效，光衰小。超高亮大功率LED光源，配合高效率电源，比传统白炽灯节电80%以上，寿命是传统钨丝灯的50倍以上。

7. 低温吸附式热泵系统。低温吸附式热泵利用机房设备等产生的低品位余热、废热，通过工质吸附热交换之后进行制冷，输出冷气。减少了机房过多的热量，又为机房提供了冷气，是一项重要的节能技术。

四、广东节能建筑发展趋势

未来节能建筑应充分将节能材料、节能技术与建筑结构设计、建筑外观设计紧密结合。目前主要有几个发展趋势：

1. 墙体材料：采用加气混凝土或空心混凝土砌块等新型隔热墙体材料。
2. 屋面材料：采取聚苯乙烯保温层、陶粒隔热砖隔热措施。
3. 外窗材料：采用中空玻璃、Low－E玻璃以及新型玻璃等节能玻璃。
4. 节能技术：组合应用太阳能（光热、光电）技术、地源热泵、绿色照明等节能技术。

5. 建筑设计：充分将结构、外观、材料、能源技术及其职能控制紧密结合。

6. 观念转变：逐步从建筑节能的被动节能，走向发展节能建筑的主动节能。

五、结语

广东正在建设低碳示范省，面对突出的建筑能耗，应重点支持、引导，优先发展节能建筑事业。发展节能建筑产业，需要进一步加大专业人才的培养力度，改革现有教育模式，培养更多的既掌握建筑设计又熟悉节能技术的专门人才。

结合《广东省民用建筑条例》的规划要求和相关应用实例，发展节能建筑，还应进一步完善相关政策法规，出台激励机制；重视建筑结构设计，以人为本，因地制宜，充分利用自然通风和自然采光，并加强施工安装过程监督；注重应用节能建材，推广太阳能、热泵、LED、节能玻璃等绿色能源与节能技术和智能控制技术的应用，着重发展建筑一体化，形成传统技术与高新科技应用的有机结合。

（作者：陈勇，国际欧亚科学院院士，中国科学院广州分院院长，广东科学院院长）

参考文献

[1] 杨仕超，吴培浩，等．广东省建筑节能现状概况［J］．建筑监督检测与造价，2008，2（1）：67－71.

[2] 徐天平，易和，等．广东科学中心建筑节能技术应用［J］．施工技术，2011，2（4）：21－23.

[3] 陈伟青，周孝清，刘芳，等．广州某商场空调系统能耗状况与节能性分析［J］．广州大学学报，2008，7（4）：91－94.

[4] 杨仕超，吴培浩，周荃，等．广东省既有建筑现状及节能潜力［J］．建筑监督检测与造价，2008，3（2）：59－63.

[5] Borg，N. J. C. M. van der，Wiggelinkhuizen. Building integration of photovoltaic power systems using amorphous silicon modules：irradiation loss due to non－conventionalorientations［R］．Netherlands：Energy Research Centre of the Netherlands. 2001.

[6] 李水生，何韶瑶，张敬农．太阳能光伏电池在建筑幕墙上的应用研究［J］．华中建筑，2009，27：115－117.

观察篇

2011 全国“两会”城乡规划建设热点问题综述

2011 年 3 月 3 日至 3 月 14 日，十一届全国人大四次会议和全国政协十一届四次会议（简称“两会”）在北京召开。本年度“两会”是我国进入“十二五”规划开局之年的“两会”，对于国家经济社会发展具有重要战略意义。本文针对“两会”代表、委员关心的城乡规划建设问题进行整理，以期对今年乃至今后几年的城乡规划建设提供有意义的指导。

国务院总理温家宝在《政府工作报告》中提出要“积极稳妥推进城镇化”，“完善城市化布局和形态，不断提升城镇化的质量和水平”，同时要“深入实施区域发展总体战略和主体功能区战略，逐步实现基本公共服务均等化。促进城乡、区域良性互动，一、二、三产业协调发展。”关于 2011 年的重点工作，温总理在报告中要求“促进区域协调发展，全面落实各项区域发展规划”，“积极稳妥推进城镇化”，“坚持走中国特色城镇化道路，遵循城市发展规律，促进城镇化健康发展”，“坚持科学规划，严格管理，加强城市基础设施和公共服务设施建设，增强城镇综合承载能力，提高管理和服务水平”……参加“两会”的代表和委员就上述问题进行了讨论，并提交了大量的提案和议案。主要内容涉及十几个方面，本文按以下五大类进行综述。

一、区域开发和城镇建设

2011 年“两会”代表委员们关注的主要是首都经济圈、成渝经济区、中原经济区、天津滨海新区以及革命老区的开发和建设。

“十二五”规划草案中“打造首都经济圈”进入了国家战略。郭金龙代表提出北京市要摆正位置，提高服务、辐射的能力和协作能力。张工代表提出北京市要实现三个转变，加强交通等基础设施建设，研究完善相关利益分配格局和空间规划，从多个方面向外围地区辐射。刘学库代表提出河北要在紧邻北京、交通便利、基础较好、潜力较大的县重点突破，以点带面建设“环首都绿色经济圈”。刘永瑞委员认为应借鉴国际大都市经济圈的发展经验，重点加快“京津一体化”进程，包括基础设施、产业和生态建设等。

“两会”前国务院批准了成渝经济区规划，王康委员认为在成渝经济区发展内陆开放型经济必将为西部其他地区发展起到示范作用。黄小祥代表、谢开华委员认为应充分发挥川、渝两地在产业方面的优势，加快区域合作，使成渝经济区真正成为中国未来经济发展的一个重要增长极。李铀委员提出成渝发展应向同城化努力，应加大产业互补。

关于中原经济区建设，吕清海代表认为中原经济区是相对独立的区域经济综合体，具有承接东部产业转移的良好基础和优势条件，他建议国家在中原经济区设立承接产业转移示范区。释永信委员提出中原经济区建设应提升为国家战略。

农工党中央针对滨海新区开发建设提案，建议“十二五”期间国家继续在区域规划、大项目建设、自主创新、生态保护、财税支持、综合配套改革等方面应给予大力支持，帮助滨海新区建设成为高端产业聚集区、科技创新领航区、生态文明示范区、改革开放先行区、和谐社会首善区，成为全国经济第三增长极。

关于目前正在探索和推进创新模式的横琴新区，林金城委员提出，未来将以合作创新和服务为主题，在推进粤港澳紧密合作中发挥制度创新、先行先试的先导作用。他建议粤港澳三方应加强研究、共同协商、提出方案，中央政府及各个主管部门应给予政策指引和实质支持。

针对大别山地区这几年发展较慢的问题，王少阶委员、陈世强委员建议“十二五”期间国家要采取特殊的措施，以区域发展为指导思想推动大别山地区与周边地区的一体化发展，改变当前地理“高地”经济社会“洼地”的格局。胡茂成代表联合鄂湘渝陕60名代表共同建议尽快启动安恩张衡铁路（安康—恩施—张家界—衡阳）建设，他认为这条铁路不仅将填补区域铁路网空白，也为沿线贫困地区和川陕、鄂豫、湘鄂西、湘鄂川黔革命根据地的开发起到积极作用。赵合代表也提出拉林（拉萨—林芝）铁路应早日动工，铁路建成后将大大带动林芝乃至整个藏东南地区的城市发展，加速城镇化进程。

周国允代表提出今后要大力发展县域经济。建议：一是要解放思想，转变观念；二是要改进县域金融支持力度；三是培育特色经济，促进产业升级；四是提升劳务经济，提高劳务竞争力；五是发展民营经济，增强发展活力。

二、城市规划和建设

近30年来我国城市建设取得了史无前例的大发展，但潘祖尧委员认为城市建设中的痼疾非但没有得到根治，反而又有新的发展，主要存在规划缺乏充分合理论证、首都效应、千城一面、高大全思想盛行、建筑师缺乏话语权、非洋莫取、近现代建筑被破坏和假古董不断被复制、建筑的质量不高、献礼工程、政绩工程、标志性工程仍大量存在等方面的隐忧。他建议国家有关部门尽快研究和总结城市规划、城市建设的经验教训，找出解决问题的办法。

胡葆森代表针对当前二、三线城市文化设施建设发展明显滞后的问题进行了分析，建议要从城市总体规划出发增加中小城市文化基础设施硬件总量，减少对有“形象工程”之嫌的大型公共设施、带有商业运营性质的文化旅游设施的投入，兴建更多贴近市民、顺应民心、方便民用的社区图书馆、小型演出厅等小型设施。

荣海委员关于《严格限制高尔夫球场建设》的提案中提出由于缺乏有效监管，近几年在国家明令停止新建高尔夫球场的政策环境下高尔夫球场的建设却逆向增长，高尔夫球场违法用地和浪费土地现象十分严峻。他建议国家应该尽快出台政策严格审批管理，严查和严惩违法征地，大幅提高征地补偿标准，同时对高尔夫球产业布局进行整体规划，制定明确的准入门槛和用地限制。

针对今年的保障房建设，代表委员们提出了规划建设方面的建议。李瑾代表提出要完善保障性住房的公共交通、小区绿化、水电煤气供应等配套设施和服务，让人“住得舒心”，同时他认为保障性住房的布局应当分散，这样既能实现广泛覆盖，解决职住分离问题，同时又可避免很多社会管理问题。贾康代表提出保障房建设不能大面积集中连片，应该和其他社区进行搭配，采取“插花式”建设。顾云昌代表认为在专门的一个地区集中建设保障性住房，容易形成国外常见的“贫民窟”，影响社会和谐。陈国强认为在各地安排年度建设用地指标时，应优先确保保障性住房用地，并通过盘活存量土地资源、加大开发力度、集约建房等方式，确保土地供应。张复明代表认为目前地方政府大量用地建设工业和基础设施，保障房用地毕竟是小头，土地问题是可以解决的。于炼代表认为不能把保障房建设仅仅当做一项任务，健康的保障性住房体系建设必须走产业化之路，用产业立法确立用地优先保障机制，同时每个城市应将交通、教育、就医等资源较为便利的用地优先满足保障房建设。茅永红委员提出应把农民工住房纳入城市规划，采取多项措施逐步解决农民工的住房问题。他认为公租房是解决农民工住房条件的一个较好途径，国家可采取减免税费等措施，引导鼓励企业建设公共租赁房和员工公寓，放宽公租房申请标准，适当降低门槛，扩大公租房提供范围。同时政府也可以建设或收购一定数量的公租房提供给农民工居住。

三、城镇化、城乡统筹和新农村建设

2011 年“两会”代表委员对于城镇化、城乡统筹和新农村建设问题的讨论依然十分激烈。迟福林委员建议国务院把海南作为国家推进城镇化综合改革试验区，全岛按照“一个大城市”进行统一规划，重点推进中心城市建设和城乡一体化，推动城乡管理社区化。同时，他认为国家有关部门应当在总体规划、行政区划体制改革、城乡一体化体制机制创新、行政体制改革和重大项目建设上给予海南支持。

刘江委员认为城镇化与新农村建设不可偏废，“双轮驱动”、协调推进才能促进城乡共同繁荣。他建议应将县城和中心镇作为重点，认真处理好城镇化过程中的土地问题，新农村建设应突出产业发展、基础设施建设和促进农民增收，应加快促进“空间城镇化”向“人口城镇化”转变，同时他认为推进城镇化过程中要善待农民，尊重农民意愿，维护农民权益。

蔡继明委员认为目前在政府主导型的城市化模式之外，应该考虑允许农民自主的推进城市化，让土地进入市场，与国有建设用地同权、同价，使农民在土地所有制、集体所有制这个属性不改变的情况下分享到工业化、城市化带来的土地增值、土地红利。

吴焰委员认为农村城镇化不仅是农民居住形态的变化，还将带来农民生产方式和生活方式的改变。为此政府应建立相应的保障机制，可从土地收益中拿出一部分资金，共同建立农民个人账户，以保障后续生活。

李成贵委员认为应把中小城市和小城镇作为吸纳农民工的一个主战场，更多地鼓励和支持就地城镇化。对于拆迁并居问题，李委员认为建立新型农村社区要本着几条原则：一是要充分尊重农民的意愿；二是要搞好规划；三是拆并出来的土地应归农民，土地所得的绝大部分收入也要归农民。

许家印委员认为加大老城区城中村改造力度既可以改善城中村村民的生活水平和居住环境，更重要的是可以缓解房地产市场的供需矛盾。同时他也认为当前城中村改造存在着诸多问题，他建议政府应加强指导和介入，包括在土地拍卖、规划条件申领、改造资金的专款专用等方面，从而提高市场化水平和工作效率。

王小同代表认为农村污水处理问题成为新农村建设的一个瓶颈，建议把农村污水处理作为一个系统工程来抓，国家应制定法规、投入资金和加强研究，并将其作为新农村建设的一个重要考核内容。

四、城市交通拥堵与规划

2011 年“两会”上，针对北京、上海、广州等特大城市的交通拥堵问题，代表委员各抒己见，纷纷建言献策。潘皓炫代表指出，交通拥堵本质上是经济发展和交通规划的矛盾，城市化不应该把城市边界无限制扩大，一方面实现城市化进程，让服务业和第三产业更活跃，另一方面，要积极发展中心城市，把中小城镇适当做大，各个城市之间用交通系统连接，完全能够解决城市病问题。

王东代表指出交通问题深层次的原因是中国城市化非常快，城市人口增加的速度比城市交通功能提高速度要快。他认为城市大的结构和布局要比较合理，才能减少很多的不必要的交通量或交通需求。另外他提出交通设施的供给也是解决城市拥堵的重要努力方向。王代表指出广州提出紧促舒展网络型的空间结构，每一个外围的点要优化，完善公共服务设施和生活配套设施，这样就会减少很多的所谓潮汐的交通。同时他认为不应限制买车，但应鼓励上下班少开车。

九三学社中央提交的《关于缓解我国大城市交通拥堵的提案》认为规划和管理是疏堵的关键所在，应避免在中心城区规划建设过多的大型商场、写字楼、宾馆饭店等高层建筑。同时在交通管理方面我国长期重主干道、轻小辅路，建议可通过地方立法，要求所有的小区在上下班高峰时段必须开放所有车辆通道。

九三学社中央的提案还提出对于紧缺的公共资源——市区道路，向占用者收取一定费用是合理的。提案建议借鉴发达国家的做法，即限制小汽车的使用量而非拥有量，划定一定区域收取交通拥堵费，并通过不同的收费标准来引导车辆流量。

邢克智代表认为目前的公共交通系统远远没有发挥其应有的作用，城市交通设施建设滞后与群众出行要求矛盾凸显。为此建议确立城市“公交优先发展”的战略地位，科学制定和实施城市“公交优先发展”规划，严格控制私家车数量，加强道路交通智能化建设和管理。

李立新委员认为交通拥堵的根本原因决不能完全归结于车多，而在于城市缺乏科学规划。他借鉴香港以“空中连廊”为代表的“步行系统”提出建议，各地应确立“路权分配”理念，因地制宜建设“步行系统”，从根本上医治交通拥堵的“城市病”。

五、其他热点话题

除上述几个比较集中的议题外，今年“两会”还有一些话题值得重视，包括城市防震、地下空间开发、历史文化遗产保护、低碳城市建设和城市资源保护、生态建设等方面的内容。

（一）城市防震

地震频发，如何加强防震减灾能力，陈骏委员认为现阶段人类还做不到地震的预测和预知，只有做好预防工作。戴雅萍委员建议，城市还应当多建一些应急避难场所，将市区里的公园、绿地，都改造成应急避难场所。葛剑雄委员则提出地震多发区在考虑整体建设规划的时候需要兼顾。他举例认为，在地震灾区发展旅游，就得考虑好地震发生后游客怎样以最快的速度疏散，对外联系的道路至少要有两条以上，要有足够的接待能力，建筑强度应达到一定的等级。

许志琴代表提出应加快健全和完善科学的灾害评价、监测预警、防治预报和应急体系。建议：一是对大城市尤其面临灾害威胁的大城市要进行地下结构勘查；二是对重点灾害地带的居民要进行搬迁和避让；三是对危险地带的建筑物进行防震加固。

（二）地下空间开发与建设

陈百成代表认为我国对“地下空间”的开发与建设重视不够，规划严重滞后，很多城市地下管网建设与城市总体建设不同步，燃气、热力、雨水排放、污水处理、电力、通信、有线电视、地下商城等各自为政，缺乏统一筹划，缺乏协调统一。他建议政府应集中人力、资金、物力建设一流的地下基础设施，编制规划要超前、实用、可行，广泛征求意见，同时要形成强有力的协调联动机制，打击对“地下空间”的非法侵占和利用，以及破坏地下设施的行为。

（三）低碳城市建设

去年国家启动低碳省和低碳城市试点工作，但由于低碳城市规划发展所需关键技术尚不明晰，相关部门也很难进行有效的引导、管理和评价，因此试点的效果并不十分理想。为此民建中央建议未来的突破口放在能源低碳化、经济低碳化、社会低碳化、排放低碳化四个方面，并以制度创新推动低碳城市发展、以科学规划引领低碳城市发展、以低碳技术支撑低碳城市发展。牛文元委员建议由国家发改委、工业和信息化部、交通部、铁道部、住房和城乡建设部、环境保护部、科技部组成“一委六部”跨部轮值机构，共同制定出工业、交通、建筑三大高耗能领域与中国50个最大城市的“低碳发展国家行动方案”，设计相应的调控总量和约束性细则，并作为国家“十二五”规划的执行附件和政绩考核的重要内容之一。

(四) 历史文化遗产保护

单霁翔代表认为20世纪遗产与古代文化遗产相比十分年轻，但对其历史价值的保护不容忽视。他建议将人民大会堂、国家博物馆、中国人民革命军事博物馆、民族文化宫、民族饭店、钓鱼台国宾馆、华侨大厦、北京火车站、全国农业展览馆和北京工人体育场等“国庆十大工程”申报全国重点文物保护单位，这些工程内涵丰富、形象直观，具有极其重要的历史、艺术和科学价值，应纳入文物保护法的保护范畴，让北京这一历史文化名城的内涵更加丰富多彩。

(五) 城市资源利用和生态建设

冯新柱代表提出处理好资源就地转化与资源输出的关系，对于促进资源型城市生态环境根本好转、实现可持续发展意义重大。他认为统筹推进资源转化，延长产业链，提高资源综合利用水平，构建资源开发利用的良性循环机制，是实现资源型城市可持续发展的必然选择，国家应在产业政策、金融政策、财税政策等方面继续给予资源型城市支持和倾斜。赵顷霖代表认为我国资源型城市转型，既关乎国民经济发展大局，又事关资源型城市自身的发展前途。国家应该进一步关注、支持资源型城市的可持续发展。

朱以庄代表提出在城市建设的过程中，要把城市与生态建设结合起来，这不仅符合城市发展的需要，也更符合老百姓的利益。他提出城市是人口的密集区，除了创造生态比较好的环境以外，还要创造比较优美的环境。

(作者：王建军，广东省佛山市南海区国土城建和水务局总规划师)

1998年以来我国保障性住房建设与政策研究

保障性住房是指一个国家或地区政府根据相关的国家政策以及法律制度的规定，为满足中低收入家庭的基本住房需求，限定建造标准、销售价格、租金标准，起社会保障作用的住房。保障性住房是社会保障体系的重要组成部分。中国现阶段的保障性住房主要是指经济适用住房和廉租住房。经济适用住房是政府提供优惠，限定建设标准、供应对象和销售价格，具有保障性质的政策性商品住房。廉租住房是城市政府向具有本市非农业常住户口的最低收入家庭提供的租金补贴，或者以低廉租金配租，具有社会保障性质的普通住宅。本文对我国1998年后新的公有住房制度改革、市场经济体制下的商品房和保障性住房发展以及有关政策演变进行梳理与反思。

一、我国保障性住房发展历程与政策演变

1998年，我国取消了新中国成立初期建立的住房福利制度，全面进入了住宅建设市场化和住宅消费商品化的时代。在过去的12年间，一方面，住房建设快速持续增长，城市居民居住条件有了很大改善；另一方面，住房私有化率的大幅提高固化了计划经济下福利住房制度的不公，同时对市场的过度依赖使很多问题凸现、矛盾激化。随着“福利性住房”退出我国城市福利体系，中低收入家庭的住房困难逐渐成为严重的社会问题，仅仅依靠市场这只“无形的手”显然不能解决中低收入家庭的住房问题。(表1)

表1　1998年以来我国保障性住房政策的演变

颁布日期	颁布部门	文件名称	政策内容
1998.7	国务院	关于进一步深化城镇住房制度改革加快住房建设的通知	对不同收入家庭实行不同的住房供应政策。最低收入家庭租赁由政府或单位提供的廉租住房;中低收入家庭购买经济适用住房;其他收入高的家庭购买、租赁市场价商品住房
1998.10	国务院	关于加强房地产价格调控加快住房建设的意见	切实解决目前存在的问题,扩大国内需求,促进住房建设成为国民经济发展的新的增长点,必须在改革住房供应体系、停止住房实物分配、发展住房金融服务的同时,加强和改善房地产价格调控,调整住房价格构成,保持价格合理稳定,促进住房建设的发展

续表 1

颁布日期	颁布部门	文件名称	政策内容
1999.4	建设部	已购公有住房和经济适用住房上市出售管理暂行办法	规定了上市补缴土地出让金和其他收益的操作程序
1999.7	建设部	已购公有住房和经济适用住房上市出售土地出让金和收益分配的若干规定	对已购经济适用房上市交易的条件、程序、必备文件、具体政策等做出了明确规定
2000.9	建设部	关于进一步规范经济适用住房建设和销售行为的通知	根据当地房价、中低收入家庭的支付能力,合理确定本地区经济适用住房在整个住房建设中的比重,更好地解决中低收入家庭的住房问题
2003.1	国家计委 建设部	经济适用住房价格管理办法	规范了经济适用住房价格管理,明确了经济适用住房价格实行政府指导价,规定了经济适用住房基准价格构成以及销售管理办法
2003.8	国务院	关于促进房地产市场持续健康发展的通知	加强经济适用住房的建设和管理。经济适用住房是具有保障性质的政策性商品住房。要通过土地划拨、减免行政事业性收费、政府承担小区外基础设施建设、控制开发贷款利率、落实税收优惠政策等措施,切实降低经济适用住房建设成本
2004.5	建设部 发改委等	经济适用住房管理办法	规定了经济适用住房的优惠政策、开发建设、价格的确定和公示、交易和售后管理、集资建房和合作建房、监督管理
2006.6 转折	国务院	关于调整住房供应结构稳定住房价格意见的通知	有步骤地解决低收入家庭的住房困难;加快城镇廉租住房制度建设;规范发展经济适用住房;积极发展住房二级市场和房屋租赁市场
2007.8	国务院	关于解决城市低收入家庭住房困难的若干意见	提出以城市低收入家庭为对象,改进和规范经济适用住房制度
2007.11	九部委	新的经济适用住房管理办法	调整购房对象及其他建筑规定,进一步改进和完善
2008.1	中国人民银行、银监会	经济适用住房开发贷款管理办法	修订完善
2009.5	国土资源部	关于切实落实保障性安居工程用地的通知	一、充分认识实施保障性安居工程的重大意义;二、加快保障性住房用地供应计划的落实;三、加强和规范保障性住房用地供应管理;四、加强用地的批后监管和监督检查
2009.10	七部委	关于利用住房公积金贷款支持保障性住房建设	为加快保障性住房建设,拓宽建设资金来源,提高住房公积金使用效率。"实现住房公积金与保障性住房接轨"
2009.12	国务院	促进房地产业健康发展"国四条"	第四条要求"继续大规模推进保障性安居工程建设。力争到 2012 年末,基本解决 1 540 万户低收入住房困难家庭的住房问题"。对于 1 000 万户国有工矿和林区、垦区的棚户区居民,要加大力度进行改造,计划用 5 年左右时间基本完成城市和国有工矿集中成片棚户区改造,有条件的地方争取用 3 年时间基本完成
2010.4	住房和城乡建设部	关于加强经济适用住房管理有关问题的通知	明确对违规出售、出租、闲置、出借经济适用住房,或者擅自改变住房用途且拒不整改的,按照有关规定或者合同约定收回,并取消其在 5 年内再次申请购买或租赁各类政策性、保障性住房的资格
2010.6	六部门	关于做好住房保障规划编制工作的通知	贯彻落实《国务院关于坚决遏制部分城市房价过快上涨的通知》(国发〔2010〕10 号)、《国务院办公厅关于促进房地产市场平稳健康发展的通知》(国办发〔2010〕4 号)精神,指导各地做好 2010—2012 年保障性住房建设规划和"十二五"住房保障规划编制工作。

到目前为止，我国保障房的发展大致可分为两个阶段：第一阶段为 1998 至 2005 年底，是保障性住房建设的起步期；第二阶段为 2006 年至今，是保障性住房建设的快速发展时期。

（一）住房体制改革的宏观背景

我国的房地产业大规模发展始于 1992 年。由于当时开发和销售的市场化价格与较低的职工工资收入分配体制不相匹配，商品房的购买者主要是实力雄厚的企业，集团购买成为房地产的主要消费方式[1]。1997 年亚洲金融危机爆发后，为了刺激内需、拉动经济增长，党的十五大报告中提出，把住房列为拉动内需的重要方面。在此背景下，1998 年国务院出台《关于进一步深化城镇住房制度改革加快住房建设的通知》（国发〔1998〕23 号）这一里程碑式的文件。文件以稳步推进住房商品化、社会化为指导思想，明确规定到当年底，停止住房实物分配，要求单位不再建房、不再买房、不再分房，结束了全国长达几十年的泛福利住房制度。2003 年，国务院再次发布《关于促进房地产市场持续健康发展的通知》，将房地产业定位为拉动国家经济发展的支柱产业，提出“完善住房供应政策，调整住房供应结构，逐步实现多数家庭购买或承租普通商品住房”，进一步加强了市场在住房发展的地位。这些措施直接刺激了房地产业发展，住房供给基本实现市场化，大规模的公有住房出售使我国住房私有化率跃世界较高的水平。有学者认为，至 2003 年，城市居民家庭住房私有化率超过 80%[2]。

（二）经济适用住房政策的演变

国家首次提出经济适用房是在 1991 年国务院发布的《关于继续积极稳妥地进行城镇住房制度改革的通知》。文件指出，大力发展经济适用的商品住宅，优先解决无房户和住房困难户的住房问题。当时单位福利房仍是城镇住房建设的主要形式，所以经济适用房的对象主要是针对城镇中难以从单位渠道解决住房的那部分居民，如大量的区属企事业单位，效益不好的市属单位企事业单位以及无业人员等。

1992 年，随着社会主义市场经济体制的逐步建立，商品房迅速发展，房价也随之成为社会关注的热点问题。为了适应这种新形势，1994 年，建设部、国务院住房制度改革领导小组、财政部印发《城镇经济适用住房建设管理办法》，这可以看做是与商品住宅发展政策相平行的政策考虑。虽然当时以经济适用住房为主的保障性住房建设开始提上日程，但由于中央和地方政府财政拮据，未出台实质性的措施，大量城镇居民仍然依赖福利分房，经济适用房发展缓慢。这种状况甚至延伸到 21 世纪初。据统计，截至 2005 年年底，仍有 13 个省（区）没有将廉租住房制度建设纳入省级人民政府对市（区）、县人民政府工作的目标责任制管理，70 个地级以上城市没有建立廉租住房制度，部分城市财政预算安排资金不足，没有建立稳定的廉租住房资金来源渠道[3]。

1998 年，在积极的财政政策推动下，我国开始实行住宅货币化制度，同年国务院在《关于进一步深化城镇住房制度改革加快住房建设的通知》中提出，对不同收入家庭实行不同的住房供应政策：最低收入家庭租赁由政府或单位提供的廉租住房；中低收入家庭购买经济适用住房；其他收入高的家庭购买、租赁市场价商品住房。

2004年，建设部、发改委等4部委印发了《经济适用住房管理办法》，规定了经济适用住房的优惠政策、开发建设、价格的确定和公示、交易和售后管理、集资建房和合作建房、监督管理。这些规定，明确了建立以普通商品住房为主的住房供应体系，完善了经济适用住房和廉租住房保障政策。

从国家宏观背景来看，自1998年房改到2004年的经济适用政策的日益完善，这一时期正是我国居民储蓄高速增长的时期，巨额的民居储蓄被认为是可能引起通货膨胀的巨大隐患。有学者指出，20世纪90年代至今，我国储蓄率大体维持在38%至40%左右，而同期的日本、韩国储蓄率则处于31%至32%左右[4]。所以，积极推动商品房和经济适用房被视为回笼货币、减少储蓄的重要经济手段（表2）。可见，住房发展的第一动力是与其相连的经济意义，而不是住房问题本身。

表2　城乡居民人民币储蓄存款1998—2004

单位:亿元

年份	年底余额			年增加额		
	总计	定期	活期	总计	定期	活期
1998	53 407.5	41 791.6	11 615.9	7 127.7	5 564.8	1 562.8
1999	59 621.8	44 955.1	14 666.7	6 214.4	3 163.5	3 050.8
2000	64 332.4	46 141.7	18 190.7	4 710.6	1 186.6	3 524
2001	73 762.4	51 434.9	22 327.5	9 430.1	5 293.2	4 136.9
2002	86 910.7	58 788.9	28 121.8	13 148.2	7 354.1	5 794.1
2003	103 617.7	68 498.7	35 119	16 707	9 709.7	6 997.3
2004	119 555.4	78 138.9	41 416.5	15 937.7	9 640.2	6 297.6

资料来源：根据1998至2004年各年《中国统计年鉴》整理。

从地方政府来看，自1992年推行土地有偿使用以来，很多城市的财政收入相当一部分来自房地产业的发展。从1998年到2004年这一段时间，地方政府对住宅商品化和房地产市场的发展格外重视。尤其是2002年实行土地招、拍、挂制度后，土地市场一路上涨（见图1），提高土地收益是城市政府增加财政收入、吸引投资、推动GDP快速增长的最重要手段（见表3）。

随之推动了房价的过快上涨。与此同时，由于经济适用房需要无偿划拨土地、并辅以一些减免政策，很多地方政府不愿多投入，致使经济适用房整体发展缓慢。据统计，2000年我国经济适用房销售面积为3 760万平方米，占普通住宅总面积（当年为16 570万平方米）的23%。到2009年，我国经济适用房销售面积为3 012万平方米，只占普通住宅总面积（85 294万平方米）的4%。1998—2009年，经济适用房投资额占住宅总投资额的比重从13%下降到了4.4%[5]。以北京为例，1998—2006年，经济适用房建设历年占新增房屋建设总量的 6.5% ~16.5% 之间，但总体呈逐年下降趋势。到 2007 年 2 月，经济适用房仅解决了 19 万户家庭住房的问题，与政府保障 45.7 万户中低收入家庭的目标相去甚远[①]。见图 2。

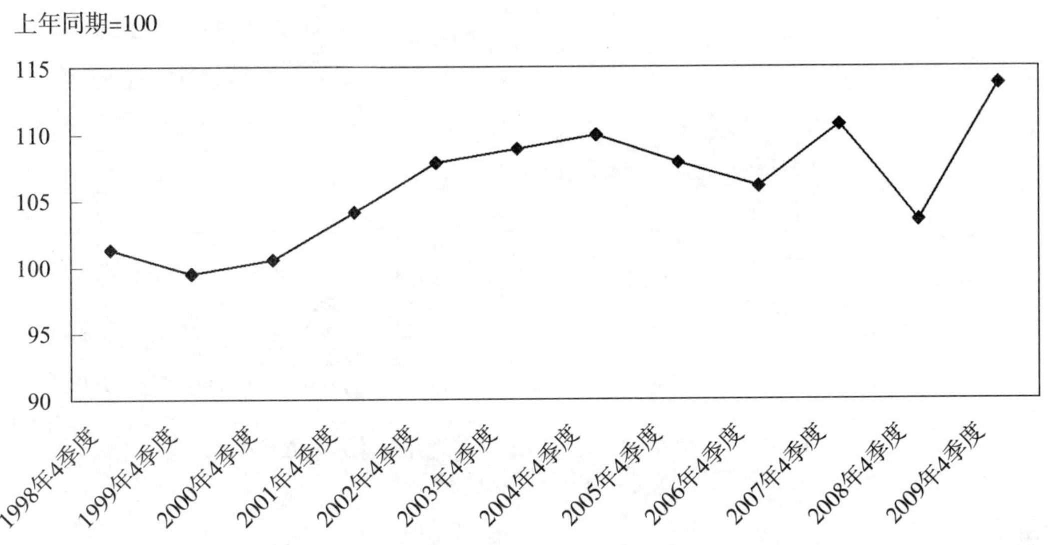

图 1　1998—2009 年全国土地交易价格指数变化情况

资料来源：中国房地产信息网．www. realestate. cei. gov. cn。

表 3　2008—2010 年地方土地出让收入情况

单位：亿元

年份	土地出让收入	土地出让占地方财政收入的比重(%)
2008	10 375. 28	36. 2
2009	13 964. 76	42. 9
2010	29 109. 94	71. 7

资料来源：根据 2009 至 2011 年各年《中国统计年鉴》整理。

即使开发了经济适用房，但由于希望快速回笼资金，地方政府在操作上往往以“好卖”为原则，对经济适用房的面积标准、受益人群等缺乏有效监管，导致经济适用房政策的社会效益大打折扣。按照政策初衷，只有收入较低、居住条件不佳的居民才可以申请购买经济适用房。但实际中，一些不符合条件的人却可以通过购买审批。以北京为例，据统计，到 2001 年初为止，在购买经济适用房的人群中，26% 为高收入家庭，2005 年经济适用房自住率为 51.34%[②]，经济适用房的保障功能极大地弱化（表 4）。

① 北京市规划委颁布的《北京市“十一五”保障性住房及“两限”商品房用地布局规划（2006—2010 年）》将保障对象范围定位为城镇户籍比例的 13.7%，约 45.7 万户。

② 资料来源：《2005 年二季度中国房地产市场报告》，由中国工商联住宅产业商会和中国城市房地产开发商策略联盟下属的 RE100 工作室于 2005 年 8 月发布。

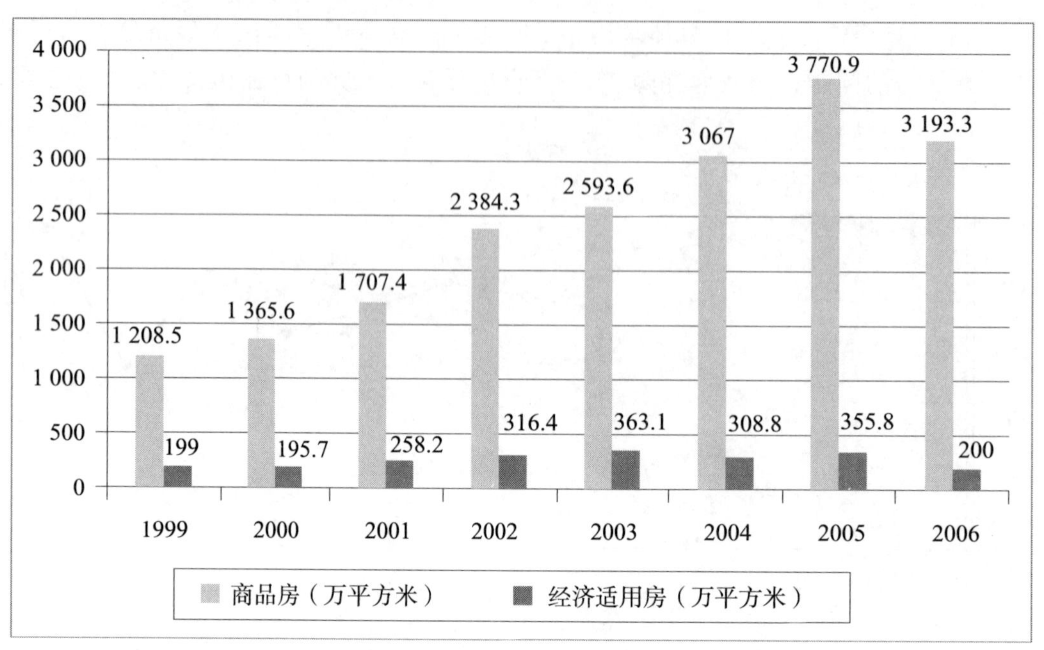

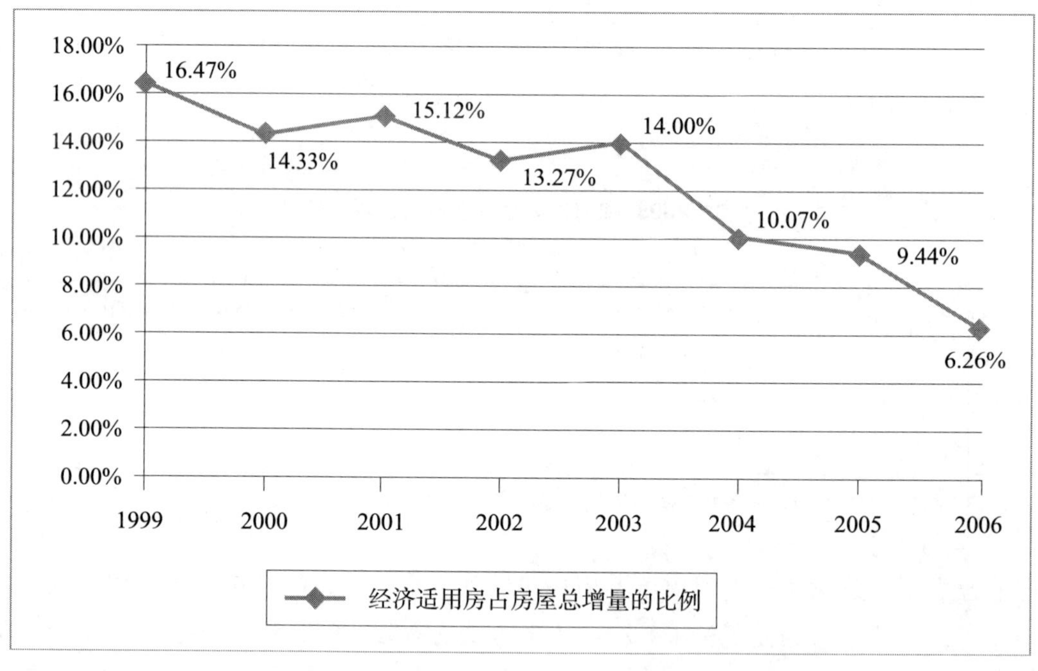

图 2

资料来源：《北京市统计年鉴 2007》，北京市统计局编。

此外“适用”名不符实，超大面积的户型不少见，甚至包括跃层（表 5）。这种情况从 2008 年才开始有所改变。

单套价格不断攀升，与中低收入家庭的支付能力脱节，致使许多符合标准收入上限的家庭也难以购买。在实际运作过程中，新建经济适用房自 2005 年起就不再面向普通申购者，仅定向供应拆迁户，从制度上排除了一部分中低收入住房困难群体。

表 4　1999—2009 年北京市经济适用住房价格与北京城镇居民收入统计

年份	平均售价（元）	户均面积（平方米）	套均价格（元）	北京城镇居民户均收入（元）	房价收入比
1999	2 664	91. 7	244 266	27 549	8. 87
2000	2 739	112. 8	308 697	31 050	9. 94
2001	2 975	111. 5	331 489	34 734	9. 54
2002	2 894	111. 5	322 415	37 392	8. 62
2003	2 847	116. 3	330 890	41 647	7. 94
2004	2 953	109. 2	322 415	46 913	6. 87
2005	3 560	105. 5	375 550. 8	52 959	7. 1
2006	3 606	108. 1	389 760	59 934	6. 5
2007	3 746. 6	107. 3	402 013. 8	61 569. 2	6. 53
2008	3 769. 1	80. 5	303 413. 7	69 230	4. 4
2009	3 800	76. 3	290 000	74 866. 4	3. 9

资料来源：根据 2000 至 2010 年各年《北京市统计年鉴》整理。

表 5　1999—2009 年北京市经济适用住房销售面积与套型统计

年份	销售面积（万平方米）	销售套数（套）	户均面积（平方米）
1999	45. 8	4 995	91. 7
2000	168. 2	14 924	112. 8
2001	185. 3	16 630	111. 5
2002	220. 7	19 810	111. 5
2003	320. 0	27 533	116. 3
2004	306. 3	28 054	109. 2
2005	304. 0	28 821	105. 5
2006	176. 3	16 311	108. 1
2007	100. 1	9 324	107. 3
2008	108. 3	13 461	80. 5
2009	82. 2	10 777	76. 3

资料来源：根据 2000 至 2010 年各年《北京市统计年鉴》整理。

再以福州为例，2007 年 5 月，福州市房管局推出 394 套经济适用房，单套建筑面积在 110 平方米至 180 平方米之间，总价在 30 万元至 40 万元的有 8 套；40 万元至 50 万元的有 105 套；50 万元至 60 万元的有 109 套；60 万元至 70 万元的有 83 套；70 万元至 80 万元的有 58 套；80 万元至 90 万元的有 27 套；90 万元以上的有 4 套。虽然每平方米单价较市场低，但是总价高导致真正需要购买低价房的低收入市民无能力购买①。

(三) 廉租住房政策的演变

如果说经济适用住房是我国在建设社会主义市场经济的同时，试图利用市场力量发展低造价住房的话，那么1998年7月，国务院在《关于进一步深化城镇住房制度改革加快住房建设的通知》中，正式提出的建立廉租房住房供应体系的构想，则是对市场经济中政府在解决社会住宅方面责任的硬性规定。紧接着，1999年国务院发布《城镇廉租住房管理办法》，提出以经济适用房、廉租房为主体的保障性住房体系。2003年，国务院在《关于促进房地产市场持续健康发展的通知》（国发〔2003〕18号文）中提出，“以财政预算资金为主，多渠道筹措资金，形成稳定规范的住房保障资金来源”，明确了廉租房建设的资金来源。2005年，国家又相继出台《城镇廉租住房租金管理办法》和《城镇最低收入家庭廉租住房申请、审核及退出管理办法》规定了城镇廉租住房管理办法，使我国廉租住房租金标准的确定有章可循。

虽然廉租房制度逐步得以完善，但地方财政对土地和房地产业的高度依赖，使廉租房与经济适用房一样，成了住房建设大家庭中的“灰姑娘”。

二、2006年至今，保障性住房建设快速发展期

(一) 住房体制改革的宏观背景

随着房地产业的大发展，造成住房供给对市场的过度依赖，引发诸如房价高涨、户型面积结构不合理、居住用地扩张过快、居住服务配套设施滞后等问题，这些问题在2004年后开始激化。特别是高房价导致大多数中低收入者买不起房，而保障性住房建设力度不够，满足不了他们的住房需求，产生了一些比较严重的社会问题。

为了有效调控和引导房地产市场健康发展，国务院于2005年发布两个“国八条”，2006年再发“国六条”，试图在改革发展中稳定房价，控制用地，优化住房供应结构，促进房地产业的健康发展。这两个文件中提出了建立多层次的城镇住房供应体系和住房保障制度的目标，确定了重点发展中低端住房的方针。2007年出台的新政策更是要求地方政府建立健全城市廉租住房制度，规范经济适用住房制度，强调完善“政策+市场”的双轨模式，以扭转过度市场化的住房发展趋向。可以说，2006年是我国保障性住房制度发展的转折年。

(二) 保障性住房政策的演变

针对房地产价格和投资增长过快，城市经济适用住房和廉租住房制度建设相对滞后，部分城市中低收入家庭住房还比较困难的现象，国务院加大力度强化保障性住房政策，把保障

① 资料来源：http：//baike. baidu. com/view/58124. htm.

性住房建设提到前所未有的高度。

2006 年，国务院在《关于调整住房供应结构稳定住房价格意见的通知》提出，加快城镇廉租住房制度建设；规范发展经济适用住房；积极发展住房二级市场和房屋租赁市场。2007 年，国家相继出台《新的经济适用住房管理办法》和《廉租住房保障办法》，首次将廉租住房保障资金纳入年度预算，规范廉租住房保障资金的管理，确保专款专用，并将廉租住房的保障对象由以往的城市最低收入住房困难家庭扩展到了城市低收入住房困难家庭。这些政策产生了一些积极效果。比如，2006—2007 年，我国经济适用住房完成投资额大幅度上升，分别为 696. 8 亿元、820. 9 亿元，远高于 2005 年的 519. 2 亿元[6]。

2008 年，为应对国际金融危机的影响，国家推出了“四万亿”计划，9 000 亿住房保障安居工程随之出炉，即 2009—2011 年，将增加 200 多万套的廉租住房、400 多万套的经济适用住房，另外还有 220 多万户林业、农垦、矿区的棚户区的改造，总投资达 9 000 亿元[7]。

2009 年 3 月，全国保障性安居工程工作会议提出，3 年内解决 750 万户城市低收入家庭，240 万户林区、垦区、煤矿等棚户区居民的住房困难[8]。随后，住房和城乡建设部、发改委、财政部等部门发布了《2009—2011 廉租房保障规划》，称用 3 年时间解决 747 万户城市困难家庭住房。2010 年 4 月，国务院出台的“新国十条”指出，要继续大规模推进保障性安居工程建设。“十一五”期间，中央累计安排保障性安居工程专项补助资金高达 1 336 亿元，我国保障房建设呈不断加速趋势，通过各类保障性住房建设，解决了 1 140 万户城镇低收入家庭和 360 万户中低收入家庭住房困难问题[9]。可以说，保障性住房建设已经进入了快车道。

2010 年 9 月 29 日，为防止房地产再次过热，住房和城乡建设部、国土资源部、监察部联合出台了《对各地进一步贯彻落实国务院坚决遏制部分城市房价过快上涨通知提出四项要求》，对楼市实施第二轮调控，指出“房价过高、上涨过快、供应紧张的城市，要在一定时间内限定居民家庭购房套数。住房和城乡建设部、监察部等部门将对省级人民政府稳定房价和住房保障工作进行考核与问责。对政策落实不到位、工作不得力的，要进行约谈，直至追究责任。”在此背景下，各地限购令纷纷出台。截至 2010 年底，北京、上海、天津、深圳、广州、厦门、杭州、宁波、南京、福州、三亚、海口、大连、兰州等 14 个城市已相继出台限购令。

与此同时，中央加大了保障性住房建设力度。据报道[10]，2010 年住房用地供应大幅增长，供地计划总体执行情况较好。30 个省区市（不含西藏和新疆生产建设兵团）住房供地计划 18. 47 万公顷，实际完成 12. 54 万公顷，比 2009 年住房供地增加 4. 9 万公顷，同比增长 64. 1%。其中，保障性住房用地 2. 47 万公顷，同比增加 124. 5%。与前几年的供地情况同口径相比，保障性住房、中小套型普通商品房和其他住房实际用地 10. 89 万公顷，同比增长 42. 5%。从计划完成情况看，全国住房供地计划实际完成 67. 9%。其中保障性住房用地完成计划的 65. 2%；棚改房用地 1. 47 万公顷，完成计划的 40. 2%；中小套型商品房用地 6. 51 万公顷，完成计划的 80. 9%；其他住房用地 2. 96 万公顷，完成计划的 68. 5%。主要热点城市住房用地供应计划落实情况普遍较好。上海、宁波、北京住房用地供应计划完成比例分别为 105.6%、103.4%、101.0%；南京、杭州、厦门完成比例分别为 94.5%、87.2%、85.2%。深圳和广州保障房用地完成比例分别为 228.0% 和 163.8%。北京、上海、杭州、宁波、南京、青岛、厦门、广州和深圳 9 城市保障性住房、棚户区改造住房和中小套型商品房实际用地占全年住房实际用地比重均达到或超过 70%。

三、当前我国保障性住房政策存在的问题及原因分析

（一）总体供给不足

在保障性制度实施过程中，地方政府缺乏无偿提供土地用于保障性住房建设的积极性。有的地方片面强调依靠市场手段解决住房问题，而对经济适用住房和廉租住房的保障作用不够重视，导致近年来全国保障性住房投资额占房地产开发总投资额的比重有所下降。根据 2009 年国家下达的保障性住房建设计划，全国共需投入 1 676 亿元，其中中央投入 493 亿元，占 29.4%；地方配套 1 183 亿元，占 70.6%。而 2009 年全国财政支出决算表显示，2009 年全国财政用于保障性住房支出为 725.97 亿元，为上年的 313.3%；其中中央财政投入 550.56 亿元，但地方财政仅投入 175.41 亿元，只占计划的 15%[11]。

（二）经济适用房购房者多，廉租房政策覆盖面小

目前经济适用房表现出了“不经济”现象。一是房价“不经济”，经济适用房价格超过了低收入家庭的购买能力，因此购买经济适用房的往往是城市中等收入甚至是高收入家庭。二是建设标准“不经济”，开发商以市场为导向，导致经济适用房面积过大，远远超出了中低收入家庭的合理需求。加之国家对经济适用房购房者身份审核不严密，于是出现了开着豪车购买经济适用房的现象。

廉租住房的分配对象主要是具有城市户口的双困难家庭户，即享受低保的同时，人均居住面积低于标准的家庭。实际情况是全国只有一少部分的家庭得到廉租住房，相当一大部分家庭尚未得到保障。

（三）经济适用房用地规划不合理，廉租房建设资金来源不稳定

由于经济适用房是免征土地出让金的，因此减少了地方财政收入，所以许多地方政府为了减轻损失，就把大多数的经济适用住房建设用地规划在地价便宜的城市郊区，影响了城市交通以及中低收入者的就业。另外，我国廉租房的资金来源主要有财政预算、公积金增值收益、土地出让金净收益、出租廉租房的收入、社会捐赠和其他来源。由于出租收入很少、捐赠和其他来源有限且不稳定，仅靠这些资金来源难以支撑廉租房的各项支出。根据审计署 2010 年 11 月公布的 19 省市 2007 年至 2009 年廉租住房保障情况审计调查报告，在审计调查的 32 个城市当中，有 22 个城市没有按时足额计提土地出让纯收益的 10% 给廉租房建设使用。2007 年到 2009 年，22 个城市共计少提土地出让纯收益 146.23 亿元。在审计署重点调

查的 32 个城市中，有 1.5 亿元廉租房保障资金被挪用，34 个项目套取补助资金6 129 万元[12]。

（四）监督机制不完善，法律法规制度不健全

由于国家对经济适用房申购者的资格审查制度具有较大缺陷，对违反规定的情况又缺乏明确的惩罚措施，致使经济适用房适用对象不清，受益人频发偏差。到目前为止，我国还没有一部专门法律来解决中低收入家庭的住房问题。

（五）对住房属性的认识不清晰

我国住房体制改革之路可以说是对住宅属性的重新认识之路。住房是一项具有复杂双重属性的物产，不但具有商品属性，同时具有福利属性。1998 年的住房体制改革之前，由于我国的计划经济体制等原因，住房体制属于泛福利性住房。可以说，当时的住房只具有单一的福利属性，而不具备商品属性。当我国经济体制从计划经济体制转变为市场经济体制之后，住房单一的福利属性就违背了市场经济的一般规律。

1998 年，我国取消了住房福利制度，进入了住宅建设市场化和住宅消费商品化的时代。从 1998 年至今，12 年的住房改革历程使得住房供给基本完全实现市场化。不能否认，这 12 年的改革之路中确实伴有保障性住房政策的颁布，但实施效果的确有限。保障性住房制度建立之初，建设经济适用住房的主要目标是推动住房制度改革，拉动经济增长，保障性住房政策制定和实施具有明显的趋利性特征。因此，一旦在实施过程中与经济效益发生冲突，就会出现变相的让步，从而导致经济适用住房成为福利保障与商品的混合体。这反映出我国住房政策在社会福利与经济利益取向上的模糊性。另外，由于地方政府难以从保障性住房建设中获得土地收益，所以缺乏大规模建设保障性住房的动力。所以，在住房改革的 12 年间，我国的住房分配体制被完全市场化。这又使得我国住房从 12 年前的单一福利属性转变为单一的商品属性，这同样违背了市场经济的一般规律。

在市场经济体制下，由于马太效应的存在，人们的收入逐步层次化、阶层化。这种阶层差异导致仅具有商品属性的住房无法有效满足所有人对住房的需求。这意味着，住房的完全市场化，或者说单靠市场不能妥善解决不同阶层人士的住房问题。

（六）住房改革遗留问题

1998 年的住房改革，停止了住房实物分配。在此后的 12 年间，当年未分配到住房的人员只能以高于数倍的市场价购买住房。改革的遗留问题经过 12 年的沉积，加剧了计划经济体制下福利住房制度的不公，引起了不容忽视的社会问题。

四、关于进一步完善保障性住房政策的建议

（一）增加保障性住房的土地供给，鼓励开发商以量取胜。要从国情国力出发，重点保

障群众的基本住房需求，主要是提供小户型、齐功能、质量可靠的住房。要扩宽廉租房的覆盖面，适当考虑外来务工人员的住房问题。

（二）在普通商品房小区应按一定比例配建经济适用房，避免城市“贫民窟”的出现，以便提升城市形象。在保障性住房建设中，要通过招投标等方式，选择技术力量强、社会信誉好的企业进行开发，严格执行项目建设程序和建设标准，使保障性住房不仅从数量上，而且从质量上与商品房同标准建设。

（三）扩展保障性住房建设资金来源渠道。要发挥保障性安居工程专用融资平台作用，吸引金融机构贷款，调动企业投入建设的积极性等，满足大规模建设保障性安居工程的资金需求。提高土地出让金用于保障性住房建设的比例、征收房产税等，健全保障性住房资金管理机制，确保专款专用。

（四）制定相应法律法规，用法律手段切实维护受保障人群的利益。要强化住房分配监督管理，实行保障房源、分配过程、分配结果“三公开”，接受社会监督。做好人口、住户、房屋、收入、就业等方面的基础工作，掌握基本情况，推进信息共享。对保障对象、保障标准、保障方式、保障资金来源、保障性住房管理机构、进入和退出机制、监督机制、出发机制等做出相应的规定，做到有法可依，有法必依。

（五）从政策层面出发，遵循住房的商品与福利的双重属性，对于中高收入阶层的人口限量提供商品住房，而对于中低收入阶层的人口政府提供更具针对性的保障性住房。

（六）1998 年住房改革后的住房体制在体现住房商品属性层面是成功的，1998 年之前的泛福利性住房体制在住房福利属性层面也有许多可取之处。政府应当融合我国在两种住房制度下所取得的经验，注重发挥市场机制的作用，使保障性安居工程既能如期完成建设任务，又能持续运转。在项目实施中，要调动各方面参与投资建设的积极性，增加资源供给，提高资源配置效率，让住房的双重属性实现有机的结合，更好地满足人们住房需求。

（作者：张杰，清华大学建筑学院，教授；张军，清华大学建筑学院，博士后；焦杨，清华大学建筑学院，博士生）

参考文献

[1] 陶美珍．扩大住房消费的对策探讨［J］．消费经济，2001（6）．

[2] Paul Jenkins，Harry Smith，Yaping Wang. Planning and Housing in the Rapidly Urbanizing World［M］. Routledge，2007：291.

[3] 资料来源：《建设部关于城镇廉租住房制度建设和实施情况的通报》，2006 年 3 月 29 日。

[4] 国研网宏观经济研究部．高居民储蓄率给我国经济发展带来哪些方面的影响［R/OL］．http：// wenda. tianya. cn/wenda/thread? tid = 55a6afab3187df4c.

[5] 时代周报．建一千万套保障性住房 地方政府动力不足［N/OL］．搜狐焦点网，［2010 - 12 - 17］．http://house. focus. cn/news/2010 - 12 - 16/1133642. html.

[6] 资料来源：《中国统计年鉴》。

［7］吴婷．4 万亿投资账单公布 民生和基础设施建设占大头［EB/OL］．中国新闻网，［2009 - 05 - 22］．

［8］周政华．高房价逼出 1000 万套保障房 1.3 万亿资金从何来［EB/OL］．中国新闻网，［2011 - 01 - 07］．

［9］亢舒．回眸“十一五”展望“十二五”保障性安居工程建设加快推进［N］．经济日报，2011 - 02 - 19．

［10］黄晓芳．2010 年保障性住房用地同比增加 124.5%［N］．经济日报，2011 - 01 - 30．

［11］刑少文．保障性住房落差［J］．财经，2011（3）．

［12］刑少文．保障性住房落差［J］．财经，2011（3）．

教育制度改革观察

——广州改革的尝试和实践

教育领域在“十一五”期间取得的成就引人注目的同时，其制度性制约亦已成为社会的共识。“十二五”规划期（2011—2015 年）被普遍认为是中国二次转型的开端期。社会各界众多有识之士对教育领域的关注不断升级，寄望于教育制度改革能达到“学有所教”。教育制度改革从 20 世纪 70 年代中期开始酝酿，到改革开放 30 多年的不断改进，到《国家中长期教育改革和发展规划纲要（2010—2020）》的出台，不可谓不成效显著。广州的教育事业也取得了长足的发展。随着城镇化进程的加速，广州作为沿海相对发达地区，成了众多农民工的首选。大量人口涌入城市，适龄儿童的教育问题、职业教育、终生教育问题也随之浮出水面。教育这一公共服务的公平性、公益性、广泛性和有效性，成为市民关注的焦点。改革是教育发展的动力所在。本文从教育制度改革的理论分析入手，简要介绍广州市在教育制度改革领域所作的尝试和实践，分析指出教育制度改革中存在的显著问题，并尝试提出建议。

一、教育制度改革的理论分析

教育制度的改革是适应当代社会经济发展的必然要求。讨论教育制度改革，绕不开的概念必然有“制度”和“教育制度”。

（一）教育制度改革的概念

舒尔茨把制度（institution）定义为：“一种行为规则，这些规则涉及社会、政治及经济行为”①。格雷夫将制度定义为“由规则、信念、规范和组织构成的系统”。② 诺斯认为，“制度是一个社会中的一些游戏规则；或者，更正式地说，制度是人类设计出来调节人类相互关系的一些约束条件”③。一般认为，制度是可以影响行为的系统的行为规则、约束条件

---

① 科斯·财产权利与制度变迁［M］．胡庄君，译．上海：上海三联书店，1991：253.

② 阿夫纳格雷夫．大裂变：中世纪贸易制度比较和西方的兴起［M］．郑江淮等，译．北京：中信出版社，2008：27.

③ 诺斯．制度、制度变迁与经济绩效［M］．刘守英，译．上海：上海三联书店，1994：3.

和组织。

康永久（2003）认为，教育制度就是用于支配人们教育行为的规则，是一种“游戏规则”，是人们相互影响的行动框架。[①] 他强调“规则”。还有学者认为，“所谓教育制度，是指旨在实现教育目的的社会公认的组织系统（人与物的系统配备）。教育制度由得到社会公认的依据法令组织成的法制性的教育制度（义务教育制度等）和出于社会生活需要而自然产生并固定下来的社会惯行的教育制度组成（预备学校和各种徒弟制）”[②]。这种说法的核心在于教育制度是组织系统，包括法制性和惯行性制度。因此我们可以下一个定义，教育制度是教育运作的组织和规则系统，规则系统包括正式规则（法令性或法制性的制度）和非正式规则（自然产生并固定的）。非正式规则包括习俗、习惯、道德、伦理和宗教规范、思想信仰等，一般不在教育制度改革的讨论范围内。

潘懋元（1995）认为教育体制是一组制度体系，他在著作中提到：“高等教育体制是根据国体形式和社会发展需要确定的一种以高等教育的领导管理制度为核心的制度体系，是由国家权力机关和领导机构制定的、相对稳定的高等教育体系结构模式。[③]”这是将体制等同于制度体系和结构模式（或组织形态）。因此我们可以说，教育体制是教育领域内的系统化的制度加上组织形态；教育制度是教育运作的组织和规则系统。从这个意义上来说，教育制度与教育体制是两个可共用的概念。如今出现在公众视野中的教育体制改革与教育制度改革两个词，并没有严格地区分开来。常见的现象是“体制改革和制度创新”相提并论。在《教育大辞典》中，顾明远将教育体制等同于教育管理体制来解释，认为教育体制是“国家组织和管理教育的形式、方法和制度的总称[④]”。事实上，在讨论教育体制或教育制度时，默认的讨论范围是教育管理体制，包括宏观的教育行政和微观的学校管理。

国际著名教育改革理论专家哈维洛克（R. G. Havelock）教授曾对“教育改革”作过如下定义：“教育改革就是教育现状所发生的任何有意义的转变”。教育改革是一个系统工程，应该包括各级各类教育[⑤]，从学前教育、初等教育、中等教育到高等教育，从普通教育到职业教育、终生教育、特殊教育等，都应该涵盖进来。

（二）教育制度改革的背景与趋势

1985年，《中共中央关于教育体制改革的决定》的颁布标志着我国教育体制改革的开始。基础教育逐步形成了以县、乡为主管理的格局，中小学实行校长负责制，高等学校试行校长负责制，办学自主权逐步扩大。

1993年，《中国教育改革和发展纲要》的颁布初步建立起与社会主义市场经济体制相适应的教育新体制。推进的教育体制改革主要包括：适应市场经济改革要求，建立政府对教育

① 康永久．教育制度的生成与变革仁［M］．北京：教育科学出版社，2003：99.

② 筑波大学教育学研究会．现代教育学基础［M］．钟启泉，译．上海：上海教育出版社，2003：176.

③ 潘懋元，王伟廉．高等教育学［M］．福州：福建教育出版社，1995：66.

④ 顾明远．教育大辞典（上）［M］．上海：上海教育出版社，1997：749.

⑤ 百度百科．教育改革［EB/OL］．（2011－10－24）［2011－12－07］．http：//baike. baidu. com/view/43819. htm.

事业宏观调控的管理体制，鼓励社会力量参与办学，形成多元化办学和投资体制，扩大高等学校的办学自主权，改变高等教育的部门办学体制，等等。①

1999年，《中共中央国务院关于深化教育改革全面推进素质教育的决定》，把体制改革、制度创新作为核心内容。

2010年，《国家中长期教育改革和发展规划纲要（2010—2020年)》颁布，将体制改革单列出来，提出人才培养体制改革、考试招生制度改革、建设现代学校制度、办学体制改革、管理体制改革等，强国先强教。

2010年，国务院办公厅印发了《关于开展国家教育体制改革试点的通知》（国办发〔2010〕48号)，从专项改革、重点领域综合改革和省级政府教育统筹综合改革三个层面，确定了改革试点的十大任务：建立健全体制机制，加快学前教育发展；推进义务教育均衡发展，多种途径解决择校问题；推进素质教育，切实减轻中小学生课业负担；改革职业教育办学模式，构建现代职业教育体系；改革人才培养模式，提高高等教育人才培养质量；改革高等教育管理方式，建设现代大学制度；适应经济社会发展需求，改革高等学校办学模式；改善民办教育发展环境，深化办学体制改革；健全教师管理制度，加强教师队伍建设；完善教育投入机制，提高教育保障水平。

可以看出，新中国成立后教育体制改革和制度创新中，教育领域正在变得越来越开放。教育领域的去行政化、逐渐脱离政府的具体管理，逐渐重视教育对人的发展的促进作用而非压制，都是显而易见的趋势。在一些不良现象的冲击下，比如贵族学校、转制学校、择校、教育资源和机会配置的不均衡等问题的出现以及部分学生因负担不起学费而辍学等，公平性（让教育公平促进社会的公平)、公益性（政府主导办教育)、广泛性（让更多的人能享受教育服务）和有效性（使教育资源得到最合理的配置)，成了社会近年来越来越明确的公众诉求。

二、广州市教育制度改革的尝试和实践

广州市是比较典型的相对发达地区，经济社会发展结构的变化、教育需求的变化必然要求与之适应的教育制度改革。社会在学前教育、义务教育、职业教育、公平教育等方面的需求和之相对应的对管理体制、办学体制、投入体制、政府职能、考试招生与就业等方面改革的需要，迫切需要教育领域在整体上不断变革。近年来，广州高度重视教育体制机制建设，积极引导体制机制改革的不断创新，促进教育的公平与发展，致力于将广州建设成为国家中心城市、区域文化教育中心和创新型城市。

（一）大力发展学前教育，切实保障和改善民生。印发了《广州市学前教育三年行动计划（2011—2013年)》，部署了未来三年内学前教育改革发展各项工作。2010年底，广州市有幼儿园1 532所，在园幼儿342 728人，在园幼儿总数位居全国中心城市第三。其中，非

① 范文曜，王烽．体制机制创新推进教育跨越发展［J］．复旦教育论坛，2008，6（6）．

本市户籍幼儿13.6万人，占在园幼儿总数的39.75%；民办园在园幼儿27.2万人，占在园幼儿总数的79.34%。入园率逐年提高，“十一五”期间，广州市学前三年（3~5岁）儿童毛入园率一直保持在98%以上。此行动计划要求到2013年，学前教育全面普及，资源加速优化，力争公办幼儿园占比达到30%以上，规范化幼儿园达75%以上，专任教师大专及以上学历的达60%以上，专任教师70%以上具备相应的从业资格。[①] 要求新建住宅小区的配套幼儿园要与小区同步规划、同步建设、同步交付使用。设立学前教育专项经费，对公办园、农村幼儿园、集体办园、普惠性民办幼儿园及学前教育教科研发展予以支持。建立学前教育资助制度，保障户籍家庭困难儿童、孤儿、残疾儿童及其他优抚对象接受普惠性学前教育。落实学前教育教师待遇，确保专任教师工资逐步提高到当地平均工资水平。[②]

（二）健全义务教育管理体制。一是明确政府对教育的职责，保障义务教育的经费投入。加大财政转移支付力度，健全各级政府分项目、按比例分担的义务教育经费保障机制。继续完善基础教育管理体制，落实义务教育以区、县级市管理为主的职责，健全教育经费保障机制，加大教育投入，落实教师待遇。加快推进中央、省属、市属国有企业办中小学移交地方政府管理的工作。二是完善农民工子女入学政策。健全制度，科学规划，更好地解决农民工子女的义务教育问题。三是认真贯彻执行《关于基本解决义务教育阶段“择校”问题实施方案》，促进教育公平。合理划分小学招生地段，公办初中招生不与学生评价挂钩（特长生除外），逐渐取消推荐生制度。严禁义务教育学校通过组织各种形式的考试、考核、测试选拔学生，严禁捐资助学与入学挂钩。均衡配置校内教育教学资源，实行常态编班，严禁以各种名义设重点班、实验班等，严格控制教学班额。签订关于基本解决义务教育“择校”问题责任状，建立义务教育“择校”问题专项督查制度，会同市纠风、监察、财政等部门，开展对各区、县级市义务教育“择校”情况专项督查。[③]

（三）改革民办教育管理体制，深化办学及投入体制改革。一是探索建立“政府宏观管理、学校自主办学、社会评估监督”民办教育管理机制，通过建立委托授权机制和政府购买服务制度，为民办教育协会承接政府事务性管理、专业服务创造条件。[④] 二是出台《广州市贫困家庭学生免费中等职业教育实施办法》（以下简称《办法》），完成广州市政府2011年“免收贫困家庭学生中等职业教育学费”的承诺。于2011年秋季学期开始实施。2004年至2010年广州市共投入1亿元，资助了7 500名贫困家庭学生免费接受职业教育，其中2010年广州市中等职业学校（含技工学校）共有3 603名广州市贫困家庭学生享受了此项惠民政策。《办法》施行后，测算2011年将有6 117名本市贫困学生享受免费中等职业教育，财政

① 参照《广州市学前教育三年行动计划》（2011—2013）.

② 万庆良. 大力发展学前教育促进幼儿健康成长［N］. 广州日报，2011-11-24.

③ 广州市人民政府办公厅. 二〇一〇年广州教育工作要点［EB/OL］.（2010-08-25）［2011-12-07］. http://www.yuexiu.gov.cn/yxxxw/xxgk/pop.jsp?catid=9290&id=99991.

④ 广州市人民政府办公厅. 二〇一〇年广州教育工作要点［EB/OL］.（2010-08-25）［2011-12-07］. http://www.yuexiu.gov.cn/yxxxw/xxgk/pop.jsp?catid=9290&id=99991.

共投入免学费资金 2 500 万元，与《办法》施行前相比享受免学费人数增加 1.7 倍。[①] 三是规范民办教育的财务管理。设立民办教育发展专项资金，制定实施《广州市民办教育专项资金管理办法》、《广州市民办学校财务监督管理办法》和《广州市民办学校财务审计技术规范》。启动专项资金的资助和奖励工作，改善民办学校的办学条件，进一步规范民办学校的财务管理。规范“名校办民校”行为，切实做到“独立法人、独立财务和人事管理、独立校园舍、独立教育教学和独立颁发学业证书”。健全民办学校年检制度，加大对无证办学的清理整治，规范民办学校的办学秩序。四是成立广州市民办教育研究中心，探索民办教育的行业协会自治的试点工作。各区、县级市全部要求建立民办教育协会，形成通过协会促进民办学校自主管理、自主约束、共同发展的工作网络，促进民办学校良性竞争。

（四）完善学校内部管理体制。一是建立现代学校制度，落实办学自主权。完善中小学校、中等职业学校校长负责制。完善党组织发挥政治核心作用，教代会进行民主管理和民主监督的体制机制，不断提升学校管理的科学化、民主化、规范化水平。探索建立自主管理、自我发展、自我约束、社会监督的科学运行和人文关怀相结合的现代学校制度。二是完善以岗位管理为核心的人员聘用制度，推进人事制度改革。按照国家、省、市有关人事制度改革的工作部署，稳步推进行政机构改革、事业单位机构改革及工资待遇改革等工作。建立与岗位职责、工作绩效相关的和向优秀人才、关键岗位倾斜的分配激励机制。强化编制管理，严把教师“入口”关，按核定的编制数及时足额配备教职员。会同有关职能部门积极稳妥解决代课教师问题，组织面向代课教师的招聘考试，将符合条件并经考试合格的代课教师聘用为公办教师，杜绝出现空编和代课教师并存的情况。[②]

（五）稳步推进招生考试制度改革。广州市坚持义务教育阶段学校免试就近入学，完善小学学校地段划分；完善初中对口直升和电脑派位入学制度，逐步取消初中生招收推荐生制度；完善初中毕业生综合素质评价和初中毕业生学业水平考试办法，继续完善普通高中招生考试评价制度；中等职业学校实行自主招生或注册入学。[③]

三、教育制度改革中存在的问题

（一）各级教育发展中存在的问题

学前教育“入园难”。政府对学前教育的投入不足，城乡发展不均衡。学前教育的保障机制、管理体制不尽完善。部分公建配套幼儿园未实现按小区规模足额同步规划、建设和交

① 广州市教育局．我市出台《广州市贫困家庭学生免费中等职业教育实施办法》［EB/OL］．（2011－09－30）［2011－12－07］．http：//www.gzedu.gov.cn/gov/GZ04/201109/t20110930_16400_105.htm.

② 广州市人民政府办公厅．二○○九年广州教育工作要点［EB/OL］．（2009－08－25）［2011－12－07］．http：//zwgk.gd.gov.cn/007482532/201103/t20110331_33049.html.

③ 广州市人民政府办公厅．二○○九年广州教育工作要点［EB/OL］．（2009－08－25）［2011－12－07］．http：//zwgk.gd.gov.cn/007482532/201103/t20110331_33049.html.

付使用，适龄幼儿好入园、入好园的矛盾日趋凸现。特殊儿童学前教育率有待进一步提高。部分公办幼儿园教职员编制尚未核定，民办幼儿教师社会保障尚未完全落实、收入水平不够高、素质不够高。①

初等教育“择校”。各个学校的设备条件和师资水平参差不齐，家长望子成龙望女成凤心切，希望将子女送入较好的学校，学校从不吝于“补充办学经费”，因此一个愿打一个愿挨，择校风潮越来越劲。“奥数班”、“培优班”应时而生。甚至在幼儿园，为了上一所好点的小学，会提前教授小学的课程。择校本质上是教育消费双轨制，拉大了义务教育阶段学校生源和经济收入的差距，引发学校不规范的办学行为，更违背了教育公平的原则，阻碍区域义务教育的均衡发展，破坏了正常的教育秩序，助长了教育腐败的蔓延。

中等教育片面追求升学率，学生负担过重。对应试教育的批判由来已久，全社会都在呼唤素质教育，但同时也都成为应试教育的奴隶。在考试依然是重要且唯一的机会的背景下，学生的负担恐怕无法减轻。虽然各级管理机构将素质教育作为一个监控的指标，但往往素质教育并没有一个显而易见的评价尺度和标准。对学校的整体评价，依然是将分数放在首位。

高等教育“现代大学制度”缺失。高等教育的任务是培养“高质量、高素质”的人，着重培养人的创新能力、实践能力和创业能力。现代大学制度一般有三个重要特征：大学自主、学术自由、学生自治。在事业单位行政化管理的背景下，大学无从选择自己的领导人，经费从行政机关拨发，“大学自主”只是一种提法，根本没有自主的基础。学术也远远没有达到欧美等国家的院校的自由氛围。大学生依然是在学校的管控之下，学校没有意识、学生也没有意识要“自治”。更常见的现象是，高等教育只是为学生提供了基础教育后的“疯狂”空间和时间，疯狂玩游戏，疯狂恋爱，疯狂踢球看球……等到临近毕业，学生们才发现几年时间下来什么也没剩下，除了面前的一纸文凭。但如今的一纸文凭已然只是一张纸，不能承载任何的保障和承诺。就业也成了一道绕不过去的坎。

（二）各类教育发展中存在的问题

职业教育在整个教育体系中属于最薄弱环节。义务教育和高等教育一直是改革的重点领域。相形之下职业教育虽然有政策和法规上的不断完善，投资渠道和办学主体也呈多样化，但实质上，在高等教育扩招的大背景下，尤其在近年来学生总数减少的前提下，职业教育的规模是逐年萎缩的。与之相对的是，劳动力市场却缺乏大量的技能人才。在传统观念中职业教育总是排在普通教育之后，人们往往不仅希望能通过受教育找到工作，更关心工作后在社会中的地位。社会上重普教轻职教、重学历轻技能的问题比较突出；职业教育的质量也差强人意。职业教育经费紧张，投入不足，相当多的学校办学条件简陋；师资严重不足，特别是缺少“双师型”的教师；中等职业教育和高等职业教育、普教和职教的沟通还有若干不畅通的地方；职业教育必须有企业参加，但是学校和企业的合作缺乏制度的保障，一些企业参与职业教育的积极性不高；职业教育现在还是多头管理，需要系统地整合，达到最优化管

① 参照《广州市学前教育三年行动计划》（2011—2013）.

理，这有待于进一步优化管理的体制、机制。[①]

建立终生教育体系的工作进展缓慢。主要原因在于人们的观念还没有完全转过来，还存在着学历文凭教育比较重要的想法。教育信息化虽然已经取得长足的发展，但依然没有普遍的受众。而且，终生教育体系的火车头——成人教育也在盲目地贩卖文凭，出售打折的高等教育。加上至今为止，没有建立起有利于终生教育发展的法规，社区教育的发展也极度缺乏。因此，总体上来说还谈不上终生教育体系的建成。

（三）教育系统与外部关系的问题

1. 政府与教育的关系

教育是重大的民生问题。在教育投入上，要强调政府的责任。在管理上，政府应该注重各级教育、各区域教育的均衡发展，促进和保障教育公平。但这并不意味着政府需要事事管控。目前政府可以决定学校的领导者、可以决定学校的经费来源等，但事实上这与现代的教育制度改革要求是不相适应的。学校应该成为办学的主体，而不是政府。政府该管的是宏观，微观的具象的管理应该下放到各个学校。政府和教育角色之间的互换将是一个长期的过程。

2. 学校与市场的关系

学校与市场有没有关系，这个问题在10年前也许不成为一个问题。10年前生源是政府分配的，出路也是政府根据需要固定的，学校的唯一作用就是教学。因此，学校不需要考虑是否能招到生，能招到什么样的生源，同时也不需要担心学生毕业之后能干什么，干得了什么。因此，学校就成了一个独立的可封闭的系统。但10年后的今天，教育面向未来面向现代化之后，经济社会的发展全球化与国际化，使中国的教育制度受到了严重的挑战。可预见的未来几年，学生数量的大规模减少，许多学校会面临招不到学生的局面。而大量的学生毕业后面临是否能学有所用，找到工作的问题。因此，是否市场化已经不是一个问题，而是学校被迫必须面对的挑战。但依然普遍存在的现象是，学校大多没有意识到他们必须市场化。

（四）教育系统内部的问题

1. 人事制度

教育领域一直属于事业单位，编制的问题引起很多人同工不同酬的感慨。代课教师和假聘任一直是教育系统人事制度绕不过去的坎。由于历史的原因，一些边远地区或师资极度缺乏地区选择了请人代课，也就是不给事业单位编制，同样承担教学任务，身份和薪酬待遇不同。近年因为教育的普遍发展，代课教师成了一个想要被取缔的名称。教育系统试行聘任制也不是一天两天的事情，但往往都流于形式。公立学校依然不会因为合同到期去辞退任何一个教师。因此，聘任都成了形式上的聘任，假聘任。即使试行之初，希望几年后学校内都变

① 王佐书．全国人大科教文卫委员会调研：职业教育存7大问题［EB/OL］．新华网，2009－04－22［2011－12－07］．http：//www.gxnews.com.cn/staticpages/20090422/newgx49eef2f8－2013274.shtml.

成聘任制，但大多最后的解决之道依然是编制内纳入现行体制。

2. 分配制度

分配制度在基础教育领域的问题主要表现在“大锅饭”，干多干少一个样，干得好与不好一个样，在高等教育领域的主要问题是分配不均衡，收入差距大。从个人来说，高等教育系统内，国家没有明确科研人员和高校教师究竟应该获得什么样的报酬，却默许灰色收入的存在。科研经费几乎是灰色收入的唯一来源。学术欺诈往往也由此引发。而分配制度应该有的“效率优先，兼顾公平”原则，按劳分配、优劳优酬，面对什么叫有效率什么叫无效率，什么是“优劳”的问题时，并没有一个客观的标准。因此只能以拿到课题与否、科研的结果或贡献来发放薪酬，在行政主导下配置科研资源。从各高校来说，现有教育资源的分配政策中，各种类型的重点课题、重点学科、重点实验室、重点基地、重点项目、直至高级职称比例、办学自主权限等额度和机会几乎无一例外地都倾向于重点的研究型大学，如 985 高校、211 高校等，由此又决定了经费投入、荣誉地位直至行政级别的不同待遇。

四、教育制度改革的对策建议

教育制度改革一直是广受社会关注的话题。尤其在义务教育和高等教育领域，牵涉广大家庭，也是政府需要考虑的重大民生问题。但政府在教育领域最主要的功能，除了保证投入的增长，就是促进教育的公平从而促进社会的公平。因此，在教育制度改革中，均衡和协调是关键之处。

（一）均衡发展各级教育

如上所言，学前教育和义务教育、基础教育和高等教育等领域都存在一个均衡发展的问题。

学前教育由于之前都没有作为一个门类纳入政府的保障体系，相对来说投入就比较薄弱。但随着企业、高校、政府机关等精简机构，幼儿园的经费来源就成了一个问题。学前教育同样也是关系千家万户的大事，政府还是应该合理地投入保障学前教育的发展。政府用于幼儿教育的财政性经费支出应该实行普惠制，区域内的全部适龄儿童、经评估合格取得办学许可证的各类幼儿园、各类幼儿园中具有任职资格的教师都享有得到政府财政保障机会的权利。由于民办幼儿园所占比例过大，因此政府在加大投入和监管的同时，要建立区域开放、公平竞争、优胜劣汰的幼儿教育市场调节机制，提供必要的扶持和指导，使之成为幼儿教育的主体。

义务教育的投入相对来说占所有教育领域投入的比例高，但地区差异、各校差异明显。应明确各级政府对义务教育的投入责任。地方政府不仅要做到预算单列，而且要确保“三个增长”。不仅要按照教职工的工资标准，学校的建设标准和学生人均公用经费标准拨付经费，而且要向农村学校、特殊学校和薄弱学校倾斜。在保证投入的前提下，坚决制止收取“择校费”，严格追查违规者的行政责任。提高农村学校公用经费标准，促进城乡教师流动。

制定并严格执行合理的工资标准，使同一地区的各个义务教育阶段学校之间教师收入水平更加公平、合理。

政府的投入是应该更倾向基础性教育，而高等教育可以让受益者本身承担一定比例的费用。高等教育的投入体制，可以逐步推进经费来源的多样化。首先保证政府是公立高校的主导投资者，其次可以通过吸引社会各界捐助办学，最后是可以大力发展高校自身优势创收，比如开展来华留学教育，产学研结合开设校办企业等。高等教育的管理体制，应该逐步实现政府宏观管理，管办分离；高校独立自主，面向市场争取发展。办学主体可以多元化，逐步放开教育市场，吸收社会力量办学。学校内部的管理，应该将人事权归还给学校，让教授治校，学生自治。加强对学生大学生活的规划和引导，提供高质量的课程，培养高素质的具有实践能力和创业能力的人才。

（二）协调发展各类教育

构建一个开放、灵活的职业教育体系。从政府层面来说，应该放松对职业教育的管制，改变多头管理的格局。放松管制包括降低门槛，使其能够从需求入手，因地制宜，灵活发展。改变多头管理应明确劳动保障部门不再直接管理技工学校，由教育部门统筹管理各类职业学校，明确以市为主统筹高职，以县为主统筹中职。从职业教育自身来说，与普通教育相比，大众的观念还是停留在普通教育好过职业教育的层面上。这要求一方面要加强对社会舆论的引导，使得人们意识到职业教育的空间和发展，满足劳动力市场对技能型人才的需求。另一方面也给我们提示要加强职业教育的质量管理，保证职业教育培养出来的人在劳动力市场的适应性。这必然要求进一步加强校企合作，甚至让行业来主办职业教育，培养自己需要的人才；要求大力加强“双师型”师资力量，使学生能学有所用。

终生教育目前最主要的在于教育大众，引导改变人们的观念，以终生教育观代替学校教育观。终生教育在实践方面的成熟程度尚不及理论，现行教育主要还局限于学校，还不能很好地走上社会，更没有把社会办成一所大学校，多数青少年学校毕业后，继续受教育的机会还不是很多，特别是文化程度低的人学习机会更少，虽说成人教育势头较好，也大多局限于学历教育和专业证书教育，真正的岗位培训很少。因此改革最主要的方向在于，一方面着眼于人一生的发展与成长，另一方面引导舆论重视发展学习型社会。

（三）协调教育制度与其他社会制度之间的关系

协调教育制度与其他社会制度之间的关系主要包括三个方面：一是要正确处理学校和政府的关系。要确保学校自主办学的法律地位、权力和责任；要制定学校法，从整体上界定学校的法律地位，把政府和学校的关系建立在法律基础上。二是解决好学校和社会的关系，加强学校和社会的双向参与。学校要积极参与社区建设，成为学习型社区的中心机构；同时，学校要吸收社会、社区人士参与学校管理，如建立社区委员会、家长委员会等。[①] 三是要解

① 谈松华．制度创新：深化教育体制改革的重点［J］．中国教育学刊，2009（6）．

决好教育与市场的关系。从总体来看，教育制度改革会越来越开放，越来越需要脱离政府的附属机构地位自行治理，因此，首要解决的就是财源问题和效率问题。要练好内功，直面市场的冲击，吸引最好的生源和师资，提供有保障的教育质量。

总体而言，教育制度改革的理论已先于实践，要关注教育各个领域尤其学前教育、义务教育、高等教育、职业教育等的制度改革，更要关注各级各类教育改革的具体操作和实践，以及对制度改革的监控。

（作者：谢少华，华南师范大学教育科学学院教授、现代教育研究与开发中心兼职教授；王永秀，华南师范大学教育科学学院教育领导科学专业博士研究生）

老龄化背景下的城市化策略应对研究[①]

——以江苏省为例

中国已成为世界上老年人口最多的国家。根据第六次全国人口普查（以下简称六普），我国60岁及以上人口比例占13.26%，其中65岁及以上人口比例占8.87%，中国已经全面迈入了老龄社会。关注新型城市化背景下的老龄化问题是促进社会和谐和推进“以人为本”的新型城市化的重要体现。中国自1999年以来开始进入老龄化社会，社会学、地理学、经济学等多学科都已经高度关注这一问题，城市规划学者也从老年住宅、老年活动场所等微观领域研究养老问题。实际上，老龄化问题已经渗透到城乡规划的各个层面，需要我们从整体上树立建设老年友好型城市的理念，将老龄化问题作为当前重要的城市问题，从一个原先“托底型”的社会保障问题延展成一个全社会的问题来思考，将规划建设关注点从“养老服务”向“为老服务”转换，研究应对老龄化的城市化策略。

一、江苏省城市化面临的老龄化挑战

2009年，江苏省65岁及以上老年人口达929.3万人，老龄化水平为12.0%，是全国老龄化最严重的省份之一。其主要特征有老年人口基数大、增速快。在2000—2009年间江苏省老年人口年均增长率高达4.0%，远高出全国的平均增长水平。作为经济先发地区的江苏省有着研究老龄化问题的迫切需要。

江苏省城市化的发展面临着老龄化的严峻挑战。一方面城市化进程中面临着质量提升的问题，我国现行国家政策提倡是以居家养老为基础、社区养老为依托、机构养老为补充的养老方式，依据预测，老年赡养比将从1964年的6%、1994年的10%快速上升到2020年的20%、2030年的30%左右，依靠现有的城市公共设施难以实现养老目标。另一方面在人口老龄化的成熟阶段和稳定阶段，劳动力资源将出现下降的趋势，农村剩余劳动力向城市转移的增速将下降，城乡统筹过程中如何更好地考虑“留守”老人的权益也将更加受到关注。

① 江苏省建设系统科技计划项目，项目编号：JS2010JH03

（一）老年人口分布的空间特征

江苏省老年人口数量存在城乡分布不均衡状况。2009 年，江苏省城、镇、村老年人口分布比重分别为29.2%、20.2%、50.6%，农村地区老年人口占全省老年人口总数的一半以上，成为江苏老年人口的主要承载地。

从省内三大区域老年人口分布情况来看，苏北地区绝对数量最高，苏中老龄化水平最高，苏南则介于苏北和苏中之间。从老年人口的城乡分布来看，城市老年人口分布与城市经济水平密切相关。城市老年人口分布比例由苏南、苏中、苏北依次递减，其中南京、苏州、无锡城市老年人口比重最高，分别占全省城市老年人口总量的19.9%、13.9%和11.3%。镇老年人口分布则以南通为集聚中心向沿海轴扩散。乡村老年人口主要分布在沿海地区和以徐州为代表的苏北腹地。其中盐城和徐州乡村老年人口占全省比重为12.9%和15.1%，表明苏北农村地区“空心化”和“空巢现象”形势严峻。

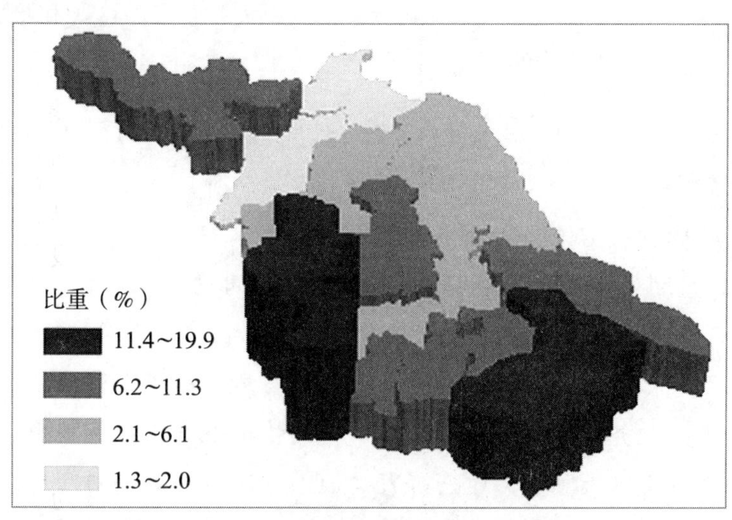

图1　江苏省城市老年人口分布比例

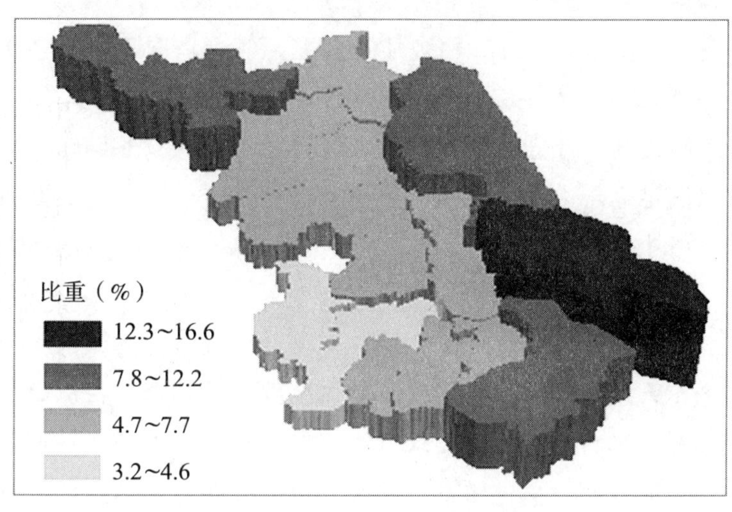

图2　江苏省镇老年人口分布比例

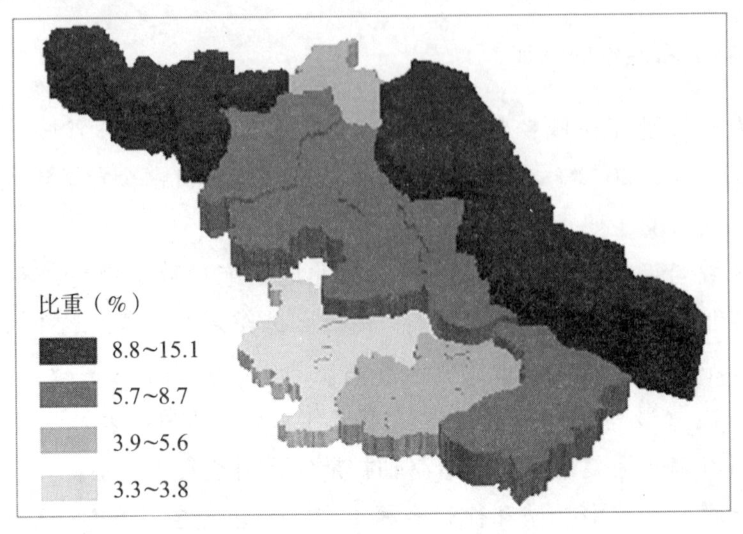

图3　江苏省乡村地区老年人口分布比例

（二）城市“为老”服务设施的不足

根据《江苏省老年人口信息和老龄事业发展状况报告（2009）》统计，截至2009年末，全省共有老年福利院、敬老院、老年公寓、护理院2 053所；社区居家养老服务中心（站）2 000个，其中城镇1 050所，农村950所；老年活动中心（室）15 852个；老年学校3 687所，其中市级13所、县（市区）108所、乡镇3 560所。从江苏全省来看，2009年末60岁及以上老年人口达1 258. 81万人，全省机构养老床位达25万张，占老年人总数接近2%。而从各地的问卷调查来看，有7%的老年人有入住养老机构的愿望，养老服务需求与供给矛盾突出。

设施布局不合理，服务范围有限。随着城市化的快速发展，江苏各市区域城市化不平衡现象日渐显现，中心城市规模和能力迅速提升，但外围区域发展相对滞后，经济和人口空间分布呈现出明显的圈层式“中心—边缘”结构，老年服务设施也呈现出区域不平衡的现象。

设施类型单一，结构性供给矛盾。目前养老公共服务设施主要以民政部门救助对象为主，养老院、老年公寓等多数为民办，服务质量参差不齐。在医疗服务方面，课题组调查访谈发现，老年医院保健机构缺乏，综合医院普遍存在老年人集聚的现象。随着经济社会发展，人民生活水平不断提高，社会各层次老年人群对老年公共服务设施需求呈现多样化，当前老年服务设施难以满足老年人生活照料、护理、康复、文化娱乐等多方面和多层次的服务需求。

（三）城市“宜老”空间环境的缺失

在社区层面，老年人生理机能的衰退以及宅域范围活动频繁等特点，都决定了与老年人相关的公共服务设施有着其特殊的布局要求，必须考虑到老年人使用的便利性，尤其是与老年人日常生活紧密相关的商业、文化体育公共服务设施。课题组通过调查发现，老年人普遍认为市场、便利店和文化体育设施的距离应该在5分钟之内，即服务半径300米之内，但多数老人对于相应设施的布局感到不满意，认为不能满足日常使用的需要。

现有的养老设施建设关注点也仅仅集中在“福利托底型”的养老设施建设，而从空间上创造一个老年人舒适的城乡环境，是当前城乡规划的缺失。如绿地公园等用地布局上考虑老年人群就近休闲要求、在交通设施建设上未考虑老年人群对公共交通的较大依赖性和无障碍交通工具的要求，在医疗设施布局上应结合患有慢性病与长期卧床老年人群的需求考虑社区级医疗设施和养护院的配置等。

二、发达国家养老模式和养老服务体系借鉴

（一）北美模式：以市场化运营为核心的多元化养老

美国的养老服务体系以覆盖面广、养老模式多样化而著称。根据美国社会保障署的资料，全美96%的在职人员参加了社保体系。在职人员通过在职期间缴纳“社会保障税”以获得退休后的由政府担保提供的相应社保福利（获得多少视其工作时间长短、缴纳社保税额度及退休年龄而定）。社保体系起到提供最基本生活保障的作用，在此基础上美国还通过由社会和个人共同承担等多样化养老供给措施，来提高老龄人群的养老服务水平。美国营利性的私立服务机构占到66%，非营利机构私立养老服务机构27%，政府举办的服务机构仅为7%，社会在养老服务中起着主导作用。

美国的养老服务设施大致可以分为公寓型服务、日间照料型服务、护理康复型服务、社区居家养老型服务。从1970年代美国开始大量兴建各类老年居住建筑和独立老年社区等养老设施，一些社区中还包括各种专门为老年人服务的配套设施，形成老年产业基地。这些设施的建立扩大了老人自主选择养老居住方式的范围。如美国太阳城是运作比较成功的社区养老的典型案例，于1960年开始建设，经过20年的发展基本建成，占地37.8平方公里并拥有1 200亩的高尔夫球场。它明文规定：所有居民必须55岁以上，这个年龄以下的，即便是亲属子女也没有居住权。

（二）欧洲模式：以社会福利制度为核心的独立居家养老

除了瑞典、芬兰等高福利国家完全依靠政府和社会来提供养老之外，欧洲其他国家大都借鉴他们，建立起了以社会福利制度为核心的独立生活居家养老体系。以英国为例，英国的养老服务体系是由国家级的退休年金制度、国家卫生服务体系和地方政府对照料资源的配置，以及整合后的社区医疗、护理、照料机构构成。该体系以老年人为中心，以老年人的实际照料需求为出发点，在科学评估的基础上，结合老年人的经济承受能力，提出合理的照料方案。对于经济困难的国民，政府提供补贴乃至全部免费的照料服务。该系统兼顾公平与效率，以公平为主，以老年人为中心，以人性化服务为主。

英国老年人的养老服务主要分住家照料和非住家照料。其中住家照料比较受欢迎，大约有80%的老年人在家中得到照料。尽管住家照料不是唯一的选择，但是英国政府还是鼓励

老年人尽可能住家养老。政府通过在各社区建立不同的老年照料组织，他们向老年人提供住家照料、日间照料、单一的住院生活照料和住院护理照料，以及临时服务如送餐、户内和户外活动等。各照料机构和人员要按需向老年人提供医疗、护理、照料、康复、家政服务。所有服务都要得到老年人（或家人）许可，并经老年人的自主选择。同时，英国还有形式多样的慈善组织、社工组织、志愿者组织向老年人提供照料服务。老年人在社区得到的服务有免费、优惠价、市场价服务。对于经济特别困难的老年人来说大多数是由政府购买向其提供服务。

（三）新、日模式：以社会福利政策为支持的多代共居居家养老

新加坡实行以强制储蓄模式为特色的社保制度以利于老年人的社会保障，并开发多代同居或亲子近邻居住的多代同堂组屋。新加坡建屋发展局从1978年起，开始实行联合抽签配屋政策，优先考虑多代人联合申请，方便已婚子女与年老父母为邻来实现居家家庭养老。

日本实行以多重养老保障的居家养老体系，全面覆盖所有国民。“国民年金”规定20至60岁的国民强制加入，“厚生年金”则以企业职工为主体也具有一定强制性。同时日本还有养老保险，但申请前提是必须加入前两种社保。同时，日本以宅养老为重点，开发供几代人居住的住房；加强社区服务；鼓励亲子家庭互助网络的形成；政府在经济上予以资助；此外长寿型住宅（预留年老后所需要的如增加扶手、增加门或过道的宽度以便于轮椅通过等潜伏性设计）也很普及。日本居家养老的比例达96%。

从以上其他国家的养老经验所见，这些先发国家的养老服务主要选择了与国民养老意愿和国家发展能力相符合的养老模式，并通过一系列养老设施体系建设来保障设施的可达和服务的可享。我国的养老服务体系的建设，应该在尊重东方传统文化的基础上，选择适合我国当前经济水平、发展阶段的养老模式，再建设与之相匹配的养老服务设施体系，促进实现以养老设施提供养老服务。参考欧洲和日本等老龄化国家的经验，我国应对老龄化的关注点要从基本老年保障问题延展为全社会问题，养老服务设施建设的理念应该由“养老服务”转向“为老服务”，应该大力支持“在宅养老”（包括社区养老和居家养老）。

三、应对老龄化的城市化策略思考

（一）明确老年友好型城市指标体系，促进和谐城市化

根据人口老龄化发展趋势，结合小康社会、基本现代化的发展目标，参考国外发达国家的养老服务体系经验和中国老年学学会编写的老年人宜居城市指标体系，本课题提出了建设老年友好型城市的指标体系，包括经济社会发展、城市基本为老与基本养老服务。其中，经济社会发展是指城镇居民收入和支出情况，包括养老支出占比和反映城乡居民消费能力和收入差距的相关指标；基本为老服务包括城镇设施建设和城市空气、绿地等反映城镇公共活动环境的指标；基本养老服务是指为老年人提高配套服务的基本公共服务设施和养老保障情

况，包括每千名老年人拥有医疗卫生技术人员数、每千名老年人占有养老床位数等能反映老年人使用城市公共服务设施、交通设施和享受养老服务的指标。

表1　老年友好型城市指标体系

评估目标	序号	分类指标	单位	推荐值
经济社会发展	1	养老支出占社会保障财政支出比重	%	30
	2	基尼系数	—	0.28
	3	恩格尔系数	%	30
基本为老服务	4	人均住房建筑面积	平方米	30
	5	人均期望寿命	岁	80
	6	城市安全指数	%	100
	7	城市道路无障碍设施达标率	%	90
	8	公共交通站点300米半径覆盖率	%	90
	9	公共交通出行比例	%	30
	10	建成区绿地率	%	15
	11	人均公共绿地面积	平方米	10
	12	环境空气质量优良率	%	70
基本养老服务	13	每千名老人拥有医疗卫生技术人员数	人/千人	20
	14	每千名老人占有养老床位数	张/千人	50
	15	居家养老服务体系城乡覆盖率	%	80
	16	老年大学(校)的入学率	%	3
	17	老人免费乘公交年龄	岁	60
	18	城乡基本医疗养老保险覆盖率	%	100
	19	城镇社区养老综合服务达标率	%	90

注：1. 养老支出占社会保障财政支出比重：包括社会养老保险、社会养老救助、社会福利养老和社会养老优抚。主要目的在于确保老年人的基本生活权益。目前日本老龄化率接近20%，其养老支出占日本社会保障财政支出比例在50%以上。

2. 环境空气质量优良率：指空气污染指数API小于100的天数占全年总天数的百分比，即空气质量指数优或良的天数占全年总天数的百分比。标准值为70%～80%。

3. 城市安全指数：城市安全指数包括城市人口安全、城市政治安全、城市经济安全、城市文化安全、城市生态安全、城市交通安全、城市景观安全、城市信息安全、城市安全应急系统、城市安全评价与规划。

4. 每千名老人占有养老床位数：指每一千名老人拥有的养老床位数。其中养老床位数指的是城市各类老年养老机构拥有的养老床位总和。

5. 居家养老服务体系城乡覆盖率：指"以家庭为核心、以社区（村）为依托、以专业化服务组织为载体"的养老服务体系。既包括以老年日间照料服务中心、托老所、老年居家养老服务站等为代表的各种居家养老服务设施（针对特殊老年群体开办的敬老院、福利院不能包含在内）；也包括社区上门护理服务、社区提供家政服务、社区为老服务等各种居家养老服务。

6. 老年大学（校）的入学率：老年人参加老年学校的人数占申报城市老年人总人口百分比。一般发达市（县级）标准值为3%～5%；非发达市（县级）标准值为3%。

7. 城乡基本医疗养老保险覆盖率：已参加城乡基本医疗养老保险的人数占城乡居民总人口百分比。

8. 城镇社区养老综合服务达标率：指社区内自理老人、介助老人、介护老人及其家人对社区养老设施建设和配套水平、生活照料服务人员与社区医疗卫生技术人员的服务满意程度。考虑到设施配置标准应与社会经济发展水平差异、老年人群需求多样性差异，达标率较难达到100%，宜以大于90%为标准。

以先发地区和老龄化严重的江苏省为例，可以依据老年友好型城市指标体系，积极推进全省老年友好城市评比，促进政府关注民生幸福工程。

（二）落实老年友好型城乡规划理念，提升城市化质量

老年友好型城乡规划应引导城乡建设由“养老服务”向“为老服务”转变，统筹考虑为老年人打造基本养老服务设施和有尊严生活的城乡空间环境。规划建设首先应以“为老服务”为核心，改变传统的面向三无五保老人的“政府托底型”养老院建设，重点加强面向老人的普惠型设施建设，实施以医疗服务设施、文化娱乐设施、教育设施等为重点的城乡为老服务体系建设，推进以居家养老为基础，社区服务为依托，机构养老为支撑的养老模式；其次规划应注重老年公共服务设施的无障碍设计、老年交通设施与公共活动空间等居民共享型设施的通用设计，侧重居住和休闲消费空间的邻近，塑造老年人享受高品质生活需要的整体城乡空间环境。

以江苏省为例，可以率先将老年友好型要求落实到法定规划编制审查中，促进老年友好型规划理念落实到城市空间。城乡规划编制过程中，应把为老年人群创造宜居环境作为重要规划目标之一，落实“老有所养、老有所医、老有所为、老有所学、老有所乐”等五个老有目标。老年友好型规划要求要贯穿区域城镇体系规划、城市（镇）总体规划、详细规划和村庄规划城乡规划编制的全过程，注重老龄化趋势对城乡发展中人口结构、城市化发展、产业结构、交通模式、居住模式、公共设施、公共空间等带来的影响，关注宜老社区、机构养老设施、老年公共服务设施、老年交通设施和老年公共活动空间等五类设施规划建设，这既包括了机构养老设施和老年公共服务设施等老年人群单独使用的专享型设施，又涉及了宜老社区、交通设施与公共活动空间等共享型设施，规划在关注养老、为老服务设施服务公平的同时也要注重资金效益和服务效率。

（三）加快城乡养老设施建设，推进城乡统筹发展

社会养老服务体系是政府当前应对老龄化的抓手工程，而与城市化紧密相关的是养老设施建设问题。城市要统筹老城更新和新区建设，差别化建设养老服务设施。借鉴欧洲的多层住宅加电梯改造经验，逐步对老城区内现有多层住宅加电梯以方便老年人出行交通；借鉴新加坡“三合一家庭中心”建设，将“托老所”和“托儿所”有机结合起来，通过增设托老所、社区老人活动中心等为老服务设施和社区公共绿地、广场等老年人活动场地，打造老年人健康生活圈。在城镇新区或新建居住社区的规划建设过程中，一方面按照公建配套要求规划、布局和建设养老设施，解决资金问题和增强服务便利性；另一方面通过合理的老年住宅建筑布局、老年住宅户型设计、住宅电梯化设施配套等来满足老年人居住需要。在当前城乡统筹发展的阶段，应加强乡村地区的养老设施体系建设，充分考虑农村留守老人的权益。日本在经过30多年的探索之后，仍然在2002年确立了“尽最大可能在自己家里生活”作为老年人居住政策的目标。从我国的城市化特点来看，一方面半城市化人口存在着返乡养老问题，另一方面乡村也成为留守老人的聚居地。

对江苏省而言，城乡规划应落实近期（2015年）全省社区居家养老服务中心（站）覆盖城市所有社区和80%以上农村社区（村）的设施建设目标，推进乡村地区的机构养老设施建设，缓解现状养老设施严重不足的状况。一方面应分类型供给养老设施，满足自理老人、介助老人、介护老人等多种健康状况的老年人养老需要，重点推进各级养老型居住社区养老服务设施建设，满足自理老人生活需要；重点推进社区日间照料中心建设，满足介助老人居家养老需要；积极建设全护理型养护院等养老服务设施建设，满足介护老人需要。按照介助老人人均社区日间照料中心建筑面积0.3平方米和介护老人每千人养护院床位数20张标准进行建设，推行每个居住社区至少建设一个社区日间照料中心，促进就近居家养老模式的推行。另一方面分级别配套养老设施，建立（县）市级、社区（镇）级、基层社区（农村社区）级的医疗服务设施、文化娱乐设施、教育设施等城乡养老设施级配体系。加快（县）市级和社区（镇）级福利型养老服务机构建设，满足老人的集中养老服务需要；重点加强基层社区级日间照料中心、托老所等养老服务设施建设，满足城乡居民就近养老服务需要。重点推进乡村养老设施建设，以城镇地区养老院、养护院和大型养老设施，满足县（市）域基本养老服务需求；以中心城镇为据点建设养老院等社区（镇）级养老设施，满足周边乡镇养老服务配置；以规划保留农村居住社区为中心，配建日间照料中心等社区级养老服务设施。

（作者：陈小卉，江苏省城市规划设计研究院，副总规划师，教授级城市规划师；杨红平，江苏省城市规划设计研究院，城市规划师）

参考文献

[1] 柴彦威．中国城市老年人的活动空间［M］．北京：科学出版社，2010.

[2] 陈慧．现代老年人居住空间行为需求研究［D］．天津：天津大学，2005.

[3] 冯燕，林晨，高莺．老龄化社会与城市规划：从加强城市社区老年设施建设谈起［J］．北京规划建设，1999（1）．

[4] 郭堃．老龄化社会的交通安全问题研究［D］．西安：长安大学，2006.

[5] 何鹏．试析我国养老模式在居住社区规划中的发展趋势［D］．北京：清华大学，2002.

[6] 黄少宽．广州市社区老人服务需求及现状的调查与思考［J］．南方人口，2005（1）．

[7] 江苏省基本养老服务体系建设“十二五”规划纲要（2011—2015年）．

[8] 老年人宜居城市指标体系［R］．北京：中国老年学学会，2010.

[9] 老年友好型城乡规划研究［R］．南京：江苏省城市规划设计研究院，2011.

[10] 韦亚平．人口转变与健康城市化：中国城市空间发展模式的重大选择［J］．城市规划，2006（5）．

[11] 中国发展研究基金会．中国发展报告2010：促进人的发展的中国新型城市化战略［M］．北京：人民出版社，2010.

国内外生态城镇发展以及对中国生态城市的批判性分析

引　言

进入21世纪以后，“全球暖化”和“控制排放”等问题成为国际间讨论和关注的主要事件。因为这两个问题与日俱增地威胁着人们的生存，气候的变化将波及地球上每一个国家的每一个居民，甚至会改变人类的生存方式（于立，2009年a）。2010年英国气象局哈德莱中心（The Met Office Hadley Centre）提交了对24个发达和发展中国家进行的研究，其中包括中国。他们分析和研究认为，在中国大陆除了西南地区，因为污染、缺水和土地的退化，大多数地区都将受到水安全的威胁。

城市，以及生活在城市的人群是不可再生资源的主要消费者，他们的生活和生产产生了大量二氧化碳。为了改变目前城市居民的生活方式和生产方式，已经有不少国家和地区开始了生态城镇的规划建设工作。从20世纪末到21世纪初短短的10多年间，生态城镇已经逐渐成为一个全球性的、主流的现象。创新的生态城市的建设和发展已经遍及各大洲。许多创新的生态城市项目正处在规划或建设的实施中。生态城镇已经从开始一些较少的、且相对不太严谨的概念，或探索性的实验发展到了目前出现大量明确的、实践性的新举措。

虽然世界上不少国家和地区都在开展生态城镇的建设，但是世界各地的生态城镇的发展模式和内容标有一定的差异。这是因为各国和各地区由于气候、地理位置、发展阶段等原因所面临的问题不同。虽然生态城镇在总目标和发展方向是可能达成共识的，但在具体定义上，以及相关的内容和发展模式上，很难在世界各国和各地区之间达成一致的意见。因此迄今为止，什么是生态城镇，并没有明确的、统一的定义。

虽然如此，根据对目前国内、外文献的检索，可以发现，普遍的意见认为，生态城镇必须是经济、社会和环境一体化的可持续发展；城镇物质形态的建设必须适应自然环境，与自然协调。以此为基础，人类的生产和生活必须考虑社会的发展目标，例如人类的健康、就业和生活水平质量的普遍提高，以及公平与和谐，特别是人与人之间的公平与和谐，城乡之间的公平与和谐，社会、经济发展与生态环境保护之间的和谐。生态城镇目标的实现和城镇的建设应当是在不超越自然界所能供给的范围之内（于立，2009年a）。

本文将分析和介绍不同国家，包括中国在生态城镇的规划和发展，并在此基础上批判性地分析中国生态城市建设存在的主要问题。

一、国际生态城镇建设实践

（一）英国生态城镇的建设

2008 年英国中央政府的“生态城镇：规划政策文件”（Eco-town：Planning Policy Statement）（DCLG，2008 年 a）草稿出台，开始在全国征求意见，允许各地方政府和开发商组织力量编制生态城镇规划，通过规划的编制和政策的制定，向中央政府申请获得生态城镇建设的许可。消息颁布之后收到了 57 份申请。经过初步审议，有 15 个进入短名单，这 15 个生态城镇集中在英格兰地区，分布很广（DCLG，2008 年 b）（图 1）：

- Pennbury（Stoughton）
- Manby
- Curborough
- Middle Quinton
- Bordon（Whitehill）
- Weston Otmoor
- Ford
- St. Austell（China Clay Community）
- Rossington
- Hanley Grange
- Coltishall
- Marston
- North East Elsenham
- Rushcliffe
- Leeds City Region

但是由于英国生态城镇项目受到利益团体和居民的质疑和反对，项目的选择和确定受到延误，2009 年 7 月中旬，通过专业委员会审查，最后确定了 4 个生态城镇，它们是

1. 诺福克郡（Norfolk）的 Rackheath；
2. 牛津郡（Oxfordshire）的 north-west Bicester；
3. 东汉特斯郡（East Hants）的 Whitehill Bordon；
4. 孔窝郡（Cornwall）的 the China Clay Community near St. Austell.

但保守党与自由党联合政府上台之后，英国的生态城镇建设处于停顿的状态。虽然如此，英国确定了生态城镇的标准和相关的要求。

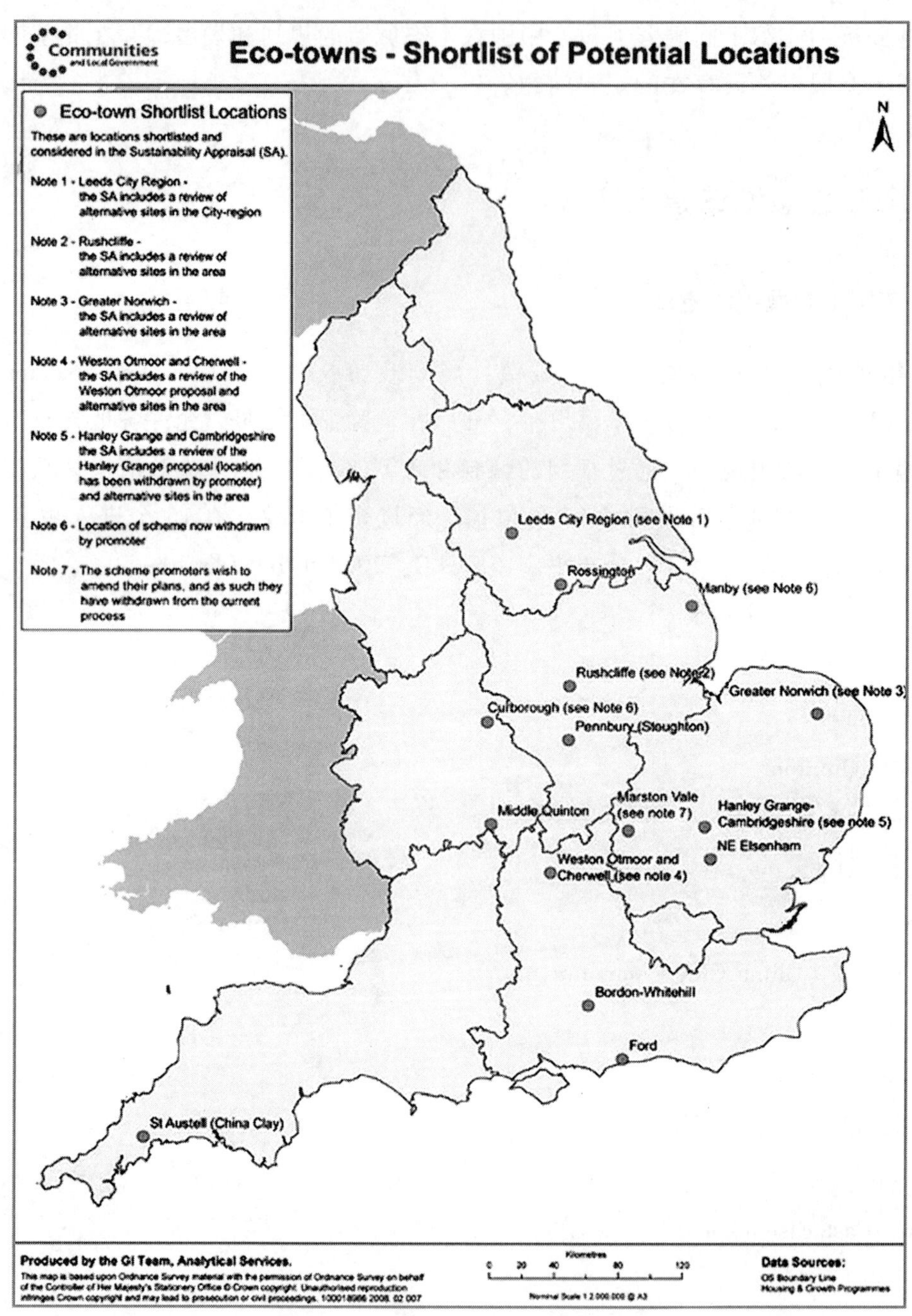

图 1　英国申请生态城镇建设的地区

资料来源：DCLG，2008 年。

1. 英国生态城镇的发展模式与标准

英国生态城镇的建设参考了早期英国新城的开发和建设的模式。实际上，2007 年英国中央政府负责规划的部门，“社区与地方政府部”（Department of Community and Local Government）就曾提到，英国生态城镇的建设可以借用 1981 年的《新城法》作为执行新城开发建设政策的依据。英国政府对生态城镇定义的第一条就明确提出，生态城镇必须是一个新的城镇。

为了生态城镇的规划和建设，特别是为了有效地指导各地方规划部门和开发商编制生态城镇的规划，英国中央政府特别制定了生态城镇的规划和建设标准，具体的内容包括（DCLG，2007年）：

1）生态城镇必须是一个新的住区（新城），每个生态城镇至少应包括5000～10000个家庭。这些新城的发展目标是能够实现零碳排放的开发和建设的新型城镇，探究实现零碳排放的开发和建设城镇的可能性和可操作性；

2）整体的发展应以“零碳排放”为目标，每个生态城镇应当至少在环境可持续的某一个领域具有模范示范意义；

3）每个生态城镇应当配备一所中学，一个中等规模的零售业、商业中心，高质量的商务空间和娱乐设施；

4）全城镇所有住宅中的30%～50%是可支付性住房（低、廉价住房），同时在购房与租房的配置上具备合理的比例；具有面积大小适宜的住宅，以及多样化的、混合型的住区，能够满足不同的需要；

5）设立一个实施机构，负责对生态城镇进行有效的管理，负责生态城镇的开发建设管理工作，为城镇居民、商业和社区提供各种服务。

英国政府还规定：生态城镇必须通过良好的设计，建设一个具有吸引力的、且具备良好的服务和各种设施的生活区；应当与周边的中心城镇有着很好的联系。生态城镇独有的性质应当通过整体的设计，实现整个城镇，包括商业、服务业和住宅等，零碳排放地开发建设。英国政府希望通过生态城镇的规划和建设具体的实践，吸取相关的经验，引导全国其他地区实现城镇生态的建设与发展。

2. 英国生态城镇的规划政策

由于英国规划体系的原因，英国的规划仅有具体的政策要求，但缺乏具体的技术层面的规范。在生态城镇的规划和建设上，也一样没有具体的技术层面的规范。因此给规划编制留下了很大的自由发挥的空间，允许各地区根据自己的实际情况进行规划的制定。因此规划具有相当的灵活性，不过也带有很大的不确定性。虽然如此，英国生态城镇的规划与发展方案在政策层面上要求十分的具体。内容比较全面，具体内容包括（DCLG，2009年）：

- 在环境与碳排放问题上，通过采用创新的、覆盖全城镇范围的可再生能源系统，全面实施可再生的能源的利用，将家庭、学校、商店、办公室和社区设施全部都纳入可再生能源的系统中。通过这个系统的运作，实现零碳的排放；同时鼓励零碳排放的生活方式，特别是尽可能减少交通所产生的碳排放；改变以往对水资源的使用无任何控制的习俗，要求每个家庭和机构都实施高标准的节水措施；
- 在具体的设计问题，要求无论是出售或出租住房，无论是商业的或社区功能的建筑都必须通过高质量的建筑设计；无论是街道、公共场所、公园或公共空间都应实现高水平的城市设计。生态城镇的规划设计的目标是能够至少减少50%的小汽车的出行。并且在“建筑与建成环境委员会”（CABE：the Commission for Architecture and the Built Environment）所制定的“为生命进行建设的规范”和“街道设计原则”指导下，制定城市设计的标准，有效指导生态城镇在开发建设过程中通过对交通的控制减少碳排放。这些设计和控制内容必须纳入生态城镇社区远期规划管治的范畴，长期监控和指导生态城镇的发展和建设；

• 在交通上，要求编制覆盖整个地区的交通规划，将提高步行、骑车和使用公共交通出行的比例作为生态城镇的整体发展目标。为了实现这个目标，每个住宅的规划和区位设置的标准具体地规定为：①10分钟以内的步行距离能够抵达发车间距较密的公共交通车站；②邻里社区服务设施，包括卫生健康、社区中心、小商店等设施。在生态城镇各种设施的整体布局规划上，要求尽可能减少居民依赖使用小汽车的规划模式和空间布局；

• 在住宅上，目前应首先依据英国的建筑节能标准进行建筑，要求在房屋内配置实时的能源监控系统，配置实时的交通信息和高速度的宽带。在建筑材料上必须体现和显示高标准的节能性。与此同时需要考虑到2016年将采用新的、更高要求的节能标准。相关具体的要求包括：通过综合节能，在当地生成低或零碳排放的能源；通过开发低或零碳排放的供暖系统等措施，实现在现有建筑标准基础上再至少减少70%的碳排放。住宅建设的另外一个具体要求是提供不低于全部住宅数量30%的低价、可支付住宅（包括社会保障性的廉租房和过渡性的出租房）；

• 在就业问题上，要求生态城镇内部应当实现混合的商务和居住功能，尽可能减少非可持续的通勤出行的产生。为此，各生态城镇必须制定一个经济发展战略，明确阐述如何解决本地的就业问题，说明将采取哪些具体措施促进生态城镇内部就业岗位的增加。同时还要求保证每一个新的住宅与就业岗位有良好的可持续公共交通联系，能够很便利地通过步行、骑车或使用公共交通实现工作的出行；

• 在服务设施上，要求建设可持续的社区，能够提供为人民的富裕、健康和愉快地生活有所帮助的设施。这些设施必须是具备高标准和高质量的。具体的设施要求包括：娱乐、健康和社会护理、教育、零售业、艺术与文化、图书馆、体育和游玩、社区和志愿者相关的设施等；

• 在绿色基础设施上，要求生态城镇总面积的40%为绿色的空间。这40%中，至少有50%是公共的、管理良好的、高质量的绿色/开放空间网络。要求将生态城镇的绿色空间与更为广阔的乡村地区衔接在一起。绿色空间要求具有多功能性和多样化，例如可以是社区森林、湿地、城镇广场等；可以用于游玩和娱乐，可以安全地步行和骑车，也能够提供野生憩息的功能；可以是城市纳凉之处，也可以是排泄洪水之地。另外，要求重视保护用于生产本地食物、农产品的土地，允许和鼓励当地社区种植农作物，开展副业生产或商业性园艺；

• 在水资源上，生态城镇必须在节水方面制定更为远大的目标，特别是在那些严重缺水的地区。开发建设应当在考虑未来发展的同时解决和改善供水的质量；明确水循环战略；要求生态城镇的开发建设不会对地表和地下水产生影响，不会恶化水源质量；要求生态城镇必须实施“可持续的排水系统”（SUDS）；

• 在防洪风险管理上，要求生态城镇的区位、布局和建设应当设置在避免或尽可能减少洪水侵袭的区位上；在规划生态城镇的同时，应解决本地区洪水的威胁问题；应当避免因为生态城镇的建设给其他地方带来潜在的洪水威胁和影响；

• 在废弃物处理问题上，生态城镇必须根据2020年的标准和目标，实施市政垃圾的处理程度和回收水平；所有的开发建设应当通过规划设计实现这一既定的目标；在处理本地区的垃圾废弃物时，应当考虑如何将其作为燃料，获取生态城镇的热能和电能资源。

（二）法国国家生态城镇发展项目

法国的生态城镇项目始于2008年10月22日。法国生态城镇的目标是促进全国性的大规模的城市可持续发展议程。通过在全国建立可持续发展的共识，实现建筑、社会和能源领域的创新。法国的生态城镇采用在现有的城市地区内部或接邻城市的地区进行生态城镇的开发建设。法国生态城镇的开发建设引入了生态社区的理念，即在分割的公共交通走廊和在城市内建设和促进自然环境的保护性发展。

对于生态城镇建设，法国政府采取各地自我决策的方式。各城镇自己决定是否参与生态城镇项目。但是一旦一个城镇或地区决定参与生态城镇的项目，这个城镇就需要编制生态城市的规划和发展建议书，并向中央政府提出申请。法国政府根据所制定标准审核生态城镇的申报，这些标准的具体内容包括：

• 生态城镇项目需要是在有一定规模的现有城市地区，现有的城市人口应当在10万人以上；

• 这个地区的人口在未来的20～25年中将有一个可持续的人口增长，例如，人口增长的规模不能低于30%或5万人；

• 生态城镇项目需要与城市政府所组织编制的城市规划的内容相结合。

所有参与申请生态城市项目的城镇和地区必须提供有关城镇创新、公共参与、分阶段发展的计划和财政安排等方面的资料信息。同时还需要说明生态城镇的发展项目如何与现有的城镇以及正在进行的项目有效地结合。

1. 13个生态城镇的选定与资金安排

全法国有19座城镇递交了项目申请书。所提交的生态城市发展建议书的内容以及深度有很大的区别。经过筛选，最终确定了13个城镇作为法国生态城镇项目。这13个城镇是：波尔多（Bordeaux），克莱蒙费朗（Clermont Ferrand），格勒诺布尔（Grenoble），马赛（Marseilles），梅斯（Metz），蒙彼利埃（Montpellier），南特/圣纳泽尔（Nantes/St-Nazaire），尼斯（Nice），阿尔泽特（Pay de haut d' Alzette），平原市（Plaine Commune），雷恩（Rennes），斯特拉斯堡（Strasbourg），以及法属岛屿留尼旺（TCO-La Reunion TCO）（图2）。

为了促进生态城镇项目的实施，法国政府安排了350亿欧元的经费。在这13个生态城镇项目中，每个城镇能够获得大约6千万欧元的经费，显然这6千万欧元的经费对生态城镇的开发建设是远远不够的，这些城镇还需要从其他资源获取资金的支持。包括申请国家对其他一些具体生态项目的支持，例如发展电力小汽车项目等；或从法国350亿欧元的“巨额贷款”中获得借贷资金。这笔借贷资金可以运用于5个重要的生态城市发展的领域：

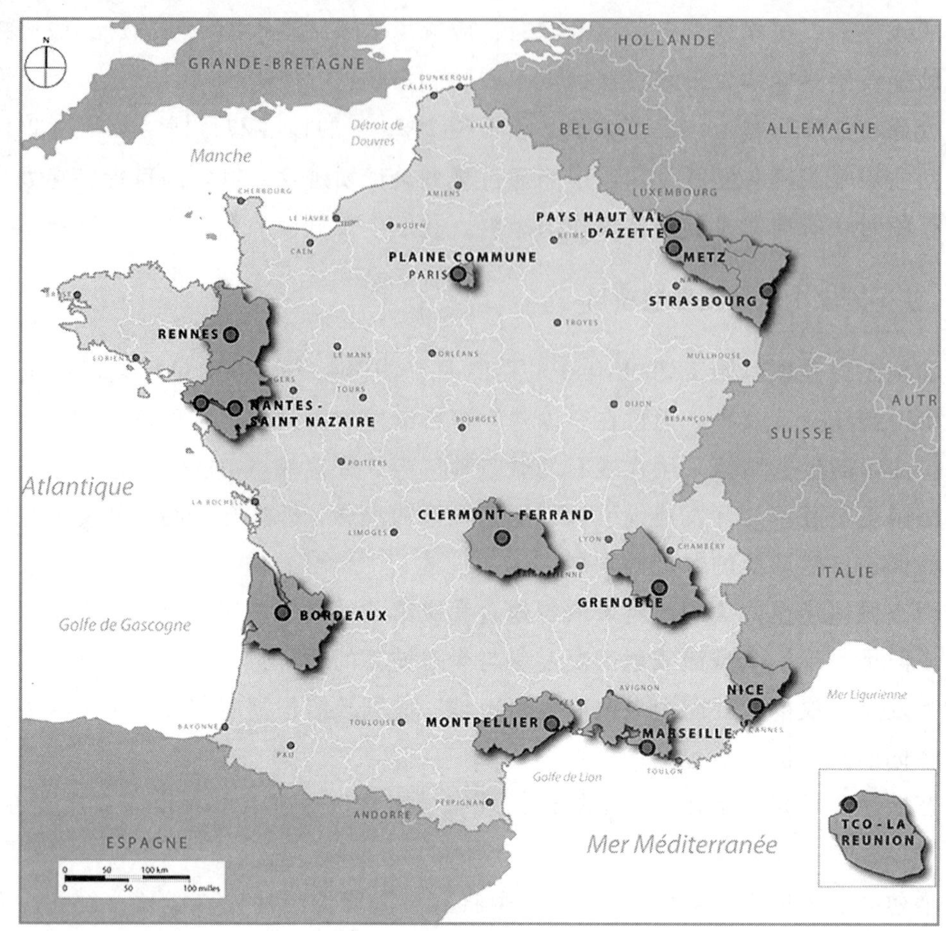

图2 法国13个生态城市

资料来源：巴顿·威尔莫国际公司。

- 高等教育
- 培训
- 科研
- 生态产业发展
- 小型企业发展

2. 具体生态城镇的评估机制

法国政府实施生态城镇的一个主要的目的是推行“创新”，因此每个生态城镇都要求有若干个重点的创新项目，以此作为法国中央政府资助的内容。很显然，法国政府的生态城镇项目具有宣传、政治和商业的目标。法国生态城镇项目是为了寻找一条“后石油”时代世界各国都将面临的问题的解决途径，减少对小汽车的依赖必将是一条出路。法国政府希望通过法国生态城镇项目中对创新技术研发的重视，使法国成为能够引领全球可持续城市发展，并成为相关技术的领先者。

为了有效地评估生态城市发展所涉及交通、基础设施、住宅、能源和生态保护等领域各种不同的生态发展内容广泛的目标，法国政府创建一个项目评估矩阵表，这样可以确保所有相关的和具体的发展和建设目标指标都包括在内。通过这种方式使每个具体的生态项目能够为生态城镇整体的可持续发展和其目标的实现做出贡献。评估矩阵表包括了6组不同的目标指标，即管治、交通、资源与环境、经济和社会。

这个评估矩阵表成为法国中央政府与各生态城镇申请者就其城镇发展建议书的详细内容和项目进行谈判和研讨的基础。通过评估矩阵表分析和审核这些生态城镇的项目和内容与全球气候变暖、控制排放等主题的关联度，并以此作为确定相关具体技术的使用。通过评估矩阵表的分值系统，法国中央政府可以追踪各生态城镇的发展建议书的强项，及其可操作性和具体的运作绩效，并以此作为提供资金的依据。

（三）马斯达尔生态城：实现能源转型，引领新能源研究

2006年4月，阿拉伯联合酋长国的阿布达比邦决定通过启动“马斯达尔创始”（Masdar Initiate）项目，目标是创建第一个以碳氢化合物生产型为经济发展模式的城镇—马斯达尔。该项目希望提供一个全球性的平台，共同探讨人类面临的最紧迫问题，包括能源安全、气候变暖，以及人类可持续发展的相关技能。

马斯达尔生态城的建设不仅仅是建设一座零碳排放和零废弃物的城镇，更重要的是通过投资各种不同的新能源技术，以及建立研究院和成立碳管理单位，以及其他的创新活动为可持续的新产业发展奠定基础。

1. 马斯达尔生态城建设的目标之一：加强对“碳“的管理

马斯达尔生态城的碳管理机构以开发了温室大气减排项目为主要的方向，通过联合国领导的“清洁发展机制”条款（Clean Development Mechanism - CDM)），实现温室大气减排的货币化。

马斯达尔生态城将自己定位在全球快速发展的碳交易市场中能够发挥长久作用的角色。作为全球温室大气减排项目的开发者，无论是在阿布达比邦的天然气加工项目，还是在北美的发电厂项目，马斯达尔碳管理机构为能源产业客户提供低碳文化和从可持续发展中获得经济效率的多种方式选择。

2008年2月，马斯达尔生态城开始建设具有世界先进水平的，能够捕获自然界二氧化碳的网络项目，通过这个项目将大大降低阿布达比邦的碳足迹。这个网络的第一期工程将从2013年开始，从阿布达比邦的发电厂和工业设施中捕获650万吨的二氧化碳。捕获的二氧化碳将重新注入油库，经过处理获取高附加值的再生油。

2. 马斯达尔生态城建设的目标之二：发展新能源技术和产业

阿布达比邦通过马斯达尔生态城发展加大在再生能源产业领域的投资。希望通过促进这项新型产业的发展，使马斯达尔生态城能够成为再生能源价值链中一个重要的环节，并从此能够在再生清洁能源领域成为全球领导者之一。

目前马斯达尔生态城一个重要的“旗舰投资项目”是建立于2008年的“马斯达尔光电”公司。该公司的目标是成为世界前三位的薄板光电公司。“马斯达尔光电”公司是中东地区第一个采用先进的半导体纳米制造技术的企业。这项技术的采用明显加强了阿布达比邦

作为技术领导者的地位。项目第一期6亿美元的投资将建设位于德国和阿布达比邦的生产厂家，开工生产后，每年的产量达到210兆瓦。

“马斯达尔光电”公司是阿布达比邦太阳能高科技制造业的一个核心组成部分。整个产业链完成之后，将成为世界最先进的生产中心。产业链形成的产业将布局在一个4平方公里的产业园区内，园区将包括3种主要的光电技术，其一是结晶体光电，其二是薄板光电，其三是高容量集约光电；以及其他的配套和支持产业。

太阳能高科技产业的发展将帮助阿布达比邦经济的多样化发展，并且通过发展最新技术的产业，实现阿布达比邦经济的转型。阿布达比邦高科技制造业产业园已经进入建设阶段，与规划的马斯达尔生态城市紧靠在一起。

由于阿布达比邦高科技制造业产业园在区位、经济的发展和低成本的优势，产业园区不仅仅吸引来自太阳能产业的企业，同时还吸引了相关的供给和辅助产业，例如天然气和玻璃等领域的企业。马斯达尔生态城在阿布达比邦高科技制造业产业园的建设和运作过程中所发挥的主要作用是为产业园区提供基础设施，促进园区的发展。

3. 生态城建设

马斯达尔生态城发展的理念包括创新、科技和可持续发展。这座生态城的建设目标是完全通过再生能源供电，包括风力、水力、太阳能与氢气发电并行，并计划未来进一步提高太阳能发电的比例（若光能转换电能的效率再提高，80%建筑屋顶将改设太阳能板）。马斯达尔生态城建成之后将拥有4万居民；每日的通勤人数将达到5万人次。马斯达尔生态城的城市规划和设计主要以步行为主。狭窄的、有树荫的小道将公共广场与住宅、餐馆、戏院和商店全部连接起来。城市内的建筑都采用传统的麦地那式的建筑风格。城市内将设置阿拉伯式的露天市场、风塔等，充分体现当地民族的特色和象征。

整个城市都将采用清洁能源。这座城市不仅仅实现零碳排放和零废弃物；同时还将是零关税、零税收、零资本流动的限制，以此吸引具有世界水平的研究者、学者、学生、企业家、金融家等的入住，预计将有1 500多家公司入住马斯达尔生态城。

根据总体规划，一个人的步行出行距离在200米以内就能够抵达基本的设施。虽然如此，整个城市将建设一个全自动的，以电力为动力的个人捷运系统（Personal Rapid Transit）。以此系统取代私人小汽车，作为可选择的出行工具。马斯达尔市与周边地区，包括阿布达比市中心和机场的交通将通过轻轨连接。因此马斯达尔生态城将是一个紧凑的、高密度的城市。整座城市将禁止小汽车的通行，所以也就不存在汽车尾气的排放问题。与其他相似规模的城市进行比较，马斯达尔将减少75%的石化燃料的消耗量，减少300%的用水，减少400%的废弃物。自行车和步行将是主要的交通工具。

马斯达尔生态城的建筑将全部采取以坐东北朝西南的走向兴建，以获得最佳采光及蔽荫效果。建筑的高度控制在5层楼以下；街道限制在三公尺宽、七十公尺长，以维持微气候稳定并促进空气流通。城市内将通过大量的植栽与水景设施以及风塔设施将凉风引入城内以达到降温目的。

水对于阿拉伯联合酋长国是十分宝贵的资源，马斯达尔生态城所需水的来源将以太阳能作为电力对海水进行淡化而获得。另外还通过可持续的排水系统（SUDS）大量回收雨水，而且使用高效率的污水回收与再利用设施，循环使用废水。在水资源的利用将尽能够采取各种措施和规划手段，降低对水的需求。预计全城每日仅需 8 000 吨的饮用水，为现有同等规模城市的五分之二（约 20 000 吨）。

（四）日本生态城镇项目

1. 日本生态城市发展的内容与目标

根据日本相关的研究资料（Bettina 和 Raimund，2007 年），日本生态城镇项目的启动原因之一是由于日本的土地资源很有限，可进行废弃物填埋的土地严重不足。但是日本社会的废弃物却在大幅度增长。为了解决这个问题，日本政府希望启动生态城镇的项目，采取提供资金创建具有创新意义的物质材料循环利用的设施和体系，促使居民、研究机构、企业和地方政府在材料的循环利用上进行合作，减少废弃物的产生。

日本的生态城镇项目始于 1997 年，由原来的国际贸易和工业部与健康和福利部共同发起，同时为了鼓励社区居民一起参加到环保型的城市发展项目中，政府还提供了一些资金奖励和援助计划。

日本的生态城镇是在一个定义的地区，通过城市/区域和环境协同规划，实现资源投入、废弃物管理和环境保护一体化，并且同时促进工业和经济快速的发展（图 3）。在所定义的地区内，产业、经济、社区和居民通过与政府和私营的合作伙伴关系的建立，在生产过程中实现循环利用；在工业企业和家庭之间开展循环材料的交换，实现最优化的资源使用。实现所有的领域和行业，以及所有的产品都能够与生态城镇发展规划相结合。

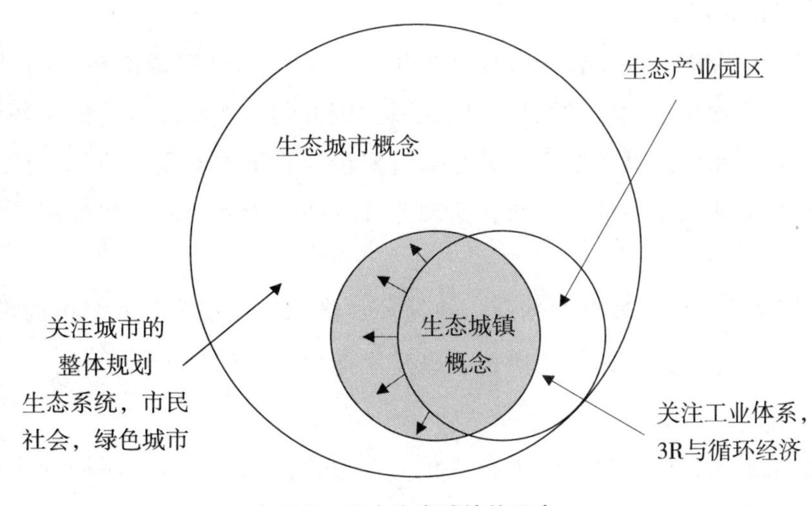

图 3　日本生态城镇的理念

资料来源：WUPPERTAL Institute for Climate，Environment and Energy，（2007），Eco Town Program。

生态城镇项目立足零废弃物和零碳排放的理念。该理念源于联合国大学最早提出的零排放模式。该模式根据自然界食物链的原理建立的。在自然界食物链中，不存在任何的废弃物。因为一个废弃物将成为链中下一个环节有机体的资源或养分。日本生态城镇就是根据此进行组织，即一个产业或家庭所产生的废弃物将是另外一个企业、产业的材料资源，形成一个区域资源循环经济的社会。

2. 日本北九州生态城案例

北九州市的面积为485平方公里，位于九州地区的北面。北九州市曾经以钢铁和制造业为主，是日本重型工业最重要的一个基地。钢铁产业为北九州的发展和繁荣做出了很大的贡献，但是也带来严重的污染问题。

根据有关机构的研究（APEIS和RISPO，2005年），20世纪50年代至70年代初期是日本经济的快速发展阶段。但是70年代以后日本的钢铁业在全球激烈的竞争下开始衰败。北九州市的钢铁产业也出现滑坡并最终衰败。然而由于钢铁产业和制造业生产所带来的严重污染问题并没有因为污染产业的衰败而消失。钢铁和制造业给北九州市带来的污染随处可见，到处是工业废弃物和生活废弃物，海水也被严重污染。

为了解决污染问题，恢复北九州市的蓝天碧海，同时实现北九州经济和产业的转型，日本政府于1997年首先将北九州市列入生态城镇项目的名单之列。为了帮助地方政府实施生态城镇的项目，日本政府在高科技循环技术的开发和使用上，以及在市场的营销和开拓上提供了资金的支持。北九州生态城市项目战略明确提出将通过引入各方的力量，特别是加强专业研发机构与商业的结合，寻找一条具有示范性的、有推广意义的环境产业发展之路。

北九州市生态城镇项目的具体政策是实施3R措施，即减排（reduce）、再利用（reuse）和循环利用（recycle）。整个过程分为两个阶段：第一个阶段是1997年至2002年，这个阶段主要执行“循环利用”（Recycle）的方针；第二阶段是2002年至2010年，这个阶段的重点是“再利用”（Reuse）。

由于日本是一个资源和土地都十分稀缺的国家，无法满足资源消耗型的经济发展模式，也不可能长期提供土地用于垃圾的填埋，因此减少废弃物，实施废弃物的循环利用是生态城市的重要任务。北九州生态城镇的宗旨就是通过对废弃物的再利用，将一个产业或企业的废弃物变成另外一个产业或企业的原材料，实现零废弃物。为此，北九州确定了生态城镇发展的目标，即，

- 促进环保/循环产业的发展和创新，使循环经济和产业成为北九州市的新产业；
- 通过企业、商业、地方政府和消费者以及本地居民之间的大力协作，建立一个物质循环利用的社会。

在实施生态城镇项目中，通过若干利益相关者的合作和各自发挥不同的作用，实现生态城市的发展目标。这些利益相关者包括地方政府、商业团体、研究机构和市民们。

地方政府：北九州市政府在生态城镇项目中的作用包括：

- 提供硬件，即基础设施和其他公共设施，包括给排水、道路以及土地等；
- 提供软件，即资金支持和人力资源的支持；
- 提供一站式服务，加快速度；

• 通过学习和借鉴其他城镇的废弃物分类方法，举办展览、会议，向市民们进行介绍，并且为研究机构提供研究的机会。

私营的商业和企业：商业企业机构将主要承担从重型工业向复合型的产业结构转型的任务，同时还需要设法解决废弃土地和产能过剩问题。私营企业将这次生态城镇项目中的经济转型看作是一次复兴公司运作的机会，也愿意承担投资新型产业的风险。

研究机构的目标是与产业界、学术界和政府合作，开展对废弃物管理，循环利用和污染控制技术等领域的研究，并推广相关的技术和知识。

消费者与当地市民是项目的积极参与者。北九州市的“生态城市中心”是唯一的公共设施，也是当地居民相互交流的场所，同时还是海外和其他地区此地游览的游客中心。成立这个中心的目标是为了使当地市民对生态城市有一个更好的了解。政府要求商业界和研究机构将他们的设施和信息在“生态城市中心”向市民们进行展示。

市政府还成立了北九州委员会。委员会的主要目的是考虑如何减少和循环利用废弃物。在这个委员会中，市民们发挥了积极的作用。他们举办各种与环境保护有关的展览和活动，还举办“零排放”旅游，通过旅游介绍废弃物的分类和处理，使广大的市民了解生态城市发展的目标和要求。每个人从自己做起，减少废弃物。

3. 北九州市生态城产业园区建设

北九州市生态城市项目建设的第一期内容包括建设“综合环境产业园区”、“Hibiki 循环园区”和“实践型研究区”（图 4）。

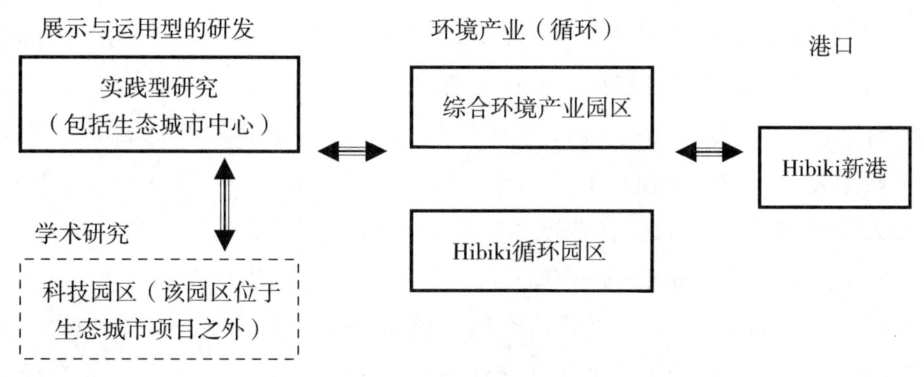

图 4　日本北九州生态城市的内容构成

资料来源：APEIS 和 RISPO，2005 年。

综合环境产业园区（19 公顷）：该园区位于 Hibiki-Nada 地区，在城市的滨海沿岸。这个园区建立的目的是为了在园区建设一个循环系统实现在能源和材料领域建立循环产业链。

Hibiki 循环园区（5.5 公顷）：循环园区与综合环境产业园区接邻。建立这个循环园区的主要目的是为了支持中、小型高科技的环保型循环产业企业。这个园区内的中小型企业基本上都是本地区的公司，市场也在本地区。该园区分为汽车循环产业区与新领域园区。

实践型研究区：设立这个园区的目的是为了促进具有前沿性的环保技术的研发。通过园区内研究机构在环保技术上的研发，特别是废弃物的循环利用和废弃物的处理技术等，然后通过技术的展示和推荐，实现其市场化和商品化。这个园区集聚了许多的科研机构，包括福冈大学工程循环与生态技术研究中心。由于该中心的建立，还吸引了一些私营的循环经济的研究机构。到2003年3月，已经有19家研究机构入住该园区。

（五）库里蒂巴：公交导向发展的生态城市

库里蒂巴在世界以其规划，特别是快速公交系统及其公交导向的发展而著名。库里蒂巴在这个方面的努力为其赢得了城市发展和建设的典型范例，成为世界上最宜居的城市之一。1990年，库里蒂巴作为唯一的发展中国家城市，与加拿大的温哥华、法国的巴黎、意大利的罗马和澳大利亚的悉尼一起成为世界上首批被联合国命名的五个“最适宜人类居住的城市”（李忠东，2009）

1. 公共交通、土地利用以及建设指标一体化的规划

20世纪60至70年代，巴西的工业化带来大量人口向城市的迁移。库里蒂巴曾经是工业化最快的城市之一。20世纪50年代，库里蒂巴的人口仅20万人，但随着工业化带来的城市化进程，库里蒂巴在30年的时间内，以每一个10年人口翻番的速度增长。到20世纪80年代，库里蒂巴的人口达到100万。其中的30%是农村向城市的移民（Macedo，2004）。

为了解决库里蒂巴的城市扩展问题，库里蒂巴的城市规划师和政府官员们曾经试图通过物质规划，从城市的结构和布局着手解决城市的问题。但是城市快速的发展所带来的问题并没因为物质规划而得到解决。与大多数发展中国家在工业化和城镇化过程中发所出现的问题一样，库里蒂巴同样面临高企的失业率、无家可归人数的增加、高犯罪率和交通拥挤等现象。在库里蒂巴快速的工业化和城镇化的初期，快速的发展并没有为库里蒂巴带来好的形象，当地居民的生活质量也并没有因为发展而得到改善。

1971年到1975年，库里蒂巴城市研究与规划院的一名负责人，盖默·勒那（Jaime Lerne）被军政府任命为库里蒂巴市的市长。在这之后，他又在1979年至1983年，以及1989年至1992年两次出任市长。在盖默·勒那出任市长期间，特别是在1975年至1979年间，他大力推行Jorge Wilhelm于1966年所制定的库里蒂巴总体规划，特别是运用这个规划所提出的土地利用、道路系统和公共快速交通一体化的规划发展理念。同时将土地利用方式及其相应的控制性的指标与道路等级和公交网络综合地联系起来进行空间的布局（Macedo，2004），形成主要交通干道，特别是快速公共交通走廊沿线混合型的、高密度的开发。这些快速公共交通走廊因此成为城市的主要发展轴。Wilhelm的土地利用、道路系统和公共快速交通一体化的规划理念，以及公交走廊与城市发展轴的一体化的方式在盖默·勒那第二任市长期间的1975年至1979年得到完整的体现。也正是这个规划和发展理念的实施，为库里蒂巴带来了国际声誉。

2. 解决低收入阶层的住宅

在库里蒂巴，城市房管局负责低收入阶层住宅的筹资、规划、建设、分配和管理工作。除了来自中央和州政府所提供的低收入住宅建设资金，库里蒂巴市政府利用城市规划管理权利，通过“开发权转移”机制，为低收入阶层的住宅筹资建设资金。开发商可以通过为低

收入阶层住宅建设基金提供资金，作为获取规划许可或提高一定的容积率的条件。

库里蒂巴市政府为低收入阶层提供住宅的努力获得一定的成效。1998 年在库里蒂巴市房管局登记为低收入家庭，申请低收入住宅的家庭有 7 万户，2002 年，这个数字减少到 52 824户（Macedo，2004）。登记为低收入阶层的家庭中，有 50% 是来自农村地区的移民。库里蒂巴市房管局所提供的低收入家庭住宅并不仅仅为城市居民服务，也为进入城市的农村移民提供住宅。

3. 交通

库里蒂巴没有地铁系统，主要依靠导向型、隔离式的快速公共汽车体系。城市主要的发展地区基本上是沿着公共交通走廊进行布局。与其他车辆分离的公共汽车专用道使公共汽车的速度得以提高。其他常规的公共汽车将周边其他地区与快速公共交通走廊衔接起来，形成全市范围的一个整体的公交网络。目前库里蒂巴全市拥有 2 160 辆公共汽车，日载客量达到 190 万人次（Macedo 引用 URBS 数据，2003）。

虽然库里蒂巴是巴西比较富有的城市，也是巴西人均小汽车拥有量很高的城市，小汽车拥有率占全市人口的 40%（Macedo 引用 Detran - PR 数据，2003）。但由于库里蒂巴公共交通的高效率、通达性和便利性，促使当地的居民放弃私人小汽车的使用，日常的工作出行基本上以公共汽车为主要的出行工具。目前城市 80% 的出行是依靠公共汽车完成的，库里蒂巴的燃油消耗仅是同等规模城市的 25%。其污染却远低于同等规模的其他城市的水平（秦柯，李利，2008）。

另外，为了保证公共交通的“社会性”，政府综合考虑了低收入阶层出行的需求，特别是针对那些居住在城市外围，或城市边缘地区的低收入阶层出行的需要。库里蒂巴的公共汽车采取一票价制的模式，即无论路程的远近都是一个票价。购买一次票可以乘坐约 70 公里的距离。这种机制为居住在城市外围的低收入阶层的交通出行提供了便利。

4. 社会化的废弃物处理

库里蒂巴市政府从 1983 年开始实行垃圾分类。据统计，99% 的家庭都购置了专门用来回收垃圾的容器，主动地对垃圾进行分类。现在，全城五分之一的垃圾可以得到分类回收，垃圾回收率令人瞩目，在巴西名列前茅（李忠东，2009）。

库里蒂巴引入“绿色交换”（green exchange）的项目，目的之一是实现社会的包容性。这个项目既有利对环境的保护，也为低收入或失业群体提供了生活的基本保证。生活在棚户区的低收入，或无业群体由于收垃圾的车辆无法进入棚户区，政府因此启动了这个项目。居住在棚户区的居民可以将装着垃圾的垃圾袋送往社区中心。在社区中心用垃圾袋换取公共汽车的车票或食物。这带来多重的益处。第一，通过垃圾的收集并兑换食品与车票，人们不会到处乱扔垃圾，特别是不会往河流倾倒垃圾，因此城市的垃圾减少了，疾病的威胁也降低；第二，通过为低收入阶层或无业群体提供食品，避免了他们出现饥荒，产生营养不足或其他的疾病，也稳定了社会；第三，有利促进当地农业的发展，“绿色兑换”所兑换的食品都是从当地农民购买的，这个项目使农民的粮食有了销路，也因此增加了农民的收入。

在“垃圾不应就是垃圾”（garbage is not garbage）运动中，城市 70% 的废弃物得到居民们的回收处理。每周都有两辆车到居民区回收废弃物，其中一辆是废弃物回收车，回收纸张、纸板、金属、塑料和玻璃；另外一辆车装着食品，用于兑换给居民。这个项目使库里蒂巴每天所回收的纸张等同于保护了1 200根树木。这项运动还深入到学校，让孩子们每天将可回收的废弃物带到学校，换取学习用品、巧克力或文艺演出票。回收的物品还可出售，获得的资金进一步投入社会或医疗卫生保障项目中。

这些简单、讲究实效、成本很低的社会公益项目旨在成为库里蒂巴生态环境保护的一部分，并使得城市在环境和社会方面走上了一条健康的发展之路。

二、中国生态城市的实践

（一）天津

天津生态城以生态修复和保护为目标，力求建设自然环境与人工环境共融共生的生态系统，实现人与自然的和谐共存。目前，天津生态城的4平方公里起步区正在抓紧建设中，作为重点工程国家动漫产业园已经完工并即将投入使用。经过一年多的施工，已经有7座廉租房拔地而起，主体建筑外观清晰可见。首期工程于2011年6月底竣工。天津生态城已经安装了大约700盏具备“风光”互补系统的路灯，最终此类路灯将达到约2 400盏，占生态城路灯总量的60%。天津滨海新区污水处理厂已在2010年10月投入运作，开始为生态城和周边地区服务，解决了区域工业污水及生活污水的处理问题，并对穿越区域的蓟运河水环境改善起到重要作用。

（二）唐山

唐山曹妃甸生态城建设开展至今，已经完成总投资300亿元，谋划项目100个。目前已开工项目89个（完成项目21个），11个项目正在进行前期准备中。曹妃甸生态城的基础设施和城市项目建设已经全面铺开。

曹妃甸生态城倡导建设交通宁静区。通过自行车推广运动和新传统邻里的城市设计的方法以及低污染公共汽车、无轨电车、现代有轨电车、轻轨为导向的公共交通运输等措施，从而解决交通污染、实现资源环境的可持续发展。目前，曹妃甸工业区至生态城有轨电车可行性研究报告已经完成并通过专家论证，正在进行批复工作，BRT专用道路车行道已施工完成。

（三）海南

1999年7月海南省二届人大常委会第八次会议审议批准了《海南生态省建设规划纲要》。2005年海南省政府根据形势发展的要求，提请省人大常委会审议并通过了《海南生态省建设规划纲要（2005年修编）》。文件中提到，海南省将认真处理好保护和开发的关系，在海南实现经济社会可持续发展，人与自然和谐发展。通过大力发展生态经济和循环经济，努力构建资源节约型社会。建立生态补偿机制，改善人居环境，提高生活质量，使生态省建设惠及广大人民群众。

海南在推进生态省建设过程中，依托自然生态环境优势，积极发展环境与经济“双赢”的生态型产业，同时按照合理布局，借鉴先进技术，有效控制了资源型产业所产生的污染。海南省的生态省发展是一个综合的发展模式，涉及农业、工业和旅游业。在农业领域，积极规划和发展生态农业，制定无公害农业和生态农业的发展规划，优化农业结构；同时推进工业生态化建设，推行清洁生产，实施糖胶等传统工业的生态化改造工程。例如海南马村生态产业链以制糖业作为马村生态产业的龙头。但糖厂可分布在其他区域，制糖业的主要副产品，糖蜜废液则集中到马村酒精生产基地进行综合利用，实现海南省制糖业清洁生产和废弃物资源化。在这个生产过程，充分利用海口电厂的副产品余热和蒸汽，作为糖蜜酒精厂的能源。糖蜜酒精厂的有机废水采用厌氧发酵法处理和利用生产沼气，经脱硫处理后可提供电厂作为能源，代替部分燃煤；剩余的沼液量排至生物稳定塘沉淀、氧化、稳定水质，然后根据农田灌溉需要进入土地处理系统。电厂的固体废弃物可用于生产建材；糖厂的糖蔗废渣经处理之后是农业的有机肥料，可以生产绿色、有机的食品（欧阳志云等，2004 年）（图 5）。

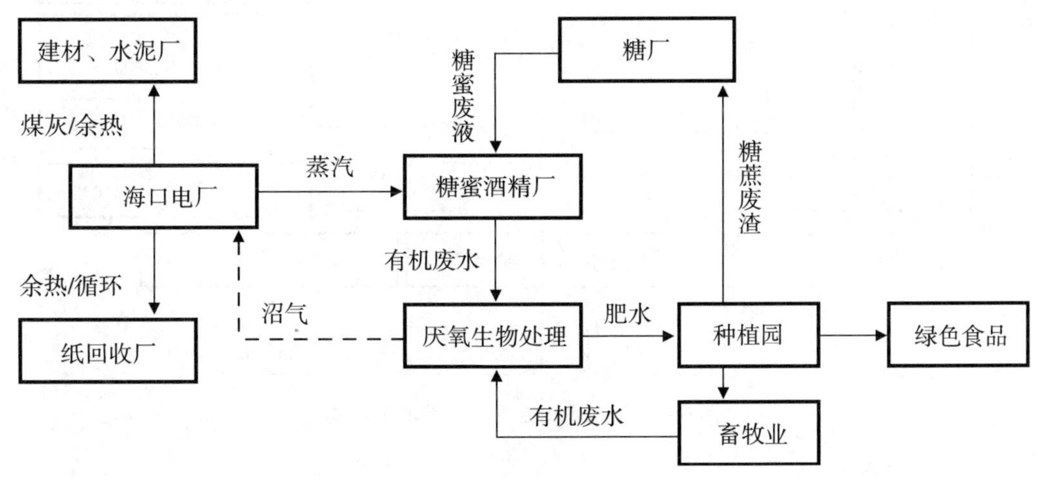

图 5 海南马村生态产业链

在“十一五”期间，海南省投资 90.15 亿元用于环保项目，其中新建项目约 25.25 亿元，老工业污染源治理环保投资约 4.5 亿元，环境基础设施建设投资约 60.4 亿元。

（四）武汉

中国仍然是一个正在快速城镇化和工业化的国家。发展经济，实现工业现代化仍然是大多数城市未来 10 多年，甚至数十年的主要目标。如何实现工业现代化，或生态工业化，即在发展工业的同时，同时实现节能减排的任务是摆在多数城市面前的一个难题。生态产业园区的建设是一个可行之路，实现产业的共生。在这个方面，武汉已经开始做一些尝试。武汉是中国中部地区一个重要的工业基地，工业化和城镇化是重要的发展目标。武汉是中国目前快速工业化和城镇化的一个缩影。解决工业发展带来的污染和废弃物的问题，开展循环经济是武汉“两型社会”建设的一个重要问题和主要目标。武汉如果能够实现产业的调整，以不搬迁为前提，通过技术升级和创新处理好能源和污染问题，实现节能减排，将对中国许多重型工业和化工城市起示范的作用。

作为武汉重型工业的产业基地，武汉青山区人民政府于2008年出台了《武汉市青山区循环经济试点实施方案》，青山区的GDP占全市的9.91%，在武汉13个区中位居首位。青山区的重化工产业结构特色鲜明。辖区内拥有武钢、一冶、武汉石化、武汉船厂等大、中型企业百余家，形成了以武钢为龙头的钢铁制造业板块和以武汉石化为重点的石油化工板块。

武汉青山区根据生态城市发展规划，将整个地区划分为生态产业区、生态宜居区和生态保护区。武汉青山区着力构建以生态产业园区位载体，形成企业、产业园区和区域经济三个层面的循环经济体系。其中的物质流主要包括武钢、武汉石化、青山热电厂等核心企业，其他相关的以其副产品为原料的附属企业和资源再生企业共同构成了产业共生集群，并通过群落之间的物质联系形成了整个产业园区具有多样化的生态产业链（图6）。

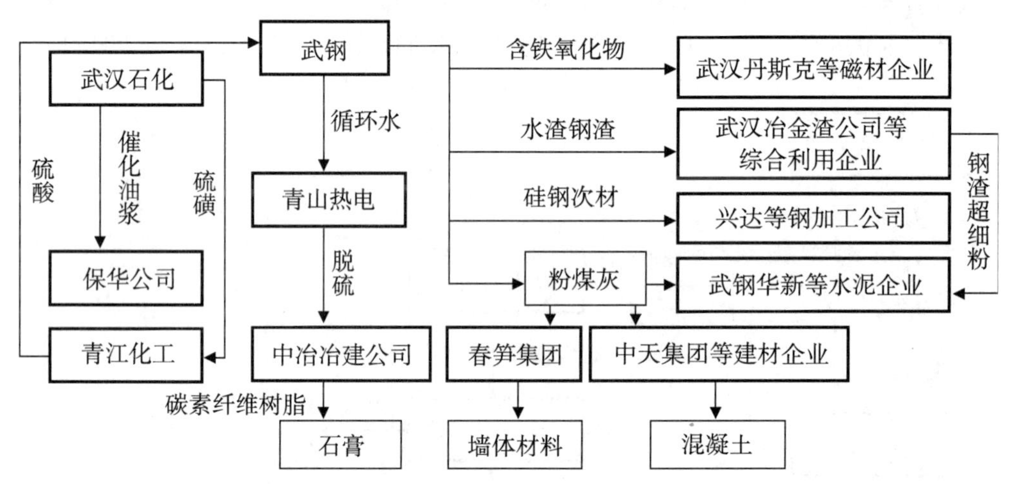

图6　武汉市青山区循环经济物质流图

资料来源：《武汉市青山区循环经济试点实施方案》。

能量流主要以青山电厂的电力供应、武汉石化的燃气供应，及通过对其他企业的余热回收，既满足自身热量需求，又为其他机构和生活居住区提供热源，实现有效的能量循环使用（图7）。

青山区计划到2012年，工业废水的处理率达到80%以上，冷却水循环利用率达到85%，区域中水利用率达到10%以上；工业固体废弃物的综合利用率达到98%，工业危险废弃物的处理将达到100%的处理，废纸、废塑料回收利用率保持在80%，生活垃圾处理率达到90%。

这些案例显示了中国中央政府和不少地方政府正在与世界其他国家的人民及其政府一起共同采取措施，减少全球气候变化，降低碳的排放；正在逐渐改变过去粗放的和耗能型的经济发展模式；同时在人类住区上实现生态发展和生态城镇的建设，并制定了相应的发展目标。

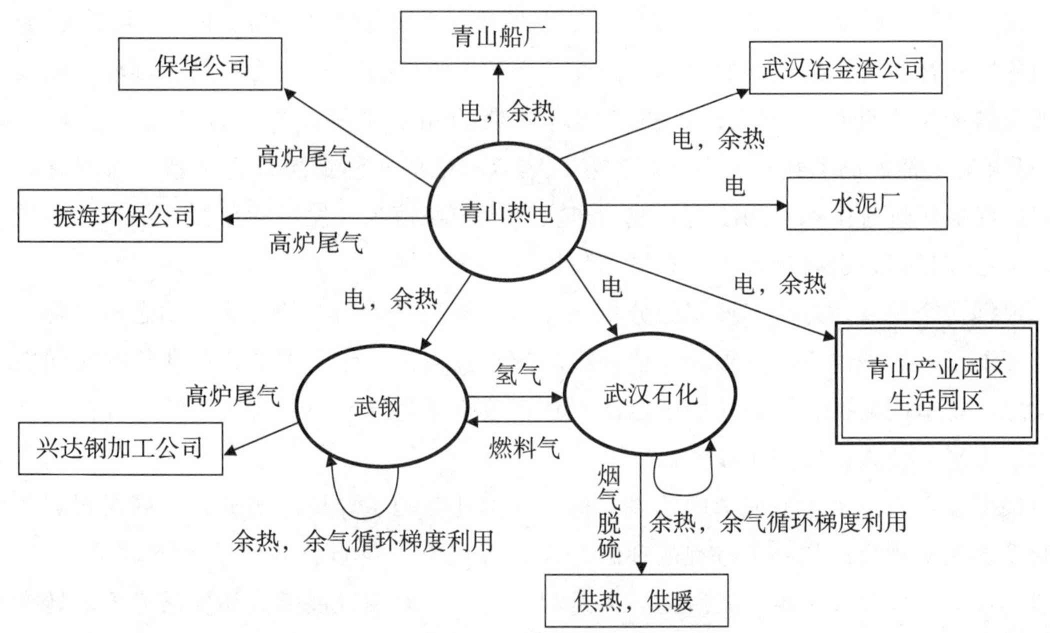

图 7　武汉市青山区循环经济能量流动图

资料来源：《武汉市青山区循环经济试点实施方案》。

三、对中国生态城镇发展现状问题的分析

中国生态城镇与世界其他国家的生态城镇一样都是在进行着新的城镇发展方式的探索。调研显示中国城镇既有与世界其他国家生态城镇建设所面临的相似的问题，也有自己独特的问题。中国的生态城镇与世界其他生态城镇一样展开了多样化的建设形式。调查的数据显示在开展生态城规划和建设的城市中，所确定的生态城覆盖范围各不相同，53% 的城市将全市域纳入生态城的建设范围。27% 的城市采取有针对性地解决本地区所存在的问题，因此，生态城建设的目标是老城区的生态复兴改造和生态新城的建设；另外 13% 的城市将生态城的目标锁定在新城建设上。还有一些城市在生态产业的发展和循环经济领域做了很好的尝试。

作者认为，根据中国的国情和目前所必须面对的发展中的问题，中国生态城镇的发展目标是实现经济、环境和社会一体化和可持续发展；生态城镇的基本任务是实现发展模式和生活方式的转变；而生态城镇所面对的主要挑战是进行制度和技术等各方面的创新。作者还认为要实现生态城镇的发展目标，即经济、社会和环境可持续的、一体化的发展，世界上任何国家和城市要在短期内建设成一个能够获得公认的、名副其实的生态城镇都不容易；更何况生态城镇的发展与一般城市的发展一样，在市场经济条件下的社会和经济发展过程中，发展面对着是未来众多的不确定性。即使生态城镇初步实现了既定的目标，仍不可避免地还需要面对各种的变数。所以生态城镇是一个过程，是实现生态城镇目标，并以目标为导向的一个过程。生态城镇的发展和建设需要持续监控和调整其具体和实际的发展过程，还需要管理好生态城镇，保证生态城镇的发展继续沿着全面实现经济、社会和环境可持续的目标迈进。

如果生态城镇的发展是一个过程，生态城镇的发展就需要分阶段、分层次逐步实现经济、环境和社会可持续发展的目标。因此一个生态城镇可以表现为在某些领域，或某个地区实现低碳的生产和生活方式；或初步实现社会的相对平等；或改善环境，或减少对石化（不可再生）能源的消耗；或利用新技术，结合本地的实际情况进行创新，对现有的产业和现有的建成区进行生态化的改造；或初步实现生态城镇综合发展的目标。如果一些城镇初步实现了这些目标，也就进入了生态城镇发展的初级发展阶段。

根据这个论点，对生态城镇的分析和评估也应当采用动态的方式。动态地看待一个城镇是否开展了生态城建设和发展。评估一个城镇在过去的几年，例如5~10年的时间内，是否持续地实现节能减排，同时发展了经济；是否改善了生态环境；是否持续地提高了当地居民的生活水平，使人民安居乐业。

根据以上对中国生态城镇的发展目标、基本任务和主要挑战的分析；同时根据对生态城镇的发展是实现目标的一个过程的理解，作者提出三个论点：其一，生态城镇是实现经济、环境和社会一体化和可持续发展的一个过程；其二，实现发展模式和生活方式的转变是生态城镇之本；其三，创新是生态城镇的发展与建设之魂。

以这三个论点为基础，作者展开对中国生态城镇发展中的现状问题进行分析。

（一）生态城镇是实现经济、环境和社会一体化和可持续发展的一个过程

1. 中国生态城重视技术和经济发展，忽略生态城市社会和环境问题

虽然生态城镇目标的实现任重而道远，是一个相对漫长的过程，但“千里之行始于脚下”。正如前面已经提到的，在中国政府推行发展生态（绿色）经济，推动生态城镇建设的政策引导下，中国不少地区已经展开了多种形式的生态城镇探索。中国生态城镇的建设在规模、范围、领域和主要解决的问题都不一样；在不同的领域也尝试做了不少的工作。一些生态城在国内、外已经引起了不少的反响，例如天津和唐山曹妃甸的生态城。但调研发现，中国生态城市在实际运作上存在一些问题，这其中主要表现在重视技术层面的改造，以求实现经济的发展，但却忽略了生态城镇需要经济、环境和社会一体化的发展。目前生态城的发展对社会问题，特别是对民生问题的解决不够重视。调研发展，多数的城市在建设生态城时，虽然政策上谈到促进社会和谐的发展，在生态城发展指标体系构建上也确实包括了相关社会进步的问题，但没有具体的工作，基本停留在口号或指标上。还有的认为社会和谐的工作就是提高市民的素质，加强管理和预防，进行生活废弃物的处理等。这显示不少城市对生态城镇中要素构成之一的社会和谐发展并没有深刻的认识和考虑。

有些生态城在社会和民生问题上做了一些工作，但存在一些矛盾。例如，天津生态城的发展目标提出建设20%的廉租房（“公屋”），解决低收入阶层的居住问题。这应当是生态城镇的一个重要目标之一。但是天津生态城入住“公屋”家庭的各项标准中，除了收入标准之外，另外一个标准就是必须在生态城内工作。天津生态城的产业构成包括发展节能环保、科技研发、总部经济、服务外包、文化创意、教育培训、会展旅游等现代服务业；形成动漫园、影视园、科技园、产业园、信息园和总部园的高科技产业。根据生态城的产业构

成，又能有多少人成为廉租房（“公屋”）的受益者？这个疑问需要通过未来具体的实践找到答案。

在生态环境的保护方面，有些生态城甚至出现假借生态之名，行破坏生态之实！一些地区的生态城镇建设的选择就是在生态保护区或生态敏感区内。任何的开发建设，无论规模的大、小都将对原来的生态环境产生影响。当然生态城镇的开发建设，并不仅仅涉及生态环境的问题，而是实现社会、经济和环境的一体化发展。但这三位一体中，环境是另外一项要素构成。生态城镇的建设本应当避开生态敏感地段进行建设。沿河道或在山体生态敏感区进行所谓的生态城镇建设，不仅对现有的生态环境造成破坏，还可能带来洪水、山体滑坡、泥石流等自然灾害的风险。生态城镇建设中一个标准是提高防范自然灾害的能力和等级，在防洪风险管理上是国外政府制定生态城镇政策和标准的重要内容之一（于立，2009 年 a）。但现实是某些生态城的选址存在很大的问题，选择占用了原本就是很好的生态用地。

例如，用地面积约 66 平方公里的武汉花山生态新城，位于武汉新闻媒体所描述的“山体众多，湖泊环抱，植被茂密，风景宜人，自然环境优美”的东湖、北湖和西湖的交汇处（武汉视界网，2010 年 6 月 2 日），是武汉城市楔型保护绿地。虽然武汉花山生态新城规划中提到了对遭受破坏的生态环境进行修复。但是又为什么要首先对良好的生态环境进行破坏，然后再修复？生态城开发建设应当避开生态敏感地区。这种现象并非仅武汉花山一个地区，还有不少类似的项目。调查显示，生态城建设占用农业用地的占 60%，占生态用地的占 7%。这种模式的生态城建设是对生态环境带来严重的负面影响。

海南省中、日合作的乐城太阳与水示范区项目，规划在万泉河流域进行开发建设。该项目由两个部分构成，即乐城岛和大乐城。初期规划面积约 2.8 平方公里，远期规划面积约 19 平方公里。海南乐城太阳与水示范区项目提出的目标是构建低碳社会，希望所需能源全部通过太阳能、风能、水能等可再生能源解决，希望乐城岛成为首个“零碳排放”的生态城。该项目在生态城镇建设上尝试采用“民间平台，政府后台，国际舞台”的形式，这是一个很好的探索型的发展模式。但是调研了解到，目前的防洪还是二十年一遇的标准。远远低于一般的城市的防洪标准。随着全球气候的变化，西方国家一般城市的防洪标准已经提高到百年一遇，更何况一个生态城镇的建设。过去的几年，所出现的自然灾害的危害级别都已经是几十年，甚至上百年一遇。一个生态城镇如果没有充分考虑防灾问题，或防灾的标准太低，以致在未来造成灾害。这是不可饶恕的，也将成为一个大笑话！

减少交通的生成，减低交通带来的碳排放是生态城的一项标准。因此世界各国生态城建设的目标之一就是混合的土地利用。但是目前中国一些生态城显然在这个方面考虑不够。天津生态城的规划仍然采用了传统的土地分区的方式，而且仅 10% 的用地是产业用地，多数的土地使用功能是居住用地。这 10% 的产业用地将提供多少就业岗位？是否可能实现生态城镇“职住平衡”的要求？

根据“中新天津生态城总体规划专题研究：中新天津生态城人口规模测算”研究，中、新天津生态城的研发产业用地占 10%，约 3 平方公里。预计约可以提供 5 万人的就业岗位。研究认为，根据台湾新竹等地区的经验，产业人口带动服务业的系数为 0.8，那么服务业人口为4万人，因此估算生态城内部可以提供的就业岗位9万人。研究还提到，考虑到生态城内居住人口年轻化特征，按照每人的平均带眷系数为1.8计算，估算生态城内部16.2万人将可以达到职住平衡。而根据《中新天津生态城总体规划纲要（2008—2020）》估算生态城人口规模约为35万人左右。另外就业与居住的分布不一定能够按照规划的设想方案实行，市场发挥的作用更大，至今为止，各国新城建设还没有出现根据规划实现“职住平衡”的。因此解决这个问题需要更多地分析居民职业的构成，以及提供更多本地区就业的岗位机会，在土地利用上为就业岗位的用地需求留出更大的空间。天津生态城人口规模和就业分析的结果显示天津生态城建设成为“卧城”的可能性是极大的。

唐山曹妃甸生态城与工业园区是分离的。界定的生态城内的产业有部分的三产，主要以居住功能为主。另外居住与就业的分离带来两个问题：第一，每天将形成大量的潮汐交通流和交通量，就近就业无法实现；第二，一个缺乏产业的城镇，很难说就是一个真正的城镇。

在生态城镇的发展政策上，还出现相互矛盾的现象。生态城镇的发展政策是推行“绿色交通”鼓励使用自行车、步行等慢性系统，实现节能，减少污染。中国曾经以“自行车的王国”而闻名于世。过去在以自行车交通为主的年代，我国城市的道路系统形成了著名的“三块板”的格局，有独立的自行车道路网络。这种道路形式曾经让世界其他国家那些倡导环保和自行车出行的人们十分的羡慕。令人遗憾的是，随着小汽车拥有量及其使用的快速增长，在短短不到10年的时间内，在我们城市“三块板”的道路系统中，留给自行车的车道逐渐地被机动车道所侵蚀、或成为停车场。生态城镇的建设，推行“绿色交通”，一个行之有效、且无需很高成本的是将我们城市中的自行车道网络重新恢复起来，并与快捷的公共交通网络实现换乘节点的便利联系。

2. 重视大城市的新城，忽略中国城镇化的主要问题，小城镇发展和城乡协调发展

中国还在快速城镇化的进程中，以减少对环境的破坏，降低对资源和能源的消耗，避免社会问题的产生，以及实现城乡协调发展为主要目标的生态城镇化是中国可持续发展的道路。重视和促进城市与农村之间的经济联系网络的建立，这是生态城镇化的一项重要的核心问题。

中国的“三农”问题仍然是当前城镇化和工业化面临的重要问题之一。中国仍然有大量的农村人口，生态城镇的发展需要同时考虑农村问题，考虑如何实现生态发展模式，帮助和促进农业经济的发展，并解决城乡收入差距的问题。经验已经证明如果我们忽略了农村经济的发展，仅仅一味发展城市，特别是大城市，将可能面临经济和社会巨大的风险。因此，生态城镇的规划和建设必须顾及乡村地区，实现城乡协调和一体化发展。需要制定相关的政策和措施促进农村社区之间政治和社会网络的建立，及其与生态城镇的联系。在世界不少国家的生态城镇的规划和政策的制定上基本都涉及与农村协调和共同发展的问题，很遗憾国内的生态城镇多数不考虑这个方面的问题。调研的数据显示，仅7%的城市在生态城镇的发展目标和需要解决的问题中提到了农村问题和城乡协调发展的问题。

能够促进城市与农村之间的经济联系网络的核心是建设生态型的小城镇。生态型的小城镇应当成为中国生态城镇发展的政策导向中最重要的组成部分。需要从资金、土地和制度上

着手，解决小城镇既不是农村又不像城市的现状。生态城镇应当发挥小城镇在我国城镇体系中、在城乡经济发展中所应发挥的承上启下的功能，实现小城镇服务于乡村，联系城市的枢纽作用，发挥小城镇传递大中城市向农村经济辐射的功能（仇保兴，2006 年）；解决几个亿农民的流向大城市所带来的严重的社会和城市问题，包括城市的交通、每年春节的民工潮、农村里的留守老人和留守儿童等。

虽然生态小城镇的建设是中国生态城镇化和有效处理城乡差距的重要途径，但是至今为止，中国生态城镇建设针对小城镇，特别是对现有小城镇进行生态化的规划，促进其生态经济发展的并不多见。主要的原因之一，犹如 2010 年 11 月 25 日《南方周末》报道“中国生态城迷失”中所提到的，“在无人识得生态城真面目的时候，谁的方案先采纳不仅仅意味着不菲的咨询费，也意味着在业界的强大话语权”。目前多数生态城的建设无非是为了建立一个“标本”。因为 21 世纪城市发展的语境必然是气候变化和可持续发展。这两个内容都与生态城镇有直接的关联。因此，生态城镇或冠于其他名称的城市发展，如可持续的城市或绿色城市等的规划与建设将是一个重要的主题。世界上已经有不少国家在进行生态城镇的规划和建设。所以如果能够成功的建立一个生态城的标本，将直接影响一个城市或一个规划和建设的咨询机构在这一轮城市可持续发展过程中的作用与影响力。而能够显示在生态城规划和建设领域成就的莫过于从一无所有的平地开始的新城的规划与建设，这是为什么国外咨询公司对中国的生态新城趋之若鹜的原因。

现有小城镇进行生态规划与建设所获得的成就感和表现力远远不如新城的建设，而且规划咨询费用与大城市周边的新城规划相比较，就低得太多了。因此虽然生态小城镇的规划和建设本应当是中国生态城镇发展的重点之一，但目前的问题是，现有小城镇的生态规划和建设既吸引不了国内主要的规划机构的重视，更不用说国外的咨询机构了。

生态新城建设是必要的，特别是在某些特大城市地区。但中国生态城镇的工作重点应当是针对大、中城市建成区的生态社区建设和生态化的改造；以及发展与农村有密切联系的、生态型的小城镇。

3. 生态城镇发展建设成本问题研究不足

对于发展中国家，如何通过挖掘现有的资源，改善环境，提高人民的生活水平，减少碳的排放，但又尽可能采用低成本的方式实现目标是非常重要的。因为只有这样才可能做到可持续的发展。

中国城市科学研究会的调查结果显示 57% 的城市十分担心生态城镇建设的成本问题。认为这是制约生态城镇发展的一个重要的因素。

实际上生态城镇的建设不一定必须都是高成本的。一些国家的经验值得我们借鉴。

巴西库里蒂巴在建设其生态城市过程中，既有技术的创新，更有制度的建设和创新。他们通过“建筑权的转移”（transfer of building right）及其购买，通过制度的建设，解决了对历史建筑的保护、维修和提供可支付住宅（廉租房问题）等资金的问题。

库里蒂巴还实施了“绿色交换”（green exchange）的项目，开展了“垃圾不应就是垃圾”（garbage is not garbage）运动。

巴西库里蒂巴这种简单、讲究实效、成本很低的生态城镇的项目很值得我们借鉴和学习。

实际上，中国传统建筑的一些简单的措施就能够在住房的节能问题发挥重要的作用。例如楼房的南、北朝向和通透性、形成穿堂风等。当然这就要求城市设计和景观设计能够发挥作用，通过合理的设计减少建筑和小区布局呆板、缺乏美感的问题。

节能建筑还可以通过一些低价的措施提高节能的效率，这其中包括建筑的外墙采用隔热层，窗户采用双层玻璃，提高房间的防透气能力就可以实现保持室温的效果。在生态城镇的建设过程中，对于如何节约成本、降低造价、充分利用本地区的自然条件，目前相关的研究开展的不是很多。

（二）实现发展模式和生活方式的转变是生态城镇之本

1. 当前的政绩评估体系影响发展模式的转型，价值导向影响生活方式的转变

实现发展模式和生活方式的转变作为生态城镇发展的基本任务，是生态城镇之本。但是当前的政绩评估体系不利于促进发展模式的转型，而目前社会上的价值导向影响了生活方式的转变。

生态城镇的发展需要实现节能减排，可持续发展的目标。中国的生态城镇发展需要变革过去的发展模式。

改革开放30多年，中国的经济发展和城市建设取得了举世瞩目的成就，人民的生活水平有了巨大的提高。2010年中国成为世界上第二大经济体。然而我们应当清醒地看到，这些成绩的获得所付出的代价以及中国仍然是一个发展中国家这个事实。

改革开放以来所采用的粗放型、出口导向型的和劳动密集型的发展模式，为中国的发展做出了重大的贡献。但是这种发展模式造成的是资源大量的耗费和严重的污染问题。更为重要的是在这个发展的过程中，我们有意或无意地忽略了社会平等和城乡协调等社会问题，

中国未来的发展还面临一个巨大的挑战，这就是资源的问题。住房和城乡建设部副部长仇保兴博士的研究（2009）表明中国正以全球7%的耕地，7%的水资源，4%的石油，2%的天然气推动全球21%人口的城镇化。中国的城镇化和工业化显然遭遇到巨大的资源缺口。中国不可能走西方国家，甚至其他发展中国家所经历的、常规的工业化与城镇化道路。由于庞大的人口与短缺的资源之间所存在的矛盾，中国不得不走一条生态城镇化和生态经济发展的道路。过去30年所走的粗放型的道路不具备可持续性。若继续沿这条道路发展，中国的未来将受制于他人。

中国经济发展所产生的污染问题已经不仅仅是生存条件和生活质量的问题了，它还涉及国际政治问题。“全球暖化”和“控制排放”这几年一直就是国际间讨论和关注的事情。在当今国际议事日程上的众多问题中，没有任何问题比气候变化与日俱增地威胁着人们的生存，因此也更具有全球的影响。这种气候变化所带来的影响，将波及地球上每一个国家的每一个居民，甚至会改变人类的生存方式。正因如此，全球气候变化已经成为世界各国政府、学术界和人民普遍关注的问题。

如果我们不采取措施控制污染，减少排放，开发新能源改变我们现有的发展模式，其结果不仅仅严重影响了当代中国人的身心健康，破坏了我们当代人和后代的生存条件，而且加速全球气候变化的速度；更为重要的是，我们自己国内的能源和资源，无法持续满足供给，我们的发展将受制于他人；全球的能源和资源也无法满足所有的人都像美国人的那种生活方式，这是现实。因此，我们的发展模式需要变革！

但是目前整个政府的评估体系、方式、模式与生态城镇发展所要求的发展模式的转变并不配套，存在很大的距离。另外目前的财税和投资体系所产生的地方政府的“土地财政”问题对生态城镇的建设也有很大的影响。解决的前提是实现地方政府、领导现有的这种评估方式和政绩要求的转变，进行制度的创新。

在生活方式转变上，主要的制约因素是价值观的导向出现很大的误区。

中国改革开放使全体人民的整体生活水平有了很大的提高。随着人民收入的增加，人们的生活方式与过去相比有了很大的变化，特别体现在城市居民的吃、穿、住、行和生活方式上。但是中国毕竟还是一个发展中国家，还有不少居民的收入仍然很低，城乡收入差距很大，甚至我们经常挂在口中的 GDP，一按人均进行计算，就远远落后世界上许多的国家。

虽然过去的 30 多年，中国为世界减少贫困做出了榜样，成为减少贫困人口最多的国家之一。但是在中国人们整体生活水平得到提高的同时，中国仍然存在不少贫困人口。按照中国 2009 年确定的 1196 元的标准，中国仍有 3597 万绝对贫困人口；如果按照世界银行的标准（1.25 美元/人/天），中国还有 1.5 亿人贫困人口（全国人口的 11.5%）。中国社会的变革，还带来相对贫困人口增长的现象，贫富差距在加大，城乡差距更趋严重。这带来了许多潜在的和隐性的社会不稳定的因素。中国要可持续地发展，就必须实现全社会的平等和全体人民公共的富裕，巨大的贫富差距问题必须要得到解决。

然而，一些先富裕起来的人们在生活消费上开始追求奢侈、浪费和讲排场。生活方式追求欧美发达国家居民的形式。追求大排量、排放污染严重的汽车；追求一掷千金、浪费资源的消费方式。

根据“新华网”的消息，中国已经成为世界顶级奢侈品的重要市场，在上海举办的顶级奢侈品展览。组办方将法、意、英、美等国众多顶级品牌参展，从私人飞机、豪华游艇，到钻石珠宝、时装名表，以及世界著名投资理财公司、贵族百货，凡与有钱人沾边的应有尽有，其规模、奢侈度可与著名的摩纳哥顶级私人物品展媲美（新华网，2005 年 3 月 4 日）。根据英国《金融时报》的报道，在短短 1 年内，上海曾连办 3 次奢侈品展，这是全世界任何城市都未曾经历过的奢华体验（《金融时报》，2006 年 5 月 12 日）。而这种现象越演越烈，继上海、北京、深圳、厦门、南京后，开始向西部城市延伸，目前已经进入成都（中国经济新闻网，2011 年 1 月 7 日）。2010 年上海胡润百富（Hurun report）公布了对 401 位中国富翁的调查结果。结果表明中国亿万富翁每年的平均支出为 250 万元人民币，他们青睐于少数高端奢侈品牌，根据胡润的报告，受到中国富裕人群欢迎的多数奢侈品牌都是外国品牌（《金融时报》，2011 年 1 月 8 日）。《金融时报》的报告还提到，2010 年，中国成为宝马 7 系、5 系、X6、5 系 GT 全球最大市场。在中国富人的狂热追捧下，宝马车型售价最高的几个细分市场，中国已经全部包揽全球第一的位置。奔驰公司2010年在中国市场售出各种品牌车型147670辆，同比增长115%（《金融时报》，2011年1月30日）。

在目前的中国，这样的生活方式和追求对一些人来说，特别是富裕起来的一批人并非是不能，而是是否应当的问题。与全国的人口相比较，富翁仍然还是少数，农村还有上千万人生活在贫困线下，城市失业下岗不在少数，巨大的贫富差距尽人皆知，已经带来不少社会问题。中国社会科学院曾经在“2010年《法治蓝皮书》”中提到，中国的贫富差距加大，相对贫困人口增加，各种社会矛盾引发各种群体性事件多发。当前某些阶层、群体这种挥金如土，一味贪图奢侈与虚荣，炫耀比阔，宣泄物欲的现象本不应在中国出现。

中国每年的中秋节奢侈型月饼的包装及其他各种华丽的礼品盒不仅仅造成大量资源的浪费和树木的砍伐；还产生大量垃圾的排放。造成这些现象，其中有社会风气的原因，也有社会价值观导向的因素。

过去几年，中国的汽车产业得到快速的发展。汽车产业的发展有利提升中国机械制造业、钢铁等产业的综合水平，提高中国的经济发展能力，同时带来不少的就业岗位。但是汽车产业的发展，特别是汽车进入家庭带来大量石化能源的消耗却带来很大的隐患，中国对石油和钢铁的需求依赖进口。小汽车进入家庭了，对石油的需求也开始增加。我们的能源命脉开始被他人掌握。而且汽车排放的污染问题，城市交通的拥挤问题日趋严重，中国的几个大城市已经成为世界上交通最拥堵的城市之一。

10多年前在中国多数城市，“节约每一滴水”和“节约每一度电”的宣传到处可见。这几年这种类型的宣传从许多城市，特别是一些大城市消除了。我们的一些专家、学者和媒体更多考虑和宣传的是人均用水量和人居用电量如何追上西方国家，向西方国家的水平看齐。这种现象在许多城市编制生态城市指标体系的过程中表现得更为明显，存在着生态型节约用水标准和向西方国家人均用水标准看齐，美其名为生活质量提高的矛盾和争论。作者认为，无论是用电，还是用水，中国没有必要向西方国家看齐。因为每个国家，甚至每个城市的气候条件不一样，资源构成也不一样。中国许多城市属于严重缺水的城市，而西方国家，甚至国内的一些城市不一定存在这个问题。另外生活方式也不一样。西方国家用水量高，其中一部分水耗的构成是用于浇花，浇自家院里的草地。中国城市的多数居民没有自家院子。作者认为用水和用电等应当是以能够满足需求，实现舒适度为标准。在缺水型的城市，减低用水量不一定就不能实现舒适的生活。“节约每一滴水”和“节约每一度电”的宣传应当重新出现在所有的生态城镇。

2. 社会成本建设尚未起步，社会各群体的参与有待加强

社会资本是指一个地区合作做事的能力，强调做事情的协作方式。实施这种方式需要建立一种能够鼓励每个人、团体、组织开展合作的机制和氛围（于立，2009b）。

生态城镇的基本任务，发展模式和生活方式的转变需要逐步实现整个社会的变革。使人们意识到生产与消费是密切联系在一起的活动。建设生态城镇需要从更大的、更广泛的社会体系上进行考虑。这个系统包括产业的活动。在全社会实现全面的低碳。这其中要解决的问题包括城市与区域规划，消费模式，节能，能源的保护，上游的产业链，产品的再利用、整修利用和循环利用，并将这些活动与本地区产业的生产活动结合起来。

建设真正意义上的生态城镇，需要得到社会所有人的认同和支持，其中包括各级的政府、居民和市场的力量，需要得到广大消费者和开发机构的合作。因此建设和增加社会资本，提高社会生态发展的意识和共识是目前我们开展生态城镇的一项重要的任务。然而在这个方面，无论是政府机构，或社会团体、学术部门、媒体在宣传导向上存在误区，至少做的很不够。

提高社会资本的方式可以是开展社区物质文化生活建设；加强社区的参与和凝聚力，增强地方的自我管治能力；实现居民对本地（文化）的认同感；并通过建立、增强和协助地方的自我管治机制，以及完善社区活动的基础设施等措施。应当通过减少犯罪率，提高居民的安全感；更重要的是避免各领域存在的不平等，包括教育、就业、医疗等领域存在的不平等。社会资本的建立还应当鼓励居民们转变生活方式，例如减少对商品过度包装的需求，更多选择本地农产品和食品等。

生态城镇需要各方的参与，生态城镇的和谐需要社会的共建。因此只有在全社会上达成共识，才有可能解决中国生态城镇发展存在的问题，实现发展模式和生活发展的转变，建立真正意义上的生态城镇。具体的手段应当通过提高社会资本的方式，这是实现社会和谐以及实现全社会参与生态城镇建设的一个有效的方法。

（三）创新是生态城镇的发展与建设之魂

1. 创新能力，特别是制度创新的缺失制约生态城镇的发展

生态城镇与一般常规城镇的一项重要的区别体现在社会和技术领域以及制度上的创新。创新是生态城镇之魂，但也是中国生态城镇面临的主要挑战。没有了创新，生态城镇的建设与一般城镇就没有太大的区别。

中国城市研究会调研发现，40%的城市认为制约生态城镇发展的一个重要因素是制度的问题。因此，有57%的城市提出制度的创新是生态城市发展的必须。当然技术的创新基本上是所有城市一致的观点。有50%的城市深感现有城乡规划的理论和技术手段远远落后于社会经济的发展，特别是生态城镇发展建设的要求。另外6%的城市提出产业和经济发展模式的转型也需要有创新的意识和理念。还有3%的城市提出了对文化发展的创新。

在新能源开发上和运用同样也需要考虑结合本地区的气候条件，并非所有的地区都适合风能或太阳能。生态城镇的建设不能完全照搬他人的做法。别人的经验可借鉴，但不能照抄。

但是，中国城市科学研究会的调研发现，多数生态城镇在谈到创新时，特别是绿色建筑和再生能源等领域，只有少数几个城市考虑了在运用绿色技术的过程中与本地的气候、地形和环境特点相结合，进行本地化调整，使绿色建筑具有地域性，并体现当地的风土民俗和传统文化。

中国经历了30多年快速的发展和城镇化，但是我们的创新能力一直很弱，盛行的功利主义使很多的产业和地区一直采取模仿和拿来主义。科技进步和创新是富强之基和发展之

本。中国的经济与社会发展已经到了必须将科技进步和创新作为加快转变经济发展方式的重要支撑。这一点同样适应生态城镇的发展需求。没有创新就不可能建设真正意义上的生态城镇，而且创新领域不能仅仅局限在技术，还包括管治或制度的创新。目前生态城镇的创新考虑基本上针对技术层面的问题，管治或制度领域的创新展开的不是很多。而制度的创新对于发展模式转型和生活方式的转变至关重要，调查中多数城市的反馈意见说明了这一点。

另外需要强调的是在考虑创新时我们有必要意识并牢记一点，建设生态城镇，创建一个更为和谐的社会，推行低碳、节能的发展，实现社会、环境和经济一体化地发展是我们的目标。技术的创新是一项重要的手段，但不是目的。

2. 规划理论和手段缺乏创新，滞后于社会经济的发展

与技术的创新一样，中国的城乡规划的手段和理念需要创新，目前开展的生态城镇规划需要引入新的规划理论和方法。

但是很遗憾的是目前中国规划界多数的机构对于生态城镇的规划建设有点麻木不仁，生态城镇的规划理论和手段滞后，规划界疑惑生态城镇的方向。对这个生态城镇的规划理论和技术手段的探讨和尝试非常缺乏，除少数一些机构，大多数的规划编制机构基本没有太多的举措，如果规划行业不迎头追赶，使规划适应社会经济的发展，落伍的规划将可能面临边缘化的危险。

目前无论是中央政府还是地方政府，参与或牵头生态城镇建设的部门不少。根据中国城市科学研究会开展的问卷调查，在各开展生态城规划和建设的城市中，由城市领导直接负责的综合性领导小组，包括管委会等类型的机构占10%；由环保局负责牵头进行生态城建设的城市占30%；由发改委、规划局和建设局协作负责生态城建设的城市占13%；由规划局和建设局合作牵头的占13%；规划局负责的城市占17%；由建设局牵头负责生态城建设的城市占7%。

无论是哪个部门负责生态城的建设，都需要有具体的措施能够协调并引导城镇的发展。生态城镇的发展涉及经济、社会、文化、历史、人文、环境等问题，需要实现经济、社会和环境一体化和可持续的发展，相关的政策需要落实到空间上，因此需要具备手段和措施，能够协调社会各阶层，统筹各行业和各领域之间的合作。世界各国的生态城镇建设都以城乡规划作为协调和统筹的主要工具。中国生态城镇的发展也需要城乡规划的创新，适应社会和经济的变革，有效引导各地生态城镇的发展和具体的建设。

规划的创新是多层面的。在理论上，需要重新审视规划的意义和作用，根据当今世界全球化所导致的复杂的、不确定的环境，构建适应中国城乡发展的规划程序理论和方法，科学地、有效地进行城乡规划的编制和实施（于立，2008年）

在区域规划和总体规划的层面上，需要分析和发掘一个区域的物质流的走向，需要控制一个地区物质的数量和质量，需要考虑物质在得到利用之后，其废弃物能够成为另外的资源，得到进一步的利用和处理。这对于现有的规划模式提出了新的目标。

在城乡规划的微观层面上，可持续的城市设计手法是生态城镇建设的一个重要的工具。生态城镇应当很好地利用城市设计的手段，在考虑城市美学的同时，考虑风向、阳光等自然

环境的因素进行布局，实现建筑的节能和环保。生态城镇建设，不应当也不一定就必须是高成本的，首先应当考虑低成本的运作。城市设计和景观设计能够发挥很大的作用。

在土地利用上，规划需要重视混合的发展，提高密度，空间布局应当有利公共交通的使用。同时应当考虑变革传统的产业用地与生活休闲用地严格分区的方法。虽然目前在一般城市，以及生态城镇的规划中也经常提到混合的土地利用。但在进行土地的分区时，规划师们情不自禁地又在将土地划分为住宅、商业、工业等不用的土地利用性质。

混合的概念应当是大概念的混合，产业、商业、住宅、休闲等混合在一起。以此减少各种类型的出行需求，减少交通的生成，实现碳的减排，交通污染的减少。

在规划管理上，对于住区进行绿色建筑、绿色照明、绿色出行和其他绿色基础设施的建设等要有控制性和鼓励性的措施，以及相应的补偿机制。例如，对于每个居住区开发和建设项目，在规划审批时，应当对于绿色建筑、绿色照明和绿色基础设施的配置有一定的比例要求，这是控制性的内容。在此基础上，如果开发商或居民有意提高这个比例，应当给予鼓励，并相应有补偿措施，例如可以考虑在容积率方面有一定的补偿等，推行奖励性容积率，这是规划在制度上所需要考虑的创新问题。

四、结论

根据对国外生态城镇的研究，可以发现生态城镇的产生，有一个宗旨上的共识，即针对“全球暖化”问题，为了控制碳的排放，同时提高人民的生活水平；生态城市的发展与建设需要通过规划引导的方式实现社会、经济和环境的协调发展。城镇体系中的物质形态的确立和建设必须遵循自然规律与自然协调，或模仿自然运作规律，减少废弃物的生成，这不仅仅与人们日常的生活方式息息相关，也涉及产业的发展和经济的增长模式。另外生态城镇的规划和建设需要解决所在国家和地区所面临的问题。也正因为如此，在具体的操作上，每个国家和地区都体现了自己的特点。由于所面临的问题各自不同，因此每个生态城镇具体的规划和发展模式，生态城镇的标准和内容也有差异。这也是生态城镇的定义很难有单一的答案，很难形成一个为各国家或城市效仿的模式的原因。

但是从国际间各国生态城镇规划和发展的一个共识和一个共同点思考，对我国的生态城镇发展目标和宗旨，及其相应的规划和建设内容，显然具有一定启示和借鉴的意义。第一，从生态城市的发展目标和规划建设的内容角度分析，要求对我国目前的城乡规划体系和理论进行变革与创新；第二，在确定生态城镇发展目标前，需要确定我国城乡发展所面临的主要问题，并以此作为我国在生态城镇项目的开发建设中应当考虑解决的重要问题之一。

在过去的几年，中国有不少城市在生态城镇的发展上进行了探索，取得了一定的成绩和经验，特别是在产业园区的技术领域，引入了循环经济的新技术和新理念，也进行了一定的创新。这些有利于促进经济可持续的发展。但是调研发现对于生态城镇建设的另外两个主要的目标，社会和环境方面，所做的工作和相关的研究显然与促进经济的发展，特别是新技术的运用上有很大的差距。一些地方甚至有借生态城之名，对现有生态环境产生破坏的。生态城镇是经济、社会和环境的一体化发展，缺了任何一个环节的发展，就称不上为一个真正的生态城镇。

另外，由于当前的政绩评估体系和社会价值导向等问题，对发展模式的转型和生活方式的转变造成制约性的影响。社会上存在追求奢侈、浪费，讲排场的生活方式。对资源造成很大的浪费。这与生态城镇的发展理念是不相吻合的，给社会的发展带来潜在危险。生态城镇的发展需要全社会的共同参与，需要在全社会建立资源节约的共识，否则生态城镇的建设就是一句空话。然而在这个方面我们做得远远不够。政府和各级官员的评估方式需要变革，相关的研究和呼声早已经是学术界和媒体的热点，在此不再重复。但社会价值观的引导问题，中央政府虽然提出过，但在媒体的导向上有偏差。需要引导全社会对当今的价值观进行广泛的探讨，恢复我们曾经有过的节能、节约型的社会。

作为一个发展中国家，中国的生态城镇的发展之路应当更重视探索一条讲究实效、成本低廉的道路。中国曾经有过不少行之有效的经验，恢复这些传统对于中国生态城镇的发展有事半功倍之效。生态城镇的开发建设有必要加强对如何结合并利用本地区的气候、地形和环境等特点的研究，找到一条低成本的发展道路，实现发展的本地化，体现地方特色，避免千城一面的现象。

生态城镇的建设必须重视防灾问题，但是在生态城镇的具体实践中，这个问题往往被忽略。

创新是生态城镇之魂。技术的创新是当前中国生态城镇发展的主要方向。但是目前生态城镇在制度上的创新，在城市建设规划方法和理念上的创新却相对落后。一些生态城镇的规划仍然采用了传统的土地分区的概念，有效的、适合实际情况的混合型的用地规划模式还需通过实践和创新的手段创建起来，特别是在工业、商业、居住、娱乐、教育等不同的土地利用之间建立混合的模式。生态产业园的建设，通过节能、减排、废弃物循环利用、减少污染和新技术的利用等措施对打混合的理念提供的前提条件。

小城镇和城乡协调发展是中国城镇化和发展过程中有待解决的主要问题，生态城镇的建设应当解决中国所面临的主要问题，小城镇本应当是生态发展和建设的主要载体。但是对咨询费用，以及对市场份额和声望等功利型的追求，造成目前的生态城镇主要集中在大城市地区，进行新城的开发建设。

生态小城镇的建设提高到中国生态城镇建设的重要议程上，生态小城镇的建设更有可能实现从“低碳”的排放逐步过渡到“零碳”排放的目标。通过生态小城镇的建设解决城乡协调发展，加强和促进城市与农村之间的经济、文化和交通联系网络的生态型的城乡协调发展。通过制定相关的政策和措施促进农村社区之间政治和社会网络的建立，及其与城镇的联系。在经济领域，通过农业食品联系链的建立，特别是绿色的、有机的农副产品与城镇市场之间联系链的建立，形成城乡互动的，一、二、三产联动的，城乡一体化的发展纽带。生态小城镇的建设同时也有利解决我国城镇化过程可能产生的对环境和不可再生资源所造成的威胁。

本文通过“生态城镇是实现经济、环境和社会一体化和可持续发展的一个过程”，“实现发展模式和生活方式的转变是生态城镇之本”和“创新是生态城镇的发展与建设之魂”

三个论点对中国生态城镇发展过程中所存在的问题进行分析，可以得出七个结论，它们是：

1）重视技术和经济发展，忽略生态城市社会和环境问题；

2）重视大城市的新城，忽略中国城镇化的主要问题即小城镇发展和城乡协调发展；

3）生态城镇发展建设成本问题研究不足；

4）政绩评估体系影响发展模式的转型，价值导向影响生活方式的转变；

5）社会成本建设尚未起步，社会各群体的参与有待加强；

6）创新能力，特别是制度创新的缺乏制约生态城镇的发展；

7）规划理论和手段缺乏创新，滞后于社会经济的发展。

然而，无论从中国发展的外部环境，还是从自身的需要来看，生态城镇的发展是中国当前以及未来的必由之路。虽然中国生态城镇在发展过程中存在这样或那样的问题，但作为人类住区的生态城镇，这是一项人类历史进程中的创新事物，是人类探索人与自然之间、人与人之间、发展与生态环境保护之间和谐共存的过程。

（作者：于立，英国卡迪夫大学规划和研究国际中心主任）

参考文献

［1］APEIS（Asia-Pacific Environmental Innovation Strategies），RISPO（Research on Innovative and Strategic Policy Options）. *Good Practices Inventory:Kitakyushu Eco-Town Project.* Asia-Pacific Environmental Innovation Strategies，Research on Innovative and Strategic Policy Options［R］. 2005.

［2］Bettina，B.，Raimund，B.. *Eco-town Programme*，UNEP/WUPPERTAL Institute Collaboration Centre on Sustainable Consumption and Production［R］. 2007.

［3］DCLG（Department of Communities and Local Government）. Planning Policy Statement：Eco-towns-A Supplement to Planning Policy Statement 1［R］. 2009.

［4］DCLG（Department of Communities and Local Government）. Draft Planning Policy Statement：Eco-towns-Consultation.［R］. 2008，a.

［5］DCLG（Department of Communities and Local Government）. Eco-towns Prospects［R］. 2007

［6］DCLG（Department of Communities and Local Government）. Eco-towns：living a greener future：Summary of consultation responses［R］. 2008，b.

［7］Macedo，J. City profile Curitiba［J］. *Cities*，2004，21（6）：537－549.

［8］The Met Office Hadley Centre. *Climate*：*Observations*，*projections and impacts*［R］. 2010. http：//www. metoffice. gov. uk/media/pdf/4/p/China. pdf.

［9］WUPPERTAL Institute for Climate. Environment and Energy［R］. Eco－Town Program.

［10］仇保兴. 我国城市发展模式转型趋势：低碳生态城市［J］. 城市发展研究，2009，16（8）.

［11］仇保兴. 小城镇发展的困境与出路［J］. 城乡建设，2006（1）.

［12］金融时报，2006－05－12［2011－01－06］http：//www. ftchinese. com/story/001004346.

［13］金融时报，2011－01－08［2011－01－06］http：//www. ftchinese. com/story/001036528.

［14］金融时报，2011－01－30［2011－01－30］http：//www. ftchinese. com/story/001036693.

[15] 李忠东．最适宜人类居住的城市．库里蒂巴 [J]．国土绿化，2009 (10)．

[16] 南方周末，2010-11-025 [2010-12-28] http：//www.infzm.com/content/52790.

[17] 欧阳志云，赵同谦，苗鸿，王如松，王效科．海南制糖2酒精2能源2农业生态产业模式设计 [J]．环境科学学报，2004，24 (5)：915-921.

[18] 秦柯，李利．库里蒂巴的可持续发展规划实践及对我国城市规划和建设的启示 [J]．现代农业科技，2008 (19)．

[19] 武汉青山区人民政府．武汉市青山区循环经济试点实施方案 [R]．2008年．

[20] 武汉视界网，2010-06-02 [2011-02-11] http：//pic.cnhubei.com/sjshow/201006/t20100602_6546.shtml.

[21] 新华网，2005-03-04 [2011-01-06] http：//news.xinhuanet.com/collection/2005-03/04/content_2646634.htm.

[22] 于立．创立一个中国式的生态发展模式：安吉研究 [J]．城市发展研究，2009，B (10)．

[23] 于立．构建适应我国城乡发展的规划框架：新城乡规划法到来之前对规划程序的一些思考 [J]．城市发展研究，2008 (5)：73-79.

[24] 于立．中国生态城镇发展目标和实施措施初探 [J]．国际城市规划，2009，A (6)．

[25] 中国经济新闻网，2011-01-07 [2011-02-08] http：//www.jjxww.com/html/show.aspx? id=183343&cid=209.

我国城市综合交通问题评述

我国城市交通发展依然处在挑战与机遇并存、危机与希望并存，复杂、敏感而困难的关键时期。城镇人口与客货运输需求还在持续快速增长，城市机动车特别是私家车增长更为迅猛；尽管城际和城市交通基础设施建设还在加快推进，但区域与城市交通供求矛盾依然突出；尽管各城市正在加大力度、加快实施公交优先和拥堵治理，但城市交通拥堵状况依然严重；尽管从立法和执法、管理和治理等多方面加强了交通安全工作，但重特大交通事故频发势头并没有得到有效遏制，总体交通安全形势依然不容乐观；尽管绿色交通、慢行交通等得到了明显重视和加强，但交通节能减排、和谐交通环境依然任重道远。这一切都意味着处在城镇化、机动化联动高速发展时期的我国城市交通问题高度复杂性、高度敏感性，需要采取更加科学、更加理性和更加智慧的态度与方式去认识、理解和处理。

一、拥堵治理初见成效，发展趋势不容乐观

近年来，随着我国经济持续快速增长，城市化进程持续加快，机动车特别是小汽车呈现爆发式增长，引发了从沿海到内陆、从南方到北方、从东部到中西部，全国各大城市道路交通拥堵日趋严重，成为社会各界日益关注的热点和焦点。

2011 年全国两会期间，“治堵”成为代表委员们提案建议的重点，包括公车改革、轨道建设、公交优先、完善路网、交通管理、调控车辆发展等[1]。全国人大代表张育彪表示：治理交通拥堵，首当其冲是进行公车改革，限定公车的购买和使用；建议国家应该尽快出台公车使用规定；建议公车号牌向社会公开，鼓励群众举报公车私用，严惩公车私用行为。九三学社中央在提交全国政协十一届第四次会议的一份提案中建议，大力发展最具效率的地铁交通，发挥其在公共交通中的核心作用，有计划地增加城市中心区的地铁密度，完善地铁中心枢纽和配套服务功能，结合产业布局和人口流向原则使地铁在城区内四通八达；坚持实行低廉票价。同时，九三学社中央也认为，政府应建立低廉、方便、快捷、高效的公共交通系统，增强公共交通对市民的吸引力。同时努力缩小乘客候车时间。进一步优化公交线路设计，做好换乘设计、站点规划和乘车付费手段管理，科学设计公交站台，进一步优化运行时间。全国政协委员李立新建议各地应确立“路权分配”理念，因地制宜建设“步行系统”，从根本上医治交通拥堵的“城市病”。他认为香港以“空中连廊”为代表的“步行系统”，

在治理城市交通拥堵上最具优势。内地的大部分城市比香港拥有更为有利的地质自然条件，所以，李立新委员认为，内地大中城市完全可以因地制宜，选择最经济、最合适的“步行系统”建设方案。十届全国人大代表周厚健建议：用软投资改善交通环境，大城市的交通问题解决之道不仅在于“建”，更在于“管”和“控”。并指出要向西方学习，努力提高国民的交通意识和加强建设城市的智能指挥控制系统。代表委员们提出的这些建议都经过了认真调研、深入分析、深思熟虑，具有很强针对性，大部分建议都是正确和可取的，值得各级政府认真采纳、积极实施。

事实上，城市交通拥堵治理已经引起了各级党委和政府的空前重视，列入了党委和政府的重点议题和中心工作。北京市政府继2010年底公布实施《关于进一步推进首都交通科学发展加大力度缓解交通拥堵工作的意见》，取得较明显成效后，再次推出了《缓解北京市区交通拥堵第八阶段（2011年）工作方案》：（一）从加快交通基础设施建设，提高承载能力；（二）继续实施交通疏堵工程，提高通行能力；（三）加强交通精细化管理，提高交通管理水平；（四）着力实施5项重点措施：公交提速、地铁运力保障、道路交通秩序整治、停车秩序综合整治小客车数量调控；（五）文明交通建设。从上述5个方面提出了66项任务综合措施。广州市发布了《广州中心城区缓解交通拥堵方案》，从加强交通基础建设、调节交通量、加强交通管理3个方面提出了30项措施；深圳市以建立“公交都市”示范城市为目标，探索缓解城市交通拥堵之道，并发布了《深圳市城市交通白皮书》和《关于进一步转变交通发展方式加大力度缓解交通拥堵工作的意见》。其他大城市如天津、沈阳、长春、大连、郑州、贵阳、兰州、沙市、许昌、呼伦贝尔等城市的市委、市府先后发布治理城市交通拥堵的实施方案、意见或计划，或进行专题研究部署。这些拥堵治理措施的积极推进实施，不同程度上对缓解城市交通拥堵取得了一定的成效。北京市自实施治堵系列措施以来，2011年本市交通拥堵指数下降了12%，早晚高峰平均速度提高了13%，拥堵路段和拥堵持续时间减少了50%[2]。广州中心城区高峰期干路平均车速达到23公里/小时，轨道交通日均客运量突破400万人次，公交出行占机动化比重超过60%，而私人机动化出行比重比上年下降了3.6个百分点。

冷静客观地认识和判断未来一段时期（至少10年左右时间内）我国城市道路交通发展趋势，情况不容乐观。大城市的交通拥堵正从高峰时段向全天候扩大，从市中心向外围扩大、从局部地区局部节点路段向网络化扩大。许多大城市道路交通负荷已接近甚至超过路网极限容量，道路交通运行正处于极为脆弱、极不稳定的状态。经济发展较快较好的中小城市也将出现较严重的交通拥堵。其一，机动车特别是私家车还将持续快速增长。近5年，我国机动车保有量保持较快增长速度，年均增量达1 591万辆。2011年全国机动车保有量达到2.25亿辆，新增加1 773万辆，汽车保有量突破1亿量，新增加1 493万辆。全国共有23个城市的机动车保有量超过100万辆，其中，北京、重庆、成都、上海、广州、杭州、天津7个城市的机动车保有量超过200万辆。拿北京市来说，即使自2010年开始推行汽车总量控制、摇号上牌之后，每年新增汽车还在20万辆以上，每5年还要新增100万辆小汽车！这对几乎已经处于极限饱和状态的北京来说，无疑还在火上浇油！而对于其他机动车保有量突破100万辆或者200万辆大关的大城市来说，它们的轨道交通规模、公共交通系统远没有北京好；它们的道路网条件特别是快速路网条件也远不如北京好，如果持续以每年10多万辆、20多万辆甚至30多万辆的速度增长，那么这些城市的道路交通负荷与压力必将迅速加剧！其二，“公车治理”、“公车改革”已经喊了近20年了，虽不能说毫无成效，但遗憾而不争的事实是，公车越改越多，越治越乱！各城市“合规”注册的公车规模相比20年前已经增长了数倍甚至数十倍了，而违规使用的“公车”则更是很难统计道明了。公车的失控不仅仅是涉嫌违规腐败，不仅仅是公共财政的巨额浪费，更是妨碍和影响公平理性、有效治理城市交通拥堵的重要根源之一。其三，多重结构性问题短期内难于得到改善。包括均质蔓延的城市空间结构问题，比例失衡的综合交通体系结构和道路网体系结构问题，缺乏统筹的交通建设投资结构问题等。这些极为重要而关键的结构性问题是导致道路交通拥堵产生和不断加剧恶化的本源性问题。这些本源性问题绝非一朝一夕就能解决的，需要相当长的时间。其四，治理交通拥堵的制度环境和舆论环境还有待改进。在缺乏制度化的理性论证、决策、执行机制的情况下，城市政府很难形成连续的、长效的、持之以恒的拥堵治理政策与策略。来自不同岗位背景、专业背景、行业背景的决策者、参谋者和社会舆论，对交通拥堵的根源和治理拥堵的正确方向、路径和措施的认识存在极大差异甚至误区。许多涉及采用经济、行政和技术等手段对小汽车拥有和使用进行限制调控的政策措施均受到领导、专家、舆论的多重质疑和反对。相反，“修路治堵”这条已经被世界先进大城市交通发展经验证明收效甚微或者基本无效的治标之策，在国内却依然有着很大、很强的舆论基础和支持群体。导致那些本源的结构性问题的更是本源性的历史、政治、体制、机制等方面的问题，更非一蹴而就能解决的，需要时间和耐心，更需要智慧和勇气。

二、城际交通更加快捷，科学决策与管理还需加强

2011年全国铁路完成基本建设投资4 690亿元，铁路新线铺轨3 176公里、复线铺轨2 468公里，投产新线铁路2 022公里、复线1 752公里、电气化铁路2 647公里。2012年投产铁路更要达到6 300余公里[4]。2011年全国高速公路网建设继续推进，重点在国家高速公路网、国家区域发展战略确定的交通基础设施、特大城市圈、大中城市群交通基础设施以及省际“断头路”建设，重要运输通道扩容改造，完善疏港高速公路等方面取得重大进展。全国新增公路通车里程7.14万公里，其中高速公路1.10万公里。长江干线南京以下12.5米深水航道和中游荆江河段航道治理、京杭运河航道改造升级和西江老口航电枢纽建设等有序推进。民航基础设施建设加快推进，全年完成固定资产投资690亿元，新增机场5个。这一大批区域与城际重大交通基础设施建成投产，进一步改善了我国国际、区际和城际交通间联系的快捷性和总体运输能力与水平，加速了城际交通进入高速网络化时代的步伐，对支撑和促进国家、区域和城市经济社会持续平稳快速发展发挥了极为重要的作用。

2011年6月30日，举世瞩目的全球距离最长、标准最高的高速铁路——京沪高铁于中国共产党建党90周年前正式开通运营。同日，青岛胶州湾大桥和胶州湾隧道同时建成通车，

这“一桥一隧”是目前世界上最长的跨海大桥和中国最长海底隧道。2011 年 11 月 1 日“神州八号”飞船成功发射，11 月 3 日“神州八号”与“天宫一号”空间实验室首次实现成功对接。这些标志着中国在高速铁路、宇宙飞船等高端载运工具综合制造技术、超长距离高精度高速铁路建造技术、特大型跨海桥梁隧道建造技术等领域再次获得了重大突破，在国际上取得了领先水平。

本轮交通基础设施建设高潮始于 2008 年下半年中国政府为抗击全球“金融海啸”而推出的 4 万亿元投资拉动“扩内需、保增长”计划[3]。当年，铁道部拟定了 3 年内新建 4 万公里铁路、总投资 3.5 万亿元的投资计划；交通运输部推出了 3 ~5 年内投资 3 万亿 ~5 万亿元用于公路、港口等建设的投资计划；国家民航总局则出台两年内投资 4 500 亿元用于机场航空建设的投资计划。另外，2009 年国务院批复 22 个城市的轨道交通建设规划，总投资达 8 820亿元。这一波交通基础设施大投入、大建设中的众多交通基建项目从 2011 年开始陆续进入收官投产阶段。

如此高投入高速度交通基建，必然带来资金、人才、技术、安全、监管等多方面巨大压力。2008 年中央政府在宣布 4 万亿元投资拉动内需时，温家宝总理就要求要加强投资项目和资金的监督管理，提高工作的透明度，保证资金用好，发挥效益。不少全国人大代表和政协委员也纷纷提出议案建议，希望科学理性用好 4 万亿元巨资，严格科学论证、严格审批程序、严格审计监督。然而，百密难免一疏。第一，工程质量问题与运输安全事故凸现。投资 87 亿多元建设的甘肃省天水至定西段高速公路，是连接我国东、中、西部的骨干道路即连霍高速公路的重要组成部分，通车约半年就出现了坑槽、裂缝、沉降等重大病害，部分路段不得不铲除重铺。被称为“世界最长跨海大桥”的青岛胶州湾大桥通车 5 天后，这座有着“世界之最”名头的大桥就被曝出存在质量问题：很多隔离护栏的螺栓没有拧紧，有些地方甚至还没有安装隔离护栏。有“亚洲第一站”之称的京沪高铁南京南站开通不到 10 天，其北广场已有数千平方米的地砖需重铺。从 7 月 10 日至 14 日短短 5 天时间里，京沪高铁连续发生 5 次因故障影响正常运营的事件。7 月 10 日的故障主要原因在于滕州东站内，下行上海侧接触网附加导线，也就是供电线故障，中断供电 1 小时 37 分。另外两次故障也是因为列车在运行过程中电器元件发生故障而导致运行受到影响。2011 年 7 月 23 日 20 时 30 分 05 秒，甬温线浙江省温州市境内，由北京南站开往福州站的 D301 次列车与杭州站开往福州南站的 D3115 次列车发生动车组列车追尾特别重大事故，造成 40 人死亡、172 人受伤，中断行车 32 小时 35 分，直接经济损失 19 371.65 万元[5]。经调查认定，“7·23”甬温线特别重大铁路交通事故是一起因列控中心设备存在严重设计缺陷、上道使用审查把关不严、雷击导致设备故障后应急处置不力等因素造成的责任事故。京沪高铁建设工期由原设计确定的 5 年，先后被缩短为 4 年、3 年，而实际施工工期仅为 2 年 7 个月。如此重大举世瞩目的世纪工程，施工工期被如此一压再压，其工程风险可想而知！第二，巨大的资金压力在 2011 年也已经充分暴露。年初铁道部官员披露的建设计划是 2011 年中国铁路安排基本建设投资 7 000亿元，新线铺轨 7 935 公里，复线铺轨 6 211 公里，新线投产 7 901 公里，复线投产 6 861公里，电气化投产 8 800 公里[6]。年底实际完成的投资额、铺轨里程数、投产铁路里程数等却大大缩水。在2011年12月23日在京召开的全国铁路工作会议上，铁道部部长盛光祖首次证实铁路建设中存在的规模过大、标准过高、盲目压缩工期等问题。铁道部总负债已达1.8万亿元。受铁道部债务高企、资金短缺影响，江西境内包括沪昆客专、合福铁路等在内的多个铁路项目，从2011年8月份以来陆续处于停工或半停工状态，建设脚步放缓。这种情况并非只发生在江西。在湖北，包括汉宜、石武、武咸、武黄等铁路均已宣布推迟通车；在广东，厦深、南广、贵广等跨省铁路均停工或缓建。江苏境内的沪通铁路、宁安城际铁路、宁启铁路复线电气化改造等也被停工或缓建。由于银根紧缩，湖南、云南、陕西全国部分省市高速公路也出现了停建的现象[7]。第三，工程建设领域贪污腐败、违规招投标、偷工减料等现象依然相当严重。2011年，从原铁道部部长刘志军，原铁道部运输局局长、副总工程师张曙光等7名铁路高官被双规，到河南省交通运输厅第四任厅长董永安再度落马，原湖南省交通运输厅党组成员、湖南省高速公路管理局局长冯伟林涉嫌严重违纪被立案调查等，表明交通运输领域依然是贪腐案件重灾区。2011年4月审计署披露4万投资事后审计报告表明，发现部分项目以违规方式获取中央投资资金，未严格执行国家土地和环境保护政策，先行建设，未进行相关的招投标工作等问题。其中，18个项目以违规方式获得中央投资13 915万元人民币。出现以上一系列问题，说明重大交通基础设施建设科学决策科学管理还必须引起高度重视，要真正将科学发展观在工程建设领域贯彻到位。必须更加严格执行国家基本建设程序，合理确定重大交通基础设施的建设规模、建设时序、建设工期；必须更加严谨科学地编制和论证重大交通基础设施工程选址、规划方案、设计方案、施工方案；必须更加严厉预防和查处重大交通基础设施建设领域的贪污腐败、质量事故、运行安全事故。

三、公交优先渐入佳境，务实推进还需加快

2011年是大部门制改革公交行业管理划归交通运输部管理后的第三个年头，也是正式实施“十二五”公共交通发展规划的第一年。为贯彻落实国家城市公共交通优先发展战略，提高城市公共交通服务水平，满足人民群众基本出行需求，缓解城市交通拥堵和资源环境压力，交通运输部以交运发〔2011〕635号文发出《关于开展国家公交都市建设示范工程有关事项的通知》，明确在“十二五”组织开展国家“公交都市”建设示范工程，2013年年底前，启动30个城市示范工程试点工作。这是继2005年国务院办公厅转发建设部等六部委《关于优先发展城市公共交通意见》的通知（国办发〔2005〕46号）以后，中央政府层面又一次实质性地倡导和推进公共优先发展的一项有力举措。

中央政府的倡导激励，加上城市交通拥堵的日益加剧，各城市党委、政府也纷纷将公交优先发展列入议事日程，人大、政协也将公交优先作为议案建议和监督的重要题材。2010年12月23日，北京市再次公布了《关于进一步推进首都交通科学发展，加大力度缓解交通拥堵工作的意见》，提出要继续加大优先发展公共交通力度，实现跨越式发展。2011年2月26日，哈尔滨市政府召开全市优先发展城市公共交通领导小组第一次会议。会议明确了该

市实施公交优先发展战略的紧迫性和重要性，针对当前公交基础设施建设的五大任务，进行全面安排部署。4月11日无锡市人民政府办公室发布“关于印发《无锡市区落实城乡常规公交优先发展行动计划（2011—2013年）》的通知”。6月16日，广州市人民代表大会常务委员会作出《关于进一步优先发展公共交通的决议》。8月30日，杭州市人大常委会专题听取审议市政府《关于杭州市实施“公交优先”战略情况的报告》。10月31日，南京市政府召开常务会议研究南京公交优先发展五年行动计划方案和公交企业改革有关问题。11月11日，交通运输部和深圳市政府在深圳正式签署《共建国家“公交都市”示范城市合作框架协议》。12月23日深圳市交通运输委日前正式发布《深圳市打造国际水准公交都市五年实施方案》。11月21日，天津市第十五届人民代表大会常务委员会第二十五次会议，听取和审议该市优先发展公共交通情况。2012年元月召开的南京市第十四届人大第五次会议决定将加快实施南京城市公共交通优先发展列入2012年市人大常委会两件议案之一。

从各地推行公交优先发展的认识与举措看，第一，对公交优先发展的重要性、必要性和紧迫性等认识与决心更加统一、更为坚定；第二，公交优先发展规划更加系统、更为科学；第三，公交优先发展行动计划与实施方案更加务实、更为全面。如《南京市公交优先发展五年行动计划方案》提出要按照“十二五”南京公交优先发展目标要求，统筹规划，快速推进。主要内容包括：加快公交线网规划建设，加快轨道交通、地面公交、换乘中心等基础设施建设，推动公共交通资源有效整合，实现公交体系全市域覆盖。要优化公交、地铁与快速路网线路配置，构建完善的换乘体系，科学配置资源，提升运行效率。要加快改善车辆设施和管理水平，合理规划配套设施选址，科学研究更新车辆选型，大力引进新能源公交车辆，推动公交绿色清洁发展。同时提出，公交改革发展要打破传统模式，既要坚持公共服务产品的公益性、准经营性原则，又要坚持市场经济取向，构建现代企业制度和经营模式，通过整合资源，完善机制，增强公交企业内生发展活力，提升公交整体运营服务水平。

在公交优先战略得到广泛重视和加快推进的背景下，2011年，我国大城市公共交通建设和发展取得了相当大的进展和进步，主要体现在：

轨道交通。截至2011年底，全国城市轨道交通通车里程约1 800余公里，线路58条，运行车站数1178座。除2010年已有北京、上海、广州、天津、重庆、南京、武汉、长春、深圳、大连、成都、沈阳12座城市，又新增了西安、佛山两座城市。目前中国内地共有36座城市向国家主管部门上报了城市轨道交通建设发展规划，其中有31座城市得到了国家批准。计划至2015年前后规划建设96条轨道交通线路，建设线路总长2 500多公里，总投资超过1万亿元。

快速公交。截至2011年底，全国已经有北京、杭州、苏州、郑州、大连、常州、济南、枣庄、合肥、昆明、厦门、广州、重庆、乌鲁木齐、盐城15个城市开通了BRT线路运营。另外武汉、长沙、深圳、沈阳、南昌、常德、黄石、奉贤、柳州等城市也在计划和筹建中。在2011年美国交通运输研究委员会（TRB）年会上，广州由于在中山大道快速公交（BRT）系统、公共自行车系统、绿道系统等方面的突出建设成就，获得了可持续交通奖委员会颁发的“2011年可持续交通奖”，这是中国城市首次获得该项荣誉。从2011年5月至11月历时

6个月，乌鲁木齐快速公交1号线、2号线、3号线三条BRT线路建成开通。BRT 1号线和3号线开通仅一周，运量已经超过设计之初预测的数据，日均载客量超过20万人次。至2011年底，3条BRT线每天客流达33.3万人次。“大容量快速公交系统（BRT）开通运营”入选2011年乌鲁木齐十大新闻。2011年8月，国内第一条城际BRT线路——山东枣庄至台儿庄BRT线路正式开通。随着2011年9月23日B支4线的开通，盐城市规划的“一主一环五支”快速公交网络历时一年4个月全部建成通车，公交出行分担率由2009年BRT开通前的2.34%迅速提升到2011年的7.1%。

新公交系统。佛山市在2010年完成《新型交通系统规划研究》基础上，2011年，新型公共交通系统试验段（桂城至三山枢纽段）建设全面进入设计实施阶段。沈阳浑南新区、海口滨海旅游带、南京河西新城等现代新型有轨电车线路工程相继完成立项审批和工程调研，即将开工建设。

公交专用道。2011年6月，成都新增8条公交专用道，从2011年到2015年，每年还将新增公交专用道20公里以上。8月，广州新划设的公交专用道将集中在13个主要路段70公里公交专用道。南京新增4条共计8.5公里公交专用道。北京在城市放射线、拥堵路段增加施划公交专用道50公里。拉萨开辟4条公交专用车道。深圳将新增公交专用道150公里以上，至2015年底，全市公交专用道规模将达到780公里以上。沈阳新增公交专用道30公里。

换乘枢纽与公交场站。2011年全国交通运输工作会议上，李盛霖部长指出，“十二五”全国重点建设与铁路衔接的综合客运枢纽100个，在36个中心城市重点建设现代化综合客运枢纽，完善集疏运基础设施。江苏省交通运输厅厅长游庆仲提出，江苏把有机衔接作为构建综合运输体系的重要切入点，加快综合客运枢纽建设。依托铁路客运站规划建设一批综合客运枢纽，加强铁路与公路长途客运、城市公交、地铁、出租车等多种交通方式的有机衔接，努力实现客运“零距离换乘”，方便群众出行。北京市“十二五”期间，将重点建设四惠、宋家庄、苹果园、望京西、北苑北5个综合客运交通枢纽，还将规划新国展、丰台火车站、木樨园、奥体中心、通州新城、芍药居等一批新的综合性交通枢纽，打造“立体化”公交换乘系统。南京市继开工建设高铁南京南站、南京火车站、禄口国际机场和马鞍机场4个大型对外综合客运枢纽基础上，将结合城市轨道交通换乘枢纽规划12个城市区域性综合换乘中心。哈尔滨市2011年建设3个停车换乘枢纽，3个公交接驳枢纽，20座公交首末站，200座港湾公交停靠站。重庆2011年建成4个综合换乘枢纽，建成15个公交站场和6个公租房公交车首末站。

另外，2011年城市公交体制改革、换乘优惠、智能公交、绿色公交等方面也取得了一定进展和进步。新一轮城市公交体制改革以地级市、县级市为主，如河北廊坊市、浙江温州市、余姚市、乐清市、山东招远市、安徽宁国市、陕西延安市等，也包括了省会城市江苏南京市等。改革的主导方向是保障公益、国有主导、规模经营、适度竞争、加强监管。上海、南京、苏州、重庆、厦门等城市出台或酝酿出台公交（含轨道交通）换乘优惠政策。成都、沈阳、南京、合肥、厦门、福州、苏州、无锡等城市正在积极推进智能公交和绿色公交规划建设。

由此可见，公交优先发展和公交都市建设在我国正在渐成大势、渐入佳境，并已经取得重要进展。尽管如此，公交优先是一项复杂的系统工程和长期艰巨的任务，不可能一蹴而就。第一，与发达国家和国际先进城市相比，我国城市公共交通在综合交通体系中的主体地位和作用还远远没有真正确立。公交出行在全方式出行中的分担率还很低，绝大部分城市都没有达到30%，与国际先进40% ~60%的公交分担率相比差距很大，短期内要取得明显提高难度极大。第二，小汽车拥有与使用正在高速增长，已经采取调控的手段和成效都很有限，城市道路交通面临空前压力，对公共交通健康发展造成严重冲击。第三，公共交通供应能力、服务水平还远远不能满足广大市民选择公交出行的实际需要。大部分城市的公共交通体系还很不完善，层次单一、标准偏低、能力不足；大城市特大城市轨道交通快速公交建设发展需要巨大的资金投入和相当长的建设周期；路面公交供应能力与路权优先保障远远没有到位；公交枢纽场站建设还严重滞后，不能满足无缝衔接便捷换乘的出行要求；智能公交发展也还刚刚起步。第四，城市公共交通系统管理与运行体制改革还在摸索之中，公共性、公益性、服务性与市场性、竞争性、效率性等关系依然没有完全理顺协调；公共交通发展中的政府主导责任与财政能力，企业的服务目标与财务支撑，乘客的服务要求与承受能力等依然没有完全平衡协调。而城市化与机动化联动快速发展，则迫切要求城市公交优先和公交都市建设必须务实推进、加快发展，可以说时不我待，任务十分艰巨、时间极为紧迫。

四、交通转型引起关注，规划落实更为紧迫

“转型发展”是贯彻落实科学发展观的重要抓手，已经成为新一轮改革和发展的主题。转型发展包括了经济增长方式转型、发展动力与机制转型、产业结构转型、城市发展模式转型、百姓消费和生活方式转型等。毫无疑问，城市与区域交通发展也同样面临转型发展的重大课题，包括综合运输体系协调发展、交通引导产业和土地集约节约发展、交通节能减排与清洁能源技术、公交优先与低碳出行等。为此，2011 年从中央到各地方各城市也都做了积极探索研究和实际推动。

住房和城乡建设部提出 2011 年中国城市无车日活动的主题是：绿色交通 · 城市未来。确定这一主题，旨在鼓励人们更多关注和选择低能耗、低污染和低排放的绿色出行方式，传递政府应对资源环境约束，发展绿色城市交通的决心。

2011 年 9 月 20—22 日，中国城市规划年会在南京隆重举行。大会主题是“转型与重构”。中国城市规划学会理事长仇保兴就年会主题“转型与重构”发表了主旨发言，强调了城市空间与土地应当紧凑发展、混合利用，要合理安排步行、自行车、轨道、公交和小汽车各类交通用地，构建以绿色交通为主的城市综合交通体系。本次年会恰逢“世界无车日”。为实践低碳、低排放的规划理念，本届年会中所有参会人员，包括住房和城乡建设部、省市领导和国内外专家共 3 500 多人全部乘坐地铁参会，将会议公务与接待用车减少到最低程度。

2011 年 11 月 17—18 日，“中国城市交通规划 2011 年年会暨第 25 次学术研讨会”在武

汉召开。来自全国交通规划领域的专家学者400余人，围绕“城市交通发展模式转型与创新”主题，“城镇化与交通协调发展、交通与城市布局统筹规划、大众出行与公共交通、交通拥堵治理、交通管理机制创新”5个方面主要议题，展开了广泛深入的交流研讨。东道主武汉市副市长孙亚作了典型经验交流。为促进土地利用与交通协调发展，武汉市明确将推行以公共交通为导向的城市开发模式，在主城与6个新城组群间构筑由14条轨道交通、18条快速路组成的“多快多轨”复合交通走廊，以复合交通走廊促进和支撑城市“1+6”轴向跨越式发展。武汉市大力推进“低碳、环保”的绿色交通，绿色、环保的公共自行车系统建设全面展开，目前已经建成公共自行车租赁站点1 218个、自行车5万余辆，建成380公里自行车道和95座人行过街设施。同时，“一环、两带、六片”集通勤、运动、休闲和旅游等多种功能绿道网络体系启动，慢行交通系统不断完善，可持续发展的交通得到落实。

武汉的追求、尝试与经验近年来在国内其他大城市也在积极探索与尝试之中。由中国城市规划设计研究院承担完成的《长沙市综合交通规划》、《潍坊市综合交通规划》、《三亚市综合交通规划》等，都强调并很好体现落实了交通与城市空间、产业布局的互动协调。获得全国优秀规划设计一等奖的《昆山市城市总体规划》第一条规划理念就是“交通引导”。具体内涵是以轨道交通引导城镇空间集聚；以公共交通引导功能布局优化；以交通枢纽引导城市用地开发和服务业发展。2011年上报审批的《南京城市总体规划》与综合交通规划同步编制，突出了交通对城市总体规划各个层面的支撑和引领，承担交通规划编制任务的规划设计单位被确立为城市总体规划主编单位之一。南京提出以实现交通“畅达、绿色、和谐”为愿景，构建陆港、空港、水港、信息港“四港”合一的枢纽都市，支撑城市功能地位提升；构建国铁、城轨、城市道路公共交通等多级公交网络合一，高效率、高品质、高适应性的一体化公交都市，引导城市空间布局优化和交通方式结构优化；构建高机动性与高可达性的畅达都市，适应排堵保畅、节能减排、公平和谐的发展要求。这样的理念和目标被写入了该市党代会和“十二五”规划报告中。广州、杭州、深圳等城市总体规划与综合交通规划中都倡导和不同程度体现了公交优先、公交导向、公交都市等理念和要求。

2011年3月25日，交通运输部在无锡召开低碳交通运输体系城市试点启动会，深圳、天津、无锡等10个城市被确定为全国低碳交通运输体系建设试点。其中深圳市推出了具有典型代表意义的五大交通减碳策略：技术减碳、结构减碳、制度减碳、管理减碳以及消费者减碳，系统推进低碳、高效的交通运输体系建设。具体包括积极推进新能源和清洁车辆的推广应用；结合公交都市建设，进一步优化交通方式结构、建立公共交通主导的城市交通发展模式；加强政策调控和市场调节作用，合理引导个体交通需求；大力加强智能交通系统建设，提高交通系统的整体运输效率；积极倡导公众形成健康的交通消费理念，提高公共交通及慢行交通的分担率等。江苏省宣布推出3 000台新能源公交车投入运营。2011年7月，首届中国国际低碳交通及新能源汽车展览会在北京全国农业展览中心举行。展览内容包括了低碳交通、轨道交通、智能交通、新能源汽车、低碳城市等领域。

总之，交通转型、低碳出行的理念正在全国得到推广普及，相关理论研究、规划设计、工程实践也在积极推进之中。但是，要广泛付诸实施，并取得实际成效还有很长路要走，还有许多工作要做，如体制机制、法律法规、配套政策、关键技术、投资来源与合理分配、运营支持与监管等。从目前城市与交通发展的现实情况看，公共交通体系本身远未健全完善，无力真正引领和引导城市空间结构优化和土地集约节约使用，城市无序蔓延、土地粗放使用现象相当普遍突出。当前我国绝大部分城市的出行结构还是以步行、自行车和公交占主导，相对还是低碳的。但是个体机动化的趋势十分迅速和明显，由此造成的交通能耗、尾气污染、噪声振动等负面影响迅速显现。城市土地枯竭、能源紧张、环境恶化等刚性约束已经十分突出。这些都对我国经济增长、城市建设、交通模式、生活方式的转型转变提出了极为紧迫和严厉的要求。“倒逼机制”成为2011年党委政府和媒体网络的热词之一。国土资源部部长徐绍史在2011年2月《求是》杂志撰文指出，要控制总量、增加流量、盘活存量，形成土地节约集约利用的“倒逼机制”。2012年1月10日国家发改委副主任、国家能源局局长刘铁男在全国能源工作会议上表示，“十二五”期间将逐步建立合理控制能源消费总量的“倒逼机制”，落实能源消费总量和强度双控的要求。2011年4月，环境保护部部长周生贤在记者采访时指出，环境承载力越来越成为经济发展规模和发展空间的主要制约因素，将环境保护的“倒逼机制”传导到结构调整和经济转型上来，能更好地推动整个社会走上生产发展、生活富裕、生态良好的文明发展道路。

2011年11月，环境保护部公布《环境空气质量标准》（二次征求意见稿），将PM2.5值纳入了标准中，开始实施日期为2012年。消息一公布迅速引起各地政府、新闻媒体和网民市民的强烈关注和热议。北京、上海、天津、重庆、江苏、广东、山东、山西等直辖市和省，广州、南京、杭州、西安、郑州、哈尔滨、昆明等省会城市环保部门很快相继表态，要立即启动或在2012年开始实施PM2.5监测并择机向社会公布监测结果。PM2.5为何如此受到关注？因为这是一种可入肺颗粒物。空气中的PM2.5浓度如果超过一定限度并长期吸入人体内，将对人的健康乃至生命构成很大威胁。PM2.5的来源主要包括机动车尾气、燃油尘、硫酸盐、餐饮油烟尘、建筑水泥尘、煤烟尘等。其中，机动车尾气尘对PM2.5的贡献值达到38%，位于第一，其次是燃油尘，贡献值达23%[8]。雾霾状况下PM2.5更容易生成和集聚。而中国许多大城市由于机动车爆发式增长，工地众多扬尘得不到有效控制等多重因素作用，雾霾天气逐年增多（以山水城林交相辉映著称的江南名城南京市雾霾天气20世纪60年代每年仅有数天，而到了90年代雾霾天数达150多天，现在已经超过200天！），市民呼吸道疾病和肺癌发病率持续升高等问题，已经引起市民、媒体乃至国外来宾的强烈反响。如此严重的污染严峻的形势不得不要敲响警钟，不得不要拷问发展的终极目的是什么？不得不要“倒逼”我们调整城市与交通发展的理念、思路、模式和方式了！

五、慢行交通得到重视，示范成果应当推广

2010年9月，住房和城乡建设部城建司发布建办城函〔2010〕738号文，正式启动全国城市步行和自行车系统示范项目。首批示范城市有重庆、济南、杭州、昆明、昆山和常熟6个城市。2011年6个试点城市按照住房和城乡建设部有关示范城市项目要求，组织编制城

市步行和自行车系统专项规划，制订出台促进步行和自行车系统规划建设的政策性文件和规划设计导则，根据各自城市特色和条件选择典型区域、典型道路和公共自行车等典型项目推进实施示范工程。

2011 年，6 个示范城市项目陆续进入验收阶段。2011 年 4 月杭州公共自行车交通系统工程通过了住房和城乡建设部科技示范项目的验收。验收组认为，这个项目具有实用性、稳定可靠性、先进性、适用性和可扩展性等特点，与倡导的绿色出行、节能减排降碳理念相符合。住房和城乡建设部要求在全国各个城市推广杭州公共自行车的运营模式。2011 年 11 月中旬至 12 月初，住房和城乡建设部对重庆、济南、杭州、昆明、昆山、常熟 6 个第一批“城市步行和自行车交通系统示范项目”进行了阶段性验收。“示范项目”第一阶段均已完成规划编制、政策制定、示范工程建设等相关工作，并结合城市发展实际采取了很多行之有效的措施，在加强城市步行和自行车交通系统建设方面积累了丰富经验。济南市把保障路权作为推进步行和自行车交通系统建设的首要任务。采取的主要措施有：压缩机动车道，增加人行道和自行车道；自行车道敷设彩色沥青，设置硬性隔离，保证自行车路权和出行安全；合理设置隔离墩，防止步行和自行车空间被随意占用。常熟市以面—线—点构建步行系统规划体系。杭州市结合市区原有道路、街巷以及河岸游步道的整治，发展步行和自行车交通。重庆市提出了山城步道的理念，并结合周边环境整治，提升整个步行空间的品质，改善步行出行环境。昆明、昆山等地均依托风景区、公园、山体、主要湖泊和河流等水系建设自行车道，倡导自行车健身文化，强化了自行车交通的健身、休闲功能。昆山、常熟市采取以政府向企业租赁的方式建设与运营公共自行车系统，昆山市已建公共自行车租赁网点 150 个，停车桩 4 000 个，5 个发卡管理亭，投放 3 000 辆自行车；常熟市公共自行车系统共设 149 个网点，3 600 个停车桩，投放 3 000 辆自行车。两城市单车日使用频率均约为 7 次。通过“示范项目”的宣传和实践，城市步行和自行车交通出行条件得到了改善，城市居民绿色出行的认识得到了提高，取得了良好的社会效果。第一批 6 个“示范项目”将深入开展第二阶段工作。2011 年 10 月，住房和城乡建设部在厦门、深圳、株洲、常德、三亚、寿光 6 个城市启动开展了第二批“示范项目”。

除了以上典型示范城市之外，还有很多城市也开始重视步行和自行车交通的规划建设，努力营造以人为本、慢行友好的城市交通环境，并创造了一些特色案例和很好经验。北京市为了鼓励市民绿色出行，在环保局、首都文明办、市交通委和市公安交通管理局共同主办的“第四个文明出行推动日”活动期间，以“安全顺畅、舒适便利、公共服务、历史文化和节能环保”5 个方面评选标准让市民和专家评选出了建国门经长安街、永定门经鼓楼大街至奥林匹克森林公园等 10 条“最佳步行路线”。2010 年 11 月份在苏格兰举行的国际慢城会议上，江苏省高淳“桠溪镇”生态之旅被世界慢城组织正式授予“国际慢城”的称号，这是中国首个国际慢城。佛山市在推进古镇复兴项目“佛山名镇”中考虑了注入“慢城”概念，把佛山打造成一个国际化的、拥有强烈文化气息的“慢镇”或“步行城市”。海口推出系列旅游活动，为海口旅游品牌的打造注入新的活力，打造独具特色的海口旅游“慢城”。2011 年 9 月在从化市第十二次党代会上，从化市委书记黄河鸿提出，“温泉之都从化，从化发展张弛有度，在经济社会发展上要走得快一些，在生活上则‘慢’一些，建成广东休闲的‘慢城’，让人们到这里休闲、旅游、养生。”继广东省近几年大力推进绿道建设，取得明显成效之后，2011 年成都、武汉、青岛、宁波相继推出了城市绿道规划建设计划，并已部分付诸实施。

六、交通安全形势严峻，惨痛代价亟待遏制

根据公安部统计分析，2011 年全国的道路交通安全总体形势总体平稳。据统计，全国涉及人员伤亡的道路交通事故 210812 起，共造成 62387 人死亡，事故起数、死亡人数同比分别下降 4% 和 4.4%。从事故原因看，超速行驶、酒后驾驶、疲劳驾驶仍然是导致交通事故多发的主要原因。特别是超速行驶导致的事故死亡人数占全部死亡人数的 14.2%，这个比例还是相当高的。从事故发生的地点、道路情况看，高速公路的事故仍然呈上升的趋势。

2011 年 2 月 25 日，全国人大常委会表决通过的《刑法修正案（八）》将醉酒驾车、飙车等严重危害群众利益行为定为犯罪，规定在道路上驾驶机动车追逐竞驶，情节恶劣的，或者在道路上醉酒驾驶机动车的，处拘役，并处罚金。该刑法于 2011 年 5 月 1 日实施。

从公安部交通管理局获悉，《刑法修正案（八）》和修改后的《道路交通安全法》实施 8 个月来，公民守法意识明显增强，自觉抵制酒驾醉驾行为，取得良好的法律效果和社会效果。2011 年 5 月 1 日至 12 月 30 日，全国公安机关共查处酒后驾驶 23.8 万起，较 2010 年同期下降 45%。其中，醉酒驾驶 3.8 万起，较 2010 年同期下降 45.3%。人民法院已经对 1.2 万起醉酒驾驶机动车犯罪案件依法作出有罪判决。全国因酒后驾驶造成交通事故死亡 716 人，较 2010 年同期减少 205 人，下降 22.3%。而值得高度注意的是，2011 年醉酒驾驶造成交通事故死亡人数仍然高达 708 人，较 2010 年同期仅减少 25 人，仅下降 3.4%。从这个统计结果看，第一，酒驾现象的确得到了有效治理；第二，醉驾危害后果的确严重，治理效果却相当微弱；第三，酒驾入罪，罪不当赦，醉驾入刑，刑不当减。遗憾的是，全国人大常委会通过的《刑法修正案（八）》5 月 1 日刚刚生效，5 月初最高人民法院副院长张军表态称，并非所有醉驾都是犯罪。随后，最高人民法院下发通知，对于醉驾案件已经采取强制措施的，法院可视具体案情依法变更强制措施。最高人民法院的解释和通知立即受到公众和媒体的强烈质疑和不满！在中国酒文化原本浓厚并有日益增强的背景下，在酒驾醉驾日益猖獗、危害日趋严重，必须用重典治理的情况下，全国人大常委会响应公众长期呼声，好不容易审议通过了酒驾入罪的刑法修正案刚刚生效，最高人民法院如此急不可待出来作出这样的解释和通知，显然有违民意、有悖法理、不合时宜，而且客观上造成了相当负面的影响，为一些地区对酒驾醉驾违法行为处罚网开一面提供了方便。相反，酒驾入罪法条生效后第一位“撞枪”被判 6 个月监禁实刑的名人高晓松先生的诚恳表态与良好表现却得到了民众的谅解和赞许。

值得严重关注和令人痛心疾首的是，2011 年全国发生一次死亡 10 人以上的特大交通事故高达 27 起，造成 410 人死亡，平均一起事故死亡 16 人，另有 380 多人受伤。如此令人震

惊和痛心的特大恶性交通惨剧，其多发高发势头近10年来并没得到有效遏制，每年每月都在2起以上！2011年则特别令人伤心伤痛。因为，2011年的特大恶性交通事故中有数起校车事故，死亡大多是花样年华的中小学生，其中有两起校车安全事故特别重大，引起举国震惊！一起惨剧2011年11月16日发生在甘肃省庆阳市正宁县榆林子镇下沟砖厂门口，一辆大翻斗运煤货车与正宁县榆林子小博士幼儿园学生接送面包车迎面相撞，事故遇难人数高达21人，其中包括18名幼儿以及校车司机和1名教师。另一起惨剧2011年12月12日发生在江苏省徐州市丰县首羡镇，一辆核载52人的接送学生车辆接送47名首羡镇中心小学生回家，途中因躲避一辆人力三轮车发生侧翻滑入路边水沟，致使15名学生因溺水、窒息而抢救无效死亡。

多起震惊全国的校车交通惨剧引起了党中央、国务院高度重视。2011年12月11日，由国务院法制办牵头起草的《校车安全条例草案征求意见稿》将正式全文公布，广纳民意。《草案》对资金问题做出了这样的规定：国家通过财政资助、税收优惠、鼓励社会捐赠等多种方式，支持农村地区为居住分散的接受义务教育的学生提供校车服务。发展校车服务所需的财政支持资金由中央财政和地方财政分担，具体办法由国务院财政部门制定。为了保障校车通行和停靠安全，《征求意见稿》对校车享有的优先权作了规定，包括：校车运载学生时，应当按照公安部门规定的位置放置校车标牌，开启校车标示灯，按照经审核确定的线路行驶。公安机关应当加强对校车经过路线状况、交通流量和交通安全设施的管理。交通警察遇到运载学生的校车时，应当指挥疏导校车优先通行。校车运载学生时，可以在公交专用车道以及其他禁止社会车辆通行但允许公交车辆通行的路段行驶。校车在道路上停车上下学生时，应当靠道路右侧停车，开启危险报警闪光灯，由驾驶人将停车示意牌伸出车窗，后方车辆应当停车等待，禁止超越；道路无中间隔离带的，对面驶来的车辆应当停车等待。下车学生需横穿马路时，车辆应当停车让行等。

但愿这个条例能尽快颁布出台，但愿条例出台后能得到有效贯彻执行！

（作者：杨涛，教授，中国城市交通规划学术委员会副主任委员，南京市城市与交通规划设计研究院有限责任公司董事长）

参考文献

[1] 刘慧琴，张辉. 2011年“两会”建言分析报告：城市交通专题［EB/OL］. 中国网，［2011-03-14］. http：//news. china. com. cn.

[2] 邓杭，韩旭，等. 北京交通拥堵指数下降12% 尾号限行或继续执行［N/OL］. 京华时报，［2012-01-12］. http：//city. sina. com. cn/focus/t/2012-01-12/094526464. html.

[3] 杨涛. 2009年城市交通行业盘点与反思［J］. 城市交通，2010，8（1）.

[4] 全国铁路工作会议召开今年完成基建投资4690亿［EB/OL］. 中国网，http：//www. china. com. cn/news/txt/2011-12/23/content_ 24230959. htm.

[5] 国务院“7·23”甬温线特别重大铁路交通事故调查组. “7·23”甬温线特别重大铁路交通事故调查

报告［EB/OL］. 国家安全监管总局网站，http：//www. chinasafety. gov. cn/newpage/Contents/Channel_ 5498/2011/1228/160577/content_ 160577. htm.

［6］中国大规模高铁建设不会导致债务危机［EB/OL］. 新华网，http：//news. xinhuanet. com/fortune/2011 -01/15/c_ 12984958. htm.

［7］中国经营报. 铁路公路债务危机信号释放 多地工程出现停建［N/OL］. http：//www. shenguang. com/ news/2011 - 11/978204914172_ 2. html.

［8］梁恒. 汽车尾气：PM2.5 最大毒源［EB/OL］. 半月谈网，http：//www. banyuetan. org/gsxs/jdqs/ 111214/60780_ 2. shtml.

城市生态环境问题的诊断与对策

——以山西省临汾市为例

一、前言

（一）当前研究的基本情况

可持续发展是城市规划中的一个重要议题，受到了广泛的关注，无论是城市可持续发展现状问题的诊断还是规划对策的提出，都有了很多的理论研究和实践。

在可持续发展上面临问题的诊断方面，往往将生态环境作为诊断的重点，生态足迹法是一种常用的方法，国内已经有大量的案例研究，如蒋依依等（2005）对深圳的研究，曹宝等（2007）对天津的研究，吴承照等（2010）对义乌的研究。

指标体系也是评价可持续状态的一种常见方法。国际上在可持续发展上已经提出了若干套指标体系，例如联合国可持续发展委员会（UNCSD）于 1996 年创建指标体系，它由社会、经济、环境和制度四大系统按驱动力（driving force）、状态（state）、响应（response）模型设计的含 25 个子系统、142 个指标构成。联合国环境问题科学委员会（SCOPE）和联合国环境规划署（UNEP）提出了一套经过整合的指标体系，包括环境、自然资源、自然生态系统、环境污染 4 个层面共 25 个指标，评价的基本方法是层次分析评价法。世界银行于 1995 年从考察实际财富以及可持续能力随时间的动态变化这一宗旨出发，将可持续发展指标分为 4 个要素，即自然资本、生产资本、人力资本和社会资本，首次将无形资本纳入可持续发展评价要素之内。

国内关于指标的研究一般将可持续发展涵盖了经济、社会、环境三个方面，或者侧重于环境，大多是特定的案例研究。例如方创琳等（2010）构建了由自然资源要素、生态环境要素和社会经济要素组成的武汉城市群空间扩展的生态状况诊断指标体系，采用熵技术支持下的 AHP 模型和模糊隶属度函数模型建立了城市群空间扩展的生态状况诊断模型。李祚泳等（2001）提出了基于 GA 优化的分类单项指标的发展指数普适公式，并采用广义对比运算和层次分析法对不同层次指标赋权，建立了社会、经济和环境可协调持续发展评价模型。李莉等（2000）提出包括经济发展、社会发展、环境发展、城市法律法规管理四方面的评价城市可持续发展程度的指标体系。梁伟等（2011）提出重点反映生态环境质量的评价指标，涉及废物排放、环境治理、能耗和环境资源，共计 25 个指标。

郝翠等（2010）比较了可持续发展的各种评价方法，提出各方法适用范围和优缺点：可持续性指数法适合于国家间的综合评价，该方法信息量大，但是计算复杂；生态足迹和能值分析法适合于各种范围，包括国家、区域、地区和小系统；生态足迹法计算过程简单，但是缺失一些可持续性信息；能值分析法考虑问题全面，但是其原理涉及热力学知识，很难被一些学者认同；指标体系综合评价法对于小范围更合适，该方法变通性较大，可随着评价系统的变化而进行调整，但是主观性较强。

与研究可持续问题诊断的众多文献相比，关于可持续发展对策的研究相对较少，而且对策、方法均较为分散，当前各项研究之间的系统性不强，缺乏梳理。

一部分对策研究主要从生态角度出发，例如李卫锋等（2003）以深圳为例，运用生态敏感性与适宜性分析和景观格局整体优化的方法，将深圳市域的整体生态结构分为自然生态空间、城镇发展空间和生态廊道三部分。苏维词等（2004）对重庆都市圈生态环境问题进行分析，结合三峡水库安全运行的需求，提出了加大都市圈生态环境建设力度和绿地景观整治工程，优化产业结构与布局，扶持循环经济和生态环保产业发展，控制主城区规模、积极发展周边卫星城市，增加环保投入、加强重点环保基础设施建设、实施“净空”和“碧水”工程，建立都市圈生态环境信息管理系统和预警系统、实施都市圈生态系统管理等 8 条治理途径与措施。

另一部分研究提出包括环境、经济、社会领域的综合性对策，其中大部分是针对具体案例的，例如杨国华等（2007）以地处广东省北部山区的东源县为例，提出充分发挥当地的资源环境优势，寓生态建设于经济建设之中，抓好绿色产品开发，加快以生态旅游业为龙头的第三产业的发展，以专业镇带动农业产业化等措施。王海飞（2011）针对白银市资源枯竭的现状，指出应积极融合于兰白都市经济圈中，进行区域发展战略的创新，通过圈内产业联动打造核心工业基地和沿黄特色农业带、城市联动规划进行城市再造、生态联动创建生态文明、行政联动实现兰白行政一体化等战略，完成白银市的经济和社会转型。鲍超等（2006）对我国矿业城市提出了 9 种可持续的资源开发利用模式，即“细水长流”模式，“黑绿置换”模式，“优势组合”模式，“优势延伸”模式，“地企融合”模式，国有 J 民营的“双轮驱动”模式，公有 J 非公有的“双轨并行”模式等。李莉（2008）对矿业城市提出发展新产业、绿色矿城、开源节流、产业复位、税制改革、财政补贴的措施，帮助矿业城市摆脱困境。王志宪等（2005）对长三角提出明确其在全国区域经济分工中的地位，在提高产业发展层次的同时，不可放松对劳动密集型产业的发展，加强土地资源和能源的管理，加速环境保护和生态修复工作的进程等可持续发展的对策。

还有一些研究关注了空间在可持续发展中的作用，例如王正等（2010）针对重庆都市区的可持续目标，提出通过持续强化“多中心、组团式”城市空间形态实现与自然共生、通过紧凑型混合土地利用的组团组织减轻对资源的消耗、通过绿色交通系统的建设降低对小汽车的依赖、通过绿色开敞空间控制保护自然生态基础等城市形态组织对策，达到城市可持续的空间建设目的。任绍斌等（2011）从城市区域、城市/片区、城市住区三个层面，对可持续城市空间的规划准则进行结构性、系统性的整理。张新生等（1997）探讨了城市可持续发展的时空复合调控动力学理论模型，并在地理信息系统、空间分析和可视的空间表达支持下，建立了城市空间增长动力学过程模拟系统。

（二）当前的研究的主要缺陷

总体而言，可持续发展是一个受到普遍关注的议题，相关的研究成果丰富，而且跨越了多个领域，但是从能否支撑规划实践的角度来看，仍然存在很多缺陷。

缺陷之一是，问题诊断与空间规划对策脱节。

已有关于问题诊断的研究对帮助我们认识城市有很大的帮助，但是许多研究通常并不指向特定的规划对策，多数流于为诊断而诊断，虽然有其认识层面的价值，但是仅限于描述现状或者分析原因，与解决可持续发展的对策之间是脱节的，诊断也就失去了操作层面上的价值。

其中一种常见的情况是关注于各城市之间的可比性，或者过于强调方法的统一性（尤其是使用生态足迹等国外引入的方法时），指标和诊断方法并没有针对本城市的特定情况，更加重要的是看不出这些指标将引出何种对策措施。另一种常见的情况是诊断过于偏重于环境和产业，但是忽略了空间问题。对空间问题的忽略导致相关的研究难以转化为规划的语言，在空间方案中很难找到切实的抓手，规划措施也往往沦为对其他领域相关文献的简单引用而无法形成规划本领域的突破。

缺陷之二是，空间规划对策与现实操作性之间的脱节。

许多对具体城市的对策研究具有对该城市的针对性，但是缺乏对经济社会问题的深度思考，空间和经济、社会、环境之间的连接是断裂的，空间对策过于宽泛和偏向原理。例如在可持续发展压力很大的资源型城市的研究中，常见的规划对策大多从一般的空间规划原理出发，以改善城市环境为主要目标，使用的技术手段也为规划师所熟悉，但是规划在空间模型的同时，却没有构筑一个配套的产业转型模型，并建立两者之间的关联。这些规划往往在实际中难以实施，原因在于可持续发展仅考虑环境改善是不够的，如果不能在改善环境的同时提出保障经济平稳过渡的方案，任何政府都很难接受和实施。

缺陷之三是，对策之间缺乏内在的逻辑关联。

许多研究提出的一揽子对策，包括了经济社会环境等诸多因素，貌似全面，但从逻辑上看是并行罗列几项措施，它们之间相互孤立。规划在城市可持续发展问题的成因分析中没有剖析经济社会环境与空间之间相互关联，对策中也看不出这些措施之间的逻辑关系，规划的对策也就失去了说服力。

二、可持续发展问题诊断与规划对策的基本框架

城市的可持续发展是一个很宽泛的概念，通常需要兼顾环境、社会、经济三个主要领

域，而每个领域内又可以从多个角度和指标对城市的可持续状况进行评估，这很容易导致问题诊断流于宽泛和简单的罗列。但是从城市规划这一特定角度出发的问题诊断实际上需要进行筛选。筛选的标准主要有两个，一是重要性标准，即某个问题应该在本城市影响重大，是可持续发展的主要障碍之一；二是空间相关性标准，即这个问题应当能够折射到该城市空间问题上（例如涉及环境问题时应研究环境的空间指向，如排放源的位置，环境敏感区的位置等），并且有可能通过空间规划的手段加以改善。通过筛选形成一个针对规划对策的“问题包”。

规划既需要研究“问题包”如何影响城乡空间的变化，更需要研究如何通过空间规划的技术方法反作用于环境、经济、社会等相应议题上，从而形成“对策包”，这样既保证了“对策包”与“问题包”之间的延续性，又保证了这两者与空间之间的紧密联系。对“对策包”内部各要素的关联分析与综合就可以转化成为城市可持续发展在规划上的措施。

在构建和运用这个分析框架时，应结合当地当时的工业化和城镇化背景，尤其高度关注其发展阶段和现实条件等特定情境对特定城市问题诊断与规划对策的约束作用，规划对策不应超越城市发展的现实条件。

从城市发展的全局角度来看，通过空间属性筛选后的问题诊断和规划对策不见得一定是城市可持续发展的关键，但是却保证了这样的诊断和对策在城市规划的领域内具有操作上的意义。对政府而言，这些对策无疑还需要其他政策的紧密配合形成合力，才可能促使城市走向可持续发展。

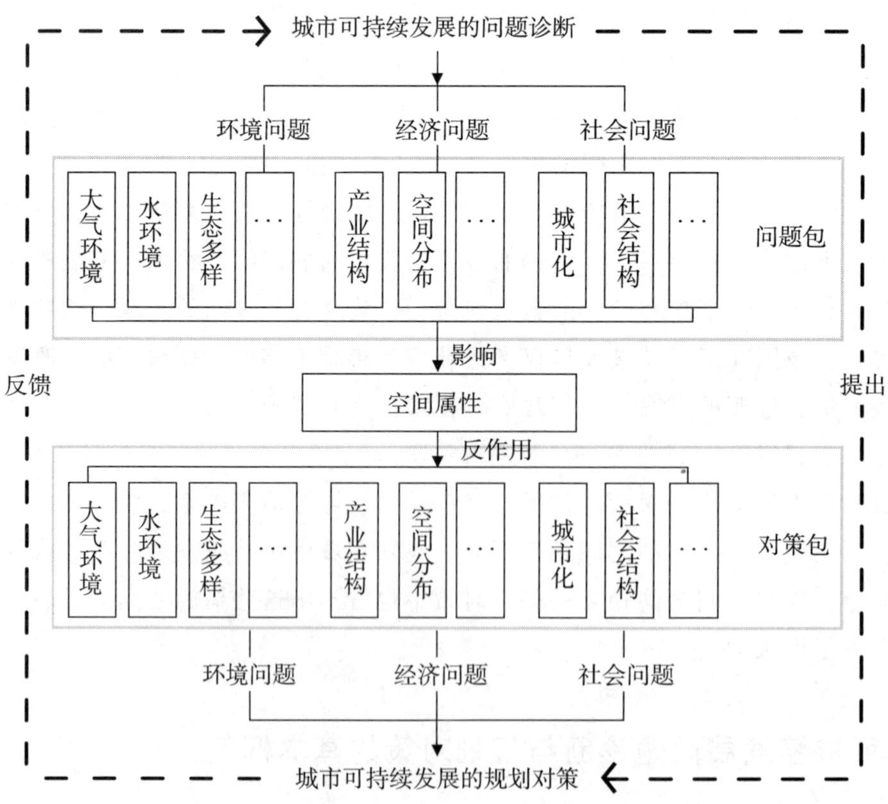

图 1

三、临汾可持续发展面临的问题与形成机制

我们通过临汾的案例对这个框架加以说明。临汾位于山西省南部，市域约 2 万平方公里，辖 17 个县市区，总人口约 420 万人，城市 GDP 和财政收入长期居于全省第二位。临汾发展不可持续的困境在环境、经济、社会上均有体现，而且相互之间存在着内在的关联，这种情况在资源型城市中具有典型性。

（一）经济问题的表现及其成因

1. 产业结构陷入严重的资源依赖

临汾产业结构很不合理，产业高度集中于工业，工业内高度集中于重工业，重工业内高度集中于资源型工业。临汾市 2008 年三次产业结构比例为 5. 11:65. 33:29. 56，一产、三产很不发达。第二产业内部结构中，轻重工业增加值比例为 1:99；重工业包括能源原材料工业和深加工工业两大部分，其产值比例为 96:4。全市钢铁冶炼、炼焦业和煤炭采选业三大行业占全部规模以上工业总产值的 85. 8%。

从趋势上看，资源型产业在全市经济的比重在过去十年来一直处于上升态势，资源依赖程度日益加深。从 2000 年到 2008 年，临汾的 GDP 增长了 563. 8 亿元，其中煤炭、炼焦、钢铁产业增长了 313. 7 亿元，占 55. 6%。

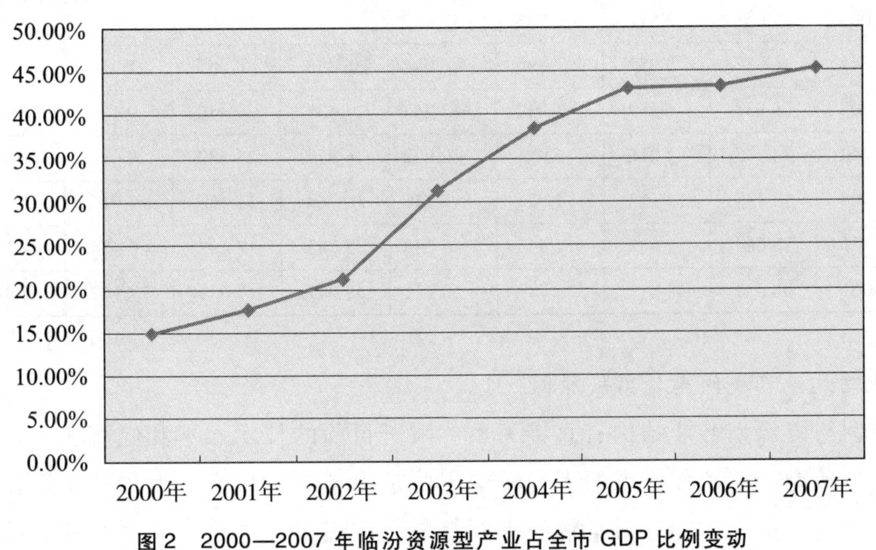

图 2　2000—2007 年临汾资源型产业占全市 GDP 比例变动

2. 环境恶化阻碍了产业结构的升级

临汾资源型产业的畸形发展带来了本地环境的严重恶化，环境的恶化损害了本地的投资环境，资源型产业由于临汾的资源优势不断发展，但新兴产业尤其是对环境要求较高的服务业和先进制造业受到了环境的明显抑制，产业结构日益锁定在原有路径上。

产业升级所需的资金在临汾其实并不缺乏。临汾资源型经济带来了巨大的利润，但问题

在于很难转化为对新兴产业的投资，反而存在着严重的投资外逃和消费外溢。资本外逃问题体现在大量的资源财富被用于异地投资和异地置业（不动产）；消费外溢主要表现为在外消费，特别是采矿权收益人的奢侈品消费、高档服务消费以及旅行消费。而导致资本外逃和消费外溢非常重要的原因正是临汾环境的日益恶化。这样，临汾资源型产业的畸形繁荣与其他产业的衰退形成了鲜明的对比，产业的资源依赖性难以摆脱，环境恶化与产业固化之间形成了难以打破的恶性循环。

（二）环境问题的表现及其成因

1. 环境污染现状

大气环境是临汾环境各类中最为严重的问题，在2003—2005年连续三年成为全国113个重点监控城市中污染最重的城市。当前临汾的平原各县市的排放量普遍超出了环境容量，如果要使大气污染控制在环境容量以内，必须要求各地削减至少一半以上的排放量。

表1　临汾市平原地区各区县环境容量

单位:吨

县市区	SO_2					TSP				
	现状排放量	理想容量	允许排放量	理想剩余容量	允许剩余容量	现状排放量	理想容量	允许排放量	理想剩余容量	允许剩余容量
尧都区	22 400	20 800	10 100	-1 600	-12 300	27 300	69 100	14 400	41 800	-12 900
侯马市	16 009	9 021	3 512	-6 988	-12 497	13 212	19 103	5 310	5 891	-7 902
霍州市	16 041	16 937	9 957	896	-6 084	36 358	46 063	21 359	9 705	-14 999
曲沃县	9 602	9 934	6 359	332	-3 243	21 437	24 458	9 130	3 021	-12 307
翼城县	7 210	14 135	4 218	6 925	-2 992	16 977	23 589	8 012	6 612	-8 965
襄汾县	14 368	12 447	7 112	-1 921	-7 256	10 764	16 156	7 313	5 392	-3 451
洪洞县	13 431	15 064	7 582	1 633	-5 849	33 293	19 182	9 438	-14 111	-23 855
小计	99 061	98 338	48 840	-723	-50 221	159 341	217 651	74 962	58 310	-84 379

2. 产业结构是环境问题的第一原因

环境问题与资源型产业结构有直接关系。限于目前的技术水平和经济实力，资源型工业多为高污染高耗能产业，临汾市的大气污染主要是由于资源型产业大量使用煤作为主要能源而造成的煤烟型污染，大部分污染物的排放都与使用煤炭或与之有关的工业有关。

但是作为一个煤炭资源丰富的城市，临汾在很长一段时期内都需要维持相当大的资源型产业总量，企图通过主要发展非资源型工业来解决环境问题的路径是不切实际的，从这个角度上说，产业结构导致环境问题在临汾是一个“伪问题”，仅仅停留在这个层次上会引向理想化但是却无法实现的政策方向。因此规划继而深入研究资源型产业空间布局机理对环境的影响，排放源的空间分析成为临汾规划上的基本方法。规划发现了排放源布局引发环境问题的三个空间机理。

3. 空间机理之一：资源型产业布局过于分散

临汾的资源型企业在相当长一段时期内以乡镇自发的小规模民营企业为主，企业空间布局分散，企业间距离较大，较高的运输费用阻碍了废弃物的资源化利用；另一方面由于企业规模较小，单个企业排放的废弃物有限，收集企业排放物的成本很高，达不到资源利用的经济规模。与成规模集中式的资源型城市比，临汾单个企业规模小、空间布局分散阻碍了循环经济发展，使环境问题日益突出。

更加深入的研究还发现，除了难以组织循环经济外，临汾过于分散的企业布局对环境污染有着致命的影响，这将在后面说明。

4. 空间机理之二：排放源分布与人口分布重叠

平川七县是临汾人口最密集的地区，它集中了全市3/4以上的人口，但同时也集中了3/4以上的污染物排放量，污染企业与人口在平川地区重叠，导致平川地区环境长期得不到改善。

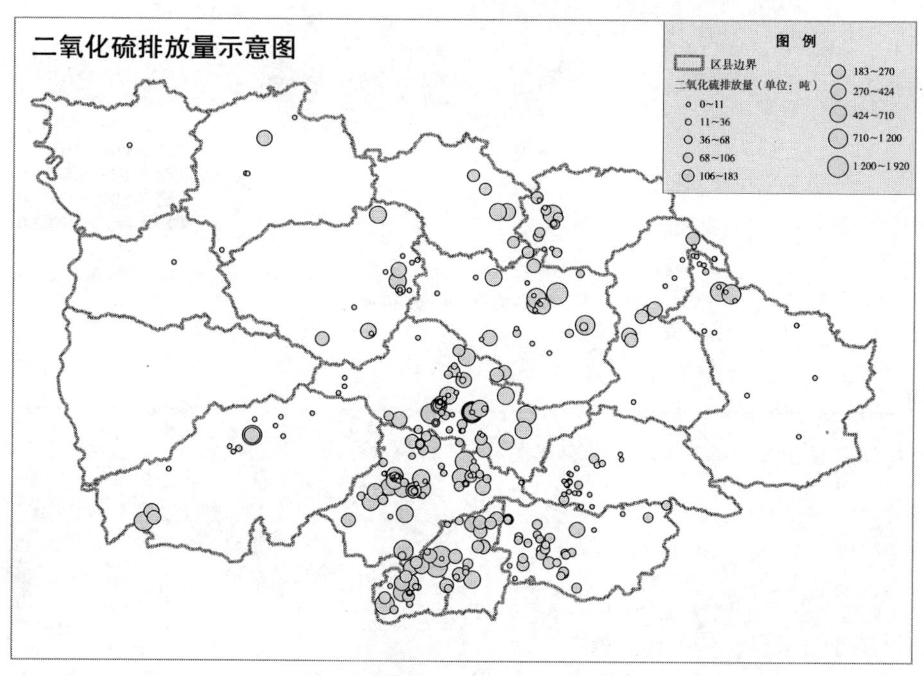

图3 临汾主要工业污染源分布

5. 空间机理之三：排放源分布与地形环境不匹配

临汾先天不足的地理环境大大加重了平川地区的大气污染。原因之一是平川地区口袋型的地势特征使外界新鲜空气很难进入河谷地带，河谷内的平均风速很低，大气扩散条件很差，静风率甚至可以达到40%。原因之二是由山谷风形成了逆温层，使大气污染物昼夜间循环往复无法排除。

从气象分析对污染源布局在全市的适宜性评价来看，平川河谷均属于最不适宜和不适宜区，因此尽管临汾的污染企业很少分布在城市之内，而是分布在农村地带，但是由于地理条件的限制，导致污染物弥漫于整个平川地区，城市环境的改善始终不明显。

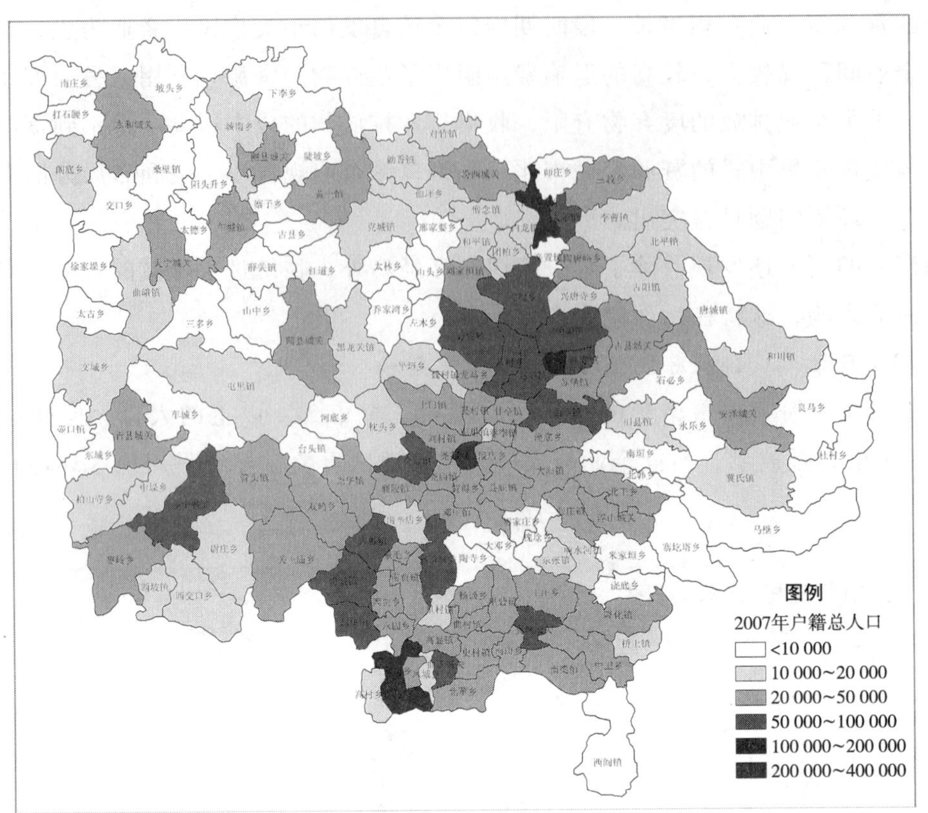

图4 临汾人口分布密度

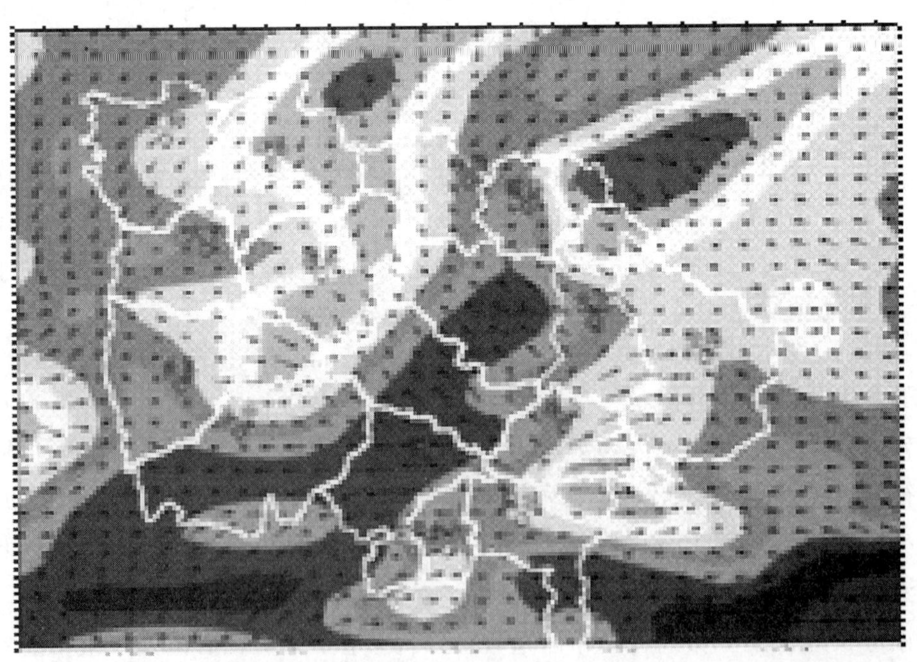

图5 气象扩散条件分析（风速模拟）

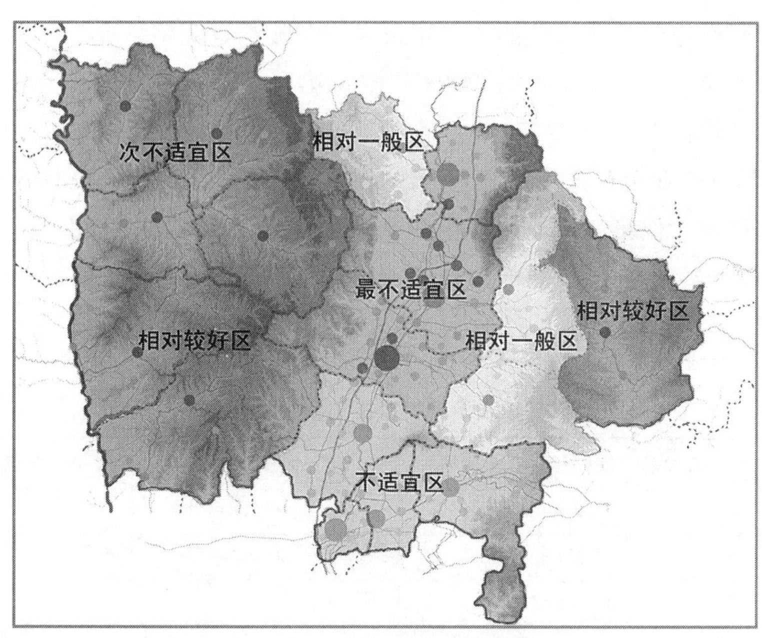

图6　基于气象模拟的污染源布局适宜性分级图

（三）社会问题的表现及其成因

1. 城镇化进程缓慢

2008年临汾三次产业从业人员结构为44.67:22.74:32.59，非农产业的从业人数比例已经达到55.33%；产业方面，非农产业占GDP的比例也达94.89%；但是城镇化水平仅为37.44%，人口城镇化水平远远滞后于经济和就业的非农化发展水平。如果以二产占GDP比例与城镇化水平的差值来衡量工业化与城镇化之间的差距，全国为4.3%，山西省为15.6%，临汾则高达28.3%。

以资源型为主的工业化对城镇化的带动非常微弱，这主要与带动就业量和就业的空间分布两个因素有关。

表2　2008年临汾城镇化水平与全国全省比较

	全国	山西	临汾
人均GDP(万元)	22 640	20 300	18 031
二产占GDP比例(%)	48.6	61.5	65.33
城镇化水平(%)	45.7	45.11	37.44

表3　2008年临汾非农化与城镇化情况比较

非农产业占GDP的比例	非农产业从业人数所占比例	城镇化水平
94.89%	55.33%	37.44%

研究发现不同产业的就业吸纳能力差距很大，在临汾资源型工业、非资源型工业、第三产业吸纳劳动力的能力基本是1:2:6。2008年临汾第二产业占生产总值的65.33%，但是吸纳的社会从业人员仅占全市的22.74%，第三产业占生产总值的29.56%，吸纳从业人员却达到32.59%。第三产业单位产值的就业吸纳能力几乎是第二产业的三倍。临汾第二产业产值远远超过第三产业，但第三产业所吸纳的从业人员从1995年起就超过了第二产业，并且持续上升，然而2007年临汾第三产业仅占GDP的29.56%，三产发育不良延缓了城镇化进程。

表4　2008年临汾规模以上工业企业吸纳就业情况

	工业总产值(万元,当年价格)	从业人员数(人)	亿元产值从业人员数(人)
资源型产业	11 497 106	149 257	129.8
非资源型产业	1 211 451	40 367	333.2
全部规模以上工业	12 708 557	189 624	149.2

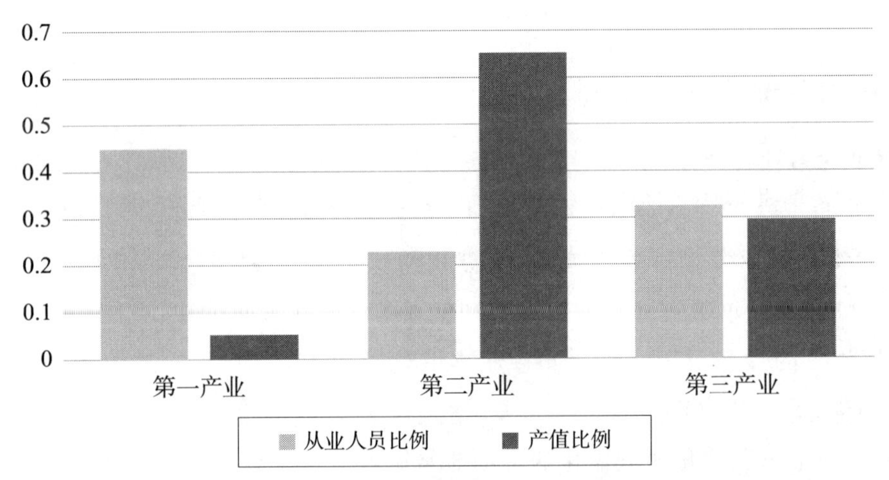

图7　2008年临汾三次产业增加值和就业结构比例

企业散布于农村导致农民离土不离乡。临汾的煤焦铁等资源型企业大多自发产生，煤矿大多分散在山区，焦化厂、炼铁厂也多分布在各个村庄，很少形成集中的片区。尽管非农就业比例已经占到46.4%，但是全部从业人员中约有70%在乡镇企业中工作，非农就业岗位中有58%在乡村地区，非农产业推动城镇化的效果不明显，这与大同、阳泉等国有企业模式的高城镇化形成了鲜明的对比。从下表中还可以发现临汾不同产业的集聚程度有很大差异：第二产业的分散程度非常高，采矿业尤其明显；第三产业则较为集中，可见第三产业更加适合在城镇集聚，只有运输业有明显的分散现象，这与各地农村依托资源型企业发展运输有关。因此，工业企业的高度分散，加上适宜在城镇集聚的第三产业发育不良，是城镇化水平低下的重要原因。

表 5　2005 年临汾城乡劳动力行业分布

单位：万人

		全市	城镇	农村
第一产业		85.09	0.60	84.49
第二产业		44.85	14.52	30.33
其中	采矿业	13.23	4.53	8.70
	制造业	21.71	8.33	13.38
	建筑业	9.90	1.65	8.25
第三产业		55.70	27.85	27.85
其中	交通运输仓储邮电	13.44	3.25	10.19
	批发零售餐饮住宿	17.04	7.57	9.47
	其他	25.22	17.03	8.19
合计		185.63	42.94	142.69

注：不含城镇登记失业人员、16 岁以上在校学生、其他劳动者。

2. 市民社会的断层

临汾的产业结构决定了其劳动力的素质结构。使用山西省第一次经济普查（2004）资料分析各行业的劳动力素质结构，从学历、职称、技术工人三项指标进行考察。总体来看，科学研究技术服务和地质勘查业，教育，信息传输、计算机服务和软件业等行业由于其行业自身特点，进入门槛较高，占有人力资源的总量也处于相对较高水平。住宿和餐饮业、仓储和邮政业等行业由于进入门槛较低，技术含量不高，虽拥有大量的从业人员，但劳动力整体素质较低。采矿业、制造业、交通运输业等行业，在人力资源配置水平上，同样处于劣势。

表 6　2004 年山西分行业人力资源分布状况表

	从业人员合计（人）	学历		职称		技术工人	
		本科以上（人）	占从业人员比重（%）	中级职称以上（人）	占从业人员比重（%）	技师以上（人）	占从业人员比重（%）
采矿业	1 146 901	23 550	2.05	50 306	4.39	9 000	0.78
制造业	1 681 795	55 616	3.31	94 567	5.62	23 670	1.41
第三产业	2 090 548	256 349	12.26	339 105	16.22	17 520	0.84

从单位产业资本人力资源配置状况可以观察在同样的资本投入下，不同产业所需要的劳动力结构。如下表所示，采矿行业的单位产业资本人力资源配置水平几乎是最低的，说明采矿业吸纳的从业人员以底层为主。制造业从业人员素质高于采矿业，分布特点为，中高素质就业者低于各行业平均水平，但是中等素质人员明显高于平均水平，说明制造业从业人员以社会中层为主。第三产业在就业结构方面有两个显著的特点。第一，多数行业属于劳动密集型产业，吸收劳动力能力强。第二，劳动者素质弹性大，呈现出明显的多样化：租赁和商业

服务业、批发零售业等传统产业的人力资源配置低；而教育、科学研究技术服务和地质勘察业、金融业、卫生社会保障和社会福利业单位资本所拥有的人力资源配置处于较高水平。通常情况下，随着经济发展水平的提高和对第三产业服务需求的转变，第三产业内部的就业结构转变趋势是传统的第三产业如商业饮食、交通运输比重稳定下降，而金融保险、房地产、社会服务趋于上升。

表7　2004年全省分行业单位产业资本人力资源配置状况表

	产业资本		本科以上		中级职称以上		技师以上	
	资本规模（千元）	比重（%）	人数（人）	单位资本人力资源配置（人/百万元）	人数（人）	单位资本人力资源配置（人/百万元）	人数（人）	单位资本人力资源配置（人/百万元）
采矿业	48 218 192	15.70	23 550	0.49	50 306	1.04	9 000	0.19
制造业	88 604 420	28.86	55 616	0.63	94 567	1.07	23 670	0.27
第三产业	116 222 378	37.83	256 349	2.21	339 105	2.92	17 520	0.15

临汾是山西省的典型地区，综合临汾各个行业的劳动力素质构成，各个行业的劳动力素质构成如下图所示，可以发现当前临汾的劳动力素质构成中，缺乏依靠管理、专业技术能力取得收入的中等收入人群，人力资本在社会收入中不明显，整体上是一种“上端高，底层大，中间小”的结构，不利于社会和谐发展，是一种结构性失调，而这个特点正是由临汾资源型产业结构所决定的。

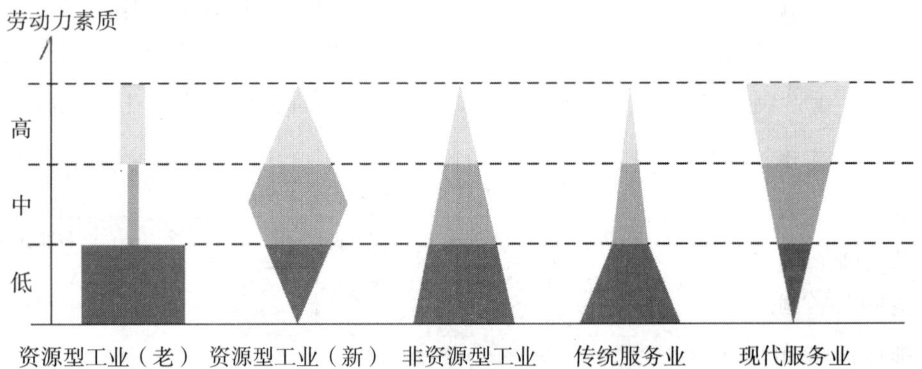

图8　不同产业的劳动力素质构成示意

3. 文化关怀和环境伦理的缺失——感觉写的不好

临汾对文化的忽视从其对历史文化的态度中得到印证。临汾是文物大市，全市现有全国重点文物保护单位28处，其中丁村古建筑群入选世界文化遗产预备案；省级重点文物保护单位67处，市级文物保护单位30处。此外临汾市还有国家级非物质文化遗产8项，省级5项。可以说临汾的历史文化资源的价值不亚于其煤炭资源。

但是城市对历史文化的关怀和保护却与城市的经济发展水平不相称，文物保护资金缺口较大，大量优秀文物没有得到充分展示，一些文物保护单位本体及其建设控制地带和环境受到不当建设的威胁（例如侯马晋国遗址、临汾市的古城墙等）。

在资源型产业带来的巨大财富面前，政府和企业都缺乏应有的环境伦理观，主要体现在急功近利式的矿产采掘造成的资源破坏和生态破坏，对后代生存环境的漠视，以及对建设过程中利益受损者补偿的漠视。

这种文化观和价值观上的缺失对临汾社会发展影响深远。其成因与现代市民社会的断层有关，暴富的顶层群体和大量在资源型发展中受惠微薄的底层群体之间形成了巨大的张力，畸形价值观在这种张力中得以无限放大。而中间阶层的难以发育除了与产业结构有关外，也与临汾城市人居环境恶劣，降低了城镇对人才的吸引力，导致高素质人口外流有关。

文化观和价值观的缺失在中心城市建设中主要表现为人居环境品质的恶化。城市空间狭小，中心城区平均人口密度超过2.8万人/平方公里；铁佛寺、古城墙等历史遗迹湮没在杂乱的建筑之中；城市至今没有城市级的文化、体育、图书馆、博物馆等设施；绿地占城市建设用地的比例和人均指标分别为1.9%和2.1平方米/人，均低于《城市用地分类与规划建设用地标准》所规定的8%和9平方米/人的下限。

四、面向可持续发展的空间规划思路

基于临汾在可持续发展中，产业、环境、社会问题与临汾的空间发展有着密切的互动关系，因此规划将空间优化作为解决临汾可持续发展的一把钥匙。规划从解决环境问题入手，通过产业空间的调整来改善环境，实现产业发展与环境优化的目的，基于环境改善和产业调整实现社会结构的优化，促成空间与经济、环境、社会之间的正向循环。

（一）调整资源型工业布局改善城市环境

规划需要探索继续发展资源型产业前提下改善环境的对策，除了提出扩大单个企业规模以提高技术水平、发展循环经济等对策外，着重研究优化资源型工业空间布局的现实方法。

首先进行了污染型工业布局对环境影响的理论研究。规划将临汾市必须达到的年排放总量、气象条件、市域面积作为固定参数；将最大污染程度、平均污染程度、污染范围作为因变量；将排放源的布局方式作为可以控制的自变量；分析工具采用ADMS大气扩散模型系统。规划研究了排放源总数量不变，但是分布范围由集中到全市域的分布范围变动对污染的影响，以及排放源始终在全市域均布，但排放源的数量逐步增加，即排放源分布密度对污染的影响。

分布范围研究的结论是污染程度随着分布范围的扩大而降低，而且排放量越大，越应当分散布局。分布密度研究的结论是污染程度刚开始会随着排放源数量的增加而显著缓解，但是存在一个拐点，排放源过多反而会加重污染。理论研究表明，污染工业应当在市域内大分散，以分摊排放量，改善整体环境，但应在县域内小集中，以推行循环经济，促进污染集中治理。临汾的现状恰恰相反，在市域内集中在平川，在平川县域内又极为分散，临汾的严重污染得到了理论上的解释。

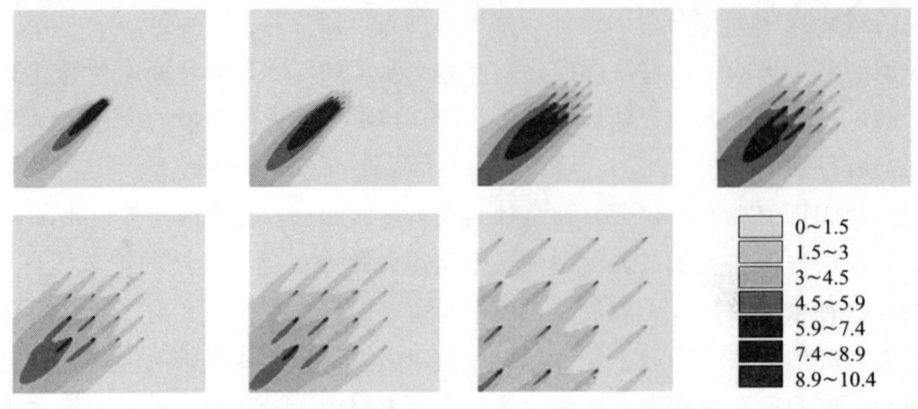

图 9　排放源分布范围研究中的布局变化

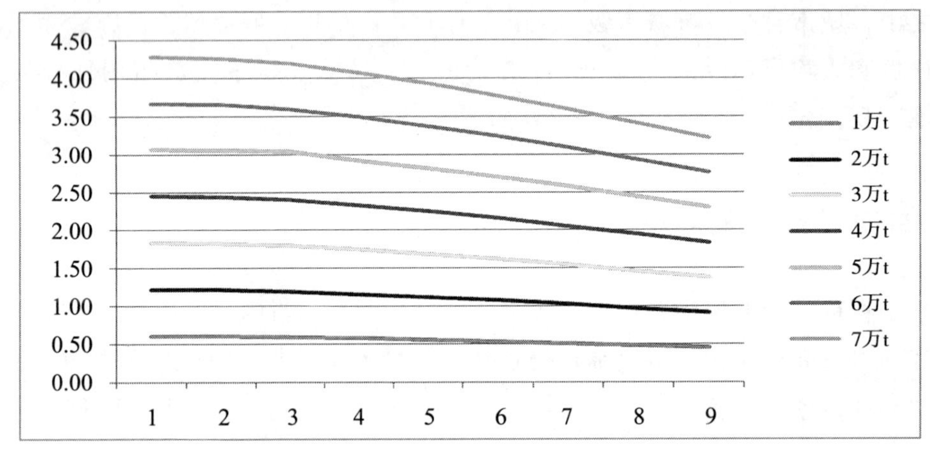

图 10　排放源分布范围研究中的平均污染浓度变化曲线

其次对临汾市域 17 个县市区进行了污染型工业区选址的可行性分析，考虑因素包括大气扩散条件分析、生态影响分析、资源型工业分布的现状基础、地形条件分析、水资源条件、矿产资源条件、交通条件等，以此将各县发展资源型工业的条件进行综合评价，分为好中差三级。

规划结合理论研究的结果以及对临汾市域发展资源型经济的实际条件评估，兼顾产业区调整的现实性，提出了资源型工业区的布局和资源型产能空间调整的建议，使排放源从目前的大集中小分散转向大分散小集中，以促进环境的改善。

（二）优化产业布局促进接替产业和市民阶层的形成

产业结构的固化与城市阶层的断裂紧密关联，而这两者都可以通过对产业布局的分类引导来加以改善。从研究的需要出发将临汾市的产业分为资源型工业、非资源工业和服务业三大类，后两者是需要大力培育的接替产业，并且是培育市民社会的主要温床。

规划利用全国投入产出表测算消耗系数，来代表三大类产业之间的经济联系，发现非资源工业和服务业联系紧密，应当空间结合；而资源型工业与其他两个联系较弱，可以空间分离。加上考虑到资源型工业的严重污染，规划提出分别建立资源型工业区和非资源型工业

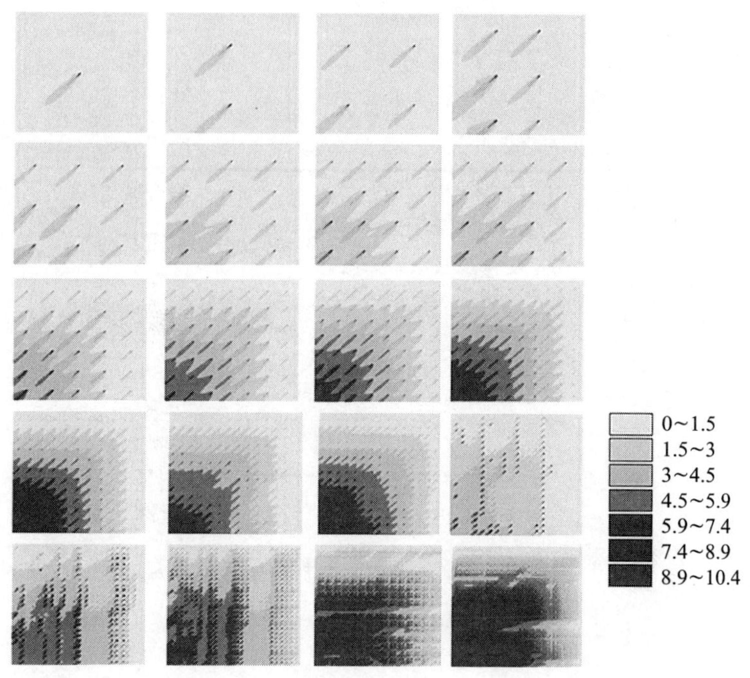

图 11　排放源分布密度研究中的布局变化

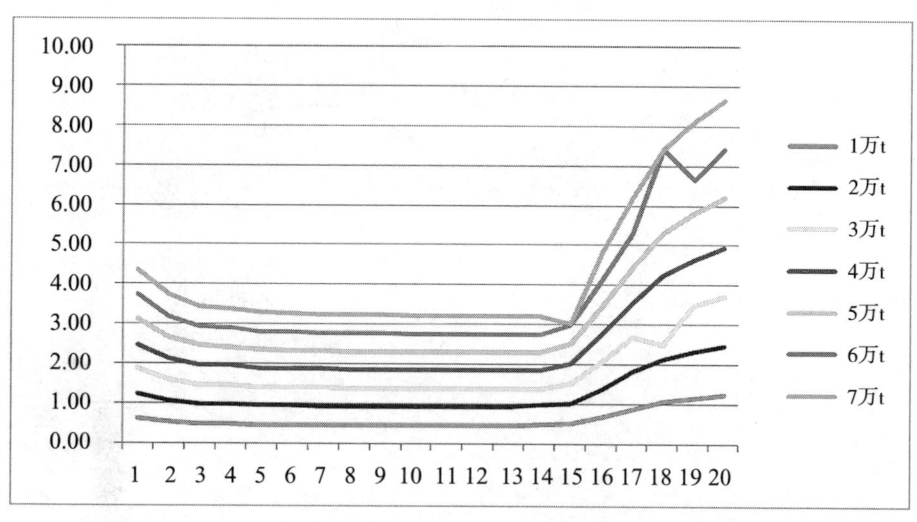

图 12　排放源分布密度研究中的平均污染浓度变化曲线

区，资源型工业结合矿产资源布局，采取产居分离方式；非资源工业和第三产业结合城市布局。产居分离条件下，将资源型工业区建设成为循环经济生态工业园，企业高技术含量的下游深加工、中高层员工的居住生活、企业所需要的产业服务依托中心城市解决，日常生活配套主要依靠临近的城镇满足。

通过区分两类工业并提出不同的布局原则，规划尽可能减少资源型工业对城镇环境的负面影响，使吸纳劳动力最多的非资源型工业和服务业能够在主要城镇集中，有利于推动城镇化进程。城镇环境质量的优化也有利于催生非资源型工业和第三产业的发展，启动接续产业的发育；而伴随着城镇人居质量的提升和产业的多元化，新的城市社会阶层尤其是中间阶层

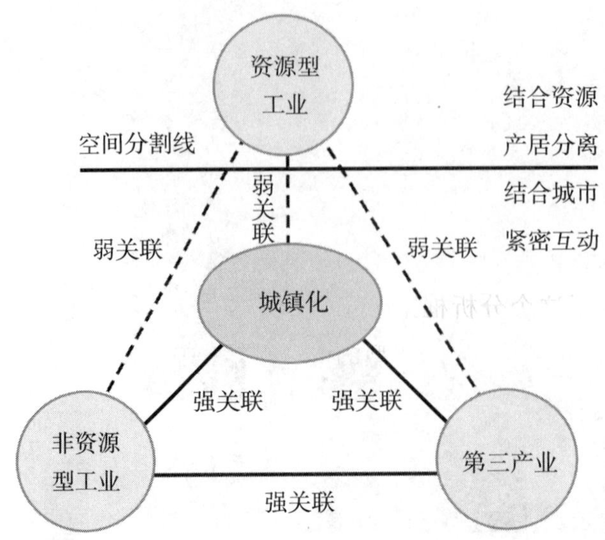

图 13　两类工业区布局原则示意

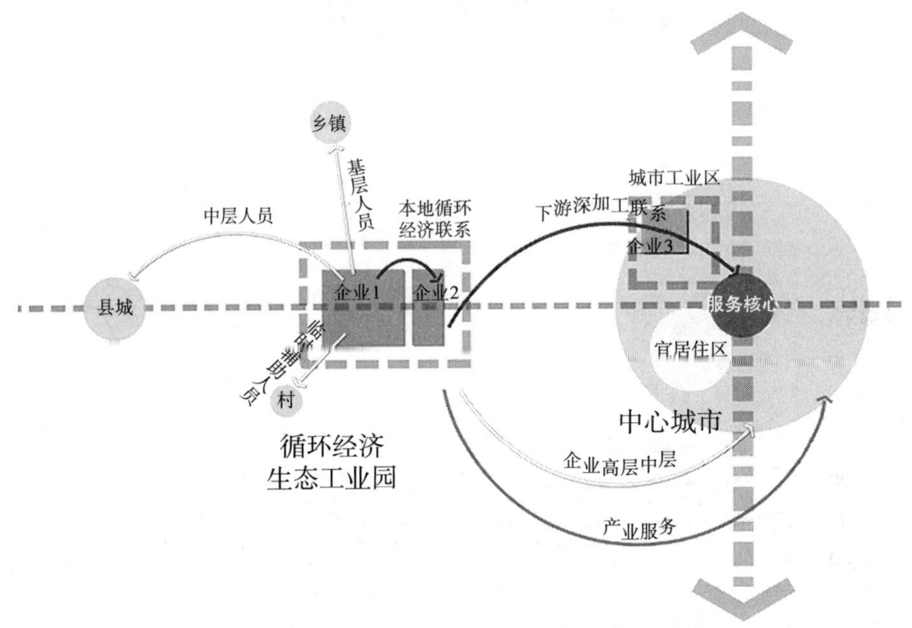

图 14　产居分离下资源型工业区与城市的联系示意

也具有了更好的发育土壤。

（三）改善城市环境促进社区再造和新文化的形成

规划通过开拓城市新区、适当疏散旧城人口、打造汾河滨河公园、增加街头绿地和休闲广场、建设公共文化体育设施、展示城市历史文化遗产等方式提升中心城市的人居环境品质，增强城市的吸引力和居民的自豪感，促进新型城市社区的形成，引导市民树立积极健康的环境观念和文化关怀。

五、小结

本文为城市可持续发展中问题诊断和对策提供了一个分析框架，即基于环境、经济、社会三个方面的分析，经过筛选后形成“问题包”，通过空间属性的折射后转化为“对策包”，再转化为可持续发展在城市规划上的对策和建议。同时以临汾这个在可持续发展上有巨大压力的资源型城市为例使用这个分析框架，基于对临汾在环境、经济、社会方面关联机制的分析，提出以空间规划促进资源型城市转型的SESE模型，即从空间优化这个城市规划的核心手段入手，启动环境、经济、社会从恶性循环走向良性循环之路。

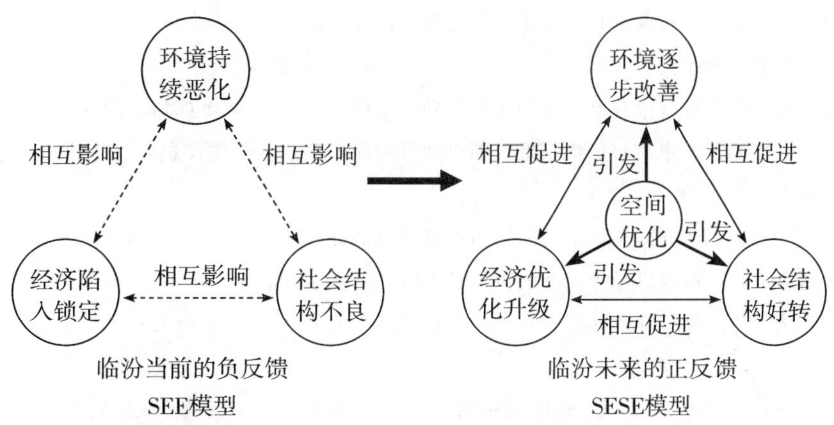

图15 以空间规划为抓手推动可持续发展的SESE模型

（作者：张兵，中国城市规划设计研究院总规划师，教授级城市规划师；林永新，中国城市规划设计研究院，城市规划师）

参考文献

[1] 鲍超，方创琳．我国矿业城市资源可持续开发利用的战略思路与模式：东营、焦作、克拉玛依市资源开发利用的经验与启示［J］．自然资源学报，2006，21（6）：900－909.

[2] 曹宝，秦其明，王秀波，朱琳．生态足迹改进模型在可持续发展评价中的应用研究［J］．生态环境，2007，16（3）：968－972.

[3] 方创琳，蔺雪芹．武汉城市群空间扩展的生态状况诊断［J］．长江流域资源与环境，2010，19（10）：1211－1218.

[4] 郝翠，李洪远，孟伟庆．国内外可持续发展评价方法对比分析［J］．中国人口·资源与环境，2010，20（1）：161－166.

[5] 黄肇义，杨东援．测度生态可持续发展的生态痕迹分析方法［J］．城市规划，2001，25（11）：26－32.

[6] 蒋依依，王仰麟，李卫锋，韩荡，牛慧恩．城市生态可持续发展量度方法探讨：以深圳市为例［J］．北京大学学报（自然科学版），2005，41（4）：612－621.

[7] 李莉，裴荣富．矿业城市的可持续发展对策［J］．中国矿业，2006（6）．

[8] 李莉，吴洁，岳超源．城市可持续发展指标体系及综合评价研究［J］．武汉城市建设学院学报，2000，17（2）：30－35.

[9] 李卫锋，王仰麟，蒋依依，李贵才．城市地域生态调控的空间途径：以深圳市为例［J］．生态学报，2003，23（9）：1823－1831.

[10] 李祚泳，程红霞，邓新民．赵晓宏．城市可持续发展的指数普适公式及评价模型［J］．环境科学，2011，22（6）：108－111.

[11] 梁伟，朱孔来．生态环境可持续发展能力研究：以长江流域为例［J］．经济问题探索，2011（8）：159－165.

[12] 林永新．资源型地区低碳化和生态化治理的现实途径：以山西临汾为例［C］．2010 城市发展与规划国际大会论文集，2010.

[13] 任绍斌，吴明伟．可持续城市空间的规划准则体系研究［J］．城市规划，2011（2）．

[14] 苏维词，罗有贤，翁才银，杨华．重庆都市圈可持续发展面临的主要生态环境问题与对策［J］．城市环境与城市生态，2004（2）．

[15] 王海飞．兰白都市经济圈视角下的白银市可持续发展战略［J］．经济地理，2011（4）．

[16] 王正，赵万民．可持续目标导向下的重庆都市区空间形态组织［J］．城市发展研究，2010（8）．

[17] 王志宪，虞孝感，徐科峰，林康．长江三角洲地区可持续发展的态势与对策［J］．地理学报，2005，60（3）．

[18] 吴承照，陶聪．城市生态足迹的地域格局：以义乌市为例［J］．城市规划学刊，2010，191（6）：46－53.

[19] 杨国华，周永章．欠发达地区实现可持续发展的创新思维；以广东省东源县为例［J］．热带地理，2007，27（1）：40－43.

[20] 张健，濮励杰．广西崇左市可持续综合发展及对策初探［J］．地理研究，2008，27（4）：938－948.

[21] 张锦高，李忠武．可持续发展定量研究方法综述［J］．中国地质大学学报（社会科学版），2003，3（6）：32－35.

[22] 张新生，何建邦．城市可持续发展与空间决策支持［J］．地理学报，1997（6）．

城市邻避性设施建设面临的困境

——以广州市番禺区生活垃圾焚烧厂事件为例

引　言

（一）邻避设施的基本概念

城市公共设施由以政府为主的公共部门提供，满足城市居民在行政、信息、教育、文化、市政、卫生、体育、交通、绿化等多方面的公共需求。城市的健康运行离不开各类公共设施的支撑。然而，并非所有的城市公共设施都能受到一致欢迎。一些公共设施如垃圾焚烧厂、垃圾转运站、公厕、加油站、高压变电站、殡仪馆、火葬场等，常常面临着负外部性而引发的公共抵制，这种现象一般被称为“邻避”。

“邻避”这一概念由西方学者在 1970 年代提出，英文为“NIMBY”（Not-In-My-Backyard），直译即为“不要在我家后院”[1]。而邻避性设施，简单而言，可以理解为“邻居希望躲避”的设施，也有学者称为“污染性设施”[2]、“不宁适设施”[3]、或“嫌恶性设施”[4]等。虽然称谓和含义有所不同，但都集中反映出此类设施的三个特征：一是具有某种满足社会需求的功能；二是具有直接或潜在的污染性和危险性；三是受到所在地居民的反对和抵制[5]。

（二）邻避冲突的普遍化

邻避性设施建设所引发的冲突和抵制由来已久并且屡见不鲜。早在 1960 年代，美国就出现了反对垃圾填埋场、毒性废弃物处理场等“污染性设施”的抗争活动。此后，愈来愈多的案例出现于其他公共建设中，如停车场、戒除药瘾医疗中心、流浪汉收容所，甚至低收入户的住宅建设，部分激进的居民通常会联合屋主团体与小区协会，共同对抗政府或开发商，使得此类建设的兴建陷入无法解决的僵局[6]。20 世纪 80 年代至今，我国台湾地区的“邻避”问题一直持续，垃圾掩埋场、焚化厂、火力发电厂等设施的建设，常常引发地方居民采取激烈的示威围堵或自力保护的方式进行抗争活动[7]。

近年来，在我国各大城市中邻避冲突也日益普遍。例如，2004 年 8 月，承担着重庆市主城区垃圾处理重任的长生桥垃圾处理场遭当地村民围堵，上百辆垃圾车被迫滞留，主城垃圾清运系统几乎陷入瘫痪[8]。2005年2月，由于担心高压电磁辐射会危害身体健康，刚开工不久的广州地铁三号线五山主变电站工程就遭到了附近居民的强烈反对，工程一度被迫停工[9]。2006年12月，北京市海淀区提出在六里屯垃圾填埋场的南侧新建一座垃圾焚烧发电厂，随后遭到六里屯居民的反对，引发万人签名的“反烧”行动，该项目最终被移址苏家坨[10]。诸如此类的邻避冲突事件不胜枚举。

（三）问题的提出

随着我国城市化进程的推进，城市人口的增加急速膨胀，对各种公共设施包括邻避性设施的需求必然持续增长。同时，在经济长期快速增长的背景下，我国城市居民对于自身居住环境质量的要求越来越高，居民的维权意识也在不断增强，这使得邻避性设施在实际建设过程中遇到的阻力也越来越大。邻避性设施的规划与建设已成为我国城市亟待解决的一大难题。邻避性设施建设究竟面临着怎样的困境？如何摆脱困境，促进邻避性设施的建设？本文试以广州市番禺区垃圾焚烧发电厂事件为例，对邻避性设施建设的困境、成因以及相应的对策进行简要探讨。

一、番禺事件的回顾

（一）区域背景

番禺区位于广州市南部。2001年，伴随广州市“北优、东进、南拓、西联”空间发展战略的提出，番禺区作为“南拓”的重点区域，开始了其快速的城市化过程，大量土地被用于住宅房地产的开发。短短两三年时间内，番禺区内就建成多个大型的居住楼盘。该区一度成为广州乃至全国都颇具知名度的住宅房地产热点板块。

（二）事件发展历程

2003年，番禺区开始着手垃圾焚烧厂的选址工作。2004年8月，沙湾河道以北的垃圾焚烧发电厂项目获广州市计划发展委员会批准立项，初步拟选址于石基镇凌边村一带，但在征地过程中因受到当地居民的坚决抵制而被迫停止。2006年，有关部门历经3年多的调研和选址论证，初步确定大石街会江村的大石简易垃圾处理厂作为新建生活垃圾焚烧发电厂的选址，并得到了广州市规划局批准和发放了《建设项目选址意见书》。

2009年2月4日，广州市政府正式发布“关于番禺区生活垃圾焚烧发电厂项目工程建设的通告”。通告称该项目为广州市重点建设项目，计划于2010年建成并投入运营。番禺区民众获悉之后提出了强烈反对和抗议。番禺区政府随后聘请相关专家并召开了新闻发布会，但由于专家的身份遭到质疑，事态没有得到平息。2009年11月，番禺区区长召开座谈会，作出“环评不通过不动工，绝大多数群众反映强烈不动工”的表态，然而有关媒体却爆料政府态度的急遽转变与承建运营商存在着利益交易关系，事态越演越烈。随着广州媒体的连续报道甚至有中央媒体的介入，“番禺垃圾焚烧事件”演化成全国性的热点事件。迫于舆论压力，当地政府开始与民众代表接触和协商，最终认可民众提出的垃圾分类方案，并决定暂停建设垃圾焚烧发电厂，选址工作被推迟到2011年1月后进行，整个选址估计要到2012年底才能完成。至此，番禺区垃圾焚烧厂事件暂告一段落。

（三）困境所在

与大多数邻避性公共设施境遇相同，番禺区生活垃圾焚烧厂项目陷入了进退两难的困境。一方面，随着番禺居住区规模的扩大和人口的增加，城市现有的生活垃圾处理设施已无法应付，存在“垃圾围城”的潜在危机，政府力推垃圾焚烧厂项目显得有理有据。然而，另一方面，番禺民众却自觉利益受损，坚决抵制项目的建设，最终导致该项目被搁置。究竟是何原因使得番禺区居民强烈反对和抵制这样一个对全体市民有利的公共设施项目？

二、邻避困境解析

邻避设施建设引发的冲突往往涉及包括居民、设备提供商、政府等多个的利益博弈。在番禺垃圾焚烧厂事件中，博弈的主体重点为两方：一方是垃圾厂项目的决策者，也是投资者——当地相关政府部门，包括广州市发改委、国土房管局、财政局、规划局、环保局以及番禺区政府等；另一方则是垃圾厂周边5到10公里范围内影响到的多个住宅小区的居民，如丽江花园、广州碧桂园、祈福新村、海龙湾等。周边居民反对和抵制项目的建设，其原因归纳起来主要包括三个方面：一是对设施的外部性存在担忧以及由此引发的强烈“不公平感”，二是对项目规划本身的科学性存在质疑，三是认为政府决策过程中有失公正、民主。

（一）设施的负外部性

作为这一类经济活动，城市公共设施的运营会对他人及社会造成利益或成本的影响，根据影响的积极或消极效果表现，可分为正外部性和负外部性。如前文提到的，邻避性设施的一个主要特征是存在直接或潜在的污染性和危险性。因此，该类设施往往都具有明显的负外部性，主要涉及环境污染对居民健康的威胁以及房地产贬值造成的居民财产损失。

在番禺垃圾焚烧厂事件中，设施存在的负外部性一直是冲突的主要焦点。拟建中的垃圾发电厂占地365亩、计划日焚烧处理城市垃圾2 000吨。番禺区的居民们在获悉了该项目后，就开始通过各种渠道收集关于垃圾焚烧厂的资料，发布到网上共享并讨论。他们了解到垃圾焚烧过程中会排放出一种剧毒的污染物——二恶英。大量网上收集的资料显示，二恶英是毒性最大的化合物之一，其毒性是氰化物的130倍、砒霜的900倍，有“世纪之毒”之称，国际癌症研究中心已将其列为人类一级致癌物。并且，二恶英不能在线检测，没有人知道它是否真的超标，因此就极可能变成一种很随性的排放。在欧洲和美国，垃圾焚烧厂备受诟病；日本甚至还发生过“垃圾岛污染事件”。众多的负面信息，使得受影响的当地居民对该项目产生了极大的抵触。居民们戴上写有“拒绝毒气”字样的口罩签名反对修建垃圾焚烧发电厂，高呼“为了孩子，我们不要垃圾焚烧带出的二恶英”。

很多在广州市区工作的市民之所以选择搬到番禺居住，是看中了郊区相对优质的空气质量和生态环境，因此，他们无法接受这样一项会对自己周边的居住环境带来威胁的设施。而且，他们也担心整个番禺区良好的城市形象会遭到破坏，使得自己的住宅物业大幅贬值。有网友就如此质疑：“将来从亚洲第一高铁大站——广州新客站出来，看到的是三根80米高的大烟囱，不知大家有何感想!”

此外，邻避设施的负外部性容易引发受影响居民强烈的“不公平感”。大部分居民都了解邻避设施对于社会全体所具有的效益，但问题在于他们会质疑为什么这项设施偏要设置在他们家“后院”而不是设置他处。一般而言，设施负外部性的大小程度与地理上的距离远近成反比，即距离邻避性设施越近的居民受到设施的消极影响越大，反之则越小。这种特征意味着邻避性公共设施会产生不对称的收益——成本分配结构：设施服务功能带来的利益由广大市民共享，但生产或运营成本也外部化，并集中转嫁给设施周边的民众[5]。因此，不难理解番禺区居民在获知垃圾焚烧发电厂项目“落户自家”的心理不平衡。这种不对称的成本—利益分配结构正是引发邻避性设施冲突的根本原因。如何平衡部分居民的“部分利益”或“局部利益”以及全体市民的“整体利益”，是解决邻避设施困境的关键。

（二）项目规划的科学性

邻避性公共设施往往涉及很强的专业性环保污染问题，这对设施的规划选址提出了较高的技术要求，如果缺乏充分合理的科学依据，很难得到社会各方的普遍认同。

番禺区垃圾焚烧厂规划选址的科学性正是受到当地居民质疑的重要方面。首先，为何选址在楼盘密集的居住区？番禺垃圾焚烧发电厂选址附近有10多个楼盘，近30万业主在此居住。发电厂选址地距最近的楼盘仅2公里，最远的也不过8公里。受垃圾焚烧厂影响的远不止30万人，该项目附近区域内居住的人口数目在100万~300万人之间。在聚集着如此众多的村镇和高档楼盘区域中兴建日焚烧量2 000吨的大型垃圾焚烧发电厂究竟有何依据？其次，垃圾焚烧厂如果建成投产，会造成多大程度的污染，污染是否可控，有无相关的安全防御措施？对于这些问题，政府方面并未给出全面而合理的解答。此外，该项目在2009年通告实施前，甚至之后已经基本完成了征地拆迁工作时，都一直未进行专业的环境影响评价。最后，该项目从2003年开始酝酿，2004年正式立项，2006年获得项目选址意见书，到2009年准备建设，经过了较长的时间跨度，这期间该区域的社会经济和空间环境都发生了很多变化。对此，政府方面并未对该项目最初的规划决策作出相应的回顾和检讨，这在一定程度上降低了规划决策的科学性。这些涉及规划决策科学性的漏洞，都是造成了周边居民对项目“不依不饶”原因。

（三）决策过程的公正性

在前述的分析中已提到，邻避性公共设施的利益冲突可以理解为受影响的当地居民代表的“部分利益”或“局部利益”与政府公共部门代表的全体市民的“整体利益”之间的一种矛盾。长期以来，在我国公共设施的规划与建设过程中，政府作为决策者处于绝对的主导地位，重视决策的效率性而忽视其民主性和公平性：没有提供真正意义上的公众参与的途径，或者即便有也徒具形式，往往只是“告知”，而不接受反馈和诉求，并惯以“服从大局”为名，牺牲部分民众的利益。2009 年 2 月广州市政府发布了题为《关于番禺区生活垃圾焚烧发电厂项目工程建设的通告》的文件，文件中这样写道：“番禺垃圾发电厂项目是广州市重点建设项目，位于番禺区大石街会江村与钟村镇谢村交界处，计划于 2010 年建成并投入运营。工程建设范围内的单位和个人应当顾全大局，积极支持和配合国家建设，不得阻挠建设工程的测量、钻探、施工以及征地拆迁工作。”而在通告下发之前，有关政府部门并未将整个垃圾焚烧发电厂项目的论证、申请、招标过程告知直接利益相关方——番禺区的当地居民，更未在此过程中征求过民众的意见。这种对于决策信息的封闭以及决策过程公正性的忽视，严重损害了居民对于政府的信任感，也是造成居民对垃圾厂项目坚决抵制的一项重要原因。

2009 年，广东省省情调查研究中心针对番禺垃圾焚烧厂项目 8 公里范围以内的小区居民展开了一项问卷调查。据调查显示，高达 97.1% 的受访居民不赞成在番禺区大石街会江村附近建设垃圾焚烧发电厂，92.5% 的受访居民对有关部门政务信息公开方面表示“很不满意”。如果垃圾焚烧发电厂通过环评，88.4% 的受访居民表示不信任此结果。由此也可窥见居民与政府之间存在的信任危机。如果不能增进民众与政府之间的彼此信任，很难协调两者的利益冲突，邻避设施的建设也难以推进。

三、对策探讨

邻避性设施的建设所遇到的困境是无法获得设施所在地居民的支持和认同。基于前述的分析，居民之所以抵制邻避性设施主要涉及关于设施的负外部性、项目规划建设的科学性以及政府决策的公正性三个方面的担忧和质疑。打破居民心理的担忧和质疑是突破设施建设的出发点。下面，针对当地居民对邻避设施抱有的主要担忧和质疑，提出几条解决之策。

第一，转变观念，尊重每个城市居民的合法利益。国家的发展体制在由计划向市场转型的过程中，城市居民的居住模式也在悄然发生着变化，由过去“单位制”主导的社区模式向“开发商”市场化主导的住宅小区模式转变。城市居民也相应从“单位人”转变为“社会人”，越来越关心自身周边居住环境的品质。同时，住宅的商品化使得自有住宅物业成为了城市居民最重要的一部分家庭私有财产，居民对于可能影响到自有财产贬值的外部因素的关注度和敏感度都在提高。而《物权法》的颁布实施，也给城市居民的越来越高涨的维权意识提供了法律保障。因此，当遇到反对和抵制诸如垃圾焚烧厂之类的“邻避设施”的建设时，作为决策者的城市政府部门不应简单将居民的抵制认为是“自私”行为，而应当顺应社会经济体制变迁，不断转变观念，看到居民反对背后的合理性，毕竟每个完全的“经济人”都是从自身利益最大化的角度来做出行为选择的。政府决策者应当学会尊重每个城市居民的合法利益，避免以“公众利益”为借口，而忽视部分城市居民的利益。

第二，降低设施负外部性给周边居民带来的不利影响。一方面是提供风险保障，即为居民提供应对可能损害的保险性措施，达到减轻居民预期恐惧与不安、弱化反抗动机的目的。例如，通过设置一定的安全间距来达到减少设施可能产生的环境污染对人体健康带来的影响，但前提是存在一个各方都能接受的环保标准[11]。或者，政府或相关机构可以和民众签订具有时效性的环保协定，明确邻避性公共设施设置后提供的安全保证、环保标准、损害赔偿及违约处罚等。另一方面则是考虑对于受影响的居民一定的回馈补偿。回馈补偿就是基于经济诱因，用金钱或其他实物的方式作为周边居民损失的补偿，以降低居民的抗争的方式[12]。回馈补偿一般分为金钱和实物或其他补偿两类：（1）金钱补偿。对邻避性公共设施周边居民直接给付金钱或提供有关赋税的减免，但这种方式涉及受损失居民及其程度界定的问题，容易引发新的争议，同时这种方式也较容易被看作贿赂而引起反效果。（2）实物补偿即以实物回馈的方式对邻避性公共设施附近的居民进行补偿，例如兴建公园、游泳池、游乐设施等受民众青睐的公共设施供其使用。从回馈补偿方式来看，以提供正外部性大的公共设施与公共服务的方式较好。

第三，提高项目规划的科学性。首先是规划的技术科学性，包括聘请具有资质的专业设计单位对邻避设施进行规划设计，对设施可能造成的各种负面影响进行全面的评估以及选址地周边情况特别是居民情况等进行深入的分析，做出具有预判性的冲突应对方案等。其次是规划过程的科学性。规划本身是一个动态的过程，并需要具备一定的前瞻性。随着时间的推移，邻避设施面对的客观经济社会环境会发生改变，需要政府规划部门适时地对规划作出检讨和修正。此外，在规划设计、项目选址、方案实施的整个过程中需要加强公众的参与，吸收各方意见，提升规划本身的合理性。

第四，加强公众参与，提升规划决策的公平性和民主性。通过公众参与的完善，为与邻避冲突有关的各方，包括民众、政府官员及专业人员等提供了解、沟通的机会，促进矛盾的化解[13]。在应对“邻避”发生时，最常使用的公众参与方式主要有以下三种：（1）信息公开。政府于事前提供充分、正确的信息使民众了解设施建设的方案、依据与行动计划，满足民众的知情权，有助于建立民众对于政府的信任。（2）问卷调查或民意访谈。这是一种收集信息的有效方式，因为人们在匿名的情况下往往更愿意表达自己的意见，同时它也提供了一种参与途径，使民众认为自己意见获得尊重。（3）公众大会。会议以面对面的沟通和讨论的方式，一方面能在短时间内让各方包括民众、决策者或专业人员表达各自的观点，一方面可以通过彼此的互动来达成妥协或协议，最后在彼此能接受的范围内得到各方都能接受的解决方案。

四、结语

邻避性城市公共设施的建设是世界各地都普遍存在的难题。番禺垃圾焚烧厂项目遭遇周边民众抵制而最终被暂停的事件充分反映了此类特殊的公共设施在建设过程中所面临的进退两难的困境。一方面，邻避性设施的建设有其客观需求，有利于城市居民生产和生活的顺利进行，但另一方面，邻避性设施具有一定的负外部性，难以获得周边居民的认同和支持，其建设实施阻力重重。

造成邻避性设施建设困境的成因非常复杂。从当地居民的角度出发进行剖析，可以看到，居民反对和抵制邻避性设施的建设主要出于三个方面的原因，包括对设施负外部性的担忧和承担负外部成本带来的巨大“不平衡感”，以及对项目规划的科学性、决策过程的公正性的质疑。针对居民的这些主要担忧和质疑，建议政府决策者转变观念，与时俱进，尊重每个公民的合法权益，平衡好“部分利益”或者“局部利益”与“整体利益”之间的关系；通过提供风险保障以及回馈补偿等措施，降低邻避设施负外部性给居民带来的不利影响；努力提高项目规划的科学性；以及加强规划建设过程中的公众参与，提升决策的公平性和民主性，从而有效化解各方的利益矛盾，找到共识。

（作者：李晓晖，广州市城市规划勘测设计研究院，高级规划师；杨海寰，香港大学建筑学院城市规划与设计系博士）

参考文献

[1] Ohare, M. . Not on My Block You Don't: Facility Siting and the Strategic Importance of Compensation [J]. Public Policy, 1977, 24 (4): 407 - 458.

[2] 李世杰．污染性设施对居住品质影响之研究：以台中火力发电厂为例［D］．台中：逢甲大学，1994.

[3] 曾明逊．不宁适设施的风险知觉［J］．人与地，1992（126）：36－40.

[4] 陈柏廷．嫌恶性设施合并再利用之研究：以福德坑垃圾掩埋场及富德公墓合并再利用为例［D］．台北：中兴大学，1994.

[5] 李晓晖．城市邻避性公共设施建设的困境与对策探讨［J］．规划师，2009，25（12）：80－83.

[6] Barry, S. . Not In My Backyard: The Sequel [J]. Waste Age, 2000 (8): 25 - 31.

[7] 丘昌泰．从“邻避情结”到“迎臂效应”：台湾环保抗争的问题与出路［J］．政治科学论丛，2002（12）：33－56.

[8] 张向和，等．重庆市垃圾处理场的邻避效应分析［J］．环境工程学报，2011，5（6）：1363－1369.

[9] 付昱．五山变电站建在小区中居民强烈反对［N］．南方都市报，2005－2－4（4）.

[10] 熊炎．邻避型群体性事件的实例分析与对策研究：以北京市为例［J］．北京行政学院学报，2011（3）：41－43.

[11] 郑卫．邻避设施规划之困境：上海磁悬浮事件的个案分析［J］．城市规划，2011，35（2）：76－81.

[12] 黄德秀．补偿对邻避现象的影响：以乌丘低放射性废料场址为例［D］．台北：台北大学，2001.

[13] 汤京平．邻避性环境冲突管理的制度与策略［J］．政治科学论丛，1999（6）：355－382.

广东“三旧”改造政策分析：背景、内容与创新

引　言

“三旧”改造，始于2007年佛山市政府出台的《关于加快推进旧城镇、旧厂房、旧村居改造的决定》，用以指代旧城镇、旧厂房和旧村庄的改造，并逐渐被政府和社会舆论沿用。直至2009年，广东省政府出台了《关于推进“三旧”改造促进节约集约用地的若干意见》（粤府〔2009〕78号），标志着广东省“三旧”改造政策正式出台并实施。

“三旧”改造政策，实际上是广东省向国家争取的特殊支持，是面向城市更新改造的一次积极的政策创新与尝试。它的出台反映了广东省这一全国发展先行地区的现实问题与主动行动，政策本身也有着不同以往的创新之处。为此，本文对“三旧”改造政策出台的背景与意义进行了分析，梳理和总结了其对原有政策体系的突破，并以广州市为例，进一步介绍和分析了“三旧”改造政策在地方层面的深化与实施，为理解“三旧”改造，也为全国其他地区的类似更新改造提供政策借鉴。

一、“三旧”改造政策的由来

改革开放以来，广东省特别是珠三角地区大力发展外向型经济，带动了大量制造业和外来人口的涌入。面对快速增长的产业与人口需求，地方政府为了不“错失发展机会”，为吸引投资而普遍提前、超前进行土地投资与开发。许多集体经济组织绕开《土地管理法》和市、镇政府，直接与投资者签订集体土地使用权出让协议，将集体土地通过挂靠、租赁等方式供其他个人和单位使用，同时，村民乱占耕地、私建房屋的状况也愈来愈普遍，结果导致政府规划引导和控制政策的失效，建设用地失控。根据相关统计数据显示，仅在2001年至2007年，广东省耕地面积就减少了416万亩，2007年建设用地总量就提前达到了2010年规划控制规模，用地矛盾突出。同时，大量涌入的劳动密集型产业也逐步引发产业结构低端、产出低效、环境污染等问题。“遍地开花”的工业、“城中村”积累了大量的低效用地、违法用地。对此，珠三角各地市也出台过有关旧城镇、旧村庄和旧厂房改造的系列政策，试图

缓解日益突出的人地矛盾。但是，由于政策的限制，在土地产权、功能置换、拆迁补偿、开发收益等问题上困难重重，难以形成有效的激励机制，导致“三旧”改造进展缓慢。

近年来，在国家保障粮食安全、严格保护耕地的背景下，广东省土地资源控制与经济社会发展的用地需求矛盾更加突出。根据《全国土地利用总体规划纲要（2006—2020年）》，国家下达给广东省2020年的建设用地指标，远远难以满足全省在新一轮发展中新增建设用地的需要。与此同时，随着我国汇率上升、出口退税政策调整、成本要素上升以及全球金融危机导致的外需急速下行等产业环境的改变，令广东外向型经济发展面临巨大压力。此外，居民对城市环境的要求也愈来愈高。土地挖潜、产业结构调整升级、转变经济发展方式成为珠三角和广东发展的必然选择。

在这些压力下，广东省政府在参考广州、佛山、深圳、珠海等地市实践经验的基础上，与国土资源部商讨，拟以省部合作方式在广东开展节约集约用地试点示范省工作。2009年2月4日，国土资源部和广东省政府共同制定的《广东省建设节约集约用地试点示范省工作方案》印发并下发广东省内各地政府、部门和机构。2009年11月23日，广东省政府印发了《关于推进“三旧”改造促进节约集约用地的若干意见》（粤府〔2009〕78号），以此文为指导，各地市随后出台了各自的“三旧”改造实施意见与办法，“三旧”改造政策及实践在广东省全面展开。

二、“三旧”改造政策的主要创新与突破

“三旧”改造是广东省以制度创新推进产业升级、空间调整的一次重要尝试。由于之前已经积累了如广州、佛山、深圳等地市的众多政策经验，因此整个“三旧”改造政策体系与之前的相关政策体系相比有了很大不同。内容涉及多方面，包括国土、规划、房管、产业、财政、税收等。根据粤府〔2009〕78号文和粤府办〔2009〕122号文，“三旧”改造主要的政策创新有以下几个方面：

1. 历史用地遗留问题处置

“三旧”改造政策规定，根据用地行为的发生时间和拆迁改造类型将“三旧”改造用地分类处理，纳入“三旧”改造范围、符合土地利用总体规划和“三旧”改造规划、没有合法用地手续且已使用的建设用地，按用地行为发生时的法律政策处理完善征收手续。此政策为之前没有合法用地手续的用地也提供了完善手续的机会。

2. 用地报批手续简化

按以往规定，“三旧”改造需按该土地使用前的地类报批，需扣减指标和缴纳新增建设用地土地有偿使用费，需占补平衡。“三旧”改造政策对纳入“三旧”改造范围的用地，不管原来是建设用地还是农用地，全部采用现状（即建设用地）报批。这样就免除了办理农转用的手续，为进一步改造降低了成本。

3. 供地出让方式灵活化

“三旧”改造政策规定，即除属于政府收购储备后再次供地的必须以招拍挂方式出让

外，其他可以协议方式出让。这一规定简化了供地方式，大大调动了使用者的积极性。

表1　各类用地手续完善方式一览表

用地行为分类	办理方式	具体规定
用地行为发生在1987年1月1日之前	直接办理国有或集体建设用地确权	由市、县人民政府土地行政主管部门出具符合土地利用总体规划的审核意见书，依照原国家土地管理局1995年3月11日发布的《确定土地所有权和使用权的若干规定》进行确权后，办理国有建设用地确权登记发证手续，不需报省以上审批
用地行为发生在1987年1月1日之后、在2007年6月30日之前的	依照旧（新）《土地管理法》办理征收	已签订征收协议并进行补偿、未引发纠纷、迄今被征地农民无不同意见，已按照用地发生时的《土地管理法》落实处理（处罚）后按土地现状办理征收手续，不需办理新增建设用地、农用地转用手续，不需缴纳有关税费、不需扣减有关用地计划指标，2004年5月1日前的，无须听证、社保、留用地

广州市“三旧”改造工作办公室．广州市“三旧”改造规划（2010—2020年），2010。

4. 改造模式多样化

按照“三旧”改造政策规定，需要改造的“三旧”项目可以根据实际情况选择适合的模式，包括政府主导改造、社会资金参与改造、集体经济组织自行改造和原土地权利人自行改造四种类型。这为吸引更多社会力量参与改造创造了制度条件。

5. 税费减免

按照以往规定，办理土地征收手续需要缴纳新增建设用地有偿使用费、耕地占用税和耕地开垦费等。按照“三旧”改造政策规定，用地行为发生在1987年1月1日前的不需要缴纳任何费用，直接确权发放证书；用地行为发生在1987年1月1日至2007年6月30日之间的，免交新增建设用地有偿使用费、耕地占用税和耕地开垦费，以减轻业主的负担。

6. 土地出让金优惠与分成

按照旧规定，建设项目申请增加容积率需补缴土地出让金。按照“三旧”改造政策规定，对现有工业用地改造后不改变原用途，申请提高容积率的，可以不再增缴土地价款。同时，“三旧”改造政策规定，对“三旧”改造中收取的土地出让纯收益可按不高于60%的比例用于支持原用地企业、原农村集体经济组织，从而有利于充分调动原使用者参与改造的积极性。这些土地收益新政策，旨在充分调动原使用者参与改造的积极性。

7. 集体土地产权的变更

“三旧”政策规定，允许村集体申请把集体建设用地转为国有用地。农村集体经济组织可经村民（代表）大会表决同意后，向区国土资源部门申请将集体建设用地转为国有用地，按程序逐级上报省人民政府批准。由于集体土地上的物业无法买卖，土地产权变更为国有，可令改造物业有条件进入市场，产生更多的收益可能，从而提高市场参与集体土地改造的积极性与可行性。

8. 关于边角地、夹心地、插花地的优惠政策

凡符合土地利用总体规划和城乡规划的，可依照有关规定一并纳入“三旧”改造范围。并允许在符合土地利用总体规划和控制性详细规划的前提下，通过土地位置调换等方式，对

原有存量建设用地进行调整使用，有利于土地的整理与集中改造。

“三旧”改造是在土地资源供需矛盾日益突出的情况下，破解用地瓶颈、拓展建设空间、保障发展用地的重要途径。

“三旧”改造政策在国内率先将旧城镇、旧厂房以及旧村庄三者改造同时纳入政策支持，通过用地手续简化、改造模式多元化、财税支持等手段，鼓励了对“三旧”用地的二次利用，有利于实现“存量”土地的盘活、整理和重新开发。同时，对“三旧”进行改造，为引进新产业、完善新功能腾出了空间，有利于产业结构调整升级，也有利于提升城市功能和改善城乡人居环境。“三旧”改造不仅是一次城市更新运动，同时也是广东省促进城市发展模式和经济增长方式转变的一个重要战略举措。

三、“三旧”改造政策在地方的深化与实施：以广州市为例

广州市，是广东省第一大城市和珠三角的核心城市，同时也是一座拥有2 200年历史的历史文化名城。一方面，经济与人口的快速增长，令广州也面临着巨大的土地、资源压力。2008年，广州市经济总量已接近万亿元，但2001年至2008年的年均建设用地增长也达到了40～50平方公里。2008年，全市土地利用强度已达到23%。根据广州市的土地利用规划，从2008年至2020年，广州市可使用的新增建设用地规模只有148平方公里，按广州市目前的土地消耗速度，仅够3年。与此同时，土地利用效率也有待进一步提高，特别是广州市农村居民点、乡镇工业用地普遍粗放，低效用地和违法用地多发的问题急需解决。另一方面，广州长期的历史积累形成了较大面积的老城区。老城区人口和建筑密度很大，交通拥挤、公共空间不足，新城推进过程中形成的大量城中村令城市二元结构突出，更淹没了具有丰富价值的历史文化遗存。在“三旧”改造政策正式出台前，广州市就已开展了以“城中村”改造、历史文化名城保护为重点的城市更新行动。可以说，广州市的“三旧”改造重“质”胜于重“量”，更关注通过土地挖潜提升城市功能与环境形象。

自从2009年全省统一部署推进“三旧”改造工作以来，广州市积极响应、大胆实践，以前所未有的力度推进“三旧”改造。2009年12月31日，广州市政府颁布了《关于加快推进“三旧”改造工作的意见》，同时还一并出台了《关于广州市推进旧城更新改造的实施意见》、《关于广州市推进“城中村”（旧村）整治改造的实施意见》、《关于广州市旧厂房改造土地处置实施意见》三个政策文件，以及一系列工作指引和标准，深化和细化了“三旧”改造政策的实施办法。2010年2月24日，广州市“三旧”改造工作办公室正式挂牌成立，作为广州市“三旧”改造领导小组日常性工作机构及统筹全市“三旧”改造工作的常设性工作部门，下属各区县也相继成立了“三旧”改造办公室，全面推进“三旧”改造工作。下文主要以穗府〔2009〕56号文及其三个附件文件为主要依据，对广州市“三旧”改造相关政策的主要内容进行梳理和介绍，以进一步反映“三旧”改造政策在地方层面的深化内容。

表2 广州市“三旧”改造相关政策文件一览表

类别	政策文件名称
广州市“三旧”改造文件	关于加快推进“三旧”改造工作的意见(穗府〔2009〕56号)
	广州市民营企业产业用地结合“三旧”改造完善用地手续指引(送审稿)
旧城镇改造文件	关于广州市推进旧城更新改造的实施意见
	广州市旧城更新成片重建改造工作流程(征求意见稿)
	广州市旧城更新改造规划指引(征求意见稿)
	广州市旧城改造方案编制指引立案标准(征求意见稿)
旧村改造文件	关于广州市推进“城中村”(旧村)整治改造的实施意见
	广州市“城中村”全面改造工作流程(征求意见稿)
	广州市“城中村”(旧村)改造规划指引(征求意见稿)
	广州市“城中村”改造方案编制指引立案标准(征求意见稿)
	“城中村”改造复建费用标准指引
旧厂房改造文件	关于广州市旧厂房改造土地处置实施意见
	广州市旧厂房改造工作流程(征求意见稿)
	广州市旧厂改造规划指引(征求意见稿)
	广州市旧厂房改造方案编制指引立案标准(征求意见稿)

资料来源:“三旧”改造:佛山创新七大模式.佛山日报,2009-11-26。

(一)旧城镇的改造

根据穗府〔2009〕56号文附件一《关于广州市推进旧城更新改造的实施意见》的相关内容,广州旧城镇改造政策结合自身实际,在改造模式、税费优惠、补偿安置等方面作了进一步深化与创新。

首先,在旧城更新改造的模式上。根据具体情况不同,旧城更新改造模式分为成片重建改造、零散改造模式和历史文化保护性整治模式。成片重建改造项目的资金主要采取区政府为主体,市场开发方式运作。而零散改造项目原则上由业主负责修缮改造,区政府可结合实际情况予以补贴。各区政府从实际出发,在会商市“三旧”改造办公室意见的基础上,结合房屋危破状况、土地利用效率、环境条件、历史文化等因素,制定的拆(成片重建改造模式)、改(零散改造模式)、留(历史文化保护性整治模式)的选址范围。

其次,在更新改造税费优惠政策上。按照“拆一免一”的原则,对于成片重建改造项目,市政府实行市级权限范围内的税费减免和返还。

最后,在补偿安置政策上。旧城更新的补偿安置方式有货币补偿、本区域就近安置和跨区域异地安置三种方式。市、区人民政府和各相关部门应当按照“先安置、后改造”的原则,多渠道筹措动迁安置房源。鼓励企业提供存量土地建设就近安置房,可调整土地用途,增加开发强度,减免土地闲置费用。

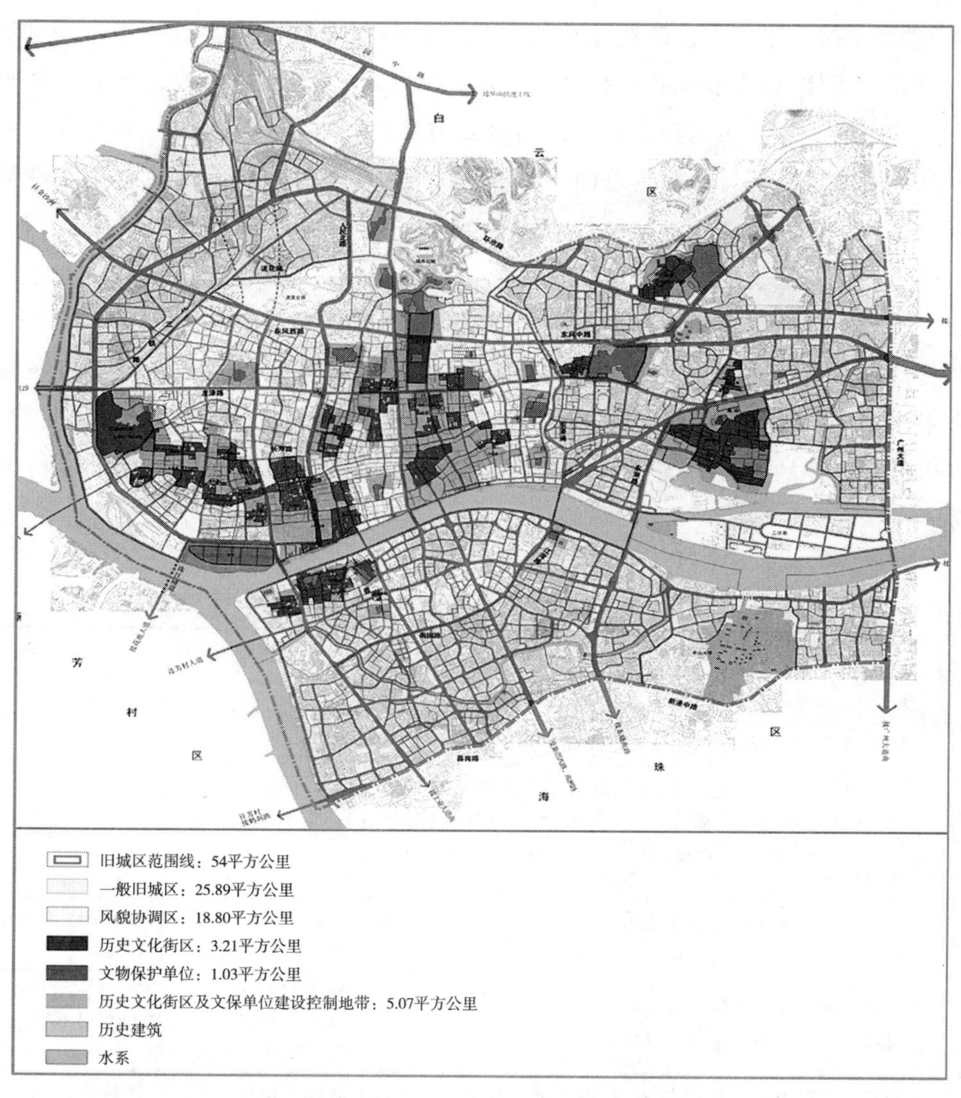

图1　广州市旧城更新改造规划分区示意图

资料来源：广州市规划局．广州市旧城更新改造规划纲要，2010。

（二）城中村（旧村）的改造

根据穗府〔2009〕56号文附件二《关于广州市推进“城中村”（旧村）整治改造的实施意见》的相关内容，广州“城中村”（旧村）改造分为“全面改造”和“综合整治”两种模式。全面改造模式主要以整体拆除重建为主，并明确提出采取全面改造的52条“城中村”。综合整治模式主要以改善“城中村”的居住环境为目的，清拆违章、抽疏建筑，打通交通道路和消防通道，实现三线下地、雨污分流，加强环境整治和立面整饰，使环境、卫生、消防、房屋安全、市政设施等方面基本达到要求。在模式的应用上还规定，未纳入全面改造计划的村，村民自愿进行全面改造的，经市“三旧”改造工作领导小组同意，可以补充纳入全面改造计划。涉及局部拆建的综合改造项目，经所在区政府同意，并报市“三旧”改造工作领导小组批准，可以使用全面改造项目的政策。

同时，“城中村”（旧村）改造在改造的优惠政策及财政支持上有许多创新和突破。包括：(1) 可完善集体（国有）用地手续，完成确权登记。(2) 全面改造项目可将原集体用地转换为国有用地（需在报送项目专项改造规划方案时一并申请）。(3) 可将单块面积不超过3亩、多块累计面积不超过改造总面积10%的“三地”一并纳入改造，国有性质的“三地”可采取协议出让，现状用地属性为农用地的“三地”需办理农转用手续。(4) 全面改造项目如村要求自主开发的，改造地块可采取协议出让，缓缴土地出让金；采取公开出让方式融资的，可以实行现状出让方式。(5) 除政府土地储备项目外，未来5年全面改造项目的土地纯收益（土地公开出让收入扣除土地储备成本及按规定计提、上缴的专项资金）的60%支出用于支持村集体经济发展。(6) 全面改造项目的安置房（含非住宅复建安置房）办理国有房地产权证的，可缓缴土地出让金，如发生交易转让，业主按基准地价的30%缴纳出让金。

表3 全面改造与综合整治政策比较一览表

	序号	改造方式	
		全面改造方式	整治改造方式
优惠政策层面	1	可完善集体(国有)用地手续,完成确权登记	适用
	2	可将单块面积不超过3亩、多块累计面积不超过改造用地总面积10%的“三地”一并纳入改造,国有性质的“三地”可采取协议出让,用地属性为农用地的“三地”需办理农转用手续	适用
	3	改造范围内地块可采取协议出让(空转),缓缴土地出让金;采取公开出让的,可以实行现状出让方式	不适用,但在符合规定的情况下可通过流转集体建设用地使用权进行融资
	4	村集体可申请将集体建设用地转换为国有用地(需在报送项目专项规划方案时一并申请)	须为1987年1月7日前已使用,或由区政府征收统筹后仍安排给本村集体作产业用地使用的才能享受该项政策
	5	安置房办理国有房地产权证的,可缓缴出让金,如发生交易转让,安置房按基准低价的30%缴纳出让金	修详规中保留的部分建筑物,经全面整治且通过市“三旧”办检查的,可办理房地产登记发证
操作层面	1	改造规划方案编制:由区政府和村一起编制全面改造项目专项规划和实施计划	改造规划方案编制:由区政府编制整治改造项目的规划和实施计划
	2	改造规划方案审批:报市“三旧”办审核,如无不妥,报市“三旧”改造工作领导小组审批	改造规划方案审批:区政府审批,只需报市“三旧”办备案
	3	资金筹措: ①市场运作。采取土地公开出让方式融资,如所融得资金超过改造成本,超出部分的60%返还村集体,如所融得资金少于改造成本,由政府进行保底 ②自主改造。由村通过集体和村民自筹,或是以部分改造地块抵押获取贷款、引入合伙企业、吸引社会资金等开发方式进行改造	资金筹措: ①政府投入。主要用于公共服务配套设施建设 ②自主融资。在符合城市规划、留用地管理政策和得到2/3以上村集体经济组织成员同意的前提下,允许村集体经济组织按照规划和“三旧”改造政策,通过旧厂房、旧商铺等低效空闲存量土地升级改造,适用集体建设用地使用权流转政策,自主进行综合整治招商融资

资料来源：广州市城市规划勘测设计研究院．广州市“三旧”改造规划设计资料汇编，2010。

（三）旧厂房的改造

根据穗府〔2009〕56号文附件三《关于广州市旧厂房改造土地处置实施意见》，旧厂房用地按照用地所有权不同，可分为国有用地和村集体用地两类，其用地处置方式及相关政策要点均有所不同。整理如下表所示。

表4　旧厂房改造用地处置方式及相关政策要点一览表

<table>
<tr><th>分类</th><th>处置情况分类</th><th>处置方式</th></tr>
<tr><td rowspan="4">国有用地的处置</td><td rowspan="3">经划拨、出让等方式合法取得使用权的国有用地、符合登记确权条件（含1987年1月1日前已使用）的历史国有土地</td><td>自行改造，补交地价：依照城乡规划，可申请单独开发、无须纳入政府储备的，企业可在补缴土地出让金后，进行商品住宅外的开发</td></tr>
<tr><td>公开出让，收益支持：具备开发经营条件的原址用地，可由土地储备机构收购土地，也可由企业自行搬迁整理土地后，政府组织公开出让。原土地使用权人可选择一种收益支持方式补偿，并根据完成搬迁、拆除的时间，追加相应的补偿比例资金</td></tr>
<tr><td>公开收益，合理补偿：原址用地规划控制为非营利性公共服务设施（占50%以上），或纳入旧城区成片改造，不具备独立开发条件的，政府依法收回，对原土地使用人支付补偿款</td></tr>
<tr><td colspan="2">无合法用地手续，用地行为发生在1987年1月1日之后、2007年6月30日之前（不符合历史用地登记确权），且土地实际使用人已与村集体或农户签订了征地补偿协议并进行补偿，没有引发纠纷，农民迄今无不同意见且符合土地利用总体规划和改造规划的，按照用地发生时的土地管理法律法规落实处理（处罚）后完善用地手续，再按以上三种方式进行处置</td></tr>
<tr><td rowspan="7">村集体用地的处置</td><td rowspan="4">用地行为发生在1987年1月1日之前，或已取得《同意用地通知书》或《建设用地批准书》的集体建设用地</td><td>自行改造：村集体可依规划进行除商品住宅开发外的经营开发项目改造；自愿申请转为国有土地的暂缓收取土地出让金，转让时补缴；集体用地规划功能为商品住宅，想进行开发的，应转为国有用地（政府统一组织，公开出让）；其中如连同村一并改造的，可补办协议出让手续，按规定计收土地出让金</td></tr>
<tr><td>公开出让，收益支持：土地公开出让后按照出让成交价格的60%补偿给村集体</td></tr>
<tr><td>依法流转改造：保留集体土地性质的，按照集体建设用地流转的相关规定办理；转为国有用地后转让的，转让前须按规定计收土地出让金</td></tr>
<tr><td>依法征收：原址用地规划为非营利性公共服务设施用地的，政府依法收回，并按现行征地补偿的有关规定给予补偿</td></tr>
<tr><td rowspan="3">无合法用地手续，用地行为发生在1987年1月1日之后、2007年6月30日之前的，结合村留地管理和“城中村”改造完善手续</td><td>补办手续的用地用于兑现留用地指标；留用地指标额不足（含无留用地指标）改造项目用地面积，但项目符合现代产业发展要求，且仍有未征用的农用地可预支留用地</td></tr>
<tr><td>纳入“城中村”改造范围与旧村改造一并规划、平衡成本、统筹实施</td></tr>
<tr><td>由区政府征收后统筹使用。统筹后仍安排给本村集体做产业用地使用的，办理协议出让手续，并按规定计收土地出让金</td></tr>
<tr><td rowspan="4">其他规定</td><td colspan="2">按城乡规划需整合旧厂房用地以外的边角地、夹心地、插花地的，应一并纳入改造范围（单块面积不超过3亩、多块累计面积不超过改造总面积10%的“三地”可一并纳入改造，国有性质的“三地”可采取协议出让，用地属性为农用地的“三地”需办理农转用手续），由改造主体承担相应的改造费用</td></tr>
<tr><td colspan="2">经原土地使用权人同意，政府可先行组织地块出让后再实施搬迁</td></tr>
<tr><td colspan="2">原土地使用权人和实际使用人不一致时，双方达成补偿协议后，再向有关部门提出土地处置申请</td></tr>
<tr><td colspan="2">原址用地已补办出让手续并已缴纳土地出让金的，补缴土地出让金时，剩余年期的土地出让金可作抵扣；采用公开出让、收益支持方式处置的，剩余年期的土地出让金另行返还</td></tr>
</table>

资料来源：广州市城市规划勘测设计研究院．广州市“三旧”改造规划设计资料汇编，2010。

四、结语

广义而言，新、旧都是相对而言，那些落后于时代，不适应现代社会、经济的发展要求，土地利用方式粗放、效率低下，对城市生态、景观、人居等各方面环境造成不利影响的城镇、厂房和村庄都可以视为“三旧”。“三旧”改造政策是广东建设节约集约用地试点示范省的重要举措。政策出台的背后是珠三角乃至整个广东土地资源紧缺和产业结构急需调整的困境，也由此为广东省转变土地利用模式，促进产业升级和结构调整以及城市化发展提供了新机遇。

“三旧”改造与以往土地开发不同，是靠原有建设用地的二次开发、拆旧建新，而不是靠新占农用地或生态用地来达到发展经济、更新功能、改善环境的目的。“三旧”改造政策是对粗放用地进行整体二次开发的有益探索和尝试，有利于破解土地供需矛盾、盘活土地资源，促进产业调整升级，提升城市功能、改善城乡环境，同时破解城乡二元结构，推动城乡统筹发展，对于现今处于高速发展中的城市具有普遍意义。

（作者：李晓晖，广州市城市规划勘测设计研究院，高级规划师）

参考文献

[1] “三旧”改造：佛山创新七大模式 [N]. 佛山日报，2009-11-26.

[2] 广东省人民政府. 关于推进“三旧”改造促进节约集约用地的若干意见（粤府〔2009〕78号）. 2009.

[3] 广州市“三旧”改造工作办公室. 广州市“三旧”改造规划（2010—2020年）. 2010.

[4] 广州市城市规划勘测设计研究院. 广州市“三旧”改造规划设计资料汇编. 2010.

[5] 广州市规划局. 广州市旧城更新改造规划纲要. 2010.

[6] 梁学斌. “三旧”改造激活广州新动力 [J]. 房地产导刊，2010（4）.

[7] 卢轶，陈韩晖. 广东破解土地瓶颈制约，先行先试初见成效 [N]. 南方日报，2009-04-15.

[8] 舒涓. 提升城市功能，加快“三旧”改造 [N]. 广州日报，2009-09-29.

[9] 杨明，刘海健，黄蓉芳. “三旧”改造政策广东独享，大拆大建扩内需今年见效 [N]. 广州日报，2010-01-07.

最具幸福感城市评述

一、概述

为了弘扬中国民生幸福成就，推介幸福城市，新华社《瞭望东方周刊》与中国市长协会《中国城市发展报告》工作委员会联合主办了中国最具幸福感城市调查推选活动，2007年至2011年已连续举办五年。活动采用美国芝加哥大学奚恺元教授提出的城市幸福学评估体系，通过公众调查及城市材料申报的方式对居住在城市的人们幸福感进行调查的活动，旨在全面彰显党的十七大以来科学发展与和谐社会建设成果，展现民众的幸福生活。推选幸福城市典范，推介幸福案例。活动凭借其公正性、权威性、广泛性已成为中国最具影响力的活动之一，当选城市的形象得到了进一步的提升，成为新华社和中国市长协会的品牌活动之一。

二、幸福感城市评价体系解读

务实与发展是当今世界发展的主旋律，经济的发展程度常常决定了一个国家或地区在世界上的话语权。国家追求经济发展，企业追求经济回报，个人追求经济地位，但是经济就真的是一切的终极目的吗？大部分人思考一下应该都会否定这种说法。经济只是一个手段或过程，我们追求的终极目标应该是人生的幸福。幸福是一种对生活的满足和感到生活有巨大乐趣并自然地希望持续的愉快心情。就如马斯洛需求理论一样，对于一些发展比较落后的国家或地区，经济的提高当然能够提高幸福度。但是当经济发展到一定阶段的时候，经济与幸福之间的关系会大大减弱，比如，在美国过去的50年中，人均GDP翻了3倍，但主观幸福感却没有提高。

经过几代人的努力，中国的经济飞速发展，GDP年均增长近10%，即使在经济危机的大环境下仍然能够保持8%的增长率。但与此同时，对于幸福感的质疑却越来越明显，流行的词汇也都是像“房奴”、“杯具”（与“悲剧”同音）这样的负面性词汇。人们对于幸福感的质疑却越来越明显。

我们不禁反思到，经济增长与否、经济增长快慢并不能代表社会和谐、健康发展的程度，我们应该更加关注社会总体幸福感的增长程度。而人们主观幸福感的高低在很大程度上取决于很多和经济无直接关系的因素，例如情感状况、社交关系、生活环境。为了探求我国全民的主观幸福度现状及改进方向，我们对全国各地的幸福感进行客观的调研及分析，把研究重点放在调研对象的主观感受，即当他们想到城市某个方面的主观感受如何，研究采用直接调研和侧面了解两种方式。一方面了解居民对自己所在城市的感知，另一方面了解居民对其他城市的感知，并结合两个方面进行对比分析。具体调研方式采用网络调研、实地调研、传统媒介调研等多种方式进行。

研究采用的是美国芝加哥大学奚恺元教授提出的城市幸福学评估体系。奚教授是最早系统地将幸福学和幸福指数引入中国，并在中国倡导研究城市幸福感的学者。

（一）研究目的

1. 采用入户调查、网络调查和报纸调查三种方式探索地级市和县级市不同城市市民的生活总体幸福度和城市具体幸福度；

2. 探索市民对其他城市的幸福度的预期；

3. 探索市民对其他城市的幸福度预期与该城市的实际幸福度的异同点。

针对上述研究目标，本次研究主要分为三个部分，即地级市和县级市市民对自住城市幸福度的评估、市民对其他城市的幸福度的预期、对于其他城市幸福度的投票结果与自住城市幸福度的调查结果比较。考虑到地级市和县级市在经济、人口等因素上的差别，本次研究所有的比较研究都对两者分别研究。

（二）生活总体幸福度

一个城市的市民是否觉得自己幸福是多方面的，它涉及诸如交际、职业发展、生活等多个方面。为了相对准确地衡量出他的生活总体幸福度，需要考虑到多个方面的影响。本次研究测量了市民在人情味、交通状况、医疗的便利程度和质量、教育质量、文体设施、餐饮及娱乐设施、购物便利性、治安状况、气候、污染程度、自然环境、城区建设、赚钱机会、房价、房价以外的物价、经济发展、生活节奏、工作压力、市民文明程度和文化底蕴具体方面的幸福度，最后采取将各个指标的分数加总从而得到总分的方式获得总体幸福度，虽然简单但是客观，同时回避了一些问卷设计的偏差和受调研者对问卷感知的偏差。

表1　中国幸福感城市评价体系

序号	评价指标	指标解释
1	人情味	受调研者对当地人情味浓厚感到的幸福程度
2	交通状况	受调研者对当地整体交通状况感到的幸福程度
3	医疗的便利程度和质量	受调研者对当地医疗的便利程度和质量感到的幸福程度
4	教育质量	受调研者对当地学校质量、教学质量等感到的幸福程度
5	文体设施	受调研者对当地文化体育设施等感到的幸福程度

续表 1

序号	评价指标	指标解释
6	餐饮及娱乐设施	受调查者对当地的餐饮设施,以及娱乐设施的便利感到的幸福程度
7	购物便利	受调研者对购买各种生活相关产品的便利程度感到的幸福程度
8	治安状况	受调研者对当地整体的治安状况感到的幸福程度
9	气候	受调研者对当地的气温及天气舒适度感到的幸福程度
10	污染程度	受调研者对当地的空气、水质及道路干净程度等感到的幸福程度
11	自然环境	受调研者对当地的绿化、山水等感到的幸福程度
12	城区建设	受调研者对当地的建筑、街道设计建设等感到的幸福程度
13	赚钱机会	受调研者对当地就业机会与赚钱机会感到的幸福程度
14	房屋价格	受调研者对当地房屋价格感到的幸福程度
15	房价以外的物价	受调研者对当地除房价以外的其他物价感到的幸福程度
16	经济发展	受调研者对当地近年来经济方面发展感到的幸福程度
17	生活节奏	受调研者对当地的生活节奏感到的幸福程度
18	工作压力	受调研者对当地工作的压力感到的幸福程度
19	市民文明程度	受调研者对当地居民整体文明程度感到的幸福程度
20	文化底蕴	受调研者对当地的历史、传统等感到的幸福程度

三、对“幸福”几点共识

如果说“十一五”期间的热词是“和谐”，那么从 2011 年开始的“十二五”，“幸福”毫无疑问成为又一个热词。2011 年春，在各地方两会上，提升居民幸福感已经成为各级政府转变发展思路的新抓手。北京决心“让人民过上幸福美好的生活”，广东“把保障和改善民生作为建设幸福广东的出发点和立脚点”，重庆则宣布要成为全国“居民幸福感最强的地区之一”。温家宝总理在与网民交流时，将“幸福”解读为“四心”——“让人们生活得舒心、安心、放心，对未来有信心”。“幸福”已经正式列入政府的责任清单之中，甚至可以说已经上升为全民意志。人们都知道，幸福是一种主观的心理感受，一个人幸福或不幸福，是诸多因素综合作用的结果。那么，作为执政者，应该怎样看待“幸福”这个执政目标？怎样把握百姓心中的“幸福指数”？要提升人民的幸福感，着力点又在哪里？

通过连续五年调查，数万个问卷调查样本，我们发现，幸福感并非难以捉摸，政府可以通过很多抓手，改变一个城市的“幸福环境”，调配一个城市的“幸福底色”。当然，在我们这个许多人自认为是弱势群体、抱有“弱势心态”的社会，建设“幸福中国”谈何容易。一谈到幸福感、幸福指数，声音总是很杂乱。因此，作为执政者，有必要凝聚关于“幸福”的几点共识，以便于廓清认识、明确方向、坚定信心。

共识之一：“幸福”不是“工程”，不是技术手段，而是一种执政理念，是一种价值观。

近来，我们时常能在媒体上看到这样的新闻：“优化城市环境增强市民幸福感”，“用提高劳动者幸福感来留人”，“抓紧教育、卫生、社保等七项民生工程，努力提升百姓幸福感”，等等。政府关注人民的幸福感，这是好现象。但是，幸福感不是一只时髦的“筐”，什么都能往里装；幸福感也不是一枚闪亮的标签，贴到哪里哪里亮。有的地方还提出了“幸福工程”。有学者评价：中国最当警惕“工程”，一提“工程”就有可能跟形象联系在一起，往这个方向发展，就可能偏离决策者的价值追求，甚至导致民众对“幸福”的反感。从科学发展观到和谐社会，再到幸福中国，从以人为本到统筹发展，再到注重成果的共赢、共享，这是一种执政理念和价值观的递进，是我们面对复杂的利益格局、面对多重的社会矛盾、面向中国未来道路的必然选择。从这个意义上说，“幸福”不是赶时髦，不是一种创意；不是一种技术手段，而是一个需要深刻理解的理念。每一个重要理念的提出，都为我们提供了新的执政资源，如果不加珍惜，滥用误用，很快就会变成套话、空话，让百姓厌烦，让政府公信力减退。我们也看到，一些地方尝试推出“幸福指数”，用来考核干部政绩。如何防止“幸福指数”重走“GDP崇拜”的老路，关键在于不能把“幸福”简单化，并仅仅看做一个技术指标。GDP是好东西，“幸福指数”也是好东西。指标本身无关对错，重要的是我们如何使用这些指标，想用它们达到什么目的。比如GDP原本作为制定政策的依据，但却成为考核干部政绩的唯一指标。“幸福”有自己的特殊规律。从我们连续几年的调查结果看，收入不高未必不幸福，收入很高也未必幸福；有些中小城市，幸福感高于大城市；有些地方，GDP连年上升，幸福感却在下降。因此，“幸福指数”并不适于对不同地区的经济社会发展程度进行排队和比较，更不宜像关注GDP那样片面地强调“幸福指数”的增长幅度以及不同地区所处位次的变化。尤其要注意克服期望“幸福指数”长期保持线性增长的不切实际的心态。提倡幸福感，是从单纯追求发展速度，转向把更多的政策和资源投向民生，这原本是要增强地方在转变发展方式中的自觉性，希望科学发展观更加深入人心。如果和GDP考核一样，用这个指标来排队，数字高的就能表彰提拔，就容易重新陷入“数字陷阱”，让幸福感贬值。

共识之二：民生是通往幸福的重要台阶，但是民生不等于幸福。

2011年两会前，公众纷纷在网上“晒”出幸福观。第一点是基本生活保障。有网民提到，在影响个人幸福的最重要变量中，前三项分别是就业、婚姻和教育。有调查显示，在影响中国居民幸福感的19个因素之中，前五名依次为家庭和谐、健康、子女教育、生活安全和医疗服务。这一结果表明，要提升幸福感，政府首先要为居民创造良好的社会保障条件。强调“幸福”并非否定GDP，正相反，经济发展是幸福的保障。我们多年的调查结果显示，入选幸福城市的，东部地区明显多于中西部。今年，长三角等经济发达地区逐步调低了GDP预期，但退出GDP竞赛并不等于不发展，而在中西部地区，幸福指数与GDP的相关度仍然较高。因此，从执政者的具体操作来讲，一是要尽可能地出台各方面的政策推动经济发展，并使广大民众在改革与发展中得实惠。二是要出台各种政策保护好弱势群体的切身利益，采取措施缩小各类差距，最大限度地减少跨越式发展中部分民众可能产生的强烈被剥夺感。目前中国一部分人中的不幸福感，和贫富差距有极大的关系。幸福不幸福，都是相对的，主要来自比较，一些屡屡被曝光的垄断企业的高工资高福利、豪华吊灯、天价烟酒等个案，就严重影响了人们的幸福感。在基本生活保障之外，公众的幸福观还包括更多非民生因素：比如公民权利行使，包括知情权、表达权、监督权；比如民主诉求表达和利益协调渠道顺畅；比如社会公平正义。如果一个社会的大多数人把自己划入弱势群体，幸福从何谈起？几年来的调查让我们强烈地感受到，幸福内涵丰富，超越了经济增长；幸福基于民生，但不能止步于民生。幸福学研究显示，当一个国家中的大部分人尚未解决温饱问题的时候，发展经济无疑会提高人的生存率和幸福感；而当经济发展到一定程度之后，经济与幸福的边际效应就会减弱。连续几年的城市幸福感调查显示，城市的经济增长速度并不能完全体现社会和谐、健康发展的程度，当经济发展到一定程度，人们主观幸福感的高低，往往取决于很多与经济无直接关系的因素。人情味、赚钱机会、生活便利程度、建筑美观程度、自然环境等不直接被经济指标所囊括的“软性”因素，对一个城市幸福感都有重要影响。比如人情幸福感每增加 1 个单位，城市总体幸福感就会增加 0. 3 个单位；而赚钱机会、生活便利、建筑美观、娱乐、城市发展等因素，每增加一个单位，对城市总体幸福感的贡献是 0. 15 个单位。做好民生工作能够为提升幸福感创造条件，但是不能完全等同。幸福是一个人的主观感受，政府不能单方面决定公众的幸福程度，但能够创造包括民生、政治、文化等因素在内的丰富环境，从而影响公众的幸福感知。

共识之三：公平，公平，还是公平。

观察近些年的舆论调查可以发现，民众最关心的社会问题中，排在第一位的是贫富差距。当前中国的社会流动和阶层分化提供了大量让人们比较的情境，“富二代”与“贫二代”，天价楼盘与蜗居强拆，让不少人体会到不公平的焦虑。判断收入分配公平程度的基尼系数，1994 年达到 0. 434，超过了警戒线，2010 年已接近 0. 5。除了基尼系数，还有 CPI，以及波动式下降了 30 年后在 2010 年重新上涨的恩格尔系数。《人民日报》说：“公正规范的行政行为，完善平等的公共服务，对人们幸福感的影响至关重要。如果人们在社会生活当中感到自己没有受到应有的尊重，感到机会不平等，甚至常常遇到权力滥用的情况，那么收入提高带来的幸福感，会因尊严、机会受损而被冲淡或抵消。”收入分配公平、发展机会公平、司法公平……公平是一种社会氛围。很多人即便没有直接遭遇不公平事件，也会受到这种氛围的感染。有了基本的社会公平，才有尊严，才能谈到幸福。特别需要执政者注意的是年轻群体。比如“蚁族”、“新生代农民工”，他们对幸福不幸福的感受更加敏锐。理想与现实的冲突，社会结构板结化阻塞上升通道，可能使他们成为社会不稳定的酝酿群体。比如，每年沉淀上百万的大学生待业大军，对于“富二代”、“官二代”的行为非常敏感。席卷长三角、珠三角的民工荒，富士康的“十三连跳”，背后是年轻人幸福观的改变：不要流水线上枯燥而看不到前景的原子化劳动，不要赚钱回老家、盖房娶媳妇，他们希望融入城市，改变人生。在对这些人群的调查中，他们会把自己的处境与社会不公联系起来，而这个人群在网络上也相当活跃，因此他们的幸福感影响力更强大。

共识之四：幸福感之本在于价值观重建。

如果把财富追求放在第一位，把物质满足作为价值尺度，相信绝大多数人不会幸福。因为财富追求受种种外部条件的限制，物质满足永无止境，而我们面对的又是一个资源短缺的世界。实际上，幸福感的一个重要来源，是精神领域的满足，是价值观的认同，和谐的人际关系、真实的情感交流、良好的社会风尚、健康的生活方式，是人们获得幸福的保证。有人说，造成中国一些人缺少幸福感的一个重要原因是信仰缺失，传统的伦理道德被撕裂，新的金钱崇拜又让人疲惫空虚。因此，必须像抓经济建设一样推动文化和价值建设，为促进人的全面发展创造良好的条件和氛围。从“两手抓”之一的精神文明建设，到先进文化教育，再到核心价值体系，相对物质文明建设而言，精神文明建设还是显得弱效。原因在于，幸福感、尊严等精神层面的东西，需要自下而上自发体会，不是单凭思想教育、媒体导向就能实现的，也不是搞一些一笑而过的小品就能送来的。执政者所能做的，是营造一个宽松的氛围，给“异质思维”以空间，同时从自身做起，在政府工作中首先实践诚信、公平。

共识之五：幸福来自愿景，来自对未来的稳定预期。

幸福感不仅仅来自现实处境，还有一个重要因素是对未来的期待和“信心”。在我们以往的调查中，“发展预期”是提升幸福感的重要因素。在2009年，我们将县级市也列入幸福感调查序列之后，有一个意外的发现：“逃离北上广”的年轻人，在发达地区的小城市里，找到了更实在的发展期待，而这些小城市的幸福感和活力，也因此大大增强。

30多年来，改革开放之所以能够成功，正是因为大家对中国的发展有共识，对中国的前景有认同。今天的中国社会，虽然有种种不同的利益诉求，有不同的期望和想法，但聚合我们认同的东西客观存在，那就是中国在向前发展，任何个人都只会在中国的发展之中找到自己的位置和机会。

有学者称之为“中国梦”。没有这个梦想，我们对于幸福感提升的努力就不可能获得切实可行的路径。如果对社会发展方向缺少共识，难免会出现幸福感的低迷和消极“抱怨文化”的盛行。

对于政府和社会而言，要找到不同诉求和期望的“最大公约数”，要告诉每一个成员：社会正在向什么方向走，有可能给你提供怎样的空间，让你自己去追求个人的发展；你的付出、你的贡献，将会获得怎样的回报。我们要给个人明确的信息：幸福并不意味着任何期望都可能得到满足，但它意味着你的期望有实现的可能和路径，正在召唤和期待你的努力。执政者有责任激励并呵护人民的愿景，保持明确的发展方向、稳定持续的政策、公开的信息披露，公众就能回报以信心和良好预期。而信心，比黄金还珍贵。

共识之六：民众是建设幸福社会的主体。

在2011年两会上热议幸福的同时，有一条网民的微博这样说：“我怀疑他们在密谋策划要让我幸福。”一些人担心“被幸福”，是因为我们的一些政策措施，有时有些一相情愿。

在幸福社会建设中，要特别注意处理好“政府主导”与“民众主体”之间的关系。幸福不幸福，每个人心中都有一把尺子。执政者如果在幸福感、幸福指数上自说自话，甚至造假，它的后果可能要比GDP造假更恶劣，更容易让政府失掉公信力。

民众是幸福社会建设的主体，幸福不幸福，关键看老百姓怎么评价。现在一些地方用来考核干部的“幸福指数”，是由很多现成的统计数据构成的，比如经济发展速度、人均GDP、工资收入等，都是拿已有的统计数据重新排列组合，做做加减法。而幸福不幸福，不是由统计指标评价出来的，应该由公众来打分，应该对每一个调查对象的满意度进行调查。

建设幸福中国，离不开广大民众的积极参与。中央高层近来多次强调提高社会管理水平，其中一个重要支点，就是政府要充分让渡权力和利益，不断提高非政府组织的公共服务能力和水平，相信群众能够实现自我管理。我们每年搞城市幸福感调查，问卷上的每一个问题，都是让群众就城市的某一方面打分，是满意、基本满意、还是不满意；给幸福城市的市长颁奖的，也是普通市民代表。可以说，民意是幸福感的决定因素。

附：历届中国最具幸福感城市调查推选活动获奖名单

2007 年获奖城市：

杭州、沈阳、中山、宁波、青岛、台州、珠海、上海、北京、成都

2008 年获奖城市：

杭州、宁波、昆明、天津、唐山、佛山、绍兴、长春、无锡、长沙

2009 年获奖城市：

地级及以上城市：西安、南京、昆明、宁波、杭州、成都、银川、长沙、南昌、长春

县级市：山东邹平县、江苏宜兴市、江苏吴江市、湖南长沙县、江苏江都市、浙江余姚市、云南安宁市、四川都江堰市、辽宁海城市、广东增城市

杭州、成都获得建国六十年特别大奖

宁波获金奖

2010 年获奖城市：

地级及以上城市：杭州、成都、长沙、昆明、南京、长春、重庆、广州、通化、无锡

县级市：江阴、宜兴、长沙县、余姚、滕州、铜梁、海城、太仓、莱州、胶州

杭州、成都市获得最高荣誉奖——民生贡献特别大奖

昆明、长沙、长春市获得金奖

宜兴、余姚市获得民生贡献大奖

长沙市获得民生满意大奖

2011 年获奖城市：

2011 中国最具幸福感城市地级及以上城市获奖名单：

天津市、重庆市、珠海市

地级及以上城市 2011 中国最具幸福感城市金奖城市：

南京市、无锡市

中国最具幸福感城市五周年特别荣誉大奖：

杭州市、成都市、宁波市、昆明市、长沙市

2011 中国最具幸福感城市县级市获奖名单：

江阴市、吴江市、昆山市、江苏武进区、太仓市、重庆云阳县

其中宜兴市、余姚市、长沙县、海城市获得 2011 中国最具幸福感城市金奖

幸福乡镇：

重庆（云阳县）迎龙镇、江苏（吴江市）震泽镇、江苏（江阴市）新桥镇、江苏（太仓市）城厢镇、湖南（长沙县）榔梨镇、辽宁（海城市）腾鳌镇

中国城市民生贡献奖：

重庆市江津区、重庆市渝北区、重庆市永川区、重庆市云阳县、重庆璧山县

（作者：中国市长协会）

专题篇

粤港澳合作示范区的开发与建设

引 言

改革开放30多年来，广东发挥毗邻港澳的地缘、人缘优势，依托中央赋予的“特殊政策、灵活措施”，不断加强粤港澳合作，有效促进了三地经济社会发展。当前，粤港澳合作上升为国家战略，粤港澳合作的战略地位大幅提升、发展目标日益明确，合作共识不断增强、互动联系更加紧密，特别是从更紧密合作到融合发展、再到经济一体化发展的合作思路层层递进，合作内涵不断深化，在思想认识、发展定位、社会民心上有了新变化。为了应对新的变化，通过设立粤港澳合作示范区作为创新合作的空间载体进行先行先试、探索经验，不断推动三地繁荣发展。

一、粤港澳合作示范区的建设背景

（一）粤港澳合作由“民间合作”走向“政府合作”

广东改革开放30多年的历史就是一部粤港澳合作的历史，经历了从“前店后厂”到“共同市场”，从“经济合作”到“全面合作”，从区域战略到国家战略的过程，逐步实现从依靠劳动力资源优势参与国际低端竞争向利用创新和核心技术参与国际高端竞争转变，共同探索制度创新的区域经济一体化发展新模式。

1. 经贸合作从“前店后厂”向“共同市场”转变

改革开放以来，港澳商人在深圳和珠海等经济特区“窗口”示范作用影响下，开始在广东特别是珠三角地区大规模投资开办“三来一补”企业。此举促使广东一跃成为亚太地区重要的劳动密集型产品生产基地，实现了地区经济的快速增长。截至目前，港澳在广东直接投资项目超过10万个，实际投入1 200多亿美元，占广东实际吸收外来资金的三分之二。在优势互补的基础上，粤港澳形成“前店后厂”的合作方式，即以广东为加工制造基地、港澳为购销管理中心的产业跨地域分工格局。

紧密的社会和经济联系为深化区域合作提供了深厚基础。2003年，CEPA协议的签署进一步落实了区域合作的制度安排，促进三地产业合作从“垂直分工”的“前店后厂”模式走向“水平分工”的“共同市场”模式。一方面，是减少和最终消除各种粤港澳区域内有形和无形的经贸壁垒，为商品、人员、资金、技术、信息等商品和要素的自由流动创造更加便捷和有效的制度环境，携手打造更具竞争力的“经济共同体”。另一方面，在“港主服务”、“粤主制造”的大格局下推进粤港澳产业融合与互补，重点促进高技术产业和高端服务业的发展。如在制造业方面，广东近年在提升传统制造业技术水平的基础上积极发展重化工等资金密集型制造业，港澳则大力发展知识密集型制造业。在科技研发方面，可将香港的商业化研发和广东的基础性研发相结合，共同为粤港澳地区产业升级和技术创新提供支撑。在高端服务业方面，香港可将其中的后台操作环节向广东转移，广东则重点发展满足本地制造业升级急需的生产性服务业支援体系。

2. 合作层面从地方自主协调上升为国家战略

香港和澳门回归后，在“一国两制”方针的指导下，粤港澳合作的重点、领域、机制、范围都发生了深刻而重大的变化，粤港澳合作机制在实践中不断巩固和完善。2008 年，由国家发改委组织编制、国务院审议通过的《珠江三角洲改革发展规划纲要（2008—2020年)》颁布，赋予珠三角地区发展更大的自主权，并提出珠三角发展要实现四个“率先”。这标志着粤港澳紧密合作、构建世界级珠三角都会区有了制度保证，也昭示粤港澳合作从区域战略上升为国家战略。此后，《粤港（澳）合作框架协议》、《中华人民共和国国民经济和社会发展第十二个五年规划纲要》（以下简称《国家十二五规划纲要》）等系列政策和规划也明确提出粤港澳合作内容，彰显了中央对深化推进三地合作的重视和支持。

（二）粤港澳空间发展与规划合作的深度和广度不断加强

在中央以及粤港澳三地政府引导下，粤港澳合作除继续推进经贸合作外，逐渐开始关注民生领域，探索道路交通、能源等基础设施，教育、卫生等社会公共服务设施、生态环保等的深度合作，寻求由生产合作向全方位合作的转变。适应粤港澳走向更紧密合作的趋势，按照加快转变经济发展方式的要求，以共建全球城市区域为目标，粤港澳三地政府联合开展《共建优质生活圈专项规划》、《粤港澳基础设施建设合作专项规划》、《环珠江口宜居湾区建设重点行动计划》等规划合作，重点关注资源、环境问题以及社会民生的改善，强调经济、社会和环境保护的平衡协调，将追求优质生活和宜居区域确立为区域发展的新目标，通过提升生活质量和营商环境，吸引全球人才和资金，从而在国际竞争格局中保持优势。

1. 《共建优质生活圈专项规划》

为应对大珠三角区域面临的经济发展模式不可持续、区域环境质量面临严重威胁、公共服务和社会管理水平的滞后严重制约了人民生活质量的提升等严峻挑战，《共建优质生活圈专项规划》明确提升居民生活质量的核心主题，提出了不断深化区域合作，将区域协调和融合不断推向新高度。《共建优质生活圈专项规划》的发展愿景是将大珠三角地区建设成绿色、宜居、低碳、可持续发展的世界级城市群，在为居民提供一个洁净、舒适、便捷、高效、人本的优质生活环境的同时，提升大珠三角地区的整体竞争力和吸引力。并从环境生态质量、低碳发展、文化民生合作、空间协调发展、绿色交通和便利通关共五个领域构建了区域多主体共同行动的策略性框架，作为对三地政府部门相关行动的指南。

2.《粤港澳基础设施专项规划》

为促进区域生产要素更便利流动，适应打造全球最具竞争力都市圈发展的客观要求，扩大粤港澳都市圈辐射空间，制定《粤港澳基础设施专项规划》。规划以交通、水利、能源、口岸、信息等基础设施为重点，突出强调空间、时间、功能上的衔接，通过对区域经济协调发展具有重要影响的重大基础设施项目建设上的合作，加快建设和完善区域对外及内部基础设施系统，构建具有整体发展能力，合作紧密、分工协作的基础设施体系，推进粤港澳地区基础设施的全面现代化，适应粤港澳构建世界级大都市圈的需要。

3.《环珠江口宜居湾区建设重点行动计划》

为推进“一国两制”框架下的区域合作创新，增强环珠江口湾区和大珠三角地区的国际影响力，实现粤港澳三地人民共享国际水准的优质生活，制定《环珠江口宜居湾区建设重点行动计划》。规划围绕粤港澳三地共同关注的环境和民生问题，从发展优先向生态优先转变，从关注生产向关注生活转变，提出了开展“绿网”、“阳光水岸”、“区域公交网”、“文化街区”、“特色公共空间”、“公共服务网”、“宜居社区”、“步行城市”、“便捷通关”和“跨界环保合作”十大重点专项建设，以及南沙、前海、横琴等环珠江口七个重点合作发展地区的行动计划，把环珠江口湾区建设成为“粤港澳共建优质生活圈的精华区”和“引领大珠三角转变经济发展方式的示范区”。

除以上落实《珠三角规划纲要》和粤港、粤澳高层会晤共识的三大规划外，《澳珠协同发展规划》、《珠江口西岸地区发展规划》、《澳门与广州南沙合作规划》等规划研究也在积极制定当中。

二、粤港澳合作示范区开发建设探索

《珠三角规划纲要》、《粤港合作框架协议》以及《国家十二五规划纲要》都将横琴、前海和南沙作为加强粤港澳合作的空间载体。三大新区作为粤港澳合作的“三颗棋子”，以及国家为广东经济的转型升级提供的重要平台，将形成以南沙新区为主体（开展粤港澳三方合作），以前后海地区、横琴新区为两翼（重点开展深港合作和珠澳合作）的“一主两翼”新格局，为珠三角地区“科学发展、先行先试”创造经验，为维护港澳长期繁荣稳定，促进澳门经济适度多元发展，打造“中华民族共同家园”做出贡献。

（一）珠海横琴新区——“谋而后动”

横琴新区位于珠江口西岸，面积106.46平方公里。1992年，横琴被广东省定为扩大对外开放的四个重点开发区之一；2006年，“泛珠三角横琴经济合作区”的设想首次提出；2009年，国务院正式批准通过《横琴总体发展规划》，横琴新区成为继上海浦东新区、天津滨海新区之后第三个由国务院批准的国家级新区。

1. 两大政策突破

一是将横琴纳入珠海经济特区范围，享受特区的财税和立法权等优惠。二是采用“分线管理”的通关政策，延展港澳的国际自由港优势，享有比一般保税区更优惠的关税政策。两大政策赋予横琴为最便捷地联通粤港澳三地和国际、国内两大市场的重要甚至唯一的战略通道地位，极大地吸引国内外高端人流、物流、资金流和信息流的高度集聚和高效流动，有利于横琴发展成为“内地开放度最高、体制宽松度最大、创新空间最广”的地区。

2. 三大发展定位

以合作、创新和服务为主题，充分发挥横琴地处粤港澳结合部的优势，推进与港澳紧密合作、融合发展，逐步把横琴建设成为带动珠三角、服务港澳、率先发展的粤港澳紧密合作示范区。三大发展定位包括：“一国两制”下探索粤港澳合作新模式的示范区——探索建立合作方式灵活、合作主体多元、合作渠道畅顺的粤港澳合作新机制；深化改革开放和科技创新的先行区——进一步在深化体制改革和提升开放水平方面率先突破，为珠三角“科学发展、先行先试”创造经验；促进珠江口西岸地区产业升级的新平台——珠澳携手共建珠澳国际都会区，形成珠江口西岸地区新的增长极，带动珠海市以及珠三角地区的发展升级。

3. 四大城市功能

未来重点发展商务服务、休闲旅游、科教研发和高新技术等四大功能，逐步建设成为粤港澳地区的区域性商务服务基地、与港澳配套的国际知名旅游度假基地、珠江口西岸的区域性科教研发平台和融合港澳优势的国家级高新技术产业基地。

横琴规划批复两年多来，其开发建设取得四大成效：（1）粤港澳合作取得重大突破。目前，横琴岛澳门大学新校区软基处理工程全部完成，地面主体建筑正全面展开，计划2012年12月20日前交付使用。粤澳合作中医药科技产业园首期用地正在进行土地平整。香港丽新集团和世贸集团已决定在横琴进行“大手笔”投资，项目投资总额达100亿元港币。（2）产业发展取得重大突破。目前，长隆国际海洋度假区、十字门中央商务区、多联供燃气能源站等总投资超过700亿元人民币的重大项目进展顺利。（3）基础设施建设取得重大突破。顺利回收中心沟12平方公里土地，清理重大项目用地7平方公里，市政道路、海堤、共同管沟等建设快速推进，为横琴未来的发展打下坚实的基础。（4）开发体制创新。粤澳合作中医药科技产业园是粤澳合作产业园区的首个启动项目，采取粤澳双方共同规划、共同投资、共同经营、共同收益的开发模式，共同打造国际中医药产业基地。由双方共同成立的合资公司负责园区运营，总投资12亿元（澳粤双方投资比例为51:49），合资公司由澳方控股，澳方以现金出资，珠海方以土地作价出资，合资公司注册地在珠海横琴，适用中国内地法律。

（二）深圳前海地区——第三部“春天的故事”续写蛇口传奇

前海地区位于珠江口东岸，面积18平方公里。2005年，前海地区被定位为深圳最具战略意义的空间资源（《深圳2030城市发展策略》）；2007年，提出了福田中心和前海中心双城市中心的概念（《深圳市城市总体规划（2008—2020）》）；2010年，国务院批复《前海深港现代服务业合作区总体发展规划》(以下简称《前海规划》)。

1. 管理体制创新

国务院对前海作出了两条特殊的政策安排：一是建立由国家发改委牵头的前海部际联席会议制度；二是在非金融类产业项目的审批管理上赋予前海管理机构相当于计划单列市的管理权限。成立前海管理局，通过立法形式授予部分行政管理职能和公共服务职能，比如政府资助、独立运作、企业化管理，等等，成为中国内地第一个真正意义上的“法定机构”。前海管理局拥有相对独立的土地开发权、人事权和财政管理权。由前海管理局代表市政府负责前海合作区的土地监督、管理和开发；实行企业化、市场化的用人制度，享有独立的用人自主权；负责编制前海合作区财政预算和前海管理局经费预算，经市政府审定后纳入市级财政年度预算，报市人大审议批准后，由前海管理局组织实施。通过法定机构的企业化运作，营造更加公开、透明、高效的政府服务环境。

2. 法律体制创新

为落实《前海规划》、促进前海合作区现代服务业发展，《前海深港现代服务业合作区条例》规定“在不与本市经济特区法规基本原则相违背的前提下，可以制定有关规章、决定和命令在前海合作区施行，并报市人大常委会备案”，“借鉴香港经验，制定促进现代服务业发展的有关规则、指引等，在前海合作区施行”，“鼓励深港合作建立法律查明机制，为前海合作区商事活动提供境外法律的查明服务”，“鼓励前海合作区引入国际商事仲裁的先进制度”，“鼓励香港仲裁机构为前海合作区的企业提供商事仲裁服务”，“鼓励深港民间调解组织合作，为前海合作区的企业提供商事调解服务”等一系列措施，打造与香港接轨的营商环境。

3. 重点合作领域

前海作为粤港现代服务业创新合作示范区，主要通过推动以跨境人民币业务为重点的金融领域创新合作、深港资本市场合作等，发展金融业；通过打造区域生产组织中枢和国际供应链管理中心、积极发展港口航运配套服务，发展现代物流业；发展信息服务业、科技服务和其他专业服务。

一年来，前海开发建设取得阶段性成果：(1) 立法工作取得了重大成果。《前海深港现代服务业合作区条例》正式颁布实施，《前海深港现代服务业合作区管理局暂行办法》和《前海湾保税港区管理暂行办法》也已原则通过。(2) 土地整备工作稳步快速推进。目前已完成填海和软基处理用地10.76平方公里，占区域面积的72%，正在施工的有1.47平方公里，剩余2.67平方公里已基本完成勘探设计等前期工作。(3) 招商引资工作取得初步成效。已经明确意向投资金额的重点项目累计11个，意向投资金额达585.5亿元。

(三) 广州南沙新区——“深化粤港澳合作，建设中华民族共同家园”

南沙位于珠江出海口，面积803平方公里。1993年，国务院批准成立国家级经济技术开发区，揭开其大规模开发的序幕；2002年，广州明确提出“南拓、北优、东进、西联”的空间发展战略，南沙成为南拓的重要节点；2010年，省委、省政府决定在南沙成立

“CEPA 先行先试综合示范区”；2011 年，《国家十二五规划纲要》明确将南沙发展成为“服务内地、连接港澳的商业服务中心、科技创新中心和教育培训基地，建设临港产业配套服务合作区”；汪洋同志提出了“以南沙新区开发为突破口，打造一个新广州”的战略构想，赋予了南沙新区新任务和新使命。

目前，《广州南沙新区定位与发展战略研究》、《南沙新区实施 CEPA 先行先试综合示范区规划》、《南沙新区粤港澳合作发展规划》、《南沙新区总体概念规划》等一系列规划研究已陆续开展并发布；《南沙新区发展总体规划》正积极编制准备上报国务院；《广州南沙新区城市总体规划（2011—2030）》正在开展；2011 年 10 月 11 日，省委、省政府在南沙召开广州南沙新区开发建设现场会，确立“科学开发，从容建设”的核心理念，打造成经得起历史检验的“伟大作品”，并签约 10 个重点项目，投资达人民币 110 亿元。

三、粤港澳合作示范区未来发展方向

粤港澳合作示范区承载着推动粤港澳更紧密合作和促进广东产业转型升级的重任，必须坚持以创新为核心的发展战略。南沙、前海和横琴必须以目前的开发建设为基础，在“一国两制”框架下，有效整合粤港澳三地力量，在国家的体制创新上发挥带动作用，开展“政策先导，体制创新”，通过政策创新建立新型经济体制，以体制创新带动发展创新，寻求新的发展路径，推动粤港澳“打造更具综合竞争力的世界级城市群”。

（一）构建决策与利益协调机制

目前，三大新区虽然在制度框架及其项目报批政策上有所创新，但与现行行政管理制度存在着诸多矛盾，而且缺乏一个基于粤港澳三方共识并能有效协调各方权益、加大国家相关部委支持力度、真正保证示范区作为国家战略有效运作的高层决策机构，使国家战略层面上的新区定位，在实际操作过程中有意或无意地降低到了升级版的经济开发区层面上。

作为“十二五”国家重大区域规划项目，以探索“一国两制”下粤港澳紧密合作示范区为使命的横琴、前海和南沙，必须建立一个以追求国家利益最大化为目标，同时能够促进多方合作共赢的利益机制，这一利益机制要能协调社会制度不同、愿望诉求不同的粤港澳三方和中央政府之间的利益平衡、利益差异和利益互补，能够调动起各方在示范区开发中的价值追求和参与冲动。当无法兼顾各方利益的时候，包括中央政府在内的各方要能够给予承担损失的一方以公正的利益评估和合理的利益补偿，实现不同利益主体的共同利益和共同繁荣。

（二）加强产业对接和错位发展

香港的发展必须依托内地的市场和资源优势；澳门经济适度多元化的一条新的出路，就是积极参与区域合作。三个示范区的发展必须要加强与港澳的产业对接和错位发展，支持和维护香港国际金融中心、国际贸易中心和国际航运中心地位；支持澳门建设世界旅游休闲中心，以及中国与葡语国家商贸合作服务平台，推动经济适度多元化。重点是加强金融、物流、会展、商务、科研、信息、专业服务、旅游等现代服务业和物联网、生物医药、新能源、新材料、环保、航空制造、海洋等高新技术产业的合作。

（三）自由宽松的通关管理模式

作为粤港澳经济合作的重要区域，必须得到国家的大力支持，特别是政策上的优惠扶持，赋予特殊灵活的配套政策，创建符合国际通行规则的制度环境，一是原政策区域基础上，支持享受国家级经济技术开发区、高新技术开发区和保税区等国家重点扶持区域的优惠政策；二是在CEPA框架下，支持服务业扩大开放，在企业税率、税收减免期限、外汇进出、货物进出口、地区总部认定等方面给予更加优惠的政策；三是在“一国两制”体制下，支持享受香港和澳门自由港的各项政策，充分利用港澳的政策优势、制度优势和示范区的区位优势、土地优势，吸引国际资源参与示范区开发；四是在条件成熟时，探索实行自由贸易区出入境管理特殊政策，真正实现人流、物流、资金流和信息流的自由往来。

（四）构建粤港澳金融共同市场

当前，我国金融改革开放迈入了新的阶段，如何进一步发挥粤港澳区域作为“试验田”和开放门户的作用，在“十二五”期间，加快我国金融改革创新步伐，增强参与国际金融事务的能力，是关系全局、影响长远的重大课题。在示范区创建粤港澳金融共同市场试验区具有非常重要的意义，也具有很强的可行性。一是推动金融服务业向港澳开放先行先试，探索建立粤港澳区域金融合作的新模式，如开展外币离岸金融业务试点、支持港澳地区非银行金融机构落户等；二是针对区域经济转型升级的金融服务需求，搭建粤港澳三地科技与金融资源的对接平台，如建立各类股权投资基金、设立知识产权质押融资试点等；三是围绕人民币区域化和国际化战略，建立内地与港澳地区人民币跨境双向流动的试验场，如全面推广跨境贸易人民币结算业务、开展人民币跨境直接投资试点、开展粤港澳银行机构人民币银团贷款合作试点等；四是配合港澳旅游业发展，推进支持旅游业发展的金融服务创新，如探索开展非现金支付工具创新试点、引入港澳地区货币兑换经营模式等。

（五）探索港澳自主开发模式

探索在示范区内建设香港自主开发区和澳门自主开发区，赋予港澳在各自区域内一定的经济、社会管理权限，借鉴粤澳合作中医药科技产业园的开发模式，采取“共同投资、合作开发、共同发展、利益共享”的合作思路，以“港澳自主开发区”作为战略性平台开展产业、科技与社会管理等的全面合作，共同探索开发建设、口岸通关等制度对接，实现三地共赢，促进三地融合发展。

（六）解决不同法域的法律冲突

“一国两制”是我们国家为实现祖国和平统一而做出的创新之举，而粤港澳合作示范区的开发建设突破了"一国两制"的理论界限，将带来一系列法律问题，这些问题关系到"一国两制"理论在新时期如何发展和创新，也关系到香港和澳门特别行政区未来的繁荣和稳定，因此急需完善理论并建立制度，将其纳入法制化轨道。一是处理特区租赁内地土地的问题上应该本着相互促进发展的角度来对待；二是需要法律对授权主体作出明确的规定或授权，这个主体只能是全国人大及其常委会；三是在法律制度建设方面，全国人大应当尽快制定相关的程序法律，规范特区政府向内地租赁土地应当履行的程序和提出请求的对象。特别行政区租赁内地土地应当向国务院提出请求，并由国务院负责具体事宜的办理，然后报全国人大常委会批准。还要对基本法的相关内容作出修改，规定特区政府的管辖地域包括特别行政区范围内的地域和经全国人大常委会授权管理的特别行政区外的地域，属于内地的土地经全国人大常委会授权给特区政府管辖后，内地法律的效力自特区政府开始行使管辖权之时中止，从而解决法律空间效力的冲突问题。

四、结语

根据国家的战略部署，南沙将发展成为"服务内地、连接港澳的商业服务中心、科技创新中心和教育培训基地，建设临港产业配套服务合作区"；前海将通过推进粤港澳现代服务业紧密合作，打造"粤港现代服务业创新合作示范区"，逐步建设成为现代服务业体制机制创新区、现代服务业发展集聚区、香港与内地紧密合作的先导区和珠三角产业升级的引领区；横琴将以合作、创新和服务为主题，发展成为"一国两制"下探索粤港澳合作创新模式示范区、深化改革开放和科技创新先行区以及促进珠江口西岸地区产业升级发展新平台。通过三大粤港澳合作示范区的建设，推进粤港澳紧密合作，实现区域经济一体化，共同打造亚太地区最具活力和国际竞争力的城市群。

（作者：广东省城市发展规划研究中心）

参考文献

[1] 广东省城乡规划设计研究院，广东省城市发展研究中心，横琴总体发展规划，广东省人民政府，2008.

[2] 广东省城乡规划设计研究院，广东省城市发展研究中心，环珠江口宜居湾区重点建设行动计划（公众咨询本），广东省住房和城乡建设厅，香港特区发展局，澳门特区土地运输工务司，2011.

[3] 广东省城乡规划设计研究院，广东省城市发展研究中心，粤港澳地区空间发展战略规划，广东省住房和城乡建设厅，2008.

[4] 广东省社会科学院广东发展研究数据库．横琴新区开发建设调研报告，2011.

[5] 国家发展和改革委员会．前海深港现代服务业合作区总体发展规划，2010.

[6] 国家发展和改革委员会．珠江三角洲地区改革发展规划纲要（2008—2020年），2008.

[7] 中华人民共和国国务院．中华人民共和国国民经济和社会发展第十二个五年规划纲要，2011.

近年国内城市防灾规划发展综述

一、对城市防灾规划的理解

（一）城市防灾规划的社会需求

城市作为国家经济社会发展的中心和重心，具有人口集中、财富集中、生产活动集中、基础设施集中等特点。一方面，随着我国经济和社会的快速发展，城市扩张的速度越来越快，集中程度越来越高。虽然现有的城市规划和建设法规对城市建设有具体规定，但总体而言，缺乏建立安全城市、安全社区的概念，缺乏对城市防灾、避灾的系统要求。近年来城市时常发生的雨雪冰冻、地震、泥石流和洪涝等灾害更折射出我国城市目前的防灾体系建设远不能适应现代城市发展的需求。

另一方面，现代城市在呈现越来越强大功能的同时，其脆弱性也不断暴露，潜伏越来越多的风险。城市内部各系统相互依存、相互影响，当城市遇到突发灾害时，子系统间的影响作用十分明显，尤其是作为城市生命线系统的道路、供水、供电、供气、通信等设施，任一系统的损坏，都将影响其相关系统的运行，甚至影响到整个城市的安全运行。这些特点，使得城市灾害的影响常常表现为次生、衍生灾害的重复叠加，表现为相关连带和放大作用，形成所谓的“灾害链”、“灾害群”。

在城市化进程快速发展的背景下，城市防灾规划的出发点正是为城市安全保障提供重要的防灾建设指导，通过用地安全选择，建立安全的布局形态，建设灾害应急管理体系和避灾设施系统，有准备、有计划地预防和应对灾害，减少城市的灾害损失。

（二）城市防灾规划坚持的理念

1. 从构建和谐社会的高度推动城市防灾减灾

把城市防灾作为构建社会主义和谐社会的重要内容，坚持“以人为本”的施政理念，保证灾时最大限度地避免和减少人员伤亡，尽可能降低人民群众的生命财产损失，保障人民群众的安全。

2. 确立综合防灾安全观念

综合防御灾害是城市应对各种灾害的基本思路，突破传统的单灾种防御形式，从局部安全保障发展为能够全面抵御各类灾害，实现全面安全保障。

3. 构建城市防灾与应急体系

综合考虑城市防御大灾、巨灾的要求，强调应急管理和防避灾设施的有机结合，建立以应急管理为主导，防灾与避灾设施为基础的城市防灾与应急体系。

二、当前城市防灾规划的构成

（一）防灾规划的分类

现有的城市防灾规划大致有两种类型，一类是城市总体规划中的防灾专业规划，另一类是独立编制的防灾专项规划，而专项防灾规划中还可以区分综合防灾规划和单灾种防灾规划。

根据2006年实施的《城市规划编制办法》第三十一条第十五款规定，总体规划要“确定综合防灾与公共安全保障体系，提出防洪、消防、人防、抗震、地质灾害防护等规划原则和建设方针”。由此，城市总体规划中的防灾专业规划包括防洪规划、抗震规划、地质灾害防治规划、消防规划和人防规划5个项目。城市总体规划中防灾专业规划的任务是原则指导未来城市的防灾与避灾设施的建设，对城市的防灾与避灾设施进行总体安排。

防灾专项规划是在总体规划的指引下，指导城市防灾与避灾设施具体建设的规划，要求核实设施规模、形式和数量，进行设施布局，落实建设用地，明确配置和设计要求，制定实施计划，提出投资估算。专项规划方案具体，项目明确，可操作性强，是城市防灾建设不可或缺的技术指导文件。

城市综合防灾规划的任务主要从城市防灾救灾体系建设的高度来进行规划，基于城市主要灾害的风险评估，从安全性角度提出用地布局的调整建议；在城市防灾救灾体系建设方面，需要综合考虑应急指挥系统、救灾专业队伍、疏散救援通道、避难场所、应急物资设施和应急基础设施的建设，并提出防灾避灾宣传教育组织体系，整体提高城市灾害应对能力。

城市单灾种防灾规划大多由相关管理部门组织编制，规划的任务相对单一，局限在某一灾害防治和应对的范围内。单灾种防灾规划针对性较强，消除灾害威胁的效果显著，实施周期和投入相对较小，对专项防灾设施建设作用很大。

根据城市灾害环境和经济条件的不同，城市防灾规划的标准也不同。灾害种类多、经济实力强的城市应偏重于防灾救灾体系建设；灾害种类简单、经济实力弱的城市可先从单灾种防灾做起，解决主要问题，逐步完善防灾救灾体系。

（二）城市防灾规划的基本框架

现有城市防灾规划的内容主要包括现状条件分析、灾害危险性评估、用地安全布局、防灾避灾设施布局、防灾避灾设施建设技术要求、规划实施建议和近期建设7部分，基本涵盖了城市防灾避震机构和设施建设的各方面，对指导相关系统建设具有较明确的意见。梳理近年各地编制的城市综合防灾规划和主要的单灾种防灾规划，其基本框架构成如下表所示。

近年编制的城市综合防灾规划和主要单灾种防灾规划内容框架

序号	综合防灾规划	单灾种防灾规划		
		抗震专项规划	防洪专项规划	消防专项规划
1	规划范围和期限	地震地质环境	流域概况	规划范围和期限
2	规划依据和目标	规划目标	防洪现状与问题	规划目标和原则
3	灾害危险性评估	地震危险性评估	规划目标和原则	火灾危险性评估
4	用地安全布局	建筑抗震防灾	防洪总体方案	消防安全布局
5	应急指挥系统建设	次生灾害防御	防洪工程设施建设	消防站布局
6	救灾专业队伍建设	基础设施抗震防灾	非工程措施	公共消防设施建设
7	防灾避灾宣传教育	避震设施布局	规划实施建议	实施保障与建议
8	建筑加固改造	规划实施保障		消防建设投资估算
9	疏散救援通道建设	近期建设规划		近期建设规划
10	避难场所建设			
11	应急基础设施			
12	救援物资设施			
13	实施建议			

三、城市防灾规划的发展与进步

（一）近年城市防灾规划概况

我国在城市灾害管理方面起步比较晚，从城市层面关注防灾减灾始于20世纪90年代联合国“国际减灾十年”活动。随着社会各界对城市防灾减灾的认识不断加深以及相关法律法规的不断完善，各级政府对城市防灾规划越来越重视。近年来，不少城市已开展了城市防灾规划的探索和实践，一些城市已经编制完成或正在开展防灾专项规划的编制工作，取得了一定的进展，防灾规划已经成为城市规划体系中一个十分重要的组成部分。当前城市防灾规划编制主要有以下特点：

1. 传统领域与非传统领域的均衡发展

长期以来，城市防灾规划只是作为城市总体规划的一个章节编制，涉及内容主要是抗震、防洪、消防、人防和地质灾害防治等传统防灾减灾领域。随着社会对于城市防灾减灾认识加强，城市防灾规划的地位不断得到提升。很多城市防灾规划已经发展成为独立编制的防灾专项规划，如泉州、厦门、海口、福州、武汉、合肥、淮南、廊坊、无锡等城市纷纷开展了抗震防灾、消防、人防等方面的防灾专项规划编制。

2003年"非典"危机以后，城市应急管理、避灾设施等非传统领域的建设内容逐渐成为城市防灾规划的内容之一，越来越受到关注和重视。随着各省"十二五"应急体系规划颁布，应急体系规划已经成为各级政府五年发展规划的重要组成部分。在避难场所规划方面，北京市①于2006年率先完成了应急避难场所规划纲要的编制，重庆②、成都③、攀枝花④、深圳⑤、西安⑥、南昌⑦等城市已经编制完成应急避难场所规划，上海、杭州、济南、昆明等城市则纷纷开展了应急避难场所规划方面的研究。城市防灾规划正逐渐向传统领域与非传统领域均衡发展过渡。

2. 单项防灾规划向多灾种、综合性防灾规划发展

当前城市总体规划中的防灾专题研究和防灾专业规划，已逐渐从单灾种规划向多灾种、综合性防灾规划发展。2004年完成的《北京市城市总体规划（2004—2020》首次提出了综合防灾减灾规划的理念，增加了应急体系、避难场所设施、应急物资等内容的规划。随后，济南、重庆、武汉、南京等地的城市总体规划纷纷加入了综合防灾减灾规划的内容。一些城市开始了综合防灾专项规划的探索，如成都⑧、哈尔滨⑨、厦门⑩、烟台⑪、淮南⑫、海口⑬等城市纷纷开展城市综合防灾减灾规划的编制和研究工作，从防抗单一灾种的防灾专项规划向多灾种、综合性的防灾专项规划发展。

3. 防灾规划向科学性发展

随着新的规划方法、技术理论及规划理念的引入，防灾规划正不断向科学性、系统性、可操作性方向发展。

在城市风险评价中，借助先进的评价模型、分析软件，对城市风险进行更科学、合理的定量评价。在防灾对策制定中，基于重大灾害的情景模拟和事故推演仿真，分析不同灾害情景下的应急策略及其效果，作为制定不同灾害情景下防灾对策的依据。在防灾设施布局方面，结合地理信息系统（GIS）分析和优化选址模型，对防灾设施的空间位置、数量等进行

---

① 《北京市北京中心城地震及应急避难场所（室外）规划纲要（2006—2020）》.

② 《重庆市主城区突发公共事件防灾应急避难场所规划（2007—2020）》.

③ 《成都市中心城应急避难场所布局规划（2008—2020）》.

④ 《攀枝花市应急避难场所总体规划（2007—2025）》.

⑤ 《深圳市应急避难场所专项规划（2009—2020）》.

⑥ 《西安市城区应急避难场所规划（2009—2020）》.

⑦ 《南昌市中心城区应急避难疏散场所规划（2011—2020）》.

⑧ 沈莉芳，陈乃志．城市公共安全规划研究——以成都市中心城公共安全规划为例［J］．规划师，2006，22（11）：27-30.

⑨ 于亚滨，张毅．城市公共安全规划体系构建探讨——以哈尔滨市城市公共安全规划为例［J］．规划师，2010，26（11）：49-54.

⑩ 厦门城市建设综合防灾规划（2006—2020）.

⑪ 烟台开发区综合防灾规划（2007—2020）.

⑫ 淮南市城市综合防灾规划（2009—2020）.

⑬ 海口市城市综合防灾规划研究.

优化，达到合理配置资源的目的。在规划内容上，既体现防灾工程设施的硬实力规划，又重视防灾信息系统、应急管理、防灾教育等软实力规划，使规划更符合地方发展规律，体现以人为本、公众参与的新理念，操作性更强。

（二）城市防灾的法规与标准建设

城市防灾规划的实施需要法律法规的保障。早在 20 世纪 80 年代，《中华人民共和国城市规划法》（1989 年）就提出了在城市规划中需要考虑城市防灾减灾的要求。之后，相继出台的《中华人民共和国人民防空法》（1996 年）、《中华人民共和国防震减灾法》（1997 年）、《中华人民共和国防洪法》（1997 年）、《中华人民共和国消防法》（1997 年，2008 年修订）和《地质灾害防治条例》（2003 年），分别提出了编制抗震防灾、防洪、消防、人防、地质灾害等防灾规划的要求。2007 年颁布的《中华人民共和国突发事件应对法》强调“城乡规划应当符合预防、处置突发事件的需要，统筹安排应对突发事件所必需的设备和基础设施建设，合理确定应急避难场所”的要求。2008 年 1 月 1 日实施的《中华人民共和国城乡规划法》明确提出，城市总体规划中应“确定综合防灾与公共安全保障体系”的要求。国家法律法规的要求，提高了城市防灾规划在城市规划体系中的地位，更为城市防灾规划的编制和实施提供了法律保障。同时，为进一步规范城市防灾规划，我国还出台了《城市抗震防灾规划标准》、《地震应急避难场所场址及配套设施》、《防洪标准》、《城市消防场站建设标准》（修订）等国家标准、规范，同时《城市消防规划规范》、《城市防洪规划规范》、《城镇防灾避难场所设计规范》、《城镇综合防灾规划标准》等国家标准和规范正在编制。

随着城市防灾减灾领域的有关规范、标准体系的建立和不断完善，城市防灾规划也必将不断向标准化、规范化、科学化发展。

（三）城市防灾规划的主要应用技术

城市规划设计和研究人员从不吝惜利用科学技术来支撑城市规划工作。近年来，在城市防灾规划方面应用的技术，主要包括以下几个方面。

1. 空间信息技术

地理信息系统（GIS）、遥感（RS）、全球定位系统（GPS）等空间信息技术在城市防灾规划的灾害识别、风险评估、用地安全性评价、设施布局等方面都有很广泛的应用。利用 GPS 技术，可以准确定位和标记灾害源及周边要素，如在淮南市综合防灾规划中，利用 GPS 技术，对淮南市重大危险源及周边信息进行了精确的定位；RS 技术可以在不同空间和时间尺度范围内快速提取地理要素，进行危险源识别、灾害影响区识别等，如在海口市综合防灾规划研究中，利用 RS 技术提取研究区域地形、土地利用等信息，并对洪水淹没区进行了分析；GIS 技术强大的空间分析、网络分析、数据统计等功能，在风险评估、用地安全性评价、设施布局等方面提供了有力的支撑，如淮南市抗震防灾规划、福州市抗震防灾规划、北川羌族自治县消防规划分别采用 GIS 技术进行地震次生火灾风险评估、抗震防灾用地安全性评价、消防站选址布局优化等过程。GIS、RS、GPS 等空间信息技术在城市防灾规划中的利用，不仅提高了防灾规划的工作效率，也提高了防灾规划的有效性和科学性。

2. 情景模拟和事故推演仿真技术

通过灾害情景模拟和事故推演仿真，实现对灾害空间和时间数据进行有效的集成管理和时空分析，动态地显示已发生的和未发生的状况，使得一个在多种因素的影响下往往要经过若干年才可能发生的灾害，在计算机上只需几分钟即可得出和看到类似的结果。这种跨时间的模拟能够发现隐藏的事实，为防灾规划提供可靠的依据。

在厦门抗震防灾规划中，通过构建地震次生火灾模拟模型，考虑地震作用、建筑破坏、火源、时间、气象等因素，利用 GIS 和离散事件动态系统仿真技术实现了震后起火、火灾蔓延、消防扑救的模拟，为地震次生灾害防治规划提供了有力的技术支持。淮南市综合防灾规划中，借助 HEC-RAS 模型和 DHI 的 MIKE 模型进行河流洪水的模拟和评估，实现对城市不同降雨重现期下的洪水进行模拟，得到不同重现期下的洪水淹没区域、深度和持续的时间，并可以生成动态的模拟结果，取得非常直观的成灾情景，实现洪水淹没模拟的可视化，对洪涝灾害可能造成的影响范围和程度作出准确的判断，对洪水灾害防治规划提供了有利的依据。

3. 重大危险源风险定量评估技术

重大危险源灾害风险的定量评估技术主要是借助一些较为成熟的软件，对常见的各种危险化学品的存储和输送设备进行风险的定量计算，并借助 GIS 平台，将其风险落实到空间上，从而得到不同空间的风险情况，为防灾规划的制定提供定量支持依据。例如，淮南市综合防灾规划中，利用 ALOHA（Areal Location of Hazardous Atmospheres）软件对重大危险源事故后果进行定量评价，并根据评价结果确定重大危险源的风险等级，作为重大危险源防治规划的依据。ALOHA 软件储存了近千种常用化学品的物理化学性质和毒性参数，还可以根据需要添加新物质参数，计算中采用的数学模型包括：高斯模型、重气扩散模型、蒸汽云爆炸、BLEVE 火球等成熟的事故后果计算模型。评价过程中，由分析人员提供气象资料和分析对象的实际设备参数和事故变量等，选择合理的事故模型，即可对毒气溃散、火灾和爆炸等事故造成的毒性物质浓度、热辐射和冲击波影响范围和程度进行定量评价。

（四）城市防灾规划的方针和对策

当前城市防灾规划主要从对灾害的“防、抗、避、救”四个方面开展，各类防灾规划重点对灾害发生前和灾害发生时提出对应措施，大多做到了对灾害风险进行分析，评估现有灾害防范设施的状况和水平，确定城市建筑和设施的抗灾建设标准和技术要求，提出避灾和救灾设施的规划方案和建设要求。

1. 灾害预防和抵御

灾害预防和抵御的基本方针是以灾害防范为主，基本对策有：

（1）调整用地安全布局，迁出可能发生灾害危险地段的居民，调整城市重大危险源布局。

（2）实施建筑加固计划，加强防洪排涝、消防等防灾设施建设。

（3）保持防灾设施的水平，加强防灾设施的运行管理。

2. 灾害应对和避灾救灾

灾时应对的基本方针是以避灾救灾为主，基本对策有：

（1）建立灾害监测和预警系统，做到预先发现灾情和信息传递；

（2）完善应急指挥机构和运行机制，辅以信息技术手段，谋求有效地组织发挥各类应急资源的效能；

（3）落实应急通道、避灾场所、应急基础设施、救灾物资保障设施的建设，建立避灾救灾体系；

（4）培养公众防灾安全避灾意识和技能，提高公众防灾避灾的能力。

（五）城市防灾规划待解决的相关问题

目前城市防灾规划的编制和实施尚未形成完善的机制，存在的问题主要表现在以下方面：

1. 综合防灾规划的实施主体不明确

目前，城市单灾种防灾规划分别由其主管部门负责组织编制和实施，如消防、人防、防洪和抗震规划分别由消防、人防、水务和地震等主管部门负责编制和实施。城市综合防灾规划一般由规划主管部门委托编制，政府应急主管部门单独委托或应急主管部门与规划主管部门联合委托编制的情况均较少。但城市综合防灾涉及众多部门，即使是承担防灾减灾管理与协调工作的应急主管部门，由于体制、机制、权限等多方面的原因，在灾害信息掌握、防灾资源调配和防灾设施组织建设等方面可发挥的作用尚有限，城市规划主管部门的职责和权力更难以整合全社会的防灾救灾资源，这使得综合防灾规划在编制过程中与应急、防灾等专业主管部门的参与和配合非常有限，在规划实施阶段则缺乏明确的主体部门，严重约束了城市综合防灾规划的编制和实施。

2. 城市综合防灾规划的地位不高

我国在城市防灾减灾法规标准体系建设方面虽然开展了不少工作，但与城市规划建设水平相比，还远不够完善。虽然2007年颁布的《中华人民共和国突发事件应对法》明确提出“城乡规划应当符合预防、处置突发事件的需要，统筹安排应对突发事件所必需的设备和基础设施建设，合理确定应急避难场所”的要求，但对于城市防灾规划并未作出规定。近些年来，虽然有学者呼吁我们尽快出台类似于日本的《灾害对策基本法》的防灾减灾方面的法律，并希望确定防灾减灾规划尤其是城市综合防灾规划的地位和作用，赋予防灾减灾规划法律地位，提高其权威性，但目前依然没有这方面立法的相关消息。

由于缺少应有的法律地位，现有城市防灾规划从编制到实施都不是强制性的。目前，城市防灾规划是否需要编制主要取决于地方领导对防灾减灾的认识和兴趣。而对于已经编制完成的综合防灾规划，实施过程中无法统筹各类资源，部分与其他城市规划有冲突的内容难以协调，严重限制了综合防灾规划作用的发挥。

3. 防灾规划技术标准缺乏

城市综合防灾规划在我国尚属于起步和探索阶段，规划内容一般包括灾害源识别、灾害风险评估、防灾减灾目标与对策、防灾避灾设施规划布局、防灾避灾设施建设要求等内容。但由于缺乏统一的技术标准，不同的规划编制单位完成的城市综合防灾规划在内容和深度上都有很大差异。

城市总体规划中的防灾专业规划本应通过重大灾害源识别和城市灾害风险评估，引导城市规划在用地布局和设施布局的安全性考虑，为城市总体规划、控制性详细规划以及其他各专项规划提供有效的指导意见。由于缺乏技术标准，目前的灾害风险评估只能形成定性描述的结论和意见，可落实内容较少，无法充分发挥作为规划依据的作用。

四、国家“十二五”城市防灾规划简述

2011 年 11 月 26 日，国务院发布了《国家综合防灾减灾规划（2011—2015 年）》（以下简称《减灾规划》），将成为“十二五”期间全国防灾减灾工作的指导文件《减灾规划》的概要如下：

《减灾规划》阐述了“十一五”期间我国在 8 个方面防灾减灾工作取得的成效：①防灾减灾管理体制、机制和法制；②自然灾害监测预警体系；③自然灾害工程防御能力；④重特大自然灾害应对能力；⑤科学技术的支撑作用；⑥防灾减灾人才和专业队伍建设；⑦防灾减灾社会参与；⑧防灾减灾国际合作与交流。《减灾规划》认为，自然灾害风险会进一步加大，防灾减灾工作形势严峻，指出了未来我国防灾减灾工作面临的 4 项挑战是：①提高灾害监测、预警预报及信息传播水平；②城乡基础设施设防标准偏低，避灾设施薄弱；③应急救灾物资供应、救灾应急设施比较落后；④需加强防灾减灾专业队伍建设、协作机制和防灾减灾宣传教育。面对“十二五”期间的灾害形势和挑战，开展防灾减灾工作也并存着诸多机遇：①中央将防灾减灾工作列为政府工作的优先事项，防灾减灾的地位和作用凸显；②我国经济实力为开展防灾减灾工作奠定了物质基础；③社会各界积极支持减灾工作，具有良好的社会氛围。

《减灾规划》提出了我国综合防灾减灾工作的 4 项工作原则：①政府主导，社会参与；②以人为本，依靠科学；③预防为主，综合减灾；④统筹谋划，突出重点。明确了防灾减灾工作的 8 项目标：①基本建成国家综合减灾与风险管理信息平台；②因自然灾害造成的死亡人数明显下降；③将防灾减灾工作纳入各级规划；④加大受灾救助的力度；⑤全面增强国民防灾减灾意识；⑥扩大防灾减灾专业人才队伍；⑦创建综合减灾示范社区；⑧进一步完善防灾减灾体制机制。

《减灾规划》制定了“十二五”时期国家要完成的 10 项加强建设的主要任务：①自然灾害监测预警能力建设；②防灾减灾信息管理与服务能力建设；③自然灾害风险管理能力建设；④自然灾害工程防御能力建设；⑤区域和城乡基层防灾减灾能力建设；⑥自然灾害应急处置与恢复重建能力建设；⑦防灾减灾科技支撑能力建设；⑧防灾减灾社会动员能力建设；

⑨防灾减灾人才和专业队伍建设；⑩防灾减灾文化建设。

《减灾规划》还强调了“十二五”时期我国综合减灾工作要落实的8项重大建设工程：①全国自然灾害综合风险调查工程；②国家综合减灾与风险管理信息化建设工程；③国家自然灾害应急救助指挥系统建设工程；④国家救灾物资储备工程；⑤环境减灾卫星星座建设工程；⑥国家重特大自然灾害防范仿真系统建设工程；⑦综合减灾示范社区和避难场所建设工程；⑧防灾减灾宣传教育和科普工程。

为了保障《减灾规划》的实施，需要围绕防灾减灾工作采取5项保障措施：①完善工作机制；②健全法律法规和预案体系；③加大资金投入力度；④广泛开展国际合作与交流；⑤做好规划实施与评估。

（作者：朱思诚，中国城市规划设计研究院城市公共安全研究中心副主任，教授级高级工程师）

关于“十二五”加强大城市交通规划建设与管理工作的建议

当前，我国大城市规模快速扩张、汽车数量急剧增长，交通拥堵、交通污染状况严重，交通耗能持续增长。为了应对我国大城市日益严峻的交通问题，未来五年十分关键，必须以科学合理的城镇化为方向，加快推进大城市交通发展模式的转变，构建以公共交通为主体的城市综合交通体系，促进绿色、节能、低碳交通方式的发展。

一、对“十二五”城市交通发展形势的认识和判断

（一）城镇化与城市快速发展带来大城市交通需求急剧增长，城市综合交通区域统筹的作用明显加强

预计在“十二五”期末，我国城镇化率将突破50%。随着高铁、城际铁路、航空、高速公路的发展，城镇之间与区域交通联系的态势更加明显，大城市中心区功能更加集聚，城市空间扩张的压力巨大，交通需求时空分布和服务要求都将在区域层面面临深刻变化。亟需在城镇化总体发展的前提上，进行综合协调和统筹优化。

（二）小汽车发展进入快速增长阶段，城市交通出行结构调整的任务十分紧迫和艰巨

城市小汽车增长速度多年来持续超过20%，小汽车能耗占据了城市交通总燃油消耗的73%，且呈上升趋势。城市土地资源被小汽车大量占用，步行、自行车活动空间逐渐丧失。公共交通整体服务水平依然不高，居民采用小汽车出行的比例远高于公共交通。科学调控大城市的小汽车发展、优化居民出行结构的任务十分紧迫和艰巨。如何在城镇化快速发展过程中，实现两个结构性转变，即建立以公共交通引导的城市布局结构和以公共交通为主体的机动化交通出行结构，是城市规划与交通规划面临的重大课题。

（三）城市交通问题更加复杂，解决难度更大，规划、建设、管理的协同作用成为关键

短期内城市道路交通拥堵加剧的趋势难于避免，停车问题将更加突出。治理和改善大城市交通问题是一项长期而艰巨的任务，任何期望通过单纯的工程和管理措施能够彻底解决问

题的想法都是不现实的。未来五年，加强规划、建设、管理的综合协同作用，实施交通需求管理，促进绿色交通发展，对缓解城市交通问题极为重要。

二、坚持四项发展理念，实施五项发展策略

尊重客观规律有序引导城镇化发展，遏制城市盲目扩张，树立并坚持“和谐高效、服务民生、节约资源、科学决策”的发展理念，促进城市交通发展模式的转变。

和谐高效。引导城市合理布局，统筹城市交通与城市土地使用；处理好区域交通、城市交通和城乡交通的布局关系；科学安排多种交通方式之间的衔接和换乘；加强对小汽车交通需求过快增长的政策调控。

服务民生。坚持以人为本，协调不同交通参与者的交通需求和权益；保障公众通勤、通学、生活等基本出行的安全畅达；保障交通不便者和低收入人群的交通权益不受侵害；营造与人的活动相适宜的交通空间。

节约资源。扶持和鼓励占用资源少、使用效率高、人均排放低的绿色交通系统和新能源交通工具；大力发展与集约型城市相匹配的公共性、集约化运输方式及配套的交通基础设施建设，减少对小汽车出行的依赖。

科学决策。创新决策机制；推进城市交通规划、建设和管理决策的科学化、民主化；加快完善公众参与制度，进一步加快法规建设。

在坚持四项发展理念的基础上，加快实施五项发展策略：

一是公交优先策略。坚定不移地贯彻优先发展公共交通的发展战略，大城市应将公共交通发展作为城市建设的首要任务，在投资、财税、规划、建设、管理和服务等各个环节给予优先支持，大力提升公共交通出行比重。

二是需求调控策略。以优化调整出行结构为目标，加强交通需求管理，对小汽车交通需求过快增长实施政策调控。结合城市发展阶段、城市功能布局和交通需求分布，在交通设施配置、需求管理对策等方面实行有差别的调控和引导。

三是交通引导策略。加强城市规划与交通规划编制体系的整合，积极推进公共交通导向的土地开发模式，加强城市轨道交通等重大交通基础设施建设的前期研究论证，引导城市空间结构和功能布局优化。加快大城市地区的城市轨道交通系统建设。

四是综合协同策略。以促进公共交通发展为主线，服务民生为基点，改善交通为目标，加快形成规划、建设、管理各部门相互衔接、政策连贯、共同推进的综合治理城市交通的决策协同机制和保障制度。

五是公众参与策略。在城市交通规划、建设、管理各个层面，完善公众参与制度，充分发挥多层次、多方式、广泛的公众参与及监督作用，遏制并减少违背客观规律的交通建设上的“形象工程”、“政绩工程”、“献礼工程”等。

三、对策建议

针对我国城市和城市交通发展趋势，“十二五”期间要把科学引导城市布局、优化调整出行结构、转变大城市交通发展模式作为工作重点，具体建议如下：

（一）优化城市布局，加快产业结构及布局调整

加大城市总体规划实施和监督力度，推进城市布局优化、空间结构与产业布局结构的同步调整。结合城市轨道交通系统建设合理安排集约型、高密度开发地区，力求形成职住平衡、配套齐全的组团结构，避免“摊大饼”式无序蔓延。

（二）高度重视城市交通规划工作，完善规划编制工作机制和协调机制

统筹安排城市交通系统与土地使用的关系，加快推进城市综合交通体系规划的编制工作，建立独立的审查工作机制和制度。整合城市综合交通体系规划与区域交通规划、土地使用规划的衔接关系，加快解决交通规划建设条块分割、功能层次混乱、衔接不畅问题。进一步完善交通规划编制的协调机制，在城市综合交通体系规划的基础上，加快开展公共交通、停车系统、步行与自行车交通等专项交通规划编制。实施交通影响评价制度，加强对城市大型建设项目的交通影响评价工作。大城市应该组织编制城市交通发展年度报告。

（三）应对城市多元化交通需求，统筹规划建设城市综合交通体系

加快建设以公共交通为主体的公共客运设施和服务系统，因地制宜地建设快速公交系统，积极推进公交专用道建设，加强公交专用道的管理。科学安排步行、自行车交通设施，有条件的城市，推进专用的步行、自行车道路系统建设和步行街区的建设。加快完善城市各级道路网络，提升道路网整体密度，科学安排步行、自行车专用的道路设施。在路网密集的城市中心区，应慎重决策新建快速道路和高架道路。加强停车设施建设和管理，在差别化策略指导下，规范停车配建标准，合理布局社会停车场。加强交通换乘设施和配套设施建设。逐步转变出租车营运模式，推进出租车预约车系统建设。

（四）大城市实施“公交优先”和“需求管理”并重的发展政策

大城市应制定详细的“公交优先”实施方案，研究制定调控小汽车需求过度膨胀、引导其有序发展的调控政策和具体措施。加快公务车改革，严格控制公车购买和使用。建立“公交优先”和“需求管理”政策制定、执行的协同机制。

（五）加快城市交通信息化和智能化建设，提升道路交通运行管理水平

加快城市智能交通系统发展，重点加强道路交通智能诱导系统建设，以提高公交准点率为目标，推进公共交通智能化建设。加快建设面向公众的交通信息服务系统。研究制定切实

可行的交通改善综合措施，完善道路交通标线标志和指引系统，优化交通信号控制，积极利用路网条件优化交通组织。

（六）重视交通立法，充实完善城市交通规划建设技术法规

加快交通立法工作，尽快研究制定“公共交通法”和“停车法”，为公共交通发展和停车设施建设提供法律保障。补充、完善城市交通规划建设技术法规，修编、调整落后过时的技术标准，建立技术法规的定期审查和修编制度。

（七）深化城市交通的科学技术研究

增大对城市交通科技研究的投入，建立长效跟踪研究机制和研究团队，深化城市交通基础理论和应用技术研究，加强交通出行行为的研究，加快研究城市交通科普教育体系和推进机制，提升全社会的交通文明意识。

（作者：中国城市规划学会城市交通规划学术委员会）

我国中部地区城镇化发展特征与趋势的若干探讨

——基于皖北的乡镇实证研究

据统计资料，2009 年我国城镇化率为 46.6%，城镇人口达 6.22 亿人[1]。根据《国家人口发展战略研究报告》的预测，我国仍有 1.5 亿 ~ 1.7 亿农村剩余劳动力。今后 20 年间，将还有 3 亿农村人口要陆续转化为城镇人口[2]。而根据联合国《世界城市化展望（2009）》（World Urbanization Prospect, the 2009 Revision）的预测，2050 年我国的城市人口将达 10.3 亿；这意味着，未来 40 年间，还将有 4 亿农村人口迁入城市[3]。

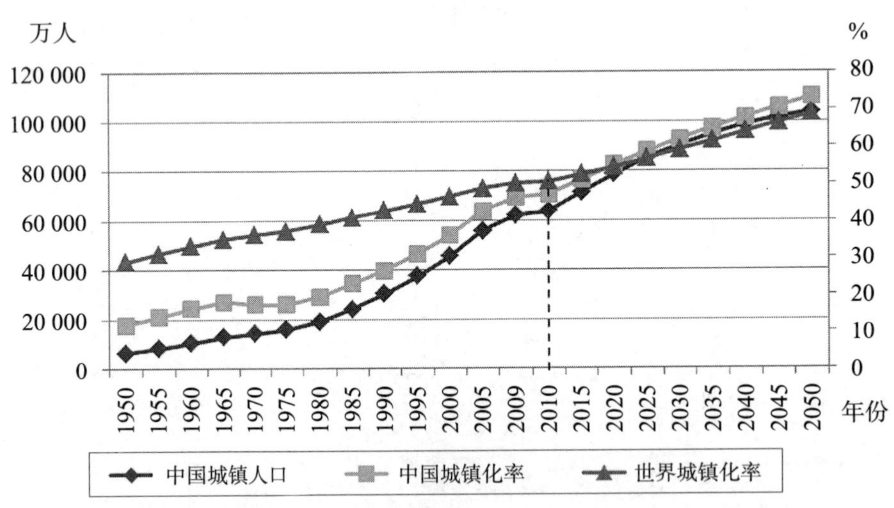

图 1　联合国对我国城镇化率的预测

数据来源：World Urbanization Prospect, the 2009 Revision。

无论这些预测准确与否，至少预示了这样一个事实——未来我国的城镇化进程关乎国民经济的整体运行，并将具有全球影响。因此，对我国现阶段城镇化特征的准确把握，以及对我国未来城镇化趋势的客观判断，其重要意义不言而喻。下文将在相关研究课题的基础上，展开若干分析和讨论。

一、关于我国城镇化的研究综述

（一）城镇化人口的相关概念

区别于多数欧美国家，我国的城镇化除了人口基数大、迁移速度较快之外，其主要特征还表现在“未改变永久居住地的流动人口”是推动城镇化的主体[4]。也正是这一大规模的劳动力迁移和流动增强了中国的经济活力，并不断创造着财富[5]。2009 年全国流动人口达 2.11 亿人。根据相关研究[6,7,8]的估计，流动人口的规模在未来 20～30 年内还将继续增加；至 2050 年，全国流动人口规模可能达 3.5 亿人。

高流动性使得中国的城镇化人口成为一个混杂而多元的群体。约翰·弗里德曼（John Friedmann）在其著作中，将中国的迁移人口分为五类[9]：第一类是由农村迁往附近的镇、再到县城、再到城市的连续迁移人口（serial migrants）/逐步迁移人口（step migrants）；第二类是重复迁移人口（repeat migrants），系指在一段较短时间间隔回乡，并再次向外地迁移的人口；第三类是季节性迁移人口（cyclical migrants），即在农忙或某一时节回乡、具有固定外出间隔的人群；第四类是长时间外出后回乡创业或退休的人口，即返回迁移人口（return migrants）；而第五类则选择定居于城市，成为永久性迁移人口（permanent migrants）。①

而在朱宇[4]、杨（YANG[10]）等学者的文章中，则把除永久迁移人口以外的迁移人口统称为“非永久性迁移人口”（temporary migrants）（基本等同于“暂住人口”/“流动人口”概念）②。

（二）我国城镇化研究中的争议焦点

1. “滞后”还是“适宜”

自 1990 年代起，国内外学者就我国城镇化水平是否滞后于经济发展水平问题展开了热烈的讨论。大多数学者认为我国城镇化发展的实际水平滞后于经济发展水平[11]。但仍有部分学者[12,13,14]指出，由于我国人口基数大、区域差异大、所处城镇化阶段特征等因素，城镇化率与经济指标的关系具有特殊性，仅凭西方的经验参数并不足以判断中国城镇化滞后与否。这些学者认为，我国当前的城镇化水平并非远低于经济发展水平，而是基本相对称的。

此外，还有少数学者认为，若将在乡镇企业就业及外出就业的农村人口及其抚养人口也计入城镇化水平，则中国的实际/隐性城镇化率非但不低，反而是“隐性超城市化”[15]。

2. “加速”还是“稳步”

与对我国城镇化现状水平的理解相对应，持两种观点的学者对于未来的城镇化趋势也有

① 其中，连续迁移人口/逐步迁移人口、重复迁移人口、返回迁移人口的翻译方式参考联合国人口司相关定义。

② 下文中，除特别指出，凡涉及“流动人口”、“迁移人口”，都特指从农村向城镇流动/迁移的人口，而忽略城镇之间或农村之间流动/迁移的人口。

着不同的判断：认为城镇化滞后的学者提出，未来我国城镇化将进入、也必须进入加速阶段，并由此推动整体经济的发展。而与之相反，那些认为当前城镇化水平尚处于合理范围的学者指出，我国的社会、经济、生态资源和环境基础皆“不能支撑这种‘急速城镇化’”[16]，且从我国城镇化发展的自身规律判断，继续提加速发展可能不妥[14]。

3. “极化”还是“均衡”

在预测未来我国城镇人口的空间分布时，国内外学者也存在分歧。目前多数学者认为[17]，过去的30多年间，我国城镇化存在极大的地区（东中西部）差异，且这一极化趋势将在未来进一步加剧。虽然这些学者不约而同地认为，针对这一不平衡趋势，应在我国区域发展政策上予以适当纠正；但他们同时也指出，“先天区位资源所导致的城镇化区域差异还将持续相当长的一段时间”[9]。

与之相对的是，针对我国20世纪80—90年代乡镇经济活跃，城镇化自下而上推进的特点，以朱宇等为代表的学者提出，我国城镇化进程应选择相对均质的“就地城镇化”（in situ urbanization）路径。即通过高人口密度乡村聚落的演变，完成乡村到城镇的就地转型[18,19]。

需要予以说明的是，“就地城镇化”的观点，与麦吉（T. McGee）等学者20世纪90年代初对东南亚城镇化的研究有某种相似性。麦吉教授把“都市延伸区”（Extended Metropolitan Region，EMR）由内至外分为城市核心（city core）、半城镇化地区（peri-urban）和农工混合地区（Desakota）三层。其中，农工混合也是所谓亦城亦乡的“第三类空间”。麦吉教授关于这些空间产生的机制分析、对其经济及社会特征的研究也为我国“就地城镇化”/“农村城镇化”（rural urbanization）等相关研究提供了借鉴。根据麦吉教授2008年对中国城市空间的研究[20]，未来50年，城市外围区域（半城镇化地区及Desakota）将成为中国城镇化的主要载体。

此外还有综合了“极化”和“均衡”的第三种观点。20世纪90年代，以辜胜阻等为代表的学者提出了“二元城镇化理论”。其核心观点是，根据不同区域和发展阶段，中国的城镇化进程是一个多元的过程：即城市化与农村城镇化并重，以大都市圈为依托的“网络发展式”城镇化与以县城为依托的“据点发展式”城镇化同步[21]。因此，这些学者主张，在不同地域宜采用不同形式的城镇化，避免“撇开农村孤立地发展大城市的‘大城建派’”，以及“盲目无序发展小城镇，实施‘村村点火，户户冒烟’的‘乡村派’城镇化”两种片面倾向[22]。

（三）小结

总结以上关于我国城镇化的主要研究方法及结论，笔者认为有以下四个显著特征。

1. 多是基于不准确的统计数据的研究

城乡之间人口的持续流动和季节性迁移，多元、复杂的迁移人口构成以及不断变更的统计口径，都影响了我国历年人口统计数据的完整性和准确性。然而，目前绝大多数的研究分析恰恰是基于这些很不完善的统计数据；由此，其所得出的结论也难免会有偏差。

诚然，部分学者已经认识到这一数据“陷阱”，并试图避免由于统计数据的局限而导致观点失误。尤其是认为我国城镇化水平基本合理的学者，往往将统计数据偏差作为其重要的立论依据之一。但不足的是，这些论证要么限于个人主观“感觉”或经验判断，缺乏微观层面的实证支撑；要么陷入为纠正统计数据而建立的新的数据分析，重又回归至“纸上谈兵”。

2. 较多是基于情景假设的研究

目前我国的城乡户籍制度尚未消失，城乡在住房、社会保障、公共服务等领域的差异仍然存在。未来，如若这些制度隔阂消失，将对我国城镇化的趋势产生何种影响尚属未知。因此，目前的相关研究只能基于情景假设，而这些假设又往往出自研究者的主观猜测，缺乏必要的社会调查支撑。

以户籍制度为例，目前相当多研究所隐含的推论是，一旦户籍制度的障碍消除，我国的城镇化将迎来新的高潮；多数流动人口的非永久性迁移将转变为永久迁移，并在城市定居[19]。然而，到底户籍门槛对城镇化有多大的影响力？如若不考虑城乡户籍限制，农民的真正迁移意向如何？对于这两个基本问题，在有关研究中尚缺乏深度探究。

3. 缺乏实地调查及微观层面支撑

如上所述，目前我国的城镇化研究所提出的假设或推论较多是基于数据分析和情景推演，缺乏必要的事实证据支撑。因此，支撑性的实证研究就显得十分必要。国内不少学者已开始注意这一点，已经有研究开始涉及微观个体在城镇化进程中的选择（例如蔡禾等一批学者就曾对外出务工人员的回迁意向做了问卷调查[23]）。

但同时仍可发现，部分研究要么又再度依赖数据分析，要么多限于社会学领域研究，较少与地理研究、区域政策分析和城市研究等领域相联系。由于研究成果偏于微观结论，其解释力的“普适性”不够。以外出回流人口定居意向研究为例，受访者选择定居城市的比例从25% ~85%不等，差异很大。这实际反映出微观研究的局限性——由于调查时间、区域、对象的限制，又加问题设计、提问方式等外部因素的影响，其研究结论往往只能反映我国城镇化的局部或片段特征。

4. 缺乏针对特定区域的系统研究

虽然我国东中西部在城镇化水平、特征、趋势等多方面存在差异，但目前尚缺乏聚焦于某一区域板块、系统性的城镇化研究。尤其对于不同区域城镇化路径的讨论尚十分缺乏。全国“均一化”的研究隐含着这样一个前提判断，即中西部地区将复制东部地区的城镇化路径；或是在城镇化的速度、水平上有所差别，但基本模式趋同。显然，这个前提能否成立是需要被质疑的。

二、研究对象与方法

（一）技术路线

本文的基础是研究课题，主要以安徽省阜阳市作为实证研究对象，通过对阜阳城镇化微观（乡镇、个体）机制的分析，认识全市（中观）的城镇化特征，并进一步形成关于中部地区①城镇化（宏观研究）的认识和判断（见图2）。

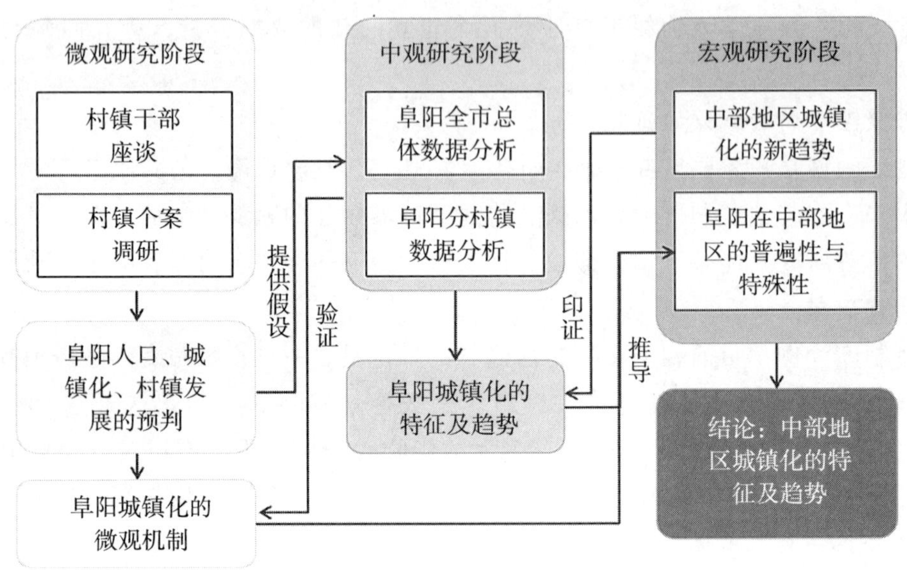

图2　本研究的理论技术路线框图

在三个不同研究阶段，主要研究方法也有所侧重：在微观研究阶段，通过对多个有代表性的个案乡镇②进行调研，并对乡镇干部进行访谈，初步形成对整个阜阳城镇化的预判和假设；在中观研究阶段，通过对阜阳全市、所有乡镇的数据分析和GIS空间分析，对微观层面的发现及所提出的观点加以检验和论证，初步形成全市性的判断；而在宏观研究阶段，则试图通过分析阜阳在中部地区的普遍性和特殊性，并观察中部地区城镇化的总体趋势（辅以在中部其他省份的所作的调研工作），以印证上两个阶段所得结论，进而推演出关于中部地区城镇化特征与趋势的观点——形成本次研究的主要结论。

（二）研究对象

阜阳市的前身是阜阳地区，目前是安徽省辖地级市建制；阜阳位于苏豫皖交界地区，在皖西北拥有较大的腹地，其“中心城市—外围区域”的结构较为稳定。

一定程度上，阜阳在是我国“人口多、密度高”的人居环境的缩影。2008年阜阳全市户籍人口987.8万人，人口密度达1 011人/平方公里。从统计数据看，阜阳的城镇化水平较低。2008年，全市常住城镇人口233万人，城镇化率为30.6%[24]，低于同时期全国水平，也低于安徽省平均水平（40.5%）近十个百分点[25]。

阜阳是人口输出大市。近五年其外出务工人数始终保持在200万人以上，是全国重要的

① 此处的“中部地区”按中国统计年鉴统计方式，是指河南、山西、安徽、湖北、湖南、江西六省。

② 调研对象分别涵盖了距离市区近、中、远距离，不同经济发展水平，重点镇和一般镇等条件的6个乡镇。

劳务输出基地。2008 年，阜阳全市外出半年以上人口占户籍人口 29.1%（287 万人），其中绝大多数（244 万人）外出务工经商[26]。

三、关于阜阳市城镇化的研究发现

1. 异地城镇化比重高，实际城镇化水平被大大低估

根据乡镇调查，阜阳市绝大部分的外出务工人员来自农村，包括集镇居住人口在内的城镇人口外出比例远低于农村。国家统计局阜阳调查队 2008 年对阜阳外出人口的抽样统计数据证实了这一点[27]：当年阜阳全市输出农村劳动力占总输出人口的 72.8%，共计 225 万人。

绝大多数农村外出人口流向地为城镇地区，常年从事的是非农业生产活动。这些人口虽然并未完成户籍身份的转换，但实际已在阜阳以外地区完成了城镇化。换言之，2008 年阜阳全市至少有 200 万人的异地城镇化人口。

但由于这部分人口的流动性较高，难以准确统计。因此，往往是按其户籍所在地被计入农村人口。为了正确认识阜阳的实际城镇化水平，笔者假设一种极端情况：即这 200 万人的异地城镇化人口全被当地统计为阜阳的常住农村人口。则在计算实际城镇化率时，或者将这部分人口从本地常住人口中减去，可得阜阳 2008 年的城镇化率为 41.4%；或者将这部分人口全部计入城镇人口，则阜阳户籍总人口中大约已有 43.8% 完成城镇化。不论用哪个数据，至少有一点是明显的，即阜阳目前的城镇化水平是被低估了的。

2. 农村空心化现象普遍

对阜阳城镇化水平的重新认识引发了另一问题——既然阜阳实际的城镇化水平可能并不低，那么，未来其进一步城镇化的潜力又有多大呢？事实上，乡镇调查表明，约三分之二的农村劳动人口（15 ~ 54 岁年龄段）选择常年外出。若按这一比例粗略估计，2008 年阜阳全市外出农业人口约 237 万人，与抽样统计数据的 225 万人基本吻合，证实了个案调查的结论。

此外，乡镇调查同样显示，阜阳现有的农村常住劳动力已经不足以完成传统的农业耕作。相当部分农业生产，尤其是如播种、收割等适于机械化的集中性生产活动，已经被外包给流动的专业生产队伍。

综上所述，阜阳农村地区空心化现象已经十分普遍，农村留驻人口多是儿童和老人，农村进一步释放剩余劳动力的潜力已经不大；另一方面，土地的全面流转和集中经营尚没有大的突破，土地对农村人口的束缚还将长期存在。

3. 乡镇发展缓慢，作为城镇化的载体作用很有限

阜阳的乡镇经济活力不强，发展缓慢。2008 年，全市建制镇人均财政收入仅为 74.23 元（安徽全省平均 409 元）。多数乡镇仍处于典型的农业经济阶段，第一产业比重较大，工业很少。2008 年，全市近三分之一的乡镇只有不到 10 家工业企业。

究其原因，是由于阜阳地处中部，产业经济发展所需的市场、资金、开放度等条件都不优越；而大多数乡镇又缺乏不可替代的比较优势，同位竞争尤为激烈；此外，比较中心城

市，乡镇经济发展还面临着土地指标无法落实、基础设施配套落后、投融资困难、人才缺乏等许多问题。据调查，目前阜阳的市/县工业园区地价甚至低于乡镇自建园区成本，大大削弱了乡镇对于企业的吸引力。就阜阳现存的乡镇企业类型而言，或是生产资料及市场依托农村的企业，或是不符合城市产业园区进驻标准的小型企业，包括一些回乡创业人员所办的起步企业。而这些企业的数量和产能都十分有限。

回顾阜阳过去几十年间乡镇经济的发展历史，除若干依靠“能人经济”或偶发机遇实现较大发展的乡镇产业集群，对于多数不具特殊资源禀赋的乡镇，其工业经济发展难以复制沿海省份的做法及辉煌成就，所以能提供的就业机会也就十分有限；缺乏经济支撑的镇区，其居住和工作环境也难以与城市相比。

总之，在阜阳这样的中部地区，就整体而言，再想要通过农村工业化来推进城镇化进程——复制沿海地区的做法，其可能性已不复存在。

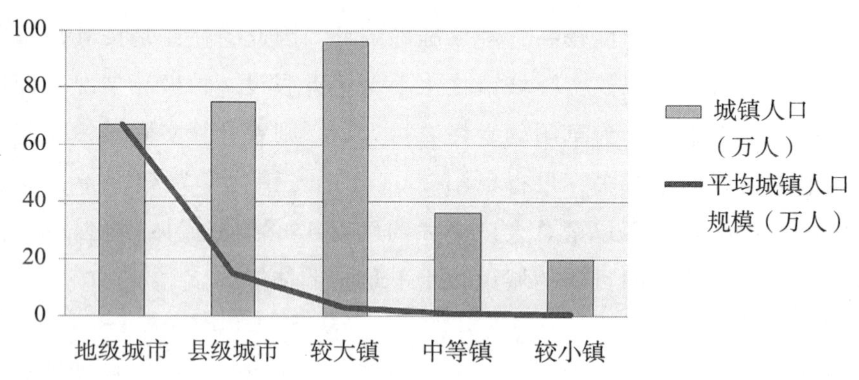

图3　阜阳分规模序列的城镇人口结构（2007年）

数据来源：根据《阜阳市城市总体规划（2007—2020）说明书》数据整理。

4. 人口逐步向城市集中

与乡镇相比，中心城市（城区及县城）在阜阳的城镇化进程中发挥了更为重要的作用。分析2008年全市乡镇非农人口变化情况①，农转非人口基本集中在市区和县城。考虑到这些人口变动中的一部分与城镇化原因无关，因此排除这部分人口单独进行分析②，发现中心市区和县级城市的优势更加明显；形成鲜明对比的是，绝大多数乡镇农转非（由于城镇化原因）的人口数则为零（见图4）。

5. 外出人口返乡比例趋于上升

2008年的抽样调查显示，阜阳市农村外出务工人口的返乡③比例为20.4%，比上年同期

① 由于数据限制原因，此处用“非农人口”代替“常住城镇人口”，间接反映乡镇的城镇化水平。

② 按照阜阳市2008年公安局人口统计年报中，农业人口转为非农人口理由包括招生、聘用、征用土地、落户小城镇、投资购房、投靠亲戚和其他七项。其中，“投靠亲戚”是指随父母、伴侣、子女等进城，不属于城镇化原因；而“其他”项由于原因不明，且人数较少，基本可忽略，因此也被排除。

③ 本文中所提及的“返乡”既包括短期、季节性回阜，也包括中、长期回阜。

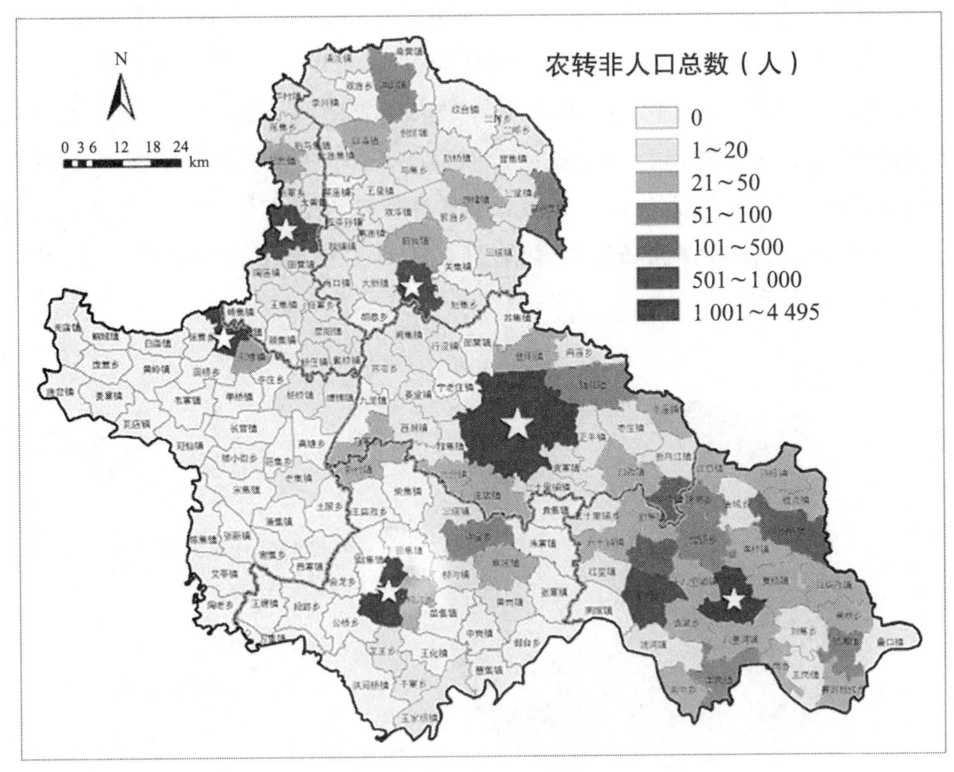

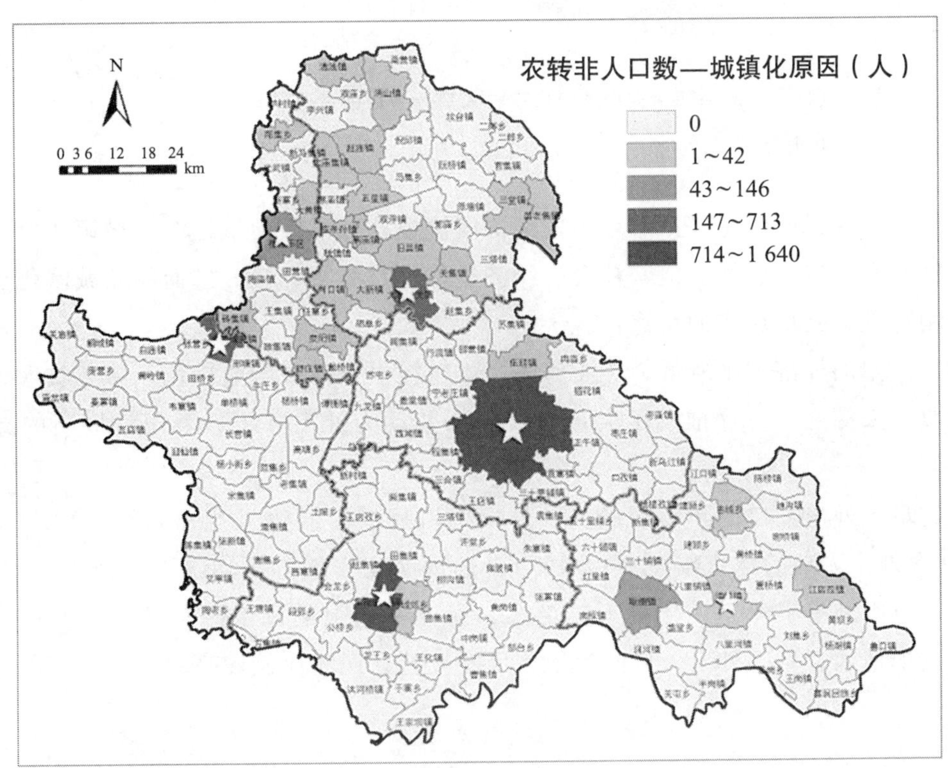

图 4　2008 年阜阳市全部乡镇农转非人口（分原因）空间分布图

注：五角星所标识区域分别为阜阳市辖区、阜阳所辖四县一市县/市政府所在地。

数据来源：阜阳市公安局 2008 年人口统计年报。

上升5.4个百分点[27]。另一份关于安徽省返乡人口的抽样调查显示，虽然超过一半（53.6%）的人员仍有打算继续外出务工，但有30%左右的人员选择留在家乡[28]。如果这一比例接近事实，2008年阜阳约有15万人原外出人口长期回流。

但需要明确的是，人口外出和回流是一个持续变化的动态过程。阜阳市2008年的返乡比例上升很可能受到了全球金融危机、天气条件①等特殊因素的影响。对此还需做跟踪调研分析。此外，在原外出人口回流的同时，仍有新的劳动力源源不断的向外输出，阜阳全市人口净输出率仍然保持在相当高的水平。

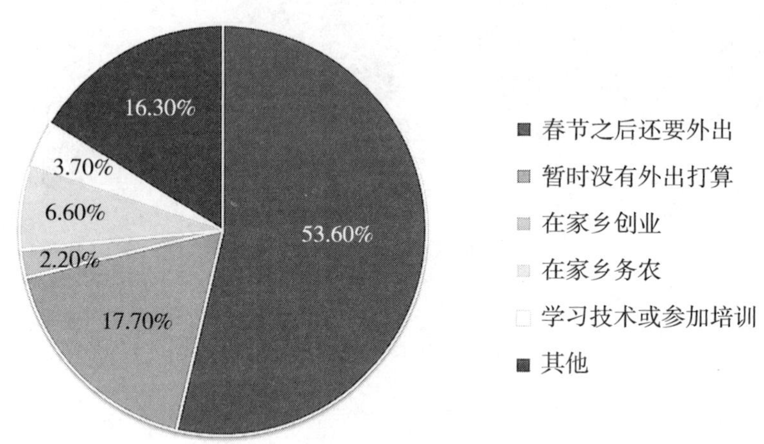

图5 安徽省外出农村人口返乡后的意愿调查

数据来源：安徽农民工返乡跟踪调查报告。

需要予以特别说明的是，虽然阜阳的经济发展模式、城镇地域组织、城镇化特征等在我国中部地区具有一定代表性。但其社会、经济条件也具有特殊性，进而使其城镇化进程呈现出不同于中部地区其他城市的特点：

首先，阜阳的经济水平较低，产业薄弱，难以提供充足的就业岗位。劳务收入成为农民最主要的收入来源之一。这推动了大量农村剩余劳动力外出务工，表现为极高的异地城镇化率。

其次，阜阳外出人口的年龄层较低、外出单次持续时间短且流动频繁。2008年，阜阳市15~19岁外出人口的比重较高（13.4%），远远高于安徽省平均水平（图6）。在外出时间结构上，阜阳外出半年至一年的人口更多，而五年以上的比例则较低（图7）。这意味，相比全国其他地区，阜阳外出人口的生根性可能较差，回流比例较高。

① 受2007年冰灾影响，一部分外出农民无法在春节回乡，所以选择2008年提前回乡。

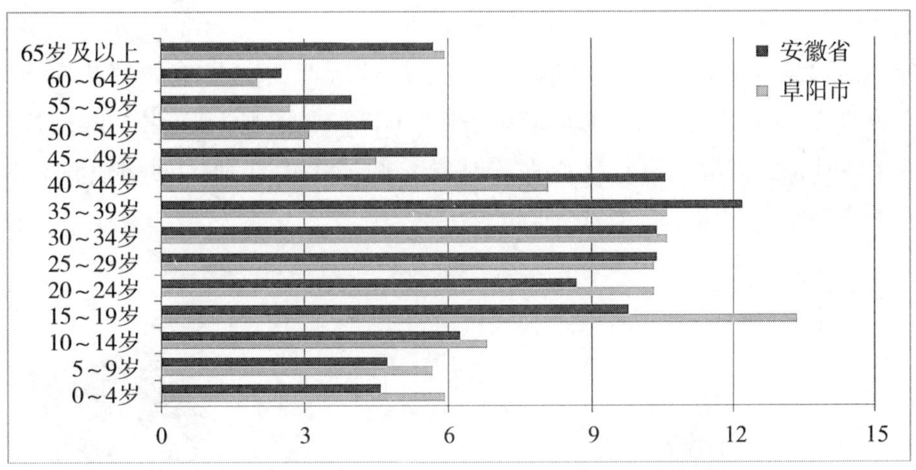

图6　2008年安徽省及阜阳市外出半年以上人口年龄结构（%）

数据来源：2008年安徽人口。

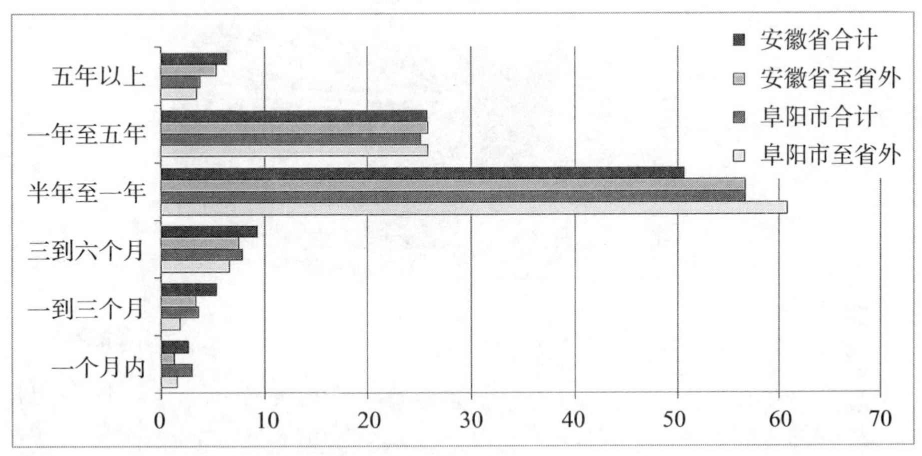

图7　2008年安徽省及阜阳市外出半年以上人口外出时间构成结构（%）

数据来源：2008年安徽人口。

四、对我国中部地区城镇化趋势的分析和推论

（一）我国中部地区城镇化的新趋势

虽然阜阳的城镇化具有其地域特殊性，无法准确地反映整个中部地区城镇化的全貌；但上文对阜阳的研究却为宏观层面的研究提供“线索”，为观察我国中部地区城镇化的一些普遍性趋势提供视角。

1. 存在大量异地城镇化人口，农村已普现“空心化”

中部地区是我国流动人口主要输出地。2008年全国跨省流出人口中，安徽占15.7%、河南占13.5%、湖南占8.3%、湖北占7.8%[6]，即，在山西、江西两省跨省流出人口尚未计入时，上述中部四省的跨省流出人口已占全国近1/2。

这些流出人口绝大多数是农村户籍人口，也就是所谓的“异地城镇化人口”。按2008年全国流动人口2.01亿[6]估计，中部地区至少有0.5亿的异地城镇化人口；若在计算城镇化率（当量）① 时将这部分人口计入，保守估计，则该年中部地区的城镇化人口占总人口46.8%左右，略高于全国水平（45.6%）[1]。

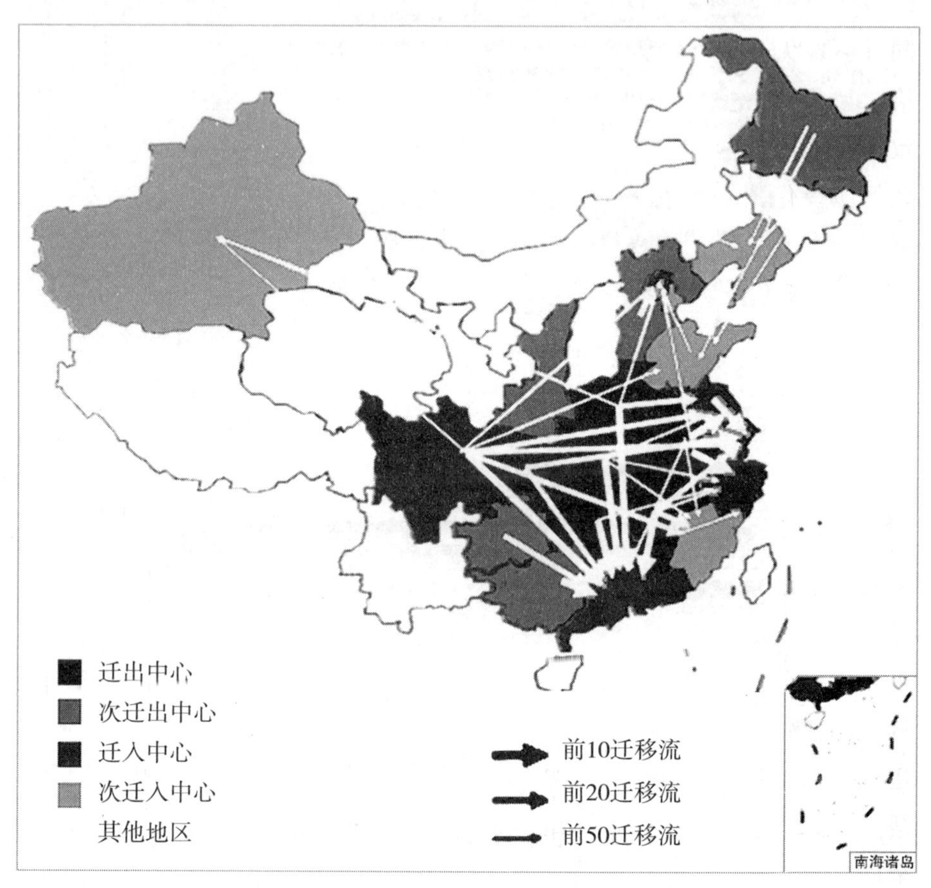

图8　跨省流动人口的分布和数量

数据来源：中国流动人口发展报告2010。

表面上，根据以上计算，中部地区至少还有3亿人口在从事农业，存在大量潜在的农村剩余劳动力；但笔者认为，这一看似与前文发现相矛盾的“现实”实际存在“数字陷阱”：

其一，国内外学者普遍认同的是，流动人口的准确数据较难统计。当前大量常年在城乡之间频繁迁移的流动人口（下文将这类人口称为“两栖人口”）已经给人口统计造成了相当的难度；加之上述数据并非出自全国人口普查数据，而是由2005年全国1%人口抽样调查估算，存在偏差可能性很大。

① 此处的城镇化率（当量）是指将异地城镇化人口视为城镇人口时，城镇人口占户籍人口总数的比重。虽然该当量并不等同于城镇化率，也并不完全准确（仍有少部分流动人口被计入城镇常住人口）。但该指标能在一定程度上反映一个地区实际的城镇化水平。

其二，所谓的“2.01亿人”或“0.5亿人”都是“流动”的概念，仅能表示在某个时间截面（或相当短时期内）的流动人口值。而在这一值的背后，是成倍的正在外出、曾经外出和打算外出人口。显然，对这一流动性极高的人群，不能囿于城乡二元的户籍分类和静态的数字统计定义。

其三，有关研究[6,29]之所以认为我国农村仍有进一步释放劳动力的空间，其原因是比较发达国家的城镇化率，我国还有近30个百分点的上升空间①。然而，我国的城镇人口与发达国家不同，存在大量的两栖人口。一方面，在城乡户籍体制下，这些人口无法平等享受城市设施供给，加之劳务收入偏低，不得不将父母和子女留在家乡（农村），以降低生活成本。这导致了在相同农村剩余劳动力水平下，城镇化率必然要低于发达国家。另一方面，我国中部地区低城镇化率的背后实际是不低的农村劳动力输出率②。

2. 乡镇经济活力下降，人口向较大城市集中成为趋势

在过去的20~30年间，乡镇经济一度成为推动我国沿海地区经济发展的重要动力。但需要认识到，我国当时尚处于“短缺经济”年代，产业经济的门槛很低；加之正处于经济全球化的高潮，大量境外加工企业在我国沿海地区登陆，以汲取“两头在外”的成本优势——某种程度上，是特殊的时代背景造就了当时乡镇经济的繁荣。而随着我国市场经济的发展成熟，乡镇经济的内在缺陷开始日益显现；在一体化的市场条件下，产业经济发展如果不依托现代基础设施、不结成产业集群，其竞争能力就不强；乡镇企业的发展遭遇瓶颈，已是许多地区的普遍现象。

乡镇经济活力下降将直接影响所谓的“就地工业化、城镇化”进程。事实上，这一概念的提出以及之后相关研究[30,31]的展开，多是针对乡镇非农经济活跃的都市区边缘地带。换言之，就地工业化、城镇化是乡镇经济在社会上的投影。后者的衰落导致乡镇地区就业岗位减少，建设滞缓，对外出人口回流并定居的吸引力也相应下降。相应地，就地城镇化进程也必然放缓。

分析全国三次1%人口抽样调查数据，近20年间，城市已经成为人口最主要的迁入地。相形之下，“镇”对人口的吸引力（见图9的“迁入”比重）在20世纪90年代中叶就已见衰减。至2000年，我国多于70%的城市人口主要分布于中等城市和大城市，远远高于其他发展中国家[32]。加之多数中部地区的乡镇经济基础尚且薄弱，当前发展又面临多重限制，欲重复东南部依靠小城镇与城市并驱来推动城镇化的可能性已相当小。

3. 户籍门槛大大降低，市场对人口资源的调配作用凸显

我国城乡二元化的户籍管理制度正式形成于1958年。此后，经历了1984年开放集镇非

① 此处是按照《中国流动人口发展报告2010》中所提出的，“所有发达国家的城镇化水平都超过70%，有的国家的城镇化水平已经超过85%”，而2009年我国城镇化率为46.6%。由此估算，得差值为30%。

② 此处的“农村劳动力输出率”是指进入城市的农村劳动力占农村劳动力总量的比重。其中，农村劳动力是指户籍所在地为农村，15~54周岁的男性和女性个人，但不包括其中的在校学生、服兵役人员，以及因身体原因不能劳动的人等。需要说明的是，有些研究将劳动力的年龄段定义为15~64周岁，但考虑到本文讨论的是外出务工劳动人口，其从事的多是重体力工作，通常在50岁左右就会选择转从他职。

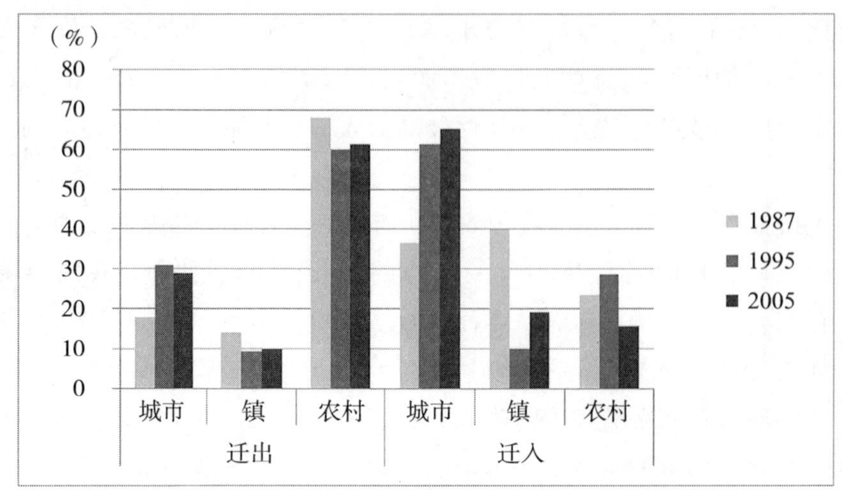

图9　1987年、1995年、2005年人口迁入地、迁出地地域构成

数据来源：Hong Yang，2005年全国1%人口抽样调查数据，2000。

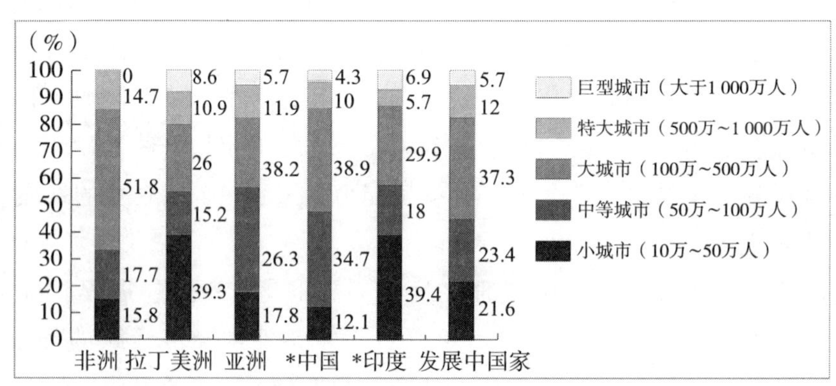

图10　2000年发展中国家城市人口分布结构（分城市规模）

资料来源：和谐城市：世界城市状况报告2008—2009年。

农业户口，以及2001年开放小城镇户籍两次重大改革①，户籍对于城镇化的影响力已经减弱。

朱宇指出[4]，“在没有户籍制度的国家，循环流动人口及其家庭的相关能力、利益和家庭资源在流入地和流出地间的配置策略；与市场需求变化相联系的流入地劳动力市场的固有波动、劳动力市场在资本密集的主要部门和劳动密集的次要部门间的分割，以及企业在此条件下的用工策略，也都是制约循环流动人口流迁行为的重要因素”。简言之，流动人口及其家庭的综合能力，劳动力市场的供需分布等成为户籍制度之外，决定人口城镇化的重要因

① 1958年1月，全国人大常委会通过并以国家主席令形式颁布了《中华人民共和国户口登记条例》。该条例以国家法律的形式对户籍管理的宗旨、户口登记的范围、主管户口登记的机关、户口簿的作用、户口申报与注销、户口迁移及手续、常住人口与暂住登记等方面都作了明确规定，标志着全国城乡统一户籍制度的正式形成。1984年10月，国务院发布《关于农民进入集镇落户问题的通知》，规定凡在集镇务工、经商、办服务业的农民和家属，在集镇有固定住所，有经营能力，或在乡镇企事业单位长期务工，准落常住户口，口粮自理。2001年3月30日国务院批转公安部《关于推进小城镇户籍管理制度改革的意见》，小城镇户籍制度改革全面推进。

素，且其重要性仍在与日俱增。

根据对阜阳的调查，包括中心城在内的安徽全省、乃至整个中部地区，除个别区域中心城市外，过去制约农业人口流入城市的户籍门槛几近消失。相对地，市场因素对于外出人口流向及其最终回流地的选择起着支配性的作用。其中，流出地与企业所能提供的岗位数量及平均收入水平相关，表现为大量流动人口集聚于东部沿海经济发达地区，尤其是这些地区的大城市、特大城市①；而回流地则与个人及家庭的经济承受能力关系最为密切[4]。

4. 农民的“身份红利”逐渐提升，较多人已不愿放弃户籍

在阜阳的乡镇调查中发现，许多农民主观上并不愿放弃农业户口。

根据《中国流动人口发展报告（2010）》中公布的两次全国性流动人口问卷调查结果，如果以交回承包地为前提，大多流动人口不愿落户于城市（图 11）[6]。尤其是“具有流动史的返乡人口”，选择“不愿意”的比重高达 66.7%。

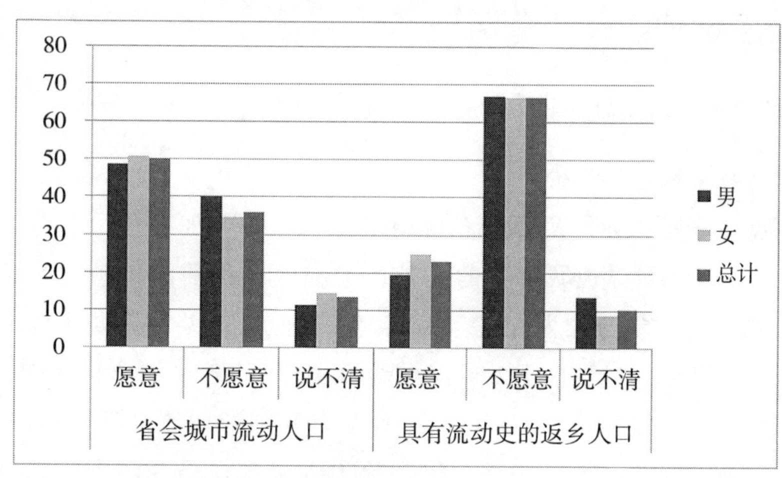

图 11　如果要您交回承包地，您愿意转为非农户口成为城里人吗（%）

数据来源：中国流动人口发展报告 2010。

此外，2010 年湖北进行的一次问卷调查②同样显示，农村居民不愿放弃农村户口的比例高达 70%；选择“进城不转户”的被访者比选择“进城转户”者多出十个百分点左右（图 12）。

造成这一现象的根源在于农业户口与土地承包权、宅基地分配、集体股份分红等利益的直接挂钩关系。一方面，近年来，随着农村土地股份合作社、集体土地流转机制等的不断探索，被城乡双轨制所抑制的集体土地价值正在不断地被释放，集体建设用地及承包地已经成为农民所掌握的最重要资源。另一方面，虽然近年我国城乡之间的壁垒和差异已经逐步消减，但不可否认的是，外出农民仍没有被完全纳入城市社会保障体系中。这使得他们不得不

① 下文将大城市、特大城市统称为“大城市”。

② 这一调查由同济大学和华中科技大学《湖北省城镇化与城镇发展战略规划研究》课题组完成。问卷调查了湖北省的 7 个小城镇、30 多个县城；总计发放 1500 份问卷，共回收 1391 份有效问卷。

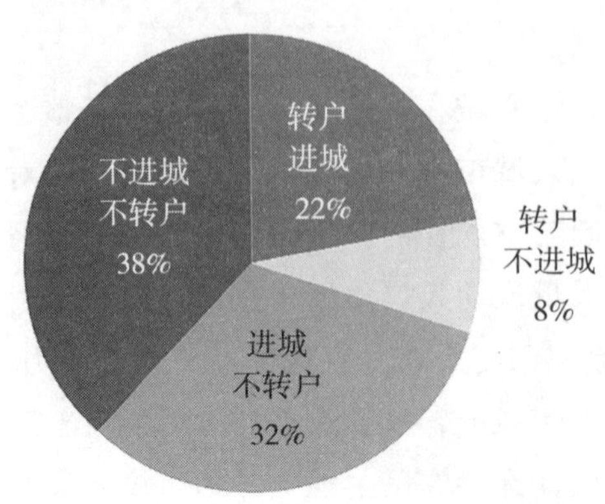

图12 湖北省农村人口迁居意向问卷调查结果

数据来源：湖北省城镇化与城镇发展战略规划研究，2010。

担心一旦失去工作，生活保障从何而来。因此，承包地成为了农民在城市难以维生时的“退路”或最后的保障[6,33]。

（二）对中部地区城镇化总体趋势的若干判断

1. 流出人口的规模增速将趋缓

综合之前观点，笔者认为，我国的农村剩余劳动力并非如有些学者认为的“近于无穷大”[34]。事实上，若计入对异地城镇化的贡献，中部地区目前的城镇化水平已经不低。此外，农村“空心化”的现象已较为普遍。因此，在当前的公共财力及个体的经济能力许可条件下，中部地区的流出人口规模不太可能再延续过去近3个百分点的年增速。

根据《中国流动人口发展报告（2010）》预测，我国新增流动人口数将在2015年前后达到高峰，之后逐渐下降[6]。鉴于中部地区的流出人口规模已经较大，农村剩余劳动力数量有限，可以判断，中部地区新增流动人口数量达到峰值并趋于下降的时间拐点将会早于全国来到。

2. 异地城镇化人口回流将成为本地城镇化的主要动力

（1）从区域经济发展趋势判断

我国大规模的人口迁移源于区域经济发展的不均衡。然而，自“十一五”以来，一方面，我国的经济发展模式以及区域发展战略已经有所调整，尤其是受到2008年的金融危机影响，中央政府开始重视内需对经济的拉动作用和区域板块的均衡发展；另一方面，受到生产成本上升等因素影响，一些原址在东南沿海的产业也已经开始逐步向中部城市转移。从2007年开始，我国中西部的发展速率已超越东部地区（见图13）。虽然由于起跑线不同，区域差异还将长期存在，但至少我国区域差异不断扩大的趋势及速度已经有所扭转。

区域发展格局的变化反映在城镇化上，即虽然目前我国流动人口主要集聚于东部地区（尤其是京津冀、长三角、珠三角三个城镇群地区）（见图14）；但未来，随着中部经济的发展，与东部地区在就业机会、城镇建设水平等方面的差距将会缩小，从而有可能吸引部分在异地的城镇化人口回流。

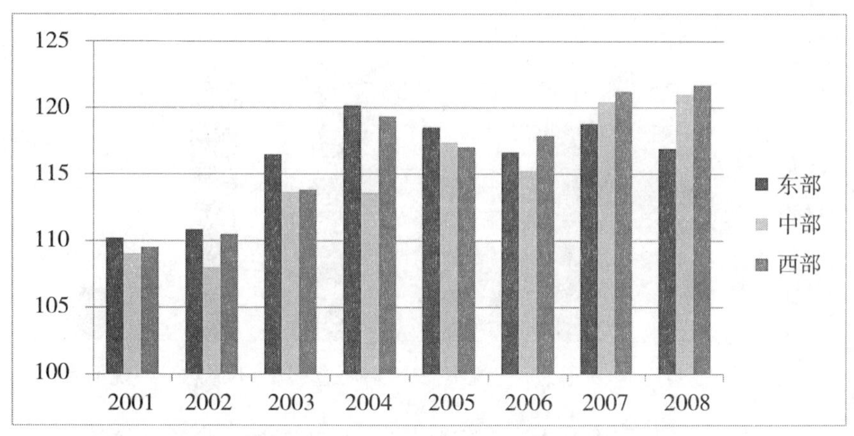

图 13　2001—2008 年全国分区域地区生产值指数（上一年 =100）

数据来源：《中国统计年鉴（2009）》。

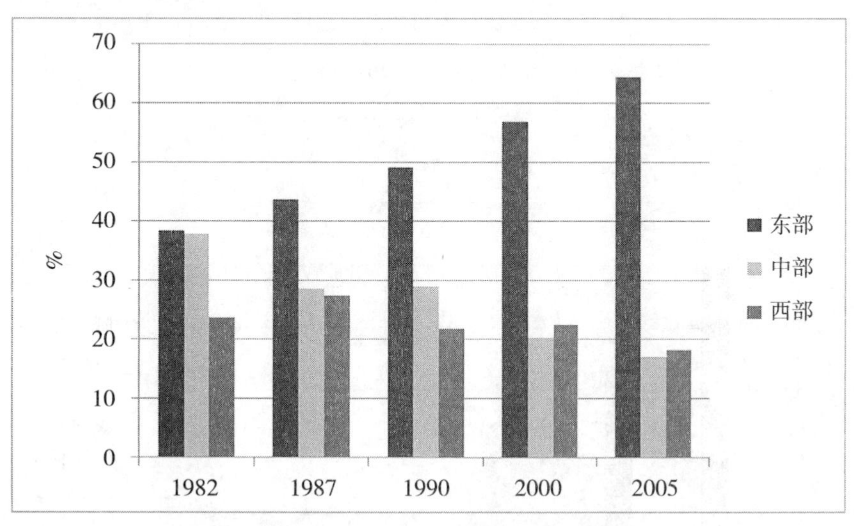

图 14　流动人口在东、中、西三大区域的分布（%）

数据来源：《中国流动人口发展报告（2010）》。

（2）从外出人口回流趋势判断

据调查，由于思想意识、生活习惯等原因，外出人口将倾向于定居至城镇地区，成为“新市民”（见图 15、图 16）。而笔者认为，虽然流动人口在选择流入地时更多考虑就业机会、收入水平等因素，倾向于选择东南沿海地区；但在定居地的空间选择上则较为均衡，相当比例的人员会选择回流中部。理由如下。

首先，如前文分析，流动人口定居地的选择极大程度取决于其经济能力。农村流出人口大部分文化程度较低，劳动技能不高，加之其他社会性因素，因而劳务收入大都偏低。据 2004 年全国 6 城市流动人口抽样调查显示，流动人口月均收入在 1 000 元以下的占 90% 以上，其中有接近 45% 的流动人口月收入在 500 元以下[35]。可以大致判断，其收入结构呈现“金字塔形”。即经济能力由低到高，人数成倍缩减。与之对应的，按“家乡附近中小城镇—中部大城市—东部中小城市—东部大城市”的顺序，选择将其作为定居地的人口数也

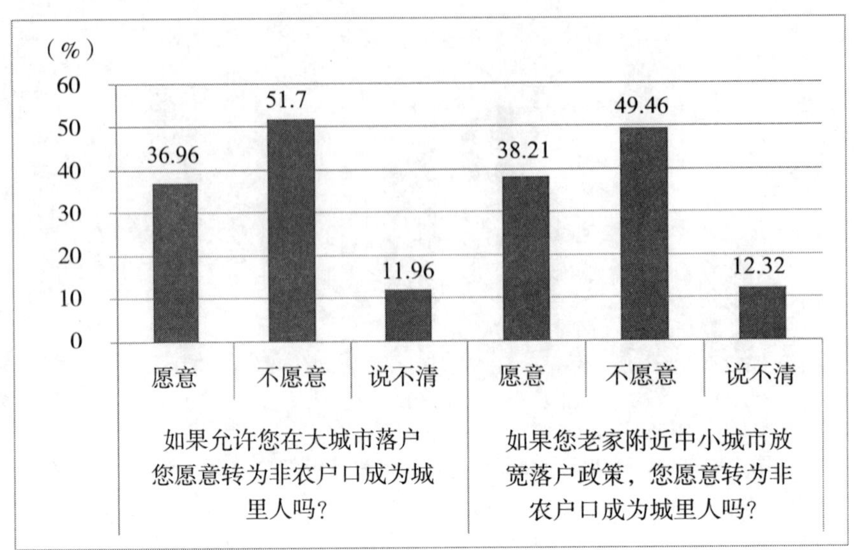

图 15　回乡流动人口的落户意愿（%）

数据来源:《中国流动人口发展报告（2010)》。

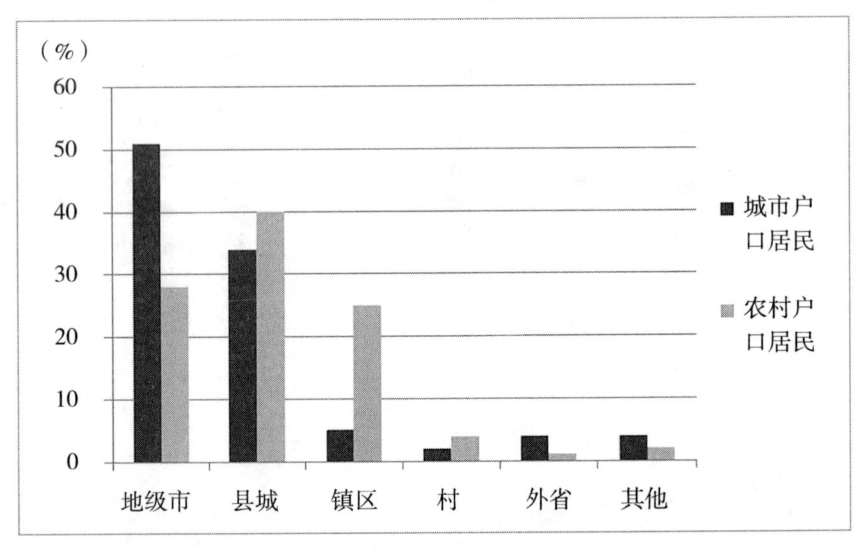

图 16　湖北省按户籍分居民迁居意愿

数据来源：湖北省城镇化与城镇发展战略规划研究。

将逐级减少。

其次，在当前城乡户籍和土地体制不发生重大调整的前提下，部分外出农民基于“身份红利”不愿放弃农村户籍、“进城不转户”的现象还将持续。而为了享受和维护自身在农村集体中的权益，尤其是土地权益，不愿放弃原来身份的外出农民将倾向于定居在家乡附近的城镇。此外，诸如“落叶归根”、“乡土情结”等社会因素也使部分外出人口选择回家乡[①]定居。

① 除特别指出外，此处及下文的“家乡”泛指外出人口原户籍所属的地级市、甚至省。

基于以上判断，笔者认为，在适当引导下，中部地区的异地城镇化人口转为“本地城镇化”人口并非不可能。自2007年起，中部外出农民回流比例持续增高已从一个侧面证实了这一判断。如截至2008年12月底，湖南、河南、湖北三省农民工返乡率分别都在20%以上，均比2007年有所上升[36]。可能有所不同的是，目前中部外出人口的回流主要源于东部地区就业机会缩减而产生的“推力”；但如若未来从中部地区自身“引力”提升着手，可以预计，将有更大规模的人口回流发生，并大大推动中部地区的城镇化进程。

3. 与沿海地区不同的城镇化模式

在过去的30年间，以东南沿海地区为代表，我国的城镇化曾探索出一条以乡镇为载体、发展乡镇企业和就地城镇化/农村城镇化的成功道路，形成了独特的模式。然而，正如之前所述，这一模式是当时特定时空背景下的产物，在现时并不一定可行。

必须正视的是，中部地区乡镇的经济活力及其发展条件都远不如沿海地区；更为重要的是，当前的发展环境已经不允许重复过去东南沿海相对粗放的、资源高消耗型的分散工业化和分散城镇化路径。在新的历史时期，中央领导高瞻远瞩，一再强调“要转变发展方式”。落实到城镇化发展上，就是要走一条资源集约型、环境友好型的健康城镇化道路。

结合前文对中部地区城镇化的特征分析及趋势判断，笔者认为，未来中部地区的城镇化将有着“异地城镇化”和“就近集中城镇化”的内在需求或趋势。

首先，需要明确的是，虽然存在推动外出人口回流的潜在机制，中部仍将是我国重要的劳务输出区域，即存在大量的异地城镇化人口。

其次，在这一地区，乡镇经济的基础尚且薄弱，未来发展前景尚不明朗。虽然不可否认，存在偶然因素可能会支持个别镇的较大发展，但总体上，小城镇所能提供的就业岗位，或对农村剩余劳动力、外出人口的吸引力和吸纳能力都十分有限，难以支撑“就地城镇化”的愿景。

再次，相比华北、东北沿海地区，中部大中城市的密度低、距离远，辐射范围难以覆盖整个区域。因此，小城市，尤其是县级城市在补充大中城市服务区域，可以在吸引回流人口等方面起到重要作用。

最后，除了已经具备中小城市能级，或有条件加以重点培育的个别镇之外，乡镇一级小城镇的职能重在服务“三农”，而不再以发展工业及作为城镇化的重要承载地为目标。

总而言之，今后中部地区要继续鼓励劳务经济及完善异地城镇化政策、从而使得相当部分流出人口能够真正融入所在城镇；同时，随着地区经济社会发展速度的加快，未来中部地区城市所承担的城镇化份额将日益扩大。其中，中小城市（包括县城）的作用尤为重要，将成为中部地区城镇人口的主要承载地之一。即，进城农民以及外出回流人口趋于选择其户籍所在地附近的中小城市，实现“就近集中城镇化”。

五、中部地区城镇化的挑战与应对

（一）城镇化路径的转型与创新

由于城镇化的模式不同，中部地区需要基于自身特点，适应宏观环境的变化，在城乡资源配置、城镇经济政策、城镇地域组织、城乡设施供给等方面有所创新，以充分体现“就近集中城镇化”原则。尤其从提高城镇化效率、减少不必要的资源浪费出发，提高城镇化的“集中度”。

具体而言，就是以县域为单位，引导城镇人口向县级市或县城集中；重视中小城市（包括县城）在城镇化中的重要作用，培育和完善中小城市体系，引导县域经济的特色发展，增强这些城市对于城镇人口的吸引力；鼓励外出人口回乡（户籍所在地附近的城市地区）创业，依托“打工经济”所获得的资金、人才、技术等资源而发展本地经济。

而在乡镇一级，规划建设中应控制“三农服务型”小城镇的人口、建设用地规模；但同时，对于其面向农村社区的公共服务能力及必要的基础设施配置则要大力加强。要实现这一目标，则有赖于合理的配置标准、相应的管理能力及财政转移支付的力度。

（二）向异地城镇化人口主动提供服务

正如上文判断，中部地区仍将存在大规模、高比例的异地城镇化人口，且这些人口中的绝大多数为“两栖人口”。

虽然从积极的方面看，这些两栖人口“外地挣钱、本地消费”，刺激了中部城市和乡镇的零售商业发展；他们“外地学艺”，有的成为家乡的“精英分子”，为中部地区带来了先进的文化、理念，并为本地经济发展做出了贡献。

但同时，大规模的异地城镇化也造成了诸多负面影响：一方面，中部地区大量的人力、资金、技术和社会资本流失，本地工业经济发展动力不足；另一方面，由于“流动人口”并未完成户籍身份转换，而被视为介于农民、城镇居民的第三类人口[7]，无法平等地享受工作所在城市提供的设施和服务，也没有被纳人工作地的福利体系中。在这一体制下，目前异地城镇化的成本有相当比例为流动人口本人及其户籍所在地的农村社区所承担，诸如与“留守儿童”、“人口老龄化”等相关的一系列社会问题的广为存在就是佐证。

因此，在未来，要实现健康和谐的城镇化，中部地区必须承认和正视异地城镇化问题。一是主动承担异地城镇化的部分成本，为农村外出人口提供专门的职业培训、就业指导、子女教育、老年人口（包括外出人口的父辈）社会化服务等。二是充分认识到外出人口的“流动性”和“两栖性”。在城镇建设、产业发展、城乡设施的供给和布局等方面要为其周期性“回乡”和长期“回流”预留空间。

（三）积极引导和应对外出人口的回流

未来5至10年，我国“第一代农民工”将面临选择定居地的切实问题①，他们的选择不仅关系到自身及其家眷的最终流向，也会极大程度地影响到“第二代农民工”（其中，相当一部分为“第一代”的子女）的选择。在这一重要的时间转捩点，中部地区必须抓住时机，积极引导外出人口回流，探索出一条与该进程相适应的城镇化道路。

但需要强调的是，外出人口的回流对于中部地区也是一把“双刃剑”。一方面，人口回流将大大推动中部地区的城镇化进程，并带回资金、技术等发展资本；但另一方面，随着回流人口及其家眷的“市民化”，将产生大量的设施、服务、福利要求。其中，还存在相当数量的因年老力衰被迫回流的人口，他们对于养老、医疗等设施及福利的要求将尤其突出。而这些都将给中部城镇带来巨大的财政负担。

因此，对外出人口回流，首先，要做到积极吸引。通过发展本地经济，加快城镇建设，改善创业环境，扩充就业机会，予以政策支持，加强宣传力度，以鼓励外出务工人员回乡创业/就业。其次，引导回流人口合理布局。基于“就近集中城市化”原则，应通过市场、政策、户籍制度等调控手段，鼓励回流人口选择在城市地区“集聚”。同时，充分预计回流人口对于城乡设施、就业岗位、城镇环境等多方面的需求，未雨绸缪而积极应对。

六、结论

如果说，20世纪80年代至今，东部地区率先发展，主导了我国经济发展和城镇化进程；那么，未来相当长一段时期，中部地区将极大程度地影响我国城镇化的发展轨迹。可以肯定的是，包括中部地区在内，我国的城镇化不可能再重复20世纪80—90年代东部地区的模式，而是必须探索出一条符合时代精神、适应资源和环境条件的新道路。

本文提出，中部地区的城镇化进程，可以“异地城镇化”和“就近集中城镇化”为基本形式，同时充分考虑人口流动因素。

总体而言，未来我国的城镇化将呈现不同区域的多元形式共存的格局。相应地，基于地区微观机制研究，聚焦于区域板块的城镇化研究显得十分有必要。从方法论角度而言，本文的意义在于从中微观的案例研究切入，辨析有关地区的真实状况，进而探讨该类地区城镇化特征、趋势与挑战。

（作者：程遥，同济大学建筑与城市规划学院博士生；赵民，同济大学筑与城市规划学院教授）

① “第一代农民工”是自20世纪八九十年代外出务工的农村人口。若按当时年龄为20岁计算，未来5～10年，这些人口将达50岁，不再适宜从事重体力工作，倾向于结束“两栖生活”，选择定居地。

参考文献

[1] 中华人民共和国国家统计局．中国统计年鉴（2001—2009）［M］．北京：中国统计出版社，2001—2009.

[2] 人口计生委发展规划司．国家人口发展战略研究报告［R/OL］．2007 - 01 - 11. http：//www. chinapop. gov. cn/fzgh/zlyj.

[3] 联合国人口司．World Urbanization Prospect，the 2009 Revision［DB/OL］．http：//esa. un. org/wup2009/unup.

[4] 朱宇．国外对非永久性迁移的研究及其对我国流动人口问题的启示［J］．人口研究，2004（3）：52 - 59.

[5] 世界银行．2009 年世界发展报告：重塑世界，经济地理［R］．华盛顿：世界银行，2008.

[6] 国家人口计划生育委员会流动人口服务管理司．中国流动人口发展报告 2010［R］．北京：中国人口出版社，2010.

[7] 吕雪莉．我国人口分布将形成“三分天下”格局［N］．共产党员，2009（5）：49.

[8] John Friedmann. The Next 400 Millions：Reflections on City-building in China［A］．全球视角下的中国范式——城市发展与规划会议论文集［C］，2010.

[9] John Friedmann. China's Urban Transition［M］．Minneapolis：University of Minnesota Press，2005：65.

[10] Hong Yang. A comparative analysis of China' s permanent and temporary migration during the reform period［J］．International Journal of Social Economics，2000（3）：173 - 193.

[11] 周一星，于海波．以“五普”数据为基础对我国城镇化水平修补的建议［J］．统计研究，2002（4）：45.

[12] 张颖，赵民．论城市化与经济发展的相关性——对钱纳里研究成果的辨析与延伸［J］．城市规划汇刊，2003（4）：17.

[13] 侯静珠，魏广君．中国城镇化快速发展期的思考［J］．小城镇建设，2009（12）：27 - 29.

[14] 周一星．关于中国城镇化速度的思考［J］．城市规划，2006（增刊）：33 - 35.

[15] 邓宇鹏．中国的隐性超城市化［J］．东莞理工学院学报，2000（1）：61.

[16] 陆大道，姚士谋．中国城镇化进程的科学思辨［J］．人文地理，2007（4）：1 - 6.

[17] 张同升．中国城镇化发展的现状、问题与对策［J］．城市问题，2009（8）：23 - 25.
刘新卫．中国城镇化发展现状及特点［J］．国土资源情报，2007（7）：42 - 46.

[18] 朱宇．城市化的二元分析框架与我国乡村城市化研究［J］．人口研究，2001（2）：53 - 59.

[19] 朱宇．城镇化的新形式与中国的人口城镇化政策［J］．人文地理，2006（2）：117 - 118.

[20] McGee，T. G.，C. S. Lin，A. M. Marton，Y. - L. Wang and J. Wu. China's urban space：Development under market socialism［M］．London and New York：Routledge，2007.

[21] 辜胜阻．中国城镇化的发展特点及其战略思路［J］．经济地理，1991（3）：27.
辜胜阻，李永周．进一步优化农村城镇化的战略对策［J］．中国人口科学，2000（3）：5.

[22] 辜胜阻，李华，易善策．城镇化是扩大内需实现经济可持续发展的引擎［J］．中国人口科学 2010（3）：6.

[23] 蔡禾，王进．“农民工”永久迁移意愿研究［J］．社会学研究，2007（6）：97 - 107.
国家人口计生委流动人口服务管理司．提前返乡流动人口调查报告［R］．人口研究，2009（2）．
梅建明．进城农民的“农民市民化”意愿考察［J］．华中师范大学学报（人文社会科学版），2006

(11).

黄振华.农民工返乡和留乡的基本态势与特征分析[J].财经问题研究,2009(7).

王哲,光钧.皖西农民工迁移与市民化意愿倾向分析[J].乡镇经济,2006(7).

施晓娟.住建部:农民工定居城镇的住房政策欲出台[N].广州日报,2010-02-26.

林玉妹,朱孟哲,林善浪.福建农村劳动力转移的行为特征[J].发展研究,2008(10).

李梅,高明国.金融危机背景下的农民工回流特征分析[J].农村经济,2009(12).

[24] 阜阳市统计局.阜阳统计年鉴(2001—2009)[M].安徽:阜阳市统计局,2001—2009.

[25] 安徽省统计局.安徽统计年鉴(2001—2009)[M].安徽:安徽省统计局,2001—2009.

[26] 安徽省统计局.2000、2001、2003、2007、2008年安徽人口[Z].2009.

[27] 国家统计局阜阳调查队.2008年阜阳农村劳务输出情况调查分析[Z/OL].http://www.ahdc.gov.cn/dt2111111144.asp?docid=2111132208,2009.

[28] 国家统计局安徽调查总队.安徽农民工返乡跟踪调查报告[Z/OL].2009-01-22.http://www.ahdc.gov.cn.

[29] 信春霞.中国人口城市化率的深层次分析[J].上海财经大学学报,2002(12):40.

朱丕荣.世界城市化与中国城镇化的发展趋势[J].世界农业,2001(4):12.

杨风,陶斯文.中国城镇化发展的历程、特点与趋势[J].兰州学刊,2010(6):76.

[30] Zhu Y. Beyond large-city-centered urbanization: in situ transformation of rural areas in Fujian Province [J]. Asia-Pacific View Point, 2002 (1): 9-22.

[31] 邵怀友,朱宇.大城市周边城乡融合区人口的就地城镇化——以福州市为例[J].市场与人口分析,2007(1):13-16.

[32] 联合国人居署.和谐城市:世界城市状况报告2008—2009[M].北京:中国建筑工业出版社,2008.

[33] 梅建明.进城农民的"农民市民化"意愿考察——对武汉市782名进城务工农民的调查分析[J].华中师范大学学报(人文社会科学版),2006(11).

王天宇.沿海发达地区农地流转中的农户意愿实证分析——以浙江省宁波市为例[J].宁波大学学报(人文科学版),2010(1):86.

[34] 周一星.中国的城镇化有别于其他国家的六大特点[N].城市规划通讯,2009(14).

[35] 王广州.当今我国的流动人口特点以及生存状况[EB/OL].2006-02-21.光明观察,http://guancha.gmw.cn/.

[36] 龙立珍.湖南农民工返乡情况跟踪调查报告[R/OL].2009-09-28.http://www.hndc.gov.cn.

海南转型跨越发展的战略与行动

——“国际旅游岛”建设进行时

引　言

经过30多年的改革开放，我国进入了发展的战略转型期。“十二五”规划明确提出了“科学发展”的主题和“加快转变经济发展方式”的主线，围绕主题、主线的转型发展成为“主旋律”，不同地区基于自身特点和国家战略要求，都在展开转型发展的探索和实践。

海南的资源特点、生态环境、区位条件和产业基础具有独特性，转型发展的要求迫切。2009年12月31日颁布的《国务院关于推进海南国际旅游岛建设发展的若干意见》（国发〔2009〕44号文），从国家战略层面明确了海南新的发展定位与要求，为海南的转型发展明确了新的发展方向。一年多以来，海南省委、省政府紧紧围绕“国际旅游岛”建设的要求，以“强岛富民”为目标，以“跨越传统工业化阶段”为基本取向，迈开了新时期海南转型跨越发展的新步伐。这一时期，中国城市规划设计研究院先后承接了包括《海南省城乡经济社会发展一体化总体规划》、《海南国际旅游岛先行试验区规划研究》等在内的，从宏观到微观的一系列规划项目，参与和近距离观察了“国际旅游岛”战略下海南转型发展逐步开展的全过程。

战略与行动相结合、整体框架与项目实施同步推进，是一年多来“国际旅游岛”建设的最大特点。概括起来，一年多以来的工作可以分为三个层面。第一，在认识层面，全省上下通过宣传、学习和讨论，统一了对“国际旅游岛”丰富内涵的正确认识；第二，结合“国际旅游岛”的发展要求，认真分析了省情，学习借鉴国外的经验，谋划了海南未来一段时期转型跨越发展的整体框架和战略路径；第三，划定了陵水黎安作为“国际旅游岛先行试验区”起步区，率先启动了具体的规划建设，先试先行、以点带面。海南的转型跨越发展探索具有很强的示范借鉴意义，本文结合项目实践，从认识、战略和行动三个层面总结对“国际旅游岛”建设的观察，以期对其他城市和地区的发展有所借鉴。

一、认识层面：系统理解“国际旅游岛”的丰富内涵

国家从战略层面，明确提出了海南国际旅游岛建设的目标是形成“两区三地一平台”，即我国旅游业改革创新的试验区、世界一流的海岛休闲度假旅游目的地、全国生态文明建设示范区、国际经济合作和文化交流的重要平台、南海资源开发和服务基地和国家热带现代农业基地。进而逐步将海南建设成为生态环境优美、文化魅力独特、社会文明祥和的开放之岛、绿色之岛、文明之岛、和谐之岛。

海南国际旅游岛上升为国家战略，其意义不仅仅是促进海南发展模式的战略转型，更表现为通过海南岛的进一步开放，为新时期国家参与全球竞争与合作探索积累新的经验，推进我国新一轮的全方位对外开放。一定程度上讲，建设海南国际旅游岛事关国家科学发展和改革开放的全局。

针对“国际旅游岛”战略出台后已经或将可能产生的认识偏差，海南省委、省政府首先通过各种途径，统一了对“国际旅游岛”战略的正确认识，较为系统地阐述“国际旅游岛”战略不仅仅是指发展旅游业，而是对海南未来很长一段时期经济社会发展全面的、综合性的战略部署，具有丰富的内涵体系，实现国际旅游岛建设的目标需要经济、社会、城镇化、城乡关系等多方面的支撑。国发〔2009〕44 号文共分为 9 个部分、28 条具体意见，内容涵盖了总体要求、生态文明建设、旅游业发展与管理、现代服务业发展、现代农业发展与城乡一体化、基础设施、社会建设、新型工业发展、政策保障措施等方面，是一个丰富的完整体系。具体可分为国际、国家和海南省三个层面的战略意义和内容要求。

在国际层面，主要是代表我国在海岛旅游、生态环境、现代服务和特色文化四个方面参与国际竞争与合作。

在国家层面，海南国际旅游岛的建设是国家的发展转型示范区，需要在经济发展方式转变、生态文明建设和旅游业改革创新方面先行先试，改革创新积累经验。

在海南层面，国际旅游岛建设的根本目的在于“强岛富民”，通过国际旅游岛建设实现区域协调、城乡协调、民生改善和社会和谐。

二、战略层面：谋划转型跨越发展的整体框架与路径

（一）着眼于空间资源的有效配置，构建转型跨越发展的整体框架

从规划和建设的角度看，“国际旅游岛”真正的内在核心是国家在战略层面对海南空间资源的优化配置提出了明确的方向和要求。具体而言，包括发展和保护两个方面，保护方面，核心是要求必须严格保护住国家唯一的热带资源和优良的生态环境；发展方面，核心是明确了资源价值最大化导向下的海南新的发展路径，即构建以旅游业为龙头、现代服务业为主导的现代产业体系。

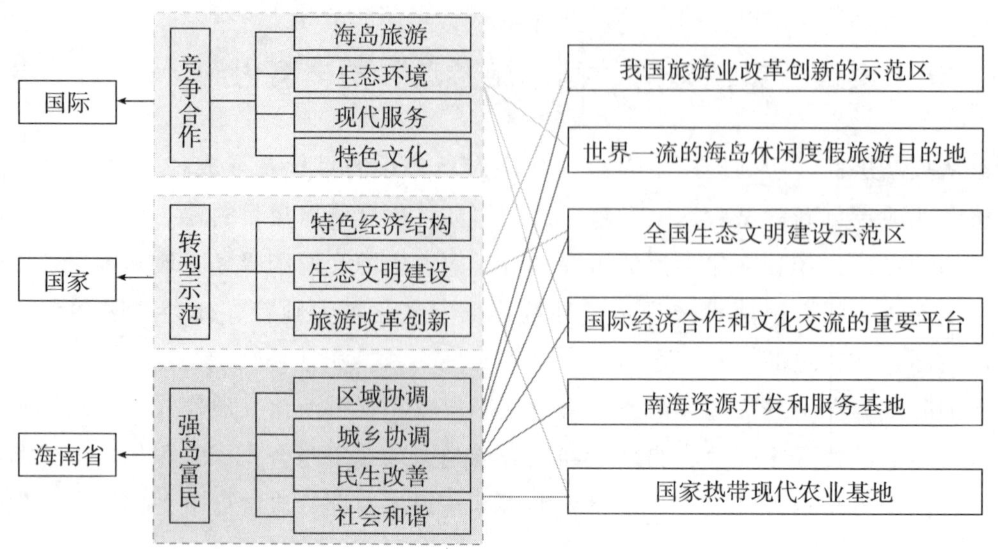

图1 “国际旅游岛”战略的丰富内涵

因此，对于“国际旅游岛”建设而言，需要构建四大核心体系作为支撑。

第一，以建设高品质的宜居环境为目标，构建生态为核心的绿色体系。首先，划定空间开发边界，严格保护住生态环境本底。对省级以上的自然保护区、水源保护区、生态敏感区和红树林保护区等由省级政府统一管理严格保护下来。其次，发挥规划的引导性，主动地构建全省的景观格局，包括依托河流水系、山体建设生态景观廊道，促进中部山区的“绿色景观”向沿海发展地区渗透，对于河口、泻湖、海湾等多类型景观密集的地区主动打造一些特色化的景观节点等，这些景观廊道、景观节点既是生态环境整体保护的一部分，同时本身也是旅游景点之一。最后，对于全省的核心资源必须从省级政府的角度进行统一规划和管理，包括海岸带、近海海域等。

第二，根据海南的资源特点与国家要求，构建绿色发展的现代产业体系。首先需要明确，对于海南而言，通过大力发展工业实现传统意义上的工业化，进而谋求海南的整体发展，无论是从现实基础，还是从未来需求看，都不是最优的选择。海南未来产业发展的重点是形成以旅游业为龙头、现代服务业为支撑的现代产业体系。

第三，资源的不可分割性以及保障全省城乡居民资源收益公平分享的需要决定了海南的国际旅游岛建设必须与推进全省城乡经济社会发展一体化相辅相成。因此，构建以一体化为特点的城乡体系也是一个重要方面。具体包括，根据国际旅游岛的功能要求，主动地强化和调整核心城市的功能；根据旅游业发展的客观需要，培育量大面广的乡村服务点；发挥小城镇承上启下的连接作用，对小城镇发展进行具体的分类引导；面向西部地区旅游业未来发展的需要，主动地选择和重点建设“新城”作为服务中心等。

第四，根据海南的特点，因地制宜地规划、建设一套设施体系作为支撑。首先，根据海南中部山区到沿海平原台地的“圈层”结构特点，有针对性地建立快慢适中、内外有别的省域交通骨架，避免高速公路穿越中部山区，一方面保护环境，另一方面节约建设成本；其次，根据海南岛面积小、通达性好的特点，采取组织“生活圈”的方式配置服务设施体系，一方面满足基本公共服务需求，另一方面满足国际旅游岛的服务要求；最后，省级政府需要从国际旅游岛建设的高度出发，对全省各个层面的基础设施建设提出标准体系，统一规划、加强管理。

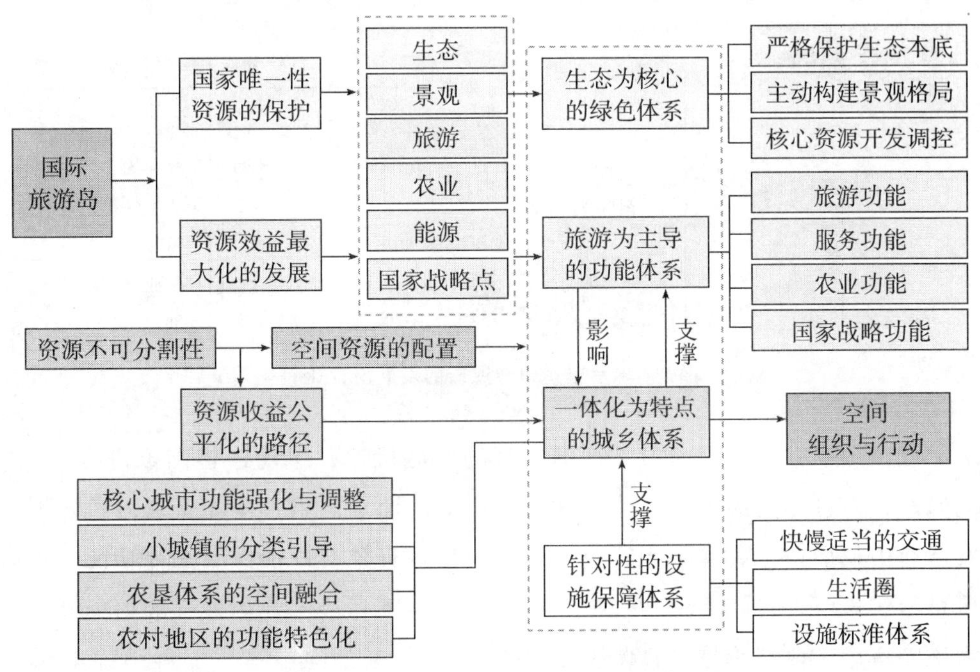

图2 “国际旅游岛”建设的整体框架

（二）吸收和借鉴国外发展经验，明确海南转型跨越的实施路径

找准参照系，吸纳和借鉴国外相关地区的发展经验，对海南谋划新的发展思路和发展路径具有重要意义。在《海南省城乡经济社会发展一体化总体规划》中深入剖析了佛罗里达州经济社会持续发展的历程阶段、动力来源及基本经验等，从中获取对海南国际旅游岛建设和转型跨越发展的相关启示。

从发展历程看，佛罗里达州先后经历了农业主导、早期旅游业发展、旅游产业拓展、军工业发展、高科技产业发展，跨越了传统工业化阶段，形成了多元化产业体系。在20世纪40年代美国已整体进入后工业化时期，而佛罗里达州依然是个相对落后的农业州。经过近几十年坚持不懈地发展旅游业、现代服务业和高新技术产业，该州实现了跨越式发展。海南发展历程也与其高度相似，目前正处于旅游产业拓展和新型工业发展阶段。借鉴佛罗里达州经验，确定海南转型跨越发展的七大实施路径。

1. 在全国整体发展格局中准确把握海南的发展定位

佛罗里达州在发展过程中，始终围绕区位、气候、生态等资源优势，在全美产业格局中准确把握自己的特色定位，抓住美国历次产业转型升级的历史机遇，坚持走以旅游业、现代服务业、高新技术产业为主导的特色发展道路，实现了跨越式发展。

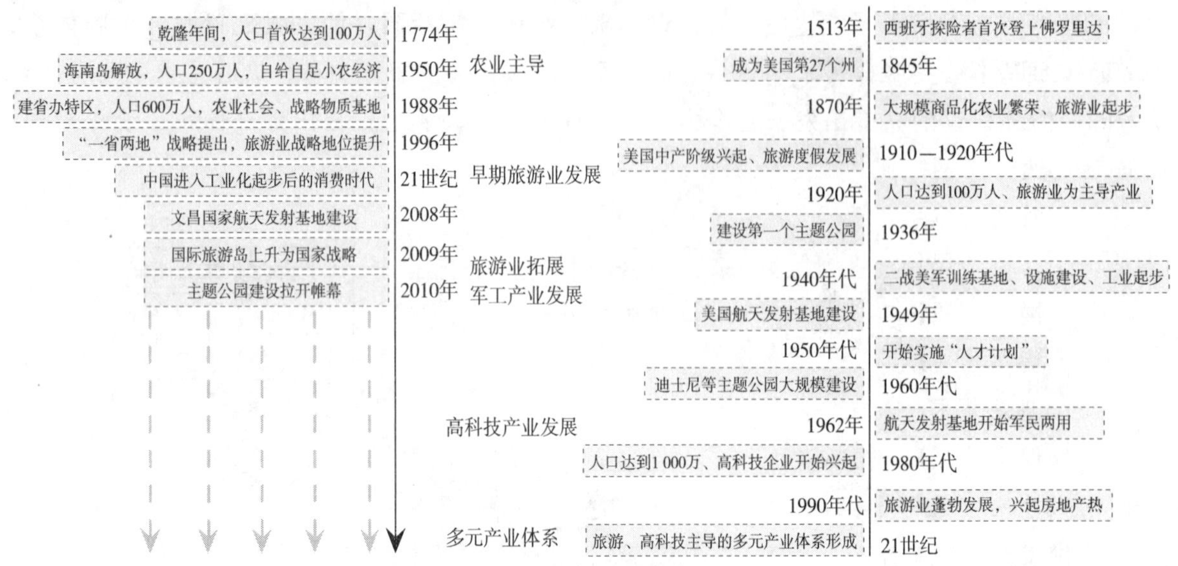

图3 佛罗里达州与海南的发展历程比较

海南应该在国家整体发展阶段下把握自身的发展机遇，主动迎接国家进入"消费时代"的战略机遇期，面对国内庞大的工业化腹地所产生的消费需求，率先实现绿色发展。在全国整体发展格局中找准特色，着眼于资源优势最大化，有针对性地发展主导功能，走海南特色的发展道路。

2. 培育以五大产业群为核心的现代产业体系

支撑佛罗里达州经济的产业门类主要包括旅游业、现代服务业、高新技术产业和现代农业等。州政府为了促进经济发展，有重点地打造了若干重点产业空间，引导产业发展。高新技术产业方面，集中、集约形成了"三核一走廊"格局，分别是西部依托交通枢纽和南佛罗里达大学的高科技产业区、东部围绕火箭发射基地的高科技产业区、东南部围绕西棕榈海滩的尖端技术公司集聚区，以及沿中部高速公路的高科技走廊。旅游业方面，加大创意性景点的开发力度，全州共有各类主题公园 335 个，形成了三大主题公园空间集聚区，分别是北部滨海地区以怀旧纪念为特色的集聚区、南部围绕迈阿密集聚的滨水主题公园集聚区、中部以奥兰多为核心的探险文化娱乐主题公园集聚区。

无论是从现实的发展基础，还是从未来的发展趋向看，海南都不会出现传统工业占据主导地位的工业化阶段。跨越传统工业化阶段，积极发展服务型、开放型、生态型经济，形成以旅游业为龙头、现代服务业为主导的特色经济结构，是海南国际旅游岛建设的重要内容。通过对三次产业重点领域，以及由融合而产生的新兴产业进行重新整合、重组，构建由现代服务业、新型工业、高新技术产业、热带现代农业和海洋经济组成的五大产业群。

3. 建立高效快捷的现代立体综合交通系统

基础设施是支撑佛罗里达州发展最重要的前提。目前，全州有 16 个国际机场、35 个国内机场，铁路全长 4 800 多公里，三条州际高速公路通往美国各州，5 个主要邮轮母港、14 个深水商港，基本实现了交通网络全覆盖。

结合海南自然资源环境特征，以对外通达性与对内便捷性为导向，建立高效快捷的现代立体综合交通系统。首先，加强对外交通发展，包括加强跨海交通建设、健全空港体系、完善以“四方五港”为基础的全省港口体系等。其次，完善省域交通系统，包括加强环岛交通，构建高速公路网络，加强全岛横向和纵向联系，改造提升国道、省道、县道等。再次，精心建设旅游交通体系，建设为专业化旅游服务的小型机场和直升机场，建设国际邮轮母港和游艇码头，科学规划环岛海上旅游线路，发展内河观光航运，改造提升公路景观，完善城市和旅游区慢行交通设施建设。最后，完善乡村地区公路配置标准和乡村公路建设，加大农村公路客、货站场建设，开通农村客运班线，推动城乡公交一体化发展。

4. 组织满足基本公共服务和国际旅游岛建设的生活圈

提供和保持高品质的生活质量，是佛罗里达州最重要的动力来源之一，对支撑旅游业发展、吸引人才集聚具有重要意义。佛罗里达州目前有 30 多所学院和大学、30 余所社区学院，保证了发达的教育服务；有 80 多个艺术长廊和博物馆、4 个主要交响乐团、4 个主要表演艺术团体、4 个著名演出场所，提供了多样的文化服务。拥有一批设施齐全的医疗、疗养、养老机构。

针对海南实际条件，综合考虑通勤半径和人口分布，从满足国际旅游岛高端服务和满足基本公共服务两个层面，组织都市生活圈和基本生活圈。以海口、三亚、琼海、儋州为核心组织四大都市生活圈，以都市生活圈为载体，配置满足国际旅游岛高端需求的服务设施。以 18 个市县驻地及乐东莺歌海镇、文昌锦山镇和儋州白马井镇为中心，建设全省 21 个基本生活圈覆盖全岛，以基本生活圈为载体，构建满足城乡居民需求的社会公共服务网络。

5. 建设高品质的绿色生态格局

在发展过程中，佛罗里达州始终将维护和保持良好的生态环境作为发展基础，通过严格立法保护和主动构建一些高品质景观格局作为重要手段。佛罗里达州划定了 3 个国家公园和 1 个国家保护区、160 个州立公园、41 个水生保护区、3 个国家河口研究保护区和一个国家海洋保护区，这些公园和保护区一方面是维护生态环境和景观格局的重要单元，同时也是佛罗里达州旅游产品体系中重要的组成部分。

首先，“国际旅游岛”战略明确要求高度重视生态环境保护和建设，坚持生态立省、环境优先。加强城乡生态保护，严格保护生态本底，划定省级层面需要严格保护和禁止开发的地区，作为空间大规模开发的边界，由省级行政主管部门管理。其次，依托河流、生态保护区、林地分布，构建十条生态绿廊，由山区向沿海渗透，促进山海联动；依托环形基础设施廊道和沿海防护林，构建环岛景观绿环，建立 12 个生态节点，形成沿海城镇外围的绿色生态背景和屏障。再次，划定海岸带功能分区，有序推进保护和开发，把全省海岸线划分为城镇生活、生态保护、旅游休闲、临港产业、农业渔业五种功能岸线，巩固和加强海岸防护林建设，严格保护沿海基干防护林带，形成海岸带功能区的绿色隔离。最后，加强生态补偿和流域补偿。

6. “小集中、大分散”城镇化道路，构建海南特色的现代城乡体系

目前佛罗里达州共有 282 个不同等级、不同功能的城市，形成了以十大重点城市为核

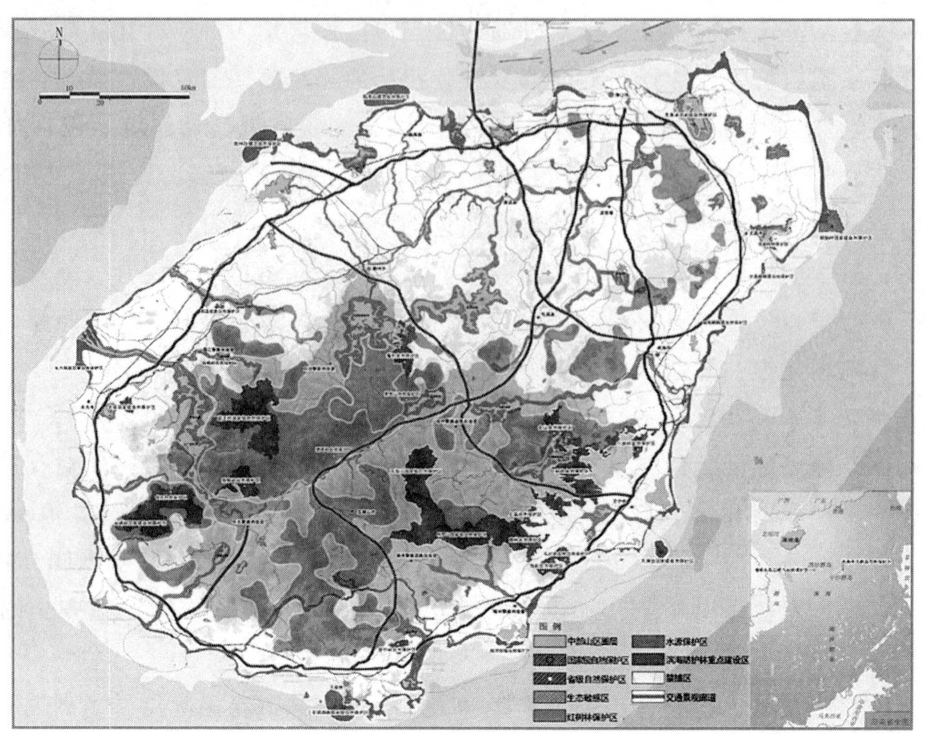

图4　禁止大规模开发建设的重点地区分布图

心、量大面广的小城镇为支撑的结构合理、功能健全的城市网络。

未来海南需要坚持“重点集中、高效分散、差异指引、加快融合”的原则，走具有海南特色的“小集中、大分散”的城镇化道路。构建以省域中心城市、区域中心城市、县城镇、中心镇为主体的四级城镇体系结构，推进旅游度假区建设，培育发展小城镇和农村中心居民点，建立“四核多心网络化”的城乡空间格局。

集中培育海口、三亚、儋州—洋浦、琼海—博鳌四大中心城市；加快建设文昌、万宁、五指山、东方市区和其他13个县城镇，成为海南现代城乡体系的重要节点和旅游服务中心；大力培育183个建制镇，构建特色鲜明、产业支撑强劲的中心镇体系，推动特色产业发展，就地吸纳农村剩余劳动力；完善旅游区功能配套，将旅游区发展成为现代城乡体系的重要组成部分。

7. 实施“人才强岛”战略，重视无空间差别政策与空间政策的结合

政策是佛罗里达州政府引导发展的重要手段，在发展过程中，推行过一系列直接或间接促进发展的政策，包括人才开发、产业发展、税收、环境等方面。

海南需要以满足国际旅游岛建设要求为目标，健全人才政策、实施重大人才工程，逐步形成支撑国际旅游岛长远发展的人才体系；加强教育，提高少数民族地区、落后地区和贫穷地区的教育水平；适应以旅游业为龙头、现代服务业为主导的现代产业体系要求，在现代服务、旅游业、生物医药、新能源、新材料、现代热带农业、海洋经济、电子信息、创意文化等方面，引进和培养一批国家级的高端人才。

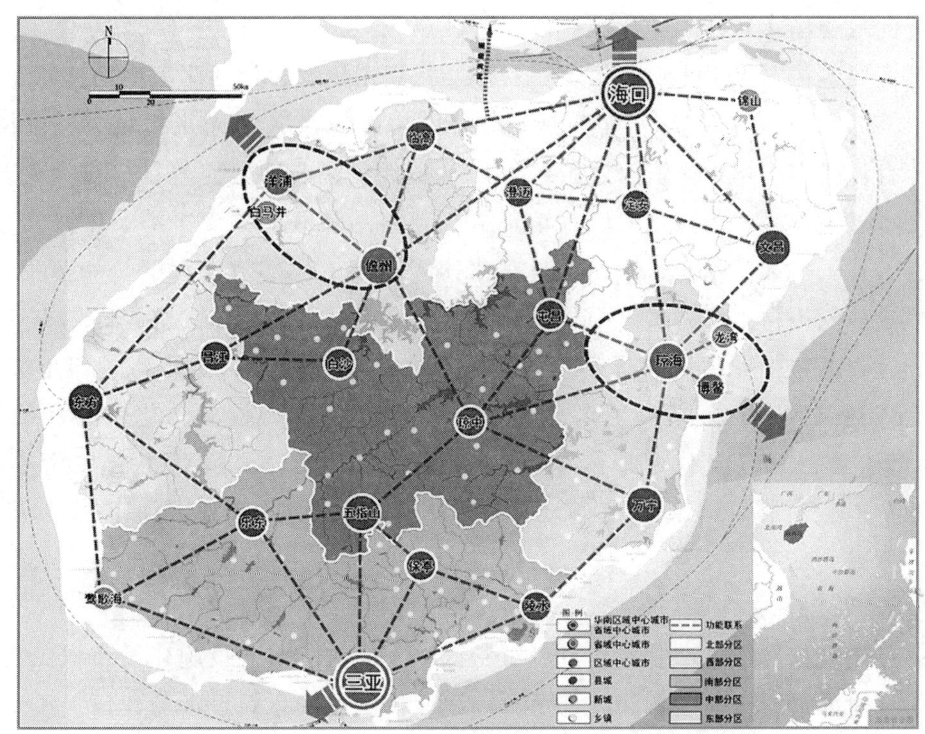

图5　海南“四核多心网络化”的城乡空间结构规划图

（三）行动层面：率先启动“先行试验区”的规划建设

为更好地探索和落实中央赋予海南国际旅游岛的特殊政策、海南省委、省政府特别划定海南国际旅游岛先行试验区，探索国际旅游岛发展经验。试验区以文化产业为重点，围绕国家赋予海南国际旅游岛的特殊支持政策、开发模式、体制机制创新、产品创新、投融资模式创新5个方面先行先试。并将陵水黎安地区作为先行试验区的起步区率先规划建设。

1. 试验区起步区：陵水黎安

试验区位于北纬18°，地处三亚东部陵水县，涉及黎安、新村和三才镇范围，规划面积约75平方公里。试验区距县城10公里，生态条件优越、自然环境优美、拥有两大天然泻湖、浅水港、生态海岛和多处优质沙滩岸线；地域文化丰富，热带海滨资源突出，气候宜人。集合了海南岛山、海、河、湖、林、湾、岛等自然魅力要素资源。

2. 规划初步设想

试验区以创新国家文化标杆为目标，以新兴文化业态、中国传统+现代文化和地方文化为三大文化元素，塑造中国现代气质、中国当代文化特色的新文化发展基地。以休闲文化旅游为平台，塑造开放包容的文化环境，突出国际文化交流活动特色，以文化创造和文化创新为两大路径，塑造海南特质的中国新文化发展标准。

试验区将落实十七届六中全会精神，立足高端要素集聚和制度创新，建构基于中国特色的、对外开放的社会信用试验地、不断完善和持续发展的文化开放体验区、新人文和科技文化鉴赏的新平台、尝试中国和国际文化要素会聚和信息传播的新标准、使之成为国际和区域间文化交流的重要场所和新兴文化产业的聚集区。

试验区主要包括五大文化功能板块：一是文化娱乐板块，包括国家南海博物馆、海洋文化主题园（海事与海权博物馆）、娱乐文化 MALL、水上商务观光飞机场、国际游艇码头、国际水陆体育竞技赛事场馆、滨海旅游综合体（最大免税购物城）等；二是文化艺术板块，包括各种艺术展览中心、民间收藏展览馆集群、奢侈品和藏品拍卖中心、中国文化主题园、热带雨林露天音乐节和国际音乐厅；三是文化休闲板块，包括陵水泻湖及海草生态保护区、猴岛自然风景区、牛白山海岛热带雨林森林公园、海南民俗文化区、特色高尔夫球场、现代渔农业观光区、风情主题街镇、疍家文化区、各种标准的度假旅游酒店；四是文化科技板块，包括低碳建筑实验区、国际旅游学院、新媒体产业城（影视文化中心和动漫体验区等）、生命健康城；五是文化产业板块，包括智库信息园、国际商贸会展中心、知识产（版）权交易中心、国际旅行社总部基地、游艇国际俱乐部基地、通用航空飞行基地和海洋经济区等。

3. 建设初步设想

为了高品质高标准推进试验区建设，试验区将率先进行基础设施建设及村民安置迁并工作，具体包括对外道路交通改善和内部道路建设，泻湖岸线景观设计与建设，排水工程系统建设，海防林带保护和完善、山体修复，清理海水养殖的规模及其养殖类别等。同时安排试验区管委会向全球招聘管理人才并尽快进驻现场，加强试验区的规划建设管理。

三、小结

明确的国家战略布局是支撑我国改革开放和现代化建设的重要内容，30 多年前的改革开放以及今天的新一轮改革开放，国家面临的整体发展阶段不同，战略空间的选择也有所不同。第一轮改革开放的背景是谋求经济发展起步，发展是明确的工业化导向。选择的战略空间，无论是“特区”、“沿海开放城市”，还是“高新技术园区”，其核心任务均是成为国家“外引内联”工业化“据点”，空间选择侧重开放的便捷性，“自上而下”为主导。新一轮改革开放，谋求工业化的深入推进和适应人的全面需求，发展具有明确的国际化、服务型导向，选择的战略空间，其核心任务是成为国家转型率先发展“高地”。空间选择侧重于发挥资源效益的最大化，“自上而下”与“自下而上”的良性互动。

“国际旅游岛”作为新时期国家整体格局中的一个战略空间，为海南转型跨越发展提供了难得的机遇，同时也承担着为国家转型发展先行先试的任务。一年多来，海南省委、省政府围绕“国际旅游岛”建设要求，从统一认识到明确思路再到行动试点，全面展开了工作，战略与行动相结合、整体框架与项目实施同步推进是一年来的主要经验，值得推广。“国际旅游岛”建设是一个长期的目标，海南的转型跨越发展也是一个长期的过程，海南发展的经验将会随着“国际旅游岛”建设的深入，越来越丰富，我们的这种观察也将会持续。

（作者：杨保军，中国城市规划设计研究院副院长，教授级城市规划师）

参考文献

[1] Florida A Time for Reckoning, National Geographic, Aug. 1982.

[2] Florida Attractions Association, 2009.

[3] Florida History, Florida Dept. of Commerce, Tallahasse, 1986.

[4] 杨保军，赵群毅，查克，徐有钢，等．海南发展的战略转型与空间应对：写在“国际旅游岛”建设之初［J］．城市规划学刊，2011，(2)：8-15.

[5] 中国城市规划设计研究院，海南省住房和城乡建设厅．海南省城乡经济社会发展一体化总体规划(2010—2030)，2011-06.

[6] 中国城市规划设计研究院．海南国际旅游岛先行试验区规划研究（初稿），2011-08.

低碳生态城市的理论发展与实践探索

建设低碳生态城市是党的十七大提出建设“生态文明”的战略部署，是城市发展的新型模式和社会共识。在城市问题日益突出、原有城市发展模式难以为继的今天，大力发展低碳生态城市，探索一条符合中国国情、文明本底的“C（Chinese Model）模式”城市发展道路，是我国当前城市发展和建设的迫切需要。我国政府明确承诺，到2020年单位GDP的二氧化碳排放量将较2005年降低40%～45%。建设低碳生态城市成为城市发展的必然趋势。

一、低碳生态城市的内涵与概念

“低碳生态城市（Low Carbon Eco-city）”概念是“低碳经济（Low Carbon Economy）”和“生态城市（Eco-city）”这两个关联度高、交叉性强的发展理念复合起来的综合概念。“低碳经济”的概念是在应对全球气候变化、提倡减少人类生产生活活动中温室气体排放的背景下提出的。这一概念脱胎于2003年英国政府在题为“我们未来的能源：创建低碳经济（Our Energy Future：Creating a Low Carbon Economy）”的《能源白皮书》中提出的“低碳经济”概念，切入点是能源的利用和气候的变化。尽管地球变暖是否由人类活动引起还有争议，但是工业革命之后，人类的发展方式对气候造成的影响是不可否认的，因此提出要从能源角度和气候角度，保护地球环境，减少温室气体排放，从而提出低碳的理念，并提出城市的发展要遵循低碳理念。“生态城市”是基于生态学原理建立起来的社会、经济、自然协调发展的新型社会关系。这个概念最早是1971年联合国教科文组织（UNNSCO）在“人与生物圈（MBA）”计划中提出的，计划中明确提出要从生态学的角度用综合生态方法来研究城市。

低碳生态城市不是“低碳”、“生态”、“城市”三个词的简单叠加或者说用“低碳”和“生态”限定“城市”，而是三者结合创造了一个新的完整的概念，并超越了原有概念的含义，是不能分开的。“低碳”不仅局限于降低碳排放，更延伸到经济产业、消费理念，甚至是城市的集约化发展道路上，从能源资源角度进一步强调了生态化。“生态”也不是传统意义上的生态，超越了原有单纯的学科意义，发展成为一种方法论，用于人们认识和改造自然的一种系统方法论。“城市”已经突破了传统意义上的城市，是在对传统城、乡辩证否定的基础上发展而来的，是城—乡复合共生系统，是人类住区发展的高级阶段[1]。

在以上理论研究的基础上，住房和城乡建设部副部长仇保兴博士把生态城市与低碳经济这两个关联度高、交叉性强的发展理念复合起来，在2009年国际城市规划与发展论坛上首次明确提出“低碳生态城市”的概念：“低碳生态城市”是以低能耗、低污染、低排放为标志的节能、环保型城市，是一种强调生态环境综合平衡的全新城市发展模式，是建立在人类对人与自然关系更深刻认识基础上，以降低温室气体排放为主要目的而建立起的高效、和谐、健康、可持续发展的人类聚居环境。“低碳生态城市”这一概念一经提出，就受到社会各界的普遍关注和认可。

从某种意义上来讲，低碳生态城市可理解为是生态城市实现过程中的初级阶段，是以“减少碳排放”为主要切入点的生态城市类型[2]，也即“低碳型生态城市”的简称。

二、低碳生态城市的策略与路径

（一）低碳生态城市发展的总体思路

大力发展低碳生态城市建设，走低能耗、低污染、低排放的城市发展道路是塑造新的国家竞争优势的重要方面。当前我们迫切需要解决的问题是反思和改变旧有的城市建设理念和发展模式，探索符合可持续发展要求的城市发展道路。总的来讲，推动低碳生态城市合理、有序的发展需要从以下几方面着手：

1. 建立不同类型低碳生态城动态评价综合指标体系，按照可持续发展程度对低碳生态城进行分级评价；引导城市政府和市民建设生态城的创新意识，逐步推动同类城市在生态城建设方面开展友谊竞赛并实现互帮互学；
2. 建立利益相关方参与的合作机制；
3. 充分借鉴中国传统的生态思路，创建有中国特色的低碳生态城；
4. 通过良好的设计和精细的管理，使城市成为景观上具有吸引力，具备良好服务、设施齐全、社会和谐的宜居城市；
5. 通过建设成本可负担、发展模式可模仿、自身发展可持续的“先锋”城市实践，引导全国其他城市转变发展模式[3]。

（二）低碳生态城市发展的引导政策

建设低碳生态城市，既是顺应城市低碳化、生态化发展趋势的重要战略抉择，同时也是转变发展方式、践行科学发展观的重要举措。2011年的“十二五”规划纲要提出了24项指标，其中关于资源环境的8项指标中有7项是约束性指标。从中可以看出，生态环境保护与节能减排已经被提到了更加突出重要的位置。未来，中国只有以转变发展方式和调整经济结构为主线，以采用低碳发展模式和建设低碳生态城市为手段，才能实现中国经济社会的转型发展和健康发展[4]。

为了落实“十二五”规划纲要提出的目标任务，国家发展和改革委员会于2010年8月15日启动五省八市低碳试点工作，并积极推进低碳试点实施方案的制定工作；同时，近期正在组织实施“十二五”节能减排综合性工作方案，这个方案重点从强化目标责任、优化产业结构，优化能源结构，实施重点工程，加强节能低碳管理，发展循环经济，加快低碳技术研发应用，完善相关经济政策，推动五省八市试点，健全体制机制等十个方面，全面推进绿色低碳发展。2011 年 6 月，财政部与住房和城乡建设部联合下发“关于绿色重点小城镇试点示范的实施意见”（财建〔2011〕341 号），在“十二五”期间积极开展绿色重点小城镇试点示范，9 月份下发了“关于开展第一批绿色低碳重点小城镇试点示范工作的通知”（财建〔2011〕867 号），公布了第一批试点示范绿色低碳重点小城镇名单[①]，推进绿色小城镇工作的组织实施和监督考核工作。

住房和城乡建设部在 2010 年正式启动了低碳生态城市的建设工作。2010 年 1 月，住房和城乡建设部与深圳市人民政府共同签署了共建“国家低碳生态示范市”的合作框架协议，深圳成为全国首个“国家低碳生态示范市”；2010 年 7 月，住房和城乡建设部与江苏省无锡市人民政府签署《共建国家低碳生态城示范区——无锡太湖新城合作框架协议》；2010 年 10 月，住房和城乡建设部与河北省人民政府共同签署《关于推进河北省生态示范城市建设

图 1 住房和城乡建设部与深圳市人民政府签署合作框架协议

图 2 住房和城乡建设部与无锡市人民政府签署合作框架协议

图 3 住房和城乡建设部与河北省人民政府签署合作框架协议

① 第一批试点示范绿色低碳重点小城镇名单：北京市密云县古北口镇、天津市静海县大邱庄镇、江苏省苏州市常熟市海虞镇、安徽省合肥市肥西县三河镇、福建省厦门市集美区灌口镇、广东省佛山市南海区西樵镇、重庆市巴南区木洞镇。

促进城镇化健康发展合作备忘录》；2011 年 1 月，住房和城乡建设部成立低碳生态城市建设领导小组，组织研究低碳生态城市的发展规划、政策建议、指标体系、示范技术等工作，引导国内低碳生态城市的健康发展。2011 年 6 月，领导小组下发了“关于印发《住房和城乡建设部低碳生态试点城（镇）申报管理暂行办法》[①] 的通知”（建规（2011）78 号），启动新建低碳生态城镇示范工作。另外，住房和城乡建设部还与美国、瑞典、英国、德国、新加坡等国家的有关部门签署了生态城市合作方面的谅解备忘录，共同开展生态城市方面的国际合作和交流。

（三）低碳生态城市发展的推行步骤

低碳生态城市的推行主要包括诊断、规划、实施、运营、评估五大步骤。规划和设计之前需进行诊断，诊断城市现状的生态制约条件和价值点。要建立一套综合实施体系，确保规划的有效实施。运营是一套体系措施，需要对城市运营状态实施信息监控和动态管理，及时验证、校准和调整城市规划。评估是检验基础，评估城市建设及运营状况，其结果将成为新一轮诊断依据。

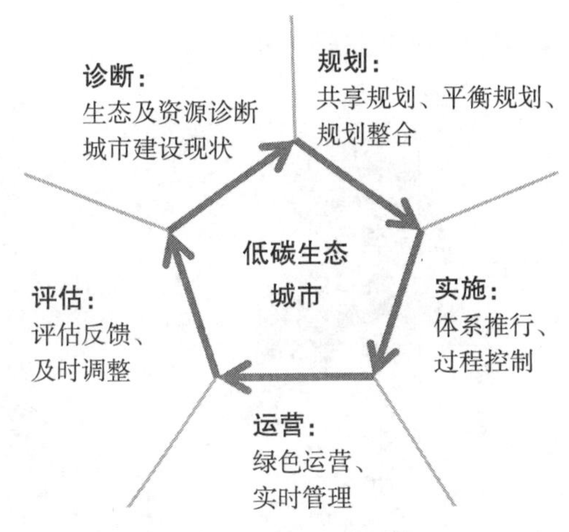

图 4　低碳生态城市推行五步骤

① 《住房和城乡建设部低碳生态试点城（镇）申报管理暂行办法》节选

第一条　为规范住房和城乡建设部低碳生态试点城（镇）申报工作，特制定本办法。

第二条　申报住房和城乡建设部低碳生态试点城（镇）的对象，应是新建的城（镇）和既有城市的新区。

第三条　申报低碳生态试点城（镇），由所在地城市人民政府提出申请，经省、自治区、直辖市住房城乡建设行政主管部门同意，报住房和城乡建设部。

经住房和城乡建设部低碳生态城市领导小组办公室组织专家审查同意后，由住房和城乡建设部低碳生态城市领导小组批准。

第四条　申报低碳生态试点城（镇）应具备下列基本条件：

（一）新建城镇（新区）规划建设控制范围原则上应在 3 平方公里以上，不占用或少占用耕地。

（二）与中心城区距离不宜大于 30 公里，在 100 公里范围内应有可依托的大城市。

（三）靠近高速公路、铁路（或轨道交通站点）、已有或者已规划建设便捷的对外交通。

（四）如已建有道路系统，其路网建设基本符合“绿色交通”的原则。

（五）有健全的工作机制。包括：成立权责相符的领导与组织协调机构，并给予资金与制度方面的支持和保障；制定了低碳生态试点城（镇）规划纲要和建设实施方案。

第五条　申报新建低碳生态试点城（镇）应提供以下材料：

（一）所在地的资源环境现状评估和经济社会发展条件分析报告。包括土地、水资源、能源利用的状况，生态环境状况，对外交通条件，经济社会发展的现状和发展目标。

（二）低碳生态试点城（镇）规划纲要。纲要应体现资源节约和环境友好的发展理念，明确试点城（镇）的功能定位和主导产业，明确提出交通、市政基础设施、建筑节能、生态环境保护等方面的发展目标、发展策略和控制指标。纲要确定的总体和人均碳排放量应低于同一区域同等规模城市的平均水平。

（三）低碳生态试点城（镇）建设实施方案。包括低碳生态城（镇）产业发展、绿色建筑推广、交通和市政基础设施建设、环境治理和生态保护等方面的行动计划和创新示范工程。

第六条　曾获得国家园林城市、中国人居环境奖、生态园林试点城市等相关荣誉或称号的城（镇）优先考虑。

三、低碳生态城市的实践与行动

（一）低碳生态城市发展的总体概述

根据中国城市科学研究会学术交流部所做的一项统计表明，截至2011年2月，中国287个地级以上提出低碳生态城市有关建设目标的城市已达259个①，占到地级市比例的90.2%，如下图5所示。

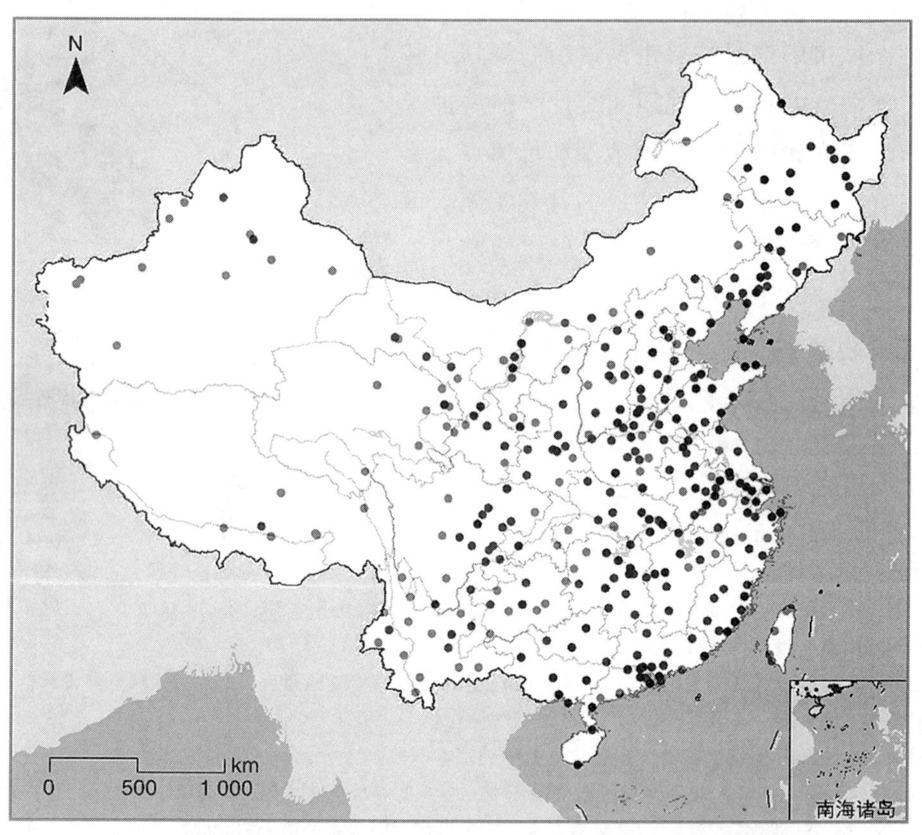

图5 全国提出低碳生态城市有关建设目标的地级市分布示意图

图片来源：中国城市科学研究会，2011。

除了地方政府在建设目标层面的积极响应和倡导，相当一部分的城市（城区）也已经开始了低碳生态城市的建设实践活动（如表1所示），这些结合各自地域特色开展的实践探索为低碳生态城市的规划建设以及运营管理积累了丰富的经验，有利于从中总结和归纳出适合中国国情的低碳生态城市发展策略。

① 由于目前对于低碳生态城市的理解尚未在定义和内涵上达到统一，且指导低碳生态城市建设的部门存在交叉，因此，城市在开展规划建设时存在“生态城市”和“低碳城市”等多种建设目标的提法，上述提法均列入低碳生态城市的统计范围。

表1　中国低碳生态城市发展的部分实践探索介绍

编号	所在省（市）	城市（地区）	地域	是否新建	生态建设特色	备注
1	北京	密云县	东部	否	新能源与节能、污水处理、生态修复工程	其他
2		延庆县	东部	否	新能源利用、生态产业、循环经济、保障机制	其他
3		门头沟中芬生态谷	东部	是	产业体系集成、规划设计布局	中芬合作
4	天津	中新天津生态城	东部	是	指标体系、能源的综合利用、绿色交通、城市安全与社会事业	中新合作 部省共建
5	上海	南桥新城	东部	否	编制专项规划和专题研究、启动指标体系研究、印发低碳要求的技术指引文件	其他
6	重庆	重庆	西部	否	保护生态本底、促进城市有机更新和改造、推进绿色出行和可再生能源示范项目试点、启动悦来生态城规划、建设	发改委 低碳市试点
7	河北	唐山湾生态城（曹妃甸国际生态城）	东部	是	指标体系、新能源和资源利用、城市安全、循环经济	部省共建 中瑞合作
8		石家庄正定新区	东部	是	新城规划和指标体系编制过程中	部省共建
9		秦皇岛北戴河新区	东部	是		部省共建
10		沧州黄骅新城	东部	是		部省共建
11		涿州生态宜居示范基地	东部	是		部省共建
12		保定市	东部	否	可再生能源利用、节能减排、低碳技术、低碳产业	发改委 低碳市试点
13	广东	深圳市	东部	否	绿色建筑、基本生态控制线、绿色交通、绿道	部省共建 发改委 低碳市试点
14	江苏	无锡太湖新城	东部	是	紧凑合理城市布局、循环高效的资源能源利用、绿色交通、原生态多样性均质化的环境	部省共建 中瑞合作
15	山东	德州市	东部	否	新能源开发利用、生态宣传教育、责任考核制	其他
16	福建	厦门市	东部		低碳生态新城规划、可再生能源城市级示范、倡导绿色建筑、发展城市林业	发改委 低碳市试点
17	浙江	安吉县	东部	否	污水与垃圾处理、生态村的创建、生态产业县、全国生态文明试点	其他
18	安徽	合肥滨湖新区	中部	是	水环境综合治理、绿色交通规划、生态社区规划、用地规划、能源综合利用规划、生态产业规划	其他
19		淮南市	中部	否	发展循环经济、瓦斯综合利用、塌陷区生态修复、棚户区改造	其他
20	湖北	武汉市	中部	否	资源节约和环境保护产业结构、城市功能、城乡统筹、土地利用和财税金融的体制机制探索	其他
21	湖南	长沙市	中部	否	区域规划与指标体系、大河西“两型”先导区、“两型”产业、保障机制	其他
22		株洲云龙示范区	中部	是	综合型的生态系统建设 多领域联合的项目组织、一体化的规划设计内容、面向实施的设计深度、八大领域技术集成与示范	其他
23	云南	昆明呈贡新城	西部	是	绿色交通、生态体系构建、土地开发控制、分层级规划建设指标体系	其他
24	新疆	吐鲁番市示范区	西部	是	指标体系、节水与节能、生态防护、历史文化保护	其他

（二）低碳生态城市发展的类型分析

综上，根据目前正在开展的低碳生态城市实践案例用地性质和开发建设模式的不同，可以将其分为三类：新建地区的低碳生态城市实践、现有城区改造的低碳生态城市实践和现有城区扩张发展的低碳生态城市实践。

1. 新建地区的低碳生态城市实践

这一类型的低碳生态城市实践是指在既有建成区以外，以低碳生态发展模式开展新城的建设。调研发现低碳生态新城的选址所占用的土地性质各不相同。其中，中新天津生态城和唐山湾（曹妃甸）生态城具有探索型的代表性，其特点为开发建设过程中尽量不占用耕地或实现占补平衡，以盐碱地、滩涂地的生态化恢复、改造为主所进行的从规划到建设的低碳生态城市实践。

相对来讲，低碳生态新城实践受到的现状约束性因素较少，规划设计和建设发展的余地较大，可以通过制定指标体系等手段来较好的和相对完整的应用低碳生态城市有关的规划设计理念和技术，全方位地开展建设活动，但同时也存在依靠政府投资、建设成本相对较高、人口集聚、产业集聚需要依托周边城市辐射力等方面的缺点。目前中国所进行的低碳生态城市实践多数属于这种类型[4]。

图6　中新天津生态城效果图

2. 现有城区原址改造的低碳生态城市实践

这一类型的低碳生态城市实践主要是指对原有城镇进行的低碳生态化改造，其特点是根据当地的现状发展水平和特色，兼顾低成本、高效益的原则，利用适宜的低碳生态技术，逐渐改变原有不合理的发展方式和生活方式，实现经济、社会、环境效益的共赢。如浙江安吉充分利用当地“竹乡”的资源禀赋，形成了从竹产业的原料供应、竹制品的初、深加工到竹产品的销售这样一条循环、高效、完整的产业链；北京的延庆、密云地区结合当地气候特

图7　唐山湾（曹妃甸）生态城效果图

点和实际需求，在国家相关政策的财政补贴和技术扶持下，在新能源利用（太阳能、生物质能、风力发电等）、生态修复、垃圾分类处理、循环产业等方面进行了建设示范和应用。相对于新建地区的低碳生态城市实践，这一类型的低碳生态城市实践相对见效慢，需要政府加强扶持和引导，但我们应当意识到，既有改造的低碳生态城市实践是我国当前最应重点推进同时也是未来发展前景最为广阔的一种类型[4]。

图8　北京密云农村太阳能浴室示范工程

3. 现有城区扩张发展的低碳生态城市实践

这一类型的低碳生态城市实践也属于新城建设，有别于原址改造型的最大特点是与主城

图9　北京延庆“德清源”循环产业园

区距离不远，属于主城区扩张发展的范围。如厦门市结合当前“统筹城乡发展，加快岛内外一体化建设”的发展战略目标，在集美、翔安、同安、海沧等四个新城的建设中，启动了低碳生态新城规划，逐步实现城市建设由岛内转向岛外，推动厦门进入“全域特区”时代。目前，集美新城（21 平方公里）、同安环东海域（114 平方公里）、东海科技创新园（4.9 平方公里）、翔安低碳研究所和低碳配套产业园（10 平方公里）已选定为低碳新城示范区，开始按照低碳要求进行规划建设[1]。

图10　厦门集美新城日建方案

图 11　厦门翔安新城 SWA 方案

（三）低碳生态城市发展的问题剖析

综上所述，无论是政府提出的建设目标还是正在开展的建设实践，低碳生态城市的发展热潮已经席卷中国大地，中国正成为世界上探索低碳生态城市最为积极和主动的国家之一。但由于当前低碳生态城市建设尚处探索阶段，其建设和发展中所表露出的问题同样也是不容忽视的，主要表现为导向不明、目标缺失、理论缺失、唯技术论四大方面[4]。

导向不明具体表现为：(1) 尽管当前地方政府已经普遍对低碳生态城市给予了高度的关注，并且进行了不同程度和规模的低碳生态城市建设实践活动，但建设过程中存在着动机不够明晰、盲目跟风，一味强调政绩工程的现象。(2) 尽管全国 90.2% 的地级以上城市均提出了建设低碳生态城市的发展目标，但从其提出时间和地理分布上来看，东部沿海地区呈现出提出时间早、分布密度高的特点。而且当前开展生态城市实践活动最为积极的多数也是经济较为发达的城市（城区），以至于造成了“低碳生态城市等于经济发展水平高”的一种错误认识。(3) 尽管新建地区的低碳生态城市实践投入成本很高，但其具有见效快的特点。因此，在多种因素的驱使下，很多城市在进行低碳生态城市实践时选择了“新城运动”，而见效慢、推动慢的建成区生态化改造则处于被当权者冷落的境地。

目标缺失具体表现为：(1) 低碳生态城市发展忽视与中国国情和客观需求的结合；上海东滩生态城和廊坊万庄生态城均是因为生态城开发占用了农用地等土地性质方面的问题造成生态城建设陷入了一筹莫展的困境。(2) 由于目前尚未出台全国性的生态城市指标体系，尽管各地出于实践建设的需要纷纷制定了地方性的生态城市指标体系，但是缺乏宏观层面的目标引导性，导致地方在制定指标体系的过程中存在目的不清、导向不明的问题。

理论缺失具体表现为：(1) 目前学术界尚未对低碳生态城市有一个明确、公认的定义和理解，其名称也呈现出多样化的趋势。(2) 低碳生态城市规划的地位、编制方法和体系等目前尚未得到明确，各地低碳生态城市的规划均属于探索性阶段，对于编制内容和深度均没有统一、明确的要求，无法对规划编制后的建设实施起到很好的保障和引导作用。

唯技术论具体表现为：（1）目前进行的低碳生态城市建设实践摒弃一些传统的低成本、高效益的手段，热衷于追求技术的新、奇、特，热衷于追求立竿见影的效果，盲目地将高投入与高回报画上等号。（2）低碳生态城市的实践中还存在着建设选址盲目性较大的问题，将地点选在自然基底良好的生态敏感区内进行开发建设，不但是对自然环境的极大干扰，同时也会破坏生物多样性、引发连锁性自然灾害的产生，对低碳生态城市的建设安全造成隐患，酿成不可弥补的损失。

四、低碳生态城市的发展与展望

在中国低碳生态城市的规划建设实践进行得如火如荼的同时，我们也应认识到，由于低碳生态城市规划与建设是一项涉及面广、综合性强的系统工程，且目前尚缺乏适合中国国情的低碳生态城市及其相关领域的理论基础、方法论、指标体系，规划设计原理、政策体系以及相关的建设技术和实践经验，中国的低碳生态城市建设仍处于起步阶段。因此，开展科学合理、因地制宜的低碳生态城市实践活动需要今后在以下方面进一步提升。

（一）低碳生态城市的理念目标需要进一步深化

低碳生态城市强调尊重过去，着眼未来，确立正确的城市发展理念，应建立科学化评估生态城市发展的指标体系；遵循平衡、共生、发展、循环的原则，顺乎自然规律的发展之道，将城市加入到整个生态系统中物质与能量循环的平衡当中，将生态学的最小干预自然、让自然做工的理念贯穿到整个规划设计管理的全过程。同时，要以人为本，把人的因素与生态并重，确立人是生态环境的保护者。通过多种方式和渠道，积极倡导低碳生活，传递生态理念，鼓励每一个公民、每一个家庭都成为低碳生态城市的宣传者、实践者和推动者，在衣、食、住、行、用等各个方面都体现绿色生活理念。低碳生态城市的目标应从资源、环境、经济和社会四个维度进行构建，最终是要通过低碳生态城市的规划建设来实现资源节约、环境友好、经济持续和社会和谐的总体目标，达到城市让生活更美好的愿望。

（二）低碳生态城市的发展思路需要进一步转变

我国当前已经进入城镇化的中后期，其发展的一个重要趋势就是重建“微循环”。从全国情况来看，许多城市在发展中已经到了转型的门槛前，其空间格局、基本框架，在经过30多年改革开放的发展建设之后，已经基本定型，各类大型基础设施也已基本建成。同时，城镇化初期大拆大建的弊端，也已充分暴露，市民对社区环境改善的愿望及提升居住舒适度的需求也愈发强烈。在这种条件下，城市的发展思路应从工业文明向生态文明转变，将传统集中式、机械式的处理方式向分散、有机化、生态化的处理方式转变，由建设大型基础设施向小型补充式设施建设转变，由集中处理排放向就地就近处理转变，由各公用设施功能分离向综合利用转变。同时，在规划建设理念方面，还应实现由自上而下向规划透明、设计透明、上下结合、充分调动民间创新积极性转变。

基于此，城市管理者应遵循“自组织”理念，抛弃初期广为流行的急风暴雨式“大开大发”、“大拆大建”，转而推行“微降解、微能源、微冲击、微更生、微交通、微创业、微绿地、微医疗、微农场、微调控”等城市微循环体系重建工作，这也将成为城市转型、低碳生态城和城市住宅规划建设的新原则[5]。

（三）低碳生态城市的规划引导需要进一步加强

低碳生态城市规划是进行低碳生态城市建设的纲领性文件，是引导城市发展的基本依据和手段。低碳生态城市规划要以其高度的综合性、战略性和政策性，在实现优化城市资源要素配置、调整城市空间布局、协调各项事业建设、完善城市功能、建设优质人居环境、维护全体市民公共利益等方面发挥关键作用。

具体来讲，各层次的规划应该注意以下几方面的内容：（1）区域城镇体系规划层面，应当重视研究区域内的城市化战略和政策，人口、产业、城镇的集聚发展，综合交通体系以及区域生态格局等。（2）城市总体规划层面，应当重视研究城市的性质与功能、规模与容量、空间与形态以及城市建设用地、基础设施和中远期发展预测与控制，尤其是通过生态运

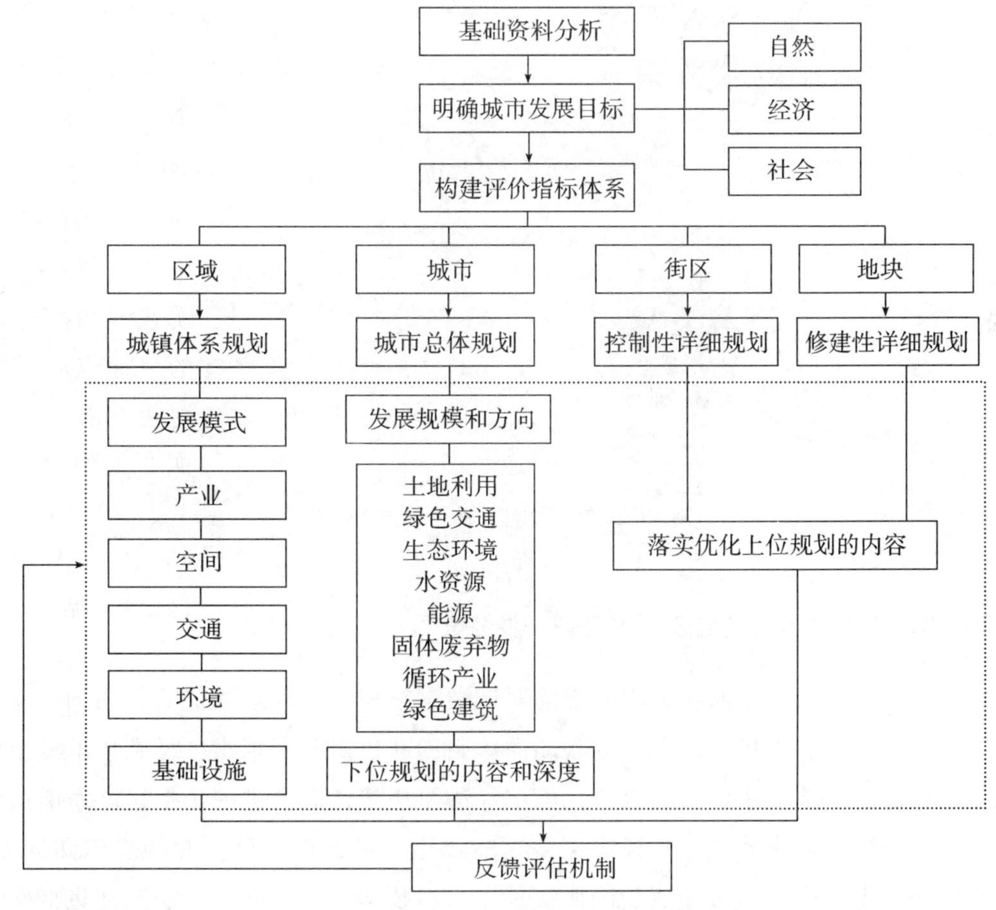

图 12　低碳生态城市规划步骤

资料来源：中国城市科学研究会．河北省生态宜居城市建设研究报告。

行模拟技术综合调配生态基础设施的配置。(3) 控制性详细规划层面，应当重视研究城区土地利用、建设容量控制、环境容量控制、建筑空间形态、市政基础设施控制以及城市规划指标落实。

(四) 低碳生态城市的技术体系需要进一步创新

低碳生态城市建设技术涉及城市规划与设计、生态环境保护规划设计、产业发展选择、绿色建筑规划设计、废弃物处理与管理、绿色交通规划与管理、能源生产与利用、水资源保护与利用、数字信息技术等方面，其研发、推广与应用是低碳生态城市建设的重要支撑。当前对于技术体系方面的应用和实践多数为单项技术的尝试，因此迫切需要对各项低碳生态技术开展系统性、整体性的尝试与整合，形成低碳生态城市建设集成技术，进一步指导低碳生态城市建设，推广低碳生态城市建设管理经验与可行模式。

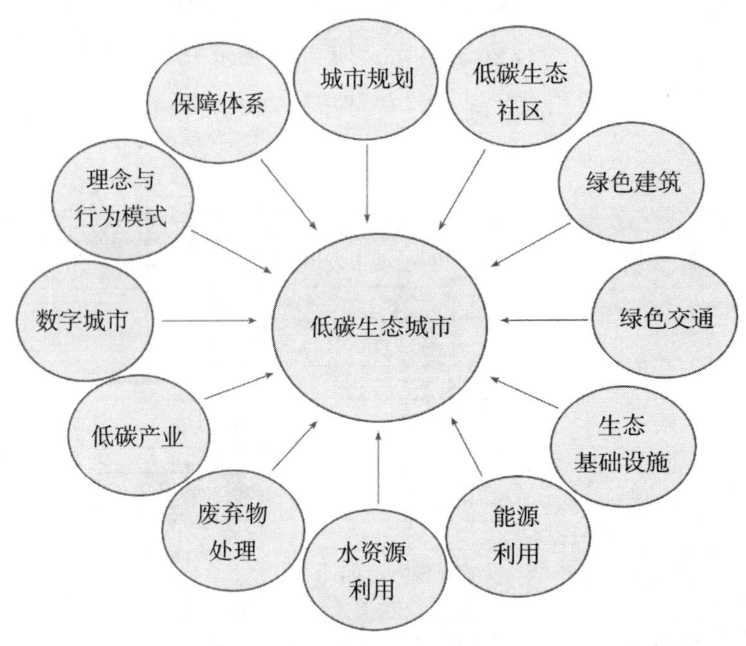

图 13　低碳生态城市的关键技术体系

(五) 低碳生态城市的发展政策需要进一步健全

低碳生态城市仍处于不断探索中，当前对低碳生态城市起促进和保障作用的法规政策体系还很不完善，政策、市场、技术三方联动的体制创新仍需不断探索。低碳生态城市建设涉及的能源、资源、土地、水、环境保护、经济等法律法规还需要进一步衔接。当前迫切需要总结国内外成功的低碳生态城市建设案例，逐渐转化为可推广、可复制的组织和运营方式，形成明确的引导低碳生态城市发展的法律法规体系和技术导则，同时，制定促进低碳生态城市发展的有关财税、产业配套政策，以城市公共政策的形式从宏观上引导和保障低碳生态城市发展，实现公共管理和服务更为周到的低碳生态城市。

（六）低碳生态城市的国际合作需要进一步拓展

低碳生态城市是一个复杂系统工程，涉及关系人类长远发展的环境、生态、资源、健康等全球性科学问题，一直以来都是各国政府和科学界关注的热点。在全球一体化的背景下，促进低碳生态城市健康持续发展的根本途径是聚集各国科学家的共同参与和努力，通过不同国家与地区、不同文化与思维方式、不同学科领域的思维碰撞，通过各国政府、非政府组织、企业、科学家之间多渠道、多形式的合作交流，共同致力于世界低碳生态城市建设的理论与实践发展。

当前，没有其他任何一种城市发展战略像低碳生态化城市发展战略这样存在如此普遍的共识，低碳生态城市发展战略必然是中国乃至世界城市未来的发展模式。低碳生态城市理想的实现，即始于我们今天的认识和行动。让我们共同关注、共同参与、共同努力，让每一个人都行动起来，携手创建我们美好的生态未来，实现人类与自然的和谐共存、永续发展！

（作者：李迅，中国城市科学研究会秘书长，教授级城市规划师；刘琰，中国城市科学研究会助理研究员）

参考文献

[1] 中国城市科学研究会．生态城市指标体系构建与生态城市示范评价（2011—2012）．

[2] 沈清基，安超，刘昌寿．低碳生态城市的内涵、特征及规划建设的基本原理探讨［J］．城市规划学刊，2010，109（5）：48－57.

[3] 仇保兴．从绿色建筑到低碳生态城［J］．城市发展研究，2009，7：1－11.

[4] 李迅，刘琰．中国低碳生态城市发展的现状、问题与对策［J］．城市规划学刊，2011，4：23－29.

[5] 仇保兴．重建微循环：生态城设计的基本原则．生态城市中国行——重庆站．会议资料，2011.

新疆吐鲁番市新区绿色交通系统规划实践

引　言

随着全球生态环境和能源问题的日益加剧，探索一条可持续的城市发展和建设之路成为当前各国努力的方向。正是基于这一思想，联合规划工作组以建设一个适合西部气候条件的可持续发展城市的思路开始了吐鲁番新区规划和建设工作。在新区交通规划方面，将以实践绿色交通系统规划为手段，结合地方特点，探索能实现新能源利用、交通可持续、环境保护等目标的绿色交通发展模式，同时，也为我国其他城市绿色交通系统的建设提供借鉴。

应该说，绿色交通并不是一个新名词，从 20 世纪 90 年代 Chris Bradshaw 提出了绿色交通体系的理念之后，绿色交通的定义就一直在演变发展中。但不管怎么样，从现有的研究共识看，绿色交通的本质是建立维持城市可持续发展的交通体系[3,4]，其基本概念是以减少交通拥挤、降低能源消耗、促进环境友好、节省建设维护费用为目标的城市综合交通系统。另外，从整个绿色交通技术发展历程看，也已经由简单的理念层面探讨发展到了现在完善的规划体系阶段。如文献[3]中详细讨论了绿色交通理念以及与可持续交通、低碳交通等几个理念的比较，并给出了基本的绿色交通规划体系框架；文献[6]和[7]以绿色交通理念为指导，开展某一城市特定功能组团的交通规划，对绿色交通系统规划体系进行了初步摸索；而文献[4]则更进一步，以城市新区规划实践为依托，建立了可操作的绿色交通系统规划平台，形成了目标规划、功能规划、系统规划三个阶段内容。本研究在充分参考和借鉴上述研究成果的基础上，更进一步深入到细致的微观设计及实施工作，使成果不仅仅停留在理念和规划阶段，更变成一个可实施的系统性工程。

一、概况

吐鲁番地区位于东经 87°41′～91°54′，北纬 41°12′～43°37′之间，辖一市二县，即吐鲁番市、鄯善县、托克逊县，地区土地总面积 67 563 平方公里，总人口 60 万人。吐鲁番市新区位于吐鲁番市区东部的戈壁滩上，距离老城区 5 公里，北依火焰山，东临土哈油田作业区，西北紧邻著名的葡萄沟景区，原 312 国道从中部穿过。

按照规划，新区将成为地区公共管理和服务中心、适宜居住的和谐生态社区以及具有国际影响的文化旅游胜地。新区规划总面积 8.81 平方公里，规划总人口 6 万人，计划用 10 年时间（2010—2020 年）分三期建设，如图 1[1] 所示。其中：一期工程用地面积 2.86 平方公里，总建筑面积 235 万平方米，计划用 5 年左右时间（2010—2015 年）完成。

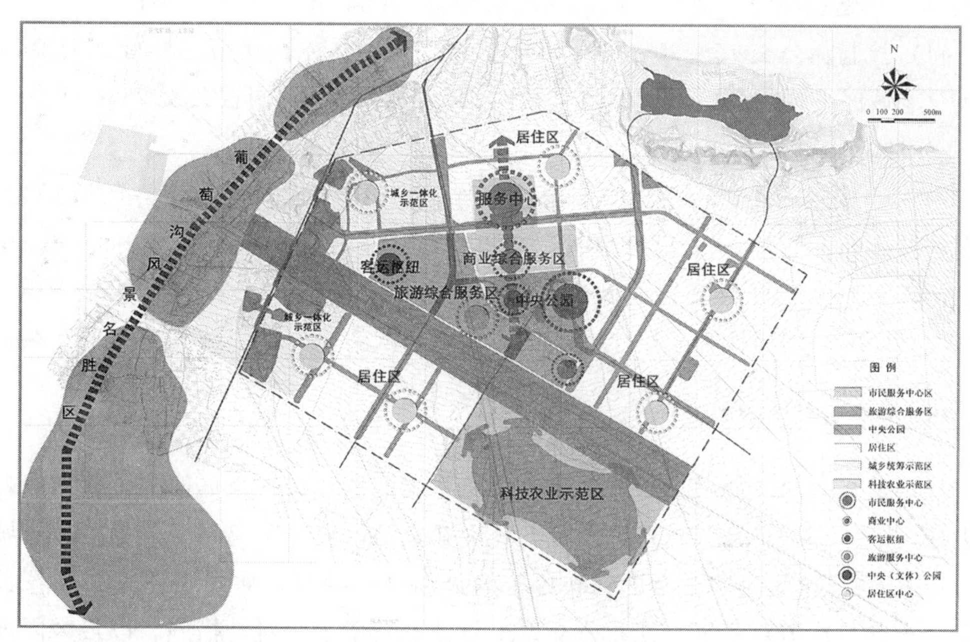

图 1　新区空间结构分析图

同时，新区针对当地气候文化特点，充分利用当地太阳能等可再生能源的优势，重点研究太阳能光电、光热等可再生能源技术在城市建筑群中的综合应用。结合太阳能发电的应用、并网等系统技术，采取创新能源管理体制，并以此为基础发展绿色交通体系，同时建立数字生态城市的管理体系，最终探索出一条充分利用可再生能源的低能耗、低排放的新型城市可持续发展模式[2]。可见，绿色交通不仅仅是自身系统建设的问题，更是城市能源管理中的重要内容。

二、系统架构

（一）规划目标确定

按照吐鲁番市新区总体发展设想，新区交通建设首先要以满足城市大多数人的出行需求为目标，并实现交通的便捷高效，为此，结合城市规模和城市出行行为研究，确定“公交优先、慢行主导”建设思路，并体现在具体目标和微观设计上。其次，综合考虑城市能源系统的建设，提出主导交通方式实现低碳低排的设想，为此，结合太阳能微电网建设，引进电动公交系统，不但实现公交的零碳排放，而且将公交充电系统作为能源储备中心起到对微电网调峰蓄能的作用，实现了新能源利用和交通的有机结合。最后，按能源消耗和环境影响控制、出行服务可靠性、交通运行结构控制等三个层面给出具体目标。

1. 目标一：发展零碳排放的绿色交通主导模式。交通出行的主导方式（慢行和公交）实现零碳排放，以太阳能利用的清洁电力为交通能源供给主体。

2. 目标二：建设集约、便捷、宜人的出行服务系统。新区平均门到门出行时间（含两端集散时间）控制在公交15~20分钟，电动自行车10分钟，其中，步行到公交站点5分钟。新区至老城区平均门到门出行时间（含两端集散时间）控制在公交25~35分钟，电动自行车20分钟。

3. 目标三：实现道路运行系统的安全、宁静、畅通。“慢行+公交”的道路空间布局，要求公交运营速度不低于20公里每小时。在出行结构指标控制上，新区内部慢行和公交出行比重不低于95%；在吐鲁番建成区内，新区对外出行慢行和公交出行比重不低于75%。慢行系统线型顺畅，连通性和便捷性高于机动车交通网络。

（二）绿色交通系统框架设计

按照规划目标，形成如图2所示的绿色交通系统框架。在这个框架中，有三点是在研究中重点去探讨的。一是出行服务系统设计。鉴于新老城区边缘距离约3公里，新老城区之间平均出行距离5~7公里；同时考虑到吐鲁番的火洲气候特点，居民不适宜在外较长时间步行和候车，为此，在道路系统设计和公交系统设计上采取了针对性措施，以最大限度减少居民步行出行距离和候车时间。二是主导交通工具，即电动公交系统的能源供给设计。新区整体上采用的是清洁太阳能能源供应，而电动公交系统要发挥整个太阳能微电网的调峰蓄能作用。为此电动公交的充电系统和太阳能储能系统如何衔接是系统设计的重要内容，也是本项目的难点所在。三是整体规划和阶段实施衔接问题。新区绿色交通系统不仅仅是一个理念，更是一个实实在在需要地方政府花大力气、长时间去做的新事情、新事物。

（三）出行服务系统设计

新区的功能定位和发展目标决定了其具有多样化的出行群体，可细分为常住居民、本市访客、地区游客和外地游客。出行主体的多样化将带来出行特征和空间分布的丰富性。家、商业中心、景点、交通枢纽将是居民出行活动的主要目的地，在空间上表现为三类出行需求：(1) 新区内部之间的出行；(2) 新区内部与老城区之间的出行；(3) 新区内部到对外交通枢纽再转换其他交通系统之间的出行。结合新区绿色交通发展目标，提出满足各类出行的主导交通模式和建设要求如下：

1. 新区内部出行：以慢行交通方式（步行、人力自行车和电力自行车）为主体，公交作为慢行的补充和延伸。具体体现在建设适宜步行尺度的高密度绿色步行道系统，直达居住社区内部；建设绿色的非机动车运行空间，提供便捷的慢行交通服务；建设高可达性的公共交通服务系统，同时设计满足弹性出行要求的辅助出行服务系统（电招或者扬招式电动出租车、租赁自行车服务）。

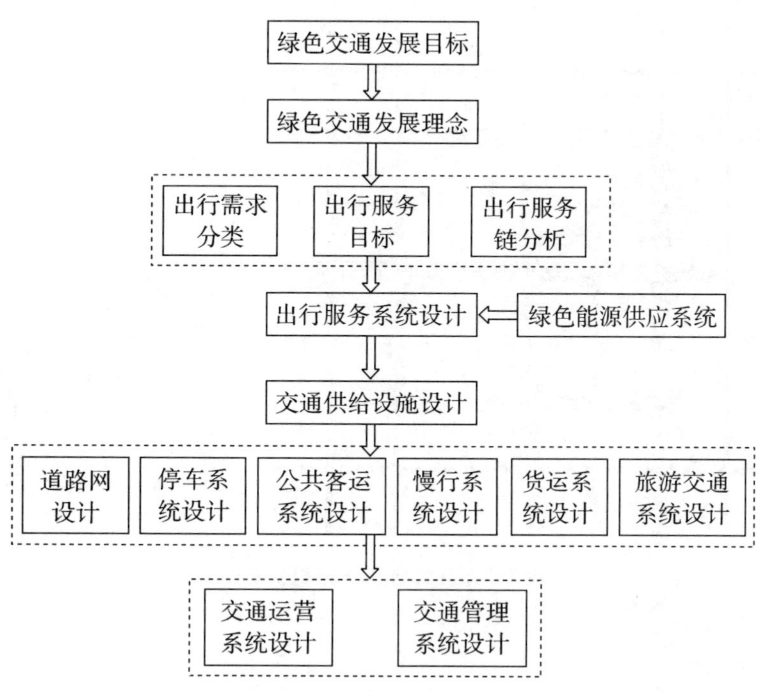

图2　新区绿色交通系统设计框架

2. 新区内部与老城区之间的出行：以直达公交为主，电动自行车为辅。以高直达性的干线公交服务新、老城区居民日常出行；通过机动车（巴士）+交通枢纽+（慢行、公交、辅助出行服务系统）完成外部游客到达新区。

3. 新区内部与外省市之间的出行：以长途巴士、其他机动车到达对外交通枢纽或“P+R”，再通过公交+慢行方式/辅助交通方式进入新区。

表1　新区居民出行结构

单位:%

范围	非机动出行方式	公交	私人小汽车	其他	合计
新区内部	75	20(电动公交)	0	5	100
新区对外	35	40(电动公交)	20	5	100

（四）绿色交通总体组织模式

如何在规划层面落实绿色交通发展理念一直是本研究的核心内容，通过对城市特点及绿色交通理念的研究，提出新区绿色交通系统将以不同交通运输方式在空间上的优化组织为切入点，也就是说，针对新区不同交通系统在实际运行中的控制性需要开展系统性设计。如图3所示。

解释如下：

1. 道路网结构设计。通过土地利用与交通的协调（这方面在总体规划阶段已经进行控

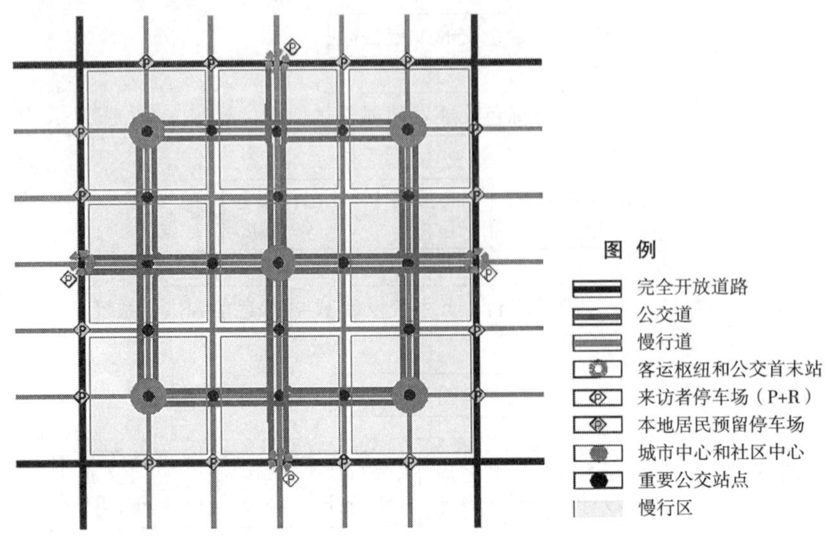

图 3　新区绿色交通组织模式图

制，从用地布局着手最大限度实现居住和就业的本地平衡），建设高密度、小尺度的道路网系统，根据道路功能划分为完全开放道路、公交道和慢行道三类。另外，为最大限度的方便居民出行和转换，规划将社区中心和公共服务中心设置在公交道和慢行道的结合处。

2. 不同性质交通流的组织。过境交通，通过完全开放道路进行交通截流，避免过境机动车进入新区。对外交通（含旅游交通及来访交通），通过完全开放道路实现新区对外、新老城区之间的交通转换，并通过在完全开放道沿线设置停车位严格控制传统机动车进入社区，乘客通过步行、公交及自行车进入社区。内部交通，通过环形公交通道和高密度站点满足公交出行需求；慢行道以慢行交通为主导方式，通过优先保障慢行设施的建设，从而实现慢行交通和机动车交通在空间上的分离。

三、核心系统规划

在本项目研究中，我们认为整个绿色交通系统的核心就是“三网”，分别是道路网，这是能够实现慢行和公交优先的基础保证；公交网，这是实现绿色交通的重要手段，同时也是整个城市能源系统的重要组成部分；慢行网，这是小城镇居民出行的首选，也是绿色交通的重要组成部分。同时，这“三网”也是本项目的特色所在。

（一）建设高密度、小尺度的道路网

文献[5]和[6]的研究表明，小街区设计、密集的街道网络、混合的土地利用方式以及基本生活设施的配置，能够使居民的出行距离最短，同时居民也更愿意选择非机动的交通方式。大多数的调查指出，小城镇的慢行交通的出行比例多数在 50% ~70% 之间，有的达到了 80% 。为此，在路网规划中，很重要的一点是要遵循这一交通出行行为特点，设计出适合慢行、鼓励慢行的路网。

1. 设计思路

主要体现在以下几个方面：改变传统以机动化方式为主导的四级道路等级体系，构筑面向慢行、公交和全部车辆使用的按三类功能划分的道路分级体系，分别为完全开放道路、公交道和慢行道等三类。道路红线控制标准适当进行压缩，采取面向步行和非机动车出行及可达尺度的道路网格设计，摒弃传统以机动车通行能力和速度为依据的路网密度和级配结构标准。按公交组织的需要（满足当地居民可以接受的步行时间要求）来设计新区内部的机动车通道系统，并在设计上充分实现慢行交通和机动车交通在空间上的分离。

2. 道路功能分级

完全开放道路。任何车辆均可进入，主要承担过境和出入境交通功能，是新区与老城区以及外省市联系的主要通道，红线规划 30 米。

公交道。主要对公交和辅助公交开放，同时慢行和部分经许可的货运车辆、特殊车辆（如工程车辆）等也可通行，承担区内组团间的机动化联系功能，是区内的综合性道路和机动车主要通道，红线规划 20 米。

慢行道。主要对步行和非机动车等慢行交通方式开放，同时作为应急情况下的绿色通道；根据功能不同又分为承担中短距离交通功能的慢行廊道（采用葡萄绿廊的建设形式并串联各社区中心和主要交通集散点）和承担短距离生活性功能的一般慢行道，红线规划 10 米。

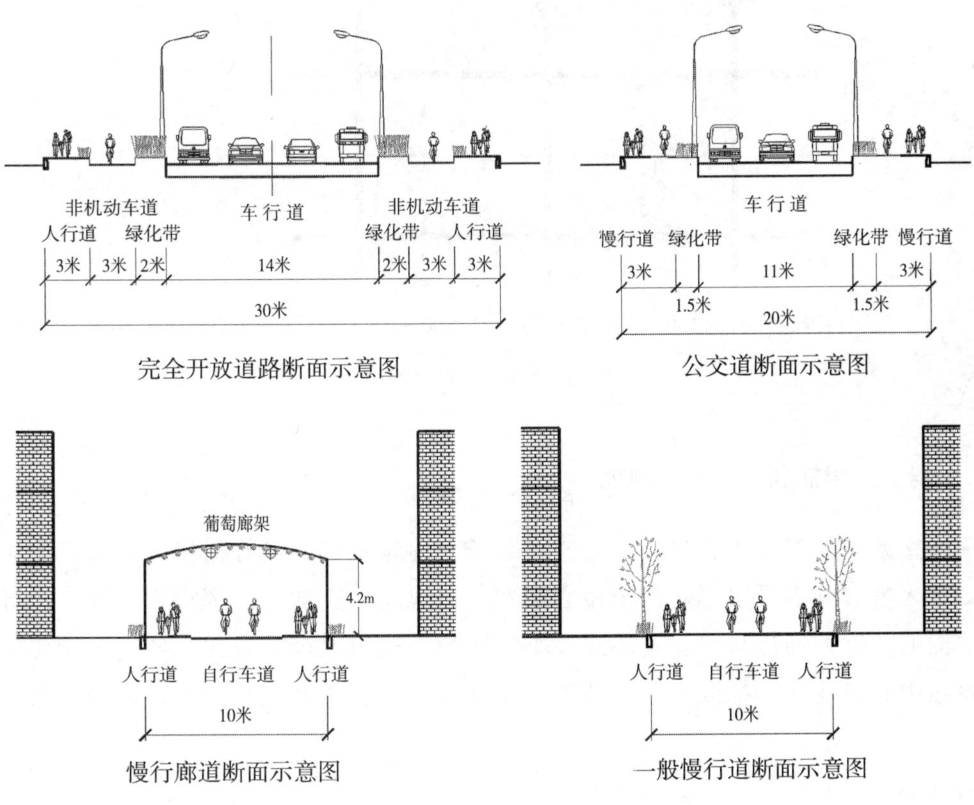

图 4 新区道路横断面设计

3. 路网尺度设计

从新区绿色交通发展要求出发，除了要做到慢行与机动车出行在空间上的分离，优化慢行出行环境外，也要充分考虑慢行与公交系统的衔接，并围绕两者相交节点形成公交社区，在满足人们多样化出行选择需求的同时，实现交通与用地的集约协调发展。

为此，新区路网尺度设计将以“步行+公交”出行为系统可靠性的衡量标准，建立合适尺度的公交社区。结合地方气候特点及居民公交出行习惯，按5分钟的步行可接受时间，1米/秒的步行速度计，步行合适的距离约为300米，即围合区域（300m×300m）可作为公交社区的适宜尺度，其中，平均步行距离200米，最大步行距离在300米以内，可完全满足新区居民公交出行对两端步行的心理可接受要求。结合慢行道的建设，将形成150m×150m的路网间隔。考虑到具体在用地安排上的差异性，慢行道路的安排可有变异。

4. 规划路网

根据路网尺度核算以及公交服务深度的测定，形成机动车道网络规划方案和慢行道路系统规划简图，经叠加后形成新区道路网规划方案，见图5，整体路网密度指标12.1公里/平方公里，其中慢行路网密度6.0公里/平方公里。

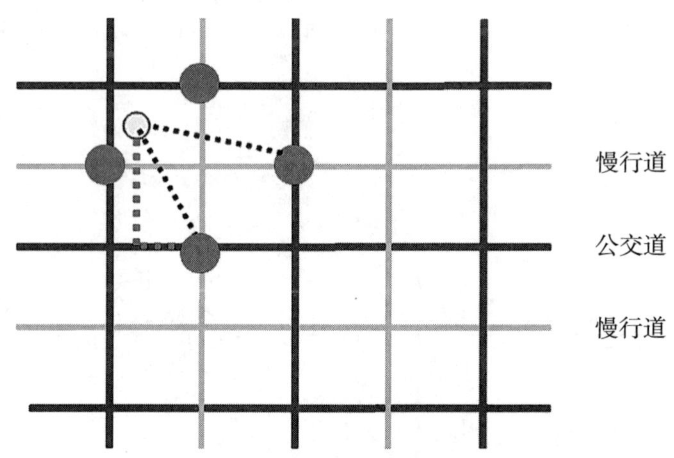

道路间隔：150m×150m；公交社区尺寸：300m×300m；平均步行距离：200m

图5　路网尺度设计简图

（二）基于太阳能利用的公交网规划

强调公交系统的便捷、直达以及与慢行系统、停车系统的良好衔接。在研究中，重点探讨了公交深入度和站点设置形式两个核心问题，这也是公交能否发挥最大效用，引导合理交通出行结构的关键。通过采用公交环线、小站距的公交组织设计方式，使得公交深入到社区中心，并在中心商业区、社区中心、外围停车截流点等城市客流集中处设置公交首末站或换乘枢纽。

1. 公交体系设计

根据新区公共交通的功能定位，规划新区公交系统分3大层次，具体分层架构如下表：

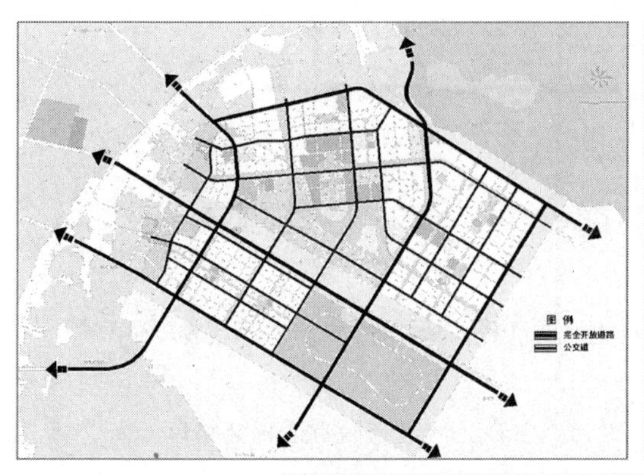

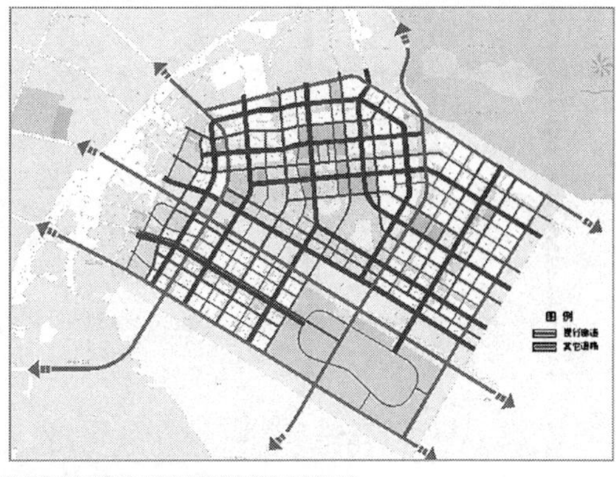

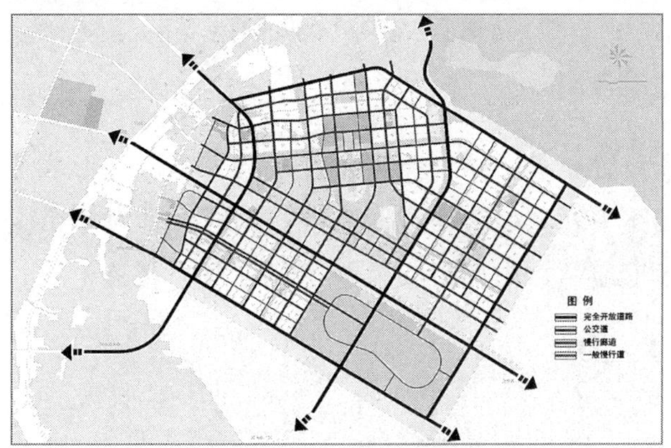

图6　道路网规划方案图

表2　吐鲁番新区公交系统体系结构

公交系统体系结构		功能定位	车型	行驶道路
长途客运		提供外省市和旅游客流到达新区的对外交通枢纽	传统巴士	完全开放道路
跨区公交		联系新老城区,高直达性线路,控制运行时间,与新区内部公交线路换乘衔接	电动巴士	公交道、完全开放道路
区内公交	环形公交	串联各发展组团,环线运行,站点固定	电动中巴	
	辅助公交	电招或扬招电动出租车服务,提供无障碍化、门到门出行服务	电瓶车、电动小汽车	
	货运系统	区内提供统一管理的货运公共服务,提前预定,统一调度货运电动车辆,安排配送	货运电动车辆	各级道路

2. 站点设置模式

模式一，传统模式，站点设置在机动车道路（公交道）相交路口，便于公交线路之间的换乘，但与慢行廊道的结合较差。模式二，站点设置在公交道与慢行道相交路口，便于居民通过慢行系统与公交系统实现转换。

本研究经过多方比较，认为应改变传统站点设置方式所带来的交叉口交通矛盾过于集中的弊端，将公交站点设置在路段与慢行道相交处。这不但减少了交叉口的矛盾冲突，也方便了公交站点和慢行道的衔接。更为有利的是，该设置模式可以便于将社区中心围绕慢行和公交节点进行布置，促进交通与土地利用的协调发展。如图7所示。

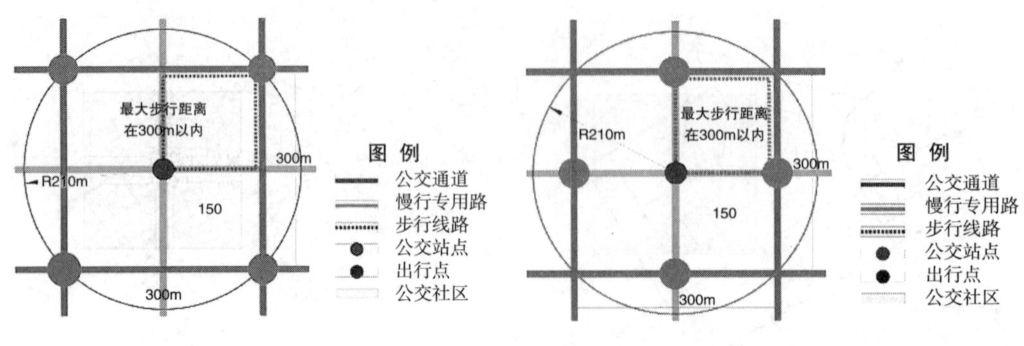

站点设置在机动车道路相交路口　　　站点设置在公交道与慢行道相交路口

图7　公交站点设置模式图

3. 公交系统规划

按照上述公交系统设置要求，结合路网尺度设计，本研究形成了以公交环线、对外联络线为骨架，一般公交线路为补充的公交线网系统。同时，针对城市空间布局及服务需求，规划设置若干个对外客运枢纽站、内部公交换乘枢纽站及公交首末站，规划方案见图 8。

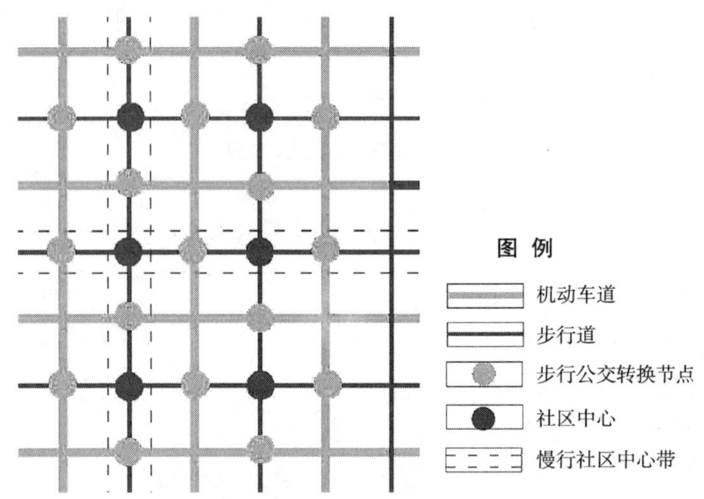

图8　公交站、慢行道、社区中心结合模式图

4. 设施保障

车辆选型。根据吐鲁番地区的公交状况和人口密度，统一采用 8 米长度的电动空调车，600V DC 250Ah 的磷酸铁锂电池配置。

充电站和充电柱。电动公交充电站和充电柱均结合公交场站进行建设。公交充电柱采用“一车一柱”的模式建设。考虑到电力调峰、公交临时充电、系统拓展的要求，每个充电柱按照快充与慢充兼容的模式建设，需直流电压 600V，慢充功率为 36kW，快充为 60kW。公交充电站按一级负荷设计，需单独设置变压器，不与居民生活、商业变压器共用。

（三）基于机非分离设计的慢行网规划

结合地方特色建设人本化的独立、完整的慢行系统。充分利用沟渠（坎儿井）、城市绿

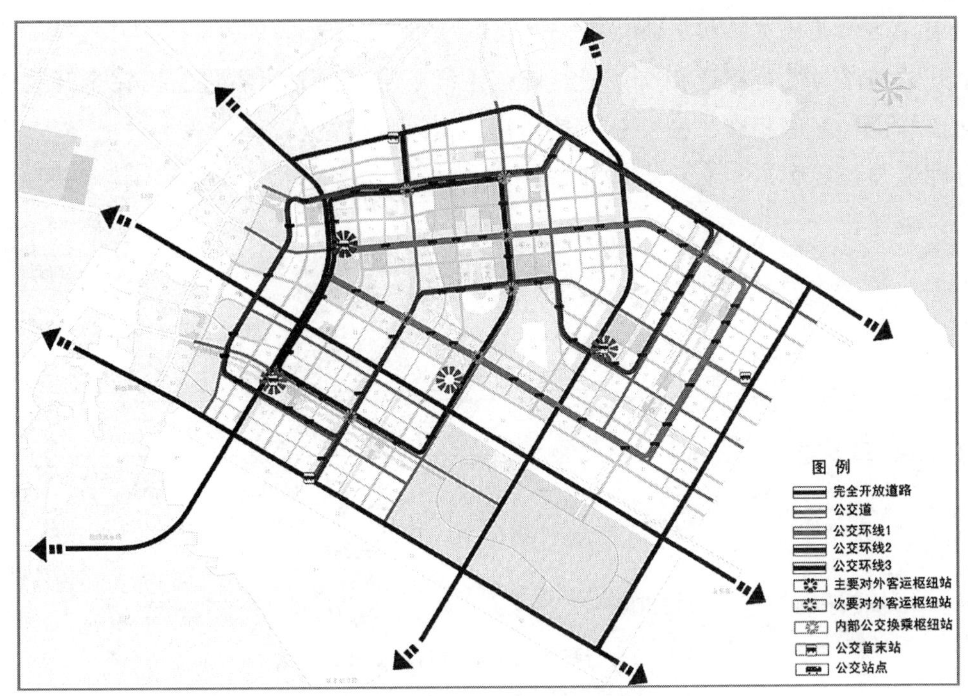

图9　新区公交系统规划图

廊（如葡萄廊）建设庭院式的慢行街道，建设空间上独立的城市慢行交通走廊和社区慢行道，串联各社区中心和主要交通集散点，引导慢行交通成为居民内部出行的首选。

1. 布局模式

路网建设方面，突出慢行路网的建设，慢行廊道优先成网，其他慢行道补充加密，深入社区。研究中充分利用具有地方特色的葡萄绿廊建设完全独立于机动车系统的慢行廊道系统和深入社区的次级慢行系统，通过慢行系统将各公服中心、主要景观节点和主要居住带串联起来，在慢行系统空间内，禁止除应急救灾情况之外的一切机动车使用。

交通组织方面，强调与公交系统的良好衔接，通过慢行系统到最近的公交站点不超过300米。

2. 功能分级

慢行廊道。与机动车通道完全分离，是慢行交通系统的主骨架，串联各公服中心、主要景观节点和主要居住带，采用吐鲁番独具特色的葡萄绿廊的建设形式。承担区内中长距离的慢行交通功能，线型连续，沿途交叉口优先通行。

一般慢行道。承担短距离生活性功能的城市慢行网络，在断面设置上部分依附于机动车行断面。

社区慢行道。深入社区内部的慢行网络，形式灵活。

休闲慢行道。滨水及绿地的健身休闲型慢行道路。

3. 慢行网络覆盖面

通过独具特色的慢行网络建设，慢行路网密度将达到6.0公里/平方公里，非机动出行方式将占新区内部出行的75%，占对外出行的35%。

4. 慢行廊道与其他道路相交的处理

完全开放道路与慢行廊道相交：慢行廊道主线下穿，同时可右进右出完全开放道路。

公交道与慢行廊道相交：公交车减速让行，黄闪灯控制。

慢行廊道与慢行廊道相交：小型环岛。

其他：减速让行。

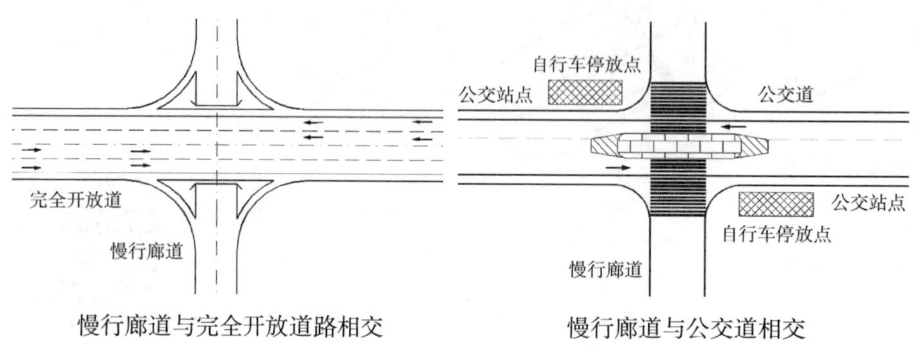

图10 慢行廊道与其他道路相交处理方式

5. 慢行网规划方案

与机动车的有限到达相比，慢行交通系统可以深入社区，与生活空间紧密结合，并实现全覆盖，将是新区居民中短途出行或换乘出行的首选和主导方式。

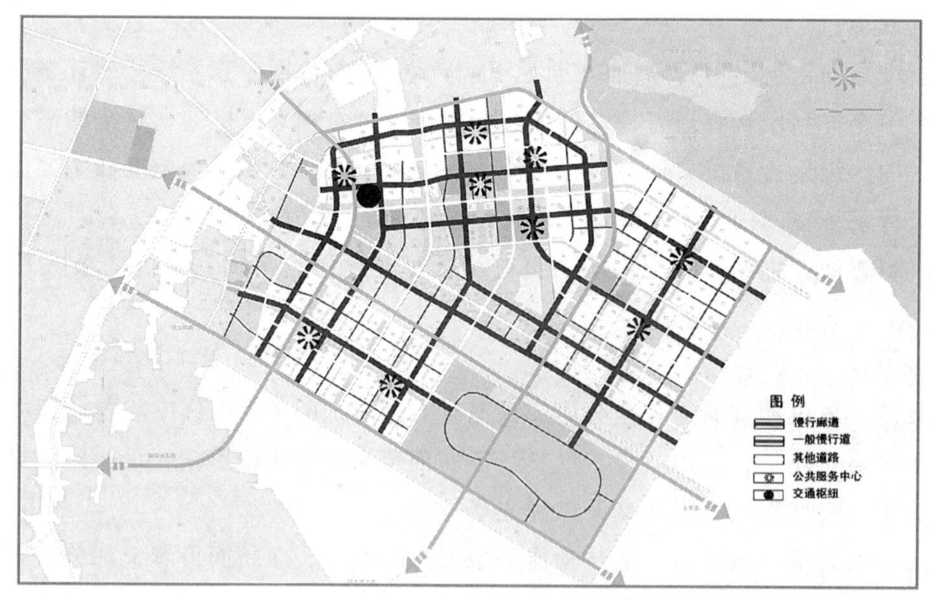

图11 慢行系统规划图

四、规划实施管理

绿色交通系统规划的建设对规划管理和实施模式提出了更大的挑战，这表现为：

（1）传统建设和管理理念上的挑战。对于绿色交通系统规划，国内大多数政府部门对此并无明确的认识和理解，自然在规划方案的解读、实施技术上存在不足，同时，规划也势必对城市政府以往的规划控制性指标要求提出挑战，这些都需要城市政府去克服。

（2）管理体制上的挑战。从本研究看，绿色交通已经涵盖了城市管理、市政电力、公交、交警等多个部门，要在各个部门之间取得认识和技术实施上的高度一致本身就是一项很大的挑战。

（3）规划实施过程中遇到的挑战。居民的接受程度是本项目能否成功的关键因素，必须在前期作好规划的解读、宣传等工作，并作好建设过渡期的各项衔接。

针对上述挑战，在规划实施和管理过程中要相应做好以下几方面的工作：

（1）加强绿色交通规划建设的宣传和解释。这不但指对城市居民的解释，也要在城市各相关职能部门开展学习和研讨，这才能保证后期实施的无障碍或少障碍。

（2）建立强有力的协调机制和协调机构。建议成立由吐鲁番市分管领导，市建设局、市科委、市财政局、市发改委、市交通局、市交警、市城管等委办负责人组成的协调领导小组，总体负责协调吐鲁番绿色交通的规划与建设事宜。

（3）完善各项管理措施，保障规划方案的实施、运营和维护。根据规划方案及实施中可能遇到的问题，应重点放在车辆通行管理、停放管理等内容上。

（4）近期结合创建国家新能源示范城市工作，以电动公交车辆的投放和普及为切入点，重点在新区电动公交示范运营的基础上，适时推进吐鲁番老城区电动公交车辆的投放和运营，并最终建立起覆盖新老城区的绿色电动公交系统，使吐鲁番建设成为国家新能源汽车应用的示范基地。

五、结语

绿色交通绝不仅仅是一个理念，一个口号，是完全可以变成实实在在的规划体系和实施性方案的。国内的绿色交通系统规划还多数停留在规划层面，而本研究从概念规划、总体规划至实施性规划展开了多阶段的工作。在目前开展的吐鲁番新区一期起步区规划建设中，除了落实研究中确定的高密度、小尺度路网，空间上独立的慢行系统，以及深入社区的公交系统等三大核心内容外，还重点研究了新能源城市太阳能微电网系统与电动公交充电系统衔接方案。

（作者：周方，广州市城市规划勘测设计研究院院长；蔡云楠，广州市城市规划编制研究中心副主任，广州市城市规划勘测设计研究院副院长；张晓明，广州市城市规划勘测设计研究院交通规划设计室负责人；周茂松，广州市城市规划勘测设计研究院规划师）

参考文献

[1] 欧亚科学院中国中心城市科学学部，广州市城市规划勘测设计研究院，新疆维吾尔自治区建筑设计总

院，北京市建筑设计研究院，北京市城市规划设计研究院．吐鲁番市新区总体规划（2009—2020）［R］．吐鲁番：新区联合规划工作组，2009.

[2] 欧亚科学院中国中心城市科学学部，北京市建筑设计研究院，广州市城市规划勘测设计研究院，中国电子工程设计院，国家气候中心（中国气象局风能太阳能资源评估中心）．吐鲁番市新区可持续发展城市项目［R］．吐鲁番：可持续城市发展研究中心，2009.

[3] 陆化普．城市绿色交通的实现途径［J］．城市交通，2009（6）：23－27.

[4] 殷广涛，黎晴．绿色交通系统规划实践：以中心天津生态城为例［J］．城市交通，2009（4）：58－65.

[5] 潘海啸，沈青，张明．城市形态对居民出行的影响：上海实例研究［J］．城市交通，2009（6）：28－32.

[6] 潘海啸，刘贤腾，John Zacharias，等．街区设计特征与绿色交通的选择：以上海市康健、卢湾、中原、八佰伴四个街区为例［J］．城市规划汇刊，2003（6）：42－48.

[7] 熊晓冬，罗广寨，张润朋．基于绿色交通理念下的广州大学城交通规划［J］．城市规划学刊，2005（4）：88－92.

以点成片　以线带线　以赛筑城

——浅析深圳大运会与城市建设

2007 年 1 月，经过多轮激烈的竞争，深圳最终获得第 26 届世界大学生运动会（以下简称“大运会”、“大运”）的承办资格，深圳也由此进入“大运时代”，2011 年 8 月 12—23 日，以“Start Here（从这里开始）”为主题口号的大运会在深圳成功举办。

回顾过去五年多的筹备工作，以承办大运会为契机，深圳从体育设施建设、公交体系完善、城市环境改善及其他一系列相关城市建设领域加大投入、系统构建，通过大运这一重大“城市事件”，真正做到了“通过‘办赛事’，实现‘办城市’，促进城市发展质量的大提升”的目标，实现了城市整体功能的大幅提升。

一、“城市事件”、城市建设与城市发展

城市事件（City Event）多指短时期内发生的一系列重要活动的总和，奥运会、世博会、亚运会、大运会等全球性盛会都属于城市事件。国内外相关研究中，“城市事件”更多的使用在主动意义上结合城市发展实际情况及阶段化的城市发展目标组织城市行为，有意识地争取的对城市发展有积极性意义的城市影响。

城市事件是提升城市竞争力的重要契机，将对城市建设和城市发展产生广泛而深远的影响，被喻为“可与 19 世纪工业革命相比的发动机”。一方面，城市事件通过新建场馆优化城市整体空间布局、完善城市基础设施、促进地区发展、提升城市景观和形象等方面重塑城市的物质环境。另一方面，城市事件通过改进城市的制度环境和服务能力、促进城市文化建设、改善城市就业、提升城市知名度和影响力等来塑造城市社会软环境。吴志强（2008）从城市事件与城市发展、城市建设的关系进行综合论述，提出城市发展的“底波率”原理，认为一个城市的发展由内生的动力和外部的流动要素驱动，城市重大事件作为“底波率”中“波”的要素，对城市发展构成阶段性跨越提升。

二、大运会筹备期间深圳城市建设概况

据有关部门统计，大运会筹备期间，深圳市政府共投入约 1800 亿元进行城市基础设施

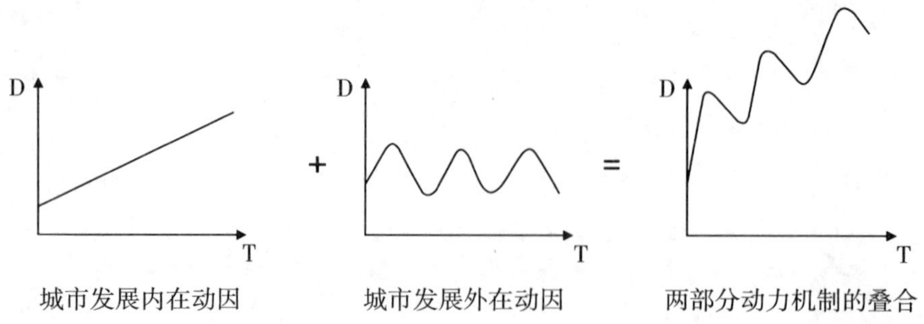

图1 城市发展机制的“底波率”原理示意图

建设改造，包括新建、改造体育场馆60余个（其中新建场馆21个、维修改造场馆29个、临时搭建场馆10个）；同时以体育场馆发展为契机，扩展到城市建设领域的各个方面。大运会后，深圳无论从体育场馆规模门类、相关基础设施建设还是城市整体功能完善等方面均走上新的台阶。

（一）以场馆建设为契机，推动所在片区的综合发展

如何充分发挥如此集中、大规模但又相对集中于体育行业的投资所带来的综合效益，场馆建设位置的选择非常重要，深圳在60余个大运场馆的布局及建设模式安排上，除满足赛事举办要求外，更充分结合城市发展要求，相对集中地将新的场馆选择在八卦岭市体育中心、龙岗大运中心、后海南山区体育中心及东部海上运动基地等片区，引导体育场馆成片发展以带动所在片区综合发展，四个片区场馆（共38个）约占全部场馆总数的63%。

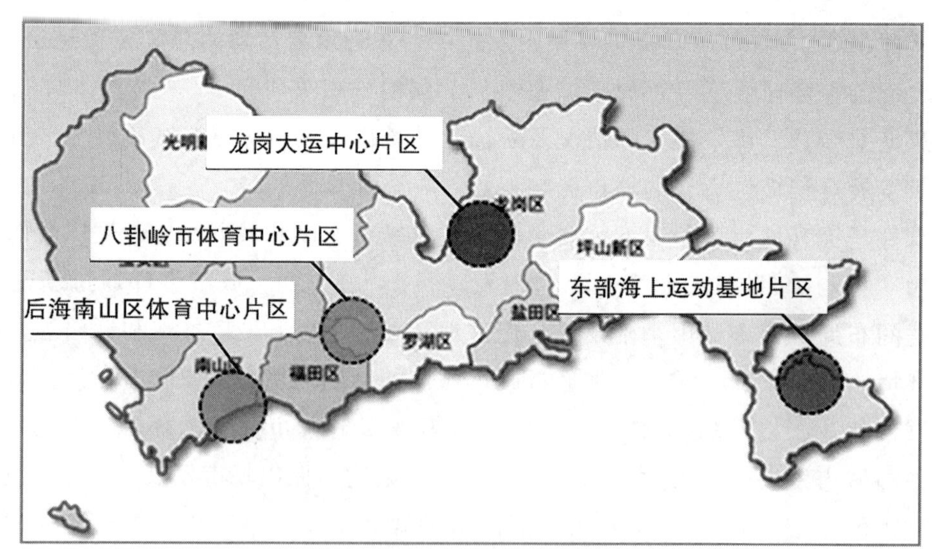

图2 深圳大运场馆布局示意图

1. 八卦岭市体育中心片区

八卦岭市体育中心片区有市体育场、市体育馆、市射击馆、市体工大队综合训练馆、市游泳跳水馆及室外池5个体育场馆，为早期深圳市市级体育中心，后新建了深圳游泳跳水

馆，主要由三部分构成：室内主馆即游泳跳水馆、附馆即戏水馆、室外水上娱乐区及其他配套设施，具备举办市内游泳、跳水等项目的各项功能，也是周边居民开展游泳健身及水上娱乐的重要场所。

2. 龙岗大运中心片区

龙岗大运中心是规划新建的深圳市级体育中心，片区有大运体育中心、龙岗体育中心、市体育运动学校及部分学校场馆等共 24 个体育场馆，涵盖可承办国际田径、篮球、排球、游泳、水球、射击、网球及自行车等门类丰富的体育场馆。

此外，大运会中心片区还规划建设了信息学院新校区、体育运动学校新校区及大运会国际广播电视新闻中心等配套项目。同时，龙岗区结合大运中心片区，新建改造大运路、鼓岭路、龙兴大道、如意路及清辉路等道路，完善周边配套市政设施，打造“大运新城”，为提升龙岗区功能定位、完善城市的综合服务水平起到了重要作用。

3. 后海南山区体育中心片区

后海南山区体育中心区有深圳湾体育中心、深圳大学及华侨城中学部分体育场馆等共 5 个体育场馆，其标志性建筑为深圳湾体育中心，即“春茧”。“春茧”作为本次大运会开幕式举办场馆，除了其“海之门”的总体构思及独特别致的建筑造型外，更是深圳在土地资源日益紧张情况下多种功能混合设置、集约利用土地方面积极探索的典范。

结合“春茧”的建设，深圳市在南山区同步开展了深圳湾 15 公里滨海休闲公园的建设。大运会结束后，从红树林生态公园——“春茧”——西部通道共约 15 公里的滨海休闲公园，各种自然景观及人文景点荟萃、植被丰富、步行及自行车专用通道完善，使南山区后海片区焕发出全新的活力，成为市民流连忘返的、新的城市休闲空间。

4. 东部海上运动基地片区及其他

东部海上运动基地片区主要承办本次大运会的海上运动赛事，包括深圳市海上运动基地、七星湾水域等共 3 个体育场馆。建设该基地的同时，深圳市对深圳东部片区道路、绿化及停车等相关设施同步进行了完善，使其具备了作为未来深圳旅游休闲集中发展片区的基础设施条件。

此外，在上述四个主要片区之外，深圳也结合各区、各相关机构现有设施情况及实际需求，通过新建、改造等方式提供其余的场馆设施。其中，位于宝安中心区的宝安体育场，其建成和投入使用完善了宝安区区级体育中心；深圳信息职业技术学院及深圳市高级中学等体育馆的建成和投入使用，使深圳在承担大运相关赛事的同时，也完善了学校体育设施的配置。

（二）以发展体育为主线，促进相关行业的系统提升

大运会筹办期间，除按照承办赛的要求重点完善体育方面设施外，深圳同步整体统筹考虑，推动了城市交通设施、环境景观等相关体系的系统提升。

1. 交通设施

为配合大运会的举办，建成了城市轨道交通二期、广深港客运专线、深圳北站、深圳机

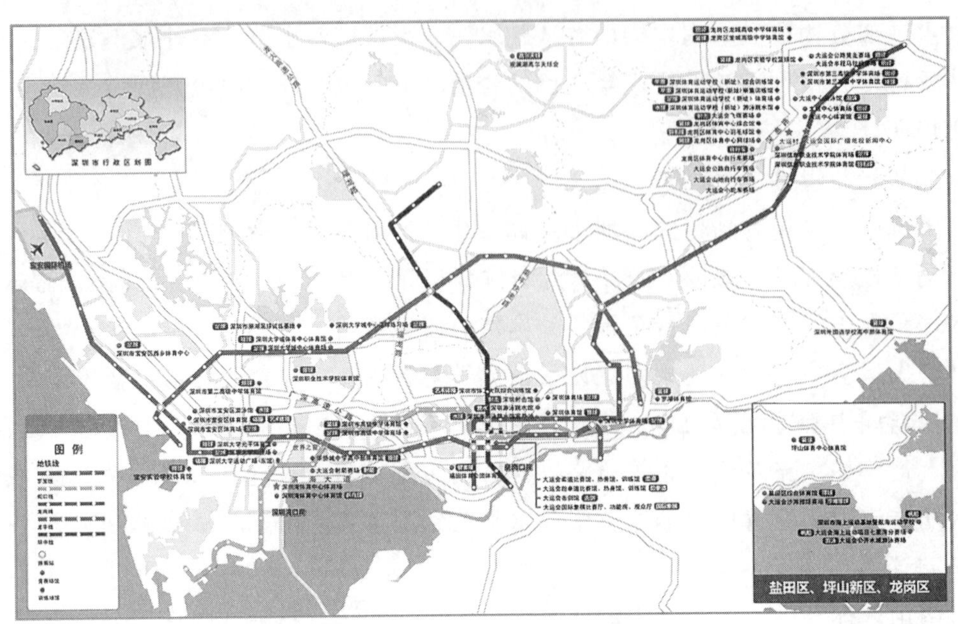

图 3 深圳大运场馆及轨道线路分布示意图

场二跑道等一批重大基础设施，先后对 280 条主次干道进行整改，拥有 500 条公交系统营运路线和 20 条快速路网，城市功能得到显著提升。

深圳市轨道交通二期线路运营后，深圳地铁线路总长从五年前的 22 公里增加到 178 公里，日均客流量达 175 万人次，最高日均客流量约 215 万人次，部分主干道车流量较地铁全网开通前下降 20% 左右。深圳市轨道交通二期共 118 座车站，其中有 13 座换乘站，形成了"四横三纵"的轨道交通网络结构，轨道交通线路几乎覆盖了深圳全市，尤其是中心区域内的各个生活区、商业区、办公区等重点地区，并将各重大交通枢纽点串联，使深圳步入了全新的轨道交通网络化时代。许多市民表示"大运会对深圳而言，最重要的就是地铁，地铁让我们出行更为方便"。

同时，大运场馆周边地区充分利用此次机会，建设或改善区内道路微循环，深圳各区交通连成一体，打造了全市任何一个地方 30 分钟可以到达大运新城的交通圈。并且，在此基础上与惠州、东莞、广州乃至整个珠江三角洲交通对接。

2. 环境景观

为迎接 2011 年世界大学生运动会，在"特色深圳、景观深圳"的总体要求下，深圳市进一步提升城市环境景观。生态风景林方面，对从广州、惠州、香港等地进入深圳境内各主干道两侧的防护绿带进行了重点改造，涉及广深、机荷、水官、南坪、深惠等 14 条干线公路，改造总面积达 566.09 公顷。休闲绿道方面，深圳初步构建起区域绿道、城市绿道和社区绿道三级绿道网，共建设约 400 多公里的绿道和公园，让市民享受到更加绿色、健康的都市生活。作为大运会标志性工程之一的深圳湾滨海休闲带项目投资约 10.9 亿元，东起红树林海滨生态公园，西至深圳湾口岸南海堤，规划总面积 108 万平方公里。

此外，深圳还启动了"市容环境提升行动"，包括建筑立面刷新和屋顶改造、街道设施清洗刷新、窗口门户地区环境综合整治、城市照明改造建设、大运场馆环境美化等内容，城市景观环境明显提升。近年来实施各类城中村综合整治项目1 608个，总投入约达20亿元，城市面貌和人居环境得到明显改善。

3. 节能环保

环保方面，投入部分资金补贴企业用于治理废气，同时新建一批污水处理设施和地下管网，全市污水处理能力比2005年提升了1.2倍，污水再生利用率从2005年的不足1%提升到目前的30%。

节能方面，深圳大运会期间投放新能源汽车达2011辆，占到大运会交通车辆总需求的一半以上，同步配套建设公交充电站31座，超过了北京奥运会和上海世博会新能源汽车投放（分别为500辆、1 147辆）的总和。

此外，大运期间深圳约25万名身着“红马甲”的义工整体转化为城市志愿者，深圳高校的大学生八成以上踊跃报名参加志愿者，全市志愿者已达127万，20%的市民以志愿服务的形式投身大运会。

（三）以大运赛事为资源，注重场馆设施的赛后利用

宋蓓（2009）通过对奥运主办城市奥运场馆再利用问题研究提出，尽管各个奥运主办城市都积极探索了奥运场馆再利用问题，但实际真正进行了再利用的场馆比例不足五成，而再利用较好的场馆比例就更低，估计不足40%。针对大型赛事场馆赛后利用不足的问题，深圳在大运会筹办之初就将场馆的赛后利用融入到场馆规划和建设中，具体体现在注重场馆混合功能设置和注重场馆赛后功能策划。

1. 注重场馆赛后功能策划

深圳市办大运的基本思路是，遵循新建场馆满足比赛需要和赛后使用相结合的原则，避免大规模建设专用场馆，尽量把新建场馆建在高校、体校、中学的校园内，为深圳市民提供长期休闲娱乐服务。

本次大运会各项比赛、训练所需要的场馆总数为60个，其中有29个场馆是对现有公共体育设施进行维修改造而作为比赛场馆使用的，另有位于学校内的场馆25个，约占场馆总数的42%。21个新建场馆中，位于学校内的场馆10个，占新建场馆总数的48%，大运赛事结束后将转交给学校使用，避免了赛后可能出现的场馆空置等遗留问题。

同时，本次大运会还搭建临时场馆10个，大运会结束后直接拆除。一方面降低了建设成本，另一方面也满足了比赛需要。

深圳大运会场馆建设还充分考虑了城市未来规划和发展的需要，将场馆布局和城市未来发展的规划紧密结合。通过完善场馆周边配套设施，打造集体育竞赛、文化娱乐于一体，提供多功能服务的市民活动中心。

2. 注重场馆复合功能设计

为了避免大型体育场馆赛后闲置，除了归属教育机构的场馆外，其他大运场馆赛后将由建设方或专业的运营机构打理，承接文体活动。采取了BOT（基础设施特许权）方式的深

圳湾体育中心，将在建设方经营期满50年后移交给政府。

坐落于深圳市南山后海中心区的深圳湾体育中心（春茧），其建筑设计注重混合功能、多用途使用，其硬件、软件等各项设施均可承办国际国内重大品牌赛事和大型演出活动。场馆在大运会结束后，不仅可用于各类职业体育竞赛活动、国家级高水平运动集训及居民健身活动等，还用于开展各项商贸展览、音乐会、演唱会、娱乐等多种大型活动。

大运村与深圳市信息职业技术学院同步规划建设是大运场馆建设的“点睛之笔”。赛后，大运村改为学生公寓交由深圳信息职业技术学院（下简称“信息学院”）使用，通过一次投入，既建成了一所综合性大学，又充分满足了大运会期间运动员的居住需求。日前该设施已移交给信息学院，并正式投入使用。

三、依托大运会促进城市发展的经验

回顾深圳大运会的赛前筹备策划、赛期城市运营及赛后资源利用，深圳在结合大运这一重大“城市事件”引导促进城市整体发展提升上，从推动重点片区建设、引导相关行业发展及促进城市整体功能提升等方面进行了一系列有益的探索，也取得了一定的经验。

（一）以点成片：依托场馆成片建设的整体发展理念及实践

总体策划上，结合八卦岭市体育中心及龙岗大运中心的现有设施进行改造、扩建并新建部分设施以适应举办大运会的要求，推动南山区级体育中心的建设及东部大鹏半岛高端旅游休闲产业的发展，形成相对集中、特色各异的四片主要赛区。

此外，其他场馆的布局上也充分考虑对周边片区的带动，大运会共使用60个体育场馆，其中新建的22个场馆有一半以上依托轨道二期工程，布局在原特区外地区，加快了特区一体化进程，改善原特区外地区的基础设施和生活品质，也大幅提升了原特区外地区的城市建设水平。

（二）以线带线：相关行业相互支撑的系统发展理念及实践

作为一项综合型的体育赛事，大运对城市的影响不仅仅在体育设施方面，更在于城市其他行业结合体育赛事积极主动应对，与体育行业获得同步发展。

首先，大运带动了与之关系最密切的交通设施、环境景观方面的改善及提升，深圳更强调了节能环保方面的探索及城市软实力方面的提升。

其次，依托大运的其他相关活动赛事的举办使深圳的文化品位大为提升，在深圳大运会期间举办的全球青年联欢节、世界大学生沙滩音乐节和中欧青年论坛等多场主题活动，都凸显全球大学生聚会的体育文化多元化和多样性；在深圳大运会赛事期间举办世界大学校长论坛，来自五大洲68个国家和地区的163位大学校长，以“21世纪大学的新使命与人才培养”为主题，分享各自的真知灼见。这也是深圳大运会在大运会历史上做出的一项创新和贡献。

最后，大运也带动外围相关产业的进一步发展。对比赛场馆和运动员村的建造修筑、对城市危旧房的改造、城市基础设施的建设以及相关配套的完善，使城市投资环境、居住环境得到改善，一方面增加投资活动，另一方面吸引了外来人口居住，增加了各相关产业尤其是服务业的有效需求。与基础设施有关的钢铁产业、水泥产业和交通产业等也受到较大影响，带来了更多的就业机会，并对周边区域乃至珠三角地区带来发展良机；以新能源汽车为主的深圳新兴产业也受到了本届大运会的直接带动。

（三）以赛筑城：城市整体功能提升的先导发展理念及实践

通过大运会的筹办，深圳以城市发展目标为导向，还重点强化了城市旅游休闲度假功能、高等教育水平和公共文化生活品质等三个方面的完善提升，使其作为国际化大都市的内涵更加全面。

完善城市旅游休闲度假功能：在城市总体规划中作为深圳最后一片“净土”、预备发展高端旅游休闲度假功能的东部大鹏半岛，在大运期间高标准展开了一系列道路、基础设施及休闲健身设施的建设，为未来的全面发展奠定了基础；深圳湾15公里滨海休闲公园的投入使用，改写了深圳作为滨海城市在主城区生活性滨海岸线不足的历史；同期建成的约400多公里绿道，适应了广大普通老百姓及游客的休闲健身需求；大运期间建成的一大批特色体育场馆、城市灯光工程及城市绿化景观等靓丽的城市旅游新景观，逐步成为深圳旅游的新亮点、新品牌。由此，完善了深圳特色鲜明、层次丰富的旅游休闲体系和度假功能。

提升城市高等教育水平：按照高校利用模式兴建的大运村，在大运会结束后，整个大运村移交给了信息学院作为新校区使用。同时临近大运村即将落户大运场馆片区的香港中文大学深圳学院，将与信息学院共同为龙岗未来的发展提供人才保障和智力支持，成为继南山大学城之后又一片高校集中发展片区，使深圳逐步向与城市人口规模及经济实力相匹配的高等教育发展规模及水平方面靠近。

改善城市公共文化生活品质：举办重大国际性体育赛事，不仅内在具有极大的经济价值，而且还可以提升一个城市的政治和文化等方面的影响力。通过大运会，迅速改善了深圳的城市公共文化生活品质，并对深圳的文化格局带来了变化；深圳建市至今仅有30多年，大部分的深圳人都是外来移民，“移民文化”是城市的主流。但随着大运会的成功举办，“市民文化”逐渐发展和强化；大运会举办之后，众多的体育场馆设施将刺激举办城市居民参与体育运动，“休闲文化”不断发展。同时，新的体育设施还可以促进城市居民健康状况的改善，加深城市居民对体育休闲活动的参与。

四、结语

与历史上“城市事件”带动城市发展和城市建设的诸多成功案例类似，2011年深圳大运会也对深圳城市发展产生了积极而广泛的影响。正如本届大运会的口号“从这里开始，不一样的精彩”，借助本届大运会，以场馆建设带动城市发展、促进相关行业系统提升、大运场馆“平赛结合”和绿色大运等理念得到贯彻和执行，城市物质环境和社会软环境得到极大提升，深圳正借助本届大运会的成功举办继续不一样的精彩。

当前，我国仍处于发展中阶段，在国家层面“城市化”战略目标的指引和几亿人进入城市的任务要求下，各城市政府一方面努力依托“分税制”的资金筹措体制及土地产权结构体系等方面尝试“做大城市”，另一方面也积极通过申办各类重大活动赛事等手段扩大城市影响力以“做强城市”。在快速发展的过程中，城市整体运营体系所涉及的法制环境不尽完善、监督机制不尽健全、公民意识不太觉醒。这种前提下，通过地方政府的积极推动，中央政府的大力支持，以政府为主导的主题性、专项性、针对性的行动，往往能在短期内集中有限的人力、物力和财力，有效突破某些政策、体制和机制方面的约束，在特定的城市建设领域取得突破性、跨越式的进展。

地方政府如果策划、组织得当，充分利用主题性、专项性行动的“触媒效应”，往往可得到除城市在特定片区、主题领域以外的协同发展，有效推动城市整体面貌的改善和城市整体功能的完善，达到事半功倍的效果。德国鲁尔工业区、日本鹿港、香港结合启德机场搬迁建设西九龙文化综合发展区、上海结合“世博会”改造黄浦江两岸旧工业区、深圳结合大运会提升大鹏半岛基础设施建设水平等专项行动，在通过城市事件促进老区的改造、引导城市升级转型方面取得了较好的效果，而广州结合亚运建设番禺体育新城、深圳结合大运发展南山后海及深圳湾片区则在通过城市事件推动城市新区建设、完善城市功能结构等方面都取得了较好的效果。

相反，如果策划、处理不当，有时不仅不能促进特定片区及特定主题领域以外的协同发展，甚至连新的建设行动本身也形成政府后续沉重的财政负担，希腊奥运会场馆片区、深圳国际自行车赛场片区不仅对周边城市片区带动不够，连场馆自身运营也成为难题。此外，为保障重大活动赛事如期举行“赶工期”而导致工程质量事故，为扩大城市影响力“举债办事”而影响事后城市正常运营的事也多有发生。

因此，从长远来看，理顺机制、完善体制，营造适宜城市长远健康发展的物质环境、制度环境和精神环境，为城市事件提供制度环境和服务能力，进而通过城市事件的发展带动城市向更高的目标发展，实现城市发展的阶段性跨越提升。

（作者：王承旭，深圳市规划国土发展研究中心，地区规划一部部长，高级规划师；李蓓蓓，深圳市规划国土发展研究中心，规划师；陈磊峰，深圳市规划和国土资源委员会第一直属管理局；郑振兴，深圳市规划国土发展研究中心）

参考文献

[1] Metropolis Commission. The Impact of Major Events on the Development of Large Cities [N]. Working Paper. 2002.

[2] 吴志强．重大事件对城市规划学科发展的意义及启示［J］．城市规划学刊．2008（6）：16－19.

[3] 郑曦，孙晓春．以城市事件为推动力的城市发展与环境景观建设［J］．风景园林，2006（2）：72－77.

案例篇

上海轨道交通基本网络与世博低碳易达模式

1995年上海建成第一条轨道交通线路——全长16公里的轨道交通1号线。进入21世纪，上海加快轨道交通建设步伐，2001年至2010年的十年间建成近450公里（含磁悬浮）的基本网络，年均建成38公里，2007年、2009年、2010年年均建成90多公里。基本网络的建成使轨道交通逐渐成为居民重要的出行方式，在城市客运中发挥主导作用，尤其在世博会高强度客流集散中发挥关键作用。同时，轨道交通线网的快速发展促进了上海城市用地、空间结构的调整和优化，初步形成了基于轨道交通网络、线路和车站的土地利用模式。

一、450公里轨道网络使轨道交通逐渐成为上海公共客运主导交通方式

（一）450公里轨道交通网络基本特征

截至2011年10月底，上海拥有轨道交通线路11条，机场磁浮专用线一条，运营线路总长450公里。换乘站按照不同线路不同站台计算，共有轨道交通车站275座；换乘站按照一座实体车站计算，共有轨道交通车站241座。上海外环内中心城区轨道交通线网总长约280公里，车站182座（换乘站算一座实体车站），线网密度约0.4公里/平方公里，站点密度约0.3座/平方公里。上海轨道交通基本为单一地铁制式，提供中心城出行服务的同时兼顾郊区出行需求，因此线路较长，如2号线全长达60公里。2010年，轨道交通（不含磁浮）全网工作日日均开行载客列车近4280列次。轨道交通服务范围随着网络规模扩大显著扩大，以车站600米服务半径计算，2010年中心城轨道交通车站覆盖中心城26%土地面积，直接服务中心城55%的人口和67%的岗位。

表1　2010年上海轨道交通线网规模

线路	运营线路长度(km)	运营线网长度(km)	车站数(个)			
			地下	地面	高架	小计
1号线	36.9	36.9	15	6	7	28
2号线	60.3	60.3	27	1	2	30
3号线	40.2	40.2	1	4	24	29

续表 1

线路	运营线路长度(km)	运营线网长度(km)	车站数(个)			
			地下	地面	高架	小计
4 号线	33.8	22.3	17	0	0	17
5 号线	16.6	16.6	0	1	10	11
6 号线	31.1	31.1	19	0	8	27
7 号线	43.9	43.9	28	0	2	30
8 号线	37.0	37.0	21	0	7	28
9 号线	44.7	44.7	18	0	5	23
10 号线	35.2	35.2	31	0	0	31
11 号线	43.8	43.8	11	0	8	19
磁浮线	29.1	29.1	0	1	1	2
合计	452.6	441.0	188	13	74	275

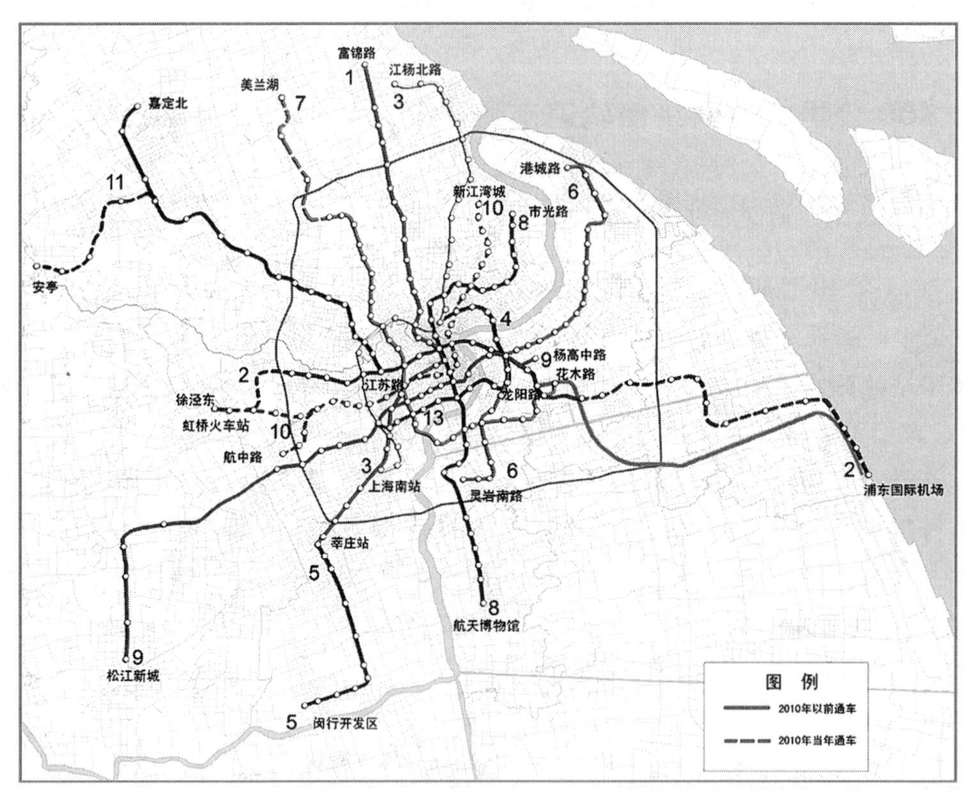

图 1　2010 年上海 450 公里轨道交通基本网络

2010 年上海轨道交通 11 条线路配备列车 442 列，平均每条线路配备列车 40 列。其中，2 号线配备列车最多，达 67 列。

表2　2010年上海轨道交通运营列车配备情况

线路	配备列车数(列)	线路	配备列车数(列)
1号线	53	7号线	42
2号线	67	8号线	46
3号线	28	9号线	52
4号线	28	10号线	37
5号线	17	11号线	40
6号线	32	磁悬浮	3

（二）轨道交通客流特征

2011年上海轨道交通工作日日均进闸客流约380万人次，站台上客量约600万乘次（换乘系统约1.6），客运周转量约5 200万人公里。虽然地面公交上客量（800万乘次）高于轨道交通，但轨道交通客运周转量高于地面公交（4 700万人公里），占公共交通（不含出租车）比重达53%，逐渐成为上海公共客运主导交通方式。2007年以来，地面公交日均客流量基本保持稳定，轨道交通日均客流量年均增长百万乘次，直接拉动上海公共交通客流量增长。

上海轨道交通工作日日均客流量最高的是开通较早的1号线和2号线，分别超过120万乘次和110万乘次。客流强度最高的是2号线市区段（广兰路—徐泾东）约3.3万乘次/公里，其次是1号线约3万乘次/公里。客流强度较低的是位于内环线外的5号线、6号线和11号线，均不到1万乘次/公里。客流强度反映了轨道线路直接延伸至郊区易导致客流强度和客流效益降低。

表3　2011年上海轨道交通工作日客运量及高断面客流

线路	工作日客流(万乘次/日)(2011年6月30日)	客流强度(万乘次/公里)	高峰小时单向高断面客流(万乘次/小时)(2011年6月7日)
1号线	111.5	3.0	52 500(漕宝路—上海体育馆)
2号线	123.8	市区段3.3	43 000(人民广场—南京东路)
		全线2.0	
3号线	49	1.2	24 600(赤峰路—虹口足球场)
4号线	72	2.1	19 600(杨树浦路—浦东大道)
5号线	12.9	0.8	12 700(春申路—莘庄)
6号线	26	0.8	15 940(源深体育中心—世纪大道)
7号线	51.4	1.2	27 480(岚皋路—镇坪路)
8号线	63.4	1.7	23 800(陆家浜路—老西门)

续表 3

线路	工作日客流 (万乘次/日) (2011 年 6 月 30 日)	客流强度 (万乘次/公里)	高峰小时单向高断面客流 (万乘次/小时) (2011 年 6 月 7 日)
9 号线	52. 5	1. 2	23 000(桂林路—宜山路)
10 号线	46. 7	1. 3	19 680(海伦路—四川北路)
11 号线	20. 6	0. 5	16 400(枫桥路—曹杨路)
合计	629. 8	—	—

上海轨道交通客流总体呈“申”字形分布，主要客流走廊上客流集聚效应凸显。随着轨道交通线网规模的扩展，网络效益日益明显，换乘客流量越来越高。目前上海轨道交通近三分之一客流为换乘客流，人民广场站、世纪大道站是换乘客流量最高的两大换乘站，日均换乘客流分别为 30. 3 万乘次和 27. 7 万乘次。

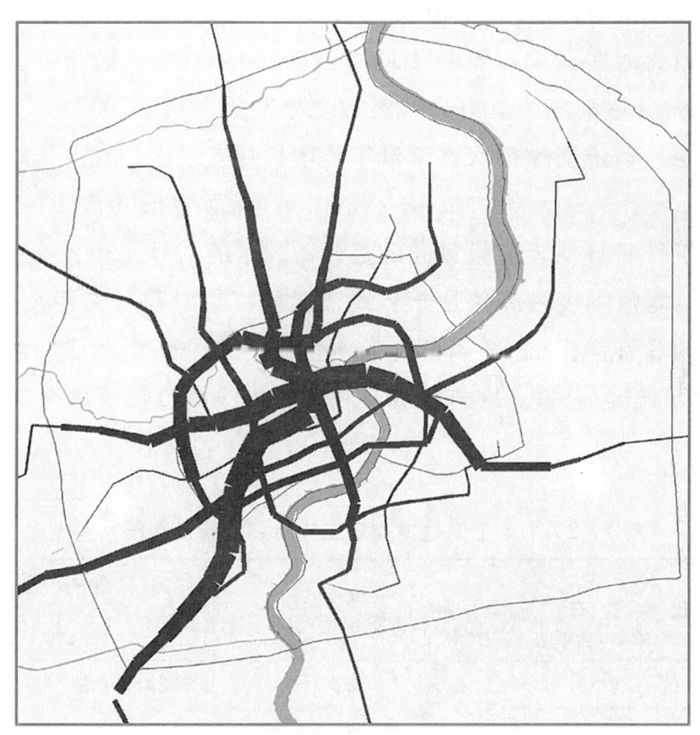

图 2　2010 年上海轨道交通客流分布

二、轨道交通网络是世博低碳易达模式的重要保证

(一)“五线九站”轨道设施顺利完成 38%的世博客流集散任务

为保障世博交通高效运转，上海在世博园周边地区布设了 5 条轨道交通线路和 9 座车站，5 条线路分别是 4 号线、6 号线、7 号线、8 号线和 9 号线，9 座车站直接对应园区 9 个

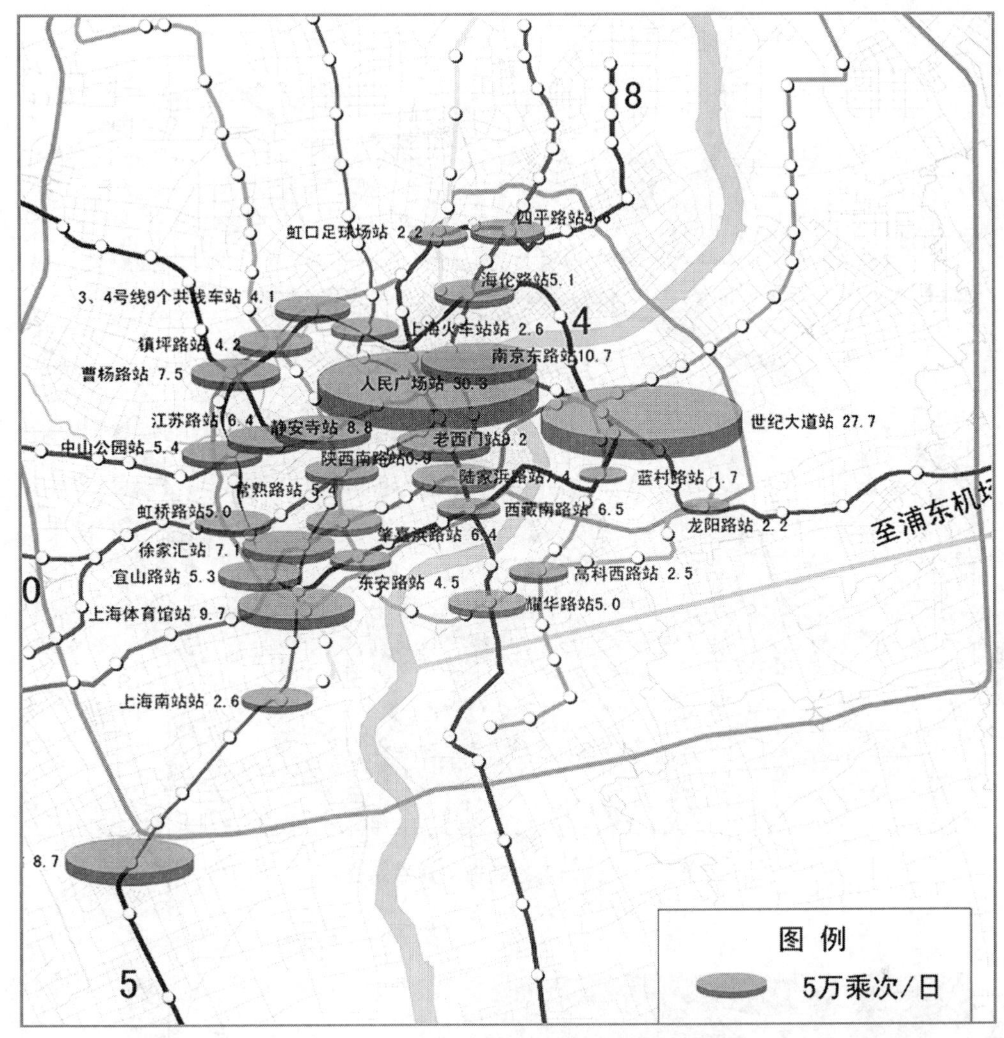

图3 2010年上海轨道交通换乘客流分布

出入口。同时，根据客流情况动态调整运营方案尽可能发挥轨道交通设施的作用，如6号线增能、涉博线路最晚班次延长到次日凌晨0:10。轨道交通设施建设和运营方案与世博出行需求相结合确保38%的世博客流通过轨道交通集散。

（二）小汽车、出租车换乘轨道交通促进世博低碳易达模式

世博会期间，上海针对小汽车和出租车采取严格的管制措施：世博园周边停车场只对团体巴士和公交车开放；周边500米范围内划定小汽车管控区；普通出租车高峰时段限制进入管控区域等。疏导结合，在城市外围区，结合轨道交通和专线公交线路设置小汽车停车换乘点，如8号线航天博物馆站、9号线松江大学城站和F1赛车场等，引导小汽车和出租车出行者就近换乘轨道交通或专线公交到达世博园，促进世博集约化出行。

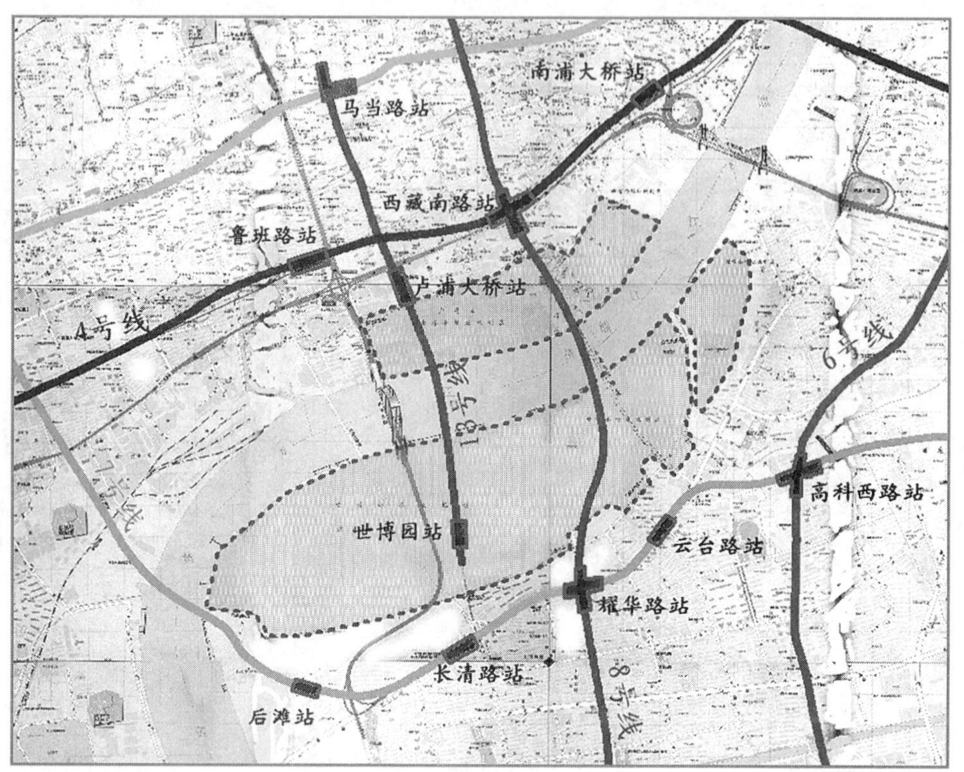

图4 世博园周边轨道交通车站分布

图5 轨道交通世博专线的大客流

表4　2010年上海世博会全日入园方式结构

交通方式	出行量(万乘次/日)	比例(%)
轨道交通	17.0	38.1
旅游巴士	15.8	35.4
世博专线	2.7	6.1
常规公交	2.7	6.1
自驾车	2.3	5.1
出租车	3.2	7.2
慢行交通	0.9	2.0
合计	44.7	100.0

（三）低碳易达的轨道交通保障世博交通运转

轨道交通由电力驱动，是一种无直接排放的交通方式。相比其他客运交通工具，能耗水平较低，2009年上海轨道交通能源消费量38万吨标准煤，个体机动能源消费量336万吨标准煤。轨道交通低碳的特征符合世博期间城市交通低碳环保运转的要求，是轨道交通成为备受鼓励的交通方式的重要原因。

轨道交通拥有较为独立的运行系统，几乎不受其他交通方式干扰，运行车速和出行可靠性较高。轨道交通易达的特征是吸引世博游客的重要原因之一。

三、轨道交通网络助推上海城市用地结构优化

（一）形成以轨道交通车站为中心的圈层用地开发模式

上海一直注重轨道交通车站顶盖和出入口周边用地的开发。1991年至1995年期间，围绕轨道交通1号线的建设，改造淮海路沿线商业、办公等建筑，实现楼宇与车站的直通。同时对外围区的轨道交通车站开展顶盖物业开发，如锦江乐园站、莘庄站等。21世纪以来，在轨道交通站点开展高建筑密度、高容积率的顶盖开发。如9号线打浦桥站顶盖开发的日月光广场；在建的13号线金沙江路站顶盖开发的月星环球博览中心，规划建筑净容积率12.9。

此外，上海还注重轨道交通车站300米至3公里范围的开发建设。如上海大宁国际广场位于轨道交通车站周边300～600米区域，建筑毛容积率4.5。城市外围区很多大型居住社区，如莲花路站周边的梅陇城、松江大学城站周边的三湘四季花城等，位于轨道交通车站周边300～600米区域。轨道交通9号线、11号线周边的许多大型居住社区及郊区新城位于轨道交通车站600米至3公里开发范围。

图 6　上海地铁打浦桥站顶盖开发——日月光广场

轨道交通开通以来，上海以轨道交通车站为中心的圈层用地开发实践推动了 2011 年《上海市控制性详细规划技术准则》的编制和发布。《准则》充分体现了基于轨道交通的土地利用模式，将地块与轨道交通站点距离作为确定其开发强度和容积率的重要依据。

（二）轨道交通逐渐改变沿线用地结构

轨道交通 5 号线 2003 年开通运营，是目前唯一基本在郊区运营的轨道交通线路。2003 年开通年份站点半径 2 公里范围内居住人口 36 万，日均客流规模 0.8 万乘次，居住用地占 21%，岗位用地占 32%；2008 年开通五年之后，站点半径 2km 范围内居住人口 52 万，日均客流规模 10 万乘次，居住用地占 27%，岗位用地占 43%。五年时间里，沿线居住人口数量增长 44%，居住用地面积增加 25%，岗位用地面积增加 33%。

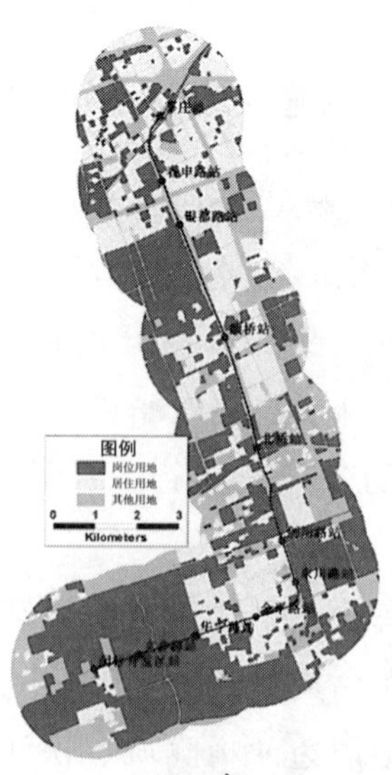

2008年

图 7　上海轨道交通 5 号线站点半径 2 公里范围内用地结构变化

四、结语

上海2010年450公里轨道交通基本网络在优化交通方式结构、保障世博会成功运转、调整城市用地结构等方面发挥了重要作用。根据《上海市轨道交通近期建设规划》，2020年上海轨道交通网络将达到800公里规模。可以预见，800公里轨道交通网络将在上海后世博时期低碳易达交通模式的形成过程中发挥更为显著的作用。

（作者：陆锡明，上海市城市综合交通规划研究所，原所长，教授级高工；王祥，上海市城市综合交通规划研究所规划室主任，高级工程师；程微，上海市城市综合交通规划研究所，工程师）

参考文献

[1] 陆锡明，陈必壮，朱洪．世博集约交通［M］．北京：中国建筑工业出版社，2010.

[2] 陆锡明，王祥．轨网功能性拓展引导空间紧凑型调整［J］．城市规划，2011（增刊1）．

[3] 陆锡明，王祥．基于轨道网络的大城市综合交通规划理念［J］．城市交通，2010（4）．

[4] 上海市城市综合交通规划研究所．上海市综合交通年度报告［R］．2011.

大珠三角区域规划：一个持续动态的过程[①]

粤港合作并非近期才开始，最近三年连续有三份有关加强粤港合作的政策性文件出台，包括2011年的《中华人民共和国国民经济和社会发展第十二个五年规划纲要》、2010年的《粤港合作框架协议》以及2009年的《珠江三角洲地区改革发展规划纲要（2008—2020年）》；粤港合作和区域规划顿然成为热点话题。本文趁机审视目前、回顾过去以及展望将来香港有关区域规划的工作，亦希望借以加深大家对大珠三角区域规划的认识。

一、区域规划合作的背景

香港是珠江三角洲自然地理区域的一部分，与广东省山水相连，而粤港社会联系亦悠久密切。内地自1978年改革开放以来，制造业以“前店后厂”模式的分工；至香港回归祖国以后，服务业以“内地与香港关于建立更紧密经贸关系的安排”模式的合作，均显示两地经济互动日趋密切。

从以下数字可以看出香港与内地社会经济的紧密互动关系：

- 2000年至2010年期间，平均每日往来香港与内地陆路跨界旅客行程数目由278 000人次增加至498 000人次，平均每年增长6%；而相应的跨界车辆行程数目则由31 000车次增加至43 000车次，平均每年增长超过3%（图1、图2）；
- 根据香港特别行政区规划署与深圳市统计局于2008年合作开展的“香港人在深圳居住状况调查”，约有61 900名香港人于深圳居住；而2010年第六次全国人口普查结果则显示有234 829名香港居民于内地居住；
- 资金方面，香港是内地最大的外来直接投资者，根据内地的统计数字，截至2010年年底，香港在内地的实际直接投资额累计4 560亿美元，占内地外来直接投资总额的42%。香港与广东省的经济联系，相对于内地其他地方远为密切。截至2010年年底，香港在广东省的实际直接投资额累计1 560亿美元，占广东省外来直接投资总额的62%。内地也是香港

① 本文的主要资料来源为香港特别行政区规划署的文件，故部分内容或已在其他有关的论坛/研讨会和文件中发表。

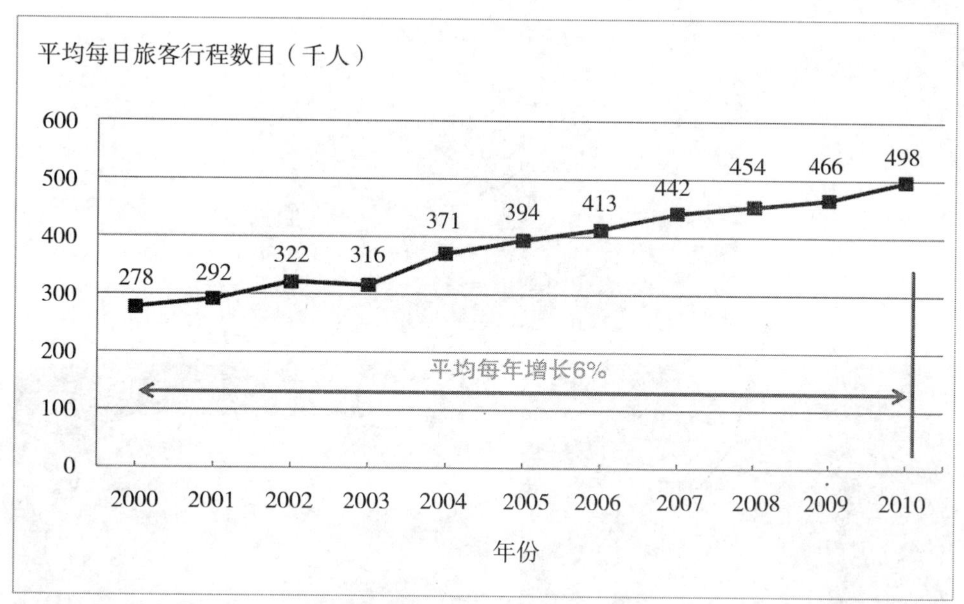

资料来源：香港特别行政区入境事务处

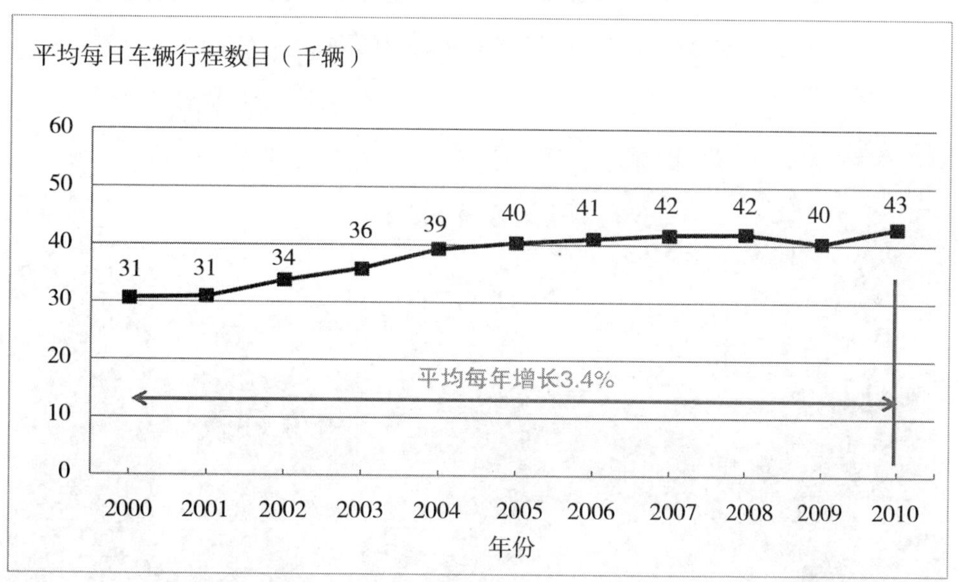

资料来源：香港特别行政区入境事务处及海关

图 1　2000 年至 2010 年平均每日往来香港与内地陆路跨界旅客及车辆行程数目

最大的外来直接投资者，截至 2009 年年底，内地在香港的直接投资市值达3 410亿美元，占香港外来直接投资总额的 36%①。

随着香港与内地的社会经济联系日益紧密，两地政府之间的合作亦在 1998 年“粤港合作联席会议”成立之后愈加紧密（图 3）。

在全球化时代以区域作为竞争主体的趋势下，大珠三角城市群随之形成。基于实际需要，时势所趋，区域之内的城市必须合作，以求增强区域整体的国际竞争力，而区域规划亦

① 资料来源：香港年报 2010。

图2　来往内地及香港跨界旅客

图3　粤港合作联席会议

图片来源：2011年8月23日香港特别行政区政府新闻公报。

必然成为其中一个重要的切入点（图4）。

有别于世界其他区域，在“一国两制”的框架内，大珠三角区域的粤港澳三地政府在行政上互不隶属，且施行不同的政治和经济制度，社会情况亦有所分别，因此，三方是采取协调的方式，进行有关的区域规划合作。

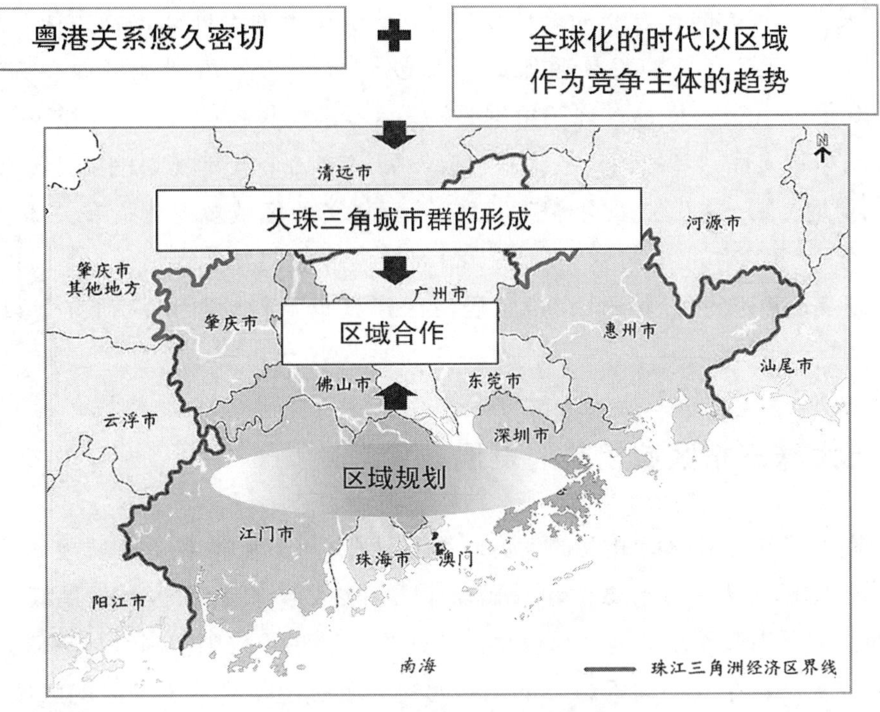

图4　大珠三角区域规划合作的背景

珠江三角洲经济区包括广东省九个城市（广州市、深圳市、珠海市、佛山市、东莞市、中山市、江门市，惠州市的惠城和惠阳区、惠东和博罗县，以及肇庆市的端州和鼎湖区、高要和四会市）。而大珠三角区域则由上述九个城市以及香港和澳门两个特别行政区组成。

二、区域规划的概念

（一）区域规划的定义

区域规划一般是指地域超越个别城市的规划工作。而地域的界定，往往考虑到一些特定的地理空间，例如河流流域范围等。在这个较大的地域空间之内，各个城市都会共同面对一些不能独力解决的问题，或须各方合作才能实现的整体发展目标，例如跨越个别城市行政界线的基础设施的整合、经济职能分工和定位、生态环境保护、空间结构优化、共同资源的综合利用等问题；规划区域为这些城市提供一个平台，共同协商处理这些问题，以促进整个区域的可持续发展。换言之，区域规划综合了经济、社会以及环境多项目标。

（二）区域规划的层面

区域规划可分为广义和狭义两个层面。广义的层面指对地区社会经济发展和建设进行总体部署；包括区际规划和区内规划，前者主要解决区域之间的发展不平衡或区际分工协作问题，后者是对一定区域内的社会经济发展和建设布局进行全面规划。狭义的层面指一定区域内与国土开发整治有关的建设布局总体规划[①]。基于这个理论框架，就大珠三角区域而言，广义的区域规划泛指有关的发展政策，主要包括《珠江三角洲地区改革发展规划纲要(2008—2020年)》(以下简称《珠三角纲要》)、《粤港合作框架协议》(以下简称《框架协议》)以及《中华人民共和国国民经济和社会发展第十二个五年规划纲要》(以下简称《国家十二五规划纲要》)这几份文件的相关章节；而狭义的区域规划泛指有关的空间规划，包括粤港澳于2009年合作完成的《大珠江三角洲城镇群协调发展规划研究》(以下简称《大珠研究》)以及现正进行的《环珠江口宜居湾区建设重点行动计划》研究(以下简称《湾区研究》)。

三、与大珠三角区域相关的发展政策

综观三份与大珠三角区域相关的发展政策文件[②]，可以归纳有关区域规划的一个前提和三项重点。前提是《珠三角纲要》和《国家十二五规划纲要》的区域发展政策只是涵盖内地珠三角的范围，提及香港的内容均以粤港合作作为表述，权限清晰，体现双方政府在行政上互不隶属的实况；在“一国两制”下，有效的区域协调须建基于各方就区域发展的愿景、目标及策略达成共识，而《框架协议》正是由粤港过去多年紧密合作交流所产生的默契和共识会聚而成的。至于重点，第一，把促进经济增长定为主要目标，亦注重以人为本的可持续的发展。第二，发展方向包括以全球视野谋划区域发展定位，形成世界级城市群；并以综合战略思维谋划区域协调发展，形成粤港澳分工合作、优势互补的格局。第三，加强深化三地合作，在恰当范畴进行区域规划合作。

(一)《珠江三角洲地区改革发展规划纲要(2008—2020年)》有关区域规划的摘要

《珠三角纲要》由国家发展和改革委员会于2009年1月正式公布。

《珠三角纲要》主要将珠三角未来的发展和改革提升到国家发展战略的层面，要求珠三角地区加强与港澳合作；对港澳的意义在于把粤港澳合作的目标、内涵和框架作为国家政策予以明确，为三地加强合作提供了政策依据[③]。

1. 主要目标

(1)要把解决当前问题与谋划长远发展结合起来，保持珠三角地区经济平稳较快发展，为保持港澳地区长期繁荣稳定提供有力支撑。

(2)形成粤港澳三地分工合作、优势互补、全球最具核心竞争力的大都市圈之一。

2. 区域发展

(1)推进交通基础设施建设，形成网络完善、布局合理、运行高效、与港澳地区紧密

① 资料来源：全国科学技术名词审定委员会。

② 广东省以至个别城市如广州和深圳的《十二五规划纲要》亦有提出与大珠三角区域规划及与港澳合作相关的政策方向；由于篇幅所限，在此不作详述。

③ 资料来源：2009年2月19日香港特别行政区政府新闻公报。

相连的一体化综合交通运输体系。

（2）以广州、深圳为中心，推进珠三角地区区域经济一体化，形成资源要素优化配置、地区优势充分发挥的协调发展新格局。

（3）推进城市规划一体化，优化珠三角城市群的空间结构布局。

3. 粤港合作

（1）本着互惠互补的原则，加强与港澳的协调合作，充分发挥彼此的优势，支持与港澳在城市规划、轨道交通网络等方面进行对接。

（2）支持共同规划实施环珠江口地区的湾区重点行动计划。

（3）规划建设深港边界区。

（4）鼓励在协商一致的前提下，与港澳共同编制区域合作规划。

（二）《粤港合作框架协议》区域规划的摘要

2010年4月，香港特别行政区行政长官和广东省省长签署《框架协议》。

《框架协议》有三项重要的标志性意义：（1）在中央层面，由国务院批准的《框架协议》把《珠三角纲要》的宏观政策转化为有利粤港发展的具体措施；（2）在区域层面，《框架协议》是首份由国务院批准就粤港合作所签订的纲领性文件，它订下重点工作，为粤港合作提供平台；（3）在本地层面，《框架协议》为粤港合作作出清晰发展定位，列出具体政策和措施，让本地业界和公众充分掌握两地最新的经济发展和措施[①]。

1. 主要目标

以战略思维谋划粤港合作发展思路，进一步建立互利共赢的区域合作关系，推动区域经济一体化，促进社会、文化、生活等多方面共同发展，携手打造亚太地区最具活力和国际竞争力的城市群。

2. 区域发展

（1）建设世界级新经济区域。

（2）建设以香港金融体系为龙头，珠三角城市金融资源和服务为支撑的金融合作区域。

（3）打造世界先进制造业和现代服务业基地。

（4）形成更低成本、更高效率的国际航空枢纽、航运中心和物流中心，构建现代流通经济圈。

（5）建设优质生活圈。

（6）形成世界级城市群。

3. 粤港合作

（1）共同编制区域合作规划，发挥协同效益，促进区域融合发展；包括优质生活圈规划、基础设施规划以及环珠江口宜居湾区建设重点行动计划。

（2）重点合作区包括落马洲河套地区。

① 资料来源：2010年4月7日香港特别行政区政府新闻公报。

（三）《中华人民共和国国民经济和社会发展第十二个五年规划纲要》有关区域规划的摘要

2011 年 3 月第十一届全国人民代表大会第四次会议批准《国家十二五规划纲要》。

《国家十二五规划纲要》就国家未来五年的经济和社会建设事宜制订发展方向、战略及指标，具体说明政府的工作重点，是国家的发展蓝图和行动纲领①。

其中港澳专章凸显了中央对保持香港长期繁荣稳定的支持，为香港的未来发展提供了历史机遇，同时让香港在“一国两制”下，配合国家的整体发展策略，按《香港特别行政区基本法》自行订定自身的发展方向、政策和措施。②

1. 主要目标

（1）坚持科学发展，促进区域良性互动、协调发展。

（2）促进经济社会发展与人口资源环境相协调，走可持续发展之路。

2. 区域发展

（1）构筑区域经济优势互补、主体功能定位清晰、国土空间高效利用、人与自然和谐相处的区域发展格局。

（2）积极支持东部地区率先发展，发挥对全国经济发展的支撑作用。

（3）推进珠三角区域经济一体化发展。

（4）在东部地区打造更具国际竞争力的城市群。

（5）科学规划城市群内各城市功能定位和产业布局，推进大中小城市基础设施一体化建设和网络化发展。

（6）城市规划和建设要注重以人为本、节地节能、生态环保、安全实用、突出特色、保护文化和自然遗产。

3. 粤港合作

（1）加强内地和香港、澳门交流合作。

（2）落实《粤港合作框架协议》，促进区域经济共同发展，打造更具综合竞争力的世界级城市群。

（3）加快共建粤港澳优质生活圈。

（4）加强规划协调，完善珠江三角洲地区与港澳的交通运输体系。

四、大珠三角的区域空间规划研究

粤港澳三地在行政上互不隶属，然而关系悠久密切，个别地方的发展均可能影响邻近以至整个区域，故此必须注重区域协调，就共同关心及影响区域发展的问题进行规划研究。这些研究为三地提供了一个打破行政区界障碍的平台，增进彼此讨论交流，一同较有系统地探

---

① 资料来源：香港特别行政区政制及内地事务局网页。

② 资料来源：2011 年 3 月 16 日香港特别行政区政府新闻公报。

索有利于发挥协同利益、促进区域整体发展的路向。在研究过程中，三地都是在平等的基础上合作；而研究所提出的建议，只供三方制定各自规划时作为参考。在考虑有关建议时，三方须根据各自的社会情况，并遵从各自的既定机制，策划其行动纲领和计划，以落实研究的目标和方向。

（一）《大珠江三角洲城镇群协调发展规划研究》（《大珠研究》）

《大珠研究》是粤港澳三地规划主管部门首次合作进行的策略性区域规划研究，亦是中国第一个跨不同制度边界的空间规划协调研究。研究于2006年3月开展，成果于2009年10月由三方共同发布。

《大珠研究》旨在于“一国两制”的框架内，以前瞻性的视野考虑和分析大珠三角发展的机遇与挑战，以“粤港澳合力建设充满生机与活力、具有全球竞争力的、协调可持续的世界级城镇群”为总体目标，借此提出可促进区域整体经济发展、社会融合和环境改善的空间发展策略，主要包括空间结构优化策略、高可达性策略以及优质环境策略。在这基础上，研究建议了涵盖多个范畴的近期重点工作，包括打造可持续发展的宜居区域和构建优质生活环境的跨界地区合作，以及跨界交通合作等。研究提供了纲领性的策略建议，作为三地政府制定区域合作及跨界政策的参考①。

（二）《环珠江口宜居湾区建设重点行动计划》研究（《湾区研究》）

《湾区研究》是《大珠研究》的其中一项跟进工作，继续由粤港澳三地规划主管部门统筹，于2010年4月正式开展。研究的目的是从一个宏观及区域性的角度，制定以“宜居”为目标规划策略，建设“环珠江口湾区”成为大珠三角内一个既有优质生活、又有利经济发展的核心地区。研究参考了有关“宜居”的文献及国际经验，归纳宜居区域的特征和标准，评估湾区的机遇和挑战，融合粤港澳三地优势，提出初步建议，包括以保护环境资源、保育历史文化、优化休闲空间等重点的规划行动方向，促进“宜居湾区”建设；例如建议中的“绿网”、“蓝网”、“绿色交通”、“低碳住区”、“跨界环保合作”等行动，分别从保育环境生态、串联地域文化、鼓励公共运输和高效集约的发展模式，以及改善大气和水质等重点改善区域环境，提升居民生活质量。研究预计可于2011年年底至2012年年初大致完成②，并就经修改的建议进行第二阶段的公众咨询。

五、现时大珠三角的区域规划

细看与大珠三角区域相关的发展政策与空间规划研究的时序（表1），《大珠研究》早于2006年（即是三份有关的发展政策文件公布之前）已经开展，其中建议进行的《湾区研

① 详情可浏览规划署网页：http：//www. pland. gov. hk/pland_ en/misc/great_ prd/gprd_ c. htm。

② 详情可浏览规划署网页：http：//www. prdbay. com/ft/home. asp。

究》亦被2009年公布的《珠三角纲要》及2010年签署的《框架协议》列为区域合作规划项目。《湾区研究》于2010年展开，所建议的优质生活方向亦于今年公布的《国家十二五规划纲要》港澳专章内有所提及。

《大珠研究》旨在提出可促进区域整体经济发展、社会融合和环境改善的空间发展策略，而《湾区研究》旨在制定以“宜居”为目标规划策略，促进建设“环珠江口湾区”成为大珠三角内一个既有优质生活又有利经济发展的核心地区；两项研究正好符合了区域规划的理论性目的：综合经济、社会、环境多项目标，同时呼应了有关发展政策的主要目标：促进经济增长之余，亦注重以人为本/可持续的发展。

表1　与大珠三角区域相关的发展政策与空间规划研究的时序

年份	发展政策	空间规划研究	其他有关区域规划的项目
1996			《跨境通道研究》探讨港深西部通道的方案
1999			进行《1999年跨界旅运统计调查》
2000			《铁路发展策略2000》建议兴建广深港高速铁路香港段
2001			首次进行《香港居民在内地居住的情况及意向调查》 进行《2001年跨界旅运统计调查》
2003			进行《香港人在珠江三角洲居住和工作状况调查》 进行《2003年跨界旅运统计调查》 进行《香港居民在内地居住的情况及意向调查》 《香港与珠江西岸交通联系研究》建议兴建港珠澳大桥
2005			进行《香港居民在内地居住的情况及意向调查》
2006	公布《国家十一五规划纲要》	展开《大珠研究》	进行《2006年跨界旅运统计调查》 展开《深港兴建莲塘/香园围口岸前期规划研究》
2007			进行《2007年跨界旅运统计调查》 进行《香港居民在内地居住的情况及意向调查》
2008			进行《香港人在深圳居住状况调查》
2009	公布《珠三角纲要》	展开《共建优质生活圈专项规划》	展开《落马洲河套地区发展规划及工程研究—勘查研究》 进行《2009年跨界旅运统计调查》
2010	签署《框架协议》	展开《湾区研究》	
2011	公布《国家十二五规划纲要》		进行《2011年跨界旅运统计调查》

注：香港规划署负责或参与大部分上述的空间规划研究以及其他有关区域规划的项目。

《大珠研究》以建设具有全球竞争力的、协调可持续的世界级城镇群为总体目标，提出三大空间发展策略；而《湾区研究》参考国际经验，融合粤港澳三地优势，制定以“宜居”为目标的综合发展策略，两者均与有关发展政策的两大重点：“以全球视野谋划区域发展定位”以及“以综合战略思维谋划区域协调发展”吻合。

综观现时的大珠三角区域，广义和狭义两个层面的区域规划兼备，而且两者之间又紧密互动，目的和重点更是一致，有效发挥协同效益，促进区域协调发展。

六、回顾以前香港有关区域规划的工作

以前，香港有关区域规划的工作以应付当前跨界问题、单一项目、个别范畴和专责性质为主。随着香港与内地的社会经济发展更紧密的互动，区域规划范畴渐趋多元化，包括跨界活动调查、跨界交通基建规划、个别发展规划项目以及区域规划研究。性质亦由单一解决当前跨界问题的项目演进至主动谋划综合、宏观和前瞻的整体区域发展策略。区域之间的沟通和交流更迈向制度化，例如“粤港合作联席会议”下设立的专责小组和个别合作项目的协商机制；模式亦日趋多样化，例如交流会、研讨会及专家评审会；关系也逐渐多边化，例如省对特区、市对特区、特区对特区，甚至省、市和特区多方协调、交流和合作。

七、香港城市规划工作的区域因素

区域视野不应只限应用于跨界的区域规划，在 2007 年完成的《香港 2030：规划远景与策略》研究（以下简称《香港 2030 研究》）中，亦已确立加强与内地的联系、把握内地快速发展的机遇为香港三大策略规划方向之一。随后，香港规划署近年所进行的城市规划研究，即使只是涉及境内范围，也充分考虑了区域因素。

（一）《边境禁区的土地规划研究》（以下简称《边境禁区研究》）

2010 年完成的《边境禁区研究》旨在为将从禁区范围释出的地区提供土地用途规划指引。禁区北沿深圳河、东临沙头角海、西至后海湾、南近规划中的新界东北新发展区，当中大部分土地为高生态价值及环境易受影响的地区，故建议土地用途应以保育为主，并可保留为港深两个高密度城市之间的“绿色地带”。这一方面有利香港境内的环境生态保育，另一方面为两地发挥视觉调剂作用，减低城市热岛效应。简而言之，《边境禁区研究》考虑到禁区处于策略性的位置，可为区域发挥保护环境的功能。

另外，由于《香港 2030 研究》已把新发展区及在市区和新市镇内腾空及未予充分运用的土地订为优先发展区，禁区内的研究范围并无迫切进行大型发展的需要。况且禁区现有的交通基建及公用设施有限，故采用了可持续发展模式：研究范围建议以保育和康乐用途为主；但在适当的位置如口岸及主要交通干道附近则会预留地方作相关的发展走廊，并会善用空置的土地或荒废的农地作不同程度和性质的发展。例如，在马草垄兴建生态旅舍，在缸瓦甫和恐龙坑进行住宅发展，在发展走廊设置跨界贸易/物流、商业和购物、娱乐、休闲和旅游等用途。整体规划布局可谓因地制宜，同时亦为下一代保护区内珍贵土地资源。这样的安排可因应香港长远发展需要的转变，在未来有需要的时候，重新审视有关地区的功能，再作切合当时情况的恰当用途[①]。

---

① 详情可浏览规划署网页：http：//www. pland. gov. hk/pland_ en/misc/FCA/frontier_ chi/frontier_ c. htm。

（二）有关新界新发展区及落马洲河套地区的研究

现正进行的《新界东北新发展区规划及工程研究》[①] 利用新界北部邻近珠三角的位置，把握跨界交通基建带来的契机，为多项优势产业或其他经济活动提供发展空间。根据初步建议，古洞北新发展区拟以“多元化发展中心”作为发展主题，主要用途包括住宅、商业中心、科研发展等；将会容纳约65 000人及提供26 000个就业机会。粉岭北新发展区拟发展成“河畔市镇”，主要用途为住宅及政府设施；将会容纳约48 000人及提供6 200个就业机会。坪蚌/打鼓岭发展区拟发展成“优质产业区”，主要用途为特殊工业、优势产业及住宅；将会容纳约18 000人及提供13 000个就业机会。

而刚于 2011 年 8 月展开的《洪水桥新发展区规划及工程研究》[②] 亦会善用新发展区优越的地理位置，配合并推进港深跨界基建合作，开拓经济发展机遇。

此外，根据正进行的《落马洲河套地区发展规划及工程研究—勘查研究》[③]，河套地区将会凸显港深边界区的优势，发展以高等教育用途为主，辅以高新科技研发及文化创意产业用途，建造跨界人才培育与知识科技交流区；容纳约24 000名学生及提供约29 000个就业机会。

以上三项研究善用区位优势，既可配合区域的发展愿景，同时为香港应付房屋需求，扩大新界地区经济活动的规模并且提升其发展定位，改善香港先进产业及职位大多集中于市区的现况，促进均衡的经济发展空间布局，务求惠及香港广大市民。

展望将来有关香港境内的城市规划工作，“因地制宜”这一原则须重新定义，就是当中的“地”除了指本地的地理因素外，还须包括区域层面的区位优势，这样才能确保区域的可持续发展，而且不会错失借助区域发展之势解决境内问题之机。

八、结语

综观大珠三角区域规划合作，是在“一国两制”的框架下进行，当中并无既定程序或模式，粤港两地均持务实自主、互利共赢的态度，不断深化和扩阔合作领域。

随着两地的社会经济联系逐渐紧密，过往区域规划的工作经历了“因事、因地、因时制宜”的演进：事项由单一变成综合，地域范围由跨界扩展至区域，时期由当前伸延至前瞻，务求与时并进。而现时大珠三角区域兼备发展政策与空间规划研究，两者之间紧密互动，目的及重点互相紧扣，有效促进区域协调发展。展望将来，两地应会一如过往在构建多年的合作平台上就影响区域发展的事项进行讨论交流，因应区内实际状况及区外宏观形势，以项目把握当前的合作机遇，以研究统筹未来的发展策略，共同营造世界级城市群。至于有

---

① 详情可浏览规划署网页：http：//www. nentnda. gov. hk/。

② 详情可浏览规划署网页：http：//www. pland. gov. hk/pland_ en/p_ study/prog_ s/hsk_ nda/index_ b5. html。

③ 详情可浏览规划署网页：http：//www. lmcloop. gov. hk/chi/。

关香港境内的城市规划工作，则须继续放眼区域，以至世界，才能有高瞻远瞩的视野。

从上述的实际情况分析，区域规划既要与时并进，有关的发展政策与空间规划研究之间又要互相配合，城市规划的工作更要应用“因地制宜”演进中的定义；这恰恰显示了大珠三角的区域规划工作是一个持续动态的过程（Process），重点并不是要制订一份区域规划图则（Plan），而是要因事、因地、因时不断考察思量，以应对当前共同面对的问题，以及谋划一个互利共赢的未来。

（作者：凌嘉勤，香港特别行政区规划署副署长；陈巧贤，香港特别行政区规划署高级城市规划师；杨倩，香港特别行政区规划署城市规划师）

广州地下空间开发与利用立法研究

2011 年 12 月，广州市政府正式公布政府规章《广州市地下空间开发利用管理办法》（以下简称《管理办法》），并定于 2012 年 2 月 1 日开始实施。《管理办法》的出台标志着广州市的地下空间开发与利用立法取得了阶段性的成果。本文拟围绕该《管理办法》，重点介绍立法的主要思路和内容，并结合国内其他城市的相关立法，对地下空间开发与利用立法的一些问题进行分析，以期对今后立法的进一步深化和完善提出意见和建议。

一、立法背景

（一）广州市地下空间开发利用和规划管理现状

城市地下空间开发是城市社会经济发展到一定阶段的产物。与国内外城市的发展轨迹相类似，目前广州的地下空间开发建设已进入了大规模开发时期，“十一五”期间，广州每年新开发的地下空间达 100 万平方米，计划在“十二五”期间还要翻一番。促进目前广州地下空间大规模开发的具体原因可归纳为以下几个主要方面：

一是地下空间开发是城市空间资源集约高效利用的现实需要。随着城市的社会快速发展，城市建设用地紧缺，地下空间已成为城市发展的重要空间资源。国际经验表明，人均 GDP 达到 5 000 美元时，地下空间将进入黄金开发期。广州市作为国家中心城市、综合性门户城市和区域文化教育中心，2010 年人均 GDP 已达到 11 695 美元，在经历了改革开放 30 多年的经济社会快速发展后，一方面广州面临着土地和空间资源紧缺的问题，另一方面广州已进入追求高质量的城市化发展阶段，城市建设用地和空间发展也已从过往的追求粗放型、外延式的增量拓展模式向集约型、立体式、内涵式的存量优化模式转化。科学、有序、合理地开发利用地下空间资源成为现阶段城市空间政策的关键词。

二是追求高质量城市化阶段精细化规划和管理的需要。这意味着要以人的全面发展为城市发展的根本目的，意味着要实现城市经济社会环境文化的协调发展。在这方面，广州以城市中心区地下空间的综合利用为切入点，进行了大胆尝试。在珠江新城 CBD 区的最核心、地价最昂贵的区域，将 56 万平方米用地规划建设为大型开敞式公共绿地广场，同时，把广场地下全部掏空，综合开发了总建筑面积约 50 万平方米的地下空间并充分利用。不仅建立起人、车和轨道交通相结合的立体化综合交通体系，还为CBD区提供了15万平方米的地下公共商业休闲服务设施和解决了派出所、变电站、集中供冷等公共设施的配套问题，实现了疏导交通与土地资源有效利用双赢的有效结合。另一方面，广州历史文化资源丰富，近年提出了建设世界文化名城的定位和从实力到魅力的城市发展战略，规划确定了20.39平方公里的历史城区、45片历史文化保护区（街区）以及约4 690处各级文物保护和线索单位需要保护。既要保护如此大量的历史文化遗存和城市风貌，又要兼顾城市发展的客观需求，合理挖掘地下空间资源以完善旧城区基础设施和公共服务设施配套，解决交通问题等成为一种较重要的手段。

三是轨道交通快速发展直接带动了地下空间的线性开发。近年来，广州市轨道交通进入了快速建设的时代，轨道交通的发展直接引领了城市地下空间的线性开发。目前，已建成运营里程222公里，线路包括一号线、二号线、三号线、四号线、五号线、八号线、广佛线及APM线共8条线路，轨道车站135座，在建线路里程26.1公里，包括六号线工程（浔峰岗至长湴段）和八号线西延线（凤凰新村至文化公园）。依附地铁站的地下商业街、地下商场，与地铁站连通、平战结合的地下人防工程吸引了大量的人流，使得地下空间以地铁站点为中心不断向外围拓展。地下空间的建设将成为城市建设的重要组成部分。

然而，相对于地下空间的开发现状和开发趋势，广州市关于地下空间的规划编制和规划管理相对滞后。国家基本法律中关于地下空间建设的有关管理制度不够明确，广州市又没有相关的地方性法规作为依据，政府对地下空间的开发行为缺乏有力地控制和引导，难以调动社会资金参与地下空间开发利用的积极性，每个地下空间项目在办理土地管理、工程管理手续时都需要作为个案经过多次会议进行协调和讨论才能做出决策，在一定程度上阻滞了城市地下空间的开发建设。

（二）国内有关地下空间开发利用立法的情况

从国内立法情况来看，基本可以说，地下空间开发利用立法是以《物权法》和《城乡规划法》的颁布实施作为分水岭的。在此之前，有关地下空间开发利用的立法很少。而在此之后，相关立法蓬勃发展，如雨后春笋般大量涌现。究其原因，在于《物权法》首次在立法上明确规定了建设用地使用权可以在土地的地表、地上或者地下分别设立，为地下空间建设用地使用权的单独设立提供了法律依据，也为地下空间房地产权登记奠定了基础。

《物权法》出台以前的地下空间开发利用立法以建设部规章《城市地下空间开发利用管理规定》为代表。早在1997年，建设部就公布了这个管理规定，并于2001年作了一次修订。《城市地下空间开发利用管理规定》中明确了城市地下空间的概念，地下空间规划的体系、内容、基本原则以及编制和审批的程序，地下空间工程建设的审批程序等内容。应该说，在这些已经规定的内容方面，该规章是具有相当预见性的，和我们今天新出台的许多地方立法相比内容相差无几。但是，它有一个很大的缺陷，那就是对于地下空间建设用地使用权没有作出规定。从民法的角度，过去一直是“土地法”的理念占主导地位，也就是认为土地所有权、土地使用权的空间范围上及天宇，下至地心。在这种情况下，如果地表土地已经设定建设用地使用权，能否再许可第三人对地下空间进行开发利用；或者反过来，如果已经对地下空间进行开发利用，还能否许可第三人开发利用地表土地，对此，理论界一直存在争议和疑虑。因此，地下空间建设用地使用权的取得方式、办理程序缺乏法律保障，地下空间开发利用就难以实施。这一硬伤的存在，导致地下空间开发利用的立法名存实亡，地方政府普遍感觉对地下空间开发利用的行政管理特别是土地管理无法可依，政府部门的自由裁量权较大，地下空间建设用地使用权的授予只能是“犹抱琵琶半遮面”。这样的状况，一定程度上制约了地下空间的发展。

2007 年《物权法》的出台，首次在立法上明确规定建设用地使用权可以分层设立，这打破了过去土地使用权的范围上及天宇，下至地心的传统理解，解除了认识上的禁忌和瓶颈，为地下空间的开发利用提供了物质基础：政府可以为地下空间单独设立建设用地使用权，而不妨碍在地表进行建设行为；对地表设立了建设用地使用权，也不妨碍对地下空间再单独开发利用。另外，2008 年 1 月 1 日开始实施的《城乡规划法》，再次明确了城市地下空间开发和利用的规划管理原则，即要“符合城市规划，履行规划审批手续”。因此，《物权法》和《城乡规划法》出台后，有关地下空间开发利用的地方立法大量涌现，其中包括两部地方性法规，分别是《天津市地下空间规划管理条例》(2009 年 3 月 1 日起实施) 和《东莞市地下空间开发利用管理暂行办法》(2011 年 9 月 1 日起实施)；多部地方政府规章，例如《深圳市地下空间开发利用暂行办法》(2008 年 9 月 1 日起实施)、《韶关市地下空间开发利用管理办法》(2009 年 10 月 1 日起实施)、《上海市地下空间安全使用管理办法》(2010 年 3 月 1 日起实施) 等；另外，还有众多行政规范性文件。

广州市的《管理办法》正是在上述背景下应运而生。

二、立法的主要思路和内容

地下空间开发利用涉及规划、土地、建设、权属登记、使用管理等诸多方面，针对该活动的管理立法也是一个系统工程，因此，广州市政府决定由市国土资源和房屋管理局牵头，成立由规划、建设、民防、地铁等单位参加的立法起草工作小组，共同开展起草工作。各职能部门分别负责各自职能范围内的条文起草工作，最终由牵头部门汇总形成规章草案。

(一) 主要思路：全方位规范地下空间的开发利用

立法的总体思路是在现有的法律法规的框架下，比照地上建筑的法律规范，着力解决当前存在的地下空间利用零散、效率低，权属不清影响开发积极性，多头管理与无人管理并存等突出问题，从规划、用地、建设、权属登记、使用管理等全方位对地下空间的开发利用进行规范。

当前，我市亟须着重解决阻碍地下空间开发的关键性制度难点和遗留问题。在国家和省对地下空间开发利用法律法规还未完善的情况下，为稳妥推进我市地下空间开发利用管理政策的制定工作，构建我市地下空间开发利用制度框架的工作思路是政策起草应立足于解决当前制约广州市地下空间开发利用的突出问题，在不突破“红线”的前提下进行创新，确保重点地下空间项目能顺利实施。

按照以上思路，起草工作小组解放思想，先行先试，勇于突破，基本明确了地下空间开发利用的基本原则，细化了规划管理，明晰了供地制度和供地审批程序，厘清了权属界定。

（二）主要内容

《管理办法》分为八章，包括总则、规划管理、用地管理、工程建设管理、产权登记、使用管理、法律责任、附则。《管理办法》的主要内容如下：

1. 明确地下空间的规划制定、管理程序和基本原则

在规划管理方面，《管理办法》主要规定了以下几方面的内容：

一是明确了地下空间规划的体系及编制、审批程序。《管理办法》基本延续了2001年建设部规章的规定，将地下空间规划划分为地下空间开发利用规划和地下空间建设规划两个层次，前者是城市总体规划的专项规划，后者是依据前者对地下空间开发利用的具体规定。在审批程序上，地下空间建设规划与城市控制性详细规划的审批程序相比相对简化，即由城乡规划主管部门审查后报市政府批准，未明确要求须经规划委员会审议。同时，《管理办法》规定城市控制性详细规划对地下空间开发利用已作出具体规定的地块，不再编制城市地下空间建设规划。

二是规定了地下空间规划的基本原则，包括合理分层及优先安排城市基础设施和公共服务设施等原则。一方面，规定规划编制要明确地下空间的分层以及各类项目之间的同层、相邻、连通要求，以便于清晰地界定地下空间权主体的权利和义务，充实了以往土地分宗概念的内涵；另一方面，通过立法体现地下空间开发的公共优先原则，保障公共利益，从法理上占据主动。

三是对地下空间开发利用的规划管理程序作了原则性的规定。考虑到地下空间建设工程的特殊性，《管理办法》列出了地下空间建设用地规划许可和建设工程规划许可的具体内容。其中，地下空间建设用地规划许可应当明确地下空间使用性质、水平投影范围、垂直空间范围、建设规模、公建配套要求、出入口、通风口和排水口的设置要求等内容。地下空间建设工程规划许可应当明确地下建（构）筑物水平投影坐标、竖向高程、水平投影最大面积、建筑面积、使用功能、公共通道和出入口的位置、地下空间之间的连通要求等内容。与地表建设工程相比，主要增加了“垂直空间范围”、“出入口、通风口和排水口的设置要求”、“竖向高程”、“地下空间之间的连通要求”等内容。

四是针对实践中的地下空间设施的地面出入口、通风口和排水口等与地面建设的协调难问题作了规范。《管理办法》规定建设单位应当按照规划条件提出的设置要求，在修建性详细规划或者建设工程设计方案总平面图中明确出入口、通风口和排水口等的具体位置，并且在申领地下空间建设工程规划许可证前取得需利用地表的建设用地使用权，或者与地表建设用地使用权人订立书面地役权合同。

2. 明确地下建设用地使用权及有偿使用的管理规则

一是确定了地下建设用地有偿、有期限使用的基本原则，避免了地下空间资源的流失和浪费，为地下空间的有序开发利用筑起了第一道防线。

二是明确了地下建设用地使用权的具体设立方式，即地下空间的具体供地方式。根据《物权法》第一百三十七条有关工业、商业、旅游、娱乐和商品住宅等经营性用地以及同一土地有两个以上意向用地者的应当采取招标、拍卖等公开竞价的方式出让的规定，《管理办法》对经营性单建地下空间实行公开出让的基本原则，并在以下几个方面进行了特殊规定：首先，针对停车难问题，延续我市的历史做法，对新供地的用于社会公共服务的单建地下停车场，规定如果只有一个意向用地者的，可以采用协议方式。从国内其他城市的经验看，深圳、南京、上海也允许协议出让，杭州还可以实行划拨。其次，根据地铁建设的特点，针对我市当前地铁建设资金需求大的突出矛盾，参照深圳、杭州、上海的做法，《管理办法》明确规定地下交通项目可以协议出让不可分割的经营性地下建设用地使用权，有利于促进我市地下空间与非营利性公共设施统筹开发利用。最后，历史用地进行经营性地下空间开发利用，地表建设用地使用权人可以协议取得地下建设用地使用权，深圳也有类似条款表述。实践上，实行公开出让也很难操作，地表原使用权人协议取得也有利于地表地下空间的统一规划和综合开发。

三是明确了办理供地手续的具体程序。由于基本建设的批准程序是围绕建设用地使用权设立方式展开，明确了地下建设用地使用权的设立方式，也就基本理清了相关的行政管理程序。《管理办法》在明确了供地方式的基础上，区分结建地下空间和单建地下空间规定办理供地手续的程序，结建地下工程随地面建筑一并办理用地审批手续，单建地下空间则区分公开出让、协议出让、划拨及自有用地再利用等几种情形分别规定了具体的用地审批程序，有利于规范和引导用地单位顺利办理各项审批手续。

3. 规范地下建设工程与地表建设、相邻建设主体的义务和责任

地下建设工程涉及面比较广，其中一个很重要的内容就是要处理好与地表及周边现有建（构）筑物的关系问题。《物权法》第一百三十六条规定新设立的建设用地使用权，不得损害已设立的用益物权。对此问题，《管理办法》主要从工程建设管理和法律责任两方面进行规范。从工程建设管理方面，《管理办法》有三个条文涉及这一内容，一是规定地下工程建设应当保护地面及周边现有建筑物、市政设施、地下管线、人防工程、文物、古树名木、公共绿地的安全，要求建设单位对上述情况进行调查、记录，制定应急预案和防护措施，开工前，将保护措施告知相关产权人或者管理人；二是规定地下工程的施工图设计，应当包含保护设计专篇；三是规定施工单位编制的施工组织设计中应当具备相应的质量、安全技术措施。这些主要是从最基本的安全的角度，作出的事前预防的规定。从法律责任方面，《管理办法》规定：“地下空间开发利用过程中对已经依法设立的用益物权、建筑物或者构筑物造成妨碍或者实际损害的，应当依法承担相应的民事责任。”这是一种事后救济方式。

为解决我市地下工程缺乏连通的突出问题，更大限度发挥地下空间的效用，《管理办法》强调了建设单位的地下连通义务，以及先建单位预留接口、后建单位后续连通的义务。

4. 简化和规范地下空间产权登记

在现行房地产权利登记制度框架下创新地下空间登记制度，简化了登记流程：一是明确了历史上已建成的地下空间，可以凭规划报建及验收等办理房地产权登记，其中地下轨道交通站场和专用人防工程，可以凭符合国家规定的建设、验收证明办理房地产权登记。二是规定地下建设用地使用权及地下空间的房地产权利登记应当在登记簿和权利证书中注明“地下”，属人民防空工程的，还应当注明“人防工程”，并记载平时用途。

5. 规范地下空间的使用管理

一是对地下空间建筑物、地下车位、车库以及单建社会地下停车场的租售管理作出规定。

二是根据地下空间使用上的特殊性，从配合公共利益、日常管理和维修、公共安全、环境保护、卫生要求、空气质量、防水排涝等方面对地下空间的使用管理进行了规定，加大了地下空间使用的安全性。

三、关于几个问题的探讨

（一）关于地下空间规划与现行法定城市规划的关系

《管理办法》虽然划分了地下空间规划的层次，但就如何编制地下空间规划，特别是如何处理地下空间规划与现行城市规划之间的关系问题上，还有待在今后编制地下空间规划的实践中不断总结、完善。

在这一问题（特别是地下空间控制性详细规划与现行城市控制性详细规划的关系）上，《天津市地下空间规划管理条例》和《东莞市地下空间开发利用管理暂行办法》各代表了一种模式。

《天津市地下空间规划管理条例》的做法可以概括为“分离模式”，即地表、地下各编一套控制性详细规划。具体而言，将地下空间的详细规划作为与现行城市详细规划并行的一套规划，也就是在编制城市控制性详细规划之外，再单独编制地下空间的控制性详细规划。

《东莞市地下空间开发利用管理暂行办法》的做法可以概括为“统一模式”，即地表、地下共用一套控制性详细规划。具体而言，将地下空间开发利用的具体规划作为现行城市控制性详细规划内容的一部分，要求“在城市地下空间总体规划确定适宜开发利用地下空间的地区，城乡规划管理部门在组织编制或者修改控制性详细规划时，应当依据城市地下空间开发利用规划对城市地下空间开发利用作出具体规定”，“现有城市控制性详细规划应当逐步补充和完善有关城市地下空间开发利用的内容”。即将地下空间开发利用规划的内容融入现行城市控制性详细规划中，而不再另行编制单独的地下空间控制性详细规划。

上述两种模式各有利弊。“分离模式”有利于单独组织编制地下空间的控制性详细规划，而不致对现行控制性详细规划大动干戈，但是不利于地表和地下建设行为的整体把握。相反，“统一模式”有利于对地表和地下建设行为的整体把握，但是对控制性详细规划的编制水平提出了更高的要求。广州的《管理办法》是在上述“分离模式”的基础上略有折中处理，即要在现行控制性详细规划之外，另行编制地下空间建设规划，但同时规定控制性详细规划已经对地下空间开发利用作出具体规定的地块，不再编制城市地下空间建设规划。

实际上，无论是旧的《城市规划法》，还是新的《城乡规划法》，以及建设部的《城市规划编制办法》，都不曾规定一个城市有地表、地下两套规划。一个城市的建设行为，无论是发生在地表之上，还是地表之下，都应当在一部统一的城市总体规划的框架内，统一编制控制性详细规划进行规划控制。

（二）关于地下空间开发利用的规划管理技术标准

《管理办法》中对于地下空间开发利用的规划技术标准缺乏明确规定，这一方面是因为该管理办法是一个综合性的规章，留给规划方面的篇幅有限，另一方面也是因为地下空间开发利用尚未形成成熟、稳定的规划技术标准，难以写到规章中去。这为今后进一步深化和完善立法留下了空间。首先需要研究的可能是地下空间的规划管理技术标准体系，与地面的建设有何不同，地面的哪些技术标准同样存在于地下空间，哪些则不存在。确定了标准体系后，再作进一步的研究。例如，地下空间的规划许可要求明确垂直空间范围、竖向高程等内容，这对相关规划测量技术、规划用地红线图的表现形式等提出了新的要求，急需进一步立法进行规范。再如，地下空间的使用性质分类、退让标准、配套要求等也都与地面建筑不同，有待进一步的研究。

从国内其他城市的立法来看，对于地下空间的规划管理技术标准也只有一些零散的规定。例如，《天津市地下空间规划管理条例》对地下空间的使用性质作出了限制，规定地下空间不得建设住宅、敬老院、托幼园所、学校等项目，医院病房不得设置在地下，但法律、法规另有规定的从其规定。《东莞市地下空间开发利用管理暂行办法》对结建地下空间项目地下室外墙距离用地界线的距离作出了规定，要求“不得超出建筑红线，且该距离的最小值不得小于5米；如需超出地表建设用地使用权红线范围的，超出部门应申请办理用地手续。”

总的来看，有关地下空间开发利用的规划管理技术标准仍有待系统的研究和规范，以便指导地下空间规划的编制，规范规划许可、审批行为。

（三）关于地下建设用地使用权设立问题

关于地下建设用地使用权的设立，值得注意的问题是，《物权法》第一百三十六条虽然规定建设用地使用权可以在土地的地表、地上或者地下分别设立，但是过去在设定建设用地使用权的时候，通常都没有明确其纵向空间范围，理解上包括了全部纵向空间范围。那么，在土地上已经存在一个普通的建设用地使用权的情况下，是否可以再就其地下空间设定一个地下的建设用地使用权？

《深圳市地下空间开发利用暂行办法》第十四条第一款规定：“本办法实施前，地表建设用地使用权已经出让或者划拨并由同一主体结合地面建筑一并开发建设地下工程的，视为地表建设用地使用权人已经取得该宗地表以下建设工程规划许可明确的结建地下建（构）筑物外围实际所及空间范围的地下建设用地使用权。”该条规定可以理解为：设立地表建设用地使用权的时候虽然没有明确其纵向空间范围，但并不意味着其权利范围就及于该土地的全部纵向空间，而仅限于建设工程规划许可所明确的地下建（构）筑物外围实际所及空间范围。如此一来，当然可以再就其权利范围以外的地下空间范围再设定一个地下的建设用地使用权。

我们认为，新中国成立几十年来，城市的国有土地使用权大部分已出让，如果认为这些国有土地使用权的范围包括了土地的全部纵向空间范围，那意味着国家如果需要出让某地块的地下空间的使用权，只能收回土地再行出让，则《物权法》有关建设用地使用权可以分层设立的规定失去意义。深圳的做法比较切合实际。

四、结语

广州市的《管理办法》虽已出台，但其主要就当前最急需解决的矛盾和问题作出了规定，很多具体的问题仍有待下一步在实践中不断完善和解决。我们将以此为基础，不断学习和借鉴国内其他城市的成功经验和做法，继续研究和深化，从而为地下空间的科学、合理、有序的开发利用提供制度保障。

（作者：夏利芬，博士，广州市规划局；廖绮晶，广州市规划局，处长）

参考文献

［1］广州市规划局，广州至信交通顾有限公司．广州市城市地下空间开发利用规划管理规定研究［R］．2010.

［2］广州市人民政府．广州市地下空间开发利用管理办法．2011.

太原历史文化名城保护

太原，山西省省会，国家历史文化名城，国家园林城市，是全省政治、经济、文化、交通中心。政区面积6 988平方公里，其中市区面积1 460平方公里，辖6区1市3县，常住人口420余万人。

据考古发掘，太原旧、新石器文化遗址丰富，从久远的古代起，太原的先民便在此繁衍生息，创造了特色鲜明的史前文化。据文献记载，太原，曾是唐尧故地、战国名城、秦汉重镇、北朝霸府、盛唐北都、明廷九边、清之晋商故里，是华夏文明的重要传承之地。

一、历史悠久的建城史

公元前497年，晋国卿赵简子在西依龙山、东临汾河、南傍晋水的太原盆地北部，版筑城垣，以狄篙为墙骨，铸铜为柱础，创建了晋阳城。之后，赵、韩、魏三分晋室，赵国都城晋阳也成为春秋战国之际华夏最早形成的7个中心城市之一，至今已有2 500多年的建城史。

公元前246年，秦始置太原郡，郡治晋阳。公元前206年，汉高祖为了防御匈奴南侵，改太原郡为韩国，都晋阳，晋阳成为北陲军事重镇。北朝时，晋阳又以其优越的军事地理位置，先后成为北魏之“霸府”，东魏和北齐的“别都”。

公元617年，李渊、李世民父子从太原起兵，建立了强大的唐王朝。武则天临帝位，又以晋阳为北都，置太原府。古城晋阳扩建为横跨汾水之上，环周42华里，号称“太原三城”的古都，进入历史上的鼎盛时期。

公元979年，宋太宗赵光义克晋阳，灭北汉，火焚古城，至此，历经近1 500年的晋阳城夷为废墟，演变为今日之农田。

公元982年，潘美在唐明镇基础上兴建周长十里之太原城，作为并州治所。公元1059年，升置太原府，并进行了较大规模的修建，著名的晋祠圣母殿就于此时建成。宋代太原府，地处北陲边防，常年与辽、金、西夏对垒，成为北宋国之屏障。

明洪武初年，晋王开府太原，太原位列九边重镇，大规模扩建宋代以来的城垣，建成环周24里，城高3.5丈，大楼12座，小楼92座，垛口逾万的雄伟古城，名甲天下。

清承明制，太原府为山西省巡抚的治所，太原发展成为我国北方的重要商埠。

从1911年至1949年，在30多年的反帝反封建的革命斗争中，太原先是在辛亥革命中起到重要作用，而后作为山西省传播马列主义、发展革命组织的中心，为新中国革命的胜利做出了巨大贡献。

近代是太原发展变化较大的时期，工业、交通等方面的建设有了质的飞跃。1927 年设立太原市，到 1949 年建成区面积达到 30 平方公里，人口约 21 万人，初步形成门类比较齐全的工业城市，是中国北方的重镇。

1949 年 4 月 24 日太原解放，太原市成为山西省省会，“一五”期间成为首批国家重点建设的城市，11 项重大建设项目在太原落地，各项建设事业得到了突飞猛进的发展，成为国家重要的工业城市。

二、积淀深厚的历史遗存

（一）底蕴丰厚的文物古迹

太原历史底蕴深厚、文物古迹众多，现有各级文物保护单位 279 处，主要分布在太原市区。由古遗址、古墓葬、石窟、寺庙组成，具有典型的历史特征和清晰的时代脉络，文化史迹完整，是太原历史文化的重要物化载体。

其中全国重点文物保护单位 13 处，有晋祠、天龙山石窟、龙山石窟、晋阳古城遗址、王家峰北齐墓群、永祚寺等。省级重点文物保护单位 32 处，有督军府旧址、高君宇故居、山西国民师范革命活动旧址、纯阳宫、文庙、山西大学堂旧址等。市级重点文物保护单位 47 处，有革命烈士陵园、皇庙、山西省立一中旧址、牛驼寨战斗遗址、太原旧城墙遗址、开化寺民居等。此外还有县区级文物保护单位 187 处，文物单位 29 处，已公布历史建筑 58 项、232 处。

（二）风貌犹存的历史文化街区和风貌区

虽历经风雨沧桑，太原市仍保留了一批内涵丰富的历史文化街区和历史文化风貌区。

1. 历史文化街区

2009 年，山西省人民政府公布了南华门、东三道巷、明太原县城、太原矿机宿舍、太原重型机器厂苏联专家楼 5 处历史文化街区。各街区保存有大量的历史文化遗产，展现了太原明清时期、民国时期和解放初工业建设时期的历史发展脉络，反映了地方文明的进步历程。

南华门历史文化街区，经历了明晋王府、清精骑营、民国民居、新中国成立初期市级行政中心的变迁，保留有明晋王府遗址格局、清精骑营街巷格局以及赵树理旧居、牺盟会旧址、徐永昌公馆等民国及解放初期传统民居院落，反映了明清以来太原的城市文化功能和历史风貌。

东三道巷历史文化街区，街区传统格局、肌理尚存，拥有多处历史民居，这些民居为传统四合院建筑，多建于民国初年，院落形制完整、细部装饰精美，在太原现存传统民居中具有一定的代表性。

明太原县城历史文化街区，创建于明洪武年间，曾作为明、清、民国县级政权治所。县城建筑布局独特，如同头北尾南、振翅高翔的凤凰，有着“凤凰城”美誉，城内保留有大量的传统民居、北城门、西城门等城垣遗址和历史传统街巷，基本保持了明清县城传统街区风貌和空间尺度，具有鲜明的地域特色。

太原矿机宿舍历史文化街区，是太原市最早的产业工人聚居区。居住建筑仿照苏联样式建造，为“苏式三层起脊闷顶式住宅区”，建于1954年至1956年，是新中国太原城市建设发展的重要见证。

太原重型机器厂苏联专家楼历史文化街区，街区内有多栋建于20世纪50年代的住宅楼，建筑以苏式为主，细部雕刻精细，是目前太原市保留最完好的苏式住宅。太原重型机器厂苏联专家楼是新中国成立初期同为社会主义阵营的苏联对我国给予人员、技术的援助，大力推进工业化建设的重要历史见证。

2. 历史文化风貌区

为了更好地保护太原府城（明清太原城）的整体格局和传统风貌，2009年市政府公布了文庙—文瀛湖、督军府—钟楼街、城西水系、迎泽大街、小东门街五处历史文化风貌区。

文庙—文瀛湖历史文化风貌区，保存有文庙、崇善寺、纯阳宫、皇庙等重要礼制、宗教建筑，有孙中山纪念馆、山西大学堂旧址、文瀛湖辛亥革命活动旧址等近现代革命活动的遗存，是太原府城传统风貌的重要体现。

督军府—钟楼街历史文化风貌区，督军府片区包括督军府及周边的府东街东花园、玉堂春等文保单位，建筑具有典型民国中西合璧建筑特征。钟楼街片区延续太原传统商业特色，老字号云集。

城西水系历史文化风貌区，曾经南北连通黑龙池、黄河套（现黑龙潭）、西泽河、文漪湖（现饮马河）、西海子、南海子等，是标识宋、明、清太原府城西侧城池的重要地标性空间，也是构成宋以来太原城城池格局特征的重要内容。

迎泽大街历史文化风貌区，迎泽大街建成于1956年，之后的十余年间，迎泽宾馆、并州饭店、财贸大楼、电信大楼、工人文化宫相继建设，具有较鲜明的时代特征，是新中国太原城市建设的集中体现，整条大街呈现承前启后的时代氛围。

小东门街历史文化风貌区，区域内有省保单位山西国民师范文保单位、文物单位太原工程队旧址，有现代工业太原面粉二厂的主体建筑，具有鲜明的工业厂房建筑特色，也是当前太原府城周边仅存的几处集中连片的工业建筑片区。

（三）悠久传承的古村镇

太原市内还分布着省级历史文化名镇晋祠镇、省级历史文化名村店头村及王郭村、峰岭底村等众多各具特色的古村镇，这些古村镇保存了大量文物和具有地方特色的传统建筑，不仅反映了不同时期的乡村风貌、社会生活和文化景观，而且为研究太原古代的军事、经济等功能体系提供了物证，是构成太原历史文化遗产的重要内容。

（四）数量众多的古树名木

古树名木是城市的记忆，市区内现有古树名木586棵，最古者距今约3 000年，亦有为数不少的唐槐，涉及29类树种，以松、柏、槐、杨、柳等适生性乡土树种为主。这些古树与自然景观和人文景观融为一体，传达着历史的古老气息。

（五）光耀千秋的历史名人

并州大地，人杰地灵，涌现出许多彪炳史册的著名人物，赵简子、刘琨、高欢、李渊、李世民、武则天、狄仁杰、白居易、王之涣、王昌龄、米芾、罗贯中、傅山、高君宇等都出生在这里或在这里留下了不朽的业绩，创造了璀璨的历史文化。

（六）丰富多彩的非物质文化遗产

古城太原是中华文明的发祥地之一，孕育了丰富的非物质文化遗产。有清徐老陈醋酿制技艺、晋剧、太原锣鼓、六味斋酱肉、传统面食制作技艺等15项国家级非物质文化遗产，有小店牺汤、太原秧歌、九大套、水母娘娘的传说等33项省级非物质文化遗产，有并州歌、码头调、东于架火迎鼓艺术等87项市级非物质文化遗产。

三、历史文化价值与特色

（一）古代中华民族融合历史的独特载体

历史上太原地区处于我国农耕文明与草原文明的融合地带，在春秋战国、魏晋南北朝、五代十国三次大的割据时期成为各民族争雄称霸的基地，晋阳城肇建至毁城的近1 500年间，有9个独立王朝在这里建立国都或陪都，集中表现出“多民族文化与政权交替融合”的特点。娄睿墓和徐显秀墓以及虞弘墓等都是中原汉族、草原游牧民族及西域民族在太原融合的真实写照。

（二）中国传统文化多层积淀的青山沃土

太原市区传统文化遗存时间跨度由东魏北齐至明清，囊括宗祖文化、佛教、道教、天主教、伊斯兰教等各类宗教文化、礼制建筑等，现存有西周初期宗法制度的实物佐证——晋祠、我国北方佛教文化和石窟研究的重要反映——天龙山石窟等、国内现存最大的道教石窟——龙山石窟、明初山西佛教最高管理机构——崇善寺等。这些重要文化遗存反映了相应时期太原城市社会文化特点，反映出太原传统文化的多层深厚积淀。

（三）中原北门控扼四方的军事重镇

太原北踞雄关，南跻中原，是历史上许多王朝的“京师之左右，首都之辅弼”，是护卫中原的北陲战略要地。古晋阳城、宋太原城、明清太原城的格局都反映出太原军事重镇的格局特点。唐晋阳城北部边城由牙城、子城、罗城组成，筑有羊马城、壅门、瓮城、角楼、马面等军事设施。宋太原城分为内外两城，四门三街，后又陆续增建三座关城，"以处屯兵"。明太原城设八个城门，八门四隅设门楼12座，城周建小楼92座、敌台多座等防御设施，其规模和规格仅次于北京和南京，是明代省城的典范。

（四）中国近代化历程中的先锋省府

太原是北方洋务运动早期中心之一，张之洞成立桑棉局、发展纺织工业，胡聘之开办太原火柴局、兴办山西兵工厂，阎锡山创办西北实业公司、发展工商业，使太原成为近代中国新式工业重镇。

太原具有悠久的革命历史。山西是全国继湖南、江西、陕西之后第四个响应武昌起义的省份，太原是辛亥革命在北方继西安革命成功的第二个城市。诚如孙中山先生所评价"使非山西起义，断绝南北交通，天下事未可知也"。1919年6月阎锡山开办了山西省立国民师范学校，在第一、二次国内革命战争时期和抗日战争时期，成为中国共产党在山西著名的活动基地之一，是"大革命的摇篮"。

（五）新中国成立初期的重工业基地

新中国成立初期，太原被列为首批国家重点建设的城市，"一五"期间国家156项重点工程有11项落户太原。目前太原制药厂、太原变压器厂、汾机、晋机等还保留有20世纪50年代建厂的规划布局及厂房、办公楼。

"一五"期间，为配合工业项目的建设，太原以苏联规划模式于1954年编制了第一版城市总体规划，这个具有千年悠久历史的城市开始用规划来科学引导城市的发展建设，成为新太原发展建设史上的里程碑。

四、卓有成效的历史文化名城保护工作

太原历届市委、市政府都非常重视历史文化名城的保护、建设和管理工作，并以此作为推动经济、社会、文化发展的重要举措，确立了围绕"改造一个环境友好、文化繁荣的宜居老城，打造一个理念先进、绿色宜居的现代新城，开发一个唐风晋韵、绿水青山的晋阳古城"的"三城联动"发展思路，以"发掘文化遗产、传承历史文脉、营造文化氛围、提升城市品位"为主线，开展了一系列卓有成效的保护工作。

（一）建立完善工作机制

成立了太原市历史文化名城保护委员会，全面负责全市名城保护重大事项的协调、指导、监督工作，强化名城建设决策权的法制化和民主化，保证名城保护规划建设的科学制定和全面贯彻落实。

在市规划局设立名城处，负责组织历史文化名城保护相关规划的编制，负责历史文化街区、历史文化风貌区、历史建筑的登记建档、挂牌保护等保护管理工作，负责名城保护的日常管理工作等。

市规划、文物、建设等部门建立了城市建设项目中涉及文物保护审核的工作机制，建立了项目方案审查联席会议制度，使太原市历史文化遗产的保护力度得到进一步提升。

（二）健全法律保障体系

为使我市的历史文化名城保护工作严格按照《中华人民共和国城乡规划法》、《中华人民共和国文物法》、《历史文化名城名镇名村保护条例》等有关法律法规健康有序地开展，市政府相继制定出台了《太原历史文化名城保护办法》、《太原市晋阳古城遗址保护管理条例》、《太原市晋祠保护条例》、《太原市文物保护和管理办法》、《太原市崛围山景区建设和管理办法》、《太原市市级非物质文化遗产保护与管理暂行办法》等一系列规章制度，逐步构建了历史文化名城保护的法律体系。

（三）编制科学的保护规划

为了切实加强名城保护规划的控制力度，市政府近几年陆续组织编制了《太原历史文化名城保护规划》、《晋祠天龙山风景区总体规划》、《崛围山风景区规划》、《南华门历史街区保护详细规划》、《明太原县城历史街区保护详细规划》、《晋祠名胜区详细规划》等一批保护规划，涵盖了名城保护的点、线、面，形成了保护规划体系。

编制的《太原历史文化名城保护规划》已成为太原市名城保护工作的重要技术文件，围绕太原历史文化名城的历史文化价值和特色，实施多层次、多类型、多途径的系统保护，形成总体格局保护、历史城区保护、历史地段保护、文物保护单位及非物质文化遗产保护为主要内容的保护框架，突出“三山环抱、汾水中流、双城错峙”的城市总体环境格局。

（四）加强保护修缮工作

近年来太原市逐步加大了保护资金的投入，完成了蒙山大佛、拱极门城墙遗址、国民师范纪念馆、唱经楼等的修复工程，完成了晋祠景区综合整治、青龙古镇一期改造、中华傅山园建设等工程，启动了窦大夫祠景区、双塔景区建设、钟鼓楼地区改造、晋阳古城遗址公园建设等工作，进行了太原晋商博物馆、太原博物馆的建设，开展了北齐徐显秀壁画馆、三畛古村农耕博物馆建设的前期工作，启动了明太原县城历史文化街区、南华门历史文化街区保护整治工作。

（五）提高宣传保护意识

市政府对历史文化名城保护的宣传工作非常重视，对各类规划方案在城市规划展示大厅、太原市规划局网站进行公示，征求广大群众意见和建议；太原电视台、《太原日报》、《太原晚报》等媒体推出了历史文化名城系列专题报道，宣传太原历史文化，进一步激发了广大群众热爱龙城太原、保护历史遗存、弘扬三晋文脉的积极性。

社会各界有识之士也积极挖掘和弘扬晋阳历史文化，研究出版了《太原赋》丛书、《龙城太原》丛书、《名都自古并州》、《太原文物名胜录》、《太原城市规划建设史话》、《晋商古韵老字号》、《晋祠志》等一批反映太原历史文化的著作，翔实、全面地展示太原深厚的文化底蕴。

通过举办太原面食节、晋商文化艺术周、晋剧展演艺术周、卧虎山庙会等形式，使得丰富多彩的民俗艺术等非物质文化遗产得到了进一步的传承和展示。

随着名城保护宣传工作的不断深入，全体市民的保护意识在不断增强，保护热情不断高涨，保护历史文化遗产已成为人们的自觉行动。国家历史文化名城的称号为我们增加了一份责任，一份保护历史文化遗产的重任，我们将按照国家法律法规和名城保护的相关规划，积极组织实施，努力建设一座历史文化独特、社会经济繁荣的历史文化名城！

（作者：高辉，太原市规划编制研究中心主任，高级规划师）

广州城市水环境建设的实践与探索

改革开放30多年来，广州的城市发展大致经历了三个阶段：第一个阶段以发展商贸业和轻工业为特点。20世纪80年代，广州依靠政策优势和体制改革，率先引入市场经济，创造了“广货”神话，形成了城市的初步繁荣。第二个阶段以招商引资、开放搞活为特点。20世纪90年代，广州较早地形成了较为成熟的市场经济规范，重型工业形成规模，城市工业体系逐步完整，成为经济快速增长的“不设防的城市”，经济规模位列全国前三。第三个阶段以大规模的城市基础设施建设为特点。21世纪的第一个十年，随着广州市辖范围的扩展，开始大规模建设和完善城市基础设施，尤其是城市交通设施，新机场、南沙港、轨道交通、高速公路和城市快速路的建设，逐渐形成了枢纽型、功能性、网络化的现代交通体系，城市骨架逐渐拉大并形成“大广州”的城市格局，广州国家中心城市和南中国门户的地位更加凸显。

长期以来，广州以其“六脉皆通海，青山半入城”的自然形态与人文特色闻名于世。嵌入城市肌理之中、与城市有着紧密血肉联系的水系，是广州最重要的要素和最鲜明的城市特色。除三江交汇于此，仅中心城区河涌就有231条。丰富的水资源及悠久的水事实践形成了典型的岭南水城特色，得天独厚的水环境塑造了广州独特的文化内涵和精神气质。在20世纪八九十年代，随着广州工业化和城市化的飞速推进，广州的水环境遭到破坏：一是城市水域面积大幅减少，岭南水城特色逐步消失；二是水体污染严重，水质恶化。恶劣的水环境造成了人水关系的疏离，不仅严重影响了广州水城的美誉度，也大大降低了城市生活的品质。

2010年前后，广州市将水环境建设作为城市建设的重中之重，进行了一系列的实践与探索。

一、治理目标

早在1988年，广州就开始大规模建设污水处理设施。1998年，提出珠江整治“2003年初见成效、2005年不黑不臭、2010年江水变清”三个阶段性目标。经过不懈努力，到2005年基本消除了珠江黑臭现象。特别是从2008年年底以来，广州以迎办第16届亚运会和首届亚残运会为契机，以中央政治局常委李长春同志提出的广州城市环境面貌“到2010年一大变”为目标，按照中央政治局委员、省委书记汪洋同志关于亚运举行时实现“水更清”的要求，把治水作为民生一号工程，举全市之力全面系统开展污水治理和河涌综合整治。

二、机构建设

2008 年 1 月，“广州市水务局”挂牌成立，这是广州水环境建设最重要的里程碑。这一全新的涉水事务综合管理部门，整合了原先分散的各项水务职能部门，改变了“城乡分割、职责交叉、多头治水”的弊端与瓶颈，扩展了原有水系的功能和内涵，将原有水系建设的概念扩展到经济、文化和社会效益等建设上来。

三、工作思路

广州在治水工作中形成五点成功经验。一是坚持以人为本、治水为民；二是必须坚持综合治理、标本兼治；三是必须坚持统筹协调、形成合力；四是必须坚持改革创新、攻坚克难；五是必须坚持拼搏奉献、大干实干。在市委、市政府的统一领导下，各级各部门按照“污水治理为主，调水补水为辅，突出重点，综合治理，城乡统筹，全市治污”的思路，巩固、优化和提升治水成果，重点抓好污水截流、污水管网完善、污水处理系统扩能、城区内涝治理、雨污分流、河道清淤和调水补水等工程建设，进一步提高城镇污水处理率，全市以超常规的投入、超常规的力度和超常规的大干精神推进治水工作。

四、资金投入

广州市举全市之力，仅在亚运前就投入 486 亿元进行水环境综合治理，在亚运后 5 年内将持续投入 872 亿元进行治水。水环境综合治理的效果非常明显。

在投融资体系方面，2008 年 12 月，广州市水务投资集团有限公司正式挂牌成立。今后在广州，治理城市水污染将成为一种“产业”，水投集团还将通过发行公司债券、开发濒水土地等方式向社会融资，使治污不再单纯依靠财政投入。

五、显著成效

亚运会前后，广州在不到两年的时间里完成了 580 项治水工程，治水工作取得了阶段性显著成效。

在污水治理方面，通过近几年的努力，有效地削减了排向珠江的污染物，珠江广州河段生态环境有了较大程度的改善。时隔 30 年后，省、市领导与广大市民共同验证了珠江水质的好转。2006 年 7 月 12 日及 2007 年 7 月 15 日，连续两年成功举办了市民横渡珠江体育活动，到 2007 年 6 月底，广州市完成了猎德污水处理厂三期工程（新增日处理量 20 万吨/

日)，建成东濠涌泵站等污水提升泵站28座，敷设完成污水收集管网608公里，广州市总污水处理能力为165.3万吨/日。到2010年，广州市中心城区建成污水处理系统10个，泵站45座，管网1 050公里，中心城区及开发区污水能力达到276.3万吨/日，并对116条河涌进行截污。全市污水处理能力显著提升，城市生活污水集中处理率从2008年的75.9%提高到2011年的85%，中心城区达到90%。

在防洪排涝方面，城市抗洪排涝能力明显增强，有效缓解了中心城区水浸内涝问题，经受住了特大暴雨的考验。

在水生态方面，通过采取截污、清淤、补水、水体循环、堤岸绿化等整治措施后，城区新河浦涌、沙基涌、赤岗涌、马涌、小洲村、荔湾涌等河涌不但改善了水质，而且两岸环境得到优化，河涌生态逐步得到恢复。主要河涌水质明显好转，水环境生态修复效果初显，河涌两岸景观及生态环境显著改善。

在供水方面，西江引水工程顺利实现通水，600万市民喝上了放心的优质水，全市自来水水质提前两年多达到新国标。

对广州治水取得的显著成效，省委、省政府给予充分肯定，广大市民群众普遍表示欢迎。实践证明，广州开展大规模集中治水的决策是正确的，措施是有力的，效果是明显的，成为广州治水史和城市发展史上的重要里程碑。2006年9月12日，国家建设部在世界水大会上授予广州市“中国人居环境（水环境治理优秀范例城市）奖”。2006年11月20日，广州市创建国家环境保护模范城市通过了考核验收。2009年，广州市荣获世界水资源论坛水环境治理奖第一名。广州市污水治理工作取得了阶段性成效。

六、广州水环境治理的重要实践

在广州中心城区的231条河涌中，涌现出一些水环境治理的样板工程，成为城市的亮丽风景和人文中心。

（一）水秀花香的都市型河流景观工程——大沙河整治工程

大沙河综合治建设工程由水利工程和绿化景观两大部分组成，打破了过去水利工程与景观绿化工程不和谐、功能单一、设计呆板、缺乏观赏性的做法，是一个将河涌整治与城市总体发展相统一、水利工程与城市建设相融合、防洪排涝工程与城市园林景观相协调的都市型、生态型、景观型、休闲旅游型的综合性河涌整治工程。

过去，由于受到过境水道污染等影响，曾经美丽的大沙河变成了一条“臭水沟”。广州市将大沙河列入重点整治河涌。为了整治大沙河，政府关闭年产值3 000万元的鹤洞水泥厂。在大沙河治理工程中，改造了原有的供排水系统，利用水生植物芦鸢对污水进行吸附，达到净化水质的效果，使大沙河常态地保持三类水质。为更有效地解决花卉博览园的排涝和水质问题，水务部门还重新建设了两条排涝渠，新建和改造了四座水闸和两座泵站，通过调控景观水位，既保证了花卉生产需要和景观对水位的要求，又可达到防洪排涝的目的。整个大沙河绿化景观整治工程，紧紧围绕具有荔湾特色的“水秀花香”为主题进行规划、设计和施工，通过“花影飘舞”、“花溪流香”和“花雨缤纷”等景观来体现，并采取各种不同风格的树种、花草进行有效地配，使整段河岸形成既有不同特色、又相互协调的多种变化的视觉效果。

整治后的大沙河

经过绿化景观建设和综合治理的大沙河，水清、岸绿、景美，是一项具有生态观赏性、休闲旅游特色的都市型河流景观工程，现已成为广大市民节假日出游的好去处，也是广州花卉博览园内一道亮丽的风景线。

（二）水环境治理与遗产保护和利用完美结合的典范——大冲口涌整治工程

位于荔湾区芳村大道的大冲口涌整治工程，是将河涌治理与文物保护、继承和发展，以及现代社区人文环境建设完美结合的典范工程之一。由于在历史上濒临交通要道，是商业、人文密集之地，大冲口涌周边遗留了不少历史古迹：涌面上横跨有200多年历史的“毓灵桥”，周边有民国初期规划整齐的聚龙村古村落，中国最早的机械厂“协同机械厂”，河涌两岸还保留了不少古树。除历史古迹外，由于城市的发展，不同年代的社区也散布周边。因此在大冲口涌周边，形成了一个古迹与人居，自然与非自然人文因素复杂交错的城市环境，而大冲口涌，则成为联系该地区大部分历史文化、自然景观和城市景观的中轴线和主要风景带。

因此，大冲口涌的整治建设，不仅仅是工程建设的问题，更是要考虑如何将其负载的传统历史文脉进行延续，必须将水文化元素引入到的河涌整治建设中。2008年以来，大冲口涌整治工程开始分期实施，其中，一期工程已经实施完毕。河涌沿线打造了四个文化节点。

其中，在一期工程内的文化节点为两个：第一个节点为“珠水沧浪”，该节点是河涌连接珠江的入口。在具体的改造中，重点表现珠江沿岸聚落的变迁，从小渔村经历沧海桑田的历史过程，将工业厂房、码头、船屋等要素保留改造，并与木桩、礁石、芦苇等景观元素相结合，建立滨水休闲广场、码头区等功能设施。第二个节点为“毓灵流芳”，这一节点聚集了“毓灵桥”、“中国第一台柴油机生产地协同机械厂”、古树等不少历史、文化资源。在河涌整治的过程中，节点设计主要通过营造硬地景观和植物景观，在灵巧的古桥和刚健的工业

大冲口涌北出口段整治前

大冲口涌北出口段整治后

建筑之间取得平衡，同时在地面雕刻等小尺度的雕刻的设计中，融合河涌沿线的历史事件、历史名人，为河岸景观塑造增添地域色彩，使之成为河涌沿线居民认同的根源之地。在河岸古树四周，塑造小型活动广场，周边配以历史名人路等装饰，打造一个生动活泼、具有生命力，同时又具有历史厚重感的公共滨水空间。

在节点改造中，古树的保护尤其值得一提。在大冲口涌最初的施工方案中，河涌堤岸为直线设计，照此方案，两岸的十余棵古树都得迁移或者是砍掉。看着这些根深叶茂的古树，荔湾区水务局的专家一致决定：修改施工方案，把大树都留下来，哪怕堤岸弯一点也不算什么。当他们把这一想法跟上级报告时，得到同样重视本土文化保护的区政府相关领导的肯定。这种因地制宜的方案结果是，大树保留下来了，而弯曲的堤岸设计，反而给河涌增添了一份自然的曲线美。

大冲口涌整治工程不仅仅是河涌整治的技术问题，还是一个将文物保护、土地利用开发、景观建设、文化传承、园林绿化、社区环境规划等多方面融为一体的综合性整体。如今，改造后的大冲口涌，小桥流水，古树婆娑，逐步显现昔日的岭南水乡风情和人文美景。

（三）时尚、现代的城市水景名片——白鹅潭酒吧街亲水景观建设工程

白鹅潭——珠江河段在广州的起点，具有广州得天独厚的人文气息。数座跨江大桥灯饰分明、音韵悠扬的美景一直为人们所传颂。而白鹅潭风情酒吧街位于荔湾区芳村花地街长堤路，东起芳村下市涌，西至花地河口。作为体现广州特色休闲娱乐的地方之一，白鹅潭不仅彰显了广州时尚新潮的一面，也浓缩了广州城深厚的历史人文气息。而作为“广州市十大特色街”之一，有人把它和北京三里屯、上海新天地相媲美，白鹅潭酒吧街在广州、珠江三角洲乃至港澳地区都享有很高的品牌知名度。

在21世纪前，珠水西岸原芳村长堤路沿江地段仍然被各式各样凌乱的民居、厂房占据，残旧而破败，与身旁秀美的白鹅潭畔、富有异国情调的沙面显得格格不入。正是在这样的背景下，广州市政府启动了白鹅潭酒吧街项目的建设。1999年，广州市“三年一中变”工程之一的珠江两岸环境景观整治正式启动，原芳村长堤路段珠江堤岸整治工程是其重要的组成部分。之后，为了凸显文化内涵，体现沿江堤岸的亲水性，市政府又加快了珠江沿岸现有场

白鹅潭风情酒吧街

地设施的立面整饰，调整原有工业、仓储用地的规划，对原芳村沿江的部分旧厂房实施功能置换，将旧厂房、工厂改造为公共绿地或者高档商务写字楼，使珠江沿线逐步转型，重点突出文化、旅游和商贸等功能。白鹅潭酒吧街根据不同地域的实际情况，共划分了四个功能区，两个区主要经营酒吧及餐饮业，另两个区则进驻了多家旅业及创意工作室。不得不说，白鹅潭风情酒吧街是一处独特的亲水景观，不仅完成了环境整治，还通过滨水空间的建设充分发掘了其土地资源优势，达到了一举两得的目的。目前，白鹅潭酒吧街亲水景观，整体营造出浓厚的江畔风情，原有的古建筑文化、优良的滨江水岸线资源以及酒吧街风情十足的时尚感，对市民散发出诱人魅力，是难得的黄金滨水地段，成为广州城市水文化的名片，折射出广州市的另一番风味。

（四）现代高雅滨水社区——二沙岛社区亲水走廊

二沙岛是珠江中的一个沙洲，珠水环岛而过，是最具有广州现代风情的宝地之一。新中国成立以来这里一直是广东省的体育训练基地，先后培养出不少世界冠军，现在已建设成为以“绿、静、美”为特色的高雅文化艺术、体育娱乐中心和高尚住宅区。

二沙岛

广州市政府在二沙岛社区亲水走廊的建设中，打造形成了一个连续的公共休闲亲水绿带。这条绿带与二沙岛独有的人文环境相协调，同二沙岛社区一起，体现了时代感以及广州地域特色的文化内涵，亲水走廊的建设使得二沙岛成为一个现代高雅的水文化社区，带给人们更加开阔的观景视线，成为一个能够尽情欣赏珠江两岸美景的绝佳位置。

改造后的二沙岛，星海音乐厅，广东美术馆，一片片高尚的生活住宅小区和体育训练基地一起掩映在广阔的绿地中，各种艺术雕塑散布周围，文化艺术氛围扑面而来，是一处心灵的回归地。市民和外来游客在欣赏星海音乐厅的高雅音乐或广东美术馆的前卫艺术作品的同时，也在不经意之间欣赏到高品位的岭南水文化特色。

星海音乐厅

（五）生态人文的岛屿堤岸建设典范——大学城生态绿堤

广州大学城坐落于番禺区新造镇小谷围岛及其南岸地区，西邻洛溪岛、北望生物岛、东接长洲岛，与琶洲岛瀛洲生态公园隔江相望，总规划面积43平方公里，外江堤防总长26.33公里。小谷围岛四面环珠江，具有天然的相对独立性，地貌为低丘陵冲积平原，岛上风景如画，文物古迹众多。由于以前长期没有路桥与广州市区相连，必须通过轮渡才能到达，但也正是如此，成全了小谷围岛原汁原味的乡土气息，民风淳朴、生态良好、环境优美。

大学城堤岸整治前

大学城堤岸整治后

小谷围岛环岛堤岸结合“生态绿堤”的理念，在缓坡上布置了园林绿化景观，在风浪大时也可以起到消浪的作用。堤岸的设计在确保防洪安全、经济和环保的前提下，贯彻穿插人文、生态、亲水的理念，强调地域性、现代性、文化性，淡化了工程痕迹。新堤不但能抵御两百年一遇的洪潮水，而且堤岸形式结合了大学城的功能要求，根据地形、地貌确定，做到多样化，体现亲水性，这也是广州珠江干流上的第一道生态型堤岸。

小谷围岛的堤岸工程在剖面设计上有意识采用滨水广场绿地做法，突出共享与亲水性、塑造滨水区特色与品质，以体现“人文、江岸、生态、水利”。在堤岸线的布置上，力求各堤段平顺相接，不使景观视觉上有过大的落差，并且尽可能保留原有自然山体和古树。同时经过筛选比较，最终选用耐淹而且叶附泥较少的香根草作堤岸护坡的绿化。针对飞翼快船和大型货船经过附近江面时，会对堤身、堤脚产生淘蚀、冲刷，因此在江岸结合部有规划地分段种植水生灌木、芦苇科植物和水杉、竹林、红树林等，起到消浪促淤的作用，尽可能减少风浪爬高，同时也形成一道道漂亮的风景线。最令人叫绝的是水岸下藏着一列沉箱堤防，箱外还有低一级的垒石围堤，沉箱盛泥，上面种植大量的水草作为岸边的缓冲，由于中午涨潮，水平面恰到好处地漫到草皮边缘，掩盖了沉箱，堤围“消失”了。这种生态自然型的设计隐藏了人工构建的痕迹，在保证人堤安全的同时，回归了河岸的原始面貌，甚至能吸引鱼类的聚集，体现了较好的生态性。

如今，漫步在大学城河岸与蜿蜒的步道之间，随处可见大片的阔叶草坪和树群，河岸斜坡以三维网固定的草皮，人们可以在岸边直接玩水。局部地区采用阶梯式堤岸，人们可以席坐在宽阔的阶梯上，体验珠江涨潮时逐级漫到脚上的感觉。

（六）集调蓄、生态、景观于一体的多功能水利工程——白云湖

位于白云区石井镇的白云湖工程既是一个集防灾减灾、调蓄雨洪等多功能的水利工程，

又是一项生态工程、景观工程，其丰富的水文化内涵是广州市补水引水工程中的典范。

作为2010年前广州市治水任务的四大调水补水系统工程之一，白云湖的破土动工，标志着西航道引水工程进入全面建设阶段。它既是一个防灾减灾的水利工程，可调蓄雨洪，提高水安全标准；也是一个生态工程，建成后可引水入涌，补充下游河涌景观用水，实现石井河流域水体循环，改善水环境；同时还是一个景观工程，规划总面积2.07平方公里，水面面积1.05平方公里，大于市区现有四个人工湖的总和，是未来广州的第一大湖，这里将建设滨水景观带，为广大市民提供一个新的休闲、游览场所。未来的白云湖将形成一个集水安全、水生态、水景观于一体的综合性水利工程，对改善广州北部城乡水环境和建设生态广州都有着深远的意义。

白云湖工程共分两期实施，近期首先满足引水和调蓄等水利功能，并形成基本生态格局。白云湖地块大部分由原有低洼水塘、河网与农田构成，地势平坦、水源丰富。但现在河网、水塘水质很差，需大力整治。建成后的白云湖首要功能就是调蓄雨洪、防止水淹。广州是全国重点防洪城市，洪涝灾害一直是城市发展的心腹大患。如果不解决排涝问题，一遇强降雨，常常受水淹。白云湖工程设计控制集雨面积近10平方公里，库容200万立方米，其中防洪调蓄库容51万立方米。2012年白云湖将实现自身通水和向石井河补水，具体做法是，与北江大堤“两涌一河”构成一个完整的引水系统，远期规划兴建北江最下游的横岗梯级枢纽工程以提高北江水位，利用白云湖经两涌及白坭河引入的北江水，近期将西航道珠江水引入白云湖，连同经左干渠引入的流溪河水以及汇集石井河流域的天然降水，补充给下游河涌，从根本上改善石井河流域的水环境。

从远期考虑，主要是完善白云湖的景观、休闲功能。在区内中部与东北角分布着几座丘陵，林木丰茂，是景区的重要景观资源；同时还有丰富的地理历史信息的遗留，纵横交错的堤塘、曲折弯绕的河涌、繁盛藏密的树林、农田阡陌、野生鸟类等，都是几千年来的人文积

白云湖效果图

淀。广州市充分挖掘了这些资源文化。在不远的将来，白云湖将呈现“一轴一链两湖八景”的布局结构，成为一个开放性的滨水公园。新建的这个2平方公里的湖区，相当于增加城市湿地2平方公里，广州市中心区水面率也因此提高到0.2%，沿湖地区的生态环境、局部气候因水而得到改善。值得一提的是，以水文化、水景观、水生态为主题的城市滨水风景区和8.6公里滨水景观带，不仅为广大市民提供了一个新的文化旅游观光场所，而且还以独特的水景观带动北部城区的开发建设。

乘着游艇欣赏白云湖美景，看着北江清流汩汩注入珠江……广大市民期盼的这一美好景象，已变成现实。

（七）滨海沙田湿地水文化案例——万顷沙沿海湿地生态系统

位于南沙区的万顷沙湿地是广州最后一片大面积湿地，有不可多得的生态功能，每年入冬都会飞来成千上万的珍稀候鸟。万顷沙有着人工围垦而成的21涌，每隔一公里就有一条涌，这21涌方方正正排列整齐，呈现出独特的沙田水乡自然风貌。

万顷沙湿地实景图

2004年，广州市政府经过两年多的反复论证，提出在万顷沙18涌以南地区不再安排建设项目，并在19涌万顷沙湿地建设一个“广州湿地森林公园”，这是广东省乃至全国首个以湿地为主题的公园。占地约200公顷，属于河口湿地，被围垦的堤岸围起来，有闸口与珠江连接。东面是隔着珠江已初具规模的南沙港，北面是正在建设中的珠江钢厂，西南方是一个热闹的渔码头，南面向着水天一色的珠江出海口，湿地的主体为约半米深的水体。

为了保护万顷沙自然风貌而兴建了生态廊道。在万顷沙规划的五大工业组团之间，有三个生态廊道，包括东部的蕉门水道水域生态廊道、中部的农田生态廊道、西部的洪奇沥水道水域生态廊道。针对东部的蕉门水道水域生态廊道和西部的洪奇沥水道水域生态廊道，在水道两边沿岸种植百米绿化带并建设海滨公园，沿岸滩涂将种植红树林，以保护水道水域的生态环境。而中部的农田生态廊道，种植岭南名优水果、优质蔬菜和发展咸淡水养殖，其中在6涌至8涌之间，还建有一个两公里宽的现代农业示范区，面积近1 333公顷。

工业防护湿地林区的建立，这充分体现了广州市政府持续关注湿地保护的战略发展思想。为了保护南沙珍贵的湿地资源，2007年广州市政府决定在位于万顷沙的湿地公园旁边建设一个面积达867多公顷的工业防护湿地林区，这也是广州市“青山绿地”工程二期建设的重要组成部分。这块湿地林区北部以15涌下为界，南部以19涌上为界，东部以洪奇沥水道为界，西部以蕉门河为界，其中，19涌西300多公顷面积建成具有旅游观光功能的湿地林区，成为南沙的第二个湿地公园。湿地林区内以乔木为主，沿水面种植不同类型的湿地植物，在湿地内营造出不同深度的水域，以吸引不同生活习性的鸟类和其他生物。而21涌将成为一个核心生态保护区，根据影响和功能侧重的不同分为抗污减污林和湿地景观林两个功能区。其中抗污减污林区由靠近工业基地的地块整合而成，在靠近工业基地的沿线设置不少于两百米的防护林带，在树种选择上以抗风抗污染、耐盐碱、耐水湿树种为主；而湿地景观林区与旁边的湿地公园相结合，打造具有岭南水乡特色的景观。

如今，“世外桃源”、“鸟类天堂”都是人们给万顷沙湿地公园的赞誉。每逢周末，市民纷至沓来，驾一叶扁舟，轻轻划入红树林深处，绿树葱茏，波光潋滟，仿佛置身江南水乡一般。这种人与自然和谐之美正是生态湿地工程中水文化的最有力体现。

（八）内陆自然湿地水文化的挖掘和保护——万亩果园果树保护区湿地生态系统

海珠区果园果树保护区又称“万亩果林”，由珠江和海潮共同冲积而成，保护区内河网水系发达，蜿蜒曲折，尤其在东南部区域，水面率更高达33.1%，呈现出典型的河流湿地特征。同时，也承担着调节气候、净化空气、防洪调蓄、保持水土、涵养水源、净化水体、保护传统水果品种和生物多样性、改善生态环境等众多作用，被誉为广州的“南肺”、“市肾”、“氧吧”。但是近年来由于经济发展带来的水质污染、土壤污染，导致果林生态系统遭到破坏。病虫害严重，部分果树死亡，产量降低，果树品种单一，使得果林生产、生态的功能衰减，“南肺”的功能减弱。区内文化资源丰富，有珠江三角洲地区唯一风貌保存完整的果林型岭南水乡，有广州地区最具岭南水乡特色的古村——小洲村，已被列为广州市首批14个历史文化保护区之一，并被评为广东省生态示范村。还有梁氏大宗祠、陈氏大宗祠、简氏大宗祠和西溪祖祠、民居古码头和渡口等古迹，有庙宇、古牌坊、古书院等。

由此可见，对“万亩果林”的整治与保护，仅仅解决截污、清淤等工程问题是远远不够的，而必须将水文化的建设理念引入其中，而这一区最重要的水文化则体现在“生态”和“人文”。21世纪，广州市政府以建设水流顺畅、碧水萦绕、绿荫环抱、果树飘香、人与

万亩果园的小洲古村依然保留着原始的果林型岭南水乡风貌

自然和谐的城市生态绿心为目标，通过综合治理及行之有效的管理，实现果树保护区城市湿地的可持续发展。在规划中，通过对自然条件、地域特征、人文景观、市政建设、城市规划等因素的综合分析，在水务部门提出的海珠果树保护区城市湿地实施方案中，初步划分为城市湿地核心区、岭南水乡风貌区、果树生态园区三个功能区。三个功能区相对独立又相互联系，突显果树保护区的城市湿地系统，发挥城市湿地的综合功能。目前市有关部门正在组织国际招标，高标准进行规划和建设该城市湿地。

规划和改造后的“万亩果林”最大的特色可以归纳为两个方面。一方面，“万亩果林”是自然湿地与人工类湿地的有机组合。果树保护区灌、排渠系统完善，自然的潮灌潮排构成果林——潮道生态系统，发挥了自然河流湿地与人工湿地的生态功能，使得广州“南肺”的美誉失而复得。另一方面，“万亩果林”还形成了具有以生态保护、科普教育、游览观赏为主要内容的自然景观和人文资源区。区内水道随潮起潮落而枯盈，独特的潮成风貌具有重要的观赏价值和科学考察价值；果树成片，果园品种繁多，形成由果园和珠江水系的滘涌河网等组成的自然景观；岭南水乡民居风情融于其中，古桥蚝屋、流水人家，富蕴岭南水乡和广府民俗风情。

（九）城市古村落的保护与水环境整治案例——小洲村

小洲位于海珠区东南端，南临珠江南河道，隔江与番禺相望，东临牌坊河，峙对官洲岛和仑头，西北与土华村相接。小洲是珠江几千年来冲积形成的，面积达400公顷，境内河涌长达10公里。

小洲村古桥遍布

小洲村四面环水，形似小岛，故称“小洲”，始建于元末明初，是具有一千多年悠久历史的古村。得益于在改造中对古文化的保护，如今的小洲村，并没有被现代化的洪流所淹没，传统的东西仍然得到传承。在村落里，河涌蜿蜒交错、造型各异的小桥枕溪流之上，庄重的祠堂规整有序，古老的宫庙朴实淡雅，传统的民居参差错落，在绿树婆娑的掩映下，像一幅画有小溪、绿树、灰垣、素瓦等具有岭南水乡特点的水墨画。区内的小洲古村是广州地区最具岭南水乡特色的古村，保存了历史悠久地岭南水乡文化。在城市湿地建设的同时，对岭南水乡文化加以保护和弘扬，将人水和谐、人与自然和谐理念与岭南水文化融为一体，进一步提升广州城市形象。

在小洲村水文化资源的保护中，临水特色街道的保护是其重点。划定的历史文化保护区面积为5.1公顷，保护区建设控制地带面积为9.2公顷，环境协调区面积为15.9公顷。重点保护的小洲村街巷为“街—河—街”、“街—河—屋”、“屋—河—屋”三种临水空间特色的街道，其中包括拱北大街、登瀛大街、登瀛外街、细桥大街、新路大街等。针对小洲村自身丰富的水网格局，也着重保护西江涌水系及沿岸的原生水网形态，保护河涌与两岸的自然生态格局，以此形成围合的环状、通畅水网，保持保护区内河涌的水位。

（十）城市历史水系的修复案例——东濠涌

东濠涌，发源于白云山的甘溪、文溪，止于今天的法政路附近，古时的东濠涌涌宽水深，可以通船。“东濠涌”在广州城市的历史上非常重要，不仅是广州仅存的旧城护城河，也是广州城东的交通要道，其水质良好，是当时广州居民的主要供水渠之一和最主要的排水渠道。因其重要的地理位置，在河涌周边密布着大量的水文化资源和古遗迹，如当铺、贡院、古桥等，记录着这个水城的历史和当时人们的生活情况。东濠涌民国时期修筑海珠路时，改为暗渠，后开挖后，改革开放后修建高架桥，原有的河涌风貌被破坏殆尽，加之整治前河涌污染严重，东濠涌沿线居民低收入家庭和住房困难群众多，人居环境较差。

东濠涌博物馆再现东濠涌历史风貌

东濠涌一期整治工程涉及八大工程。一是调水补水工程。在珠江前航道江湾桥西侧新建补水泵站，抽取珠江水对东濠涌进行补水，东濠涌南段水体实现了良性循环。二是景观、堤岸工程。改造和加固堤岸、修建桥梁、建设“绿道”等。三是两岸建筑物立面整饰工程。四是配套停车场工程，进一步缓解了该区域停车难问题。五是机电安装工程。对环市路到沿江路3.19公里的河涌进行光亮工程和视频监控工程。六是高架桥体涂装工程。七是水质净化工程。在越秀桥附近建设净水厂，日处理能力约10万吨。八是东濠涌管理中心和博物馆建设工程。将越秀北路和豪贤路交界处、紧临越秀桥和东濠涌两栋民国时期的旧别墅改造为“东濠涌管理中心和博物馆”。记录和展示河涌历史文化和整治成果。

改造后的东濠涌，绿色生态全面恢复，净水技术使河涌水标准达到可以亲水戏水的标准，这在城市中心区是非常难得的。

在景观建设方面，按照“修旧如旧”的原则，运用现代建筑工艺，恢复东濠涌越秀桥、小东门桥、筑横沙桥、东华桥等6座历史名桥原貌，新建4座现代小桥，还沿水脉设置越秀桥叠水瀑布、越秀广场治水主题雕塑、荷花池、景观石、水堰、凉亭、驿站等景观10处。

在水文化的利用上，在整治中把文化建设贯穿河涌治理全过程，挖掘水文化、桥文化、石文化、广府文化、名人文化等人文历史内涵，进一步擦亮“广府文化源地、千年商都核心”品牌，提升城市文化品质。河涌边设立的东濠涌博物馆是我市第一座以河涌为主题的博物馆，展示河涌沿线历史文化遗存及古今治理河涌史实，在博物馆中，以高科技的手段再现了东濠涌历史和现代的生活景象。

改造后通过河涌连接了周边的鲁迅故居、宋庆龄故居等名人名居景点，塑造浓郁细腻的水系概念。在糙米栏桥附近和永曜北小学墙壁各设置人物雕塑2组、壁画4幅，重塑民国时期广州普通百姓人家生活场景，栩栩如生地反映老广州的风俗人情。

如今，东濠涌，这一条城市内部的河涌已成为与城市居民生活、娱乐、休闲密切相关的一部分，也成为体验城市历史和文化的重要场所，这不能不说是一种成功。

（十一）水景与民俗风情的完美结合案例——荔枝湾涌

荔枝湾涌严格来说不是一条孤立的河流，而是原广州城西，现今的荔湾路、中山八路、黄沙大道（北段）、多宝路（西段）、龙津西路一带的江畔湿地中纵横交错的水系的总称，这里就是旧时的老西关，原本水系蜿蜒，水网如织，是人们游玩的好地方，素有“小秦淮”之称。到了20世纪40年代，随着广州城区的扩展，城市人口逐渐增加，荔枝湾河溪两面成为菜农、贫民聚居之地，居民为建房屋砍掉了荔枝树，再加上40年代末期荔枝湾附近成为了广州市近代工业的基地，造成了河涌污染，水质持续恶化，再也难以适应荔枝树的生长。1958年，荔湾湖公园的建设，保留了荔枝湾部分湖泊和水道，河道仍能北通逢源桥，南至多宝桥，但水系的各条支流被填平变成街道；随着周围的工厂建立和人口聚居，荔枝湾水系已经沦为大污水池，1985年前后，荔湾湖至多宝桥的水道被覆盖；1992年，随着泮溪酒家至逢源桥的最后一段水道被覆盖，荔湾涌的名称彻底成为历史。

1999年，荔湾区政协提出了关于“复建荔枝湾故道”的提案，并在2009年正式实施，1992年填埋的最后一段河道重见天日。2010年10月16日凌晨，荔湾湖的湖水被引入河涌，曾经消失的荔枝湾涌迎来新生，曾经的荔枝湾从历史变成现实。在荔枝湾涌的改造中，政府借把暗涌打开之机，重新整治了周边环境。改造后，富有老广州特色的花艇于河涌之上来回穿梭，结合文塔、仁威庙、古桥、古树等老建筑，复原了原旧西关的繁华风貌。周边的建筑改造富有合原有的西关古建筑的特点，并与历史街区的改造融合起来。最

充分整合水文化资源是荔枝湾涌改造的一大特色

有特点的是，河涌周边的西关大屋，演唱粤曲表演，老字号和广府饮食等商号的设置，将河涌游与街巷游结合起来，使该地富有浓厚的人文气息，人流如织的景象，仿佛回到旧西关的繁华盛地。

（作者：黄石鼎，广州市社会科学院城市管理研究所所长；宁超乔，广州市社会科学院城市管理研究所助理研究员）

民生为本　规划先行

——广州市北部山区镇扶贫开发实践

引　言

经过改革开放30多年的快速发展，广州经济已相对发达，2010年全市GDP首超万亿元（全国第三个），达到1 074.83亿元，人均GDP达到12 882美元。但同时，城乡区域发展不平衡、不协调也已成为当前制约广州科学发展的最大短板，是率先加快转型升级、建设幸福广州必须首先破解的一大难题。尤其是北部8个山区镇，长期以来由于现实条件限制和生态保护要求，经济发展滞后、公共服务资源匮乏、内生增长动力不足、镇村面貌普遍缺乏特色，与农村群众日益增长的物质文化需要相比存在很大差距。

因此，广州市在充分认识自身实力与责任的基础上，做出主动解决自身城乡协调发展问题的决策，于2010年年底提出开展北部山区镇扶贫开发工作，并将其作为“十二五”开局之年的重点工作，列为2011年要办好的“十件民生实事”中的第一件和人大一号议案，以加快北部山区脱贫奔康步伐，为全市科学发展、转型升级打下坚实基础。

本文首先分析广州市北部8个山区镇的发展情况，然后总结山区镇扶贫开发的主要举措和2011年取得的实施成效，最后给出几点主要启示，以期为中国其他发达地区解决城乡协调发展问题提供借鉴参考。

一、广州市北部8个山区镇发展情况

（一）8个山区镇概况

广州市北部8个山区镇指花都区梯面镇、增城市正果镇、派潭镇、小楼镇和从化市吕田镇、温泉镇、良口镇、鳌头镇，均属于广州的欠发达地区。

8个镇总面积2 298.9平方公里（其中山地面积的比例接近70%），占全市总面积的30.9%；耕地总面积324 661亩，占全市的21.5%；共有227条行政村，2 100多条自然村，占全市行政村总数的20%。2010年总人口44.8万人，其中农业人口40.8万人，分别占全市总人口和农业总人口的 4.3%、17.4%。

可以看出，这 8 个镇无论是土地面积还是人口规模，在全市都占有很重要的位置。它们的发展关乎整个广州的发展全局。

（二）发展存在的主要问题

8 个山区镇在发展中主要存在以下 6 个方面的问题。

1. 基础设施和公共服务设施建设严重滞后

目前 8 个山区镇仍有 30% 左右的自然村未实现通水泥路、通洁净水，有近 600 公里的自然村道亟待建设；103 条行政村（占 45%）未开展污水治理，190 条行政村（占 84%）未安装路灯，77 条行政村（占 34%）需要进行二次改水，部分镇水厂和供水管道老化严重。同时，文化、教育、医疗、体育等基本公共服务设施配置缺口较大，不少设施尚未达标，建设陈旧。

2. 农民收入水平偏低

近五年来广州市农民人均收入以两位数速度增长，年均达到 12.06%，而 8 个山区镇农民人均收入年均增长仅为 8.06%，比全市平均增幅低 4 个百分点，收入差距持续拉大。2010 年 8 个镇农民人均收入为 7 741 元，仅为全市平均水平 12 676 元的 61%。

3. 产业基础较差

长期以来山区镇经济以工农业为主，近年来由于生态保护的限制，工业发展呈负增长，从工业化初期阶段直接进入到了去工业化的阶段。2009 年 8 个山区镇工农业总产值 58.85 亿元，占全市的 0.47%，比 2005 年占全市的 0.56% 下降了近 0.1 个百分点。而山区镇乡村旅游等第三产业的发展刚刚起步，发展壮大受到较多的制约。

4. 镇级财力较弱，负担沉重

2010 年，8 个山区镇实现两税收入合计 9.76 亿元，镇财政可支配收入合计仅有 3.13 亿元。如增城的 3 个镇平均每年两税收入仅为 2 500 多万元，税收分成 500 多万元，而镇每年的正常运作支出就达 2 000 万元。此外，据调查，8 个镇各项社会事业项目镇级配套资金支出近 5 000 万元，平均每个镇 600 多万元。

5. 村级集体经济薄弱

8 个山区镇有 206 条行政村年集体经济收入不足 8 万元，占行政村总数的 90.7%，甚至有些村无集体经济收入。这就限制了村级层面解决各种发展配套问题。

6. 社会事业发展滞后

2010 年 8 个山区镇共有农村低保对象 8 651 户、22 724 人，占全市农村低保对象总数的近 33%；共有农村危房 12 165 户，占全市农村危房总户数的近 70%。

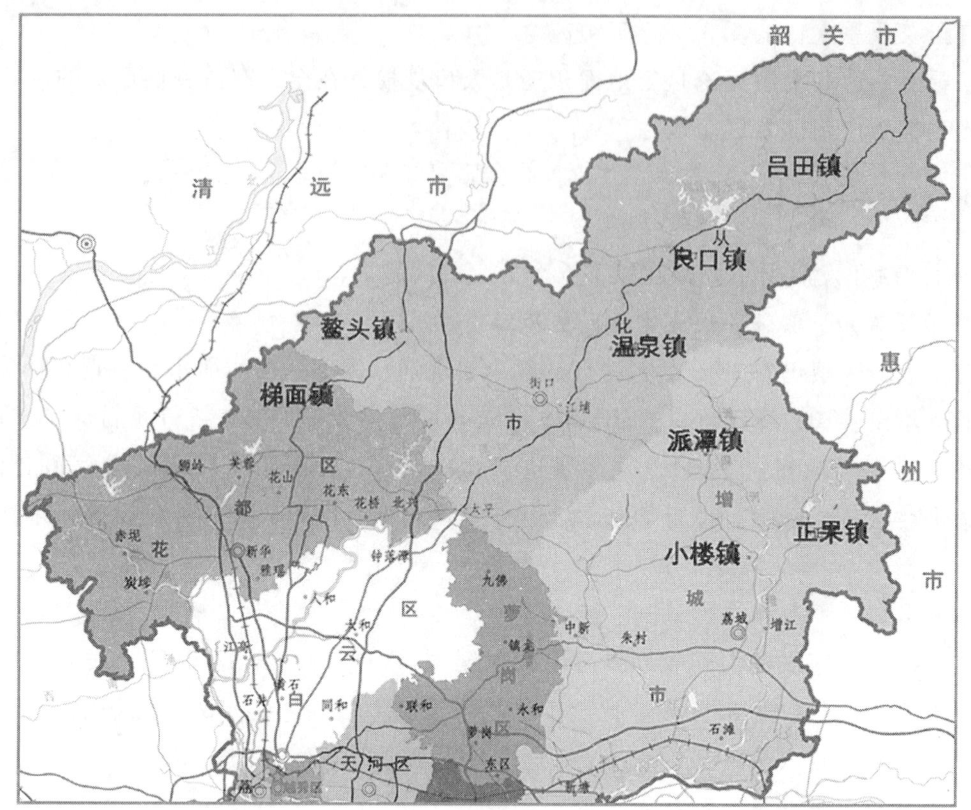

图 1　广州市北部 8 个山区镇分布

二、对口山区镇扶贫开发的主要举措

（一）实施农村扶贫开发“双到”工作

1. “双到”对象

参照广东省农村扶贫开发“规划到户、责任到人”（以下简称“双到”）的做法，确定广州市农村扶贫开发“双到”的工作对象如下：户的层面，包括有劳动能力的农村低保对象和农村低收入困难家庭；村的层面，指市委农村基层办核定的年集体收入不足 8 万元的 206 个贫困村。

2. 目标任务

从 2010 年年底开始，用 2 年左右时间实施扶贫开发“双到”工作，确保到 2012 年年底，被帮扶的贫困村年集体收入基本达到 10 万元以上，被帮扶的贫困户家庭人均年收入基本达到 5 000 元以上。

3. 具体做法

8 个山区镇的贫困村和贫困户，由广州市直机关、事业单位和市辖各有关区及国有企业，按每个村投入 50 万元，采取结对帮扶形式实施“双到”工作。

贫困村帮扶内容包括：坚持解决低收入与发展生产、增加收入相结合，变“输血式”扶贫为“造血式”扶贫，通过帮扶促进贫困村的持续发展。①管理进村。指导贫困村制定和落实科学可行的发展规划，促进贫困村建立民主的管理制度，建设坚强有力的“两委”班子。②发展经济。提供农业科技培训及信息服务，引导贫困村充分利用资源禀赋和环境优势，因地制宜发展“一村一品”特色农业和乡村旅游，发展壮大村集体经济，提高集体收入。③建设惠民设施。帮助贫困村推进自然村“五通”（通水、通路、通电、通电话、通有线电视）工程建设，开展农村污水治理、路灯、农田水利等基础设施建设；开展村容村貌整治改造，改善人居环境。④文化进村。帮助贫困村建设或改造卫生、文化、体育等设施，开展组织电影下乡、免费医疗体检服务下乡等活动。

贫困户的帮扶内容包括：在进村入户开展调查研究，摸清家庭基本情况、收入情况、就业情况和主要诉求的基础上，实施分类帮扶的措施。①就业帮扶。扶持贫困户参加相关培训，提高种养技能和就业技能；为贫困户提供就业、创业等信息和机会，帮助解决有关问题。②物质帮扶。加强宣传、协调，确保符合条件的贫困户全面、及时享受相关政策；通过提供专项生活补助、物资援助等方式，帮助贫困户渡过生活难关。③保障帮扶。资助贫困户参加农村合作医疗和农村生活养老保险，保障病有所医、老有所养；资助贫困户实施危房改造，保障住有所居。④教育帮扶。开展助学，确保贫困户子女完成义务教育阶段的学业；对考上大中专院校、普通高中的贫困家庭子女给予资助。

（二）进行“一区帮一镇、名企扶一镇”的对口帮扶

1. 目标任务

推进文化、教育、医疗、体育、市场等公共服务设施和道路、给排水等市政公用设施的标准化建设，其中中心学校的教学设施与环境达到规范化学校建设标准，中心卫生院业务用房面积和功能布局达到国家建设标准的要求。确保到 2012 年年底，实现北部贫困镇的镇容镇貌有一个大的改观，市政及公共服务设施有一个突破性的发展。

2. 具体做法

参照国家对口支援汶川地震灾后恢复重建的做法，按照“一个区帮扶一个镇”的原则，由海珠、荔湾、黄埔、萝岗、越秀、天河、番禺、花都区等 8 个经济发达区分别对口帮扶温泉、吕田、良口、鳌头、小楼、正果、派潭、梯面镇等 8 个山区镇。

同时，广州市委市政府广泛发动社会各界参与北部山区镇扶贫开发，特别是动员知名企业自觉履行社会责任，为北部山区镇加快发展提供了新动力。珠江投资集团、合景泰富集团、星河湾集团、侨鑫集团、雅居乐集团、富力集团、恒大地产、敏捷集团、碧桂园集团等 9 大知名企业纷纷慷慨解囊，积极参与帮扶 8 个山区镇建设。

表 1　“一区帮一镇、名企扶一镇”对口帮扶一览表

序号	山区镇	提供帮扶的区	提供帮扶的名企
1	温泉镇	海珠区	珠江投资集团
2	吕田镇	荔湾区	合景泰富集团、星河湾集团
3	良口镇	黄埔区	侨鑫集、星河湾集团
4	鳌头镇	萝岗区	雅居乐集团
5	小楼镇	越秀区	富力集团
6	正果镇	天河区	恒大地产
7	派潭镇	番禺区	敏捷集团
8	梯面镇	花都区	碧桂园集团

（三）着力打造名镇名村，发挥典型示范带动作用

凸显特色是加快北部山区镇发展的重要立足点，也是提高北部山区镇建设发展水平的重要标志。因此，广州市按照全省《关于打造名镇名村示范村带动农村宜居建设的意见》（粤府〔2011〕68 号）的要求，将北部山区镇扶贫开发与名镇名村建设结合起来，选择基础条件较好、文化底蕴深厚的镇和村，加大投入和建设力度，因地制宜精心打造成为具有广州特色的“名镇”、“名村”，在全市乃至全省农村宜居建设中发挥典型示范带动作用。具体来说，通过综合分析各镇比较优势和自然历史条件，整合山水景观、历史文化、传统民俗等各资源，确立打造产业强镇、文化名镇、旅游大镇等目标定位，依托自然生态环境推动绿色崛起，大力发展生态旅游、文化旅游、观光休闲等产业，带动农民实现脱贫致富。

基于此，山区镇扶贫开发十分注重塑造各镇的特色风貌，坚持“一镇一策、一村一策”，专门开展了特色风貌塑造规划，并选择重点地段进行城市设计，提出镇村的特色风貌控制要求。在扶贫项目规划建设过程中，也对项目设计方案进行严格审查把关，保证各项目能够充分体现地方特色和岭南风格。

（四）同步完善帮扶山区镇发展的配套倾斜政策

1. 切实解决山区镇经济发展需求，培育“造血”功能

①切实解决经济发展的用地问题，一方面硬性规定每年“戴帽”安排一定数量的建设用地指标给山区镇，另一方面在不破坏土地耕作层的前提下，允许乡村旅游和现代农业经营者建设必需的临时性的配套设施，并纳入规范化管理。②制定实施财政、劳动用工等方面优惠政策，鼓励和引导社会资本到山区镇投资建设道路、水、电、公共交通等基础设施，兴办乡村旅游景区（点）、旅游酒店、现代农业生产基地、农产品加工流通企业和其他工商业企业。③加大对山区镇一村一品的扶持力度，通过政策推动、示范带动、龙头牵动、专业合作

等措施，推动一村一品迅速向产业化发展。④加强项目带动、项目开发，有计划地把广州市重要战略性物资储备、大宗商品储备基地从城区向北部山区转移。⑤在山区镇开展“农民以承包土地换社保，以宅基地换住房”试点工作，盘活农村土地资源，为发展现代农业和二、三产业创造条件。

2. 有关民生政策对山区镇实行倾斜

①加大对基础教育的投入，开展城乡学校间的对口帮扶，大力培养人才。②加大职业技能培训力度，职业技能培训券的申领发放要向山区镇倾斜，积极引导农村富余劳动力根据自身就业意愿参加职业技能培训或创业培训；扩大中等职业技术教育扶贫覆盖面，免收贫困家庭学生中等职业教育学费。③加快完善农村社会保障体系，资助农民参加农村社会养老保险，减轻缴费负担；进一步提高农村合作医疗的住院报销比例和封顶线，提高村民医疗救助水平。④提高对农村危房改造的补助标准，由市本级每户补助2万元提到4万元。

三、2011年取得的实施成效

2011年2月广州市正式启动北部山区镇扶贫开发工作以来，在科学规划的引领下，开局良好、进展顺利，已取得明显成效，促进了北部山区镇发展大提速，为2012年实现目标奠定了坚实基础。

（一）从项目建设实施来看

8个山区镇共规划建设173个项目，2010年已确定由各帮扶区和各大知名企业对口援建的项目98个，投资总概算25.38亿元。其中50个项目预计在2011年年底前完成，其他项目多数也已开工建设，少数正处于深化施工图设计、招标准备或挂网招标阶段。

尤其是基本公共服务配套建设推进迅速。通过道路、路灯、供水、污水处理等市政基础设施和医院、中小学、幼儿园、文化活动中心等公共服务设施的建设，显著提高了各镇、村的基本公共服务和宜居水平，进一步强化了镇区的辐射带动和综合服务功能。

（二）从民生福利来看

从民生福利来看，在产业扶贫、就业扶贫、科技扶贫、教育扶贫、医疗扶贫等各方面摸索出一系列有效做法，解决了大量民生实际问题。206条贫困村分别制定了脱贫致富的具体工作方案和措施，截至2011年年底，8个山区镇贫困户脱贫率达到81.3%，贫困村脱贫率达到87.4%。此外，206条贫困村共梳理遴选出村级集体经济发展项目802个，投入帮扶资金2.19亿元，并建立了增强村集体经济实力的长效机制，激发村民参与发展村集体经济的动力。据初步测算，2011年年底可实现贫困村集体经济收入1 829万元，平均每村年集体收入接近9万元。

比如，广州市农业局、广州团市委以“基地＋合作社＋农户”的形式，帮扶小楼镇青迳村打造养龟专业村，为该村每年带来12万元以上的集体经济收入，并为全村贫困户带来了5万元的投资分红收入，率先在增城北部山区实现了脱贫目标。

（三）从社会影响来看

通过2011年的实践，广州市已形成全社会共同参与北部山区镇扶贫开发的良好氛围，制度优势、市场机制、社会力量互动共促的优势正逐步凸显。除8个帮扶区外，已确定由9大知名企业承担的援建项目共38个，投资概算超过13亿元。在9大知名企业带动下，越来越多的企业积极参与帮扶8个山区镇建设，2011年已确定有其他243家企业与165个贫困村签订总投资近14亿元的232个扶贫开发项目，形成了“一区帮一镇、名企扶一镇、百企助百村”的北部山区镇扶贫开发的良好局面。

此外，各类人民团体、社会组织和广大群众也踊跃参与，并通过开展扶贫济困日、慈善日等活动，组织了各类扶贫济困志愿者活动。如全市宗教界发挥大爱无疆的慈善精神，在活动中捐资扶贫达400多万元。

四、主要启示

（一）坚持规划先行，高起点谋划山区镇扶贫开发

科学规划是城乡建设的法定前提。因此，在本次山区镇扶贫开发工作尚未正式启动的2010年12月，广州市规划局已提前介入，开始编制各镇的扶贫开发规划，并于2011年3月完成规划成果，为扶贫开发工作的快速有序推进提供了有力支撑。规划坚持高起点，将近期实施需求与长远科学发展结合起来，注重空间、土地、产业、生态、人口相协调，既充分体现战略性、前瞻性和特色性，又切实满足扶贫项目实施的需求。规划内容包括发展战略规划、扶贫项目库策划、控制性详细规划深度的项目实施图则、特色风貌规划及重点地段城市设计等。

同时，为保障规划的有效实施，广州市规划局高标准做好扶贫项目建设前期的规划审查、审批工作，并指导花都规划分局、增城和从化市规划局成立专门的专家委员会或专家审查小组，对项目设计方案严格把关，确保突出特色和扶贫效果。此外，还编制了《广州市农村住宅建筑设计方案选型》，发放给农民，引导农村住宅科学、有序建设。

（二）坚持民生为本，重点完善基础设施和公共服务设施

本次山区镇扶贫开发工作以推进基本公共服务均等化为重点，把完善基础设施和公共服务设施摆在重中之重的位置，不仅切实解决当前民生问题，而且着眼于破解设施瓶颈制约，支撑长远可持续发展。具体来说，通过与《广东省基本公共服务均等化规划》对比寻找差距，筛选不达标的项目，按照“缺什么，补什么”的原则，提出扶贫开发项目，作为整个项目库的主体（以增城派潭镇为例），包括文化室、文化活动中心等文化设施，群众性体育运动场地、居民健身场所等体育设施，中小学、幼儿园等教育设施，医院、社区卫生服务中

心等医疗卫生设施，福利院、老年人服务中心等社会服务设施，肉菜市场等商业服务设施，供水厂、污水处理厂等市政公用设施，以及道路、路灯等交通设施。

表2　增城派潭镇主要扶贫开发项目概览

序号	项目名称	建设内容	概算投资（万元）	开工时间	竣工时间	对口帮扶单位
1	派潭医院	建设业务用房、公卫楼等	3 805	2011.7	2012.4	番禺区
2	影剧院改造	维修屋顶、舞台，配置舞台设备等	464	2011.7	2011.10	番禺区
3	派潭文化中心	整饰外立面，完善图书馆功能	327	2011.7	2011.10	番禺区
4	镇中心幼儿园	改造建设公立中心幼儿园	759	2011.7	2011.10	番禺区
5	镇区主干道两侧建筑综合整治	外立面整饰，功能调整等	1 320	2011.7	2011.9	番禺区
6	派潭广场周边建筑综合整治	外立面整饰，统一风貌，功能调整等	360	2011.7	2011.9	番禺区
7	派潭商业街风貌整治	完善市场功能，沿街建筑功能调整等	600	2011.8	2011.12	番禺区
8	派潭镇敬老院	拆旧建新，院内环境和绿化整治等	1 010	2011.5	2011.10	敏捷集团
9	东升村风貌整治	围屋改造，排污处理，村庄绿化等	610	2011.5	2011.8	敏捷集团
10	上九陂村山枣坛社旅游村庄整治	旧村改造成旅游特色村	3 000	2011.8	2011.11	敏捷集团
合计		—	12 255	—	—	—

（三）坚持完善机制，保障扶贫开发工作落到实处

完善的保障机制是本次山区镇扶贫开发工作取得实效的关键，包括组织保障机制、资金保障机制、责任落实机制、考核奖惩机制、督查激励机制等各方面，以实现“输血式”扶贫与“造血式”扶贫的有机结合，使受帮扶的贫困村、贫困户走上良性发展的轨道，防止蹈入“脱贫返贫，反复扶贫”的怪圈。

其中，最重要的是资金保障。只有资金落实到位才能保证扶贫开发工作切实有效推进。因此，广州市委市政府除充分调动企业和社会的资金外，尤其注重财政资金的投入。广州市本级财政2011、2012年按上年度地方财政一般预算收入的1%安排农村扶贫开发专项资金。2011年和2012年市本级财政对教育、科技、文化、医疗等切块资金的预算安排压缩10%，转移支付给从化、增城市，通过项目安排的形式，专项用于北部贫困镇对口扶贫开发建设。2011年，海珠、荔湾、黄埔、萝岗、越秀、天河、番禺、花都8个区分别对口8个山区镇投入的帮扶实物工作量，按2010年地方财政一般预算收入的1%确定；以此为基数，2012年投入的帮扶实物工作量，按照被帮扶镇的上年地方财政一般预算收入增长率同步增长。市属国有企业按每条村投入50万元实施扶贫“双到”工作。

表3 对口山区镇扶贫开发财政资金来源（2011年）

序号	资金来源	资金额
1	市本级财政上年一般预算收入的1%	“双到”资金:50万元/村,约5 000万元 政策性支出:1.4亿元 镇区基础设施建设资金:约2.2亿元 合计4.16亿元
2	各区、县级市财政 上年一般预算收入的1%	合计4.57亿元
3	市级部门切块资金10%	市本级科技、教育、文化、医疗切块资金压缩10%,共1.03亿元,转移支付给增城、从化市,用于山区镇建设
4	市属国有企业“双到”资金	每村50万元,约2 000万元

（作者：闫永涛，广州市城市规划勘测设计研究院规划师）

参考文献

[1] http://www.gzagri.gov.cn/ztzl/2011gzbbsqgzjch/index.html.

[2] http://www.gzagri.gov.cn/ztzl/2011gzncfpkfzt/index.html.

[3] 广州市规划局．关于北部山区扶贫开发规划工作情况的报告，2011-09-20.

[4] 广州市规划局．广州市农村扶贫开发专项检查工作汇报材料，2011-07-25.

[5] 广州市农村扶贫开发工作领导小组办公室．广州市农村扶贫开发简报，2011（47）.

[6] 广州市农村扶贫开发工作领导小组办公室．广州市农村扶贫开发简报，2012（1）.

[7] 汤锦华．广州市农村扶贫开发工作形势与任务，2011-03-04.

[8] 万庆良．在加快北部山区发展工作会议上的讲话，2011-02-12.

[9] 万庆良．众人拾柴火焰高：在全市加快北部山区发展工作检查现场会上的讲话，2011-09-20.

[10] 张广宁．在广州市加快北部山区发展工作检查现场会暨“百企助百村”扶贫开发项目签约仪式总结大会上的讲话，2011-09-20.

[11] 张广宁．在加快北部山区发展工作会议上的讲话，2011-02-12.

[12] 中共广州市委．中共广州市委广州市人民政府关于加强我市农村扶贫开发工作的实施意见（穗字〔2011〕7号），2011-03-02.

经济转型背景下阳朔旅游发展策略研究

一、阳朔旅游发展概况

阳朔县隶属桂林市，位于广西东北部，距桂林市65公里，总面积1 428.38平方公里，总人口31万人。县治地阳朔镇，下辖6个镇、3个乡[1]。阳朔地处北部湾经济区和泛珠三角经济圈、西南合作等多区域合作的重要节点。

阳朔是全国发展旅游业最早的地区之一。作为中国喀斯特山水风光的典型代表、桂林旅游的经典品牌，阳朔是世界旅游组织（World Tourism Organization，WTO）确定的最佳休闲度假旅游目的地，2007年被国家旅游局评为首批“中国旅游强县”。2010年接待来朔旅游者811.3万人次，同比增长11.3%；旅游产业总收入31.5亿元，同比增长30.5%[2]。旅游业已成为阳朔的支柱产业，其快速发展拉动了住宿、餐饮、运输等服务业的高速增长，2010年阳朔县直接、间接的旅游从业人员已达10万余人，约占全县总人口的三分之一。

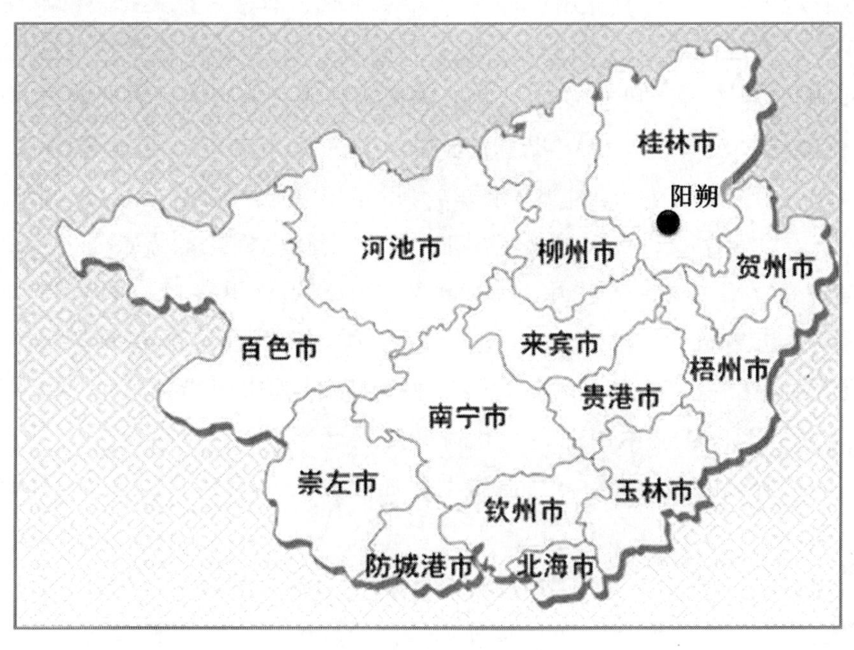

图1　阳朔县区位示意图

为进一步提升旅游业的整体实力，从竞争激烈的旅游市场中脱颖而出，自2007年起，阳朔主动推进经济转型，将高能耗、高污染的工业企业从旅游生态区中搬出，严控污染源，提升旅游环境品质[3]，推行“旅游强县”的发展策略，这也促使阳朔成为世界范围内旅游可持续发展的关注“热点”。2008年1月，国家正式批准实施《广西北部湾经济区发展规划》，极大地促进了阳朔旅游腹地的拓展。2009年10月，WTO在阳朔设立了中国首个旅游可持续发展观测点，将桂林重点推荐为世界旅游目的地。同年12月，《国务院关于进一步促进广西经济社会发展的若干意见》（国发〔2009〕42号）中明确提出建设桂林国家旅游综合改革试验区，阳朔县是改革试验的重中之重。近年来，随着北部湾经济圈的崛起，阳朔的区位优势日益明显，面临着良好的发展机遇。

总体来看，阳朔的经济转型发展思路对其旅游产业的持续发展具有重大的影响，而旅游业的发展也势必将经济转型向纵深推进。故在全国范围内经济转型的大背景下，探讨阳朔“中国县域旅游经济的标杆”，如何在既有的发展基础上，借助经济发展转型的契机，充分利用自身的优势，进一步增强自己的魅力和竞争力，实现城市的可持续发展，不仅对阳朔自己的发展具有重要的指导意义，而且对国内为数众多的旅游城市的后续发展具有重要的参考意义。

二、阳朔旅游发展现状分析

（一）优势分析

1. 旅游资源丰富多样。阳朔不仅是中国喀斯特山水风光的典型代表，而且是国内最早的乡村旅游目的地之一，拥有月亮山、遇龙河、金宝河、渔村等独具特色的旅游景点。随着旅游资源的开发，民俗民居、历史文化、生态、商务、休闲等多种类型的旅游资源日益增多，西街、“印象·刘三姐”民族表演、漓江漂流等发展成为阳朔旅游业新的“名片”。

目前，阳朔拥有5A景区1个、4A景区3个、3A景区4个，是全国A级景区最多的县[4]。此外，在旅游线路开发方面，阳朔成功开辟了多条自行车游览线路、漂流线路、徒步游线路、自驾车游览线路等，极大地满足了不同旅游群体多样化的需求。

2. 知名度较高。阳朔素有“桂林山水甲天下，阳朔堪称甲桂林”的美誉。从1973年开始，阳朔旅游发展历经近40年的历程，已成为国内接待游客量最大的县级市，2007年年底，被国家旅游局评价为“中国县域旅游经济的标杆”。其中西街被评为“中国最值得外国人去的50个地方”之一和“中国民间文化遗产旅游示范区”，而高田、兴坪、白沙和福利等乡镇拥有秀美的山水田园风光，乡村旅游发展如火如荼，吸引了大批国内外游客，享有较高的知名度。

3. 客源量规模大且稳定。几十年的旅游“积淀”不仅促成了阳朔高度的交通可达性，以及便捷、高效的宾馆住宿服务，而且具有高品质的旅游接待素质和居民文化素质，以及规范、公平的旅游市场秩序，这极大地提升了旅游的竞争力和游客们的满意度，确保了阳朔拥

图2 西街夜景

资料来源：http：//www. guilina. com/s31/。

图3 漓江山水一隅

资料来源：http：//www. 000219. com/scenic/show/1389. htm。

图4　印象·刘三姐演出

资料来源：http：//www.52uys.com/tools/photod.php？tid=797。

有大批的、稳定的“回头客”，也强有力地支撑了每年平均递增约100万游客的发展速度。

（二）不足分析

1. 缺乏长远规划，难以有效整合旅游资源

尽管旅游发展在国内起步很早，但因为观念、资金等多方面的原因，阳朔一直存在旅游规划缺位的现象。由于缺乏规划的指导，对客源市场的调查和可行性研究不够，当前全县旅游开发仍存在一定的盲目性，开发较为无序，乱建设、乱开发的现象时有发生，导致了旅游产品雷同，缺乏自身特色，影响了旅游的健康及长远发展[2]；另外，阳朔与周边的桂林、资源、龙胜等城市的旅游资源具有一定的同质性，如何进一步整合发展，形成合力，也是需要迫切解决的问题。

2. 政府、村民之间的利益需要协调

乡村旅游是阳朔旅游的“拳头产品”，也是阳朔、高田、兴坪等乡镇村民主要的收入来源。由于缺乏有效的旅游管理制度，为了争夺旅游客源，阳朔相继开拓了10条自行车游览线路、5条徒步游线路、4条民居旅游风情之旅线、8条自驾车游览线路，以及月亮山、蝴蝶泉等上百条攀岩线路[2]，发展较混乱，存在一定程度的恶性竞争。

阳朔境内的漓江段是一个整体，但由于利益分割，乡民纷纷在河道入口设置收费站，影响了游客对于旅游地的总体印象[5]。另外，当地村民与政府之间也存在利益分割的问题，以家庭为主的乡村旅游经营模式，常出现经营管理水平不高的现象，部分村民在急于获利的同时，忽视服务质量，可能会导致游客的数量下降，不利于乡村生态旅游的可持续发展[6]。

3. 开发与保护的矛盾需要缓和

高速增长的游客数量已对阳朔的生态环境造成了很大的压力。每年数百万的游客和数十

万的车辆涌入阳朔，在带来巨额经济收入的同时，也给阳朔乡村带来了巨大的污染源，当地生态环境遭受破坏的现象日趋严重[2]，往日宁和、幽静的乡野生活正渐渐远去，随之而去的是旅游产品的市场竞争力。另外，由于乡村的污水处理设施不完善，农家饭的污水不仅影响了饮食水源的供给，也严重影响了农作物的生长和收成。

4. 服务设施难以满足需求

随着旅游产业的快速发展，阳朔旅游服务设施已无法满足游客的需求，这将直接影响游客的旅游印象和体验。同时，阳朔的旅游服务设施也相对落后。虽然现有各类住宿设施数量多，但星级宾馆酒店比例低。目前五星级酒店只有1家，三星级以上酒店仅有4家，无法为高端游客提供良好的品质服务。

图5　被垃圾污染的乡村景观

资料来源：http：//act3. gongyi. qq. com/4177/work/show-id-3262. html。

三、旅游业发展趋势研究

经验数据表明，人均GDP达到800～1000美元，消费者将会普遍产生旅游动机，如果有充足的闲暇时间，他们会将想法付诸行动，观光旅游便应时而生[7]。随着消费者收入水平的提高，文化品位的逐步提升，单一的观光旅游已经不能再满足需求，商务、休闲、度假、生态等新的旅游方式成为新的市场需求[8,9]，商务旅游、度假旅游、休闲旅游等新的旅游类型浮现，旅游产业由单一的观光型旅游类型转向复合型旅游产业体系[10]，游客由仅关注物质层面的观赏逐步转向旅游地特色文化的体验和享受，旅游目的地的发展也从政府或群众单一力量的推进转向政府、企业、群众等共同推动的阶段，这是旅游业一个关键的发展趋势[11]。

在既有研究成果的基础上，结合国内外成功的发展经验，将旅游产业今后发展趋势的主要特征梳理总结如下：

表 1　旅游产业转型前后主要特征比较

	之前或现在	今后发展趋势
旅游方式	单一化(观光旅游)	复合化(观光旅游和休闲度假旅游等并重)
消费结构	吃、住、行占主要比重	游览、购物、娱乐等占主重比重
游客关注点	物质层面的观赏	文化层面的享受、体验
出行距离	短途为主	远距离(中长途)为主
旅游点腹地范围	较小	较大
旅游地品牌建设	—	重视培育、打造自身的品牌
旅游产品类型	单一	多样化
发展路径	对资源、环境等依赖严重	更加强调可持续发展
发展方式	粗放	集约
消费能级	低级	高级
发展的推动力量	政府或群众单一力量推动	政府、企业、群众等相关群体共同推动

根据旅游产业理论，每一个旅游目的地都有一个发生、发展、兴盛和衰退的生命周期过程。在此方面，加拿大学者 R. W. Butler[12] 的研究最具代表性，他将旅游地的演化分为探索、起步、发展、稳固、停滞、衰落或复苏六个阶段（图 6）。如何打造具有自身特色的品牌及实现可持续发展成为各旅游地关注的话题。

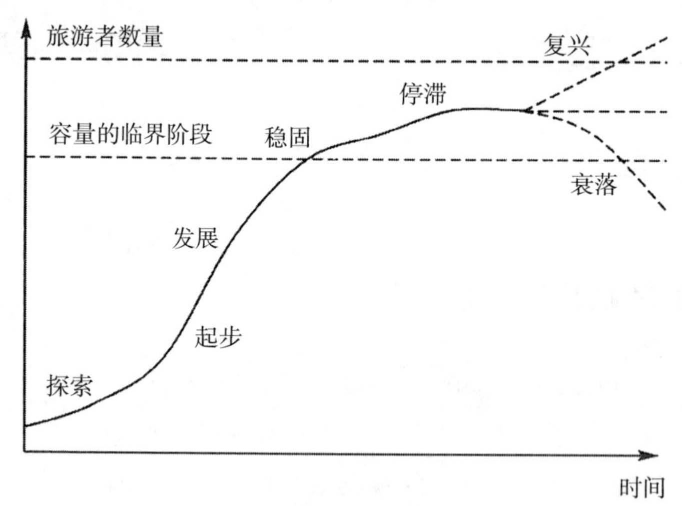

图 6　Butler 旅游地生命周期曲线

相对观光旅游而言，休闲度假等旅游的消费能级更高，在旅游目的地停留的时间较长，对其经济发展带动力度更大，故当一旅游目的地进入稳固阶段时，不仅需要在“量”上做文章，多开发几个新的旅游产品，而且需要适应市场需求，强化开发商务旅游、度假旅游、休闲旅游等新的旅游产品，注重旅游产品“质”的提升，以便能进入新的发展周期，避免过早地进入停滞、衰落阶段，是一个旅游目的地能确保持久活力的“不二法门”。

根据前文的分析，阳朔当前正处于旅游地生命周期的稳固阶段，如何在激烈的市场竞争中保持持久的生命力和竞争力是一个值得探究的问题。

四、发展策略探讨

根据阳朔旅游业发展的现状，结合旅游地生命周期理论，基于“持续发展、打造品牌、实现共赢”的发展思路，提出以下旅游发展策略：

（一）秉持可持续发展的理念，通过规划整合特色资源

针对当前景区存在的环境污染问题，建议在后续的开发进程中，应秉持可持续发展的理念，协调好保护与开发之间的关系。此外，针对当前阳朔缺乏旅游规划指导，开发无序的现状，应通过尽快编制、实施县域旅游总体规划，以及旅游线路策划、环境整治规划等专项规划[13]，有机整合全县的特色旅游资源，并与桂林、资源等周边城市旅游产业的协同发展，以指导全县旅游资源的合理开发和科学利用，确保旅游产业规范、有序发展。积极参与中国—东盟博览会，主动与环北部湾经济圈内的其他城市进行区域合作，发掘更多的资源和资金，引进国际或区域合作项目，吸引商贸、物流、信息等企业在阳朔落户，形成独特竞争力和更好的互动平台。

以规划为龙头，坚持可持续发展的理念，在旅游发展中切实遵循“先规划，后开发”，严肃纠正和制止旅游资源开发过程中“先开发后规划、边开发边规划，甚至无规划开发、无序发展”等短期行为[2]，以此来保证旅游资源的有序开发，合理利用，杜绝破坏性开发，推进阳朔旅游产业的可持续发展。

（二）以旅游发展促经济转型，打造阳朔休闲度假旅游品牌

如前文所述，阳朔当前已主动推进自身经济的转型发展，将污染型工业迁出旅游区范围，这有助于保障和促进阳朔旅游产业快速、健康地发展。而旅游业的发展，也可以带动相关产业的调整与升级，通过“一产围绕旅游调结构，二产围绕旅游出产品，三产围绕旅游现代服务业搞配套”，建立起复合型、高端化的旅游产品体系，进而推动经济的加快转型（图7）。即第一产业需要突破传统农业的限制，围绕旅游业发展观光农业、生态农业、农事参与等特色农业；第二产业注重发展旅游业相关的产品深加工业，如特色农产品加工等；第三产业围绕旅游业为游客提供精品配套服务，重点发展休闲产业，营造高品质的旅游环境，增强吸引力，延长游客滞留阳朔的时间，增强旅游产业效益。

根据旅游业的发展趋势和市场需求，阳朔应深入挖掘当地的特色文化内涵，增加游客的参与、体验环节，逐步推进旅游产业发展由观光游览等逐步向休闲度假游、商务旅游、会议旅游等过渡，逐步优化旅游产品结构，使景观文化旅游产品向体验文化产品、延伸文化旅游产品过渡，进一步增强对中外游客的吸引力[14]。设施建设，营造良好的旅游氛围和形象。一方面，阳朔需要加强旅游基础设施、服务设施的建设，不断完善旅游基础设施体系和配套

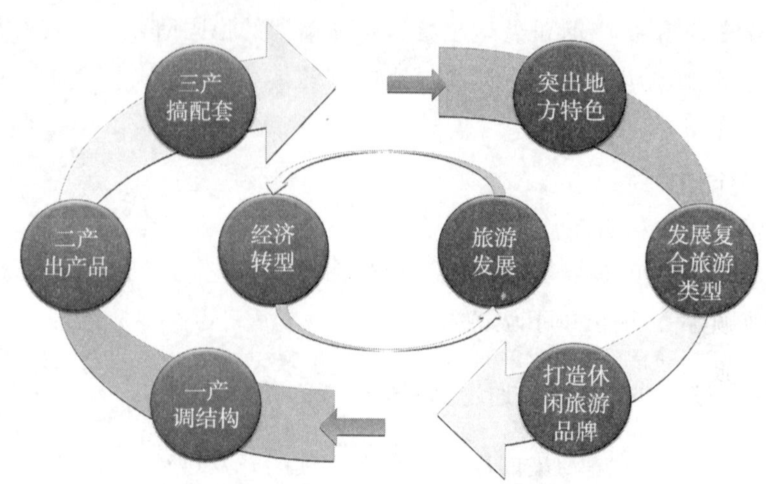

图7　旅游发展与经济转型之间的关系

服务设施体系，提高旅游承载能力；另一方面，阳朔在旅游接待设施中要增加高端星级宾馆、商务会所、度假村的数量，提高餐饮、住宿、娱乐等服务质量，提高旅游接待服务能力和品质，以适应数量日渐增长的高端游客的需求。

阳朔应结合地方特色的挖掘，注重品牌产品的开发力度，重视高端游客市场的拓展，不断构筑新的优势，增强市场的吸引力和生命力，打造具有影响力的优质休闲度假区的品牌(图8)。

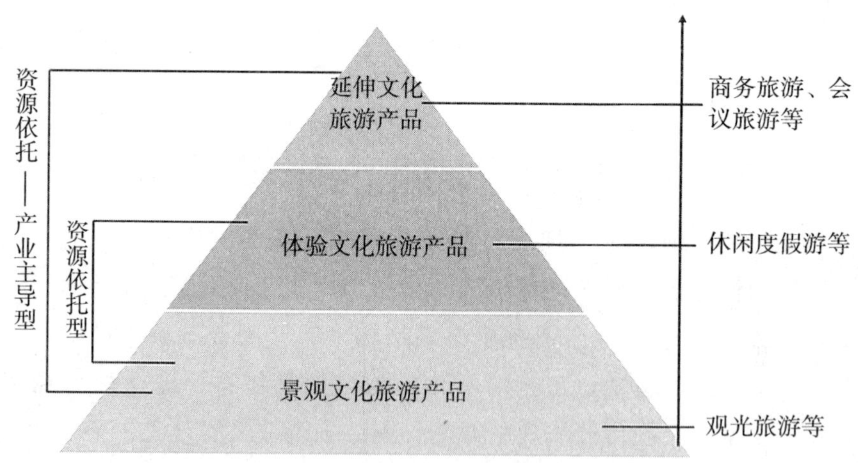

图8　旅游地发展过程中旅游产品结构演变

(三) 倡导以政府为主导，多方利益群体共同参与的发展模式

基于前文提及的政府、村民之间的利益冲突问题，应充分考虑阳朔当前所处的发展阶段，在遵循市场规律的基础上，进一步理顺当前的旅游管理机制，倡导建立政府主导，村民、旅游企业等多方利益群体共同参与的发展模式，逐步完善旅游开发格局，丰富旅游产品，规范化管理，提升区域形象[15]。

政府积极发挥在编制旅游规划，制定相关鼓励政策、投资基础设施和配套服务设施建设、提供旅游参与平台等方面的主导作用，逐步规范旅游市场秩序，增强旅游产业活力。另外，出于专业性、管理等方面的考虑，阳朔应鼓励有经验的外来资本的参与，以实现对旅游产业发展的专业化经营管理，为村民创造更多的旅游就业机会，确保经济发展的活力。

由于乡村旅游涉及的利益主体较多，建议采取多方利益主体联合开发经营模式，即在政府主导下组织当地村民、旅游经营企业联合投入，建立乡村生态旅游开发公司，共同开发乡村生态旅游，在兼顾各方利益的同时，提高经营效益和服务品质，避免各自为政，无序地掠夺性开发乡村生态旅游资源[6]。

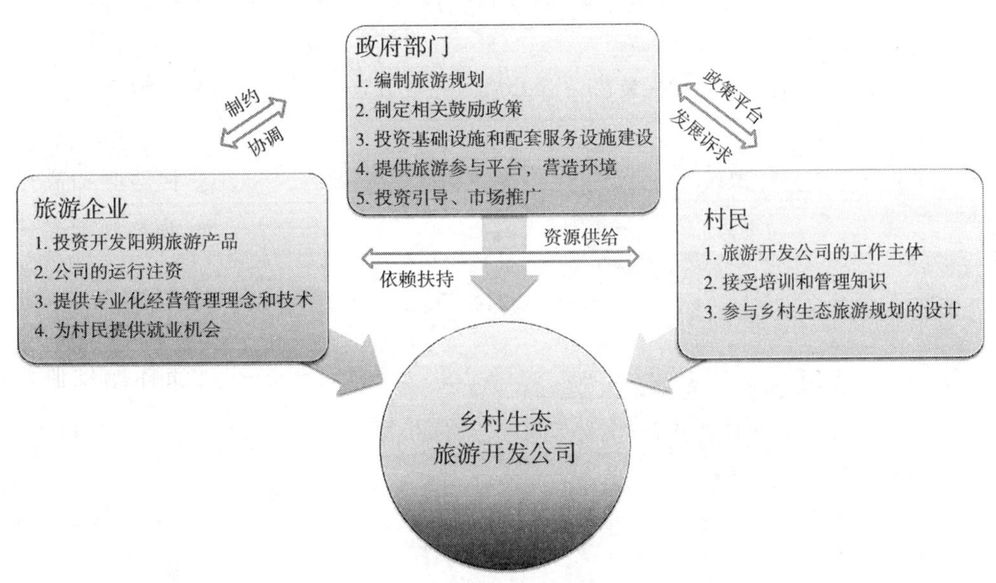

图 9　多方利益主体联合开发经营模式图

五、结论

基于对经济转型背景下阳朔旅游发展概况的分析，研究通过对其现状发展的优势和不足进行解读，结合旅游业发展的趋势，认为阳朔正处于旅游地生命周期的稳固阶段，需要遵循“持续发展、打造品牌、实现共赢”的发展思路，提出了相应的发展策略，推进阳朔旅游产业的可持续发展，并以此促进经济顺利转型：(1) 秉持可持续发展的理念，通过规划整合特色资源；(2) 以旅游发展促经济转型，打造阳朔商务、休闲度假、生态新旅游品牌；(3) 倡导以政府为主导，多方利益群体共同参与的发展模式。

（作者：廖远涛，广州市城市规划勘测设计研究院，高级规划师；魏宗财，广州市城市规划勘测设计研究院，规划师）

参考文献

[1] 阳朔县人民政府门户网站．http：//www. yangshuo. gov. cn/.

[2] 王晓丽，宋书巧．刍议阳朔乡村旅游资源开发［J］．广西师范学院学报（自然科学版），2005，22（4）：66－70.

[3] 阳朔国税．打造“绿色税收”助推地方经济发展．http：//www. gx. xinhuanet. com/fortune/. 2010－08/16/content_ 20631288. htm.

[4] 柳群．幸福阳朔活力四溢：破译阳朔经济奔跑背后的变身密码［J］．广西经济，2011（9）：53－55.

[5] 李丰生．阳朔乡村旅游规模化开发探讨［J］．经济地理，2005，25（2）：261－276.

[6] 林龙飞，陈辉．发展乡村生态旅游对策研究以阳朔为例［J］．生态经济，2007（7）：95－98.

[7] 王琪延．北京将率先进入休闲经济时代［J］．北京社会科学，2004（2），108－114.

[8] 周玲强，黄祖辉．我国乡村旅游可持续发展问题与对策研究［J］．经济地理，2004，24（4）：572－576.

[9] 王云才，许春霞，郭焕成，等．论中国乡村旅游发展的新趋势［J］．干旱区地理，2005，28（6）：862－868.

[10] 周建明．旅游度假区的发展趋势与规划特点［J］．国外城市规划，2003（1）.

[11] 郑群明，钟林生．参与式乡村旅游开发模式探讨［J］．旅游学刊，2004，19（4）：33－37.

[12] Butler R. W.，The Concept of Tourist Area Cycle of Evolution：Implications for management of Resources［J］. Canadian Geographer，1980，24（1）：5－12.

[13] 谢雨萍，李肇荣．乡村民居旅馆的开发与经营初探：以桂林阳朔为例［J］．经济地理，2005，25（3）：418－421.

[14] 廖远涛，魏宗财，陈婷婷，等．贵州西江镇千户苗寨旅游发展策略研究［J］．小城镇建设，2010（1）：94－98.

[15] 魏小安．中国旅游业发展的十大趋势［J］，湖南社会科学，2003（16）：91－98.

我国西北少数民族地区贫困县城镇化发展路径的思考

——以新疆喀什地区疏附县为例

一、前言

疏附县位于新疆维吾尔自治区西南部喀什地区，地处帕米尔高原东麓、塔里木盆地西缘的喀什噶尔绿洲，是祖国西陲重镇和交通枢纽。东邻喀什市，与伽师县毗连，西以砾石戈壁接乌恰县，南与疏勒县、阿克陶接壤，北隔喀拉塔格山、库玛塔格山和阿图什市相望。全县行政区划面积3162平方公里，辖12乡1镇，现有人口32.8万人，是一个以维吾尔族为主的多民族聚居县。疏附县城位于托克扎克镇，2009年末城镇人口3.07万人，城镇化水平9.7%。

疏附县2009年实现国内生产总值197 567万元，三次产业的比重为51.7:20.1:28.2。人均地区生产总值6 041元（884美元），是国家级贫困县。独特的生态地理环境、经济发展特征与文化传统造就了疏附县与内地迥然不同的城镇化特征。

自2010年起，国务院启动新一轮对口援疆战略，利用发达省份的财政资金转移支付、人才技术与先进的理念及管理经验，帮助新疆贫困地区实现跨越式发展，与全国同步迈入小康社会，其中决定由广州市对口援建疏附县。在此背景下，本文以疏附县为例，探讨我国西北少数民族贫困县城镇化的特征，指出制约城镇化发展的因素并结合新的发展形势提出相应的城镇化发展战略。

二、有关新疆地区城镇化的研究综述

首先，新疆城镇体系不够完善。新疆现有城市基本是在绿洲经济发展的基础上形成的，城镇分布较为分散（赵小兵，1987；陆易农，1996；李晓东，1997；李广舜，2008；李江成，龚新蜀等，2009），且城市的设置受政策环境影响较大（李江成，龚新蜀等，2009；安瓦尔·买买提明，张小雷，杨德刚等，2009；安瓦尔·买买提明，张小雷，塔世根·加帕尔等，2010），这造成了新疆的城市体系不合理，存在着城市数量少、密度低、城市首位度高、大城市缺失等问题，给新疆的城市、经济发展带来了极不利的影响，需要形成完善的多级城镇体系，支撑城镇化发展（权晓燕，王晓峰，李静等，2005）。主要表现在大城市短缺，辐射作用相对较弱（司正家，马卿等，2001；李春华，张小雷，王薇等，2003；李广舜，2008；权晓燕，王晓峰，李静等，2005；李江成，龚新蜀等，2009；卢思佳，张小雷，雷军，许科研等，2010）。关于新疆城镇化路径，主要有三种观点，一是中心城市优先发展模式（张慧，尼哈迈提·霍嘉等，2006；聂小青，张小雷，雷军，董雯等 2008）；二是加快小城镇建设，重点发展特色小城镇模式（孙秀东，2000；王克念，2007；李广舜，2008）；三是形成“点—轴—网络”城镇体系格局（宋涛，张阳生等，2001；司正家，马卿等，2001；张平，李莉萍，刘甲金，王海云等 2002；雷军，鲁奇等，2004；朱磊，张琰等 2004；李美荣，郭宁，刘文静等，2009）。

其次，生态环境对新疆城镇化进程影响极为关键。绿洲城镇化进程中面临的生态环境问题几乎都需要用水来解决。（林紫荣，张小雷，朱自安，王慧琴等，2007；李广舜，2008；阿布都热合曼·哈力克，卞正富，瓦哈甫·哈力克等，2008；安瓦尔·买买提明，张小雷，杨德刚，侯艳军等，2011）。生态环境保护既是城镇化的基础也是目标（李广舜，2008；李美荣，郭宁，刘文静等，2009）。

最后，从产业与城镇化的关系来看，传统农业和服务业所占比重较大、城镇化滞后于工业化（刘军保，苏斌等，1994；李春华，张小雷，王薇等，2003；王克念，2007；许文倩，龚新蜀等，2010a，2010b）。要解决这一问题，一是要利用产业延伸农业产业链（毛新雅，2002）。二是依靠工业化这一推动城镇化的根本动力（刘林，贺坤，龚新蜀等，2009）。三是要发展特色产业（李美荣，郭宁，刘文静等，2009；李坤，龚新蜀等，2010）。此外，还需要加强政府引导（刘林，龚新蜀等，2011），加大资金投入，以经济发展促进小城镇建设（雷军，鲁奇等，2004；王克念，2007；高岗仓，张凤艳等，2007；刘建辉，2007）。

总体而言，目前对于新疆城镇化的研究多集中在自治区或次区域层面，很少涉及以县为单元的城镇化和城镇体系研究。而在新疆这样地广人稀中小城市数目众多的地区，以县为单元探讨差异化的城镇化路径，对于指导我国西北少数民族地区城镇化发展具有实践意义。

三、疏附县城镇化现状特征与评价

（一）城镇化水平低，城镇化发展缓慢

2009 年，疏附县按非农人口计算的城镇人口仅有 3.07 万人，按此计算的城镇化水平仅 9.7%，属于城镇化水平较低的地区。从 1999 年到 2009 年 10 年间，疏附县城镇化水平仅提高 2.6%，增长缓慢。这是因为疏附县工业化进程发展缓慢，对城镇化推动力不强。根据统计资料，2001 年至 2007 年，疏附县第二产业就业人口仅增长 4 194 人，仅占 2007 年疏附县人口的 1.35%。

（二）中心城镇发育不足，城镇规模体系脱节

第一，中心城市规模不强，辐射带动能力弱。

中心城镇托克扎克镇仅有非农人口1.9万人，需求和供给能力都较弱。从需求角度看，目前城市消费需求很小，“巴扎”（集市）一周仅开放一次，现有市场仅能满足基本的消费需求，缺乏大规模的现代市场；从供给角度看，城市缺乏规模大、关联度高的产业，也没有供给能力强的大型商贸物流业，对周边乡的辐射带动作用很弱。

第二，城镇规模普遍较小，中心城市首位度过高。

疏附县的城镇结构体系具有南疆地区城镇体系的一般特点，即：首位城市过大，次级城镇不足和小城镇相对较多。至2009年，只有中心城区托克扎克镇非农人口超过1万人，其余乡集镇人口小于2 000人，规模最小的铁日木乡仅有城镇人口205人。以“四城市指数[①]”计算的中心城市首位度高达4.7。县域城镇体系尚处于发育阶段，现状第二层级的乌帕尔乡、英吾斯塘乡、布拉克苏乡等的乡集镇规模尚不足以衔接中心城与其他乡集镇，不能传递中心城镇的辐射。这造成了城镇的聚集程度较低，规模效益较差，很难发挥城市的中心作用，城市体系经济与空间不能同步发展。

疏附县各乡镇现状非农人口

乡镇	非农
托克扎克镇	19 176
乌帕尔乡	1 446
英吾斯塘乡	1 405
布拉克苏乡	1 204
栏杆乡	1 159
阿瓦提乡	1 274
木什乡	967
塔什米里克乡	896
站敏乡	739
阿克喀什乡	400
铁日木乡	205
萨依巴格乡	696
吾库萨克乡	1 159

第三，村庄体系尚未建立，对城镇化推动能力弱。

村庄规模受到绿洲承载力的制约，差异较小，在乡镇范围内依据自然条件散乱布局，公

① 四城市指数是指首位城市规模与第二、三、四位城市规模之和的比值，公式为 $S = P1/(P2 + P3 + P4)$。四城市指数的理想值为1。

共服务设施配置不足，缺乏产业支撑，对城镇化推动能力极弱。

（三）城镇职能单一，综合服务能力有待加强

第一，城镇职能单一，综合服务能力有待加强。

与多数南疆城市一样，疏附县城镇专业化职能不突出。县城和一般乡集镇皆是以行政职能为主，为农业和人民一般生活服务的小区域中心城镇。城镇功能类同，缺乏个性和特色。除了基本的文化教育、医疗卫生、商业零售等公共设施外，缺乏成规模、上档次的商业商务、会议展览、休闲娱乐设施，城市活力不足。

第二，产业基础薄弱，城镇化动力不强。

历史上，疏附县城镇的建立、布局与发展受行政性因素的影响较大，属于典型的自上而下型城镇化。疏附县产业基础薄弱，自下而上的城镇化动力不强。产业结构中，第一产业比重过大，第二产业短腿，第三产业低水平扩张。2010 年，疏附县人均 GDP 仅有 6 463 元，三次产业比重为 59. 9:11. 3:28. 8。工业产品结构单一，产品档次低，技术结构落后。表明疏附县尚处于前工业化社会时期。因为农业和第三产业吸纳不了全部劳动力，大量富余劳动力外出打工，而非在本地城镇集聚。

（四）城镇空间结构分散，缺乏规模效应

第一，城镇分布分散，联系不紧密。

疏附县是典型的南疆地区，是我国主要的干旱荒漠区，大量土地是沙漠和戈壁，人类能够居住生存的仅仅是沙漠周边的绿洲。这些绿洲主要分布在流量比较丰富的河流沿岸以及有地下水溢出的山前洪积冲积扇倾斜平原一带，被荒漠所分割和包围。因此，疏附县人口和城镇分布非常分散。各城镇布局紧紧依托绿洲呈串珠状发展，彼此相距较远，多数依靠县道连接，未形成集聚城镇的发展轴。

第二，城乡基础设施建设薄弱。

疏附县主干道路设施建设水平较高，适度超前于其城镇化水平，314 国道纵贯县域南部。但国道上交通流量小，交通工具落后。与国道连接的县乡道建设水平不高，与国道差距较大。通向主要城镇和重要旅游资源点的道路状况较差，难以带动工业、县域旅游业的发展。

四、影响城镇化发展的因素

（一）脆弱的绿洲生态

第一，水资源对城镇规模和城镇化制约明显。

疏附县主要生态特征是干旱少雨，水资源主要来自于冰川融水和地下水。冰川融水时空分布严重不均，地下水水质较差，造成水资源总量和结构性的短缺。疏附县多年平均可供水

资源量11.27亿立方米，2009年县域人口32.8万人。人均水资源占有量为3 466立方米。[①]依据生态容量研究，县域水资源承载人口为78.4万人。除了水资源总量不足以外，推动城镇化的工业化过程，也会引起严重的城市水质污染，造成结构性缺水，使供水问题更为严重。因此，疏附县城镇规模的增长和城镇化战略必须考虑水资源的制约作用。

第二，环境脆弱，易被破坏，难以重建。

疏附县域土地中，戈壁占了绝大多数，这形成了植被稀少，土地沙化，盐渍化严重等生态特征。这些特征决定了疏附城镇外部生态环境的脆弱性、不稳定性，易于受到风沙的侵蚀和人类活动的污染。而且这样的生态环境一旦遭受破坏，则难以恢复。

（二）独特的自然人文资源

第一，丰富的农业资源。

疏附县农业资源丰富，产品包括小麦、玉米、水稻、豆类、蔬菜、西甜瓜、薯类、色素辣椒、油料、苜蓿等；尤其是特色农业发展较快，有四个A级绿色食品：喀什噶尔木纳格葡萄、喀什噶尔木亚格杏干、喀什噶尔纸皮巴旦木、喀什噶尔万寿金桃；三个有机转换产品：阿瓦提乡喀鲁克村石榴、阿瓦提乡喀鲁克村红枣、塔什米力克乡热孜喀村木亚格杏。此外，经济林种植广泛，品种众多，包括杏子、核桃、红枣、石榴、巴旦木等，形成了杏子基地、核桃基地、石榴基地、巴旦木基地、红枣基地和樱桃基地等6大特色农产品基地。疏附县先后被命名为“中国喀什噶尔石榴之乡”、“中国木亚格杏之乡”、“中国木纳格葡萄之乡”。

第二，潜力巨大的旅游资源。

旅游产业已成为世界第一大产业，在经济发展中起到极为重要的带动作用。疏附县现有大量未能开发利用的旅游资源，潜力巨大。若能合理开发，形成支柱性的旅游产业，能够带动县域特色旅游产品、餐饮、酒店、交通等多种产业的发展，带动城镇化的发展。

第三，丰富的清洁能源。

疏附县具有丰富的清洁能源资源，可以为工业化和城镇化提供充足的能源支撑。特殊的绿洲生态特征对环境保护提出了很高的要求，而疏附县刚好有丰富的清洁能源资源。典型的大陆干旱气候、广阔的戈壁滩提供了丰富的风力资源，季节性的雪山融水和地形落差提供了丰富的水能资源。

（三）广州对口援建的产业支持

国家部署东部经济发达省份对新疆少数民族贫困地区实施“对口支援”行动，由广州市对口支援疏附县。在援建中，产业援助是最重要的外力，其对城镇化的推动主要体现在两个方面：

第一，充分拉动就业，将大量产业工人转化为城镇居民。基于疏附县产业现状，援助产

① 资料来源于《新疆喀什地区疏附县农田水利基本建设综合规划》。

业多为劳动密集型产业，可以吸收疏附县富余劳动力，提供充分的就业岗位，提高城镇化水平。第二，可以密切城乡联系，有助于形成合理的城镇体系。基于疏附县的资源禀赋条件，援助工业、物流、旅游等产业与疏附特色产品紧密结合，能够促进生产各类要素在城乡间的流动，改变疏附县一直以来的自上而下的城镇化发展路径，增强自下而上的发展动力，有助于形成功能分工合理的城镇体系。

(四) 富有地域特色的文化习俗

疏附县人口中，少数民族占绝大多数，其中维吾尔族人口占全县总人口的97.81%。独特的民族习俗将影响城镇化的方式。维吾尔族具有营商的文化传统，古代丝绸之路即由此经过，而现在城市中的“巴扎”（市场）也是物资交易的最重要手段之一。由于技术、资源的匮乏，当地缺少发展工业的传统。因此，选择商贸、物流、旅游等服务型的产业推动城镇化的发展较为适合本地的文化习俗。

五、疏附县城镇化战略的选择

(一) 以生态本底条件为约束，因地制宜确定城镇规模

疏附县城镇化必须坚持生态优先战略。独特的绿洲生态环境非常脆弱，人口承载能力有限，不适宜发展规模太大的城市。因此城镇不能采用摊大饼的发展模式，而适宜采用网络化的城镇体系。这体现在城市规模上就是要根据环境承载力控制城市的合理规模。

(二) 加强中心城镇建设，形成体系完善、功能合理的城镇体系

依据增长极理论，增长极是经济跨越式发展的基本推动力，从一定意义上说实现县域经济跨越式发展就是要适度超前推动增长极的发展，建立适合县情的经济空间结构，使原本均质分布的县域经济的资源、资本、劳动力等要素受极化作用形成合理的流向，促进县域经济扩大，保证其稳定、健康、快速发展。

第一，加强中心城镇的建设。

一是增强县城的规模和辐射能力。需要通过集聚人口，提高城市的需求，拉动消费需求，扩大各乡对县城农产品等物资的供给；通过集聚工业、商贸物流及其他服务业，提高县城的供给能力，向县域输送更多的货物和服务，密切城乡联系。二是提升第二层级城镇规模。疏附县现状中心城镇首位度过高，缺乏第二层次的城镇支撑，不利于中心城市功能辐射的传递。第二层次城镇可以起到联系中心城市与一般乡镇的作用。三是发展条件较好的村形成中心村，构建“中心城市—中心镇——般乡—中心村”等各个层次的中心。构成完善的城镇体系。目前，依靠疏附县自身的能力，还不足以形成强有力的中心，需要借助援建这一外部力量，促进中心城市快速成为县域增长极，加快城镇化进程。

第二，构建组合增长极。

所谓组合增长极是指两到三个城镇分担不同的功能，共同组成片区增长极。这一战略在绿洲型城镇尤为重要。在绿洲分散隔离的环境下单个城镇规模较小，服务能力不足，难以带动整个绿洲经济发展。组合式的增长中心可以形成功能互补，共同组成完善的城市职能，更好的辐射带动周边发展。

第三，多样化的城市职能。

现状城镇职能过于单一，基本以公共服务为主，缺乏活力。需要根据不同城镇的资源禀赋和区位条件，形成较为明确的职能分工，促进县域产业的多样化发展。

（三）采用“商贸先行，以贸带工”的发展路径，优先考虑农民就业问题

疏附地处古丝绸之路要冲，商贸历来在社会经济发展中占有重要地位。广州是全国乃至世界著名的商贸会展中心，商贸具有悠久的传统。两者结合，以广东商贸城为平台，将喀什、南疆乃至中亚国家的特色物产与广东的先进制造产品交换流通，搞活市场，集聚人气，并视市场需求带动相关加工业的发展，从而建立根植地方的现代工业体系。

（四）完善基础设施建设，为网络化城镇体系提供坚实支撑

第一，构建完善的基础设施，强化城镇间的联系，加快城镇化进程。疏附城镇分布不同于内地，城镇距离过远，这客观上削弱了城镇间的联系。而城镇化过程中必不可少的是人流、物流、信息流、资本流、技术流在城镇间的频繁流动。这些要素流动对城镇化起到关键的作用。因此，借助援助构建超前于城镇化水平的交通设施，有利于加快城镇化的进程。

第二，通过基础设施连接，避免城镇过度集中，保护生态。基础设施有助于构建网络化的城镇体系结构，从而避免城市连片发展，避免生态环境遭到破坏。

六、疏附县城镇化战略实施的初步绩效

（一）以中心城区建设为重点，构建产业发展平台

在《新疆喀什地区疏附县城总体规划（2010—2030）》的指导下，以中心城区建设为重点，构建了广东商贸城、广州新城、广州工业园等产业发展平台，在广州市的大力援建及推动下，2011 年招商引资项目 156 个，签订正式协议 109 个，合同投资总额 218.2 亿元，为疏附县建设现代化产业体系打下坚实基础。

（二）以基础设施建设为先导，推动重大项目建设

依照相关规划，重点完成了疏附广州工业园首期 3.5 平方公里道路、供水、排水、绿化照明等基础设施建设，新建 220kV 变电站已投入运行；完成了商贸园区 10 平方公里综合起步区市政道路及克孜河 4 公里河堤整治工程。以基础设施建设为先导，推动产业建设，目前

广州新城一期建材城、小商品城项目已全面封顶，开始招商。

（三）以改善社会民生为目标，加强住房及文化教育卫生配套建设

城镇化发展的根本目的是改善社会民生，改善人民群众的住房条件，提高文化教育、医疗卫生服务水平。在广州市援建下，启动全县13个乡镇富民安居建设工程，2011年6 000户富民安居房建设完成；同时完成了县城有线电视改造和农村无线电视覆盖项目、县电化教育中心大楼、县妇幼保健院、县计生服务站和县人民医院附属设施等建设，极大改善了人民群众的文化生活、教育培训和医疗条件。

（四）以提高人力资本为核心，加强农民的就业技能培训

结合少数民族地区的文化风俗和教育水平和人力资源特点，以提高人力资本为核心，加强农民的就业培训，以此作为推进城镇化的重要抓手。经广州市的协调安排，2011年定向职业技能培训5 491人次，4 931人获得相关职业资格证书；转移输出劳动力4.1万人次，实现劳务创收25 415.7万元。

（本文为广州市城市规划勘测设计研究院编制的《疏附县城总体规划（2010—2030）》相关研究的部分成果，在规划编制研究过程中，得到广州市规划局王东局长、刘毅东书记、李颖总工的指导，在此深表感谢！）

（作者：周方，广州市城市规划勘测设计研究院院长；赖寿华，广州市城市规划勘测设计研究院代总规划师，区域规划研究所所长，上海分院院长；黄慧明，广州市城市规划勘测设计研究院区域规划研究所副所长，上海分院副院长；唐勇，广州市城市规划勘测设计研究院区域规划研究所副总工程师，上海分院总工；傅幸之，广州市城市规划勘测设计研究院上海分院，规划师）

参考文献

[1] 阿布都热合曼·哈力克，卞正富，瓦哈甫·哈力克，等．南疆城镇化发展中的生态环境问题与反贫困研究［J］．农业现代化研究，2008，29（6）：680－683.

[2] 安瓦尔·买买提明，张小雷，塔世根·加帕尔，等．基于模糊数学的新疆南疆地区城镇化与生态环境的和谐度分析［J］．经济地理，2010，30（2）：214－219.

[3] 安瓦尔·买买提明，张小雷，杨德刚，侯艳军，等．新疆喀什地区城镇化与水资源利用结构变化的关联分析［J］．中国沙漠，2011，31（1）：261－266.

[4] 安瓦尔·买买提明，张小雷，杨德刚，等．新疆南疆地区城镇化过程对生态—环境的影响分析［J］．干旱区资源与环境，2009，23（12）：54－59.

[5] 高岗仓，张凤艳，等．新疆生产建设兵团城镇化发展的战略思考［J］．社会主义研究，2007（3）：76－78.

[6] 龚新蜀，许文倩，等．新疆城镇化发展的区域差异及决定因素分析［J］．小城镇建设，2009（11）：26－29.
[7] 贺坤，龚新蜀，等．新疆城镇化与工业化协调发展研究［J］．新疆农垦经济，2009（5）：25－29.
[8] 雷军，鲁奇．新疆小城镇发展与农村城镇化研究［J］．中国人口资源与环境，2004（6）：85－90.
[9] 李春华，张小雷，王薇，等．新疆城镇化过程特征与评价［J］．干旱区地理，2003，26（4）：396－401.
[10] 李广舜．对新疆城镇化发展问题的思考［J］．新疆大学学报（哲学·人文社会科学版），2008，36（3）：18－22.
[11] 李江成，龚新蜀，等．基于空间地域差异的新疆城镇化道路探析［J］．当代经济管理，2009，31（3）：44－47.
[12] 李坤，龚新蜀，等．新疆城镇化发展中的产业转型问题研究［J］．生态经济，2010（3）：81－84.
[13] 李美荣，郭宁，刘文静，等．基于特色产业发展的新疆城镇化研究［J］．科技与经济，2009（4）：42－45.
[14] 李美荣，郭宁，刘文静，等．新疆城镇化发展研究综述［J］．黑龙江民族丛刊，2009（3）：80－84.
[15] 李全胜．新疆城镇化问题探析［J］．新疆师范大学学报，2001（2）：1－5.
[16] 李晓东．新疆城市分等与城镇土地基准价格体系的建立初探［J］．干旱区地理，1997，20（1）：40－44.
[17] 林紫荣，张小雷，朱自安，王慧琴，等．干旱区绿洲生态环境与新疆城镇化研究［J］．干旱区资源与环境，2007，21（12）：6－14.
[18] 刘建辉．对新疆城镇化问题的思考［J］．社会主义研究，2007（6）：32－33.
[19] 刘军保，苏斌，等．新疆城镇化和农村非农化的实证分析［J］．新疆经济，1994（5）：12－15.
[20] 刘林，龚新蜀，等．福建论坛（社科教育）［J］．科技与经济，2009（2）：34－36.
[21] 刘林，龚新蜀，等．新疆城镇化的特殊性与政府的主导作用［J］．城市问题，2011（1）：12－18.
[22] 刘文静，郭宁，李美荣，等．我国内地城镇化模式对新疆城镇化的启示［J］．改革与战略，2009（7）：113－116.
[23] 卢思佳，张小雷，雷军，许科研，等．新疆城市经济区划分及影响范围［J］．干旱区地理，2010，33（2）：300－305.
[24] 陆易农．新疆城市发展战略的思考［J］．城市规划汇刊，1996（1）：49－52.
[25] 毛新雅．发展特色农业企业推动新疆城镇化建设进程［J］．新疆大学学报（社会科学版），2002（30）（增刊）：61－63.
[26] 聂小青，张小雷，雷军，董雯，等．新疆伽师绿洲经济可持续发展空间模式研究［J］．干旱区资源与环境，2008，22（11）：114－119.
[27] 权晓燕，王晓峰，李静，等．对新疆城市体系的几点认识［J］．新疆师范大学学报（自然科学版），2005，24（3）：209－212.
[28] 司正家，马卿，等．实施点轴开发战略加快新疆城镇化发展［J］．新疆师范大学学报（哲学社会科学版），2001，22（2）：6－10.
[29] 宋涛，张阳生．新疆巴州城镇化现状、特征及其发展模式初探［J］．西北建筑工程学院学报，2001，（4）：93－100.
[30] 孙秀东．关于新疆城镇化发展的思考［J］．中国民政，2000（21）．
[31] 王克念．新疆小城镇建设的思考［J］．实事求是，2007（4）：33－34.

[32] 许文倩，龚新蜀，等．新疆城镇化地域差异实证研究 [J]．技术经济与管理研究，2010 (1)：148－151.

[33] 张慧，尼哈迈提·霍嘉，等．新疆农村城镇化影响因素研究 [J]．新农村建设，2006 (12)：5－6.

[34] 张平，李莉萍，刘甲金，王海云，等．推进新疆城镇化进程的思路、途径及措施建议 [J]．新疆职业大学学报，2002 (3)：1－6.

[35] 赵小兵．新疆南疆城镇布局 [J]．干旱区地理，1987，1 (2)：41－43.

[36] 朱磊，张琰．新疆兵团城镇化建设问题研究 [J]．中国农垦经济，2004 (5)：24－25.

实事求是　探索平衡发展的城镇空间结构规划

——以温州市苍南县龙港镇总体规划为例

摘要：2010年温州市苍南县龙港镇政府以修编龙港镇城市总体规划为契机，通过空间结构优化、镇域城乡等方面的专题研究确定未来区域城镇空间发展格局，为积极应对未来龙港镇面临的确定的和不确定性的需求，系统整合城镇空间要素，尝试构建适应龙港镇更长时期的发展需求、相对稳定的城乡空间结构。既谋求独善其身，又履行县（区）域的发展战略职责，也冀望通过持续的城市发展再一次聚集浙南地区更多社会经济要素。形成这一共识的过程，经历了有利于整合资源的行政区划的调整，同时也从另一个侧面对于总体规划工作本源进行了思考和探索。

关键词：总体规划　结构效应　城镇资源　社会共识

2011年浙江省温州市苍南县龙港镇面临自1983年成立以来，最为迅猛的一次变革[①]，这次变革广泛并深度涉及自身和契合了外部发展条件的变化[②]，同时也汇聚了苍南县社会各界的需求和期盼。这次龙港镇城市总体规划修编就是在这样的背景下开展和完成的。

---

① 2011年4月温州市行政区划调整后，苍南县龙港镇将面积29平方公里的江南海涂围垦以及周边两镇一乡纳入新的行政区划范围，面积增加至176平方公里，镇域人口接近40万，成为温州南部鳌江流域第一大城镇。

② 2009年5月，海峡西岸经济区也继长三角、珠三角、环渤海、北部湾之后，成为新的国家级经济区。2009年11月，农业部和国务院台湾事务办公室批准《浙江温州苍南台湾农业创业园》、2010年11月，霞关港开展对台小额贸易首次台轮试航成功后，成为浙江杭州海关辖区内第4个正式开通的对台小额贸易点。2011年3月，《浙江海洋经济发展示范区规划》正式上升为国家发展战略规划，按照规划确定的沿海七市发展计划，温州正在不遗余力地推进其三大流域沿海区域一体化的建设进程，将会带来原本边缘的苍南县及其南部地区与北部核心地区的时空关系发生重大变化。其中甬台温高速复线、临港海涂围垦、鳌江多座跨江桥梁、温州轨道南延线等几大项目都对苍南特别是龙港镇的城市格局产生直接的作用和影响。

一、读识龙港镇的历史和现实以谋求未来

（一）龙港镇的发展历程简述

龙港镇在1982年苍南县新县城规划选址[①]的比选中首次获得关注，虽然龙港镇作为县城选址的规划（专家首选方案）并未实现，也正是这一历史偶然为日后的龙港镇“农民建城”铺垫了绝佳的时空条件。

尽管失去了县城之“名”，苍南县政府还是通过建设沿江、龙江港区引发了人们对于龙港镇区域价值之“实”的认识。1983年正式设立龙港镇，随后1984年中央政府对于城乡户籍制度松绑的政策，加速了苍南和浙南地区农村民众汇集龙港镇的速度。在创新制度、民众意愿和市场经济三者的共同作用下，龙港镇开始了中国现代史上第一个大部分依靠民间资金“自发”建设城镇的行为。龙港镇也由此得名“中国第一农民城”，今日龙港的城市空间格局和风貌大部分是在20世纪80年代中后期奠定形成的。

龙港镇在“中国农民第一城”的称号之后，又凭借其经济成就获得了“中国印刷城”、“中国礼品城”、“中国印刷材料交易中心”和“中国台挂历集散中心”等众多头衔。伴随中国改革开放的进程，龙港镇经历了三个汇聚、生长和各具特色的发展阶段，十年一个跨度，在政策环境、经济产业、空间特征等方面呈现出各自鲜明的特征[②]。

龙港镇是一个由集体自发，政府引导，以民间力量为主推进实现城镇化的典型案例。在

---

① 历史上温州市最南端的平阳县，曾是全市面积第一、人口占全市三分之一的大县，但受限于当时的社会经济发展条件，鳌江南北两岸的发展差距明显，加上浙闽文化差异以及域内多元文化的交错，管理协调难度大，1981年从加快自身县域经济发展，减轻政府行政管理难度的角度出发，平阳县地方政府结合群众意见向上级政府提出了以鳌江为界另设新县城的请求，同年6月该请求获得浙江省及国务院批准，自此鳌江以南占平阳县面积一半的七区一镇借位于玉苍山以南之名，正式成立苍南县，灵溪镇为县政府所在地。

② 80年代—90年代初：是人口政策性集聚和城镇集中建设阶段。1983年龙港建镇之初，仅由5个小渔村组成，辖区面积约5.2平方公里，人口约6 500人。到1990年年底，完成38.5公里城镇道路及市政管线、增加近150万平方米建筑、兴建了一系列基础公共设施，全镇户籍人口达4.4万人，大规模政策性人口集聚告一段落，这一阶段的产业主要以大量小规模家庭作坊式的标牌、塑编、纺织业为主，也是浙江类似地区农村工业化起步的典型代表。

90年代—2000年初：是成为小城镇改革试点和城镇经济高速发展阶段，在这一阶段，龙港镇一方面因数次行政区划整合持续地不断扩张空间规模，另一方面也在积极尝试城市行政管理制度和经济产业发展政策方面的改革，争取到了准县级的行政管理权限。至1995年，镇域面积扩至58平方公里，常住人口约达19万人，全镇工业总产值更从1990年的2.3亿元一跃达24亿元。至2000年，龙港辖区面积增至80.7平方公里，全镇常住人口已达到27万余人，全镇工业总产值达57亿元。这一阶段政府通过为私有家庭经济发展提供有利条件，刺激促进了整体经济总量的提升，但受到传统产业自身的效率与竞争力限制，90年代末期，经济增速放缓。

2000年—2010年代：是经济发展模式、产业结构以及城市格局的综合调整阶段，龙港镇产业群落的演变在这一阶段得到政府的政策支撑和引导，从自发的社会化协作和简单产业链，逐步演化到工业园区模式的小企业集群，这一时期镇政府突出以产业集聚和提升来推动城镇化协调发展。2000年初，龙港镇先后规划建设了示范印刷工业园、小包装印刷工业园、塑编工业园、城东综合工业园等4个工业园，截至2010年园区总面积接近4平方公里，两百余家企业进驻投产。至2010年年底龙港镇常住人口约达34万人，工业总产值283亿元，同比增长21%。

短短30年间，龙港镇不但在空间上从“无”到有，还实现了自身经济和社会结构的重大转变，从自然状态的小农经济社会转变为社会主义市场经济制度下的民营经济联合体。

回眸历史，与其说龙港镇是一个地方的发展奇迹，不如说是一种宏观国策与地方各种要素偶然组合共同作用下的特殊时代产物，开创了民间资本成为城镇建设主力的先河，尽显天时地利人和，也是中国当代城镇化进程中的特别案例之一。

（二）感悟龙港镇发展历史与现实

历史与现实是一个相对的话题，历史是现实的前身，现实是历史的延续。从历史中学习，对未来预判，决定今天的作为。

万事开头难，龙港镇的诞生是一件伟大的事情。人们合理的集体发展脉动和特别的社会组织形式，奠定了龙港镇后来快速发展的物质基础。当初选择的城市空间结构和发展模式，是基于建镇初期以积聚农村进城人口的基本需求为价值取向的，应该说当时的人们选择了一把合适的钥匙解开了那时候的锁。适度的空间结构满足了人们的心理和物质的承受力，也解决当时的客观需求。从今天龙港镇所面临的问题看，我们不能说是因为当时的发展规划缺少对远景的足够考虑，反倒是我们在正视遗憾的时候，要从当年的陈定模书记①决策建设规划时的胆识和勇气中感悟龙港精神的本质，为今天的规划带来有益的启示。

感悟一：实事求是。30年前的龙港镇规划面对农村紧张的人地关系②和农村涌动的进城渴求集聚发展的诉求，以客观的社会需求和制度环境为决策基础，采取力大不破皮的巧力策略，创新机制，形成了以城市空间积聚要素，化解供求矛盾，形成广泛的社会合力与集体共识，从而创造了空前的、持续的、自下而上的城镇化发展模式。这种模式对于今天的龙港镇仍具启示作用，龙港镇规划需要延续当年实事求是的态度，不搞无谓的形式主义，发展更具活力和包容的现代化城市，不仅是龙港镇持续城市化的必然，也是实现更高端社会经济要素再积聚的必要手段。

感悟二：顺势而为。如果说当年龙港镇成功化解了社会需求和资源供给短缺的矛盾，其成功正是在于其选择了恰当的预期，应时顺势，迈出了坚实的第一步，而不是采取不切实际的预判和超现实的前瞻规划。事实上在当时忐忑营城的过程中，是无法预测城市会如此超快速地发展，也无暇顾及后来出现的城市空间结构性不适应，以及小政府服务大社会不匹配等问题。反倒是因为那时的目标非常现实，就是要建设具有一定规模和运行效能的小镇。当年合理的城市空间结构，早已不能承载越来越庞大的城市社会综合体，我们只能说结构的不适应是龙港设镇成功后的遗憾。今天的龙港镇面临的规划发展问题是空间结构规模尺度超大的问题，结构不适宜是城市问题的关键，今天我们须采取更前瞻的态度，分析研究当下龙港镇坐拥的区位空间及其资源潜力和机遇，从小龙港镇到大龙港镇的空间结构变化中找寻内在关系、发展演变规律和趋势，以便及时识别问题，以结构性的布局来应对未来不同时期城市出

---

① 龙港镇镇委书记（1984）

② 1983年农村人均生产性土地面积仅为2.35亩。

现的不确定需求，顺龙港镇未来发展之势，争取对当下的城市规划结构性布局决策时产生积极有益的作用，以规避由于城市结构性不适应带来的问题。

感悟三：集体共识。如果说当年龙港设镇建城积聚了个体农民城市化的理想和发展要素，是那时的社会集体共识，那么今天龙港镇汇聚的就是苍南县域政治经济和文化的战略诉求，以及龙港镇人们源自自身更高的城市文明需求，内在动力变化了，起点也更高了，我们需要利用城市规划为手段形成新的共识。今天龙港镇城市化路径与外部软硬件环境条件更具相关性，需要充分领会和利用宏观政策背景和区域城镇发展阶段蕴藏的历史机遇，积极进取，理性看待新形势下的人地关系，人与人的社会关系以及龙港社会对提升城市文明的诉求，创新思维，以城市空间作为形成新共识的平台，有共识，才能够为龙港镇未来的发展提供持续的社会合力。

感悟四：平衡发展。当年在鳌江南平原片区积聚人口建设城镇，打破了原有的农业生产条件下的社会组织和空间要素的平衡，镇政府关注人口积聚带来的供需要素简单平衡，有效地保证了龙港镇的快速发展。今天的龙港镇为了实现苍南县域社会经济发展更大的战略意图，须在城市与乡镇（村）要素间找寻平衡发展的路径，平衡城市功能与社会复杂诉求关系，平衡人与自然环境的关系，平衡建设与保护的关系，我们还需要平衡新旧镇区的分区规划和建设标准的差异，需要平衡城乡公共服务一体化的矛盾，平衡结构性功能布局的时序关系，平衡近期与远期城市建设的合理关系，平衡城市公共服务与生产用地的比例、区位，等等。我们观察到龙港镇发展的每一个阶段都是采取平衡矛盾，协调发展的模式，积极争取及时化解发展中的矛盾。

二、实事求是——面对眼前问题与未来机遇

随着龙港镇的城镇规模不断扩张，加上百姓经济水平和生活需求的提高，人们对于龙港镇的城市空间结构和服务效能提出更高的要求，综合性的城市问题与矛盾日益显现和加剧。随着“强镇扩权”的试点和龙港镇镇域范围扩大等利好因素的出现，越来越将问题引向城市空间结构这个显性的问题上，这既是龙港镇外部环境之力的使然，同时也是龙港镇发展憋屈已久的内压力释放的结果。扩容后的龙港镇城市总体规划面对的不再只是老镇区的空间短缺和各种服务系统完善的问题，而是构建未来龙港镇全新城市空间结构体系问题，以及关联的社会结构和产业经济结构等三方面集合的问题。

（一）空间结构问题是一个内生性问题

回顾30年的龙港镇成长史，就会发现当年选择的城镇结构与快速积聚增长的需求之间出现不相适应的问题，后几版总体规划修编也尝试要解决已经出现的若干城市问题，但是由于镇的事权和空间资源有限等原因，客观地导致无法看高龙港镇未来的发展，无法从空间结构上以更前瞻的布局去疏解城市的各种问题。如果说解决内生性问题是客观的、现实的和迫切的，但来自龙港建成区之外的外源性条件对龙港镇未来的发展产生的影响却是巨大的和关

键的。2011年苍南县政府决定“两港合一”并适时调整扩大龙港镇域范围，这不但从根本上改变了新龙港镇在县域经济和区域竞合格局中的地位，更重要的是使其承载了苍南县城市发展带向东、向海发展的战略，显现出苍南县争取龙港镇在鳌江流域城镇群组合关系中更合适地位的决心，其中表现出的主动性战略思维和用于实施战略的土地空间资源是过去龙港镇发展历史上不曾拥有的。当我们不能左右和等待龙港镇外部条件变化的时候，做好满足县和镇整体发展诉求的空间结构规划工作是最现实的事情，“一屋不扫，何以扫天下”，老话讲：机会总是眷顾有准备的人。调整龙港镇的空间结构是为了迎接机会的来临。

（二）与空间结构伴生的是社会结构的问题

从城镇化的核心概念来看，人口在城市空间范围的集聚仅仅是一个最初的基本现象或指标，即便是由此带来的经济规模总量增长也无法真正地表明这一地区城镇化的真实水平。城镇化的核心意义和价值在于由个体人组成的集体城市文明化程度，也就是人口在文化价值观方面的集体变迁，因此，单纯从经济角度看龙港镇的发展不足以说明其城镇化水平，真正有利的证据是来自龙港镇社会结构的变迁和进化。龙港镇经过长期以快速经济增长为主导目标的发展引导，社会发展阶段逐步从生存型步入发展型，但社会结构变迁始终是一种经济发展的副产品和伴生物，与其经济发展轨迹类似，社会结构与制度的进步完全由自下而上的方式推进，从乡村社会结构逐步向城市社会结构转变，但明显缓慢或滞后于经济结构的演进速度。这一现象也是我国社会主义市场经济制度在建立、尝试与完善过程中的普遍问题。社会建设与民生建设也成为未来一段时间政府应重点关注和投入的领域。

龙港镇快速的城镇化和经济发展过程，使其从本地农村人口和经济要素的积聚很快就发展到对更大范围内的社会经济要素和人群的积聚，量变促质变①，城市规模化效应产生的社会生态复合性诉求，不断挑战龙港镇城市的基础性公共服务、政府事权、城市交通、社会组织等方面的能力，远较当初满足本地积聚的初始需求要复杂得多，我们把这种现象理解为城市化中高级阶段的必须匹配的社会组织和城市服务适应性的问题，这既需要城市经营者和市民观念的转变，更需要提供足够的空间与合理的结构布局来支持提升社会文明和新兴的城市功能建设。

（三）与空间和社会演变特征相生的龙港镇产业经济结构

一直以来龙港镇产业经济的发展和及时的转型升级，都是政府和市场共同的价值取向和共识，随着空间规模尺度的扩大和国家范围的经济转型，城区中的家庭作坊、工业园区（临港工业）和港口和城市日渐繁荣的三次产业相互依存，适时进退升级和转型，龙港正在

---

① 自1983年建镇以来，龙港镇的人口规模从不足2万人，发展到2010年接近40万人（含非户籍外来人口），近30年间人口规模增长20倍，人口非农化比重将近八成；龙港镇人口密度达到2 371人/平方公里，已经超出北京大学周一星教授关于中国城市实体地域的人口密度宜为2 000人/平方公里的研究结论标准，人口都市化集聚的特征十分典型。同时，根据国家城市人口规模的调查分类数据来看，龙港镇也即将到达城区50万人口常驻人口的中小城市的规模。

从工业生产阶段走向生产与消费同步发展的阶段。这个特别的发展阶段催生新的产业功能空间集群，新的产业布局一方面继续提高城市更新完善品质和数量，另一方面也会进一步拉大城市的空间结构。龙港镇在多次产业的空间结构上的重新布局将决定未来相当长时间城市产业发展的合理性。

从苍南县角度规划鳌江流域的城镇群空间结构入手，通过建构相对稳定的全镇域的空间结构来平衡产业和社会发展与空间布局的关系是影响龙港镇城市总体规划最关键的问题之一，因而，我们所关注的这三个相关联的结构问题反映了本次龙港镇城市总体规划面临的战略选择。

（四）须珍惜的龙港镇发展的新机遇期

2011年伴随着临港新城海涂围垦建设的开始和苍南县域新一轮行政区划调整，临港产业新城以及周边芦浦、舥艚、云岩等乡镇并入龙港镇，镇域面积达176平方公里，镇区常住人口接近40万人，接近中等城市规模。我们关注并充分利用“两港合一”[①] 体制改革带来的龙港镇发展的正相关前提条件，由于行政区划的调整，促成了苍南县政府的区域发展战略与苍南沿海地区的土地空间资源相结合，从空间规模上看龙港镇不再是原来的龙港镇。它承载着过去不曾有的苍南县域经济发展的战略意图；不再是那个从无到有，逐步完善功能、自我封闭完型发展的龙港镇了，我们不能再以一个常规镇的发展要求来建构龙港镇未来的发展路径。通过对龙港镇域辖区的可合法开发的土地资源规模和未来的发展趋势研判（图1），我们认为目前是龙港镇拥有难得的内外动力的机遇期，必须积极把握机遇，做好龙港镇成为更大城市的物理空间和心理准备，立足本地社会演变的趋势和特征，实事求是，不依旧习，规划统筹资源，注重形成理性的空间结构，创新规划。

三、趋利避害，寻找稳定的城乡空间结构

自平阳、苍南分县以来，从各地学者到两岸居民，始终在设想一衣带水的千年古镇鳌江和龙港之间的一体化的可能性，以期实现共建鳌江流域中等城市的理想。然而，受限于不同的行政区划，在竞争为题的区域背景下，同时缺乏上位政策的明确支撑，这些设想不仅未获实现，还构成了两岸城镇发展举棋不定的困扰。龙港原有城镇发展格局计划向南拓展结合宜山镇建设新的南部中心，然而在2007年江南海涂围垦工程开始后这一格局开始变得值得商榷，随后行政区划调整、区域重大基础设施布局都进一步表明未来龙港镇向东、向海发展的可能性。而上述的外部与内部因素在2010年前并不可知，也导致历版总体规划生不逢时。

① 龙港镇与临港工业区行政管辖合并，改分治的局面，更有助于形成实施县域社会经济发展战略的合力。

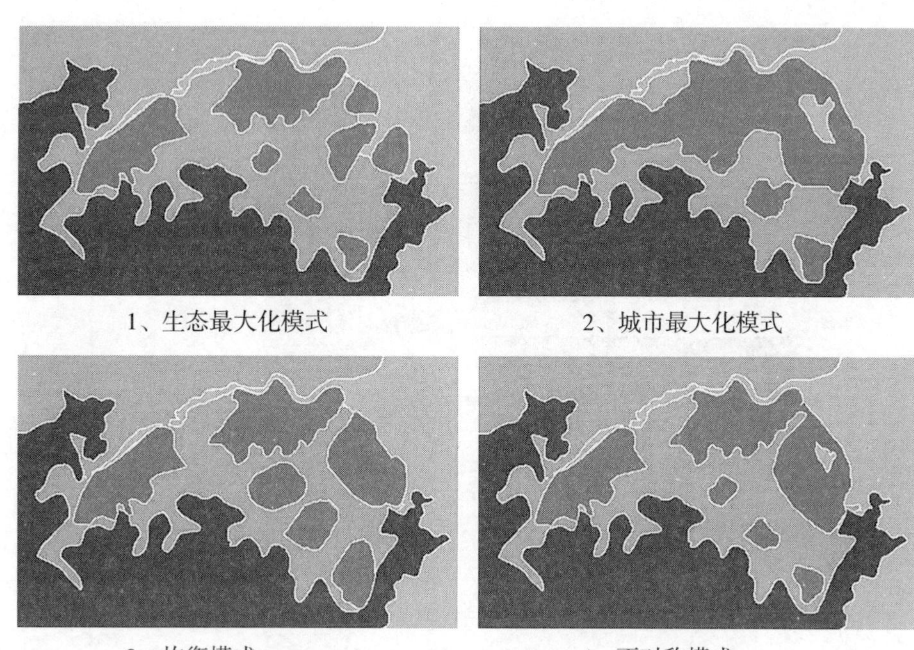

图1 鳌江南岸城镇空间发展趋势演化方案

（一）呼之欲出的全新龙港镇空间结构

2007年10月开工的苍南县江南海涂围垦工程，是温州全市最大最早的在建围垦项目之一①，提供了近30平方公里的土地增量，同时行政区划调整也整合了原舥艚镇的港口资源。由此可见，在温州乃至浙江省境内，龙港镇都占据了发展海洋战略的先机，海涂围垦实现的空间增量不但为整体的城镇空间格局提供了巨大的想象空间，更为内陆城镇化进程中举步维艰的征地工作提供了现实的解决途径。再加之舥艚、芦浦和云岩的加盟，更进一步完善了龙港镇的城市空间资源格局。借此，苍南县龙港镇通过行政区划调整在鳌江流域南侧获得了同一行政边界的扩展，其规模已经远远超出龙港镇现有的老城规模，一系列省市级别的重大基础设施选址也进一步优化了龙港镇的区位战略优势，结构性的空间转变呼之欲出。

苍南县域经济的整体布局战略和空间规模尺度改变了传统的镇总体规划的思路，虽然我们名义上是在做龙港镇的总体规划，事实上是在完型苍南县核心城区的三大功能区（灵溪、龙港和临港）的空间组织关系，重构内陆灵溪、江海龙港和临港地区的空间结构，为构建鳌江流域中心城市积极做好准备。（图2）

在龙港镇的发展历程中，政府曾经因不同时期城市发展的前提条件，就城镇自身的空间结构作出不同的选择和判断。最初龙港镇的发展主要依鳌江沿岸的空间线性快速积聚扩张。在工业化进程中，城镇空间首先开始向西拓展，形成了今日的城西产业城镇景观。随后，由

① 该工程还是《中华人民共和国海域使用法》实施后全省最早经国务院同意批准的围垦项目，也是全省上规模围垦项目中，主体工程建设进度最快的一个工程。

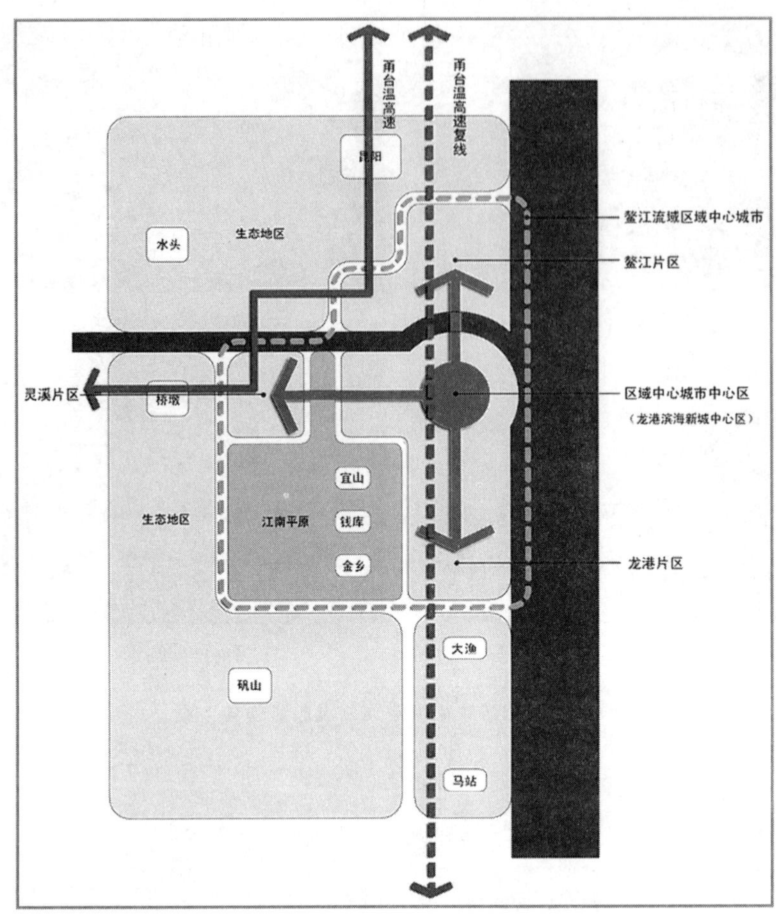

图2　鳌江流域城镇群结构设想示意图

于城镇西部空间资源的耗尽，不得不向东迁移。此外，龙港镇还试图向南侧宜山镇方向延伸。不同于以往试探性的空间尝试，今天我们面对的是一个规模聚变、城市更替、结构系统面临重塑的新龙港镇，发展的条件和需求相比从前尤为清晰强烈。

龙港镇规划面对的是30平方公里海涂围垦如何成为龙港城市的有机组成部分，如何利用突然增大的空间资源重构全新的龙港镇结构体系？如何以新的结构体系适应城市有机生长规避蔓延和离散的问题？我们十分清楚地知道：龙港镇不再是前几版总体规划面对的龙港镇了，从正常的发展趋势看，我们似乎也无法找到短期内人口规模与空间规模之间合理的平衡理由，找寻相对稳定的整体空间结构，倒是一件可以确定的重要事情。

（二）寻找龙港镇相对稳定的空间结构

如果我们基于常规总体规划的工作思路，首先考虑的会是规模问题而非空间结构问题。要么通过人口规模的推演计算出规划期限的城镇用地规模，或者从可利用的土地规模反向推导出人口规模，最终以此来完成总体规划的主体内容。事实上，无论这一规模预测的结果如何精准，土地供给如何有效，都无法弥补城镇在整体结构上的缺陷，将是一个没有整体稳定结构支撑的局部空间生长方案，从而导致总体规划很快迫于新的现实发展需求，不得不再次修编，再次预测……而实际上，这一预测也很难精准，众多城市在总体规划编制限期内突破预测人口规模，并由此导致城市空间结构整体或局部失效。这种并非针对城市“病情”刨根寻底的“治病”，而仅是针对临时“症状”采取的“卖药”式的规划，也使得城镇不断陷于盲目求诊问药的状态中。本包治“百病”的总体规划一时间成为众矢之的。

由此，本次的总体规划希望提供一个新的更加实事求是、切实有效的关于城镇空间规模和结构的解题思路。

首先，我们重新回到自然地理层面的龙港镇。温州市南部属于典型的滨海山地地区，而就在鳌江出海口整个鳌江南岸开阔平坦的冲积扇平原总面积达200余平方公里（图3），是这一地区极为难得的空间资源，县委县政府早已在县域发展规划中提出依托其北侧也就是鳌江南岸平原地带的两大城镇灵溪县城和龙港镇作为县域经济的集聚地和城镇群发展核心的整体构想，因此，龙港未来自身的规模和结构很大程度上取决于自己在这一整体镇群结构中的角色，而寻找这一地区稳定的城乡空间结构，就成了确定龙港镇自身空间结构、发展方向和可能规模的必经之路。

图3　鳌江南岸城镇分布和空间关系示意图

在这一结构中占据主体的是自然环境本底，除了灵溪、龙港两镇和建设中的临港产业新城外，也包括历史悠久的宜山、金乡、钱库三镇，此外，还有分布在河网田间的数百个村落。而稳定的城乡空间结构正是建立在这样一个相对稳定的自然地理结构基础上，建立在这一范围内人与自然、发展与保护、城镇与农田、城镇与乡村、镇群之间、镇区内部在空间上的分布状态和相互关系。并且是一种长效的平衡关系，一方面为结构中的每一个个体制定清晰的自我发展边界和路径，另一方面也为结构自身维持平衡、有效的终极规模作出整体约束。

其次，龙港镇未来的城镇人口规模预测更重视源自城市土地空间资源终极理想规模的反推，即以建立江南平原整体城镇乡村与自然要素共同形成的滨江滨海山水田园格局为目标，确定理想的龙港城镇发展边界和规模，再根据城镇空间模式确定人口密度，推导人口规模。因此，这是一个超越规划期限的理想城镇规模，也是对于龙港镇未来发展的跨越时间和行政界限的基本共识。

在从地理空间资源角度整体审视的同时，加上苍南县向海发展战略思路的支持，就使得龙港镇总体规划在“两港合一”和“行政扩容”的基础上，必须更进一步主动思考统筹空间资源，处理新老镇区整体布局关系，进行更大范围结构性和系统性的空间布局安排，为在远期建设鳌江滨海城市的目标进行战略结构性的空间准备。

而这一城乡稳定的空间结构是通过政府、社会、专家之间的讨论达成的，是一种社会共识，是将资源、社会、空间为主的相关地区视为一个发展的整体单元，基于整体表现最佳做出的统筹考虑，克服了区域不同行政主体的盲视现象，最大限度的优化区域资源，促进城乡资源要素一体化，同时不受时间要素限制。在指定龙港镇乃至更大区域形成稳定空间结构的过程中，自然要素、社会要素、文化要素、现实要素得到突出的优先重视，以弥补和修正以往快速城镇化进程中的缺失和不均衡状态。

现实是实现美好理想蓝图的必经之路，龙港城镇发展的理想空间格局不可回避本土的现实问题，更是规划实践的关键考虑因素。无论是自身的征地拆迁问题，还是区域合作的现实难度，都是影响理想格局实现的直接因素和隐性成本。在现实中规划权衡解决例如发展权利与机会、社会公平与差异等最为集中的社会矛盾问题时，立足于对现实问题的认识和理解，提出的解决方案往往比规划的理论隔空论道更具实效性。而往往地方政府作为规划的直接实践家，对于现实问题有着更加深刻和全面的了解，对解决问题的方式方法都有着独到的见解，这次龙港镇城市总体规划选择从大的空间结构入手，而不是惯常的规划手法与县镇两级政府达成共识，控制土地资源开发建设过程的理性布局和应对市场变化的时序，以有效的结构控制和引导效应为总体规划大形制控的策略，在此基础上分时分区应对老镇区更新、新中心预控和新产业集聚等不同的发展问题。

如果说苍南灵溪向东，龙港镇向外扩展，是城市整体向东、向南发展的推力，那么，从常识来看龙港老镇区南部（与宜山镇接壤）地区是城市向南发展最适宜地区，但是当涉及征用基本农田和村舍拆迁等制约门槛时，城市向南发展受阻，人们宁愿向东选择工业区更新或海涂围垦等相对容易建设地区，更符合客观的综合性价比，于是就近向南成为城市发展的特殊阻力。城市向东、向海发展是伴随着产业升级的新区建设和城东工业区更新，没有大规模的村庄拆迁、没有基本农田，有分期实施的规模化的海涂围垦造地计划，对于龙港城市空间延展生长而言就是拉力，拉动城市向东发展。一阻一拉使得龙港镇城市最容易选择沿江向东发展，形成沿江向海的整体的带型空间发展趋势。

最后，在平衡了城乡关系、龙港与临港共同发展、生态与人文、近期与远期发展的需求

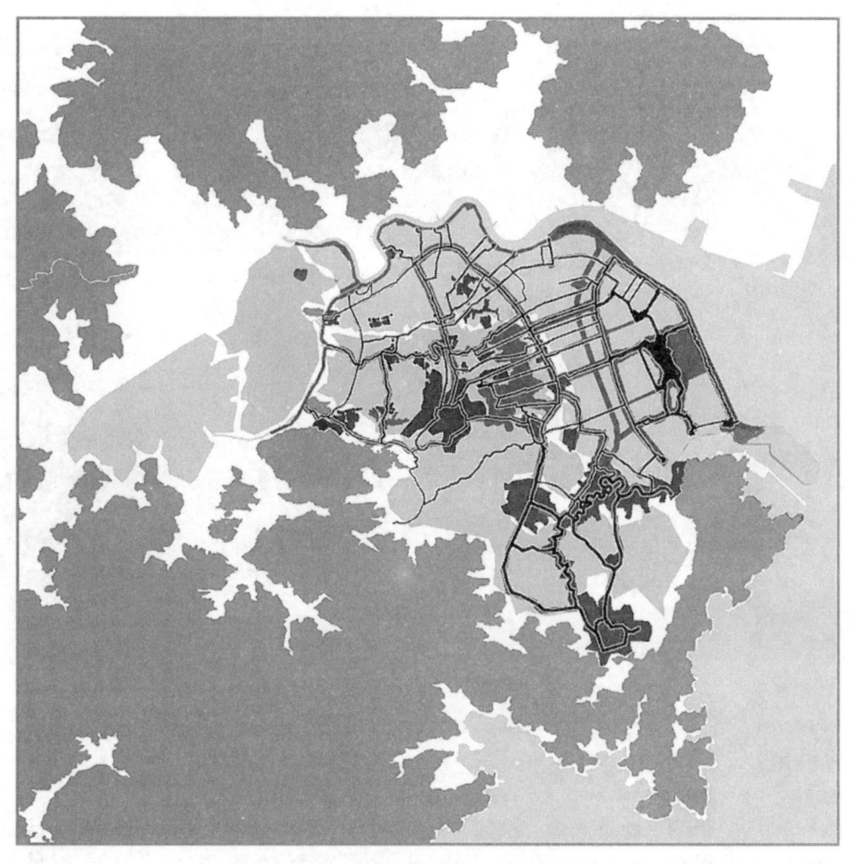

图4　鳌江出海口山水田园城镇群

后，我们构成了基于理想的、相对稳定的龙港城市与江南片区的空间结构规划，最终我们对于鳌江南侧平原地区稳定的城乡空间结构的描述是这样：一个拥有大片农田、湿地、水网密布、乡村镶嵌其中的滨江滨海城镇综合体——鳌江出海口山水田园城镇群（图4）。从全域龙港的视角，抓住城市与乡镇的组合空间结构特色，实现城市整体由滨江向滨海，由西向东的推移进程，同时收缩控制南部和西部边界，形成田园＋城市分治的空间格局，城乡边界交融有机清晰，防止城镇规模的无限度蔓延和扩展，并与周边宜山、钱库和金厢三镇保持相对的空间间隔。（图5）

实施有品质的苍南城市向东发展的战略，就不能只是局限在城市建设地区，必须包含与城市特色相关联的外围乡村地区，疏密有致不只是在城市建设区，在构成整体城乡空间结构的尺度上，我们选择构建一个集约建设的龙港镇，与江南片水乡宜山镇、钱库镇、金厢镇组合的相对稳定的建设与保护的整体格局，平衡城市与乡村，人与自然的谐调的空间关系，乡镇地区不只是大尺度湿地、蔓延的田园生态景观地区，重要的是那里还是保证城市安全的防洪滞洪功能区、城市生态环境品质的涵养区。龙港镇的城市地区不是孤立存在的，它与宜山、钱库和金厢镇有机共存，我们冀望城乡有界，城市集约与乡村舒坦的差异化空间共存。

我们将人口规模作为一个动态的与产业兴衰同步的、被城市空间所包容和服务的指标，而不是决定城市空间大结构的前提条件。龙港镇未来发展可以保持在空间结构不变的情况下，土地资源可以根据市场需求适时配给，人口规模随着城市产业和社会进步同步增加，规

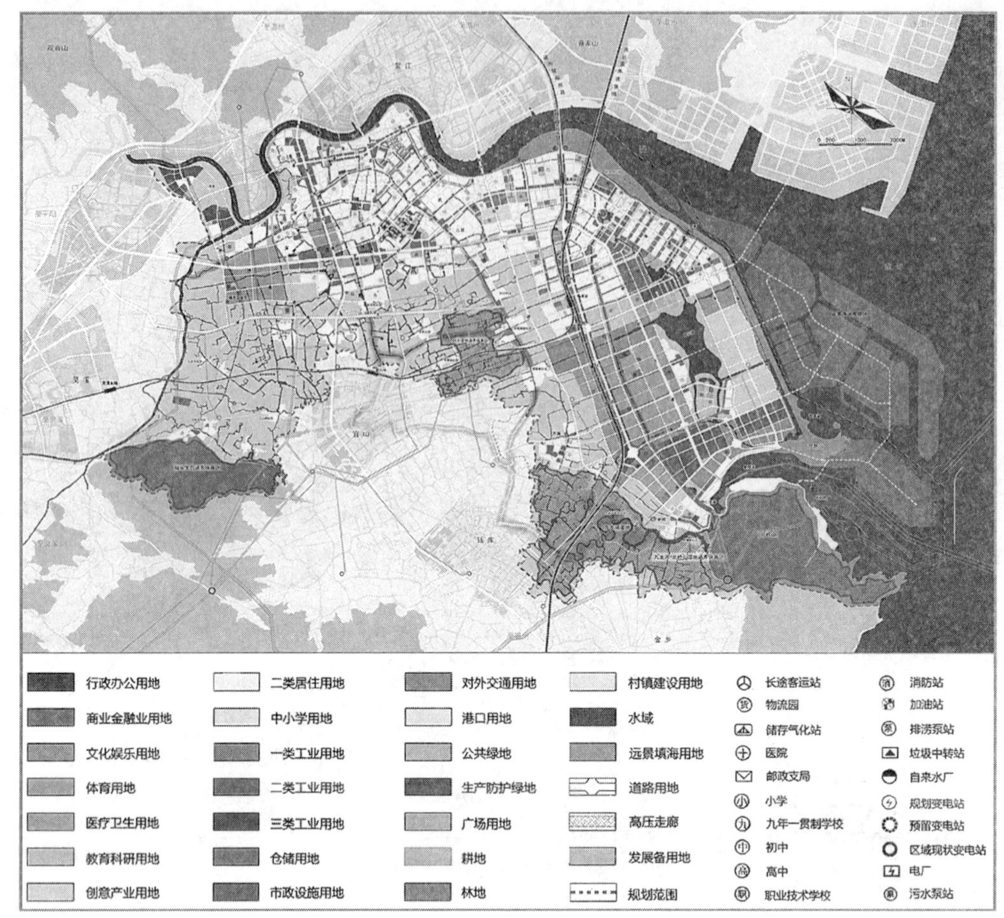

图5　龙港镇城市总体规划（2011—2030）土地利用规划图

划预设的城市公共服务设施布局体系和城乡共建生态体系将保证城市现代文明的需求。

四、几点思考

（一）实事求是，维系规划科学性的核心价值

主观规划与客观规划，如同规划的想象力与生命力，对一个平衡规划而言缺一不可。

主观性是规划的重要内容，但是如果没有切合实际的客观性，那么这样的规划要么是流于八股文章，要么易显短视。

客观性是规划的基础。当年龙港镇成功诞生的根由也是因为县镇领导正视客观的勇气和适时恰当的空间规划。龙港历史经验告诉我们，对城市未来空间结构性的预测是一项非常重要的工作，这种对于未来空间的结构性预测并不常有。随着城市发展阶段的日趋成熟，这种系统全面的空间结构预测只会越来越少，龙港镇给予我们一次难得的脚踏实地，穿越云端的展望未来理想形态和结构预体验，跨越时间探究几十年甚至百年后龙港平衡多要素发展的城乡空间结构，再回到现实，有目标、循逻辑地做今天该做的事。变的是有形的空间和需求，

但不变的是实事求是的龙港精神，今天的抉择皆由龙港的理想发展和现实境遇而生，反映了地方政府、人民群众对于发展的真实需求和共识。

龙港镇总体规划的目的，既要通过规划找到龙港镇建构理想空间结构的路径，也要有效地解决现实城镇发展过程中遇到的问题，这一现实性也是检验规划自身价值的标准。我们去除心理羁绊——没有在龙港是镇或不是镇的问题上纠结，而是直接面对空间和未来采取的控制引导措施，与县镇两级政府达成共识，重构苍南县域社会经济的空间关系，为长远的发展奠定结构性的空间基础，这是跳出镇的规划桎梏，改变习惯，感悟更真实的县域发展的诉求，施行有效的规划理念，让我们更加体会到“习惯是机会的分水岭”这句话的含义了。

（二）因地制宜，探索本土发展模式

在本次龙港镇总体规划的编制进程中，正好经历了温州市域市县行政区划调整，项目组参与了县政府以整合优化，改善城乡关系为目标的调整决策过程，不但实现了将原本独立并置的江南海涂片区纳入了龙港镇整体空间发展计划的愿望，同时也确立了县政府关于灵溪、龙港联手作为鳌江流域中心城市核心区的共识，使得总体规划工作从最初的镇政府单方委托，进一步上升为行政区划调整后的县政府联合委托，实现了对于县镇所属行政资源的主动组合。直接突破了原有鳌江南岸城镇、乡村之间的行政经济区划束缚，极大地推进了区域城镇格局的重新判定。县委县政府在处理县城灵溪与经济中心镇龙港之间关系上的空前开放和明朗态度，促使苍南县县域经济和城镇结构日趋稳定成熟，为龙港镇转变空间格局和重塑区域角色提供了绝佳的机遇。适时进行的苍南县域统筹城镇行政资源（龙港和临港合一），可以解释为本土发展模式最重要的决策，与当年陈定模书记的激情和负责任的创新营城的胆识异曲同工。本土模式有其属地化的特殊性，并不是放之四海而皆准的通则。也许今天的龙港镇如同30年前龙港镇一样注定要书写一出非常动人的故事，一定要承受一种因惯性思维围观而生的争议。

（三）时代责任，体现规划价值

总体规划作为政府落实发展意图、服务经济发展，改善民生，配置各项资源的重要公共政策，随着国家发展阶段和时代背景的变迁，总体规划从单纯政府宏观调控、管理城市土地资源的手段出发，应更多关注与长远合理的空间结构密切相关，因果互动的自然环境、城乡关系、社会结构、经济模式等领域，重视城市资源、城市个性与城市竞争力之间的关联度，关注中小城镇发展模式与社会演进过程的优化对有效改善民生和国家社会进步的影响作用。

每一次城市规划将长久、深刻和直接地影响一个城镇发展、人民幸福，这就要求规划师的服务不应该只“卖药”，更重要的是要“行医”，通过对于城镇现状的望、闻、问、切，准确地预测和发现城镇显示和未来发展中潜在的问题及其成因所在，借以规划施以疗医和补救措施。“行医”相比“卖药”，其过程固然漫长、坎坷，但也一定是充实和满足的。在这一过程中，与我们并肩给予我们信息、支持，并能产生共鸣，达成共识的是地方政府，在工作中我们感受到的是苍南县和龙港镇领导的责任和勇气，他们有整合资源的敏感性和及时

性，也有作为基层实践家的丰富经验和毅然果断。我们相信，延续实事求是、集体共识的龙港精神，促进规划从构想走向现实，推动规划从图纸成为实践，是包括规划师在内的当代人的时代责任和梦想。

（作者：朱荣远，中国城市规划设计研究院副总规划师，教授级城市规划师；梁浩，中国城市规划设计研究院深圳分院三所所长，高级规划师；王瑛，中国城市规划设计研究院深圳分院，教授级城市规划师）

参考文献

［1］迟福林．第二次转型：处在十字路口的发展方式转变［R］．北京：中国经济出版社，2010：33，54，129，210.

［2］费孝通．乡土中国［M］．上海：上海世纪出版集团，2005.

［3］李京生，马鹏．城市规划中的社会课题［J］．城市规划学刊，2006（2）：49－52.

［4］杨保军，陈鹏．制度情境下的总体规划演变［J］．城市规划学刊，2012（1）：54－62.

［5］张春霞．机会只给有准备的人［M］．北京：北京理工大学出版社，2009.

［6］朱康对．来自底层的变革：龙港城市化个案研究［M］．杭州：浙江人民出版社，2003.

附录篇

附录1　国家“十二五”规划纲要摘录

一、主要目标

按照与应对国际金融危机冲击重大部署紧密衔接、与到2020年实现全面建设小康社会奋斗目标紧密衔接的要求，综合考虑未来发展趋势和条件，今后五年经济社会发展的主要目标是：

（1）经济平稳较快发展。国内生产总值年均增长7%，城镇新增就业4 500万人，城镇登记失业率控制在5%以内，价格总水平基本稳定，国际收支趋向基本平衡，经济增长质量和效益明显提高。

（2）结构调整取得重大进展。居民消费率上升。农业基础进一步巩固，工业结构继续优化，战略性新兴产业发展取得突破，服务业增加值占国内生产总值比重提高4个百分点。城镇化率提高4个百分点，城乡区域发展的协调性进一步增强。

（3）科技教育水平明显提升。九年义务教育质量显著提高，九年义务教育巩固率达到93%，高中阶段教育毛入学率提高到87%。研究与试验发展经费支出占国内生产总值比重达到2.2%，每万人口发明专利拥有量提高到3.3件。

（4）资源节约环境保护成效显著。耕地保有量保持在18.18亿亩。单位工业增加值用水量降低30%，农业灌溉用水有效利用系数提高到0.53。非化石能源占一次能源消费比重达到11.4%。单位国内生产总值能源消耗降低16%，单位国内生产总值二氧化碳排放降低17%。主要污染物排放总量显著减少，化学需氧量、二氧化硫排放分别减少8%，氨氮、氮氧化物排放分别减少10%。森林覆盖率提高到21.66%，森林蓄积量增加6亿立方米。

（5）人民生活持续改善。全国总人口控制在13.9亿人以内。人均预期寿命提高1岁，达到74.5岁。城镇居民人均可支配收入和农村居民人均纯收入分别年均增长7%以上。新型农村社会养老保险实现制度全覆盖，城镇参加基本养老保险人数达到3.57亿人，城乡三项基本医疗保险参保率提高3个百分点。城镇保障性安居工程建设3 600万套。贫困人口显著减少。

（6）社会建设明显加强。覆盖城乡居民的基本公共服务体系逐步完善。全民族思想道德素质、科学文化素质和健康素质不断提高。社会主义民主法制更加健全，人民权益得到切实保障。文化事业加快发展，文化产业占国民经济比重明显提高。社会管理制度趋于完善，社会更加和谐稳定。

（7）改革开放不断深化。财税金融、要素价格、垄断行业等重要领域和关键环节改革取得明显进展，政府职能加快转变，政府公信力和行政效率进一步提高。对外开放广度和深度不断拓展，互利共赢开放格局进一步形成。

二、转变方式，国内生产总值年均增长7%

实现经济社会发展目标，必须紧紧围绕推动科学发展、加快转变经济发展方式，统筹兼顾，改革创新，着力解决经济社会发展中不平衡、不协调、不可持续的问题，明确重大政策导向：

加强和改善宏观调控。巩固和扩大应对国际金融危机冲击成果，把短期调控政策和长期发展政策有机结合起来，加强财政、货币、投资、产业、土地等各项政策协调配合，提高宏观调控的科学性和预见性，增强针对性和灵活性，合理调控经济增长速度，更加积极稳妥地处理好保持经济平稳较快发展、调整经济结构、管理通胀预期的关系，实现经济增长速度和结构质量效益相统一。

建立扩大消费需求的长效机制。把扩大消费需求作为扩大内需的战略重点，通过积极稳妥推进城镇化、实施就业优先战略、深化收入分配制度改革、健全社会保障体系和营造良好的消费环境，增强居民消费能力，改善居民消费预期，促进消费结构升级，进一步释放城乡居民消费潜力，逐步使我国国内市场总体规模位居世界前列。

调整优化投资结构。发挥投资对扩大内需的重要作用，保持投资合理增长，完善投资体制机制，明确界定政府投资范围，规范国有企业投资行为，鼓励扩大民间投资，有效遏制盲目扩张和重复建设，促进投资消费良性互动，把扩大投资和增加就业、改善民生有机结合起来，创造最终需求。

同步推进工业化、城镇化和农业现代化。坚持工业反哺农业、城市支持农村和多予少取放活方针，充分发挥工业化、城镇化对发展现代农业、促进农民增收、加强农村基础设施和公共服务的辐射带动作用，夯实农业农村发展基础，加快现代农业发展步伐。

依靠科技创新推动产业升级。面向国内国际两个市场，发挥科技创新对产业结构优化升级的驱动作用，加快国家创新体系建设，强化企业在技术创新中的主体地位，引导资金、人才、技术等创新资源向企业聚集，推进产学研战略联盟，提升产业核心竞争力，推动三次产业在更高水平上协同发展。

促进区域协调互动发展。实施区域发展总体战略和主体功能区战略，把实施西部大开发战略放在区域发展总体战略优先位置，充分发挥各地区比较优势，促进区域间生产要素合理流动和产业有序转移，在中西部地区培育新的区域经济增长极，增强区域发展的协调性。

健全节能减排激励约束机制。优化能源结构，合理控制能源消费总量，完善资源性产品价格形成机制和资源环境税费制度，健全节能减排法律法规和标准，强化节能减排目标责任考核，把资源节约和环境保护贯穿于生产、流通、消费、建设各领域各环节，提升可持续发展能力。

推进基本公共服务均等化。把基本公共服务制度作为公共产品向全民提供，完善公共财政制度，提高政府保障能力，建立健全符合国情、比较完整、覆盖城乡、可持续的基本公共服务体系，逐步缩小城乡区域间人民生活水平和公共服务差距。

加快城乡居民收入增长。健全初次分配和再分配调节体系，合理调整国家、企业、个人分配关系，努力实现居民收入增长和经济发展同步、劳动报酬增长和劳动生产率提高同步，明显增加低收入者收入，持续扩大中等收入群体，努力扭转城乡、区域、行业和社会成员之间收入差距扩大趋势。

加强和创新社会管理。提高社会管理能力，创新社会管理体制机制，加快服务型政府建设，在服务中实施管理，在管理中体现服务，着力解决影响社会和谐稳定的源头性、基础性、根本性问题，保持社会安定有序和充满活力。

三、强农惠农，粮食综合生产能力达到5.4亿吨以上

在工业化、城镇化深入发展中同步推进农业现代化，完善以工促农、以城带乡长效机制，加大强农惠农力度，提高农业现代化水平和农民生活水平，建设农民幸福生活的美好家园。

加快发展现代农业。坚持走中国特色农业现代化道路，把保障国家粮食安全作为首要目标，加快转变农业发展方式，提高农业综合生产能力、抗风险能力和市场竞争能力。

拓宽农民增收渠道。加大引导和扶持力度，提高农民职业技能和创收能力，千方百计拓宽农民增收渠道，促进农民收入持续较快增长。巩固提高家庭经营收入，努力增加工资性收入，大力增加转移性收入。

改善农村生产生活条件。按照推进城乡经济社会发展一体化的要求，搞好社会主义新农村建设规划，加强农村基础设施建设和公共服务，推进农村环境综合整治。

完善农村发展体制机制。按照统筹城乡发展要求，加快推进农村发展体制机制改革，增强农业农村发展活力。

四、区域协调发展，城镇化率提高4个百分点

实施区域发展总体战略和主体功能区战略，构筑区域经济优势互补、主体功能定位清晰、国土空间高效利用、人与自然和谐相处的区域发展格局，逐步实现不同区域基本公共服务均等化。坚持走中国特色城镇化道路，科学制定城镇化发展规划，促进城镇化健康发展。

实施区域发展总体战略。推进新一轮西部大开发，全面振兴东北地区等老工业基地，大力促进中部地区崛起，积极支持东部地区率先发展，加大对革命老区、民族地区、边疆地区和贫困地区扶持力度。

实施主体功能区战略。优化国土空间开发格局，实施分类管理的区域政策，实行各有侧重的绩效评价，建立健全衔接协调机制。

积极稳妥推进城镇化。构建城市化战略格局，稳步推进农业转移人口转为城镇居民，增强城镇综合承载能力。

五、转型升级，战略性新兴产业增加值占GDP比重达到8%左右

坚持走中国特色新型工业化道路，适应市场需求变化，根据科技进步新趋势，发挥我国产业在全球经济中的比较优势，发展结构优化、技术先进、清洁安全、附加值高、吸纳就业能力强的现代产业体系。

改造提升制造业。优化结构、改善品种质量、增强产业配套能力、淘汰落后产能，发展先进装备制造业，调整优化原材料工业，改造提升消费品工业，促进制造业由大变强。

培育发展战略性新兴产业。以重大技术突破和重大发展需求为基础，促进新兴科技与新兴产业深度融合，在继续做强做大高技术产业基础上，把战略性新兴产业培育发展成为先导性、支柱性产业。战略性新兴产业增加值占国内生产总值比重达到8%左右。

推动能源生产和利用方式变革。坚持节约优先、立足国内、多元发展、保护环境，加强国际互利合作，调整优化能源结构，构建安全、稳定、经济、清洁的现代能源产业体系。

构建综合交通运输体系。按照适度超前原则，统筹各种运输方式发展，基本建成国家快速铁路网和高速公路网，初步形成网络设施配套衔接、技术装备先进适用、运输服务安全高效的综合交通运输体系。

全面提高信息化水平。加快建设宽带、融合、安全、泛在的下一代国家信息基础设施，推动信息化和工业化深度融合，推进经济社会各领域信息化。

推进海洋经济发展。坚持陆海统筹，制定和实施海洋发展战略，提高海洋开发、控制、综合管理能力。

六、推动服务业大发展，服务业增加值占GDP比重提高4个百分点

把推动服务业大发展作为产业结构优化升级的战略重点，营造有利于服务业发展的政策和体制环境，拓展新领域，发展新业态，培育新热点，推进服务业规模化、品牌化、网络化经营，不断提高服务业比重和水平。

加快发展生产性服务业。深化专业化分工，加快服务产品和服务模式创新，促进生产性服务业与先进制造业融合，推动生产性服务业加速发展。包括有序拓展金融服务业，大力发展现代物流业，培育壮大高技术服务业，规范提升包括会计、审计、税务、信用评估等商务服务业。

大力发展生活性服务业。面向城乡居民生活，丰富服务产品类型，扩大服务供给，提高服务质量，满足多样化需求。包括优化发展商贸服务业，积极发展旅游业，鼓励发展家庭服

务业，全面发展体育事业和体育产业。

营造有利于服务业发展的环境。以开放促改革，以竞争促发展，推动服务业制度创新，完善服务业政策体系，优化服务业发展环境。

七、创新驱动，2012年财政性教育经费支出占GDP比例达到4%

坚持自主创新、重点跨越、支撑发展、引领未来的方针，加快建设国家创新体系，着力提高企业创新能力，促进科技成果向现实生产力转化，推动经济发展更多依靠科技创新驱动。

保障公民依法享有受教育的权利，统筹发展各级各类教育，积极发展学前教育，学前一年毛入园率提高到85%。大力促进教育公平，健全以政府投入为主、多渠道筹集教育经费的体制，2012年财政性教育经费支出占国内生产总值比例达到4%，提高教育现代化水平。

大力实施人才强国战略，坚持服务发展、人才优先、以用为本、创新机制、高端引领、整体开发的指导方针，加强现代化建设需要的各类人才队伍建设，为加快转变经济发展方式、实现科学发展提供人才保证。

八、改善民生，城镇居民人均可支配收入和农村居民人均纯收入分别年均增长7%以上

坚持以人为本、服务为先，履行政府公共服务职责，提高政府保障能力，逐步缩小城乡区域间基本公共服务差距。

坚持把促进就业放在经济社会发展的优先位置，健全劳动者自主择业、市场调节就业、政府促进就业相结合的机制，创造平等就业机会，提高就业质量，努力实现充分就业。

坚持和完善按劳分配为主体、多种分配方式并存的分配制度，初次分配和再分配都要处理好效率和公平的关系，再分配更加注重公平，加快形成合理有序的收入分配格局，努力提高居民收入在国民收入分配中的比重，提高劳动报酬在初次分配中的比重，尽快扭转收入差距扩大趋势。

坚持广覆盖、保基本、多层次、可持续方针，加快推进覆盖城乡居民的社会保障体系建设，稳步提高保障水平。

按照保基本、强基层、建机制的要求，增加财政投入，深化医药卫生体制改革，建立健全基本医疗卫生制度，加快医疗卫生事业发展，优先满足群众基本医疗卫生需求。

坚持政府调控和市场调节相结合，加快完善符合国情的住房体制机制和政策体系，逐步形成总量基本平衡、结构基本合理、房价与消费能力基本适应的住房供需格局，实现广大群众住有所居。

控制人口总量，提高人口素质，优化人口结构，促进人口长期均衡发展。

九、绿色发展，资源产出率提高15%

积极应对全球气候变化。坚持减缓和适应气候变化并重，充分发挥技术进步的作用，完善体制机制和政策体系，提高应对气候变化能力。

加强资源节约和管理。大力推进节能降耗；加强水资源节约；节约集约利用土地，单位国内生产总值建设用地下降30%；加强矿产资源勘查、保护和合理开发。

大力发展循环经济。按照减量化、再利用、资源化的原则，推行循环型生产方式，工业固体废物综合利用率达到72%，资源产出率提高15%。健全资源循环利用回收体系，推广绿色消费模式。

加大环境保护力度。以解决饮用水不安全和空气、土壤污染等损害群众健康的突出环境问题为重点，加强综合治理，明显改善环境质量。

促进生态保护和修复。构建生态安全屏障；强化生态保护与治理；建立生态补偿机制，研究设立国家生态补偿专项资金，推行资源型企业可持续发展准备金制度，积极探索市场化生态补偿机制，加快制定实施生态补偿条例。

加强水利基础设施建设，在继续推进大江大河治理基础上，积极开展重要支流、湖泊和中小河流治理，增强城乡供水和防洪能力。健全防灾减灾体系，增强抵御自然灾害能力。

关键词：改革攻坚，更加重视改革顶层设计和总体规划，明确改革优先顺序和重点任务，在重要领域和关键环节取得突破性进展。

坚持和完善基本经济制度。坚持公有制为主体、多种所有制经济共同发展的基本经济制度，营造各种所有制经济依法平等使用生产要素、公平参与市场竞争、同等受到法律保护的体制环境。

推进行政体制改革。按照转变职能、理顺关系、优化结构、提高效能的要求，加快建立法治政府和服务型政府。

加快财税体制改革。理顺各级政府间财政分配关系，健全公共财政体系，完善预算制度和税收制度，积极构建有利于转变经济发展方式的财税体制。按照财力与事权相匹配的要求，在合理界定事权基础上，进一步理顺各级政府间财政分配关系，完善分税制。围绕推进基本公共服务均等化和主体功能区建设，完善转移支付制度，增加一般性特别是均衡性转移支付规模和比例，调减和规范专项转移支付。推进省以下财政体制改革，稳步推进省直管县财政管理制度改革，加强县级政府提供基本公共服务的财力保障。建立健全地方政府债务管理体系，探索建立地方政府发行债券制度。

深化金融体制改革。全面推动金融改革、开放和发展，构建组织多元、服务高效、监管审慎、风险可控的金融体系，不断增强金融市场功能，更好地为加快转变经济发展方式服务。

深化资源性产品价格和环保收费改革。建立健全能够灵活反映市场供求关系、资源稀缺程度和环境损害成本的资源性产品价格形成机制，促进结构调整、资源节约和环境保护。

十、对外开放，实行更加积极主动的开放战略，不断拓展新的开放领域和空间，扩大和深化同各方利益的汇合点

完善区域开放格局。坚持扩大开放与区域协调发展相结合，协同推动沿海、内陆、沿边开放，形成优势互补、分工协作、均衡协调的区域开放格局。

优化对外贸易结构。继续稳定和拓展外需，加快转变外贸发展方式，推动外贸发展从规模扩张向质量效益提高转变、从成本优势向综合竞争优势转变。

统筹“引进来”与“走出去”。坚持“引进来”和“走出去”相结合，利用外资和对外投资并重，提高安全高效地利用两个市场、两种资源的能力。

积极参与全球经济治理和区域合作。扩大同发达国家的交流合作，增进相互信任，提高合作水平。深化同周边国家的睦邻友好和务实合作，维护地区和平稳定，促进共同发展繁荣。加强同发展中国家的团结合作，深化传统友谊，维护共同利益。积极开展多边合作。

（资料整理：廖远涛，陶琳，广州市城市规划勘测设计研究院）

附录 2　2011 年度中国城市规划大事记

2011 年 1 月 4 日　国务院批复《山东半岛蓝色经济区发展规划》（以下简称《规划》），这是"十二五"开局之年第一个获批的国家发展战略，也是我国第一个以海洋经济为主题的区域发展战略。《规划》的批复实施，是我国区域发展从陆域经济延伸到海洋经济、积极推进陆海统筹的重大战略举措，标志着全国海洋经济发展试点工作进入实施阶段，也标志着山东半岛蓝色经济区建设正式上升为国家战略，成为国家海洋发展战略和区域协调发展战略的重要组成部分。

2011 年 1 月 12 日　世界银行发布《2011 年全球经济展望》。报告中指出，世界经济在 2010 年增长 3.9%，发展中国家贡献了全球经济增长的近一半。预计 2011 年全球经济增速将放缓。世行警告，由于受到全球性的物价高涨影响，一些地区的经济有可能退回到 2008 年的水平。

2011 年 1 月 16 日　财政部、文化部下发了《关于推进全国美术馆、公共图书馆、文化馆（站）免费开放工作的意见》，要求各级财政建立免费开放经费保障机制，确保美术馆、公共图书馆，以及文化馆（站）免费开放工作的推进。

2011 年 1 月 17 日　住房和城乡建设部宣布，2011 年我国将开建保障性住房 1000 万套，相比 2010 年的 580 万套增长 70%，面积大体相当于 2010 年全年商品房的供应量，创历年之最。

2011 年 1 月 18 日　《成渝城镇群协调发展规划》（以下简称《规划》）由住房和城乡建设部、重庆市政府、四川省政府共同编制完成并联合印发实施。专家指出，《规划》对优化国家城镇化空间格局具有重要意义。

2011 年 1 月 19 日　国务院总理温家宝主持召开国务院常务会议，审议并原则通过《国有土地上房屋征收与补偿条例（草案）》。

2011 年 1 月 20 日　北京市编制的首个《低碳城市发展纲要》（以下简称《纲要》）正式完成。《纲要》提出从个人到家庭、从社区到整个城市的低碳生产消费模式，按照《纲要》要求，长辛店将建设北京首个低碳社区示范项目，通州正在建立低碳指标体系，延庆正在研究低碳新城规划。"十二五"期间，北京市将启动低碳城市发展策略。

2011 年 1 月 26 日　国务院总理温家宝主持召开国务院常务会议，研究部署进一步做好房地产市场调控工作。八项措施调控房地产市场。

2011 年 1 月 26 日　国务院下发房地产调控的“新国八条”政策，其中明确提出地方政府制定房地产价格控制的指标，并于一季度向社会公布；同时还提出，对于未能达标的城市，要求地方政府向国务院汇报，如果未能落实调控政策以及未完成保障性住房任务，主要行政领导将被约谈及至问责。在如此高考核、高压之下，地方政府调控楼市的行政色彩将越发浓厚。

2011 年 1 月 26 日　河南省发展和改革委员会召开新闻通气会宣布“中原经济区”被正式纳入《全国主体功能区规划》，上升到国家战略层面。《全国主体功能区规划》明确提出，中原经济区作为国家层面重点开发区域，位于中国“两横三纵”城市化战略格局中陆桥通道横轴和京哈京广通道纵轴的交汇处，包括河南省以郑州为中心的中原城市群部分地区。该区域的功能定位是：全国重要的高新技术产业、先进制造业和现代服务业基地，能源原材料基地，综合交通枢纽和物流中心，区域性的科技创新中心，中部地区人口和经济密集区，支撑全国经济又好又快发展的新的经济增长板块。

2011 年 2 月 16 日　国土资源部副部长贠小苏在增减挂钩试点和农村土地整治清查工作动员会上说，为了贯彻落实《国务院关于严格规范城乡建设用地增减挂钩试点切实做好农村土地整治工作的通知》，认真抓好城乡建设用地增减挂钩试点和农村土地整治清理和检查工作，国土资源部会同中央农村工作领导小组办公室、发改委、财政部、环境保护部、农业部、住房和城乡建设部、国务院研究室等单位和部门研究制定了《城乡建设用地增减挂钩试点和农村土地整治清理检查工作方案》已经国务院批准，城乡建设用地增减挂钩试点和农村土地整治清理检查工作正式启动。

2011 年 2 月 18 日　《文化软实力蓝皮书：中国文化软实力研究报告（2010）》在京发布。蓝皮书认为，改革开放 30 多年来，中国的硬实力发展很快，但文化软实力与硬实力相比，两者之间的落差还比较大。从国际对比来看，中国文化产业在国内生产总值中所占的比例，大大低于西方发达国家已经达到的 10% 以上的水平。蓝皮书分析认为，中国文化软实力建设出现的种种问题，是由于文化体制、国民素质等深层次原因造成的，这些原因是中国文化软实力发展的瓶颈。中国在与世界文化强国竞争的过程中，既缺乏代表性的世界级文化产业集团，又缺乏以高新技术为基础的文化产业整体性结构竞争力。

2011 年 2 月 21 日　《经济学家》信息社一年一度的世界最宜居城市报告出炉，加拿大西海岸城市温哥华，以综合得分 98 分的成绩名列第一。这已经是温哥华连续第五年蝉联榜首，中国香港此次位居第 31 位，北京名列第 72 位。《经济学家》信息社从稳定性、医疗体系、文化、环境、教育以及基础设施等 30 个方面，对全球 140 座城市进行综合评分。

2011 年 2 月 28 日　国家统计局发布 2010 年国民经济和社会发展统计公报。公报显示，2010 年我国国内生产总值达到 397 983 亿元，比上年增长 10.3%。国家统计局副局长谢鸿光在评读文章中指出，“根据日本政府公布的 2010 年年度国内生产总值数据，我国已经超过日本成为世界第二大经济体。”

2011 年 2 月 28 日　文化部命名第三批国家级文化产业示范园区和首批国家级文化产业试验园区授牌仪式在京举行。此前文化部先后命名了 2 批共 4 家国家级文化产业示范园区和

4批共204家国家文化产业示范基地，催生出一批有较强实力、竞争力、影响力和自主创新能力的大型文化企业和企业集团，培育扶持、发展壮大了一批产业集聚效应明显和特色鲜明的文化产业园区，充分发挥了集聚效应和孵化功能。

2011年2月28日 中国首部环境竞争力绿皮书《中国省域环境竞争力发展报告（2005～2009）》以及第五部《中国省域经济竞争力发展报告（2009～2010）》蓝皮书在中国社会科学院发布。省域宏观经济竞争力评价结果根据宏观经济竞争力指标体系和数学模型，对采集到的2008～2009年全国31个省、市、区的相关资料进行了整理和合成。省域宏观经济竞争力评价体系包括：经济实力竞争力、经济结构竞争力和经济外向度竞争力三个指标。

2011年3月2日 中国社会科学院城市发展与环境研究所、湖南工业大学、经济杂志社等单位正式对外联合发布了《中国低碳城市发展绿皮书》。该成果尝试从理论、实践、综合、前瞻等方面有所创新，编制整理了中国110个地级以上城市能源与碳排放数据，考察分析了中国城市低碳发展面临的困难与问题，梳理总结了中国城市低碳规划的特点与框架体系，尝试构建了中国低碳城市与城市低碳发展的评价指标体系，揭示了中国低碳城市与城市低碳发展的基本途径与主要方向，提出了推进中国城市低碳发展的具体措施与建议。

2011年3月5日 十一届全国人大四次会议开幕。《国民经济和社会发展第十二个五年规划纲要》草案明确指出，今后中国将“合理确定城市开发边界，规范新城新区建设，提高建成区人口密度”。“十二五”规划纲要草案显示，在新的五年中，中国将“优化格局，促进区域协调发展和城镇化健康发展”；规划草案还提出了“优化国土空间开发格局”“增强城镇综合承载能力”“预防和治理‘城市病’”等新概念。

2011年3月5日至3月14日 在两会召开期间，九三学社中央建议在“十二五”期间采取有力措施，加强“短命工程”治理。出台公共投资法，规范公共投资行为。对公共投资的范围从法律上予以界定，对公共投资的程序要用法律予以确定，对项目进行后期监管，对使用年限从法律上予以确定，避免“短命工程”。同时，重视规划，力求规划的科学性、民主性，严格执行已批准的规划，避免朝令夕改。时任国家文物局局长的单霁翔表示，应建立国家文物安全与违法预警系统，系统应包括以下内容：一是充分利用现代高科技手段对文物进行实时监控。二是建设电子化举报平台，加大社会公众线索供给度。三是充分发挥媒体的作用，扩大社会知晓面。

2011年3月8日 经国务院学位委员会第二十八次会议审议批准，国务院学位委员会、教育部公布了新版《学位授予和人才培养学科目录》。根据该目录，城乡规划学正式提升为一级学科，学科代码为0833。已有博士、硕士学位授权点将按新目录进行对应调整，学位授权审核及学位与研究生教育质量监督工作按照新目录进行。

2011年3月11日 国务院正式批复国家发改委上报的《海峡西岸经济区发展规划》，首次明确了“海峡西岸经济区”的具体地域范围，进一步确定了建设的具体目标、任务分工、建设布局和先行先试政策。

2011年3月13日 北京大学和中国社会科学院联合发布《中国城乡统筹发展报告》。报告称，我国农村产权制度改革势在必行，尤其是宅基地管理制度更需要改革。报告呼吁，今后法制建设应赋予农民与城市居民同等的产权落实和产权保护。为了实现城乡一体化，建议适时修订《物权法》、《土地管理法》等法律和相关法规，通过宅基地和农民住房的产权制度的改革大大激活农村经济和农村金融。

2011年3月16日 《中华人民共和国国民经济和社会发展第十二个五年规划纲要》发布。

2011年3月16日 国家发展和改革委员会宣布，按照2011年保障性住房建设目标任务，为加快廉租住房建设，国家发改委已会同住房和城乡建设部下达2011年中央预算内投资计划，安排350亿元支持地方新建廉租住房，逐步缓解城镇低收入家庭的住房困难问题。

2011年3月21日 北京市十三届人大四次会议经表决批准了北京市国民经济和社会发展第十二个五年规划纲要。北京市“十二五”规划纲要提出，将努力提升文化创意产业竞争力，整合提升30个市级文化创意产业集聚区。

2011年3月26日 “十二五”城镇化发展高层论坛举行。发展改革委秘书长杨伟民在论坛上表示，当前我国城镇化发展存在低密度和分散化的倾向，带来耕地面积减少过多过快的问题。

2011年3月31日 《中共深圳市委深圳市人民政府关于提升城市发展质量的决定》（以下简称《决定》）下发。《决定》提出，要以国际先进城市为标杆，树立以人为本、绿色低碳、集约发展、彰显特色、打造精品的发展理念，努力推动城市发展思路实现“六个转变”，以城市发展方式的转变推动城市发展质量的提升，用5至8年的努力，形成组团式、现代化、国际化的城市发展特征，打造双中心、八组团的城市发展新格局。

2011年4月2日 《国务院关于严格规范城乡建设用地增减挂钩试点切实做好农村土地整治工作的通知》播发。通知要求各地采取有力措施，坚决纠正片面追求增加城镇建设用地指标、擅自开展增减挂钩试点和扩大试点范围、违背农民意愿强拆强建等侵害农民权益的行为。

2011年4月10日 由国家文物局主办、无锡市人民政府和江苏省文物局承办、中国古迹遗址保护协会协办的第六届“中国文化遗产保护无锡论坛”在无锡举行。本届论坛以“运河遗产保护”为主题，来自国内外文化遗产、交通、规划、国土、水利、环保、法制等领域的部门领导和著名专家学者，以及运河沿线八省市文物行政部门有关负责同志，共80余人参加论坛。

2011年4月10日 北京市规划委主任黄艳表示，京津冀框架规划将于2011年年内出台，将形成北京与周边城市共同发展的一张蓝图。沿着北京周边，有七个河北城市与北京接壤，包括保定、承德、廊坊等，这些地方的规划必须成一个体系。据了解，这也是京津冀地区规划首次由政府部门提出明确落在纸面上。另据河北省发改委透露，此前面向河北及京津地区公开选拔的两名正处级领导干部已赴任上岗，河北“环首都发展协调办”已挂牌开始运行。

2011年4月11日 国务院派出8个督察组，对京沪等16个省份开展房市调控政策落实情况专项督察。按照计划，整个督察工作在20日左右结束。相关督察结果酌情对社会公布。住房和城乡建设部相关人士表示，督察情况将向国务院汇报后，再对政策和落实进行研究。在已经公布房价控制目标的城市中，西安率先进行了调整。

2011 年 4 月 11 日 国家发改委、监察部、国土资源部等 11 部委联合下发《关于开展全国高尔夫球场综合清理整治工作的通知》，针对一些地方无视国务院有关文件要求，违规建设高尔夫球场，占用大量耕地和林地资源等情况，在全国开展高尔夫球场综合清理整治工作。

2011 年 4 月 12 日 大运河保护和申遗工作会议在江苏省扬州市召开。会上宣布，世界上开凿时间较早、规模最大、线路最长、延续时间最久且目前仍在使用的人工运河大运河的申遗已进入倒计时。根据大运河申遗预备名单，大运河沿线的北京、天津、河北、山东、河南、安徽、江苏、浙江 8 个省市 35 个城市的大运河遗产将整体申报世界遗产，并争取在 2014 年列入世界遗产名录。

2011 年 5 月 1 日 汕头经济特区范围扩大至全市。此次扩容将使汕头特区覆盖全市 2 064.4 平方公里的土地，特区面积扩大近 9 倍。而在 2010 年下半年，深圳、厦门、珠海三个经济特区已先后将其范围扩大到全市。

2011 年 5 月 5 日 国土资源部日前印发了《关于下达〈2011 年全国土地利用计划〉的通知》。该计划中，新增建设用地计划安排量比去年略有增加。今年国土部计划新增建设用地 44.67 万公顷，与去年的 42.67 万公顷相比，增长 4.7%。这也是国土资源部连续两年扩大新增建设用地指标。

2011 年 5 月 6 日 我国第 10 个综合配套改革试验区——浙江省义乌市国际贸易综合改革试点全面启动。国家发展和改革委员会、外交部、商务部等 16 部委派出有关领导出席在义乌市召开的试点动员大会。国家发改委副主任彭森说，经过几年实践探索，各试验区的改革试验取得了积极进展，以国际贸易为主题在义乌开展试点，符合 2008 年国际金融危机爆发以来国内外形势发展的新变化以及转变经济发展方式内在要求。

2011 年 5 月 6 日 社科院城市与竞争力研究中心与社会科学文献出版社联合发布了《中国城市竞争力报告》。作为中国社科院关于中国城市竞争力研究的重要成果，这是该报告第九次发布。这份报告首次对中国的 294 个城市进行了幸福感指数排名。在 294 个城市中，石家庄市居民幸福感排名第一。接下来分别是临沂、扬州、承德、滨州、莱芜、鹤壁、包头、北京等地。内地城市的人们幸福感中，环渤海地区最佳，人们的幸福感打分均值为 79.48，与其他内地区域相比有明显的优势。西北地区均值最低，为 74.23。

2011 年 5 月 13 日 国务院办公厅发出通知，决定立即在全国开展征地拆迁制度规定落实情况专项检查，强化监管，严肃问责，坚决制止违法强拆行为，切实维护群众合法权益。通知要求各地区、各有关部门要认真贯彻本年 1 月国务院公布施行的《国有土地上房屋征收与补偿条例》和《国务院办公厅关于进一步严格征地拆迁管理工作切实维护群众合法权益的紧急通知》等征地拆迁制度规定，严格依法按程序办事，切实落实地方政府责任，坚决制止违法强制拆迁、暴力拆迁，从源头防范化解矛盾，做到依法、文明、和谐拆迁。

2011 年 5 月 13 日 深入实施西部大开发交通运输工作会议在宁夏银川召开，交通运输部部长李盛霖在会上披露，到2015年，西部地区高速公路（含高速化）总里程将达3.6万公里。这意味着“十二五”期间西部高速公路将比现在增加一倍。根据会议公布的《深入实施西部大开发战略公路水路交通运输发展规划纲要（2010—2020年）》，到2020年，西部地区主要公路通道的交通量将达到2010年的37倍。

2011年5月18日　国务院总理温家宝主持召开国务院常务会议，讨论通过《三峡后续工作规划》。要求妥善处理三峡工程蓄水后对长江中下游带来的不利影响，包括移民生活、生态污染、地质灾害，以及对长江中下游航运、灌溉、供水等各方面的负面影响。中央要求各地合力，8年内初步解决部分问题，实施生态修复，改善生物栖息地环境，保护生物多样性。

2011年5月23日　据北京市规划委透露，北京市城市总体规划2013年将重新编制。北京市规划委主任黄艳在近期召开的“北京市人口与产业发展规律及规划对策问题研究”专家研讨会上表示，要对北京市第六次人口普查的数据以及对首都城乡规划产生的重大影响进行分析研究，对这些数据做深入挖掘、详细分析，通过层次、结构、增量、标准等，把空间、资源、设施、产业等因素有机衔接起来，为今后的规划工作提供决策和措施。

2011年5月27日至5月29日　第二次全国对口支援新疆工作会议在北京召开。会前，中共中央总书记、国家主席胡锦涛作出重要批示，他指出：“一年来，援疆工作取得了显著成绩。要认真总结交流经验，切实贯彻援疆规划，全面实施援疆工作，务求取得扎实成效。”中共中央政治局常委、国务院副总理李克强，中共中央政治局常委、中央政法委书记周永康出席会议并讲话。

2011年5月30日　《成渝经济区区域规划》正式获国务院批复。

2011年6月1日　《非物质文化遗产法》正式施行，这是继《文物保护法》颁布近30年来文化领域的又一部重要法律。

2011年6月4日　住房和城乡建设部颁布《住房和城乡建设部低碳生态试点城（镇）申报管理暂行办法》。明确了申报低碳生态试点城（镇）应具备的条件和提供的材料。

2011年6月8日　国家发展改革委副主任徐宪平、秘书长杨伟民在国新办举行的新闻发布会上介绍全国主体功能区规划情况。《全国主体功能区规划》将国土空间划分为优化开发区域、重点开发区域、限制开发区域和禁止开发区域四类主体功能区，并规定了相应的功能定位、发展方向和开发管制原则。徐宪平就四类主体功能区的考核原则表示，优化开发区域的考核将强化对经济结构、资源消耗、环境保护、科技创新以及对外来人口、公共服务等指标的评价，以优化对经济增长速度的考核。

2011年6月8日　上海市卢湾、黄浦两区行政区划调整方案获国务院正式批复。黄浦区、卢湾区两区建制撤销，设立新的黄浦区。据介绍，两区行政区划调整有利于上海中心城区政府管辖规模趋于合理，有利于优化城市功能布局，也有利于提高行政管理效率。调整后，新的黄浦区面积达20.5平方公里，户籍人口90.9万。

2011年6月11日　时逢“世界文化遗产日”，北京中轴线申遗文物工程正式启动。

2011年6月11日　中国社科院经济所和首都经贸大学联合发布首个《中国城市生活质

量指数报告》。考量包括生活成本、医疗保障、生活环境、生活节奏、人均财富等。其中，广州、上海、南京名列前三；北京因“环境压力大”等因素影响位列第八，排在呼和浩特、石家庄等城市之后。

2011 年 6 月 13 日　国家发改委和陕西省政府在京发布《西咸新区总体规划》，西咸新区成为继上海浦东、天津滨海新区、成渝经济区之后又一个“国家级城市新区”。

2011 年 6 月 17 日　2011 城市发展与规划大会在扬州会议中心召开，围绕城市低碳转型与绿色发展的主题，与会代表共同探讨低碳生态城市的规划和建设。仇保兴理事长作主题报告“复杂科学与城市”，强调在中国的城镇化进入中后期的特殊阶段，应遵循自组织的理念，推行“微降解、微能源、微冲击、微更生、微交通、微绿地、微调控”将成为城市转型和生态城规划建设的新原则。《中国城市规划发展报告（2010—2011)》同期发布。

2011 年 6 月 30 日　京沪高铁正式通车。沿线分布着中国三大直辖市、两座省会城市和 11 座人口超过 100 万的大城市。这些地区虽然面积仅占全国的 6.5%，但人口占全国的 25.8%，而国内生产总值则占全国的 40% 以上，是中国经济发展最活跃和最具潜力的地区。这条串联中国经济最活跃板块的黄金通道，将成为经济要素快速流动的“大动脉”，将发挥协调区域平衡发展、加快产业转移优化、提升轨道交通建设能力的作用。

2011 年 6 月 30 日　全长 36.48 公里的世界最长跨海大桥——青岛胶州湾大桥和全长 7.8 公里中国最长海底隧道——青岛胶州湾海底隧道在青岛同时通车，成为中国桥、隧建设史上的一座里程碑，也为山东半岛城市群与中国北方经济一体化发展提供了新动力。

2011 年 7 月 1 日　《公路安全保护条例》正式施行。

2011 年 7 月 4 日　全国保障性安居工程推进会在内蒙古包头召开。会议要求，2011 年国家下达的保障性安居工程建设任务是 1 000 万套，要求各地今年 10 月底前全部开工，年底前确保完成 400 万套。中央下拨的资金，必须保证专款专用，各地区的配套资金也要尽快落实到位；对于工期较紧的建设项目要采取有力措施，加快进度，确保如期完成任务；要在保证工期、质量和安全的同时，把保障性安居工程建设成为廉洁工程。

2011 年 7 月 7 日　国务院正式批准设立浙江舟山群岛新区。这是继上海浦东新区、天津滨海新区和重庆两江新区后，党中央、国务院决定设立的又一个国家级新区，也是国务院批准的中国首个以海洋经济为主题的国家战略层面新区。

2011 年 7 月 7 日　国土资源部公布的数据显示，2011 年上半年，东部、中部地区违法用地面积同比分别下降了 12.5% 和 1.2%，西部地区却上升了 50.6%。随着西部大开发产业步伐升级的加快，西部地区发展对用地的需求也出现了刚性的趋势，土地需求的矛盾加剧，有些地方出现了违法计划来违法违规用地。

2011 年 7 月 8 日　2011 年度“新华—道琼斯国际金融中心发展指数（简称 IFCD Index）报告”在上海发布。报告显示，世界排名前 10 位的国际金融中心分别是纽约、伦敦、东京、香港、新加坡、上海、巴黎、法兰克福、悉尼、阿姆斯特丹。与 2010 年度相比，前 10 位城市位次没有大的变化，上海提升 2 位至第 6 位，悉尼提升 1 位至第 9 位，第 10 位的华盛顿被阿姆斯特丹取代。

2011 年 7 月 20 日　国务院总理温家宝主持召开国务院常务会议，研究部署近期加强土地管理的重点工作。会议指出，要制定并实施全国土地整治规划，加快建设高标准基本农田，力争“十二五”期间再建成 4 亿亩旱涝保收的高标准基本农田。会议还要求近期重点抓紧清理整改高尔夫球场，严肃查处违法占地、违规建设高尔夫球场的行为。

2011 年 7 月 30 日　《中国科学发展报告 2011》出炉，该报告首次完成了中国各地区的国内生产总值（GDP）质量排名，其中北京居首。该报告由中科院交叉科学中心唐山科学发展研究院编纂，独立创制了“中国 GDP 质量指数”，采用了“经济质量、社会质量、环境质量、生活质量、管理质量”五大子系统。

2011 年 8 月 1 日　《重庆市统筹城乡户籍制度改革农村居民转户实施办法（试行）》施行，据此，自主城区到远郊区县，只要是符合条件的本市农业户籍人士，均可转为城镇户口。

2011 年 8 月 2 日　《山东省国民休闲发展纲要》在济南发布。新华社称，这是我国首个以“纲要”形式颁布实施的全民休闲促进性文件。根据《纲要》，山东将把职工带薪年休假纳入考核，确保职工带薪年休假制度落实到位。

2011 年 8 月 3 日　中国社会科学院城市发展与环境研究所和社会科学文献出版社联合发布了《2011 年中国城市发展报告》。蓝皮书指出，到 2009 年我国城市中等收入阶层规模已达 2.3 亿人，占城市人口的 37% 左右。北京已经有 46% 的市民达到中等阶层收入水平，这一比例在全国排第一。截至 2009 年年底，全国城镇人口为 62 186 万人，城镇居民人均可支配收入为 17 175 元，中国目前城市合理的贫困线在人均年收入 7 500 ~ 8 500 元之间，全国贫困人口数约为 5 000 万人。报告还指出，随着中国城市化和工业化进程的加快，农村集体土地被大量征用，失地农民作为农民中的一个特殊群体，数量迅速扩大。目前，中国失地农民的总量已经达到 4 000 万 ~ 5 000 万人左右，而且仍以每年约 300 万人的速度递增，预估到 2030 年时将增至 1.1 亿人左右。

2011 年 8 月 5 日　住房和城乡建设部公布了 22 个省、直辖市、自治区上半年保障房建设的数据。其中，辽宁省的开工率最高，达到 104.6%；陕西居第二，达 101.1%。根据住房和城乡建设部提供的数据，截至 6 月底，全国保障房建设开工率为 56.6%。

2011 年 8 月 5 日　国家发改委联合国土资源部、住房和城乡建设部下发《关于暂停新开工建设主题公园项目的通知》。通知中要求，各地自通知印发之日起，至国家规范发展主题公园的具体政策出台前，一律不得批准新的主题公园项目；已办理审批手续但尚未动工建设的项目，也不得开工建设；各地规划、国土资源部门暂时办理有关主题公园建设项目的规划、用地手续。业内人士指出，三部委此次联合发文对国内主题公园市场进行摸底和规范，意在防止由于投资过热导致的重复建设，更主要的是通过“叫停”进一步调控房地产市场，防止部分企业以开发主题公园名义开发房地产项目。

2011 年 8 月 8 日　中科院地理科学与资源研究所的一套针对我国省域尺度的低碳经济发展水平评价指标体系和指数、对我国 30 个省（自治区、直辖市）进行了评价的研究成果发表。研究小组选取了社会经济资源基础、能源消费、碳排放、碳吸收能力、低碳产业发展等指标，采取定量和定性分析相结合的方法，对我国除西藏外的30个省（自治区、直辖市）的低碳经济发展水平现状进行评价，并对其进行类型划分，得出了低碳区、相对低碳区、相对高碳区和高碳区4种类型的低碳经济发展模式。结果表明，目前我国大部分省份处于“相对高碳”和“高碳”发展水平，我国发展低碳经济仍面临着巨大压力。

2011年8月11日 广东省编办正式通报：省编委已经批准通过，东莞市和中山市两个经济发达的地级市，结合本地实际，全面开展市辖镇“联并升级扁平化改革”和“撤镇建区扁平化改革”，新设立的区一级政府不再下辖镇街，而直管社区，以构建更加灵活的现代城市管理体制，探索社区治理形式。

2011年8月16日 住房和城乡建设部已经下发文件，要求各省在8月20日之前上报所辖区内各城市的上半年房地产市场调控工作情况，并给出限购五大标准。这意味着住房和城乡建设部已经在督促地方政府，预计8月份二三线城市限购令靴子落地。住房和城乡建设部给出的新增限购城市名单的建议5条标准包括：其一，根据国家统计局发布的70个大中城市房价指数，处于房价涨幅前列的城市；其二，将省内所有城市今年6月份的住宅价格与去年底的住宅价格做一个比较，涨幅较高的二三线城市；其三，今年上半年成交量同比增幅较高的城市；其四，位于已限购区域中心城市周边，外地人购房比例较高的城市；其五，群众对当地房价反应强烈、认为调控政策执行不力或不到位的城市。住房和城乡建设部建议，凡符合上述2条者就纳入到限购范围内。

2011年8月22日 安徽省正式宣布经国务院批复同意，正式撤销地级巢湖市，其所辖的一区四县分别划归合肥、芜湖、马鞍山三市管辖。区域经济学家普遍认为，这一重大行政区划调将使中国中东部继南京城市圈、武汉城市圈和长株潭城市圈后诞生又一个特大城市圈——合肥经济圈。

2011年8月28日 由钱学森先生倡导创办的中国智慧工程研究会在北京发布中国智慧城市（镇）发展指数，首次提出用幸福指数、管理指数、社会责任指数等三个指标推动中国智慧城市标准建设，促进以人为本的智慧城市创建。中国智慧城市（镇）发展指数评估体系包含3项一级指标，就业和收入、医疗卫生、社会安全等23项二级指标以及信息和网络化水平等86项三级指标和362项四级细分指标。目前我国已有上百个地区提出建设智慧城市。

2011年8月29日 文化部在北京人民大会堂举行第三批国家级非物质文化遗产名录项目颁牌仪式，第三批国家级非物质文化遗产名录包括民间文学、传统音乐、传统舞蹈、传统戏剧、曲艺、传统美术、传统技艺、传统医药、民俗及传统体育、游艺与杂技等项目，项目总计191项、扩展项目总计164项。

2011年8月30日 《加快推进厦漳泉大都市区同城化工作方案》经福建省政府研究同意，正式下发实施。此次方案发展定位是：进一步发挥厦门经济特区龙头带动作用和泉州创业型城市的支撑带动作用，增强漳州的辐射带动能力，强化分工、合作和协调，加快厦漳泉城市联盟进程和同城化步伐，实现组团式发展，构建厦漳泉大都市区，提升参与国际竞争和两岸合作的能力，充分发挥厦漳泉大都市区在海峡西岸经济区乃至在我国东南沿海的辐射带动作用，构建祖国大陆对台交往合作的平台和门户。厦漳泉同城化的时间表同时公布。

2011年9月9日　最高人民法院在其官方网站发布《最高人民法院关于坚决防止土地征收、房屋拆迁强制执行引发恶性事件的紧急通知》，通知指出，必须慎用强制手段，凡在执行过程中遇到当事人以自杀相威胁等极端行为、可能造成人身伤害等恶性事件的，一般应当停止执行或首先要确保当事人及相关人员的人身安全。

2011年9月15日　发改委、环境保护部公布通知称，对于“一地三域”的综合性规划，以及十大行业的专项规划，未编写环境影响篇章或者说明的，规划审批机关应当要求其补充；未补充的，规划审批机关不予审批。规划编制机关在报送审批专项规划草案时，应当将环境影响报告书和其审查意见一并附送规划审批机关，未附送且应要求未补充的，规划审批机关不予审批。

2011年9月16日　《沈阳经济区新型工业化综合配套改革试验总体方案》正式获得国务院批复。继一年前沈阳经济区获批为国家新型工业化综合配套改革试验区后，《总体方案》又获批复，显示沈阳经济区一年多来的“先行先试”改革实践获得了充分认可，沈阳经济区改革发展开始进入全面实施的新阶段。

2011年9月19日　国务院总理温家宝主持召开国务院常务会议，研究部署进一步做好保障性安居工程建设和管理工作。会议指出，近年来，我国保障性安居工程建设取得明显成效，为解决中低收入家庭住房困难、遏制房价过快上涨、完善住房体制和促进房地产业健康发展，发挥了重要作用。做好这项工作涉及城市规划、制度建设、资金支持、工程质量、分配机制和运营管理等多方面问题，必须坚持满足基本、保证质量、公平分配、健全制度的原则，合理确定住房保障范围、方式和标准，完善相关支持政策，抓紧形成规范的保障性安居工程投资、建设、运营和管理机制。

2011年9月20日　2011中国城市规划年会在江苏省南京市国际博览中心开幕，来自国内、国际的近4000位规划师、各级领导和专家学者参加了会议。年会的主题是“转型与重构”。整个年会倡导节能低碳理念，从所有参加会议的专家学者乘坐地铁参会等方面打造“低碳年会”。

2011年9月23日　第二届中国（天津滨海）国际生态城市论坛暨博览会在天津滨海新区举行。住房和城乡建设部仇保兴副部长在论坛上表示，面对当下良莠不齐的生态城市发展，主管部门将加强治理，建立生态城规划的审查制度和批准制度，以杜绝生态城项目中的虚假成分。将拟订5个硬件指标：紧凑混合的用地模式（1万人/平方公里）；可再生能源的占比必须要达到整个能耗的20%以上；绿色建筑占所有建筑种类比例大于80%；生物多样性；绿色交通；拒绝高能耗、高排放、高污染的工业项目等。

2011年9月27日　住房和城乡建设部举行第六批城乡规划督察员派遣仪式，将于近日向烟台、株洲、潍坊、湛江等18个城市派驻城乡规划督察员，加强对国务院审批总体规划实施情况的监督。

2011年9月28日　国务院出台关于支持河南省加快建设中原经济区的指导意见。指导意见指出，中原经济区是以全国主体功能区规划明确的重点开发区域为基础、中原城市群为支撑、涵盖河南全省、延及周边地区的经济区域，地理位置重要，粮食优势突出，市场潜力巨大，文化底蕴深厚，在全国改革发展大局中具有重要战略地位。

2011 年 9 月 30 日 《四川省人民政府关于贯彻成渝经济区区域规划的实施意见》（以下简称《意见》）发布。《意见》要求重点围绕《规划》提出的优化总体布局、提升城市功能、统筹城乡发展、夯实发展基础、深化内陆开放、建设生态屏障等要求，突出抓好 6 个方面的重大任务，具体细化为 76 个重点项目和 37 项重大政策，并逐一确定了任务实施的责任主体。

2011 年 10 月 11 日 国务院正式发布《国务院关于修改〈中华人民共和国资源税暂行条例〉的决定》（下称《决定》），并于 2011 年 11 月 1 日执行。

2011 年 10 月 15 日至 10 月 18 日 中共十七届六中全会在北京举行。此次全会提出了建设社会主义文化强国的宏伟目标，有力指引中国社会主义文化事业大步迈向大繁荣大发展的美好明天。会上审议通过《中共中央关于深化文化体制改革、推动社会主义文化大发展大繁荣若干重大问题的决定》（以下简称《决定》），《决定》围绕建设社会主义文化强国和实现到 2020 年文化改革发展奋斗目标，围绕各地区各部门各方面普遍关注的重点问题，对文化改革发展进行了战略部署，是当前和今后一个时期指导我国文化改革发展的纲领性文件。

2011 年 11 月 10 日 住房和城乡建设部公布 2011 年全国城镇保障性安居工程开工已超过 1 000 万套，提前实现了年初计划的目标。但据了解，1 000 万套已开工保障性住房中有约 1/3 还处于“挖坑待建”情况。11 月 12 日，住房和城乡建设部再次重申，2011 年开工建设 1 000万套保障性住房的开工标准是，规划设计的永久性建筑工程已进入地基基础的结构施工。对于仅是搭建施工现场围护设施，或仅是开挖基坑的，不计入已开工的项目和套数。

2011 年 11 月 11 日 社会科学文献出版社在京发布《气候变化绿皮书：应对气候变化报告（2011）》。绿皮书表示，我国“十二五”期间国内碳市场发展将有明显进展。绿皮书指出，2011 年，“十二五”规划明确提出了“建立完善温室气体排放统计核算制度，逐步建立碳排放交易市场”、“增加森林碳汇”的举措，这是中国政府首次在国家级正式文件中提出建立中国国内碳市场，表明碳交易市场建设已经进入政府工作程序。

2011 年 11 月 13 日 一批与上海世博会场馆后续利用紧密相关的“十二五”重大文化设施规划建设构想在上海市政府专题新闻发布会上正式发布。在备受关注的“后世博”文化项目中，除了已投入使用的世博文化中心，最新公布了中华艺术宫、上海当代艺术博物馆、上海儿童艺术剧场、世博会博物馆等四大文化“地标”，今后将共同构筑起黄浦江两岸恢弘的艺术“长廊”。

2011 年 11 月 15 日 全国开发区土地节约集约利用现场会在江苏省昆山市召开。国土资源部党组成员、副部长贠小苏出席并讲话，江苏省副省长徐鸣致辞。贠小苏在会上强调，要全面提升节约集约用地水平，着力推进经济发展方式和土地利用方式转变。

2011 年 11 月 16 日 国务院总理温家宝主持召开国务院常务会议，决定建立青海三江源国家生态保护综合试验区。会议指出，三江源地区是长江、黄河、澜沧江发源地和我国淡水资源重要补给地，是青藏高原生态安全屏障的重要组成部分，在全国生态文明建设中具有特殊重要地位。三江源生态保护与建设总体规划自2005年实施以来，取得明显成效。为从根本上遏制三江源地区生态功能退化趋势，探索建立有利于生态建设和环境保护的体制机制，会议批准实施《青海三江源国家生态保护综合试验区总体方案》。试验区包括玉树、果洛、黄南、海南4个藏族自治州21个县和格尔木市唐古拉山镇。

2011年11月16日　国务院新闻办发表《中国农村扶贫开发的新进展》白皮书，全面介绍了近十年来中国农村扶贫开发取得的进展。白皮书指出，20世纪80年代中期以来，中国政府开始有组织、有计划、大规模地开展农村扶贫开发，先后制定实施《国家八七扶贫攻坚计划（1994—2000年）》、《中国农村扶贫开发纲要（2001—2010年）》、《中国农村扶贫开发纲要（2011—2020年）》等减贫规划，使扶贫减贫成为全社会的共识和行动。中国的农村扶贫开发，促进了社会和谐稳定和公平正义，推动了中国人权事业的发展和进步。

2011年11月22日　《中国应对气候变化的政策与行动（2011）》白皮书发布。白皮书全面介绍了中国"十一五"期间应对气候变化采取的政策与行动、取得的积极成效以及"十二五"期间应对气候变化的总体部署及有关谈判立场。国际社会对此高度关注并予以积极评价，认为中国始终在应对气候变化的政策执行中履行承诺，不断通过国内经济发展方式的变革，为全球应对气候变化做出积极贡献。

2011年11月29日　中央扶贫开发工作会议召开。中国宣布进一步大幅上调国家扶贫标准线，从2010年的农民人均纯收入1 274元升至2 300元（2010年不变价）。此次80%的上调幅度为历史罕见，全国贫困人口数量和覆盖面也由2010年的2 688万人扩大至1.28亿人，占农村总人口的13.4%，占全国总人口（除港澳台地区外）的近十分之一。会后正式发布《中国农村扶贫开发纲要（2011—2020年）》，并发出通知，要求各地区各部门结合实际认真贯彻执行。

2011年12月1日　国土资源部发出紧急通知，严禁工商企业以各种名义圈占农地、擅自改变土地用途，违法违规进行非农建设。对此，有关专家称，这一政策的出台针对当前中国基层愈演愈烈的土地违法违规现象，有助于保护农业用地，规范土地管理。

2011年12月2日　位于北京鼓楼东大街和地安门外大街交会处的"钟鼓楼·北京时间博物馆"项目开始动工。虽然国家文物局对此项目的批复也宣告了年初设立的曾引发了文保界"地震"的钟鼓楼·时间文化城项目的正式告吹，但仍要以拆除几十所四合院为代价的时间博物馆项目引起了广泛热议、遭到了众多专业人士义正词严的批评。

2011年12月8日　中国社会科学院当代城乡发展规划院、社会科学文献出版社联合发布2011年《城乡一体化蓝皮书》。蓝皮书通过对城乡统筹发展和建设情况进行普遍调查和典型调查，系统研究了促进城乡一体化建设的理论支撑和实践创新，深入分析了各地在城乡协调、统筹发展等方面存在的共性问题、突出问题，并提出具有前瞻性和指导意义的对策建议。

2011年12月9日　中央政治局会议召开，初步勾勒出明年经济工作的主线。对于明年的宏观调控基调，中央保持了政策的连续性和稳定性，提出"实施积极的财政政策和稳健的货币政策”，但这次会议同时提出“增强调控的针对性、灵活性、前瞻性”，替代了此前“针对性、灵活性、有效性”的表述。同时还提出，“保持经济平稳较快发展和物价总水平基本稳定”。专家认为，2012 年宏观政策的重心将是“稳增长”优先，除非国内外的经济基本面出乎预料地恶化，否则货币政策将平稳推进，稳健的货币政策在 2012 年将回归“中性”。

2011 年 12 月 9 日 中国社会科学院财政与贸易经济研究所、社会科学文献出版社联合举办“《住房绿皮书》发布会暨 2011～2012 年住房形势与政策研讨会”并发布《中国住房发展报告（2011—2012）》。对中国住房市场作了全面系统的分析、预测与评价，并给出相关政策建议。

2011 年 12 月 10 日 “海上丝绸之路与世界文明进程”国际论坛在宁波举行。此次“海上丝绸之路与世界文明进程”国际论坛由中国社科院和宁波市人民政府主办、浙江省文物局协办。在论坛上，中国沿海七个口岸城市提出，将联合申报“海上丝绸之路”世界文化遗产。

2011 年 12 月 11 日 广东省在北京与重庆市、广西壮族自治区分别签署战略合作框架协议。中共中央政治局委员、省委书记汪洋，省委副书记、代省长朱小丹出席签约仪式。根据《重庆·广东战略合作框架协议》，广东省和重庆市将从经济社会发展全局高度谋划两省市合作发展，在 2009 年签订的《重庆市人民政府广东省人民政府关于加强两省市全面合作协议》的基础上，进一步创新合作机制，拓展合作领域，建立长期稳定的合作关系，共同构建合作与发展新格局。

2011 年 12 月 12 日 中国社科院发布《产业竞争力蓝皮书》，称按照 2011 年世界银行的标准，中国已经成为中上等收入国家，正面临着经济增长放缓、人均收入难以提高的“中等收入陷阱”考验。

2011 年 12 月 12 日 环境保护部发布《环境保护部关于 2010 年度全国城市环境综合整治定量考核结果的通报》，从委托国家统计局采取电话调查方式对全国城市公众随机调查结果看，全国公众对城市环境保护满意率为 62.9%。其中，城市空气污染和噪声污染是公众最为关心、关注的环境问题。

2011 年 12 月 12 日至 12 月 14 日 中央经济工作会议在北京召开。着力扩大国内需求，是中央经济工作会议作出的一项重要决策和部署。扩大内需首先要加快调整国民收入分配格局，“合理增加城乡居民特别是低收入群众收入”、“提高中等收入者比重”，这些政策被视为 2011 年中央经济工作会议致力改善民生的亮点。

2011 年 12 月 13 日 世界经济论坛发表金融发展指数。中国香港取得 5.16 分（7 分为满分），排名由 2010 年的第四位跃升至首位，超越美国（第二位）、英国（第三位）及新加坡（第四位）。这是亚洲金融中心首次名列榜首。中国内地排名从第二十二位上升至第十九位。

2011 年 12 月 15 日 国务院发布《国家环境保护“十二五”规划》。

2011 年 12 月 19 日 中国社会科学院社会学研究所、社会科学文献出版社正式发布

2012社会蓝皮书《2012年中国社会形势分析与预测》。蓝皮书指出，改革开放以来，随着政策引导和市场对资源配置作用的逐步增强，中国的城市化进程明显加快。据2010年第六次全国人口普查主要数据公报，目前中国城镇人口比重为49.68%。以目前的人口城市化速度，2011年城镇居民的比例将超过农村居民，这标志着中国数千年来以农村人口为主的城乡人口结构发生了逆转，可以说是中国现代化进程中的一件大事。

2011年12月19日 《2011年度中国社会状况综合调查》在京发布。调查结果显示，75.3%的公众认为，生活水平较5年前有所上升，同时也有近70%的公众感受到“物价上涨、影响生活水平”的压力。调查还显示，公众认为目前最为严重的社会问题前三项分别是“物价上涨”（59.5%）、“看病难、看病贵”（42.9%）和“收入差距过大贫富分化”（31.6%）。排在上述问题之后的是“贪污腐败”（29.3%）、“就业失业”（24.2%）、“住房价格过高”（24%）。此次调查由社科院社会学研究所、调查与数据信息中心联合开展，覆盖全国28个省市自治区的100个县（区、市）和5大城市、490个村（居委会），入户访问6468位城乡居民。

2011年12月21日 国土资源部公布《闲置土地处置办法（修订草案）》，并公开向社会征集意见。修订草案规定，未动工开发建设，土地闲置满2年，经批准后可无偿收回土地使用权。

2011年12月22日 中共中央政治局常委、国务院副总理李克强在全国住房保障工作会上强调，要贯彻落实中央经济工作会议精神，扎实做好明年住房保障工作，在确保质量的前提下，统筹推进新开工和结转续建项目建设，完善配套设施，力争更多竣工，确保分配公平，促进民生改善和经济发展。

2011年12月23日 全国住房城乡建设工作会议在京召开。住房城乡建设部党组书记、部长姜伟新在会上作了报告，全面总结了2011年工作，并对2012年的重点工作进行了部署。部党组成员、副部长仇保兴、陈大卫，部党组成员、中央纪委驻部纪检组组长杜鹃，部党组成员、副部长齐骥、郭允冲出席会议。会议认为，住房城乡建设系统坚决贯彻落实中央的决策部署，各方面工作都取得了较好进展，为“十二五”时期住房城乡建设事业科学发展打下了良好基础。

2011年12月27日 中央农村工作会议在北京举行。中共中央政治局常委、国务院总理温家宝在会议上阐述了在推进工业化城镇化进程中继续做好“三农”工作需要把握好的若干重大问题，对做好明年农业农村工作提出了要求。

2011年12月28日 国家旅游局正式发布《中国旅游业“十二五”发展规划纲要》，提出到“十二五”期末，旅游业初步建设成为国民经济的战略性支柱产业和人民群众更加满意的现代服务业，在“转方式、扩内需、调结构、保增长、促就业、惠民生”等战略中发挥更大功能。

2011年12月29日 国家文物局召开第三次全国文物普查成果新闻发布会，首次正式对外公布具体的普查数据。从2007年4月开始的第三次全国文物普查，经过5年调查和数据汇总，共登记不可移动文物766722处，较第二次文物普查结果增幅超过200%，其中新发现不可移动文物536001处，占登记总量的69.91%。普查显示，我国不可移动文物的保护状况不容乐观，其中保护状况较差的占到17.77%，保存状况差的占到8.43%，即约有1/4的不可移动文物保存面临重大挑战。

2011年12月30日 环境保护部部长周生贤主持召开环境保护部常务会议，审议并原则通过《环境空气质量标准》、《环境空气质量指数（AQI）技术规定》和“十二五”国家环境空气监测网建设方案，听取《全国土壤环境保护规划（2011—2015年）》编制情况汇报。

（编辑整理：金晓春，中国城市规划设计研究院学术信息中心主任工程师；郭磊，中国城市规划设计研究院学术信息中心城市规划师）

附录3　2011年度城市规划相关政策法规索引

名称	批号(文号)	发布机构	发布日期	实施日期
关于开展“十二五”期间长江黄金水道建设总体推进方案编制工作的通知	厅函水〔2011〕1号	中华人民共和国交通运输部	2011-01-10	
关于加强重点流域水污染治理项目管理的通知	发改办地区〔2011〕73号	中华人民共和国国家发展和改革委员会	2011-01-11	
关于开展第一批创建国家公共文化服务体系示范区(项目)督导工作的通知	办社文函〔2011〕22号	中华人民共和国文化部办公厅	2011-01-16	
关于加强和改进住房公积金服务工作的通知	建金〔2011〕9号	住房和城乡建设部、财政部、中国人民银行等	2011-01-19	
房地产经纪管理办法	中华人民共和国住房和城乡建设部、中华人民共和国国家发展和改革委员会、中华人民共和国人力资源和社会保障部令第8号	中华人民共和国住房和城乡建设部、中华人民共和国国家发展和改革委员会、中华人民共和国人力资源和社会保障部	2011-01-20	2011-04-01
国有土地上房屋征收与补偿条例	中华人民共和国国务院令第590号	中华人民共和国国务院	2011-01-21	2011-01-21
国务院关于同意将浙江省嘉兴市列为国家历史文化名城的批复	国函〔2011〕10号	中华人民共和国国务院	2011-01-24	
国务院关于同意将江苏省宜兴市列为国家历史文化名城的批复	国函〔2011〕9号	中华人民共和国国务院	2011-01-24	
关于组织实施太阳能光电建筑应用一体化示范的通知	财办建〔2011〕9号	中华人民共和国财政部办公厅、中华人民共和国住房和城乡建设部办公厅	2011-01-27	
关于印发《市政公用设施抗震设防专项论证技术要点(地下工程篇)》的通知	建质〔2011〕13号	中华人民共和国住房和城乡建设部	2011-01-28	
关于切实做好2011年城市住房用地管理和调控重点工作的通知	国土资发〔2011〕2号	中华人民共和国国土资源部	2011-02-05	
关于印发中关村国家自主创新示范区发展规划纲要(2011—2020年)的通知	发改高技〔2011〕367号	中华人民共和国国家发展和改革委员会	2011-02-22	

续表

名称	批号(文号)	发布机构	发布日期	实施日期
中华人民共和国非物质文化遗产法	中华人民共和国主席令第42号	全国人民代表大会常务委员会	2011-02-25	2011-06-01
水文监测环境和设施保护办法	水利部令第43号	中华人民共和国水利部	2011-02-28	
关于2010年中国人居环境奖获奖名单的通报	建城〔2011〕29号	中华人民共和国住房和城乡建设部	2011-03-01	
关于住房保障规范化管理检查情况的通报	建办保函〔2011〕106号	中华人民共和国住房和城乡建设部办公厅	2011-03-03	
关于加强"十二五"近期建设规划制定工作的通知	建规〔2011〕31号	中华人民共和国住房和城乡建设部	2011-03-03	
土地复垦条例	中华人民共和国国务院令第592号	中华人民共和国国务院	2011-03-05	2011-03-05
关于进一步推进可再生能源建筑应用的通知	财建〔2011〕61号	中华人民共和国财政部、中华人民共和国住房和城乡建设部	2011-03-08	
国务院关于同意将广东省中山市列为国家历史文化名城的批复	国函〔2011〕27号	中华人民共和国国务院	2011-03-12	
关于印发城镇污水处理厂污泥处理处置技术指南(试行)的通知	建科〔2011〕34号	中华人民共和国住房和城乡建设部、中华人民共和国国家发展和改革委员会	2011-03-14	
国务院关于同意将山西省太原市列为国家历史文化名城的批复	国函〔2011〕28号	中华人民共和国国务院	2011-03-14	
关于发布《商品房销售明码标价规定》的通知	发改价格〔2011〕548号	中华人民共和国国家发展和改革委员会	2011-03-16	
国务院关于唐山市城市总体规划的批复	国函〔2011〕29号	中华人民共和国国务院	2011-03-16	
住房和城乡建设部关于公布2011年全国绿色建筑创新奖获奖项目的通报	建科〔2011〕45号	中华人民共和国住房和城乡建设部	2011-04-06	
国务院办公厅关于发布河北驼梁等16处新建国家级自然保护区名单的通知	国办发〔2011〕16号	中华人民共和国国务院办公厅	2011-04-16	
国务院批转住房和城乡建设部等部门关于进一步加强城市生活垃圾处理工作意见的通知	国发〔2011〕9号	中华人民共和国国务院	2011-04-19	
全国人民代表大会常务委员会关于修改《中华人民共和国建筑法》的决定	中华人民共和国主席令第46号	全国人民代表大会常务委员会	2011-04-22	2011-07-01
全国人民代表大会常务委员会关于修改《中华人民共和国道路交通安全法》的决定	中华人民共和国主席令第47号	全国人民代表大会常务委员会	2011-04-22	2011-05-01
关于批准北京经济技术开发区为国家生态工业示范园区的通知	环发〔2011〕50号	中华人民共和国环境保护部	2011-04-25	
国务院关于同意将山东省蓬莱市列为国家历史文化名城的批复	国函〔2011〕49号	中华人民共和国国务院	2011-05-01	

续表

名称	批号（文号）	发布机构	发布日期	实施日期
关于发布2010年版《工程建设标准强制性条文》（水利工程部分）的通知	建标〔2011〕60号	中华人民共和国住房和城乡建设部	2011－05－06	
国务院关于支持云南省加快建设面向西南开放重要桥头堡的意见	国发〔2011〕11号	中华人民共和国国务院	2011－05－06	
关于公开城镇保障性安居工程建设信息的通知	建保〔2011〕64号	中华人民共和国住房和城乡建设部	2011－05－10	
关于印发《2011—2015年建筑业信息化发展纲要》的通知	建质〔2011〕67号	中华人民共和国住房和城乡建设部	2011－05－10	
关于加强房地产经纪管理进一步规范房地产交易秩序的通知	建房〔2011〕68号	中华人民共和国住房和城乡建设部、中华人民共和国国家发展和改革委员会	2011－05－11	
关于切实做好征地拆迁管理工作的紧急通知	国土资电发〔2011〕72号	中华人民共和国国土资源部办公厅	2011－05－16	
关于做好2011年扩大农村危房改造试点工作的通知	建村〔2011〕62号	中华人民共和国住房和城乡建设部	2011－05－17	
国务院关于哈尔滨市城市总体规划的批复	国函〔2011〕53号	中华人民共和国国务院	2011－05－17	
国务院关于海口市城市总体规划的批复	国函〔2011〕54号	中华人民共和国国务院	2011－05－17	
关于加强保障性安居工程质量管理的通知	建保〔2011〕69号	中华人民共和国住房和城乡建设部	2011－05－18	
国家级森林公园管理办法	国家林业局令第27号	中华人民共和国国家林业局	2011－05－20	2011－08－01
关于印发《"十二五"期间城镇污水处理设施配套管网建设项目资金管理办法》的通知	财建〔2011〕266号	中华人民共和国财政部、中华人民共和国住房和城乡建设部	2011－05－23	
关于命名第五批（2010年度）国家节水型城市的通报	建城〔2011〕72号	中华人民共和国住房和城乡建设部	2011－05－26	
国家发展改革委关于印发成渝经济区区域规划的通知		中华人民共和国国家发展和改革委员会	2011－05－30	
关于印发《国有土地上房屋征收评估办法》的通知	建房〔2011〕77号	中华人民共和国住房和城乡建设部	2011－06－03	2011－06－03
关于印发《住房和城乡建设部低碳生态试点城（镇）申报管理暂行办法》的通知	建规〔2011〕78号	中华人民共和国住房和城乡建设部	2011－06－04	
关于印发《全国建筑市场注册执业人员不良行为记录认定标准》（试行）的通知	建办市〔2011〕38号	中华人民共和国住房和城乡建设部办公厅	2011－06－07	
关于印发国家东中西区域合作示范区建设总体方案的通知	发改地区〔2011〕1185号	中华人民共和国国家发展和改革委员会	2011－06－08	
关于印发《国家环境保护"十二五"科技发展规划》的通知	环发〔2011〕63号	中华人民共和国环境保护部	2011－06－09	
关于进一步推进住房城乡建设系统依法行政的意见	建法〔2011〕81号	中华人民共和国住房和城乡建设部	2011－06－10	

续表

名称	批号(文号)	发布机构	发布日期	实施日期
关于做好住房保障规划编制工作的通知	建保〔2011〕91 号	中华人民共和国住房和城乡建设部、中华人民共和国国家发展和改革委员会、中华人民共和国财政部、中华人民共和国国土资源部、中华人民共和国农业部、国家林业局	2011-06-11	
关于绿色重点小城镇试点示范的实施意见	财建〔2011〕341 号	中华人民共和国财政部、中华人民共和国住房和城乡建设部	2011-06-23	
关于发布《市政公用设施建设项目社会评价导则》的通知	建标〔2011〕84 号	中华人民共和国住房和城乡建设部	2011-06-23	2011-12-01
关于发布国家环境保护标准《企业环境报告书编制导则》的公告	公告 2011 年第 51 号	中华人民共和国环境保护部	2011-06-24	
关于印发《湖泊生态环境保护试点管理办法》的通知	财建〔2011〕464 号	中华人民共和国财政部、中华人民共和国环境保护部	2011-06-30	2011-06-30
关于授予江苏省宜兴市等 27 个市(区、县)"国家生态市(区、县)"称号的公告	公告 2011 年第 54 号	中华人民共和国环境保护部自然生态保护司	2011-07-01	
关于建立保障性住房建设材料、部品采购信息平台的通知	建保〔2011〕44 号	中华人民共和国住房和城乡建设部	2011-07-07	
关于印发《国家机关办公建筑和大型公共建筑能耗监测系统数据上报规范》的通知	建科综函〔2011〕169 号	中华人民共和国住房和城乡建设部	2011-07-11	
关于印发《城市轨道交通工程概算定额》的通知	建标〔2011〕99 号	中华人民共和国住房和城乡建设部	2011-07-13	2012-01-01
关于公布第二批全国特色景观旅游名镇(村)示范名单的通知	建村〔2011〕104 号	中华人民共和国住房和城乡建设部 、国家旅游局	2011-07-15	
关于批准发布《大型公共建筑项目评价导则》的通知	建标〔2011〕108 号	中华人民共和国住房和城乡建设部	2011-07-18	2011-12-01
关于印发《农村危房改造试点建筑节能示范工作省级年度考核评价指标(试行)》的通知	建村〔2011〕106 号	中华人民共和国住房和城乡建设部	2011-07-18	
关于批准发布《城镇液化天然气厂站建设标准》的通知	建标〔2011〕113 号	中华人民共和国住房和城乡建设部、中华人民共和国国家发展和改革委员会	2011-07-20	2011-12-01
关于印发《农村危房改造抗震安全基本要求(试行)》的通知	建村〔2011〕115 号	中华人民共和国住房和城乡建设部	2011-07-25	
湖南省风景名胜区条例	湖南省第十一届人民代表大会常务委员会公告第 59 号	湖南省人民代表大会常务委员会	2011-07-29	2011-10-01
浙江省风景名胜区条例		浙江省人民代表大会常务委员会	2011-07-29	2012-01-01
关于批准发布《城市消防站建设标准》的通知	建标〔2011〕118 号	中华人民共和国住房和城乡建设部、中华人民共和国国家发展和改革委员会	2011-08-05	2011-10-01

续表

名称	批号(文号)	发布机构	发布日期	实施日期
关于印发《房屋建筑产品标准体系》的通知	建标〔2011〕119号	中华人民共和国住房和城乡建设部	2011-08-09	2011-08-09
大连市风景名胜区条例	大连市人民代表大会常务委员会公告第2号	大连市人民代表大会常务委员会	2011-08-11	2011-09-01
关于加快建设园林绿化企业资质信息核准一体化管理体系的通知	建城园函〔2011〕179号	中华人民共和国住房和城乡建设部城市建设司	2011-08-23	
关于发布《环境影响评价技术导则总纲》等两项国家环境保护标准的公告	公告2011年第64号	中华人民共和国环境保护部	2011-09-01	2012-01-01
关于印发《建设项目工程总承包合同示范文本(试行)》的通知	建市〔2011〕139号	中华人民共和国住房和城乡建设部、中华人民共和国国家工商行政管理总局	2011-09-07	2011-11-01
太湖流域管理条例	中华人民共和国国务院令第604号	中华人民共和国国务院	2011-09-07	2011-11-01
关于发布《区域生物多样性评价标准》等六项国家环境保护标准的公告	公告2011年第67号	中华人民共和国环境保护部	2011-09-08	2012-01-01
关于发布《城镇建设产品标准体系》的通知	建标〔2011〕140号	中华人民共和国住房和城乡建设部	2011-09-09	2011-09-09
关于印发《农村住房建设技术政策(试行)》的通知	建科研函〔2011〕199号	中华人民共和国住房和城乡建设部建筑节能与科技司	2011-09-09	
关于印发《绿色低碳重点小城镇建设评价指标(试行)》的通知	建村〔2011〕144号	中华人民共和国住房和城乡建设部、中华人民共和国财政部、中华人民共和国国家发展和改革委员会	2011-09-13	
关于印发《城乡建设防灾减灾"十二五"规划》的通知	建质〔2011〕141号	中华人民共和国住房和城乡建设部	2011-09-14	
关于印发《城市供热文明行业标准》的通知	建文明委〔2011〕1号	中华人民共和国住房和城乡建设部精神文明建设指导委员会	2011-09-15	
关于印发《国家环境保护"十二五"环境与健康工作规划》的通知	环发〔2011〕105号	中华人民共和国环境保护部	2011-09-20	
关于印发《工程勘察设计行业2011—2015年发展纲要》的通知	建市〔2011〕150号	中华人民共和国住房和城乡建设部	2011-09-21	
关于开展"城乡建设统计基础工作规范"试点工作的通知	建计统函〔2011〕154号	中华人民共和国住房和城乡建设部计划财务与外事司	2011-09-21	
国务院办公厅关于保障性安居工程建设和管理的指导意见	国办发〔2011〕45号	国务院办公厅	2011-09-28	
国务院关于支持河南省加快建设中原经济区的指导意见	国发〔2011〕32号	中华人民共和国国务院	2011-09-28	
云南省风景名胜区条例		云南省人民代表大会常务委员会	2011-09-30	2012-01-01
关于印发《城市轨道交通建筑安装工程费用标准编制规则》的通知	建标〔2011〕159号	中华人民共和国住房和城乡建设部	2011-10-08	

续表

名称	批号(文号)	发布机构	发布日期	实施日期
关于同意贵阳经济技术开发区等4个园区建设国家生态工业示范园区的通知	环发〔2011〕122号	中华人民共和国环境保护部	2011-10-10	
国务院关于南宁市城市总体规划的批复	国函〔2011〕121号	中华人民共和国国务院	2011-10-10	
国务院关于重庆市城乡总体规划的批复	国函〔2011〕123号	中华人民共和国国务院	2011-10-15	
国务院关于加强环境保护重点工作的意见	国发〔2011〕35号	中华人民共和国国务院	2011-10-17	
国家发展改革委、环境保护部关于印发《河流水电规划报告及规划环境影响报告书审查暂行办法》的通知	发改能源〔2011〕2242号	中华人民共和国国家发展和改革委员会、中华人民共和国环境保护部	2011-10-18	
国家发展改革委办公厅关于开展碳排放权交易试点工作的通知	发改办气候〔2011〕2601号	中华人民共和国国家发展和改革委员会	2011-10-29	
关于印发《"十二五"全国环境保护法规和环境经济政策建设规划》的通知	环发〔2011〕129号	中华人民共和国环境保护部	2011-11-01	
国务院关于同意将四川省会理县列为国家历史文化名城的批复	国函〔2011〕135号	中华人民共和国国务院	2011-11-02	
关于印发"十二五"城市绿色照明规划纲要的通知	建城〔2011〕178号	中华人民共和国住房和城乡建设部	2011-11-04	
关于印发《镇(乡)域规划导则(试行)》的通知	建村〔2010〕184号	中华人民共和国住房和城乡建设部	2011-11-04	
关于开展国家公交都市建设示范工程有关事项的通知	交运发〔2011〕635号	中华人民共和国交通运输部	2011-11-09	
关于印发《市政工程设施养护维修估算指标》的通知	建标〔2011〕187号	中华人民共和国住房和城乡建设部	2011-11-17	2012-03-01
关于批准发布《建设项目评价术语标准》的通知	建标〔2011〕186号	中华人民共和国住房和城乡建设部	2011-11-17	2012-01-01
关于发布《工程建设标准体系(煤炭工程部分)》的通知	建标〔2011〕188号	中华人民共和国住房和城乡建设部	2011-11-17	2011-11-17
关于进一步加快发展旅游业促进社会主义文化大发展大繁荣的指导意见	旅发〔2011〕61号	中华人民共和国国家旅游局	2011-11-17	
国务院办公厅关于印发国家综合防灾减灾规划(2011—2015年)的通知	国办发〔2011〕55号	国务院办公厅	2011-11-26	
发改委关于居民生活用电试行阶梯电价的指导意见的通知	发改价格〔2011〕2617号	中华人民共和国国家发展和改革委员会	2011-11-29	
关于批准发布《公共机构办公用房节能改造建设标准》的通知	建标〔2011〕197号	中华人民共和国住房和城乡建设部、中华人民共和国国家发展和改革委员会	2011-11-30	2012-03-01

续表

名称	批号(文号)	发布机构	发布日期	实施日期
关于印发住房城乡建设部关于落实《国务院关于印发“十二五”节能减排综合性工作方案的通知》的实施方案的通知	建科〔2011〕194号	中华人民共和国住房和城乡建设部	2011-12-01	
关于发布国家污染物排放标准《建筑施工场界环境噪声排放标准》的公告	公告2011年第86号	中华人民共和国环境保护部	2011-12-05	2012-07-01
关于加强国家生态工业示范园区建设的指导意见	环发〔2011〕143号	中华人民共和国环境保护部	2011-12-05	
关于批准广州开发区为国家生态工业示范园区的通知	环发〔2011〕144号	中华人民共和国环境保护部	2011-12-05	
关于印发《建设工程企业资质申报弄虚作假行为处理办法》的通知	建市〔2011〕200号	中华人民共和国住房和城乡建设部	2011-12-08	
关于批准发布《体育训练基地通用配套用房建设标准》的通知	建标〔2011〕207号	中华人民共和国住房和城乡建设部、中华人民共和国国家发展和改革委员会	2011-12-09	2012-03-01
关于批准发布《电力工程项目建设用地指标(风电场)》的通知	建标〔2011〕209号	中华人民共和国住房和城乡建设部、中华人民共和国国土资源部、中华人民共和国国家电力监管委员会	2011-12-14	2012-03-01
关于2011年中国人居环境奖获奖名单的通报	建城〔2011〕203号	中华人民共和国住房和城乡建设部	2011-12-14	
关于加强城市桥梁安全管理的通知	建城〔2011〕202号	中华人民共和国住房和城乡建设部	2011-12-14	
关于批准发布《建筑抗震加固建设标准》的通知	建标〔2011〕206号	中华人民共和国住房和城乡建设部、中华人民共和国国家发展和改革委员会	2011-12-15	2012-03-01
关于印发厦门市深化两岸交流合作综合配套改革试验总体方案的通知	发改经体〔2011〕3010号	中华人民共和国国家发展和改革委员会	2011-12-21	
国务院关于长春市城市总体规划的批复	国函〔2011〕166号	中华人民共和国国务院	2011-12-26	
围填海计划管理办法		中华人民共和国国家发展和改革委员会、中华人民共和国国家海洋局	2011-12-29	

(编辑整理：金晓春，中国城市规划设计研究院学术信息中心主任工程师；郭磊，中国城市规划设计研究院学术信息中心城市规划师)

附录 4　中国城市基本数据(2009 年)

城市名称 Name of Cities		行政级别 Admini－strative Rank	行政区域土地面积(平方公里) Area of City's Administrative (sq. km)	年末总人口(万人) Total Population (year-end) (10 thousand)	建成区面积(平方公里) Area of Built-up District (sq. km)	地区生产总值(万元) Gross Regional Product (10 000yuan)	人均地区生产总值(元) Per Capita Gross Regional Product(yuan)	污水处理率(%) Wastewater Treatment Rate(%)	生活垃圾处理率(%) Domestic Garbage Treatment Rate (%)	用水普及率(%) Water Coverage Rate(%)	人均公园绿地面积(平方米) Per Capita Public Green Space (sq. m)
北京市	Beijing	直辖市	16 411	1 245.83	1 349.83	121 530 000	70 452	80.29	98.22	100.00	12.11
天津市	Tianjin	直辖市	11 760	979.84	662.25	75 218 500	62 574	80.11	94.31	100.00	8.59
河北省	Hebei										
石家庄市	Shijiazhuang	地级市	15 848	977.41	201.06	30 012 797	30 428	83.28	100.00	100.00	11.50
唐山市	Tangshan	地级市	13 472	733.90	224.00	38 127 192	51 179	92.50	100.00	100.00	13.79
秦皇岛市	Qinhuangdao	地级市	7 523	287.24	89.48	8 045 421	27 110	89.20	96.93	100.00	13.87
邯郸市	Handan	地级市	12 062	942.77	108.01	20 152 800	22 779	84.10	100.00	100.00	13.00
邢台市	Xingtai	地级市	12 486	718.63	70.00	10 562 913	15 174	84.10	100.00	100.00	12.01
保定市	Baoding	地级市	20 584	1 155.28	130.99	17 300 023	15 770	89.02	100.00	100.00	8.67
张家口市	Zhangjiakou	地级市	36 873	462.31	82.00	8 003 407	18 948	82.28	69.80	100.00	8.62
承德市	Chengde	地级市	39 548	371.91	86.19	7 601 136	22 198	82.96	90.52	100.00	24.70
沧州市	Cangzhou	地级市	14 053	717.50	44.34	18 012 287	25 719	76.98	90.89	100.00	6.98
廊坊市	Langfang	地级市	6 429	413.33	58.63	11 474 791	27 904	85.78	94.93	100.00	12.71
衡水市	Hengshui	地级市	8 815	436.27	43.56	6 521 058	15 192	89.97	31.02	100.00	10.12
辛集市	Xinji	县级市	951	61.90	23.99			100.00	100.00	100.00	7.21
藁城市	Gaocheng	县级市	836	77.30	17.60			97.53	97.56	97.04	10.15
晋州市	Jinzhou	县级市	619	53.30	13.60			90.03	100.00	100.00	6.38
新乐市	Xinle	县级市	525	48.50	13.00			83.06		100.00	7.72
鹿泉市	Luquan	县级市	603.1	38.00	18.24			84.96	100.00	100.00	6.75

续表

城市名称 Name of Cities		行政级别 Admini－strative Rank	行政区域土地面积（平方公里）Area of City's Administrative (sq. km)	年末总人口（万人）Total Population (year-end) (10 thousand)	建成区面积（平方公里）Area of Built-up District (sq. km)	地区生产总值（万元）Gross Regional Product (10 000yuan)	人均地区生产总值（元）Per Capita Gross Regional Product(yuan)	污水处理率（%）Wastewater Treatment Rate(%)	生活垃圾处理率（%）Domestic Garbage Treatment Rate (%)	用水普及率（%）Water Coverage Rate(%)	人均公园绿地面积（平方米）Per Capita Public Green Space (sq. m)
遵化市	Zunhua	县级市	1 513	72.30	20.59			38.25	100.00	100.00	9.90
迁安市	Qianan	县级市	1 208	72.10	28.00			96.37	100.00	100.00	18.44
武安市	Wuan	县级市	1 806	76.40	26.00			80.63	100.00	100.00	10.62
南宫市	Nangong	县级市	854	47.00	12.50			89.57	97.98	100.00	9.84
沙河市	Shahe	县级市	999	47.30	14.30			83.69	100.00	100.00	10.29
涿州市	Zhuozhou	县级市	742	63.50	25.40			88.51	82.02	100.00	7.90
定州市	Dingzhou	县级市	1 274	120.60	25.21			70.06	100.00	100.00	5.37
安国市	Anguo	县级市	486	41.20	13.10			85.10	100.00	100.00	7.08
高碑店市	Gaobeidian	县级市	618	55.30	16.65			76.11	100.00	100.00	6.80
泊头市	Botou	县级市	1 007	58.50	19.72				72.60	100.00	4.64
任丘市	Renqiu	县级市	1 012	82.40	41.86			62.18	100.00	100.00	6.43
黄骅市	Huanghua	县级市	1 544.7	43.80	22.08			82.13	100.00	100.00	8.42
河间市	Hejian	县级市	1 333	80.10	17.80					100.00	3.63
霸州市	Bazhou	县级市	784	59.70	17.60			96.96	94.44	100.00	5.58
三河市	Sanhe	县级市	643	53.10	19.03			71.88	100.00	100.00	7.19
冀州市	Jizhou	县级市	917.2	36.70	15.99			81.89	81.82	100.00	9.69
深州市	Shenzhou	县级市	1 245.2	57.20	17.00			64.49	100.00	100.00	10.00
山西省	Shanxi										
太原市	Taiyuan	地级市	6 963	365.12	245.00	15 452 409	44 319	70.00	94.81	99.66	8.19
大同市	Datong	地级市	14 127	315.60	108.00	5 962 587	18 710	71.09	24.17	100.00	5.19
阳泉市	Yangquan	地级市	4 570	130.27	51.48	3 487 100	26 383	82.23	91.02	100.00	8.82
长治市	Changzhi	地级市	13 896	329.63	45.30	7 752 901	23 558	84.57	100.00	94.64	5.77
晋城市	Jincheng	地级市	9 425	216.53	31.00	6 060 499	27 108	95.00	93.11	100.00	11.67
朔州市	Shuozhou	地级市	11 066	157.37	31.75	5 613 074	36 452	95.24	67.99	98.02	9.48
晋中市	Jinzhong	地级市	16 404	320.00	38.59	6 368 106	20 335	70.98	31.66	96.50	11.93
运城市	Yuncheng	地级市	14 181	503.62	30.00	7 230 077	14 306	85.14	85.03	92.47	7.65

续表

城市名称 Name of Cities		行政级别 Admini－strative Rank	行政区域土地面积(平方公里) Area of City's Administrative (sq. km)	年末总人口(万人)Total Population (year-end) (10 thousand)	建成区面积(平方公里) Area of Built-up District (sq. km)	地区生产总值(万元) Gross Regional Product (10 000yuan)	人均地区生产总值(元) Per Capita Gross Regional Product(yuan)	污水处理率(%) Wastewater Treatment Rate(%)	生活垃圾处理率(%) Domestic Garbage Treatment Rate (%)	用水普及率(%) Water Coverage Rate(%)	人均公园绿地面积(平方米) Per Capita Public Green Space (sq. m)
忻州市	Xinzhou	地级市	25 117	306.91	21.40	3 493 072	11 292	93.44		89.39	1.49
临汾市	Linfen	地级市	20 275	437.04	37.40	7 668 659	18 215	82.84	39.83	93.23	11.58
吕梁市	Lvliang	地级市	21 240	381.09	18.00	6 115 606	16 903	47.07	100.00	95.42	12.85
古交市	Gujiao	县级市	1 584	22.00	16.50			86.25		96.32	6.13
潞城市	Lucheng	县级市	630	22.30	7.30			92.93	100.00	96.31	7.52
高平市	Gaoping	县级市	946	47.60	9.60			79.96	100.00	100.00	11.90
介休市	Jiexiu	县级市	757	40.20	17.55			94.12	90.28	100.00	12.13
永济市	Yongji	县级市	1 221	43.50	23.04			70.04	20.04	47.52	2.85
河津市	Hejin	县级市	593	39.10	18.13			80.97		63.52	10.78
原平市	Yuanping	县级市	2 556	47.90	9.57			78.39		98.32	1.86
侯马市	Houma	县级市	220.7	24.50	18.42			90.98	100.00	96.02	12.77
霍州市	Huozhou	县级市	764.3	30.60	15.40					95.00	7.50
孝义市	Xiaoyi	县级市	945.8	46.80	17.50			68.18		97.40	14.29
汾阳市	Fenyang	县级市	1 175.3	41.60	12.00					89.46	14.27
内蒙古自治区	Inner Mongolia										
呼和浩特市	Huhehaote	地级市	17 224	227.37	154.00	16 439 925	61108	56.96	95.20	95.41	16.04
包头市	Baotou	地级市	27 768	219.59	182.00	21 687 980	84 979	82.00	97.05	90.80	11.60
乌海市	Wuhai	地级市	1 754	48.06	37.51	3 115 080	64 147	68.73	81.53	100.00	9.19
赤峰市	Chifeng	地级市	90 021	459.19	79.00	9 128 888	21 037	76.00	99.69	84.54	6.82
通辽市	Tongliao	地级市	59 535	318.86	65.80	9 613 935	31 147	100.00	100.00	87.86	10.35
鄂尔多斯市	Eerduosi	地级市	86 752	149.48	109.58	21 610 000	134 400	76.87	100.00	85.11	13.19
呼伦贝尔市	Hulunbeier	地级市	253 356	271.76	28.00	7 792 653	28 882	78.79	80.56	67.65	18.39
巴彦淖尔市	Bayannaoer	地级市	64 413	173.30	38.00	5 098 658	29 384	86.15	96.50	93.26	7.36
乌兰察布市	Wulanchabu	地级市	54 492	289.72	40.75	5 000 100	23 489	97.50	100.00	93.93	20.03
霍林郭勒市	Huolinguole	县级市	585	8.20	18.00			97.50	33.69	78.57	2.61
满洲里市	Manzhouli	县级市	732	30.00	27.06			52.70	29.73	98.79	10.05

续表

城市名称 Name of Cities		行政级别 Admini－strative Rank	行政区域土地面积（平方公里）Area of City's Administrative (sq. km)	年末总人口（万人）Total Population (year-end) (10 thousand)	建成区面积（平方公里）Area of Built-up District (sq. km)	地区生产总值（万元）Gross Regional Product (10 000yuan)	人均地区生产总值（元）Per Capita Gross Regional Product (yuan)	污水处理率（%）Wastewater Treatment Rate (%)	生活垃圾处理率（%）Domestic Garbage Treatment Rate (%)	用水普及率（%）Water Coverage Rate (%)	人均公园绿地面积（平方米）Per Capita Public Green Space (sq. m)
牙克石市	Yakeshi	县级市	27 830	37.50	19.00			79.89		42.04	5.13
扎兰屯市	Zhalantun	县级市	16 800	43.00	19.20			82.26	86.87	79.84	10.11
额尔古纳市	Eerguna	县级市	28 958	8.50	10.38					42.36	8.73
根河市	Genhe	县级市	20 012	16.10	17.50					77.03	4.73
丰镇市	Fengzhen	县级市	2 704	34.10	25.00			67.67	100.00	58.74	16.15
乌兰浩特市	Wulanhaote	县级市	2 331.7	31.70	24.26			100.00	100.00	87.07	13.65
阿尔山市	Aershan	县级市	7 409	4.80	10.44					43.33	1.33
二连浩特市	Erlianhaote	县级市	4 015.1	8.90	36.00				84.51	100.00	3.01
锡林浩特市	Xilinhaote	县级市	14 592	17.00	34.00			77.71	92.08	78.51	9.58
辽宁省	Liaoning										
沈阳市	Shenyang	副省级市	12 980	716.55	395.00	42 685 137	54 654	78.59	100.00	100.00	12.77
大连市	Dalian	副省级市	12 574	584.80	258.00	43 495 050	70 781	90.40	100.00	100.00	10.86
鞍山市	Anshan	地级市	9 252	352.03	154.00	17 304 740	49 301	35.25	100.00	96.39	9.16
抚顺市	Fushun	地级市	11 272	222.61	126.31	6 986 395	31 343	57.38	100.00	98.57	8.36
本溪市	Benxi	地级市	8 411	155.46	106.50	6 883 947	44 251	43.01	100.00	99.76	9.19
丹东市	Dandong	地级市	15 222	242.64	53.40	6 075 211	25 034	46.67	100.00	93.94	6.12
锦州市	Jinzhou	地级市	9 891	310.19	70.61	7 272 951	23 447	50.65	100.00	100.00	9.03
营口市	Yingkou	地级市	5 402	235.04	97.65	7 994 827	34 104	37.59	93.41	95.56	10.60
阜新市	Fuxin	地级市	10 355	192.27	66.50	2 879 693	14 967	46.93	90.89	99.68	8.63
辽阳市	Liaoyang	地级市	4 736	183.48	93.40	6 082 597	33 151	75.23	100.00	100.00	8.46
盘锦市	Panjin	地级市	4 071	130.01	58.93	6 768 658	50 930	61.36	91.25	100.00	6.63
铁岭市	Tieling	地级市	12 980	306.06	43.96	6 057 065	19 795	85.40	86.17	97.57	9.53
朝阳市	Chaoyang	地级市	19 698	342.60	40.00	5 180 944	15 724	56.59	100.00	87.97	8.65
葫芦岛市	Huludao	地级市	10 415	282.27	72.25	4 455 816	15 856	87.36	100.00	100.00	12.21
新民市	Xinmin	县级市	3 315	69.90	18.00			100.00	100.00	90.88	10.64
瓦房店市	Wafangdian	县级市	3 793.5	102.60	32.50			83.99	100.00	100.00	10.63

续表

城市名称 Name of Cities		行政级别 Admini – strative Rank	行政区域土地面积(平方公里) Area of City's Administrative (sq. km)	年末总人口(万人) Total Population (year-end) (10 thousand)	建成区面积(平方公里) Area of Built-up District (sq. km)	地区生产总值(万元) Gross Regional Product (10 000yuan)	人均地区生产总值(元) Per Capita Gross Regional Product (yuan)	污水处理率(%) Wastewater Treatment Rate (%)	生活垃圾处理率(%) Domestic Garbage Treatment Rate (%)	用水普及率(%) Water Coverage Rate (%)	人均公园绿地面积(平方米) Per Capita Public Green Space (sq. m)
普兰店市	Pulandian	县级市	2 922	81.90	30.00			47.44	98.77	94.12	15.24
庄河市	Zhuanghe	县级市	4 086	90.80	40.00			43.71		93.73	9.59
海城市	Haicheng	县级市	2 732	114.70	32.85			60.76	100.00	96.21	5.83
东港市	Donggang	县级市	2 396	61.20	31.72				83.33	89.01	7.65
凤城市	Fengcheng	县级市	5 513	58.70	17.00				100.00	71.03	4.94
凌海市	Linghai	县级市	2 585.5	53.30	17.59				100.00	100.00	9.81
北镇市	Beizhen	县级市	1 694	52.70	14.50				100.00	77.20	2.61
盖州市	Gaizhou	县级市	2 945.9	73.20	25.00				100.00	78.37	4.16
大石桥市	Dashiqiao	县级市	1 598	72.50	30.22				100.00	100.00	6.53
灯塔市	Dengta	县级市	1 332.6	51.50	10.00				100.00	76.08	2.63
调兵山市	Diaobingshan	县级市	262	24.20	13.50			74.00	100.00	98.56	9.10
开原市	Kaiyuan	县级市	2 838.4	59.10	16.26			39.43	100.00	99.84	9.09
北票市	Beipiao	县级市	4 469	60.00	18.40					81.53	4.22
凌源市	Lingyuan	县级市	3 278	65.00	21.40					82.76	6.83
兴城市	Xingcheng	县级市	2 116	55.60	25.26			16.67	100.00	68.16	5.07
吉林省	Jilin										
长春市	Changchun	副省级市	20 604	756.50	365.28	28 485 627	37 753	88.71	88.38	99.30	13.70
吉林市	Jilin	地级市	27 126	437.42	165.63	15 004 776	34 583	90.12	100.00	97.82	11.83
四平市	Siping	地级市	14 080	339.12	45.54	6 585 947	19 468	100.00	100.00	67.39	6.86
辽源市	Liaoyuan	地级市	5 139	123.78	43.00	3 361 820	27 160	83.33	100.00	72.29	5.24
通化市	Tonghua	地级市	15 195	226.81	47.34	5 180 017	22 820		100.00	89.62	9.20
白山市	Baishan	地级市	17 485	129.72	40.00	3 566 348	27 495		100.00	83.74	8.79
松原市	Songyuan	地级市	21 090	288.33	41.56	9 008 304	31 421	60.00	60.83	92.39	10.52
白城市	Baicheng	地级市	25 745	203.17	38.11	3 533 626	17 404		100.00	91.67	7.88
九台市	Jiutai	县级市	3 375	71.10	25.20				97.22	94.62	5.43
榆树市	Yushu	县级市	4 712	129.70	35.50				100.00	69.78	5.43

续表

城市名称 Name of Cities		行政级别 Admini - strative Rank	行政区域土地面积（平方公里）Area of City's Administrative (sq. km)	年末总人口（万人）Total Population (year-end) (10 thousand)	建成区面积（平方公里）Area of Built-up District (sq. km)	地区生产总值（万元）Gross Regional Product (10 000yuan)	人均地区生产总值（元）Per Capita Gross Regional Product(yuan)	污水处理率（%）Wastewater Treatment Rate(%)	生活垃圾处理率（%）Domestic Garbage Treatment Rate (%)	用水普及率（%）Water Coverage Rate(%)	人均公园绿地面积（平方米）Per Capita Public Green Space (sq. m)
德惠市	Dehui	县级市	3 435	83.40	30.50				97.12	53.63	1.14
蛟河市	Jiaohe	县级市	6 364	45.30	13.05			99.78	87.65	98.86	14.66
桦甸市	Huadian	县级市	6 625	45.60	30.95			37.36	100.00	90.12	14.88
舒兰市	Shulan	县级市	4 557	66.30	25.00				100.00	74.83	7.71
磐石市	Panshi	县级市	3 867	54.10	13.27			95.37	100.00	72.13	5.90
公主岭市	Gongzhuling	县级市	4 028	108.80	32.58			73.57	95.15	95.28	1.56
双辽市	Shuangliao	县级市	3 121	41.70	27.48			42.69	83.38	63.36	6.66
梅河口市	Meihekou	县级市	2 174	61.90	22.00				79.41	96.92	6.21
集安市	Jian	县级市	3 342	22.50	13.79				100.00	96.51	10.70
临江市	Linjiang	县级市	3 008	17.20	8.65				80.00	100.00	8.85
洮南市	Taonan	县级市	5 031	43.80	17.40				94.48	43.78	6.54
大安市	Daan	县级市	4 879	42.00	13.90				50.00	90.89	7.50
延吉市	Yanji	县级市	1 748	50.40	34.68			98.29	98.57	98.09	8.57
图们市	Tumen	县级市	1 142	13.00	8.67				100.00	91.21	10.29
敦化市	Dunhua	县级市	11 957	48.40	17.20			92.65	100.00	93.85	21.24
珲春市	Huichun	县级市	5 145	22.30	17.89				82.50	81.00	6.33
龙井市	Longjing	县级市	2 208	18.30	9.93				98.48	92.82	7.85
和龙市	Helong	县级市	5 069	20.10	9.23				100.00	86.61	4.62
黑龙江省	Heilongjiang										
哈尔滨市	Haerbin	副省级市	53 068	991.60	345.31	31 755 391	32 053	73.94	100.00	85.15	9.42
齐齐哈尔市	Qiqihaer	地级市	42 469	571.56	115.27	6 905 169	12 714	66.10	43.98	95.68	8.84
鸡西市	Jixi	地级市	22 531	190.71	79.23	3 538 182	18 547		98.61	98.08	9.12
鹤岗市	Hegang	地级市	14 648	109.41	43.00	2 023 349	18 509			83.48	14.68
双鸭山市	Shuangyashan	地级市	23 209	150.81	58.80	2 985 082	19 817		20.46	100.00	15.92
大庆市	Daqing	地级市	21 219	280.17	206.65	21 200 036	76 068	99.95	82.29	83.10	13.30
伊春市	Yichun	地级市	32 759	127.31	161.19	1 724 616	13 530			66.86	19.25

续表

城市名称 Name of Cities		行政级别 Admini－strative Rank	行政区域土地面积(平方公里) Area of City's Administrative (sq. km)	年末总人口(万人) Total Population (year-end) (10 thousand)	建成区面积(平方公里) Area of Built-up District (sq. km)	地区生产总值(万元) Gross Regional Product (10 000yuan)	人均地区生产总值(元) Per Capita Gross Regional Product (yuan)	污水处理率(%) Wastewater Treatment Rate (%)	生活垃圾处理率(%) Domestic Garbage Treatment Rate (%)	用水普及率(%) Water Coverage Rate (%)	人均公园绿地面积(平方米) Per Capita Public Green Space (sq. m)
佳木斯市	Jiamusi	地级市	32 704	252.26	64.13	4 326 603	17 172	60.83	77.64	88.38	10.90
七台河市	Qitaihe	地级市	6 221	92.77	62.37	2 336 262	25 534		70.00	81.97	10.36
牡丹江市	Mudanjiang	地级市	40 583	270.57	65.30	6 292 848	22 645	40.84	100.00	94.07	8.10
黑河市	Heihe	地级市	82 164	174.21	19.00	2 242 095	12 882	93.52	59.09	78.01	16.74
绥化市	Suihua	地级市	34 854	580.15	30.60	6 058 790	10 471			96.46	4.02
双城市	Shuangcheng	县级市	3 112	82.20	27.70			100.00		97.78	12.16
尚志市	Shangzhi	县级市	8 825	61.60	18.30					98.39	11.57
五常市	Wuchang	县级市	7 512	98.00	21.51					90.71	8.42
讷河市	Nehe	县级市	6 648	74.10	10.69			89.20		88.59	12.53
虎林市	Hulin	县级市	9 334	16.00	10.76					98.46	12.46
密山市	Mishan	县级市	7 843	36.40	22.00					99.15	14.41
铁力市	Tieli	县级市	6 730	38.70	16.50					73.80	7.02
同江市	Tongjiang	县级市	6 300	13.20	10.00					62.70	12.38
富锦市	Fujin	县级市	8 227	39.30	16.19					76.76	7.47
绥芬河市	Suifenhe	县级市	422	6.40	15.60					57.11	3.84
海林市	Hailin	县级市	8 814	42.80	13.60			70.07		99.80	15.37
宁安市	Ningan	县级市	7 924	44.10	8.40					93.33	6.40
穆棱市	Muling	县级市	6 673	32.60	10.83					99.33	10.77
北安市	Beian	县级市	7 194	39.60	19.81					74.71	6.29
五大连池市	Wudalianchi	县级市	9 874	36.80	5.62			62.50		57.40	9.93
安达市	Anda	县级市	3 586	51.90	18.42					84.49	3.26
肇东市	Zhaodong	县级市	3 905	93.40	48.77				27.27	77.12	3.14
海伦市	Hailun	县级市	4 667	84.70	20.56					92.21	5.34
上海市	Shanghai	直辖市	6 340	1 400.70		150 464 500	78 989	88.97	78.77	100.00	8.02
江苏省	Jiangsu										
南京市	Nanjing	副省级市	6 582	629.77	598.14	42 302 608	70 377	87.50	100.00	100.00	13.60

续表

城市名称 Name of Cities		行政级别 Admini－strative Rank	行政区域土地面积（平方公里）Area of City's Administrative（sq. km）	年末总人口（万人）Total Population（year-end）（10 thousand）	建成区面积（平方公里）Area of Built-up District（sq. km）	地区生产总值（万元）Gross Regional Product（10 000yuan）	人均地区生产总值（元）Per Capita Gross Regional Product（yuan）	污水处理率（%）Wastewater Treatment Rate（%）	生活垃圾处理率（%）Domestic Garbage Treatment Rate（%）	用水普及率（%）Water Coverage Rate（%）	人均公园绿地面积（平方米）Per Capita Public Green Space（sq. m）
无锡市	Wuxi	地级市	4 788	465.65	216.50	49 917 200	115 263	93.08	100.00	100.00	13.56
徐州市	Xuzhou	地级市	11 258	957.61	205.60	23 901 600	61 699	81.46	93.12	98.46	13.64
常州市	Changzhou	地级市	4 385	359.82	133.90	25 199 300	70 138	87.75	100.00	100.00	12.20
苏州市	Suzhou	地级市	8 488	633.29	324.34	77 402 000	122 565	87.84	100.00	100.00	17.07
南通市	Nantong	地级市	8 001	762.66	93.80	28 728 038	37 642	88.62	100.00	100.00	10.53
连云港市	Lianyungang	地级市	7 500	490.64	100.00	9 411 300	19 229	80.07	100.00	100.00	11.31
淮安市	Huaian	地级市	10 072	534.16	110.00	11 217 500	20 946	81.56	100.00	99.19	10.59
盐城市	Yancheng	地级市	16 972	812.37	85.00	19 170 000	23 607	80.39	100.00	100.00	11.65
扬州市	Yangzhou	地级市	6 634	458.80	78.60	18 563 943	40 418	88.10	100.00	95.88	18.73
镇江市	Zhenjiang	地级市	3 847	269.88	104.10	16 720 765	62 084	85.25	100.00	100.00	15.64
泰州市	Taizhou	地级市	5 797	503.98	60.80	16 609 200	33 166	83.01	100.00	100.00	9.02
宿迁市	Suqian	地级市	8 555	540.60	63.42	8 268 532	15 381	82.55	100.00	98.15	11.85
江阴市	Jiangyin	县级市	988	120.30	53.20			86.08	100.00	100.00	14.45
宜兴市	Yixing	县级市	2 177	107.20	61.20			85.50	100.00	100.00	15.53
新沂市	Xinyi	县级市	1 571	102.00	30.97			69.15	96.92	100.00	8.47
邳州市	Pizhou	县级市	2 088	171.90	39.50			59.35	87.02	100.00	13.79
溧阳市	Liyang	县级市	1 536	78.10	21.31			75.03	100.00	100.00	9.37
金坛市	Jintan	县级市	976	55.00	21.72			78.59	100.00	100.00	12.34
常熟市	Changshu	县级市	1 094	106.60	97.62			86.52	100.00	100.00	30.03
张家港市	Zhangjiagang	县级市	772	90.00	63.70			87.01	100.00	100.00	18.34
昆山市	Kunshan	县级市	865	70.00	78.05			86.48	100.00	100.00	13.26
吴江市	Wujiang	县级市	1 093	79.70	32.00			87.42	100.00	100.00	14.32
太仓市	Taicang	县级市	620	46.70	93.80			83.36	100.00	100.00	10.38
启东市	Qidong	县级市	1 208	111.60	14.60			72.34	100.00	100.00	5.35
如皋市	Rugao	县级市	1 492	140.70	20.28			74.08	100.00	100.00	8.75
海门市	Haimen	县级市	939	99.80	100.00			68.39	100.00	100.00	6.31

续表

城市名称 Name of Cities		行政级别 Admini - strative Rank	行政区域土地面积(平方公里) Area of City's Administrative (sq. km)	年末总人口(万人)Total Population (year-end) (10 thousand)	建成区面积(平方公里) Area of Built-up District (sq. km)	地区生产总值(万元) Gross Regional Product (10 000yuan)	人均地区生产总值(元) Per Capita Gross Regional Product(yuan)	污水处理率(%) Wastewater Treatment Rate(%)	生活垃圾处理率(%) Domestic Garbage Treatment Rate (%)	用水普及率(%) Water Coverage Rate(%)	人均公园绿地面积(平方米) Per Capita Public Green Space (sq. m)
东台市	Dongtai	县级市	3 221	113.80	27.73			72.40	100.00	100.00	6.90
大丰市	Dafeng	县级市	3 059	72.40	15.50			68.83	100.00	100.00	6.00
仪征市	Yizheng	县级市	857	56.60	37.50			80.04	100.00	100.00	7.62
高邮市	Gaoyou	县级市	1 962	82.00	21.40			73.29	100.00	96.15	8.77
江都市	Jiangdu	县级市	1 330	106.60	30.00			82.19	100.00	96.68	11.09
丹阳市	Danyang	县级市	1 047	80.80	22.64			75.10	100.00	100.00	9.04
扬中市	Yangzhong	县级市	331	27.70	10.50			78.66	100.00	100.00	8.61
句容市	Jurong	县级市	1 387	58.00	17.32			78.52	100.00	100.00	10.72
兴化市	Xinghua	县级市	2 394	155.90	19.50			65.92	100.00	100.00	9.88
靖江市	Jingjiang	县级市	665	66.70	33.00			69.79	100.00	100.00	12.52
泰兴市	Taixing	县级市	1 172	119.70	22.15			57.50	100.00	100.00	8.20
姜堰市	Jiangyan	县级市	927	79.50	19.73			76.09	100.00	100.00	8.11
浙江省	Zhejiang										
杭州市	Hangzhou	副省级市	16 596	683.38	392.73	50 875 530	63 333	90.02	100.00	100.00	15.48
宁波市	Ningbo	副省级市	9 817	571.02	250.93	43 293 025	60 720	83.97	100.00	100.00	10.36
温州市	Wenzhou	地级市	11 788	779.11	170.30	25 273 488	32 588	62.00	100.00	100.00	6.87
嘉兴市	Jiaxing	地级市	3 915	339.60	88.08	19 180 282	44 898	78.33	100.00	100.00	12.60
湖州市	Huzhou	地级市	5 818	259.17	75.80	11 018 263	38 865	83.54	100.00	100.00	12.40
绍兴市	Shaoxing	地级市	8 256	437.74	93.44	23 757 754	54 316	83.98	100.00	100.00	15.15
金华市	Jinhua	地级市	10 941	463.68	70.58	17 760 647	34 294	72.97	100.00	99.81	12.06
衢州市	Quzhou	地级市	8 841	249.86	54.25	6 265 500	25 127	62.46	100.00	96.99	13.04
舟山市	Zhoushan	地级市	1 440	96.77	51.03	5 352 361	55 311	71.02	100.00	99.41	15.81
台州市	Taizhou	地级市	9 411	578.47	116.19	20 404 529	35 489	74.10	100.00	98.98	10.52
丽水市	Lishui	地级市	17 298	257.39	31.42	5 465 482	23 717	68.02	100.00	100.00	10.36
建德市	Jiande	县级市	2 364	51.30	8.32			81.80	100.00	100.00	9.61
富阳市	Fuyang	县级市	1 808	64.70	24.85			81.00	100.00	100.00	7.37

续表

城市名称 Name of Cities		行政级别 Admini－strative Rank	行政区域土地面积（平方公里）Area of City's Administrative（sq. km）	年末总人口（万人）Total Population（year-end）（10 thousand）	建成区面积（平方公里）Area of Built-up District（sq. km）	地区生产总值（万元）Gross Regional Product（10 000yuan）	人均地区生产总值（元）Per Capita Gross Regional Product（yuan）	污水处理率（%）Wastewater Treatment Rate（%）	生活垃圾处理率（%）Domestic Garbage Treatment Rate（%）	用水普及率（%）Water Coverage Rate（%）	人均公园绿地面积（平方米）Per Capita Public Green Space（sq. m）
临安市	Linan	县级市	3 124	52.60	12.32			90.19	100.00	99.94	4.47
余姚市	Yuyao	县级市	1 501	83.20	40.13			80.93	100.00	100.00	9.23
慈溪市	Cixi	县级市	1 361	103.50	36.50			77.94	100.00	100.00	9.52
奉化市	Fenghua	县级市	1 268	48.20	18.75			63.68	100.00	100.00	9.99
瑞安市	Ruian	县级市	1 271	118.80	22.30			60.07	92.95	100.00	4.75
乐清市	Leqing	县级市	1 174	122.50	26.00			28.22	58.50	100.00	3.08
海宁市	Haining	县级市	668	65.50	30.00			82.29	100.00	100.00	11.19
平湖市	Pinghu	县级市	537	48.50	15.80			83.07	100.00	100.00	12.12
桐乡市	Tongxiang	县级市	727	67.10	33.00			84.39	100.00	100.00	13.06
诸暨市	Zhuji	县级市	2 311	106.70	37.90			80.39	100.00	100.00	10.81
上虞市	Shangyu	县级市	1 403	77.40	22.00			68.00	100.00	100.00	11.39
嵊州市	Shengzhou	县级市	1 790	73.40	32.60			71.15	100.00	100.00	11.63
兰溪市	Lanxi	县级市	1 313	66.00	28.03			65.67	100.00	99.26	8.45
义乌市	Yiwu	县级市	1 105	73.00	83.00			80.07	100.00	100.00	4.58
东阳市	Dongyang	县级市	1 739	81.60	35.60			60.92	100.00	100.00	9.16
永康市	Yongkang	县级市	1 049	56.80	36.83			63.70	100.00	100.00	9.21
江山市	Jiangshan	县级市	2 019	59.40	15.00			79.57	100.00	97.08	10.52
温岭市	Wenling	县级市	836	118.50	30.80			81.53	100.00	98.98	10.28
临海市	Linhai	县级市	2 171	115.50	37.08			71.98	100.00	100.00	10.77
龙泉市	Longquan	县级市	3 059	28.70	11.76			53.53	100.00	100.00	15.69
安徽省	Anhui										
合肥市	Hefei	地级市	7 047	491.43	280.00	21 021 200	41 543	99.78	99.97	97.16	13.27
芜湖市	Wuhu	地级市	3 317	230.10	130.12	9 019 997	39 142	72.48	100.00	99.21	9.11
蚌埠市	Bengbu	地级市	5 952	360.64	102.55	5 320 870	14 803	83.83	100.00	97.96	7.78
淮南市	Huainan	地级市	2 585	242.52	97.45	5 087 730	22 169	87.90	100.00	97.41	11.54
马鞍山市	Maanshan	地级市	1 686	128.61	75.50	6 658 905	51 879	82.17	100.00	100.00	13.27

续表

城市名称 Name of Cities		行政级别 Admini－strative Rank	行政区域土地面积(平方公里) Area of City's Administrative (sq. km)	年末总人口(万人) Total Population (year-end) (10 thousand)	建成区面积(平方公里) Area of Built-up District (sq. km)	地区生产总值(万元) Gross Regional Product (10 000yuan)	人均地区生产总值(元) Per Capita Gross Regional Product(yuan)	污水处理率(%) Wastewater Treatment Rate(%)	生活垃圾处理率(%) Domestic Garbage Treatment Rate (%)	用水普及率(%) Water Coverage Rate(%)	人均公园绿地面积(平方米) Per Capita Public Green Space (sq. m)
淮北市	Huaibei	地级市	2 741	217.74	62.97	3 718 734	18 096	74.09	88.34	94.88	12.56
铜陵市	Tongling	地级市	1 113	73.99	47.00	3 437 300	46 765	70.23	85.99	95.16	10.78
安庆市	Anqing	地级市	15 318	615.88	72.12	7 706 600	13 811	87.58	97.64	94.99	9.53
黄山市	Huangshan	地级市	9 807	148.60	42.41	2 669 198	17 977	95.67	99.26	99.27	15.15
滁州市	Chuzhou	地级市	13 523	450.25	50.22	5 761 845	14 002	82.01	100.00	99.78	8.27
阜阳市	Fuyang	地级市	9 775	1 000.50	70.50	6 077 994	7 288	87.50	100.00	91.24	7.07
宿州市	Suzhou	地级市	9 787	635.19	50.00	5 406 000	8 526	55.11	96.98	99.25	8.21
巢湖市	Chaohu	地级市	9 394	458.60	37.50	5 293 628	12 280	83.85	100.00	77.57	8.45
六安市	Liuan	地级市	17 976	705.89	55.50	5 840 232	9 637	80.80	98.55	98.90	9.50
亳州市	Bozhou	地级市	8 374	596.93	32.00	4 319 284	8 477	92.04	100.00	96.14	10.28
池州市	Chizhou	地级市	8 272	159.88	28.18	2 455 896	17 295	68.09	85.67	93.17	16.97
宣城市	Xuancheng	地级市	12 323	277.77	38.60	4 327 700	16 774	37.42	100.00	98.56	7.01
桐城市	Tongcheng	县级市	1 546	75.40	25.22			5.83	100.00	75.47	6.95
天长市	Tianchang	县级市	1 751	63.20	25.00			81.57	41.13	89.00	0.51
明光市	Mingguang	县级市	2 359	65.50	18.50			98.00	97.67	90.10	3.49
界首市	Jieshou	县级市	666	78.10	17.08			88.27	64.80	72.95	2.86
宁国市	Ningguo	县级市	2 487	38.60	19.25			11.63	100.00	67.58	8.68
福建省	Fujian										
福州市	Fuzhou	地级市	13 066	637.92	182.96	26 040 448	38 015	80.87	100.00	99.01	10.61
厦门市	Xiamen	副省级市	1 573	177.00	212.00	17 372 349	68 938	94.05	100.00	100.00	10.90
莆田市	Putian	地级市	4 119	319.61	53.04	6 914 192	24 260	76.00	100.00	98.36	9.05
三明市	Sanming	地级市	23 094	271.06	25.85	8 002 444	30 370	79.19	95.01	99.95	11.09
泉州市	Quanzhou	地级市	11 015	680.85	87.00	30 695 003	39 227	85.20	100.00	98.69	10.40
漳州市	Zhangzhou	地级市	12 873	471.77	48.22	11 780 103	24 619	87.11	99.02	99.29	9.62
南平市	Nanping	地级市	26 315	310.10	25.76	6 216 534	21 473	75.11	98.66	98.96	11.30
龙岩市	Longyan	地级市	19 063	293.35	36.80	8 248 814	29 725	89.62	100.00	99.21	10.11

续表

城市名称 Name of Cities		行政级别 Admini－strative Rank	行政区域土地面积（平方公里）Area of City's Administrative（sq. km）	年末总人口（万人）Total Population（year-end）（10 thousand）	建成区面积（平方公里）Area of Built-up District（sq. km）	地区生产总值（万元）Gross Regional Product（10 000yuan）	人均地区生产总值（元）Per Capita Gross Regional Product（yuan）	污水处理率（%）Wastewater Treatment Rate（%）	生活垃圾处理率（%）Domestic Garbage Treatment Rate（%）	用水普及率（%）Water Coverage Rate（%）	人均公园绿地面积（平方米）Per Capita Public Green Space（sq. m）
宁德市	Ningde	地级市	13 248	335.95	17.29	6 122 829	20 174	55.01	100.00	99.07	13.38
福清市	Fuqing	县级市	1 971	125.30	30.00			70.02	100.00	99.90	10.89
长乐市	Changle	县级市	658	67.20	19.86			65.63	100.00	98.16	13.51
永安市	Yongan	县级市	2 932	32.20	18.51			65.34	100.00	99.67	10.70
石狮市	Shishi	县级市	160	31.50	18.74			67.02	100.00	99.08	4.22
晋江市	Jinjiang	县级市	642	105.00	32.50			79.53	99.68	99.75	9.17
南安市	Nanan	县级市	1 985	150.10	22.50			88.60	99.62	99.05	9.52
龙海市	Longhai	县级市	1 313	81.00	15.52			71.02	99.81	95.74	14.20
邵武市	Shaowu	县级市	2 852	30.30	13.96			65.04	98.64	100.00	18.32
武夷山市	Wuyishan	县级市	2 814	22.80	7.45			81.33	100.00	94.44	8.94
建瓯市	Jianou	县级市	4 214	53.00	9.40			66.26	100.00	99.06	10.23
建阳市	Jianyang	县级市	3 378	33.90	9.30			67.95	98.28	98.67	11.02
漳平市	Zhangping	县级市	2 975	27.70	8.30			71.15	100.00	98.70	12.99
福安市	Fuan	县级市	1 880	64.40	8.90				100.00	98.71	6.38
福鼎市	Fuding	县级市	1 526	57.60	14.78			60.31	100.00	98.33	10.10
江西省	Jiangxi										
南昌市	Nanchang	地级市	7 402	497.33	185.00	18 375 008	39 669	86.07	100.00	100.00	8.49
景德镇市	Jingdezhen	地级市	5 256	160.22	72.84	3 640 337	23 174	98.78	100.00	99.62	14.40
萍乡市	Pingxiang	地级市	3 824	186.93	42.10	4 214 862	22 685	84.74	100.00	99.72	9.21
九江市	Jiujiang	地级市	18 823	491.03	89.47	8 313 636	17 420	90.01	100.00	100.00	12.62
新余市	Xinyu	地级市	3 181	124.61	50.50	4 841 748	42 606	99.11	100.00	100.00	14.99
鹰潭市	Yingtan	地级市	3 554	119.82	23.68	2 568 020	23 106	87.82	100.00	98.73	12.08
赣州市	Ganzhou	地级市	39 379	896.99	59.23	9 406 290	11 201	55.03	100.00	100.00	9.28
吉安市	Jian	地级市	25 271	489.10	32.03	5 841 087	12 137	80.01	100.00	96.37	10.93
宜春市	Yichun	地级市	18 669	549.92	35.00	7 002 430	12 769	82.06	100.00	99.29	14.32
抚州市	Fuzhou	地级市	18 820	399.14	47.80	5 029 103	12 923	90.74	100.00	99.92	15.52

续表

城市名称 Name of Cities		行政级别 Admini－strative Rank	行政区域土地面积(平方公里) Area of City's Administrative (sq. km)	年末总人口(万人) Total Population (year-end) (10 thousand)	建成区面积(平方公里) Area of Built-up District (sq. km)	地区生产总值(万元) Gross Regional Product (10 000yuan)	人均地区生产总值(元) Per Capita Gross Regional Product(yuan)	污水处理率(%) Wastewater Treatment Rate(%)	生活垃圾处理率(%) Domestic Garbage Treatment Rate (%)	用水普及率(%) Water Coverage Rate(%)	人均公园绿地面积(平方米) Per Capita Public Green Space (sq. m)
上饶市	Shangrao	地级市	22 791	728.27	31.08	7 285 029	11 184	83.20	100.00	99.70	13.10
乐平市	Leping	县级市	1 975	86.10	16.70			37.55	100.00	98.92	13.96
瑞昌市	Ruichang	县级市	1 423	44.50	14.00			37.26	100.00	96.55	10.09
贵溪市	Guixi	县级市	2 480	59.50	20.60				100.00	99.61	16.37
瑞金市	Ruijin	县级市	2 448	65.40	19.05			12.83	100.00	94.01	18.61
南康市	Nankang	县级市	1 845	80.30	23.60			13.55	100.00	89.64	9.36
井冈山市	Jinggangshan	县级市	1 276	15.80	7.29			94.67	100.00	60.00	37.35
丰城市	Fengcheng	县级市	2 845	136.10	36.80			14.93	100.00	82.34	10.02
樟树市	Zhangshu	县级市	1 287	54.30	19.50			22.71	100.00	92.64	10.56
高安市	Gaoan	县级市	2 439	82.10	20.63			12.77	100.00	100.00	11.28
德兴市	Dexing	县级市	2 082	31.70	101.00			0.20	100.00	93.81	11.63
山东省	Shandong										
济南市	Jinan	副省级市	8 177	603.27	336.40	33 513 645	50 376	94.08	78.03	99.82	10.00
青岛市	Qingdao	副省级市	10 978	762.92	272.87	48 538 672	57 251	84.64	100.00	100.00	14.50
淄博市	Zibo	地级市	5 965	421.41	219.21	24 452 800	54 229	90.97	100.00	100.00	15.00
枣庄市	Zaozhuang	地级市	4 563	386.79	106.81	11 960 414	32 698	88.77	97.88	98.98	11.51
东营市	Dongying	地级市	7 923	184.59	103.13	20 589 700	102 370	85.14	98.99	100.00	17.34
烟台市	Yantai	地级市	13 746	652.00	235.43	37 017 900	52 683	90.76	98.75	99.89	17.70
潍坊市	Weifang	地级市	16 143	867.85	136.00	27 072 300	30 338	78.95	99.17	100.00	10.80
济宁市	Jining	地级市	11 194	831.31	88.90	22 381 300	27 979	93.52	75.87	100.00	11.93
泰安市	Taian	地级市	7 762	555.83	103.90	17 156 630	31 375	81.56	100.00	100.00	18.04
威海市	Weihai	地级市	5 797	252.97	129.00	17 803 493	63 519	89.27	100.00	100.00	24.12
日照市	Rizhao	地级市	5 348	285.76	75.62	8 646 600	31 451	91.26	84.37	100.00	20.17
莱芜市	Laiwu	地级市	2 246	126.38	57.00	4 713 000	36 907	91.38	100.00	100.00	19.01
临沂市	Linyi	地级市	17 191	1 041.54	152.00	20 691 100	20 983	91.30	100.00	100.00	20.15
德州市	Dezhou	地级市	10 356	569.01	48.00	14 760 842	28 046	81.81	92.78	99.10	19.00

续表

城市名称 Name of Cities		行政级别 Admini－strative Rank	行政区域土地面积（平方公里）Area of City's Administrative (sq. km)	年末总人口（万人）Total Population (year-end) (10 thousand)	建成区面积（平方公里）Area of Built-up District (sq. km)	地区生产总值（万元）Gross Regional Product (10 000yuan)	人均地区生产总值（元）Per Capita Gross Regional Product (yuan)	污水处理率（%）Wastewater Treatment Rate (%)	生活垃圾处理率（%）Domestic Garbage Treatment Rate (%)	用水普及率（%）Water Coverage Rate (%)	人均公园绿地面积（平方米）Per Capita Public Green Space (sq. m)
聊城市	Liaocheng	地级市	8 703	590.89	64.63	13 783 700	24 657	98.21	100.00	96.99	17.73
滨州市	Binzhou	地级市	9 454	377.49	81.00	13 549 931	36 679	89.26	100.00	100.00	15.61
菏泽市	Heze	地级市	12 239	939.44	63.40	9 573 109	11 649	72.99	92.11	94.75	10.12
章丘市	Zhangqiu	县级市	1 855	101.20	36.00			88.19	100.00	100.00	13.72
胶州市	Jiaozhou	县级市	1 313	80.00	40.09			83.89	100.00	100.00	15.87
即墨市	Jimo	县级市	1 780	112.60	51.00			87.01	100.00	100.00	14.36
平度市	Pingdu	县级市	3 167	137.60	42.70			86.90	100.00	100.00	10.22
胶南市	Jiaonan	县级市	1 802	83.70	54.00			97.47	100.00	100.00	16.99
莱西市	Laixi	县级市	1 568	73.50	30.46			94.81	100.00	100.00	16.27
滕州市	Tengzhou	县级市	1 496	167.20	44.63			85.21	93.97	100.00	10.48
龙口市	Longkou	县级市	893	63.00	40.13			93.04	100.00	99.93	10.92
莱阳市	Laiyang	县级市	1 732	87.60	32.67			93.15	100.00	99.20	10.44
莱州市	Laizhou	县级市	1 878	85.90	35.00			93.12	100.00	100.00	9.20
蓬莱市	Penglai	县级市	1 129	45.00	25.53			88.77	100.00	92.68	13.30
招远市	Zhaoyuan	县级市	1 433	57.10	27.02			94.25	100.00	99.77	17.30
栖霞市	Qixia	县级市	2 016	63.00	14.50			85.20	100.00	99.20	10.89
海阳市	Haiyang	县级市	1 887	66.70	32.00			93.92	100.00	96.94	14.06
青州市	Qingzhou	县级市	1 569	90.90	45.60			93.91	92.47	100.00	14.04
诸城市	Zhucheng	县级市	2 183	107.40	40.71			94.13	83.67	100.00	11.61
寿光市	Shouguang	县级市	2 057	103.30	36.85			94.89	100.00	100.00	20.61
安丘市	Anqiu	县级市	1 710	93.90	34.86			88.66	100.00	99.31	27.05
高密市	Gaomi	县级市	1 527	85.70	42.50			92.59	98.90	97.49	20.08
昌邑市	Changyi	县级市	1 628	58.10	24.95			92.10	98.02	100.00	18.65
曲阜市	Qufu	县级市	815	63.70	20.75			81.49	100.00	100.00	23.50
兖州市	Yanzhou	县级市	648	62.90	30.80			59.81	75.00	100.00	12.28
邹城市	Zoucheng	县级市	1 616	114.70	38.41			65.17	91.52	95.69	16.16

续表

城市名称 Name of Cities		行政级别 Admini－strative Rank	行政区域土地面积(平方公里) Area of City's Administrative (sq. km)	年末总人口(万人) Total Population (year-end) (10 thousand)	建成区面积(平方公里) Area of Built-up District (sq. km)	地区生产总值(万元) Gross Regional Product (10 000yuan)	人均地区生产总值(元) Per Capita Gross Regional Product(yuan)	污水处理率(%) Wastewater Treatment Rate(%)	生活垃圾处理率(%) Domestic Garbage Treatment Rate (%)	用水普及率(%) Water Coverage Rate(%)	人均公园绿地面积(平方米) Per Capita Public Green Space (sq. m)
新泰市	Xintai	县级市	1 933	138.40	62.00			77.30	100.00	99.96	17.75
肥城市	Feicheng	县级市	1 277	97.50	57.06			80.12	100.00	100.00	16.38
文登市	Wendeng	县级市	1 780	64.30	42.00			92.30	100.00	100.00	20.23
荣成市	Rongcheng	县级市	1 495	66.80	43.15			86.44	100.00	100.00	22.08
乳山市	Rushan	县级市	1 654	57.30	26.66			78.93	100.00	100.00	16.24
乐陵市	Leling	县级市	1 172	69.00	32.30			75.16	75.00	92.60	3.49
禹城市	Yucheng	县级市	990	52.00	24.04			83.07	100.00	98.14	12.60
临清市	Linqing	县级市	950	74.80	21.96			99.89	100.00	99.52	13.92
河南省	Henan										
郑州市	Zhengzhou	地级市	7 446	731.47	336.66	33 085 053	44 231	97.18	86.78	100.00	6.28
开封市	Kaifeng	地级市	6 444	527.14	94.24	7 787 245	16 571	88.05	100.00	98.36	5.06
洛阳市	Luoyang	地级市	15 200	694.89	165.95	20 014 846	31 170	94.34	66.50	70.97	8.28
平顶山市	Pingdingshan	地级市	7 882	532.36	62.50	11 278 100	23 018	99.73	85.18	94.06	8.50
安阳市	Anyang	地级市	7 413	573.16	75.00	11 248 807	21 578	97.46	93.97	100.00	8.51
鹤壁市	Hebi	地级市	2 182	159.79	49.00	3 636 276	25 370	77.60	82.62	97.40	11.01
新乡市	Xinxiang	地级市	8 169	597.25	95.68	9 919 801	17 992	86.71	95.43	97.17	9.18
焦作市	Jiaozuo	地级市	4 071	364.86	89.96	10 744 238	31 356	77.09	77.73	100.00	9.40
濮阳市	Puyang	地级市	4 266	404.22	36.00	6 616 319	18 855	53.42	93.73	91.06	12.36
许昌市	Xuchang	地级市	4 996	485.21	73.94	11 307 471	26 227	89.31	95.36	98.71	11.60
漯河市	Luohe	地级市	2 617	276.07	51.60	5 917 024	23 777	47.32	79.41	92.65	16.63
三门峡市	Sanmenxia	地级市	10 496	229.56	29.10	7 027 459	31 587	100.00	96.77	88.90	16.11
南阳市	Nanyang	地级市	26 509	1 167.51	87.39	17 144 914	16 997	46.84	76.12	68.16	10.61
商丘市	Shangqiu	地级市	10 704	910.87	59.00	9 955 475	12 779	95.63	67.94	62.45	5.13
信阳市	Xinyang	地级市	19 541	860.99	62.00	9 289 974	13 780	80.41	92.00	95.57	13.40
周口市	Zhoukou	地级市	11 959	1 206.76	44.00	10 653 712	10 649	69.88		91.89	9.88
驻马店市	Zhumadian	地级市	15 083	873.13	49.39	9 005 247	11 708	89.37	90.02	56.25	8.53

续表

城市名称 Name of Cities		行政级别 Admini－strative Rank	行政区域土地面积（平方公里）Area of City's Administrative (sq. km)	年末总人口（万人）Total Population (year-end) (10 thousand)	建成区面积（平方公里）Area of Built-up District (sq. km)	地区生产总值（万元）Gross Regional Product (10 000yuan)	人均地区生产总值（元）Per Capita Gross Regional Product (yuan)	污水处理率（%）Wastewater Treatment Rate (%)	生活垃圾处理率（%）Domestic Garbage Treatment Rate (%)	用水普及率（%）Water Coverage Rate (%)	人均公园绿地面积（平方米）Per Capita Public Green Space (sq. m)
巩义市	Gongyi	县级市	1 041	81.00	24.00			51.84	100.00	97.41	14.69
荥阳市	Xingyang	县级市	908	60.00	22.00			81.78	90.97	90.08	10.78
新密市	Xinmi	县级市	978	81.00	23.10			75.58	87.50	93.26	9.59
新郑市	Xinzheng	县级市	887	62.00	23.80			70.55	100.00	70.70	7.81
登封市	Dengfeng	县级市	1 219	65.50	19.20			97.95	100.00	94.21	10.49
偃师市	Yanshi	县级市	948	85.90	14.90			91.15	100.00	94.28	10.06
舞钢市	Wugang	县级市	641	31.90	13.92			64.95	21.35	88.64	10.12
汝州市	Ruzhou	县级市	957	95.10	25.00			98.91	94.71	48.49	6.77
林州市	Linzhou	县级市	2 046	104.00	19.50			69.68	61.11	90.80	10.55
卫辉市	Weihui	县级市	862	49.80	18.90			55.99	69.13	84.43	7.71
辉县市	Huixian	县级市	2 007	81.70	21.32			72.19	98.84	95.00	6.80
济源市	Jiyuan	县级市	624	49.50	30.80			85.00	100.00	99.77	9.63
沁阳市	Qinyang	县级市	542	37.90	18.50			81.67	55.91	92.97	8.75
孟州市	Mengzhou	县级市	1 461	125.70	14.32			91.58	97.22	98.57	10.00
禹州市	Yuzhou	县级市	650	70.90	32.41			88.50	82.93	96.80	11.46
长葛市	Changge	县级市	112	16.90	19.90			91.64	98.48	81.77	10.98
义马市	Yima	县级市	3 011	74.80	15.50			41.27	17.45	71.79	8.83
灵宝市	Lingbao	县级市	2 370	157.00	19.30			80.09	98.79	88.37	8.83
邓州市	Dengzhou	县级市	1 994	148.90	24.99			89.76	100.00	75.00	7.28
永城市	Yongcheng	县级市	1 083	131.00	23.30			85.23	86.73	79.16	8.89
项城市	Xiangcheng	县级市	1 894	68.20	27.19			77.52	100.00	90.24	9.68
湖北省	Hubei										
武汉市	Wuhan	副省级市	8 494	835.55	466.60	46 208 600	51 144	90.44	100.00	99.53	9.22
黄石市	Huangshi	地级市	4 583	258.56	62.00	5 715 900	23 560	72.21	100.00	99.08	11.70
十堰市	Shiyan	地级市	23 680	353.22	61.08	5 509 600	17 015	53.01	90.90	90.74	9.32
宜昌市	Yichang	地级市	21 048	401.37	85.66	12 723 300	31 476	87.17	91.01	100.00	10.84

续表

城市名称 Name of Cities		行政级别 Admini－strative Rank	行政区域土地面积(平方公里) Area of City's Administrative (sq. km)	年末总人口(万人) Total Population (year-end) (10 thousand)	建成区面积(平方公里) Area of Built-up District (sq. km)	地区生产总值(万元) Gross Regional Product (10 000yuan)	人均地区生产总值(元) Per Capita Gross Regional Product(yuan)	污水处理率(%) Wastewater Treatment Rate(%)	生活垃圾处理率(%) Domestic Garbage Treatment Rate (%)	用水普及率(%) Water Coverage Rate(%)	人均公园绿地面积(平方米) Per Capita Public Green Space (sq. m)
襄樊市	Xiangfan	地级市	19 724	588.88	80.35	12 010 100	22 071	81.32	100.00	99.53	10.04
鄂州市	Ezhou	地级市	1 504	107.24	47.30	3 237 121	31 310	74.83	100.00	100.00	11.71
荆门市	Jingmen	地级市	12 404	301.05	49.95	6 000 969	21 074	81.96	100.00	100.00	10.25
孝感市	Xiaogan	地级市	8 910	528.73	32.60	6 728 800	14 366	84.89	99.67	98.03	9.25
荆州市	Jingzhou	地级市	14 205	662.05	65.65	7 095 800	10 962	60.12	100.00	98.39	8.09
黄冈市	Huanggang	地级市	17 446	739.61	29.13	7 301 900	10 928	89.03	93.16	97.17	10.31
咸宁市	Xianning	地级市	9 861	290.63	31.30	4 051 500	16 101	42.14	100.00	96.00	10.80
随州市	Suizhou	地级市	9 636	257.77	43.00	3 419 100	15 531	90.04	100.00	94.51	9.51
大冶市	Daye	县级市	1 566	93.80	20.00			66.48	65.18	96.87	5.59
丹江口市	Danjiangkou	县级市	3 121	49.70	27.60			3.78	100.00	93.94	11.27
宜都市	Yidu	县级市	1 357	39.50	20.00			85.44	83.78	100.00	12.00
当阳市	Dangyang	县级市	2 159	48.50	20.50			16.67	87.50	99.71	6.63
枝江市	Zhijiang	县级市	1 310	50.20	14.37			78.31	95.24	100.00	13.16
老河口市	Laohekou	县级市	1 032	53.20	27.00			33.41	100.00	97.98	8.90
枣阳市	Zaoyang	县级市	3 277	111.80	24.30			81.27	100.00	93.66	13.44
宜城市	Yicheng	县级市	2 115	56.40	15.00			51.73	100.00	100.00	5.36
钟祥市	Zhongxiang	县级市	4 488	104.80	18.00			62.50	100.00	100.00	11.98
应城市	Yingcheng	县级市	1 103	68.10	19.56			20.23	97.67	92.64	8.59
安陆市	Anlu	县级市	1 355	63.00	16.20			42.60	95.82	80.85	7.75
汉川市	Hanchuan	县级市	1 663	112.10	16.00			37.30	94.41	98.01	4.33
石首市	Shishou	县级市	1 427	63.40	22.51			35.78	99.23	99.93	11.57
洪湖市	Honghu	县级市	2 519	92.50	39.52			78.31	100.00	93.94	11.36
松滋市	Songzi	县级市	2 235	84.70	28.31			58.46	66.86	97.46	14.92
麻城市	Macheng	县级市	3 747	118.00	24.03			60.32	94.62	98.36	8.80
武穴市	Wuxue	县级市	1 246	76.60	25.36			70.70	90.20	95.24	11.77
赤壁市	Chibi	县级市	1 723	51.50	23.76			41.60	74.16	94.58	7.38

续表

城市名称 Name of Cities		行政级别 Admini－strative Rank	行政区域土地面积（平方公里）Area of City's Administrative (sq. km)	年末总人口（万人）Total Population (year-end) (10 thousand)	建成区面积（平方公里）Area of Built-up District (sq. km)	地区生产总值（万元）Gross Regional Product (10 000yuan)	人均地区生产总值（元）Per Capita Gross Regional Product (yuan)	污水处理率（%）Wastewater Treatment Rate (%)	生活垃圾处理率（%）Domestic Garbage Treatment Rate (%)	用水普及率（%）Water Coverage Rate (%)	人均公园绿地面积（平方米）Per Capita Public Green Space (sq. m)
广水市	Guangshui	县级市	2 641	94.30	23.00			34.01	88.89	69.36	12.99
恩施市	Enshi	县级市	3 972	79.40	21.00			79.71	99.46	87.56	9.86
利川市	Lichuan	县级市	4 607	88.30	12.38			19.97	100.00	72.63	4.97
仙桃市	Xiantao	县级市	2 538	149.70	39.30			80.00	100.00	100.00	11.86
潜江市	Qianjiang	县级市	2 004	101.60	38.60			74.97	100.00	100.00	10.06
天门市	Tianmen	县级市	2 622	162.20	25.50				100.00	100.00	5.80
湖南省	Hunan										
长沙市	Changsha	地级市	11 819	651.59	242.43	37 447 641	56 620	79.43	100.00	100.00	9.50
株洲市	Zhuzhou	地级市	11 276	382.80	90.08	10 248 939	27 536	72.05	100.00	93.12	10.17
湘潭市	Xiangtan	地级市	5 015	285.26	73.38	7 393 818	26 608	68.99	100.00	97.31	8.72
衡阳市	Hengyang	地级市	15 299	739.80	93.00	11 680 146	17 299	46.92	100.00	100.00	8.90
邵阳市	Shaoyang	地级市	20 830	764.14	47.00	6 006 947	8 857	44.11	100.00	91.99	8.18
岳阳市	Yueyang	地级市	15 087	558.68	81.00	12 721 499	24 542	67.87	100.00	95.52	8.36
常德市	Changde	地级市	17 950	616.69	73.60	12 392 306	22 496	64.41	100.00	96.43	14.10
张家界市	Zhangjiajie	地级市	9 516	165.27	24.51	2 030 965	13 517	54.05		98.01	7.52
益阳市	Yiyang	地级市	12 144	470.55	53.00	5 916 182	14 071	68.58	100.00	93.27	6.84
郴州市	Chenzhou	地级市	19 506	473.86	49.00	8 432 283	19 059	54.78	100.00	92.09	7.59
永州市	Yongzhou	地级市	22 441	586.66	54.81	6 400 361	12 471	38.94	79.59	98.75	5.08
怀化市	Huaihua	地级市	27 624	508.88	50.00	5 594 841	12 041	67.14	100.00	94.52	7.75
娄底市	Loudi	地级市	8 117	420.53	41.80	5 683 129	14 454	51.95	100.00	95.96	8.79
浏阳市	Liuyang	县级市	4 998	140.40	22.00			72.85	100.00	99.90	5.77
醴陵市	Liling	县级市	2 157	98.30	26.38			22.31	67.23	83.32	5.66
湘乡市	Xiangxiang	县级市	2 011	89.20	20.00			32.81	93.62	87.23	6.83
韶山市	Shaoshan	县级市	210	10.10	4.72			49.48	100.00	90.74	9.81
耒阳市	Leiyang	县级市	2 656	127.50	32.00			41.66	90.38	96.06	7.07
常宁市	Changning	县级市	2 064	87.30	10.38			31.01	89.57	83.10	6.09

续表

城市名称 Name of Cities		行政级别 Admini－strative Rank	行政区域土地面积(平方公里) Area of City's Administrative (sq. km)	年末总人口(万人) Total Population (year-end) (10 thousand)	建成区面积(平方公里) Area of Built-up District (sq. km)	地区生产总值(万元) Gross Regional Product (10 000yuan)	人均地区生产总值(元) Per Capita Gross Regional Product(yuan)	污水处理率(%) Wastewater Treatment Rate(%)	生活垃圾处理率(%) Domestic Garbage Treatment Rate (%)	用水普及率(%) Water Coverage Rate(%)	人均公园绿地面积(平方米) Per Capita Public Green Space (sq. m)
武冈市	Wugang	县级市	1 549	75.70	14.21			12.65		90.42	10.54
汨罗市	Miluo	县级市	1 562	73.30	20.00			24.33	98.65	77.72	8.55
临湘市	Linxiang	县级市	1 744	49.70	15.50			59.66	100.00	88.82	4.47
津市市	Jinshi	县级市	558	27.40	10.66			31.00		91.67	9.42
沅江市	Yuanjiang	县级市	1 797	75.00	13.28			26.98	89.89	81.82	2.91
资兴市	Zixing	县级市	2 747	37.00	19.90			56.57	96.67	85.80	7.47
洪江市	Hongjiang	县级市	2 174	45.10	4.50			41.72	100.00	78.48	10.09
冷水江市	Lengshuijiang	县级市	439	37.70	19.90			32.06	100.00	86.48	7.48
涟源市	Lianyuan	县级市	1 895	112.80	12.00			26.79	100.00	80.71	4.27
吉首市	Jishou	县级市	1 059	29.20	19.50			40.00	100.00	89.55	7.61
广东省	Guangdong										
广州市	Guangzhou	副省级市	7 434	794.62	927.10	91 382 135	89 082	81.00	98.23	98.94	10.08
韶关市	Shaoguan	地级市	18 463	325.54	78.50	5 787 525	19 549	64.99	100.00	97.17	11.72
深圳市	Shenzhen	副省级市	1 992	245.96	813.12	82 013 176	92 772	68.75	94.30	100.00	16.30
珠海市	Zhuhai	地级市	1 701	102.65	118.34	10 386 627	69 890	53.84	67.25	98.96	10.19
汕头市	Shantou	地级市	2 064	510.73	172.50	10 358 687	20 385	59.95	64.13	98.80	11.76
佛山市	Foshan	地级市	3 848	367.63	151.03	48 208 972	80 686	86.26	98.48	100.00	9.12
江门市	Jiangmen	地级市	9 504	391.52	120.42	13 408 813	32 139	39.15	100.00	97.14	7.52
湛江市	Zhanjiang	地级市	12 471	763.14	78.73	11 566 678	16 647	87.14	97.36	99.36	12.73
茂名市	Maoming	地级市	11 458	735.31	69.00	12 312 519	19 979	68.12	95.25	98.42	9.20
肇庆市	Zhaoqing	地级市	15 134	413.69	74.46	8 620 048	22 415	78.09	94.42	99.90	21.11
惠州市	Huizhou	地级市	11 158	324.36	160.71	14 147 026	35 819	71.20	88.50	96.30	10.97
梅州市	Meizhou	地级市	15 870	507.36	41.50	5 192 860	12 558	62.67	100.00	95.51	11.79
汕尾市	Shanwei	地级市	5 271	340.61	14.14	3 900 405	13 363	43.01	100.00	93.06	10.27
河源市	Heyuan	地级市	15 642	348.98	27.50	4 054 956	13 928	76.00	99.21	99.63	9.12
阳江市	Yangjiang	地级市	7 946	275.67	42.36	5 272 696	22 130	60.39	100.00	100.00	9.72

续表

城市名称 Name of Cities		行政级别 Admini－strative Rank	行政区域土地面积（平方公里）Area of City's Administrative (sq. km)	年末总人口（万人）Total Population (year-end) (10 thousand)	建成区面积（平方公里）Area of Built-up District (sq. km)	地区生产总值（万元）Gross Regional Product (10 000yuan)	人均地区生产总值（元）Per Capita Gross Regional Product(yuan)	污水处理率（%）Wastewater Treatment Rate(%)	生活垃圾处理率（%）Domestic Garbage Treatment Rate (%)	用水普及率（%）Water Coverage Rate(%)	人均公园绿地面积（平方米）Per Capita Public Green Space (sq. m)
清远市	Qingyuan	地级市	19 036	408.82	56.12	8 615 921	22 797	58.25	100.00	99.17	15.42
东莞市	Dongguan	地级市	2 465	178.73	800.46	37 639 142	56 601	87.34	97.85	99.66	14.67
中山市	Zhongshan	地级市	1 800	147.86	87.30	15 664 106	62 304	87.62	100.00	100.00	9.08
潮州市	Chaozhou	地级市	3 100	257.89	41.68	4 801 815	18 681	82.09	100.00	100.00	10.30
揭阳市	Jieyang	地级市	5 240	649.11	52.80	8 160 920	14 159	13.25	82.75	97.50	12.27
云浮市	Yunfu	地级市	7 779	275.80	18.60	3 445 051	14 276	93.13	100.00	98.06	11.47
增城市	Zengcheng	县级市	1 616	83.40	24.00			59.76	86.78	66.23	12.42
从化市	Conghua	县级市	1 975	56.60	17.60			100.00	100.00	80.00	15.52
乐昌市	Lechang	县级市	2 421	52.70	12.00			52.54	50.00	84.21	8.63
南雄市	Nanxiong	县级市	2 361	46.80	11.47			79.92	72.71	95.40	12.53
台山市	Taishan	县级市	3 296	98.60	23.40			58.80	100.00	100.00	14.37
开平市	Kaiping	县级市	1 659	68.70	30.10			71.23	95.95	99.38	6.78
鹤山市	Heshan	县级市	1 083	36.50	19.93			64.14	100.00	100.00	10.29
恩平市	Enping	县级市	1 698	50.10	21.55				100.00	90.25	8.63
廉江市	Lianjiang	县级市	2 840	163.50	19.70				94.68	87.98	33.77
雷州市	Leizhou	县级市	3 662	163.20	20.88				96.64	63.20	8.03
吴川市	Wuchuan	县级市	849	108.30	69.00				96.96	73.32	11.15
高州市	Gaozhou	县级市	3 276	168.80	24.80				98.17	97.41	4.36
化州市	Huazhou	县级市	2 354	157.80	23.50				100.00	59.26	1.80
信宜市	Xinyi	县级市	3 081	137.00	74.46				98.99	85.19	6.11
高要市	Gaoyao	县级市	2 200	75.10	24.81			41.58	75.95	96.28	17.89
四会市	Sihui	县级市	1 259	51.10	160.71			60.40	80.91	93.76	9.21
兴宁市	Xingning	县级市	2 104	114.00	16.80			46.48	50.00	81.07	8.18
陆丰市	Lufeng	县级市	1 681	173.40	20.16				100.00	94.79	8.01
阳春市	Yangchun	县级市	4 054	110.70	22.13			83.26	86.63	95.06	10.93
英德市	Yingde	县级市	5 671	109.80	21.64			70.14		91.81	7.12

续表

城市名称 Name of Cities		行政级别 Admini－strative Rank	行政区域土地面积(平方公里) Area of City's Administrative (sq. km)	年末总人口(万人) Total Population (year-end) (10 thousand)	建成区面积(平方公里) Area of Built-up District (sq. km)	地区生产总值(万元) Gross Regional Product (10 000yuan)	人均地区生产总值(元) Per Capita Gross Regional Product (yuan)	污水处理率(%) Wastewater Treatment Rate (%)	生活垃圾处理率(%) Domestic Garbage Treatment Rate (%)	用水普及率(%) Water Coverage Rate (%)	人均公园绿地面积(平方米) Per Capita Public Green Space (sq. m)
连州市	Lianzhou	县级市	2 663	52.50	13.02					85.58	4.67
普宁市	Puning	县级市	1 635	225.60	26.66					97.84	0.38
罗定市	Luoding	县级市	2 327	117.60	43.00			41.00	71.89	92.54	17.50
广西壮族自治区	Guangxi										
南宁市	Nanning	地级市	22 099	697.90	189.92	15 247 144	21 945	99.42	100.00	93.89	9.90
柳州市	Liuzhou	地级市	18 617	367.56	131.04	10 460 537	28 291	87.75	100.00	99.80	13.76
桂林市	Guilin	地级市	27 809	511.63	60.79	9 405 425	18 443	84.30	90.36	77.65	6.75
梧州市	Wuzhou	地级市	12 555	316.18	36.10	4 536 513	14 776	26.73	88.35	98.94	7.33
北海市	Beihai	地级市	3 337	160.18	56.80	3 177 113	20 093	74.18	100.00	95.96	6.03
防城港市	Fangchenggang	地级市	6 222	86.92	30.33	2 510 367	29 602	10.98	31.71	100.00	7.56
钦州市	Qinzhou	地级市	10 843	371.19	63.26	3 963 669	12 212	88.95	100.00	95.45	7.51
贵港市	Guigang	地级市	10 606	509.69	53.61	4 377 331	10 215	66.10	96.93	85.75	12.43
玉林市	Yulin	地级市	12 838	653.41	53.00	6 834 915	12 032	47.22	100.00	100.00	11.02
百色市	Baise	地级市	36 202	398.57	32.52	4 528 599	12 423	13.71	100.00	100.00	9.11
贺州市	Hezhou	地级市	11 855	223.90	28.85	2 492 167	11 573	5.38	100.00	95.49	6.13
河池市	Hechi	地级市	33 508	409.55	18.30	3 827 713	9 949	87.75	100.00	99.82	3.83
来宾市	Laibin	地级市	13 411	254.50	26.00	2 993 595	12 967	34.43	100.00	97.86	7.99
崇左市	Chongzuo	地级市	17 386	241.96	18.00	3 043 555	13 921	6.35	2.00	100.00	7.37
岑溪市	Cenxi	县级市	2 783	87.50	16.05			0.64	1.07	97.89	16.66
东兴市	Dongxing	县级市	549	12.50	8.40				99.50	74.52	6.88
桂平市	Guiping	县级市	4 047	182.20	13.99			41.77	81.50	99.49	6.27
北流市	Beiliu	县级市	2 457	133.30	17.32			11.13	100.00	100.00	9.11
宜州市	Yizhou	县级市	3 869	64.90	11.94			53.14	89.05	100.00	10.11
合山市	Heshan	县级市	360	13.90	5.92				20.54	100.00	4.71
凭祥市	Pingxiang	县级市	650	11.00	8.43					93.69	8.56
海南省	Hainan										

续表

城市名称 Name of Cities		行政级别 Admini－strative Rank	行政区域土地面积（平方公里）Area of City's Administrative (sq. km)	年末总人口（万人）Total Population (year-end) (10 thousand)	建成区面积（平方公里）Area of Built-up District (sq. km)	地区生产总值（万元）Gross Regional Product (10 000yuan)	人均地区生产总值（元）Per Capita Gross Regional Product(yuan)	污水处理率（%）Wastewater Treatment Rate(%)	生活垃圾处理率（%）Domestic Garbage Treatment Rate (%)	用水普及率（%）Water Coverage Rate(%)	人均公园绿地面积（平方米）Per Capita Public Green Space (sq. m)
海口市	Haikou	地级市	2 305	158.24	91.42	4 895 519	26 366	77.41	100.00	99.77	10.54
三亚市	Sanya	地级市	1 915	55.71	28.20	1 733 198	35 750	62.87	100.00	91.23	12.14
五指山市	Wuzhishan	县级市	1 128	11.40	6.55				100.00	94.12	7.25
琼海市	Qionghai	县级市	1 710	48.90	23.00				100.00	89.22	17.20
儋州市	Danzhou	县级市	3 625	100.80	25.13				100.00	67.14	9.09
文昌市	Wenchang	县级市	2 485	57.40	14.50				100.00	64.21	2.80
万宁市	Wanning	县级市	1 884	60.10	10.00				100.00	79.00	6.39
东方市	Dongfang	县级市	2 256	45.60	16.00				100.00	85.03	6.80
重庆市	Chongqing	直辖市	82 826	3 275.61	783.29	65 300 100	22 920	88.36	98.45	94.00	11.25
四川省	Sichuan										
成都市	Chengdu	副省级市	12 121	1 139.63	439.21	45 026 032	35 215	88.45	100.00	97.09	12.79
自贡市	Zigong	地级市	4 373	328.49	68.00	5 140 487	19 256	80.24	85.16	80.35	5.90
攀枝花市	Panzhihua	地级市	7 440	111.58	54.60	4 240 750	36 562	26.24	93.94	93.90	8.64
泸州市	Luzhou	地级市	12 229	497.15	71.88	5 876 030	13 591	59.77	100.00	88.02	8.09
德阳市	Deyang	地级市	5 911	388.40	51.34	7 798 930	21 352	75.00	100.00	98.58	9.20
绵阳市	Mianyang	地级市	20 249	544.65	82.93	8 201 664	16 357	85.14	98.02	95.08	8.48
广元市	Guangyuan	地级市	16 314	312.73	33.86	2 704 803	99	71.77	75.70	90.55	8.80
遂宁市	Suining	地级市	5 325	387.05	49.34	4 120 706	11 536	78.15	92.41	82.55	7.67
内江市	Neijiang	地级市	5 386	425.61	39.00	5 608 849	14 175	39.87	44.44	66.91	5.19
乐山市	Leshan	地级市	12 826	353.22	52.33	6 190 171	18 379	51.23	95.09	91.10	7.33
南充市	Nanchong	地级市	12 479	753.51	71.00	6 862 762	10 982	44.57	82.50	97.13	8.69
眉山市	Meishan	地级市	7 186	348.07	42.20	4 653 274	15 509	72.77	82.28	90.49	10.58
宜宾市	Yibin	地级市	13 271	534.93	53.04	7 207 800	16 163	12.17	84.62	77.46	15.03
广安市	Guangan	地级市	6 344	470.02	27.00	4 503 368	12 140	88.37	99.29	74.13	15.90
达州市	Dazhou	地级市	16 591	657.56	41.90	6 827 297	11 915	86.48	82.21	94.70	17.63
雅安市	Yaan	地级市	15 302	155.15	20.40	2 396 141	15 710	62.26	86.32	99.60	7.80

续表

城市名称 Name of Cities		行政级别 Admini－strative Rank	行政区域土地面积(平方公里) Area of City's Administrative (sq. km)	年末总人口(万人) Total Population (year-end) (10 thousand)	建成区面积(平方公里) Area of Built-up District (sq. km)	地区生产总值(万元) Gross Regional Product (10 000yuan)	人均地区生产总值(元) Per Capita Gross Regional Product(yuan)	污水处理率(%) Wastewater Treatment Rate(%)	生活垃圾处理率(%) Domestic Garbage Treatment Rate (%)	用水普及率(%) Water Coverage Rate(%)	人均公园绿地面积(平方米) Per Capita Public Green Space (sq. m)
巴中市	Bazhong	地级市	12 301	401.18	16.62	2 383 161	7 548	51.32	72.95	94.25	8.82
资阳市	Ziyang	地级市	7 962	501.35	31.50	5 345 119	12 616	87.40	95.23	88.28	5.81
都江堰市	Dujiangyan	县级市	1 208	61.00	26.34			48.97	96.16	73.84	9.29
彭州市	Pengzhou	县级市	1 421	80.30	18.71			85.29	91.13	66.22	5.12
邛崃市	Qionglai	县级市	1 384	66.00	19.00			74.01	89.86	82.49	7.48
崇州市	Chongzhou	县级市	1 090	67.40	20.07			60.91	96.70	95.29	12.17
广汉市	Guanghan	县级市	549	60.10	35.08			46.13	49.22	79.04	5.31
什邡市	Shifang	县级市	820	43.50	11.00				99.68	77.42	7.20
绵竹市	Mianzhu	县级市	1 246	51.50	11.86				99.29	88.28	9.61
江油市	Jiangyou	县级市	2 719	88.70	24.08			56.19	100.00	83.94	4.21
峨眉山市	Emeishan	县级市	1 168	43.50	14.00			89.99	98.04	83.27	9.91
阆中市	Langzhong	县级市	1 877	88.30	42.20			59.13	82.28	96.53	8.24
华蓥市	Huaying	县级市	466	35.90	80.08			4.88	89.68	76.29	7.88
万源市	Wanyuan	县级市	4 065	60.40	20.40					69.63	3.60
简阳市	Jianyang	县级市	2 215	145.70	19.50				100.00	99.69	4.46
西昌市	Xichang	县级市	2 654	61.40	29.51				92.86	80.02	4.76
贵州省	Guizhou										
贵阳市	Guiyang	地级市	8 034	367.08	175.00	9 719 382	24 585	54.40	95.04	95.41	9.58
六盘水市	Liupanshui	地级市	9 946	319.35	38.50	4 301 556	14 422	84.49	100.00	100.00	2.50
遵义市	Zunyi	地级市	30 762	750.86	51.00	7 776 409	11 322	41.72	100.00	98.61	5.00
安顺市	Anshun	地级市	9 267	273.49	31.50	1 957 038	7 630	64.15	100.00	75.16	1.26
清镇市	Qingzhen	县级市	1 492	50.40	15.52				84.00	84.94	0.45
赤水市	Chishui	县级市	1 883	30.20	8.00			98.41	100.00	83.70	6.96
仁怀市	Renhuai	县级市	1 788	64.90	10.00			78.80	67.27	68.87	1.67
铜仁市	Tongren	县级市	1 514	37.70	23.00			74.80	93.33	100.00	3.82
兴义市	Xingyi	县级市	2 911	81.10	28.50			46.27	100.00	92.48	4.44

续表

城市名称 Name of Cities		行政级别 Admini－strative Rank	行政区域土地面积（平方公里）Area of City's Administrative (sq. km)	年末总人口（万人）Total Population (year-end) (10 thousand)	建成区面积（平方公里）Area of Built-up District (sq. km)	地区生产总值（万元）Gross Regional Product (10 000yuan)	人均地区生产总值（元）Per Capita Gross Regional Product(yuan)	污水处理率（%）Wastewater Treatment Rate(%)	生活垃圾处理率（%）Domestic Garbage Treatment Rate (%)	用水普及率（%）Water Coverage Rate(%)	人均公园绿地面积（平方米）Per Capita Public Green Space (sq. m)
毕节市	Bijie	县级市	3 412	141.60	20.00			97.24	94.06	77.61	8.50
凯里市	Kaili	县级市	1 306	48.50	35.00			89.15	98.99	85.93	4.59
都匀市	Duyun	县级市	2 274	48.10	14.69			43.96	100.00	98.35	8.61
福泉市	Fuquan	县级市	1 688	31.90	9.60				100.00	97.96	10.79
云南省	Yunnan										
昆明市	Kunming	地级市	21 015	533.99	285.30	18 086 467	25 826	91.31	96.48	99.24	7.88
曲靖市	Qujing	地级市	28 906	616.22	52.30	8 709 446	14 970	83.47	100.00	100.00	9.15
玉溪市	Yuxi	地级市	15 285	214.36	23.23	6 444 042	28 245	99.39	91.09	99.79	10.55
保山市	Baoshan	地级市	19 637	250.23	20.45	2 216 546	8 972	71.43	61.28	85.84	11.16
昭通市	Zhaotong	地级市	22 657	561.04	23.48	3 204 517	6 025	53.71	100.00	89.63	3.35
丽江市	Lijiang	地级市	21 219	120.53	18.60	1 206 746	9 863	74.11	84.67	93.58	26.98
普洱市	Puer	地级市	45 385	249.64	23.67	2 116 987	8 193	29.48	100.00	89.67	17.22
临沧市	Lincang	地级市	24 469	239.60	13.60	1 813 326	7 590		50.00	70.31	2.11
安宁市	Anning	县级市	1 302	26.70	19.20			86.02	100.00	100.00	8.80
宣威市	Xuanwei	县级市	6 053	145.90	26.50			90.34	98.80	87.45	7.36
楚雄市	Chuxiong	县级市	4 482	51.00	35.10			94.63	100.00	95.16	14.39
个旧市	Gejiu	县级市	1 587	39.10	12.15			80.96	100.00	100.00	12.75
开远市	Kaiyuan	县级市	1 950	27.00	19.89			97.35	100.00	91.75	6.84
景洪市	Jinghong	县级市	6 959	39.60	18.80			60.77	100.00	100.00	15.50
大理市	Dali	县级市	1 815	61.60	39.30			93.79	100.00	94.43	6.82
瑞丽市	Ruili	县级市	1 020	12.40	19.00			48.16		90.14	7.33
潞西市	Luxi	县级市	2 987	36.00	16.00			56.85	100.00	74.44	6.45
西藏自治区	Tibet										
拉萨市	Lasa	地级市		51.53	59.30	1 632 777	20 264		99.45	97.82	4.32
日喀则市	Rikaze	县级市	3 654	11.00	22.00					68.72	22.51
陕西省	Shaanxi										

续表

城市名称 Name of Cities		行政级别 Admini－strative Rank	行政区域土地面积(平方公里) Area of City's Administrative (sq. km)	年末总人口(万人) Total Population (year-end) (10 thousand)	建成区面积(平方公里) Area of Built-up District (sq. km)	地区生产总值(万元) Gross Regional Product (10 000yuan)	人均地区生产总值(元) Per Capita Gross Regional Product(yuan)	污水处理率(%) Wastewater Treatment Rate(%)	生活垃圾处理率(%) Domestic Garbage Treatment Rate (%)	用水普及率(%) Water Coverage Rate(%)	人均公园绿地面积(平方米) Per Capita Public Green Space (sq. m)
西安市	Xian	副省级市	10 108	781.67	283.10	27 240 800	32 411	80.97	90.30	104.63	7.90
铜川市	Tongchuan	地级市	3 882	85.31	38.44	1 558 600	18 548	59.02	88.39	95.17	9.49
宝鸡市	Baoji	地级市	18 131	378.78	77.11	8 065 640	21 526	91.01	100.00	99.84	14.22
咸阳市	Xianyang	地级市	10 196	516.38	60.00	8 732 000	17 429	49.66	100.00	97.59	9.80
渭南市	Weinan	地级市	13 134	556.86	38.90	6 554 980	12 069	80.90	92.35	93.67	9.83
延安市	Yanan	地级市	37 037	227.51	25.95	7 282 600	33 538	84.97	81.93	85.27	9.55
汉中市	Hanzhong	地级市	27 215	381.55	31.00	4 156 440	118 934	96.00	100.00	75.76	14.10
榆林市	Yulin	地级市	43 578	359.11	36.00	13 023 080	38 906	68.42	96.98	96.25	7.53
安康市	Ankang	地级市	23 529	303.57	30.00	2 749 450	10 341	19.35	54.62	81.60	10.06
商洛市	Shangluo	地级市	19 292	243.05	13.10	2 251 190	9 411	36.62	100.00	96.60	10.21
兴平市	Xingping	县级市	508	59.00	16.30			30.77		95.55	6.56
韩城市	Hancheng	县级市	1 621	40.00	17.72					99.23	7.99
华阴市	Huayin	县级市	817	26.00	18.00				50.85	95.33	5.14
甘肃省	Gansu										
兰州市	Lanzhou	地级市	13 086	323.59	183.85	9 259 821	27 904	60.00	99.97	92.38	8.52
嘉峪关市	Jiayuguan	地级市	2 935	20.87	44.10	1 600 500	76 087	68.19	100.00	100.00	17.63
金昌市	Jinchang	地级市	8 896	47.57	36.69	1 947 494	41 060	67.06	100.00	90.63	15.33
白银市	Baiyin	地级市	21 158	179.55	53.98	2 653 311	15 125	51.00	100.00	97.63	6.59
天水市	Tianshui	地级市	14 359	359.69	42.24	2 600 022	7 584	61.32	100.00	75.87	5.60
武威市	Wuwei	地级市	33 238	198.93	27.37	1 927 902	10 068	88.56	95.45	88.63	3.89
张掖市	Zhangye	地级市	41 924	130.37	29.17	1 920 761	14 949	80.87	100.00	92.82	18.69
平凉市	Pingliang	地级市	11 170	229.77	36.00	1 956 563	8 899	83.14	96.64	95.78	8.06
酒泉市	Jiuquan	地级市	193 974	96.42	37.10	3 210 478	31 512	47.01	89.47	100.00	8.96
庆阳市	Qingyang	地级市	27 119	560.95	19.10	3 022 211	11 973	84.88	93.78	95.54	2.95
定西市	Dingxi	地级市	20 330	299.43	22.96	1 319 394	4 491	77.46	70.00	90.35	9.15
陇南市	Longnan	地级市	27 914	279.17	10.40	14 263 400	5 428	49.43	100.00	47.75	1.26

续表

城市名称 Name of Cities		行政级别 Admini－strative Rank	行政区域土地面积（平方公里）Area of City's Administrative（sq. km）	年末总人口（万人）Total Population（year-end）（10 thousand）	建成区面积（平方公里）Area of Built-up District（sq. km）	地区生产总值（万元）Gross Regional Product（10 000yuan）	人均地区生产总值（元）Per Capita Gross Regional Product（yuan）	污水处理率（%）Wastewater Treatment Rate（%）	生活垃圾处理率（%）Domestic Garbage Treatment Rate（%）	用水普及率（%）Water Coverage Rate（%）	人均公园绿地面积（平方米）Per Capita Public Green Space（sq. m）
玉门市	Yumen	县级市	13 496	18.20	23.41			14.55	96.67	95.45	10.30
敦煌市	Dunhuang	县级市	31 200	18.40	14.89			29.61	96.15	99.90	9.09
临夏市	Linxia	县级市	88	22.30	14.20			70.94	98.48	77.93	1.04
合作市	Hezuo	县级市	2 291	8.60	8.98			69.87	100.00	81.37	5.79
青海省	Qinghai										
西宁市	Xining	地级市	7 665	193.94	65.57	5 010 743	22 865	54.47	79.68	99.35	8.62
格尔木市	Geermu	县级市	118 954	12.10	30.52			44.64	96.15	100.00	5.44
德令哈市	Delingha	县级市	27 358	7.20	16.30				62.44	100.00	5.63
宁夏回族自治区	Ningxia										
银川市	Yinchuan	地级市	9 555	155.55	115.47	5 781 483	34 453	46.52	100.00	99.50	14.60
石嘴山市	Shizuishan	地级市	5 310	74.52	94.26	2 707 801	37 050	11.18		99.29	22.20
吴忠市	Wuzhong	地级市	20 394	137.21	26.14	1 858 945	13 624	89.60	98.78	88.09	17.02
固原市	Guyuan	地级市	10 541	150.14	31.95	879 280	5 891	64.55	87.91	93.14	4.20
中卫市	Zhongwei	地级市	15 745	116.65	26.95	1 429 824	12 617	100.00	100.00	97.78	11.78
灵武市	Lingwu	县级市	4 539	23.60	7.39			100.00	100.00	78.56	17.84
青铜峡市	Qingtongxia	县级市	2 445	27.70	18.95			39.60	83.33	99.29	12.89
新疆维吾尔自治区	Xinjiang										
乌鲁木齐市	Ulumuchi	地级市	13 788	241.19	339.23	10 945 200	38 496	60.83	93.00	99.93	6.91
克拉玛依市	Kelamayi	地级市	9 548	39.35	56.77	4 802 909	87 000	91.81	100.00	100.00	8.43
吐鲁番市	Tulufan	县级市	13 589	27.00	12.36			62.75	100.00	100.00	10.39
哈密市	Hami	县级市	85 035	44.30	34.00			99.34	94.29	100.00	8.81
昌吉市	Changji	县级市	8 385	38.30	31.41			100.00	100.00	100.00	8.68
阜康市	Fukang	县级市	11 726	16.80	6.29			38.64	100.00	86.02	8.21
博乐市	Bole	县级市	7 956	26.10	14.04			100.00	70.59	99.23	16.61
库尔勒市	Kuerle	县级市	7 219	51.40	48.00			99.56	99.12	100.00	10.47
阿克苏市	Akesu	县级市	18 000	47.60	28.10			100.00	100.00	100.00	9.21

续表

城市名称 Name of Cities		行政级别 Admini－strative Rank	行政区域土地面积(平方公里) Area of City's Administrative (sq. km)	年末总人口(万人) Total Population (year-end) (10 thousand)	建成区面积(平方公里) Area of Built-up District (sq. km)	地区生产总值(万元) Gross Regional Product (10 000yuan)	人均地区生产总值(元) Per Capita Gross Regional Product(yuan)	污水处理率(%) Wastewater Treatment Rate(%)	生活垃圾处理率(%) Domestic Garbage Treatment Rate (%)	用水普及率(%) Water Coverage Rate(%)	人均公园绿地面积(平方米) Per Capita Public Green Space (sq. m)
阿图什市	Atushi	县级市	16 151	24.10	8.30			75.66	96.67	92.42	1.97
喀什市	Kashi	县级市	555	45.90	42.30			100.00	87.87	99.06	9.11
和田市	Hetian	县级市	496	29.50	17.60			80.10	82.73	96.37	9.27
伊宁市	Yining	县级市	676	45.90	36.95			70.24	98.99	100.00	8.50
奎屯市	Kuitun	县级市	1 110	15.30	24.56			67.73	100.00	100.00	8.86
塔城市	Tacheng	县级市	4 353	16.70	13.80			86.63	96.83	90.32	14.38
乌苏市	Wusu	县级市	13 729	22.40	15.99			82.83	96.00	92.83	7.17
阿勒泰市	Aletai	县级市	10 829	19.60	10.62			97.51	97.84	95.20	16.95
石河子市	Shihezi	县级市	7 762	63.50	27.05			75.53	100.00	100.00	10.70
阿拉尔市	Alaer	县级市	4 196	17.60	11.98				95.83	93.94	11.52
图木舒克市	Tumushuke	县级市	1 914	15.30	6.88			44.80		57.41	30.80
五家渠市	Wujiaqu	县级市	711	9.60	14.16					93.84	9.48

一、数据来源（Data Resources）

1. 行政级别（Administrative rank）

2. 行政区域土地面积（Area of city's administrative）

3. 年末总人口［Total population（year-end）］

4. 建成区面积（Area of built-up district）

5. 地级及以上城市地区生产总值（Gross regional product）

6. 人均地区生产总值（Per capita gross regional product）

以上数据来源：国家统计局城市社会经济调查司编，《中国城市统计年鉴—2010》，北京：中国统计出版社，2011.2。

（注：该年鉴未发表2009年全国385个县级市的地区生产总值和人均地区生产总值。）

7. 污水处理率（Wastewater treatment rate）

8. 生活垃圾处理率（Domestic garbage treatment rate）

9. 用水普及率（Water coverage rate）

10. 人均公园绿地面积（Per capita public green space）

以上数据来源：中华人民共和国住房和城乡建设部．中国城市建设统计年鉴（2009年）．北京：中国计划出版社，2010.11

二、指标解释（Data Illumination）

1. 行政级别：按行政级别分组，全国654个城市分为：4个直辖市，15个副省级城市，268个地级市，367个县级市。

——《中国城市统计年鉴—2010》，第13页

2. 行政区域土地面积：是指在该行政区划内的全部土地面积（包括水面面积）。计算土地面积是以行政区划为准。

——《中国城市统计年鉴—2010》，第443页

3. 年末总人口：是指本市本年12月31日24时的人口总数，为公安部门的户籍人口数。

——《中国城市统计年鉴—2010》，第443页

4. 建成区面积：城市行政区内实际已成片开发建设、市政公用设施和公共设施基本具备的区域。对核心城市，它包括集中连片的部分以及分散的若干个已经成片建设起来，市政公用设施和公共设施基本具备的地区；对一城多镇来说，它包括由几个连片开发建设起来的，市政公用设施和公共设施基本具备的地区组成。因此建成区范围，一般是指建成区外轮廓线所能包括的地区，也就是这个城市实际建设用地所达到的范围。

——《中国城市统计年鉴—2010》，第443页

5. 地区生产总值：指按市场价格计算的一个国家（地区）所有常住单位在一定时期内生产活动的最终成果。

——《中国城市统计年鉴—2010》，第443页

6. 用水普及率：指报告期末城区内用水人口与总人口的比率。计算公式为：

用水普及率＝城区用水人口/（城区人口＋城区暂住人口）×100%

——《中国城市建设统计年鉴（2010年）》，第622页

7. 污水处理率：指报告期内污水处理总量与污水排放总量的比率。计算公式：

污水处理率＝污水处理总量/污水排放总量×100%

——《中国城市建设统计年鉴（2010年）》，第622页

8. 人均公园绿地面积：指报告期末城区内平均每人拥有的公园绿地面积。计算公式：

人均公园绿地面积 = 城区公园绿地面积/（城区人口 + 城区暂住人口）

——《中国城市建设统计年鉴（2010 年）》，第 622 页

9. 生活垃圾处理率：指报告期内生活垃圾处理量与生活垃圾产出量的比率。计算公式：

生活垃圾处理率 = 生活垃圾处理量/生活垃圾产生量 × 100%

——《中国城市建设统计年鉴（2010 年）》，第 623 页

注：

1. 2007 年 1 月 21 日，国务院发布《国务院关于同意云南省思茅市及相关县区更名的批复》，在《中国城市建设统计年鉴（2009 年）》中已更名为普洱市；但《中国城市统计年鉴—2010》仍沿用思茅市的称谓。在本次“2009 年中国城市基本数据”的统计工作中，统一采用“普洱市”这一称谓。

2. 目前，由于各城市户籍改革步伐进展不一，一些地区已经把暂住人口完全纳入当地人口管理范畴，而另一些地区则仍维持原来的户籍人口管理办法，把暂住人口排除在外，导致各城市总人口概念差异较大。因此，本统计中的总人口及在此基础上计算出的各项人均指标均采用所引资料中的定义，可能与其他渠道统计数据存在出入，仅供参考。

（数据收集整理：毛其智，清华大学教授，国际欧亚科学院院士；厉基巍，清华大学建筑学院博士研究生）

附录5　国家历史文化名城名录

国家历史文化名城由中华人民共和国国务院确定并公布，根据《中华人民共和国文物保护法》，历史文化名城是指“保存文物特别丰富，具有重大历史文化价值和革命意义的城市”。国务院于1982年、1986年和1994年先后公布了三批国家级历史文化名城，共计99座；此后2001—2011年间陆续增补历史文化名城20个。目前国务院已审批的历史文化名城的城市共有119个。

1982年2月15日经国务院批准的首批国家历史文化名城24个：

北京、承德、大同、南京、苏州、扬州、杭州、绍兴、泉州、景德镇、曲阜、洛阳、开封、江陵（现在的荆州）、长沙、广州、桂林、成都、遵义、昆明、大理、拉萨、西安、延安。

1986年12月8日经国务院批准的第二批国家历史文化名城38个：

上海、天津、沈阳、武汉、南昌、重庆、保定、平遥、呼和浩特、镇江、常熟、徐州、淮安、宁波、歙县、寿县、亳州、福州、漳州、济南、安阳、南阳、商丘、襄阳、潮州、阆中、宜宾、自贡、镇远、丽江、日喀则、韩城、榆林、武威、张掖、敦煌、银川、喀什。

1994年1月4日经国务院批准的第三批国家历史文化名城37个：

正定、邯郸、新绛、代县、祁县、哈尔滨、吉林、集安、衢州、临海、长汀、赣州、青岛、聊城、邹城、临淄、郑州、浚县、随州、钟祥、岳阳、肇庆、佛山、梅州、雷州、柳州、琼山、乐山、都江堰、泸州、建水、巍山、江孜、咸阳、汉中、天水、同仁。

2001—2011年增补历史文化名城20个：

2001年增补2个：

增补山海关（区），2001年8月10日公布

增补凤凰县，2001年12月17日公布

2004年增补1个：

增补濮阳市，2004年10月1日公布

2005年增补1个：

增补安庆市，2005年4月14日公布

2007年增补8个：

增补泰安市，2007年3月9日公布

增补海口市、琼山区，2007年3月13日公布

增补金华市、绩溪县，2007年3月18日公布

增补吐鲁番市，2007年4月27日公布

增补特克斯县，2007年5月6日公布

增补无锡市，2007年9月15日公布

2009年增补1个：

增补南通市，2009年1月2日公布

2010年增补1个：

增补北海市，2010年11月9日公布

2011年增补6个：

增补嘉兴市、宜兴市，2011年1月27日公布

增补中山市，2011年3月17日公布

增补太原市，2011年3月17日公布

增补蓬莱市，2011年5月1日公布

增补会理县，2011年11月8日公布

（资料整理：廖远涛，陶琳，广州市城市规划勘测设计研究院）

附录 6　2010 年、2011 年中国人居环境奖名录

为在我国城镇化发展过程中充分贯彻落实科学发展观，促进经济、社会和环境协调、可持续发展，提高城镇综合承载能力，住房和城乡建设部设立“中国人居环境奖”，按照《中国人居环境奖申报和评选办法》进行评选，表彰在构建和谐社会、改善城镇人居环境中做出突出贡献的城镇、单位和个人。2010 年和 2011 年中国人居环境奖名单如下：

2010 年中国人居环境奖获奖名单：

1. 宁夏回族自治区银川市
2. 江苏省无锡市
3. 安徽省黄山市
4. 江苏省吴江市
5. 山东省寿光市

2010 年中国人居环境范例奖获奖名单：

1. 北京市通州区大运河公园建设项目
2. 天津市大板楼节能改造工程
3. 天津市天津大道绿化工程
4. 天津市梅江风景区工程
5. 上海市闵行区立体绿化建设和绿色交通项目
6. 上海市闸北区临汾路街道社区建设项目
7. 上海市农村村庄改造项目
8. 重庆市公园大渡口项目
9. 河北省唐山市中心区再生水回用项目
10. 山西省大同市富乔生活垃圾焚烧发电厂项目
11. 山西省临汾市城市公厕项目
12. 内蒙古自治区美丽草原宜居小镇项目
13. 辽宁省大连市绿色低碳住宅小区项目
14. 辽宁省锦州市东湖公园工程项目

15. 吉林省通化县既有居住建筑供热计量及节能改造项目
16. 黑龙江省大庆油田乘风湖环境综合治理项目
17. 黑龙江省海林农场生态特色小城镇建设项目
18. 江苏省可再生能源在江苏建筑上的推广应用项目
19. 江苏省昆山市锦溪镇古镇保护项目
20. 江苏省宜兴市官林镇规划建设管理项目
21. 江苏省太仓市居民住房改善项目
22. 浙江省杭州市长桥溪水生态修复工程
23. 浙江省奉化市生态滕头和谐家园项目
24. 安徽省芜湖市保兴埠城市排涝及周边环境综合治理项目
25. 安徽省阜阳市城市中心区生态环境建设项目
26. 山东省胶南市海之韵住宅小区海水冲厕示范工程
27. 山东省诸城市辛兴镇新型农村社区建设项目
28. 山东省临沂市临沂城区铁路沿线环境综合整治工程
29. 山东省德州市旧城区改造与环境提升项目
30. 河南省新安县仓头镇小城镇建设项目
31. 湖北省随州市白云湖两岸生态环境建设项目
32. 广东省深圳市南山区商业文化中心区再生水、雨水综合利用项目
33. 四川省长宁县城市绿化项目
34. 青海省西宁市餐厨垃圾处理项目
35. 宁夏回族自治区中卫市沙坡头大道景观水系建设项目

2011 年中国人居环境奖获奖名单:

1. 山东省潍坊市
2. 江苏省江阴市
3. 江苏省常熟市

2011 中国人居环境范例奖获奖名单:

1. 北京市城乡规划社区参与实践项目
2. 北京市房山区龙门台整村翻建试点建设项目
3. 天津市意式和德式风情区历史风貌建筑保护项目
4. 上海市世博会新能源公交车示范应用项目
5. 上海市普陀区苏州河(普陀段)两岸人居环境改善项目
6. 重庆市绿色轨道交通建设项目
7. 河北省邯郸市建筑垃圾资源化利用项目
8. 河北省三河市泃河城区段综合整治工程

9. 山西省大同市天然气集中发展利用项目
10. 山西省长治市澳瑞特小区供热计量改革项目
11. 辽宁省沈阳市铁西区旧城改造项目
12. 江苏省推进节约型城乡建设实践项目
13. 江苏省昆山市花桥生态保护及城市绿化建设项目
14. 江苏省常熟市古里镇小城镇建设项目
15. 江苏省苏州市吴忠区旺山村新农村建设项目
16. 江苏省扬州市城市管理与体制创新项目
17. 浙江省杭州市区危旧房改善工程
18. 浙江省杭州市老旧小区改造工程
19. 浙江省衢州市环护城河城市公园改造工程
20. 浙江省嘉兴市石臼漾水源生态湿地工程
21. 福建省宁德市东侨区环东湖生态景观建设项目
22. 山东省济南市泉城风貌恢复与保护项目
23. 山东省青岛市李沧区李村河上游片区旧村改造项目
24. 山东省临沂市屋顶绿化项目
25. 山东省德州市太阳能利用项目
26. 山东省沂南县竹泉村旧村改造工程
27. 湖北省鄂州市洋澜湖综合治理项目
28. 湖北省神农架林区九湖乡城镇综合治理项目
29. 湖南省长沙市社区公园建设工程
30. 广东省珠三角绿道网建设项目
31. 广东省广州市荔枝湾环境综合整治工程
32. 广东省深圳市建科大楼建筑节能与宣传项目
33. 四川省安县灾后城乡住房重建项目
34. 云南省昆明市地下管线信息系统建设项目
35. 云南省昆明市盘龙江整治工程
36. 云南省丽江古城历史文化遗产保护项目
37. 云南省易门县生态环境建设项目
38. 陕西省西安市大明宫遗址保护项目
39. 宁夏回族自治区隆德县城市供热计量改造工程

（资料整理：廖远涛，陶琳，广州市城市规划勘测设计研究院）

附录7　国家文明城市名录

文明城市是指在全面建设小康社会，推进社会主义现代化建设新的发展阶段，坚持科学发展观，经济和社会各项事业全面进步，物质文明、政治文明、精神文明与生态文明建设协调发展，精神文明建设取得显著成就，市民整体素质和文明程度较高的城市。全国文明城市称号是反映我国城市整体文明水平的综合性荣誉称号。

文明城市的测评体系包括基本指标和特色指标。基本指标反映文明城市创建的基本情况，共分“廉洁高效的政务环境”、“公正公平的法治环境”。“规范守信的市场环境”、“健康向上的人文环境”、“安居乐业的生活环境”、“可持续发展的生态环境”、“扎实有效的创建活动”七大项、37个子项、119个小项，分值为100分；特色指标反映城市精神文明创建工作的特色、城市整体形象。共有4个子项，分值为20分。

全国文明城市是我国城市的最高的荣誉，评选全国文明城市的目的是提高我们的生活质量，不断提升我们的文明素质，促进我们的全面发展。

第一批全国文明城市（区）于2005年10月评出，全国文明城市（区）名单（12个）：

文明城市（9个）：张家港市、厦门市、青岛市、大连市、宁波市、深圳市、包头市、中山市、烟台市。

文明城区（3个）：天津市和平区、上海市浦东新区、北京市西城区。

第二批全国文明城市（区）于2009年1月评出，全国文明城市（区）名单（14个）：

省会、副省级城市（3个）：成都市、南京市、南宁市；

地级市（6个）：惠州市、南通市、东莞市、马鞍山市、苏州市、大庆市；

直辖市城区（3个）：北京市东城区、上海市静安区、重庆市渝北区；

县级市（2个）：新疆库尔勒市、内蒙古满洲里市。

第三批全国文明城市（区）于2011年12月评出，全国文明城市（区）名单（27个）：

省会、副省级城市（9个）：长沙市、广州市、福州市、长春市、杭州市、郑州市、拉萨市、银川市、贵阳市；

地级市（14个）：临沂市、常德市、扬州市、长治市、淄博市、鄂尔多斯市、洛阳市、绵阳市、宜昌市、唐山市、江门市、嘉兴市、常州市、克拉玛依市；

直辖市城区（3个）：北京市朝阳区、上海市长宁区、重庆市渝中区。

县级市（1个）：黑龙江绥芬河市。

（资料整理：廖远涛，陶琳，广州市城市规划勘测设计研究院）

附录8 第三届中国历史文化名街

“中国历史文化名街”评选推介活动经文化部、国家文物局批准，由中国文化报社、中国文物报社联合主办。评选参照历史要素、文化要素、保存状况、经济文化活力、社会知名度、保护与管理等六大标准。旨在进一步加强中国历史文化街区的保护，促进城市经济、社会文化的协调、可持续发展，推进和谐社会建设。自2008年至今，已评选出30条“名街”。其中2011年6月评出的第三届“中国历史文化名街”名单如下：

1. 山西省晋中市祁县晋商老街
2. 江苏省无锡市惠山老街
3. 上海市徐汇区武康路历史文化名街
4. 福建省长汀县店头街
5. 广东省潮州市太平街义兴甲巷
6. 安徽省黄山市歙县渔梁街
7. 贵州省黔东南州黎平翘街
8. 浙江省杭州市清河坊
9. 河南省洛阳市涧西工业遗产街
10. 云南省大理白族自治州巍山彝族回族自治县南诏古街

（资料整理：廖远涛，陶琳，广州市城市规划勘测设计研究院）

编后语

2011年是我国第十二个五年规划的开局之年。这一年，中国共产党成立90周年、辛亥革命100周年为世人瞩目，转变经济发展方式有望取得新突破，一系列民生改革进入攻坚阶段。这一年，面对严峻复杂的国际国内形势，我国坚持以科学发展为主题，以加快转变经济发展方式为主线，牢牢把握机遇，为“十二五”时期发展开好局、起好步。为此，2011年《中国城市发展报告》（简称《报告》）的主题确定为“‘十二五规划’构建和谐社会、幸福城市”。

2011年《报告》延续了往年的基本架构。蒋正华先生撰写序言一，姜伟新部长撰写序言二，前言由汪光焘主任撰写。“综论篇”概括了2011年中国城市发展的方方面面，包括重大事件、经济发展、土地利用、交通进展、城市建设、城市信息化进程等。

“论坛篇”邀请了吴良镛、刘遵义、林珲、陈勇等几位院士和林树森、朱训、仇保兴等几位省、部级领导撰写专题文章，立论创新，内容丰富。

“观察篇”收集了除2011年两会期间人大代表、政协委员们关注的城市发展问题外，还有人民群众关注的热点、焦点问题等专述，如城市保障性住房、教育制度改革、城市综合交通评述等。其中老百姓关心的“老龄化背景下的城市化策略应对研究”和“最具幸福感城市评述”等主题文章很值得一读。

“专题篇”中，“近年国内城市防灾规划发展综述”、“关于‘十二五’加强大城市交通规划建设与管理工作的建议城市交通发展规划的建议”等文章值得参考，“粤港澳合作示范区的开发与建设”一文在践行深化改革开放方针方面有所创新，“海南转型跨越发展的战略与行动”和“新疆吐鲁番市新区绿色交通系统规划实践”等文章在低碳生态、绿色交通、节能与新能源应用等方面的经验值得借鉴。

“案例篇”中我们选择了“上海轨道交通基本网络与世博低碳易达模式”、“大珠三角区域规划：一个持续动态的过程”、“广州地下空间开发与利用立法研究”、“太原历史文化名城保护”等方面的实例和经验供广大读者参考。同时我们继续整理了有关城市规划、建设、管理方面的各类重要数据和信息作为附录资料，收辑于全书末尾，方便读者查阅。

从2006年至今，《中国城市发展报告》已经走过了6个年头。在蒋正华理事长和陶斯亮副理事长的领导下，中国市长协会和国际欧亚科学院中国科学中心精诚合作、默契互补，给市长、城市、全社会以及国际业界呈现了一份系统了解中国城市发展的白皮书，有力地推进了中国城市发展的研究，功不可没。在2011年5月30日召开的《中国城市发展报告》理事会第十三次（扩大）会议上，蒋正华理事长进一步明确了本书的定位，即“理论研究、施政分析、经验介绍、国际比较、信息服务、政策建议”，同时要求编辑部坚持“最权威、最完整地记录中国城市化的白皮书”这一属性，一方面要重视历史数据的记录和积累，另一方面应集萃当年的城市发展的理论思想，汇集重要观点，尝试开展“中国百年城市发展”专题研究，同时提出作者群应不局限于城市规划、建设、管理方面的专家学者，可加强吸收和邀请历史、经济、文化、健康、社会保障等更多城市经济社会发展领域的学者完善作者队伍。这些都是我们编委会下阶段改进编写工作、提高编写质量的目标。在此我们也恳切希望各个城市的决策者、管理者和研究人员以及广大读者多提宝贵意见，帮助我们把《报告》编写得更好。

国际欧亚科学院中国科学中心
城市科学学部副主任
戴逢院士　执笔
2012年3月30日